Praise for *Display Advertising: An Hour A Day*

The Google Display Network can be an amazing source of new customers if you do it right. However, for years it's been misused causing many to have a negative impression of display. Finally, there is a book that concentrates solely on display and tells you how to do it correctly. Display Advertising: An Hour a Day *is a must read for anyone serious about expanding their AdWords reach beyond search to finding new sources of revenue in the massive world of display advertising.*

> BRAD GEDDES, Author, *Advanced Google Adwords* & Founder of Certified Knowledge

Display advertising represents an incredible opportunity to do three delightful things: Engage consumers, deliver relevance and impact your bottom-line. In this wonderful book David and Corey provide a blueprint for going from Zero to Awesome!

> -AVINASH KAUSHIK, Author: *Web Analytics 2.0* & *Web Analytics: An Hour A Day* (Wiley/Sybex)

Dave and Corey are two of the most respected digital marketing professionals in the industry today serving some of the largest companies around the world. For a fast moving field such as Display Advertising, their new book is adding the much needed clarity on the latest development in this area. Their metrics focused approach offers the critical perspective to how to be successful in Display Advertising.

> PHIL MUI, Ph.D., EVP, Chief Product & Engineering Officer, Acxiom Corporation

Contrary to popular belief, display advertising is not dead: It's alive and well and will continue its explosive growth in the coming years. Now more than ever before, you as a business owner have more and more choices about where and how to spend your advertising budget. Dave and Corey help you navigate the complex landscape of ad networks and ad formats, and present a logical overview of the tools and techniques you need to effectively use and measure display ads. These are data-driven guys that have put together a roadmap that will help you focus your ad spend on productive display campaigns that can drive your bottom line.

> JUSTIN CUTRONI, Analytics Advocate, Google

No longer is display advertising a black art. Written by master practitioners, this book breaks down the practical details for mastering your online campaigns. Get it before your competitors do, and put it to work!

TIM ASH, CEO of SiteTuners, chair of Conversion Conference, author of *Landing Page Optimization* (Wiley/Sybex)

Winning in Paid Search Advertising has become a numbers game and proper ROI is almost impossible to achieve without a data driven attitude. Surprisingly, Display Advertising is, to this day, managed far less diligently—Dave and Corey are here to change that and their book is a great first step toward realizing that robust ROI you should demand from your display campaigns!

DENNIS R. MORTENSEN, author of *Data Driven Insights* (Wiley) and CEO and Founder of Visual Revenue Inc.

In an increasingly noisy digital marketing environment, competing for consumers' attention online is no easy task. Deciding where to allocate your advertising dollars, determining which ad networks deliver the most targeted audiences, and managing your daily operations can be overwhelming for even the most seasoned veteran. Dave and Corey take the guesswork out of display advertising with this pragmatic approach to managing your investments in time and money using sound judgment and quantifiable measurement tactics. This is a must read for anyone managing display advertising.

JOHN LOVETT, President, Digital Analytics Association, Senior Partner at Web Analytics Demystified, author of *Social Media Metrics Secrets* (Wiley)

I've been fortunate to know Dave and Corey for many years. They stand out as being truly passionate about data-driven marketing (I'm not exaggerating, they really love it) and are two of the most knowledgeable, intelligent people I know. This book shares their experience with actionable insights that will help take your Display campaigns to a new level of success and accountability.

ANASTASIA HOLDREN, Author, *Google AdWords* (O'Reilly) & President of SEM Training

Throughout its lifetime the Google AdWords Display Network has been viewed by advertisers as a dark, scary, dangerous place. Google has never done a good job of explaining the crucial differences between Search and Display advertising, and as a result many advertisers have written off the Display Network as a source of poor-quality traffic that burns cash and fails to convert. With Display Advertising: An Hour A Day, *Koberg and Booth have demystified the topic with tons of meaty, specific advice on profiting from display advertising. The ROI on this book is huge!*

DAVID SZETELA, AdWords expert and author of *PPC SEM: An Hour a Day* (Wiley/Sybex)

It's not very common to find people in the online market who understand the whole lifecycle of a digital strategy. From the mysterious realm of branding campaigns to the most concrete analysis of direct response objectives, there's no doubt that David and Corey are two of the few people who can gather it all together in a comprehensive yet easy to understand piece. In this book they do an extraordinary job explaining the high level importance of your digital strategy while providing clear, tactical steps to achieve any goal you define for your company. Whether you're starting your online business or have years of experience in the market, you'll find tons of actionable information and tips in this book. A must-read, for sure!

ENRIQUE QUEVEDO, Google Latin America

Display advertising can be complicated and difficult to master. Without a core understanding of how display advertising functions, and how to manage and optimize campaigns, advertisers are setting themselves up for failure. The day-by-day plan laid out in this book will provide campaign managers with a deep comprehension on targeting, ad messaging, and every other aspect of display advertising. If you've never done display advertising, this book is a great starting point. If you've been doing display for a while, this book can provide new ideas on how to re-vamp and optimize your campaigns.

JOSEPH KERSCHBAUM, Vice President of Clix Marketing and co-author of *PPC Advertising: An Hour a Day* (Wiley/Sybex)

This book covers the basics from the fundamentals of advertising campaigns and targeting the right audience to building and executing a campaign, measuring its effectiveness and making necessary adjustments. It's appealing in its layout and provides a step-by-step recipe for success. Kudos to Dave Booth and Corey Koberg.

FREDRIC KROPP, PhD, Professor of Entrepreneurship, Creativity and Innovation; Chair of the FisherInternational MBA Program, Monterey Institute of International Studies.

Dave & Corey wrote this book in the midst of some amazing but major changes to Google's Display Network. How quickly they reacted to those changes says a lot about their core knowledge of display advertising and this industry. The book is full of step by step instructions but it is also full of concepts that are timeless and won't change...even if interfaces, editors and user panels do.

SHELLEY ELLIS, Display Advertising and Retargeting Writer and Speaker, ContentNetworkPulse.com

Aristotle wrote 'Those that know, do. Those that understand, teach.' Corey and Dave are the kind of professionals that both know and understand, which put them in a perfect place to write an encompassing book about any subject. And since they have such a vast experience in the online advertising and analytics worlds, this is a book you should certainly read!

DANIEL WAISBERG, Founder & Editor, Online Behavior

Display Advertising

An Hour A Day

David Booth

Corey Koberg

WILEY

John Wiley & Sons, Inc.

Senior Acquisitions Editor: WILLEM KNIBBE
Development Editor: RICHARD MATEOSIAN
Technical Editor: HOWIE JACOBSON
Production Editor: REBECCA ANDERSON
Copy Editor: JUDY FLYNN
Editorial Manager: PETE GAUGHAN
Production Manager: TIM TATE
Vice President and Executive Group Publisher: RICHARD SWADLEY
Vice President and Publisher: NEIL EDDE
Book Designer: HAPPENSTANCE TYPE-O-RAMA
Compositor: MAUREEN FORYS, HAPPENSTANCE TYPE-O-RAMA
Proofreader: JOSH CHASE, WORD ONE NEW YORK
Indexer: J&J INDEXING
Project Coordinator, Cover: KATHERINE CROCKER
Cover Designer: RYAN SNEED
Cover Image: © HUCHEN LU / iSTOCKPHOTO

Dear Reader,

Thank you for choosing *Display Advertising: An Hour A Day*. This book is part of a family of premium-quality Sybex books, all of which are written by outstanding authors who combine practical experience with a gift for teaching.

Sybex was founded in 1976. More than 30 years later, we're still committed to producing consistently exceptional books. With each of our titles, we're working hard to set a new standard for the industry. From the paper we print on, to the authors we work with, our goal is to bring you the best books available.

I hope you see all that reflected in these pages. I'd be very interested to hear your comments and get your feedback on how we're doing. Feel free to let me know what you think about this or any other Sybex book by sending me an email at nedde@wiley.com. If you think you've found a technical error in this book, please visit http://sybex.custhelp.com. Customer feedback is critical to our efforts at Sybex.

Best regards,

Neil Edde
Vice President and Publisher
Sybex, an Imprint of Wiley

Acknowledgments

Throughout the journey of creating this book we've been extremely fortunate to have had the help and support of many people who have provided insight, research, and encouragement.

First and foremost, we owe a deep debt of gratitude to our wives, children, and extended family who knew better than we did what a time commitment this would be and encouraged us anyway. The late nights and weekends holed up writing added to an already extremely demanding day job, and we look forward to spending time with families who have patiently waited for Daddy's book to finally be done!

The team at Wiley are true professionals and have been beyond patient with us as we juggled travel schedules and other constraints. Throughout the course of writing this book, not a single chapter has escaped significant rewrites as the pace of this industry has continued to quicken. Willem, Pete, Richard, Howie, Becca, and the rest of the team listened to many calls beginning with, *"Bad news, there was yet another change"* and took them in stride.

We'd also like to thank our fellow Partners at Cardinal Path for their support of this project. Bringing three companies together to successfully create an entirely new type of agency is more than a full time job, and taking on a commitment such as this book right in the middle of a merger wasn't without risk. Their support and enthusiasm speaks volumes to the trust and foresight of the other Partners to have faith in our vision and embrace the project.

A huge thanks is also due to the incredible team at Cardinal Path, many of whom contributed through conversations, ideas, and words. Heather Cooan, Michael Straker, Mark Geyer, Bethany Bey, and Charlie Stone (of The Owned Agency) deserve special recognition for their direct involvement—their expertise and contributions are very much appreciated!

We are also very appreciative of the continued support from Google that has grown and grown over the years. We are particularly indebted to Rachel Greenberg, Brad Bender, and Andrea Faville for their help on this project.

Finally, we wouldn't be here without our clients, whom we consider true partners and who allow us the opportunity to use the tools and techniques in this book across a wide spectrum of industries and organizations. We'd like to give a special thanks to those who allowed us to share their stories through case studies and other examples. This is a better book because of folks like Matthew Tippins of Breezes Resorts, Stephanie Harris at Scrubs and Beyond, Richard Linevsky at Catalogs.com, David Peterson and JoLyn Laney of TravelNevada.com, and Ross Twiddy, Joe Akinc, and Evan Roberts at Twiddy & Company.

—Dave and Corey

About the Authors

David Booth is a founding partner and principal consultant at Cardinal Path as well as an author, instructor, adjunct professor, and regular speaker. As a consultant, David has advised and worked with top companies and organizations, such as Google, NPR, Teach for America, Lollapalooza, Zappos, Ethan Allen, and others across five continents in web analytics and business intelligence, statistical analysis and testing, technology selection and deployment, and online and search marketing. David is the author of *Google AdWords Essential Training* (Lynda.com, 2011) and *Google Website Optimizer Essential Training* (Lynda.com, 2010) and served as a technical editor of *Performance Marketing with Google Analytics* (Wiley, 2010) and *Google Analytics Essential Training* (Lynda.com, 2011). He also teaches a master's-level course on web analytics and online marketing at the Monterey Institute of International Studies.

As an instructor and speaker, David has keynoted numerous events and has led seminars and sessions focused on digital analytics and search and conversion marketing all around the world for audiences ranging from C-level executives to agencies and technical implementation teams.

He has been involved in web application development as an engineer and consultant since the late 1990s, beginning his career with Intel Corporation. Prior to Cardinal Path, he was a founder and Partner of WebShare, LLC, and spent two years with the United States Peace Corps developing and deploying websites and web applications to support local initiatives, attract grants, and draw international aid for Guatemalan NGOs and development organizations.

David earned his Master of Business Administration in International Management from the Monterey Institute of International Studies and holds a BS in Electrical and Computer Engineering from the University of Illinois at Urbana-Champaign. Proud husband and father, David spends his free time with his family traveling the world on frequent flier points and enjoying the outdoors on foot, bike, ropes or kayak.

Corey Koberg is a founding partner at Cardinal Path where he leads the advertising, social, user experience, development, and search optimization practices. He is a well-known speaker, having keynoted and led sessions on advertising, analytics, and optimization at conferences and events across the globe. Over the last decade he has taught thousands on the topics of online marketing measurement, statistical analysis, and optimization. He is the author of *Google Analytics Essential Training* (Lynda.com, 2011) and technical editor of several works, among them *Performance Marketing with Google Analytics* (Wiley, 2010), *Google AdWords Essential Training* (Lynda.com, 2011), and *Google Website Optimizer Essential Training* (Lynda.com, 2010).

As a consultant, he has worked with dozens of Fortune 500 companies, such as Google, Chevron, NBC, Papa John's, National Geographic, Time Warner, Universal

Music, DeVry University, and others, to improve the effectiveness of their online presence through results-oriented, data-driven optimization.

Corey holds a degree in Electrical and Computer Engineering from the University of Illinois and has been involved in Internet-related engineering and consulting for over 15 years, beginning his career in the NCSA labs that developed the world's first web browser.

Corey began his love of international travel while living in Hong Kong and covering the 14 countries of the APAC region for Intel. After a year in Germany with HP (DEC), Corey went on to design and deploy high-speed Internet backbone infrastructure for international telecom providers, banks, universities, and governments across South America, Eastern Europe, Asia, and Scandinavia. He was then part of the team at Qualcomm that deployed an advanced IP-based messaging system across the United States and Europe. As a founder and Partner at WebShare, Corey was responsible for the advertising and analytics practice prior to the merger with Cardinal Path.

Corey is a proud husband and father of three children and enjoys sailboat racing, downhill skiing, and photography. He is involved on a volunteer basis with the University of Illinois Alumni Association and the local emergency response team.

Contents

Foreword   *xvii*

Introduction   *xix*

Chapter 1   **Online Advertising**   **1**

An Overview of Search Engine Marketing 2
Search Engine Marketing   3
Pay per Click Advertising   4

Search Advertising vs. Display Advertising. 6
Search Advertising   6
Display Advertising   9

Problem Solving and Distraction. 13

Chapter 2   **Overview of Display Advertising**   **17**

The Display Advertising Landscape .18
Why We Focus on the Google Display Network   19

Identifying Display Ad Types and Formats. 23
Text Ads   24
Image Ads   24
Video Ads   25
Rich Media Ads   26

Defining Advertising Objectives 26
Defining Your Goals   27
Direct Response Advertising   32
Branding and Positioning Goals   35

Chapter 3   **Fundamental Display Advertising Concepts**   **39**

The Ecosystem: Advertisers and Publishers. 40
Display Networks Come of Age   41
Technological Advances Lead to Extreme Complexity   41

Starting Out with the Google Network 45
What Is This Page Really About?   45
Google-Owned Properties   46
AdSense for Content   48
The DoubleClick Network   53

Campaign Targeting Strategies 54
Targeting Campaigns with Keywords   54
Targeting Campaigns with Placements   54
Targeting Campaigns with Audiences   55

The Big Picture: The Process of Display Advertising 56

Chapter 4   Month 1: Planning Your Campaigns   59

Week 1: Define Your Display Advertising Goals 60
Monday: Understand the Objectives of Display Advertising   60
Tuesday: Define Your Direct Response Goals   62
Wednesday: Define Success Metrics for Direct Response Goals   65
Thursday: Define Branding and Positioning Goals   67
Friday: Create Strategies to Measure Branding and Positioning 71

Week 2: Showcase What You Do Best 74
Monday: Solve Your Customers' Problems   74
Tuesday: Look at Your Competition   76
Wednesday: Identify Your Competitive Advantage   79
Thursday/Friday: Define and Find Your Customers   81

Week 3: Take Stock of Your Resources 83
Monday: Understand the Process of Success   83
Tuesday: Identify the Campaign Implementer   85
Wednesday: Identify the Market Researcher   86
Thursday: Identify the Graphic Designer and Developer   88
Friday: Identify the Analyst   89

Week 4: Plan Your Budget 90
Monday: Choose between Bid Types   91
Tuesday: Understand How the CPC Auction Works   93
Wednesday: Understand How CPM Bids Compete in the Auction   96
Thursday: Understand How Google Spends Your Budget   97
Friday: Understand AdWords Billing Options   98

Chapter 5   Month 2: Targeting Your Audience   101

Week 5: Understand Targeting Options 102
Monday: Using Contextual Targeting   102
Tuesday: Using Placement Targeting   104
Wednesday: Using Audience Targeting   108
Thursday: Using Additional Campaign Targeting Options   110
Friday: Combining Targeting Types   112

Week 6: Find Good Keywords 114
Monday: How Google Determines Relevance   115
Tuesday/Wednesday: Using the Google Keyword Tool   117
Thursday/Friday: Using the Contextual Targeting Tool   123

Week 7: Find Good Placements 126
Monday/Tuesday: Use the DoubleClick Ad Planner   126
Wednesday: Using the Placement Tool   133
Thursday: Evaluating Placements   137
Friday: Automatic and Managed Placement Strategies   139

Week 8: Organize Campaigns and Ad Groups 141
Monday: Separating Your Display Campaigns   141
Tuesday: Organizing by Campaign Settings   145
Wednesday: Organizing by Themes   146
Thursday: Organizing by Audiences   149
Friday: Using Exclusions   150

Chapter 6   Month 3: Building Your First Display Campaign   153

Week 9: Choose Your Display Campaign Settings 154
Monday: Create a New Campaign   154
Tuesday/Wednesday: Target Locations and Languages   156
Thursday: Set Target Networks   160
Friday: Use Device Targeting   162

Week 10: Choose Your Bidding Style and Budget. 164
Monday: Learn Manual CPC Bidding   164
Tuesday: Learn Automatic & Enhanced CPC Bidding   166
Wednesday: Learn CPM Bidding   167
Thursday: Learn the Conversion Optimizer   168
Friday: Set Your Budget   171

Week 11: Configure Advanced Campaign Settings 173
Monday/Tuesday: Learn the Ad Scheduler   174
Wednesday: Understand Rotation and Frequency Capping   177
Thursday/Friday: Integrate with Google+   178

Week 12: Create Your First Ad Group 181
Monday: Add Keywords for Contextual Targeting   181
Tuesday: Add Placements for Placement Targeting   183
Wednesday: Add Audiences for Audience Targeting   185
Thursday: Exclude Placements, Audiences, and Keywords   186
Friday: Add Ads to Your Ad Groups   188

Chapter 7   Month 4: Creating Image Ads   191

Week 13: Study the Science behind Great Image Ads 192
Monday: Maintaining the Scent   192
Tuesday: Creating Strong Calls to Action   195
Wednesday: Using Enticing Imagery   197
Thursday: Writing Good Copy for Display Ads   202
Friday: Visual and Cognitive Psychology Concepts   204

Week 14: Understand the Rules. 215
Monday: Supported Formats, Sizes, and File Sizes   215
Tuesday: Flash Ad Requirements   218
Wednesday: Editorial and Graphical Requirements   220
Thursday: Content Guidelines and Family Status   221
Friday: Site-Level Guidelines   225

Week 15: Dig Deeper on Image Ads 227
Monday: What You're Trying to Accomplish   227
Tuesday: Image Ads for E-Com, Lead Gen, B2B, and
Non-Profit Scenarios   228
Wednesday: Choosing Static or Rich Media Ads   231
Thursday: Importing Your Image Ads into AdWords   232
Friday: The Approval Process   233

Week 16: Build Ads with Display Ad Builder 235
Monday: Benefits and Drawbacks of the Display Ad Builder 235
Tuesday: Browsing Your Options—Themes and Filters   236
Wednesday: Creating and Previewing an Ad   237

Thursday: Advanced Ad Types   240
Friday: Tips For Creating Unique Ads   242

Chapter 8   **Month 5: Video Ads**   **245**

Week 17: Understand AdWords Video Ads 246
Monday: What They Are, Where They Show and When
to Use Them   246
Tuesday: Click-to-Play Video Ads   247
Wednesday: In-Stream and In-Slate Video Ads   247
Thursday: InVideo Ads   249
Friday: Evaluating Video Ads   250

Week 18: Create Video Ads 252
Monday: Best Practices for Video Ads   252
Tuesday: The AdWords for Video Interface   254
Wednesday/Thursday: Creating a Campaign, Ad, and
Targeting Group   255
Friday: Guest Lecture by Charlie Stone   257

Week 19: Advertise on YouTube 258
Monday: Advertising on YouTube   258
Tuesday: Channel and Call-to-Action Overlays   260
Wednesday: TrueView In-Search and In-Display   261
Thursday: Additional Tools   262
Friday: YouTube Analytics   263

Week 20: Advertise on Television with AdWords 265
Monday: Is TV Advertising Right for You?   266
Tuesday: Networks and Targeting   267
Wednesday: Creating Your Own Ads   268
Thursday: Outsourcing Ad Production   270
Friday: Measuring the Success of a Television Campaign   271

Chapter 9   **Month 6: Launch and Measure Your Campaign's Performance**   **273**

Week 21: Launch the Campaign 274
Monday: Setting a Benchmark By Taking Stock of Where
You Currently Stand   274
Tuesday: What to Expect and Do in Your First Week   275
Wednesday: Getting Familiar with Reported Metrics   277
Thursday: Calculating ROI   278
Friday: Linking Google Analytics and Google AdWords Accounts   284

Week 22: Use AdWords Reports 285
Monday: Understanding AdWords Conversion Tracking   285
Tuesday: Installing Conversion Tracking Code   286
Wednesday and Thursday: AdWords Display Network Reports   289
Friday: Using the Dimensions Tab   291

Week 23: Use Google Analytics 295
Monday: Campaign Level Report and Clicks Tab   296
Tuesday: Campaign Tagging for Non-Google Networks   297
Wednesday: Drilling Down to Ad Groups and Using
Secondary Dimensions   301
Thursday and Friday: Very Useful Reports for Display   302

Week 24: Measure Branding and Positioning Goals 309
Monday: Dealing With Soft Metrics   309
Tuesday: Multiple Touch Point Analysis   312
Wednesday: Social Media Metrics—Traffic on Your Site   315
Thursday: Social Media Metrics—Activity Outside Your Site   321
Friday: Correlation and Causation   324

Chapter 10   Month 7: Optimizing the Performance of Your Campaigns   329

Week 25: Refine Your Campaigns and Ad Groups 330
Monday: Evaluating Performance   330
Tuesday: Optimizing Ads   334
Wednesday: Optimizing Placements   337
Thursday: Optimizing with Contextual Keywords   338
Friday: Optimizing Audiences   339

Week 26: Expand Your Reach 341
Monday: Expanding Reach with Ad Group Bids   341
Tuesday: Adjusting Keyword and Placement Level Bids   343
Wednesday: Adjusting Audience Bids   344
Thursday: Using Ad Planner to Find More Placements   345
Friday: Using Display Campaign Optimizer   350

Week 27: Test Your Ads 352
Monday: Understanding Ad Split Testing   352
Tuesday: Understanding Statistical Significance and Sample Size   353
Wednesday: Setting Up a Split Test   358
Thursday: Interpreting the Results and Tools   361
Friday: What Should I Test?   362

Week 28: Create Effective Landing Pages 365
Monday: Understanding What Makes a Good Landing
Page to Google   366
Tuesday: Understanding What Makes a Good Landing
Page to Your Visitor   367
Wednesday: The Importance of Dedicated Landing Pages   374
Thursday: A/B Split Testing   375
Friday: Multivariate Testing   376

Chapter 11   Month 8: Advanced Topics   379

Week 29: Retarget and Remarket 380
Monday: Understanding Retargeting   380
Tuesday: Using AdWords Remarketing   382
Wednesday: Creating Remarketing Lists   385
Thursday: Using Custom Combinations   388
Friday: Leveraging Remarketing Best Practices   390

Week 30: Learn Tools for Testing Landing Pages 394
Monday: Understanding Google Analytics Content Experiments   395
Tuesday: Set up a Google Analytics Content Experiment   396
Wednesday: Run a Content Experiment   399
Thursday: Reading Content Experiment Reports   401
Friday: Running a Test with Optimizely   404

Week 31: Go beyond Clickstream Analytics 411
Monday: Using Qualitative Feedback   412
Tuesday: Using Visual Analytics   416
Wednesday: Using Form Analytics   419
Thursday/Friday: Evaluating the User Experience   424

Week 32: Target Topics 427
Monday: Understanding Topic Targeting and When to Use It   428
Tuesday: Adding and Editing Topic Targets   429
Wednesday: Working with Ad Planner Codes   431
Thursday: Managing Topic Exclusions   432
Friday: Using Topic and Audience Targeting Reports   433

Chapter 12   Month 9: Using LinkedIn and Facebook Display Ads   437

Week 33: Advertise on LinkedIn 438
Monday: Understanding LinkedIn Advertising   438
Tuesday: Knowing When to Use LinkedIn Advertising   440
Wednesday: Working with LinkedIn Ad Formats   442
Thursday: Setting LinkedIn Targeting Options   445
Friday: Selecting LinkedIn Bidding and Budget Options   447

Week 34: Launch and Measure LinkedIn Campaigns 448
Monday: Launching Your LinkedIn Campaign   448
Tuesday: Using the LinkedIn Interface   452
Wednesday: Integrating with Google Analytics   455
Thursday: Optimizing LinkedIn Campaigns   458
Friday: Taking LinkedIn to the Next Level   460

Week 35: Advertise on Facebook 462
Monday: Understanding Facebook Advertising Destinations   462
Tuesday: When to Use Facebook Advertising   463
Wednesday: The Ad Format and Where it Shows   463
Thursday: Targeting Options   467
Friday: Setting Your Pricing and Choosing between CPC
and CPM   469

Week 36: Launch and Measure Facebook Campaigns 470
Monday: Launching Your Facebook Campaign   470
Tuesday: The Ads Manager   472
Wednesday: Facebook Insights Information   473
Thursday: Using the Power Editor   475
Friday: Integrating with Google Analytics   478

Glossary   483

Index   489

Foreword

I've been advertising online for well over a decade. I've written hundreds of articles, spent thousands of hours talking to companies about online marketing, and overseen more than a billion dollars in marketing spend with everyone from mom-n-pop shops to such brands as Red Lobster, YellowPages.com, and Encyclopedia Britannica.

Over the years, I've watched performance marketers dismiss display advertising as a too-expensive-time-wasting-useless inventory source. These marketers have made a mistake and missed one of the largest growth areas in effective online advertising that exists.

Years ago this was the correct decision—but not any longer.

When I started advertising online in 1998, banners were the preferred ad format. These banners were untargeted, overpriced, often quite ugly, and only bought by large companies who wanted to feel like they were participating in the new advertising revolution. They were ignored by those who wanted results, and unaffordable to those with small budgets.

A few years later, AdWords launched contextual targeting. Suddenly, you could choose a few words about your products and Google would place your ads next to website content that was based upon your keywords. The targeting was good, the idea was great, but the control was lousy.

Then Google finally understood that there was more inventory in display advertising than in search marketing. So, Google made their system transparent, took their brilliant search targeting and refined it for display advertising. This change rewrote the rules for how you can buy and manage display advertising.

Consider this: You can choose to serve an ad to someone who is viewing the New York Times Business section on their iPad, when the article is about stock brokers, it's a Monday morning, and the user is in Miami and has shown an interest in finance related content. While this example might result in little inventory, this is an unprecedented level of targeting that has never been seen before in marketing.

If you have a small budget, you can serve incredibly targeted ads to a small group of potential customers. If you have a large budget, you can redefine your 'branding campaigns' to be performance campaigns.

It requires a good teacher to take these complex subjects and break them down into understandable bits of information and then provide an action plan to make sure you can meet your display goals. Luckily, David Booth and Corey Koberg are good teachers.

I first met David when we were both teaching Google Seminars for Success, which are live training workshops that are actually endorsed by Google. It was during this time that I got to know David. I was really impressed at how well he can take the interwoven complexities of paid search and analytics, and then demonstrate how each piece fits together so anyone can understand and execute on these concepts.

Now, you can only take advantage of the new revolution in display advertising if you have both the knowledge and the time to accomplish your goals. That's what this book will give you: The knowledge of how to create successful display campaigns, and then the step-by-step, easy-to-understand action plan to implement, monitor, and optimize a successful display strategy.

In particular, Chapter 4 is invaluable because it lays out all of the possible goals of display advertising. There are many reasons to buy display ranging from direct response and brand positioning to site interaction. This chapter will help you determine what you should accomplish with display to ensure that you are ultimately successful in reaching your advertising goals.

The display revolution is happening right now—of the millions of dollars I'll oversee in marketing just this month, more will be spent in display than in search—and now with this book you have no excuse for not mastering the new rules of display marketing.

BRAD GEDDES
Founder, Certified Knowledge
Author, Advanced Google AdWords
Leader, AdWords Seminars for Success

Introduction

At training and speaking events, we're often asked if we recommend any good books for further study. For paid search, SEO, analytics, and even niches like form design, there exist many well-written volumes that we easily recommend. But we always draw a blank when it comes to display advertising—at the time of this writing, there simply aren't any.

That is somewhat shocking considering it's not new (display is the oldest form of online advertising) and it is one of the most visible and common forms of advertising in the world. It's so common that display ad impressions far outnumber search impressions, and Neal Mohan, VP of display at Google, expects display ad spend to soon exceed $200 billion annually (a 4x increase since 2010). That significant a rise in display ad activity means that it's not just for the big agencies and media buyers anymore, and there is a critical need to lay the foundation for successful display ad campaigns.

Historically, the advertising industry has not been self-serve: Businesses had to go through agencies and media desks to place any significant volume or gain a reasonable reach, but the rise of online advertising has drastically changed that model, and now businesses can reach global audiences directly in a very short time. This democratization of advertising has revolutionized the paid search arena, but the penetration on the display side has been far less prevalent. Display has remained largely the domain of large advertisers with big budgets and big agencies. We believe the new tools and technologies available today and those arriving in the near future will change that, allowing more advertisers to access and harness the power of display advertising. This book is intended to kick-start that journey.

Who Should Read This Book

While we hope this book will provide value for *anyone* interested in the topic, we do cater to certain audiences. Advanced display advertisers with large budgets and access to sophisticated real-time bidding and audience data tools will find our coverage of those topics brief at best. Instead, we wrote the book with the following groups in mind:

- Search marketers (agencies or businesses themselves) who are looking to expand beyond their paid search campaigns. Perhaps they have exhausted their audience there and are experiencing diminishing returns and thus looking to the display network to expand reach. Or perhaps an agency account manager is looking to grow the agency's advertising relationship beyond search and is interested in display as a logical and complementary next step or as a foray into branding and positioning initiatives. In many cases, we have drawn parallels and analogies to search advertisers to help ease this transition.

- Advertisers who are new to online altogether. Knowledge and experience with paid search is certainly not a prerequisite, and chapters are written so that no prior knowledge is assumed. This also includes job seekers or job switchers who are looking to educate themselves in preparation for the many career opportunities that an industry poised to grow to $200 billion and beyond will undoubtedly bring.

- Display advertisers who have previously used the medium only for branding or awareness purposes but are now interested in performance display. Many of the new tools and techniques discussed in this book are intended to pave the way for direct response advertisers to optimize for performance and deploy display ads profitably, while measurement strategies for more traditional branding and positioning objectives are also presented.

- Experienced display advertisers who are simply looking to fill gaps, reinforce their existing knowledge of the fundamentals, learn about new techniques and technologies, or simply hear another perspective.

What You Will Learn

Over the course of this book you will be introduced to the landscape and taken through the process of planning, building, launching, measuring, and optimizing your campaigns. We will take you step by step through specific examples using market-leading platforms such as Google (and YouTube), Facebook, and LinkedIn but always with an eye toward the bigger concepts that can be applied to any network or publisher you choose.

Core activities such as creating campaigns and image ads are covered in detail. Important, but somewhat tangential, topics such as landing page optimization and analytics are discussed, but they are by no means covered as comprehensively as in a book dedicated to those subjects.

A journey of a thousand miles begins with a single step, and our display ad journey is broken into 1-hour steps that will take about three months if taken one per day. However, those willing to put in the time can easily accelerate the schedule. While some "days" may take longer than one hour for large or complex campaigns, we also believe experienced advertisers may be able to accomplish some steps in less time, depending on their familiarity with the subject.

The book is designed such that you will get the most out of reading it all the way through in order, but each chapter also stands on its own to be used as a reference. When information discussed in previous chapters is required, we've tried to include references back to those earlier chapters.

The following is a quick summary of the chapters:

Chapter 1, "Online Advertising," provides an overview of online advertising, compares and contrasts search and display advertising, and discusses the advertising mindset it takes to be successful in this area.

Chapter 2, "Overview of Display Advertising," presents the landscape of display advertising, identifies the available ad types and formats, and discusses attribution and measurement of goals and objectives with respect to display ads.

Chapter 3, "Fundamental Display Advertising Concepts," discusses the relationship between advertisers and publishers, introduces the Google Network and its targeting strategies, and presents the overall process of display advertising.

Chapter 4, "Month 1: Planning Your Campaigns," starts with how to define your display ad goals and then discusses how to showcase what you do best, take stock of your resources, and plan your budget.

Chapter 5, "Month 2: Targeting Your Audience," covers some of the most critical concepts of the book, such as the available targeting options, how to select good contextual keywords, how to find good placements, and how to organize your campaigns and ad groups.

Chapter 6, "Month 3: Building Your First Display Campaign," is where we graduate from theory to practice and put your skills to use. Here you choose your campaign settings, bidding styles, and budgets and create your first ad group.

Chapter 7, "Month 4: Creating Image Ads," gets to the heart of any display campaign—the ads. This chapter covers best practices, editorial rules and guidelines, the process of building the ads, and some tools that can ease that process.

Chapter 8, "Month 5: Video Ads," dives into how display advertisers can take advantage of the exploding world of online video, via stand-alone click-to-play video ads as well as ads embedded in video sites on platforms like YouTube. We even discuss how to take those online videos and place them on traditional national television networks.

Chapter 9, "Month 6: Launch and Measure Your Campaign's Performance," brings us to that moment of truth when your campaigns have launched and it's time to evaluate performance using the various tools at your disposal.

Chapter 10, "Month 7: Optimizing the Performance of Your Campaigns," discusses how to optimize your campaigns by refining your ad groups, expanding your reach, running split tests, and improving your landing pages.

Chapter 11, "Month 8: Advanced Topics," takes you beyond the basics into topics such as retargeting and advanced testing and analysis tools that provide qualitative feedback, visual attention maps, form analytics, and other ways to gain insight around user experience.

Chapter 12, "Month 9: Using LinkedIn and Facebook Display Ads." applies the concepts and skills acquired previously on the more general networks and integrates them with the unique opportunities presented by display ads on social networks. Concepts, tactics, and best practices are presented for both Facebook and LinkedIn.

Keep Up-to-Date: The Companion Site

This industry is reinventing itself at a blistering pace. During the course of writing this book we've had to revise chapters several times because requirements changed, features were introduced, interfaces changed, and functionality was replaced or deprecated. Because change is constant, we know that certain parts of this book will become outdated over time, and we'll periodically post changes and updates on the companion site at www.DisplayAnHourADay.com.

How to Contact the Authors

We welcome feedback from you about this book or about books you'd like to see from us in the future, and we encourage you to reach out to us in the following ways:

Twitter: @davidabooth, @koberg

Google Plus: +Dave Booth, +Corey Koberg

Web: www.cardinalpath.com/contact/

For more information about what we're up to, please visit the Cardinal Path blog at www.cardinalpath.com/blog.

More information about further training opportunities in Google AdWords and Google Analytics is available at http://training.cardinalpath.com.

Readers of this book can claim a discount on many of the training programs offered by Cardinal Path by using the discount code *displaybook*.

Online Advertising

Today's world can perhaps be characterized by one thing above all others: that we as consumers are always online. As marketers, we are constantly presented with opportunities to get our message in front of the right kind of person at just the right time, and never before have we had this kind of ability to reach, target, and measure the reaction of audiences around the globe. Display advertising gives us the ability to widen our nets as advertisers and get our message out to more and more potential customers.

Chapter Contents:

An Overview of Search Engine Marketing

Search Advertising vs. Display Advertising

Problem Solving and Distraction

An Overview of Search Engine Marketing

Let's go ahead and admit it: At this point in history, we're in the middle of the digital age, and it's getting more and more difficult to find anyone clinging to the notion that the Internet is just a passing fad. This is no latest craze; it is indeed the new normal by which we live our connected lives in a connected world. The combination of ever-increasing accessibility to higher and higher speed connections and a constantly growing variety of web-enabled devices makes it just plain hard to find a place where you can't be online.

It wasn't more than a few years ago when airlines were sending out email announcements to their frequent fliers saying, "We're proud to announce Internet access in some of our airplanes!" In a completely opposite reaction than what we're sure those nice marketing folks had in mind, many of us immediately pledged to avoid those airlines at all costs. An altitude of 30,000 feet was the last remaining place on earth that a person still wasn't expected to be online, and there were more than a few of us that weren't going to book a Wi-Fi enabled flight and risk those few precious hours of freedom from the digital leash.

Times are changing, and the point is, we're now online all the time. And what are we doing? Well, as it turns out, young or old, you're probably checking your email more than anything else—at least, according to the Pew Internet & American Life Project.

Source: http://pewinternet.org/Infographics/2010/Generations-2010-Summary.aspx

These days, if when we end up on a flight that *doesn't* have Internet access, we start to exhibit signs of what we're pretty sure is clinical withdrawal after about an hour, and by the time the plane is in its descent, passengers throughout the plane are looking out the window, clutching with shaking hands a phone with a screen so big it barely fits in their pocket, desperately scanning the approaching horizon for cell towers close enough to connect to that 4G network well before the flight attendant announces that it's safe to return from the land of airplane mode. Take a look around on *your* next flight and see if you don't have a plane full of passengers with their Blackberries, Androids, and iSomethings out, downloading the last hours of life as we know it before the wheels hit the runway.

But second to email, we go online to search for something. Search engines have become our gateway to the vast and ever expanding list of things we do on the Web. It's how we keep up with our news and how we do our banking. It's how we're entertained by everything from games and 30-second videos to the latest record label-less sensation or a rant against a nameless fan of the rival team on a sports forum. It's how we shop for everything from books and televisions to groceries and cars. It's how we annoy a new generation of doctors by self-diagnosing long before we've made it to the waiting room. It's how we book our flights and choose hotels in the places we've already decided to visit based upon the reviews of thousands of other consumers. It's how we learn. It's how we share our lives among our closest 10,000 friends. And for a rapidly growing number of us, it's even how we get our work done, collaborating in real time on the latest sales numbers spreadsheet, scheduling that next meeting, or walking through the latest presentation. Sound like most of your day? Well, in the world in which we now live, that just makes you "normal."

Search Engine Marketing

Now, put on your marketing hat. If people are using the Internet to do all of these things all day long, then wouldn't it be great to get your marketing message in front of all those eyeballs? Wouldn't it be wonderful to bombard those impressionable minds with happy thoughts of your products and services at every turn?

Let's pretend for a moment that you're a loving husband to a very pregnant wife, and let's also pretend that it's 3 o'clock in the morning on a Tuesday. It's right about this time that you're made aware of an uncontrollable urge for dill pickles and chocolate ice cream, neither of which exists anywhere in the house. Being this loving husband, you realize that at this moment, you exist in this world for one single purpose: You must go out into the night and return with dill pickles and chocolate ice cream.

So you wipe the sleep from your eyes, find some pants and a pair of shoes, and find your way to the car and out into the streets. Then, you see the most perfect, unexpected, situation-saving billboard that has ever crossed your field of vision (Figure 1.1).

Figure 1.1 Billboard advertisement for dill pickles and chocolate ice cream

You pull off at the exit, walk into the Dill Pickle and Chocolate Ice Cream SuperStore, and walk out a hero. Consider the day saved.

Now, when you wake up a few hours later and head to the office of the travel agency where you happen to be the marketing manager, you're so impressed by the billboard that you drive by it again and write down the phone number of the billboard provider. You call the number, and you ask about this magical advertising product that they seem to be offering, and you're told that you can have one of these too.

"We can place your billboard on some very special roads—roads that allow *only* cars that contain people who have demonstrated an active interest in booking a vacation."

"Uh, you can *what*?"

It sounds too good to be true, doesn't it? But this is what search engine marketing has allowed us to do as marketers. We can put up our billboard anywhere on the Information Superhighway in front of eyeballs that have demonstrated their interest in our products and services. If someone goes to Google and does a search for "buy dill pickles chocolate ice cream," then we have a pretty good idea that they may be interested in what we sell if we happen to own the Dill Pickle and Chocolate Ice Cream SuperStore, so we stick our billboard up there. If someone is watching videos on how to cook lasagna and you sell pasta sauce, that's where you want your billboard. When people head over to the big screen TV buyers guide blog, well, if you sell big screen TVs, that's not a bad spot for your billboard.

In a virtual world, we can constantly adapt with minimal time, money, and resources, changing our billboard and changing the locations we put it up to find the optimal audience and the optimal messaging presented at the optimal time. And we can do this because the best part about digital advertising is the amount of data that's being collected every millisecond of every minute of every day.

Pay per Click Advertising

Now let's take this one step further. As advertisers, we can create all these billboards and put them in front of only people who have demonstrated their interest in what we're selling, but how much is this going to cost?

One of the most powerful features of online advertising is the different bidding options and cost models that are available. Depending upon your advertising goals and your budget targets, you have a few options to choose from when it comes to paying for your magic billboards, and the best part about this is the control you're given.

Cost per Click

In a pure cost per click (CPC, often referred to as pay per click, or PPC) model, you won't pay a penny unless someone actually clicks your ad. That's right. It doesn't cost you a thing to stick your billboard up in front of your target audience—you pay *only* if that set of eyeballs actually demonstrates an interest in what you're selling by clicking your ad. Try calling up your local newspaper and telling them you'd like to run an ad but you'll pay them only if people walk into your store as a direct result. Suddenly it seems pretty clear why traditional advertising media providers are struggling lately.

While Google did not invent the concept of PPC, its AdWords product has been the largest beneficiary of it: By the end of 2011, Google had already crossed into double-digit *billions* of dollars in revenue *per quarter*, the vast majority of it being made click by click. It has been so successful because for most advertisers, the model just plain works.

What's known as the Google Display Network comprises an enormous number of sites that reach over 80 percent of the world's Internet users, and that's a lot of real estate for putting up your billboards. Now, add that to targeting options that allow you to stick your ads only in relevant places, and toss in the fact that you only have to pay if someone explicitly registers interest in your ad. Last, throw in measurement capabilities that can measure ROI in near real time and tell you whether your advertising goals are being met or not.

It's no mystery why this works, and as a result advertisers are more than happy to be buying up display inventory month in and month out, shifting more and more resources from traditional media to the online space year after year.

Cost per Thousand Impressions

But if the CPC route isn't for you, and especially if you have more traditional branding or positioning goals, don't worry, there's a bidding model in the online world that offers you another alternative. Cost per thousand impressions, or CPM (which actually stands for cost per mille) allows advertisers to pay for the impression of an ad without regard for whether or not that ad draws a click.

If you're promoting a new movie that's coming out in a few weeks and your goal is to make sure that every non–cave dweller on the planet knows about it, you would do well to use a CPM model and control your costs by paying every time your ad is shown. If you were to run a campaign with a CPM of $10.00, for example, you would be paying 1 penny every time your ad appears ($10.00 / 1,000 = $0.01).

While CPM bidding is commonplace when purchasing premium display advertising inventory and third party audience data, for most advertisers it is typically not recommended for direct response campaigns, or campaigns where the marketing goal is to get a user to do something in response to having seen your ad. What we're trying to do with CPM bidding is get as many eyeballs as we possibly can on the ad itself. Remember, it's possible with CPM bidding that you'll spend all your money without a single click and not a single visitor to your website.

Cost per Acquisition

One of the newer and more exciting bidding options available to search marketers is cost per acquisition (CPA). If you have a direct response type of conversion, meaning you want something tangible and measurable to happen as a direct result of your advertising, then you may want to look at CPA bidding.

As an example, let's say you have an online store, and on average you make $10.00 profit from everyone who purchases from you. The purchase itself is your *conversion*, and you are willing to pay up to $9.99 for a conversion to stay profitable. Well, in a CPA model, you don't bid for clicks or impressions—now you're bidding for those conversions.

Google AdWords currently offers tools like the Conversion Optimizer and the Display Campaign Optimizer that will evaluate dozens of factors as your ads are displayed across a variety of web properties to a variety of users. The system begins to learn which types of users, which times of day, which language settings, and even which browsers and operating systems have a high probability of resulting in a conversion action, and the system then uses this information and tries to get as many conversions as it can for you based on your CPA bid.

Search Advertising vs. Display Advertising

Whichever way you choose to pay for it, if you're going to do online advertising, one of the most important decisions you're going to have to make is how to allocate your marketing dollars across search and display advertising.

Search Advertising

By now, search advertising is both sophisticated and mature, and it has been used very successfully by a lot of people for a lot of years. At its core, what we're talking about here is someone typing something (their search query) into some kind of search engine and receiving results containing relevant items. Mixed in with those results are advertisements, also triggered by their relevance to what that searcher is looking for.

Perhaps the most important concept to understand with search advertising is that we have *active users* who are essentially *exposing their intent*. This is not someone flipping through a magazine and possibly noticing the ads that are mixed in with the content they're casually browsing. Here, we've got laser-focused people who are actively looking for something—something that is currently at the forefront of their mind. When Sally goes to Google and types "indian restaurant san francisco," Sally is sharing her intent. Sally is actively looking for an Indian restaurant in San Francisco, right at this very moment. And if you as an advertiser happen to own an Indian restaurant in San Francisco, you can get your *extremely relevant* ad in front of Sally at *exactly the time* she's looking for a solution to her current problem: finding a good Indian restaurant to go to.

Contrast this with traditional advertising. Let's say that as the owner of this San Francisco–based Indian restaurant, you want to advertise in a San Francisco–based newspaper, and you specify that you want your ad to show up in the Food & Dining section. At this point, you've targeted this ad just about as much as you can, and in trying to find relevant potential consumers, you've been able to narrow it down to (mostly) people in the San Francisco area who have at least some expressed interest in food and dining out.

But what is the real intent of someone browsing the Food & Dining section of a San Francisco newspaper? Really, we have no idea. They might be attempting to waste some time on a bus ride or they may be interested in learning about a new recipe, but the probability that someone is looking for a local Indian restaurant to eat in is pretty low. And you as an advertiser are essentially paying for all of those people to see your ad whether they have any interest in you—or whether they even *see* your ad—or not.

Search advertising addresses this limitation by letting advertisers bid on the keywords that match the search queries people are typing in. So, when Sally searches for "san francisco indian food," she might see something like the search results page shown in Figure 1.2.

Figure 1.2 Google search results page for "san francisco indian food"

Here, advertisers are offering Sally coupons on Indian food, Indian food delivery, discounts, and even directions to Indian restaurants. Sally was targeted and shown ads based on the search query she entered into Google at the very moment she entered it.

Google Search and Display Networks

The focus of this book is display advertising and specifically, accessing the Google Display Network through Google AdWords. But this is just one of the advertising networks that Google offers, and it's important to distinguish between them. Google AdWords allows you to place your ads across the entire Google Network, which consists of two parts: the Search Network and the Display Network (this used to be known as the Content Network).

Google Search and Search Partners Networks

For all practical purposes, you can think of any site that requires you to type something into a search box to find what you're looking for to be part of the Search Network. Google.com is the easiest example: You type in "san francisco indian food" and Google gives you back results and ads. But there are many others as well. The Google Search and Search Partners Networks also include sites like Google Maps, Google Product Search, and Google Groups as well as non-Google properties like Virgin Media, AOL. com, and RoadRunner that use Google to return search results. Basically, as you can see in Figure 1.3, we're talking about any kind of search that's on a Google property or is powered by or enhanced by Google and requires users to type in what they're looking for and click the search button.

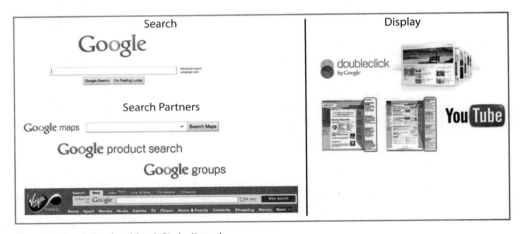

Figure 1.3 Google Search and Google Display Networks

The important part about the Search Network is that as advertisers, we're targeting potential customers by the keywords they type in. If Sally goes to Google Maps and does a search for "san francisco restaurant," advertisers targeting that keyword phrase or variations of it can bid to have their ad show up. When Sally goes over to Google Groups and looks for forums and postings by searching on "san francisco restaurant," she'll find sponsored links that were triggered by the keyword bids on the search query she typed in.

Google Display Network

The Google Display Network, or the GDN as it's commonly known, is quite a bit different. The first thing to note is that it is enormous. The GDN encompasses over two million web properties, has over half a billion users, and serves up hundreds of billions of page views every month. The GDN gives you, as an advertiser, the ability to place all kinds of ads, including text, image, video, and rich media, on virtually any kind of site you can imagine. Of course, the GDN includes many Google properties, but its real reach lies in the non-Google partners. From news sites to blogs, video sites to forums, social networks to your favorite shopping sites, weather sites, sports sites, review sites, article sites, reference sites, movie sites, and anything-else-you-can-think-of sites, the GDN has you covered.

We'll talk more about the specifics of where you can advertise a bit later in this book, but for now, the key point to remember is that with display advertising, *we're no longer responding directly to a search that our audience has just performed.*

Display Advertising

So right about now, you're probably thinking, "Wait a minute—I thought you just said the best part about online marketing is that the searchers type in exactly what they want and you can then give them what they want right when they want it. How is this going to work if users aren't typing in anything anymore?"

Well, in short, you're right. Display advertising is a very different animal from search advertising, but it also offers some incredible opportunities to us as advertisers. If you think about it, even though we use search to find just about every bit of content we're looking for, the amount of *time* we spend on search engines is actually very short. This is in part a testament to just how good search engines have gotten at figuring out what we're looking for, but also an indication of what we're *really* doing online.

Once we've done our search, we spend our time consuming the content that we just found. We do a search for "taco salad recipe" and in a fraction of a second we're given millions of options to choose from. We spend a few seconds looking through them, click on a couple, and in a very short period of time we've landed on a page with a recipe we're going to read, maybe print out, and eventually follow in the comfort of our kitchen. We end up spending a lot more time on the actual content we were searching for than we do on the searching itself, and if you don't get them to click your ad in the few seconds they spend scanning the search results page, you've lost your chance if you're not leveraging display in your marketing mix.

Extend Your Reach

You might want to think of the Display Network as a way to expand the size of the lake you're fishing in for potential customers. Now don't get us wrong; search advertising is fantastic, but one of its drawbacks is that we're somewhat limited in our "fishing grounds." We're trying to find prospective customers in the instances where they're actively searching, and that's it. This is the little pond in the city park that's regularly stocked with fish. It's where grandparents take their grandkids to make absolutely sure that something will be caught inside of a short attention span.

Just as in that city park pond, you very likely find keywords that are sure to get you the right kind of customer, but at some point, you reach diminishing returns. There just aren't any more keywords that you can profitably bid on, and it's time to look for a bigger pond.

The Display Network gives you this opportunity in the form of those millions of websites that people are *spending their time on* after they've searched. Now you're trawling the ocean. Sure, the fish are tougher to find, and there's a lot of stuff you might catch in your net that you just want to throw back, but you've now got access to all the fish in the sea.

And just as when you're fishing in the ocean, the GDN gives you lots of tools to refine what it is you're catching. On the boat, you can change your bait, swap out your nets, use different lines, move to different areas, and these days you can even get data about what's below you before you drop your first line. With platforms like Google AdWords, you can control where you're fishing, both geographically and contextually; you can change the messaging, format, and type of advertisements you're running; and you can leverage an enormous amount of data around the oceans you choose to fish in.

Another key item to keep in mind is that while we do use search a lot, there's a lot we do online *without* a search engine. For example, many of us have favorite news sources, magazines, blogs, forums, and social networks that we manage to find on a regular basis without the help of Bing or the big G. And in many cases, we're not looking for anything in particular anyway. People who go to the online version of the *New York Times* (NYTimes.com) for their daily news aren't using a search engine to get there. They've got it bookmarked and memorized. And they weren't looking for something specific— their intent in going to this news source is in large part to be told what's important and what's worth reading about. Just as we all have our favorite magazines, television channels, newspapers, catalogs, radio programs, and more in the offline world, we regularly consume content that fits our interests in the online world, and these are the kinds of opportunities available in the ocean that you just won't find in the city park pond.

If you can use search and display *together*, you get the best of both worlds. Now you're fishing in the little pond where you can find all those easy targets and take advantage of the active searchers giving away their intent, but you've also got boats out there finding more and more fish in the open ocean as well. Keep in mind that this is also one of those situations in which the sum of the parts is going to be greater than the whole. While more difficult to measure, display advertising can achieve branding and positioning goals that enhance the likelihood of your drawing that click from a search campaign when the user is finally ready to have you fulfill a need with your products and services. If you really stop to think about it, odds are good that this has happened to you at one point or another. You did a search to find something you wanted to buy, and when you had to decide which link on that page to click, you clicked one that you recognized, one you had heard of. And that recognition was very likely the result of a branding campaign that included display advertising.

Diversify Your Message

We haven't explicitly said it quite yet, but the obvious big advantage of display advertising is that you're not limited to the constrictions of text-based ads that dominate the search advertising landscape. Many of the places where search-targeted ads show up, including Google.com searches, don't let you use anything except your headline, two lines of copy, and a display URL in your ad. You get the same font, font size, and font color as everyone else, and the only control you get of your message is limited to 25 or 35 characters per line. Display advertising opens up a whole new realm of possibilities because although there are some restrictions on the file size, format, dimensions, and some editorial constraints, you can use all that creativity and take the handcuffs off of the marketing department now.

You can use imagery to connect with your audience, and you can use as much text as you can reasonably stand to fit in the space of your ad. You can use buttons and unique calls to action in your designs, and you can use animations and even video. And rich media allow advertisers to create interactivity inside the ad itself. You can leverage mobile ad formats to "talk" to your potential customers on the go or run a variety of video ad formats with creative built expressly for the medium on which it's being served.

All of these options help you convey your marketing message to the right audience in the ways you wish to convey it, giving you back much of the flexibility and richness of traditional media you don't get to take advantage of on the search advertising side.

How Display Ads Are Targeted

So back to our original question about display advertising: If we're not showing people ads based on what they type into search engines, then how are we targeting them? Well, a lot of the targeting options available with search advertising do carry over to the display side. For example, we can choose certain geographies to target or specific devices like mobile phones or tablets. But over and above the basics, there are three ways platforms like AdWords allow us to target our potential customers.

Google AdWords Targeting Options

First, we can use keywords. This time, though, we're not using keywords in the sense that users are typing them in, but in the sense that they can describe the types of pages we'd like our ads to show up on. Within Google AdWords, this has come to be known as *contextual targeting.* Those keywords can then be used to match pages on the Web that share that same context and are then deemed relevant to our display advertising campaigns. The technology that Google uses for its search engine is pretty good at figuring out what every page on the Internet is about and then returning those pages based on the search queries users type in. That same technology is used in contextual targeting on the GDN, and in early 2012, a significant improvement to this capability was released. Continuing with our example of Indian restaurants in San Francisco, if we want our display ads to show on websites that are contextually relevant to Indian food, we may target keywords like "indian food" and "healthy indian food" and "indian food calories" and "indian food blogs." These are quite different from the keywords I might be bidding on in a search campaign, and it's because I'm trying to tell Google AdWords what kind of websites I'd like my ad to show up on, *not* what user search queries I want to respond to.

The second way we can target users in the Display Network is by choosing the websites, the pages on those sites, and even the ad slots on those pages that we want our ad to show up on. These potential locations where our ads can show are known as *placements*, and we have the ability to research and specify the locations where we'd like to place our ads. In our example, instead of providing keywords as we do with contextual targeting, we can scour the Web for websites and placements that we'd like our ads to show up on and explicitly tell Google where we'd like to advertise. If this sounds like a daunting task, that's because it is. While there may be lots and lots of websites you already know about, there are many more you've never heard of before. Tools that we'll talk about later on in this book, like the DoubleClick Ad Planner, can help you to find those placements and also quickly see what kinds of advertising those sites accept. And don't forget about another powerful feature we can take advantage of as advertisers: *exclusions*. Just as we can choose which placements we *do* want to target, we can also choose which placements we *don't* want our ads showing up on.

The third way we can target on the Google Display Network is by defining specific audiences. Essentially, cookies are used to track users anonymously as they traverse the Web, and these usage patterns can help determine the kinds of categories users are interested in as well as keep track of users who visit key pages that we as advertisers identify. For example, if you as an advertiser want to target dining enthusiasts, you can choose to show your ads not based on keywords or based on the sites you think these people will visit, but to anyone, anywhere, whose usage pattern has identified them as a member of the dining enthusiasts audience. And you can get even more specific than that: AdWords allows you to create your own audiences based on things that users do on the pages of your website. For example, as that restaurant owner, we can place a snippet of code on our menu page. That code identifies that user as having seen our menu, and signs them up for a custom audience that we've just defined of people who have seen our menu. Now, wherever that person goes, and regardless of what website they're on, they can see our ad based simply on the fact that they are part of an audience we created we know has demonstrated an interest in our restaurant.

It's worth noting that there is a fourth targeting option within Google AdWords known as Topic targeting, and as it is typically best used to refine other types of targeting, we'll be discussing this in its own section a bit later in the book.

While we're focusing on the Google Display Network in this book, it's also important to understand that there are many other ad networks and many other ways to target display advertising to potential customers. Facebook, for example, offers advertisers the ability to target users based on demographic and psychographic information and even behaviors and personal information. If we want to show our ads on Facebook to 20-something college graduates in a certain city who have demonstrated an interest in food on their birthdays, we can do that through the Facebook platform. Over on LinkedIn, we can target our audience based on not just things like gender, age, and geographic location, but also by job titles, industries, and even specific companies that people work for.

Problem Solving and Distraction

Regardless of the targeting options we use, the ad types we create, the messaging we employ, or the networks we choose to leverage, our end goal as advertisers is still the same, and it comes all the way back to the first day of Marketing 101. As marketers, we don't sell products and we don't sell services. We sell *solutions* to the *problems* that people have.

Display advertising gives us a medium by which we can connect with our potential customers on the problems that we can help them solve, and this solution is what they'll ultimately see value in and trade their hard-earned money for.

Every day, we're under attack from advertisers at every turn. From the moment we wake up each morning to the moment we go to bed, we're being barraged with marketing messages. We hear ads on the radio, we see them on TV, and we drive past them on the freeway. Ads fill more pages of newspapers and magazines than the stories do, and even public restrooms are now selling ad space.

SOURCE: MAD MEDIA INC.,
www.alloverchicago.com

Figure 1.4 Advertisements running in a restroom

The result of this constant assault on consumers is that consumers have built up a wall to protect themselves; they've put together a defense. Way back in 1885, Thomas

Smith authored a guide called *Successful Advertising* and postulated that a consumer needs to be exposed to an ad 20 times before it leads to a purchase:

The first time a man looks at an ad, he doesn't see it.
The second time, he doesn't notice it.
The third time, he is conscious of its existence.
The fourth time, he faintly remembers having seen it.
The fifth time, he reads the ad.
The sixth time, he turns up his nose at it.
The seventh time, he reads it through and says, "Oh brother!"
The eighth time, he says, "Here's that confounded thing again!"
The ninth time, he wonders if it amounts to anything.
The tenth time, he will ask his neighbor if he has tried it.
The eleventh time, he wonders how the advertiser makes it pay.
The twelfth time, he thinks it must be a good thing.
The thirteenth time, he thinks it might be worth something.
The fourteenth time, he remembers that he wanted such a thing for a long time.
The fifteenth time, he is tantalized because he cannot afford to buy it.
The sixteenth time, he thinks he will buy it someday.
The seventeenth time, he makes a memorandum of it.
The eighteenth time, he swears at his poverty.
The nineteenth time, he counts his money carefully.
The twentieth time he sees the ad, he buys the article or instructs his wife to do so.
Source: Thomas Smith, *Successful Advertising*, 7th edn, 1885

And if 20 sounds a bit too high to you, there's also the commonly accepted Rule of Seven in traditional advertising, presenting a little lower threshold for exposure before action is taken. Either way, we've got our work cut out for us, and this same concept is true in the online world as well. In 1998, Jan Panero Benway and David M. Lane described the phenomenon of banner blindness that they found in their experiments, which makes it even more difficult for advertisers to get their ads noticed.

Source: www.internettg.org/newsletter/dec98/banner_blindness.html

So when we place our ads on websites around the Internet, our job is not only to attract attention from the right kind of potential customer, but to do that by *distracting* users from whatever content they're consuming at the moment. One of the most effective ways we can do this is by connecting with users on a cognitive level, recognizing their problem and then *showing* them how we can help them solve it. Let's finish this chapter with one small example as to how that might happen (see the sidebar "The Art of Distraction and Problem Solving").

The Art of Distraction and Problem Solving

Bob's Bad Day

Bob is having a rough Tuesday. He's walking back to his desk after yet another disastrous meeting, and he's about to hear from on high about how his department missed its targets yet again. Bob can already hear his boss saying, "Well Bob, the success or failure of this group is on your shoulders, and that's going to be what's looked at when it comes to your bonus."

Bob sighs and drops into the chair in which he spends the majority of his life lately and looks at the calendar on his cubicle wall. No relief there either—there's not a holiday in sight. Bob logs in, and feeling particularly unmotivated, he opens his favorite browser and all hope of productivity for the rest of the day is now officially out the window.

First stop: Check what's going on in the world. Bob knows he's going to need to have something to talk about at that dinner party this weekend, so current events it is. He opens a page and starts reading about the latest world conflict and glances briefly at a picture of a white sand beach with happy people sipping drinks. "Man, that would be nice," he chuckles to himself, and keeps on reading.

After he's armed himself with some conversation material, Bob heads over to a handful of job sites. He logs in to a couple of his accounts and polishes up that resume, then starts looking for other ways to spend the majority of his waking hours from here to retirement. He's reading a job posting when he notices another one of those ads, this time with a picture of a pool the size of a football field and a pair of snorkelers exploring some crystal clear Caribbean waters. "Well, I do have some vacation time built up," Bob thinks. "I wonder what that place is all about…" and Bob clicks the ad.

Solving Bob's Real Problem

As an advertiser, Breezes Resorts has successfully distracted Bob from the content he's working on and achieved a new visitor to its website. We've had the pleasure of working with Breezes as one of our clients for a number of years, and this kind of story is in many ways the holy grail of what we want to have happen in a display campaign. Of course we target the travel sites and people who demonstrate an interest in vacations. And we're constantly on the prowl for placements on the most relevant Caribbean tourism pages, but we also take advantage of other, more-subtle opportunities that allow us to show potential customers a way to solve their problems that they didn't even realize existed!

Continues

The Art of Distraction and Problem Solving *(Continued)*

Remember, as visitors to a website, we're trained to recognize and ignore advertising. That means your message needs to not only attract, it needs to *distract* from the content the visitor came for, and we need to dig deep into visitors' minds and appeal to the underlying problems that we can help them solve.

The bottom line here is that Bob needs a vacation. Yes, he's looking at news sites to help him get through his dinner party weekends, and yes, he's trying to find a new job to make his life a little easier. But a week on the beach is a solution to the underlying issue that Bob is facing—the poor guy just needs a break.

As you read this book, and as you learn about the ways we can target people with display advertising and the places we can show our ads, be thinking about opportunities for distraction. Always ask yourself, "How can I get Bob or Sally to stop what they're doing and pay attention to how I can solve their problems?"

Overview of Display Advertising

2

While the world of display advertising can be incredibly complex, it doesn't have to be. The everyday advertiser can use a number of different platforms to purchase display ads on a host of publisher websites in formats ranging from text and images to video and rich media. And the best part about advertising online is accountability. Whether you have direct response goals for your campaigns or branding and positioning objectives, the amount of data that we can analyze is astounding, and at the end of the day, we can measure the success or failure of the marketing dollars we're spending.

Chapter Contents:

The Display Advertising Landscape
Identifying Display Ad Types and Formats
Defining Advertising Objectives

The Display Advertising Landscape

When it comes to placing your display ads around the Internet, clearly you've got options as an advertiser. And within the murky intricacies of a convoluted ecosystem that links together advertisers, agencies, publishers, data providers, and middlemen, there are quite a few options out there that everyday advertisers can take advantage of.

Of course, there's the Google Display Network, which we discuss in greater detail later in this chapter. But beyond that, display ads can be bought and targeted by just about anyone through a number of other networks and services. The following are just a few of the most prevalent options to which everyday advertisers have access.

Facebook This social networking giant is actually the #1 player in the display advertising industry by revenue, pulling in over $2 billion a year and allowing advertisers access to roughly 700 million users. The real power of Facebook advertising lies in the amount of consumer data people provide on a daily basis. The current level of targeting is exciting, but what will almost certainly become available in the future represents an incredible opportunity.

Yahoo! Still a top 3 player in the display arena, and for advertisers spending more than $10 thousand per month, Yahoo! offers everything from banner ads to rich media and formats ranging from mobile to video along with sophisticated targeting options including retargeting and behavioral. Advertisers can also take advantage of some unique custom solutions on popular web properties, including brand-building full page takeovers and even Yahoo! home page opportunities. Most recently, Yahoo! has teamed up with Microsoft and AOL to cross-sell each other's display inventory, providing some competition to Google and Facebook.

Microsoft Advertising In 2007, Microsoft dropped $6 billion on the acquisition of aQuantive, Inc., primarily for the latter's Atlas ad exchange platform, which competes with Google's DoubleClick. More recently, partnerships with demand-side platforms like AppNexus and MediaMath have bolstered their display offerings from a targeting perspective, and at this point Microsoft is the fourth largest player in the market behind Facebook, Google, and Yahoo!. Advertisers spending more than $2 thousand per month can leverage image, rich media, video, and mobile formats across the Microsoft Media Network, which reaches an estimated two-thirds of the US online population (source: comScore Media Metrix, March 2011).

LinkedIn Targeted toward the business to business (B2B) space, LinkedIn allows advertisers to leverage the professional network that includes more than 150 million members with a handful of display ad formats, text formats, and even home page takeovers. Targeting options are tailored to professional profiles, allowing advertisers to select audiences based on job titles and functions, industries, demographic information, and even company names.

Advertising.com Picked up by AOL in 2004, Advertising.com offers display solutions that can be managed through its Ad Desk platform. Advertisers can reach popular AOL properties along with thousands of other publishers like MapQuest, MovieFone, Rhapsody, and *USA Today* through this ad network. Ad Desk allows for geotargeting and behavioral and site-level/inventory targeting and lets advertisers bid by impressions, clicks, and conversions.

ValueClick Media Another option worth mentioning is ValueClick, the owner of the affiliate marketing giant Commission Junction. This platform allows advertisers to target audiences by over 750 million consumer profiles worth of online behavioral data taken from product and comparison-shopping searches or transactions via large affiliate networks. The network itself encompasses just under 9,000 sites and reaches over three-fourths of the US Internet audience with standard Interactive Advertising Bureau (IAB) ad units, rich media, and video formats.

Retargeting solutions A number of retargeting solutions like AdRoll, Chango, Criteo, Fetchback, Magnetic, ReTargeter, Simpli.fi, and more allow access to additional inventory and the ability to retarget potential customers based on the actions that they take. For example, if a consumer does a search for a particular product or places an item in the shopping cart and then decides not to purchase, an advertiser can "retarget" that shopper and offer them a coupon for the particular item they were interested in or that they *almost* bought. While most of the major networks also offer this technology, advertisers can reach additional ad networks and get additional targeting features through these third-party solutions.

Why We Focus on the Google Display Network

If one thing is certain, it's that there are a *lot* of options out there, and we haven't even touched on the details of the current ecosystem (this is something we devote an entire section of the next chapter to). The companies and players between the advertiser and the publisher abound, and they handle everything from demand to data sourcing and from supply to the dynamic brokering of the display of an ad for a price in fractions of a second.

But here's the good news: You don't even have to read that part of this book to be successful in your display advertising campaigns. While you can certainly take a trip down the rabbit hole and dive into the ever-changing and intricate details of the products, services, networks, and technologies that drive today's display advertising ecosystem, the truth is that most advertisers probably won't want to. One of the great successes of the Google Display Network, affectionately known as the GDN, is that it has allowed advertisers to target and place their ads on *millions* of websites around the globe quickly and effectively from a single, simple, clear, and measurable platform.

The GDN shields us from the inner workings of how our ads end up on the pages that they do but at the same time provides many of the rich features we need and exposes just about all the data we could care to analyze. While it's true that you can be up and running with Google AdWords in just 5 minutes, it's also true that you can spend countless hours poring over help files and books like this one or days sitting in seminars and training and you'll still have more to do. The GDN has brought the power of display advertising into reach for just about any advertiser and has maintained many of the advanced components for those that want them.

So while Google AdWords is certainly not the only place to buy display ads these days (we cover a handful of other platforms in later chapters), the GDN is the focus of this book for quite a few reasons.

The Three Rs

Google articulates the value proposition of AdWords with the three Rs: reach, relevance, and ROI. The GDN, while just one part of the AdWords platform, exemplifies these benefits quite well. Let's take a look at what makes the Google Display Network one of the most accessible, powerful, and accountable single platforms available to advertisers today.

Reach

There is simply no other ad network that has the reach of Google AdWords: This network is so big that you can get your ads in front of more than 80 percent of the entire Internet-using world through it. Every month, over 500 million users are served literally hundreds of billions of ads. It's just plain difficult to browse the Web these days and not see "Ads by Google."

How does Google do it? Well, the Google Display Network sources its inventory of locations to show your ads from a few different places: YouTube, AdSense, and the DoubleClick Ad Exchange.

AdSense

AdSense is actually the most prevalent source of inventory for the Google Display Network, and it's also another Google program. Basically, if you own online content—content that can range from websites and blogs to mobile, video, and even online games—then you can make some space available on your pages and let Google serve ads in those spaces, taking a cut of the advertising spend in return. As a web publisher, you can determine what kinds of ads you want to show on your site and in what formats and sizes. Google figures out how to best fill those ad slots with ads from advertisers that are looking for content like yours or audiences like your visitors. So, if you run a blog all about hiking and the outdoors, through the AdSense program, you can be serving ads for advertisers wanting to reach that kind of audience.

DoubleClick Ad Exchange

The DoubleClick Ad Exchange is essentially a very large online marketplace that brings advertisers and web publishers together to buy and sell display advertisements. The Ad Exchange is a real-time auction that allows advertisers to bid for every impression available in the ad spaces across the large network of publishers and includes some very desirable ad inventory.

DoubleClick is now a subsidiary of Google after its 2008 acquisition, and as of 2009, advertisers can access the inventory in the Ad Exchange directly through the Google AdWords interface.

Relevance

Not only does the Google platform afford access to such a wide variety of sites, it also allows advertisers to specifically target the *right kind* of visitor to all of these sites, putting *relevant* ads in front of those targeted eyeballs. We dive into each of the targeting options available in the Google Display Network in much more detail a bit later, but there are essentially four ways that Google lets advertisers specify where they'd like their ads to show up.

Contextual Targeting

Contextual targeting works by taking advantage of the extremely effective technology that Google has developed for its search engine to figure out what a web page is all about. When you do a Google search, Google is able to tell you in less than a second which of the billions of pages out there are the most relevant to whatever you just typed in. It uses the same sort of system to match advertisers with web pages across the Internet.

As an advertiser, you might choose to target websites that are contextually relevant to certain keywords. When you enter these keywords into your ad group, Google finds sites that match your context, and those are the sites on which your ads show up.

Placement Targeting

Placements are really nothing more than ad spaces on specific pages that are available to you. There are two types of placement targeting options when you're using the Google Display Network:

- Automatic placements are ones that Google chooses for you, based on any other kind of targeting you've chosen to use. Here, you're letting Google choose from its wide array of inventory and show your ad wherever it sees fit.
- Managed placements are ones that you, well, manage. Instead of letting Google choose, you can identify and select each place on the Web where you'd like your ad to show.

There's one more type of placement, known as an exclusion, that we discuss a bit later. Excluded placements are those places on the Web where you *don't* want your ad to show, and you can specify these within the AdWords interface as well.

Audience Targeting

Audience targeting is the most recent of the targeting options on the GDN, and it allows advertisers to shift the targeting from the website to the actual visitor. With contextual and placement targeting, we're trying to scope out the location that your eventual prospective customers might visit. But with audience targeting, you don't really care *where* they see your ads; you care much more about what they've done to exhibit a certain behavior that qualifies them as part of your audience. There are currently three types of audiences you can define within the AdWords interface:

Interest categories As visitors browse around the Web, cookies are used to get a sense of the kinds of things they're interested in. As an advertiser, you can choose to target *visitors* that have an interest in anything from sports to cooking.

Remarketing lists Remarketing lists allow advertisers to set cookies when users do specific things on specific pages. For example, if you have an e-commerce store, you can set a cookie when someone puts something in their shopping cart. At that point, you know that they're interested in purchasing something, and if they don't check out, you can target that person around the Web.

Custom combinations Last, you can use what are known as custom combinations, and you can target your audiences using AND and OR logic to combine your lists and interest categories. A common example of this is combining two lists: first, a list of people who have put something in their shopping carts, and second, a list of those who have completed the checkout process. You can then target the combination of people who *have* put something in their cart but *have not* yet checked out with discounts or other offers that might close the deal.

Topic Targeting

Topic targeting is the broadest form of targeting available on the Google Display Network, and it allows advertisers to have their ads show on any page that is determined to match a topical theme. If you want your ads to show across any online content that has anything to do with food and drink, for example, topic targeting allows this.

We discuss topic targeting in its own section later in the book. Because this targeting is so broad, it is typically not used alone but as a refinement to the three types of targeting discussed previously.

Return on Investment

Return on investment, or ROI, is the third R of the AdWords value proposition. What this really boils down to is something that has traditionally been extremely difficult to measure: accountability in advertising.

Never before have we had the ability to track exactly what we get back for our advertising spend in such detail and so quickly. Not long ago, Google AdWords removed its separate reporting section and integrated all the collected data and metrics into the interface itself. That's how central data is to advertising on the Google platform.

Google provides the following tools for measuring the return on ad spend.

Account and campaign statistics Inside the AdWords interface, advertisers have direct access to reporting of all the data that's needed to gauge the success or failure of a campaign. Cost and impression data can be broken down to whatever level of granularity you'd like, letting you quickly see which ad creatives are drawing the clicks, which campaigns are finding the most eyeballs, and which are costing you the most money.

Conversion tracking When you add the optional conversion tracking features available in the AdWords platform, you start to see the real impact of your advertising. No longer are we defining the success or failure of display advertising by whether or not we spent the budget; with conversion tracking, we can see things like conversion rates and cost per acquisition as well as correlations between just seeing (and not necessarily clicking on) our ads and conversion actions. In select markets, Google AdWords even offers call tracking options that can be enabled directly from the AdWords interface.

Analytics Tools like Google Analytics, Adobe Site Catalyst, Webtrends, Unica, Coremetrics and more allow advertisers to measure everything that happens after the click occurs, and turning this sea of data into actionable information is the key to truly managing your advertising campaigns. Being a Google product, Google Analytics has the rare quality of having access to the cost and pre-click data collected by AdWords, and by linking the two accounts, advertisers can see everything that happens from the time the ad is displayed to the final conversion actions and repeat interactions that those ads drive. For offline conversions such as phone calls, there are a host of call tracking providers like Mongoose Metrics, IfByPhone, KeyMetric, Marchex and more that can integrate with AdWords as well as web analytics tools. You can't manage what you can't measure, and friends don't let friends use online advertising without the appropriate analytics tools in place!

Identifying Display Ad Types and Formats

We dive into the specific details of all the ad formats that many of the display advertising platforms support later in this book, but at this point it's worthwhile to understand what these ads look like and what makes them display ads.

Text Ads

First and foremost, the boring old text ads you find on all those search results pages can actually be placed in display networks. You often find these embedded between paragraphs of a news or informational article, see them as you interact with social networking sites, and even see a string of them where you think an image advertisement should be.

Figure 2.1 shows some examples of text-based ads as they might show in the Google Display Network. Display advertising is synonymous with images and video, but don't forget that textual ads can run on many display networks as well.

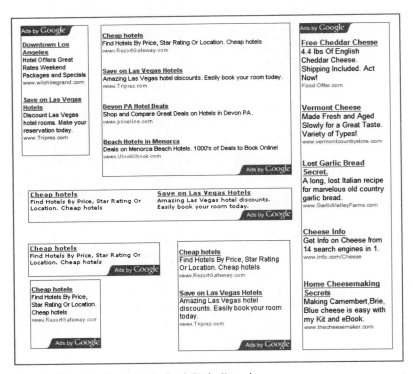

Figure 2.1 Examples of text ads in the Google Display Network

Image Ads

From the birth of the banner ad, image ads have been extremely popular and have permeated the Internet, finding their way into just about any kind of online content that exists. Popular formats for image ads include horizontal banners, vertical skyscrapers, and square or rectangular boxes.

A handful of examples of the most popular sizes are shown in Figure 2.2, and it's important to note that animated GIF files (not videos, but a few frames of animation designers can compress into an image format) are counted as image ads.

Figure 2.2 Examples of image ads in the Google Display Network

Through the years, thankfully the larger ad networks have disallowed the use of things like multicolor strobe light effects or ads that look like system pop-up windows warning you that if you don't click right now, your hard drive is about to be erased. A well-designed image ad doesn't need trickery to accomplish its goals, and we discuss what makes a good display ad in later chapters.

Video Ads

This ad format provides advertisers with a chance to leverage all of the rich sights and sounds of video, and with constant advances in compression technologies, available bandwidth, and network infrastructure, these are becoming more and more common and accessible every day.

There are quite a few different kinds of video ads out there, and in addition to showing video formats across the Google Display Network inventory, advertisers have access to YouTube, the most popular video sharing site on the planet.

You can choose to run your video ads before, during, or after regular video content. You can promote your video ads as search results or related content in YouTube, or you can place them across a wide array of publisher content. Whichever method you choose, you can reach an audience with your message much like you would with television advertising.

Rich Media Ads

Rich media formats allow advertisers to provide a more interactive experience for their target audience, and these can take a variety of shapes and sizes. Two of the most common are expandable ads and product showcase ads.

Expandable ads are ads that encourage interactivity by expanding to a larger size and offering more space for messaging, imagery, calls to action, or even video content. When users click to expand the ad, an "interaction" is logged, but in a cost per click model, the advertiser wouldn't be charged until the visitor clicks all the way through to the advertiser's website.

Product showcase style ads, such as the example in Figure 2.3, give advertisers the opportunity to provide more details and information about a number of different products or services right inside the ad. Users can interact with these kinds of ads, rolling their mouse over products to view different images and descriptions before actually clicking to the advertiser's website.

Figure 2.3 Example of a product showcase

One important note is that while technologies like HTML5 are poised to offer some incredible interactivity in the very near future, today rich media ads are typically accomplished using Flash, and Flash is not supported on devices that use iOS. So for advertisers wanting to target iPhone, iPad, and iPod devices, rich media is probably not going to be your best option quite yet.

Defining Advertising Objectives

It wasn't that long ago that companies and organizations were putting up websites just because they wanted to have a website. "Well, nobody's ever told us they saw us online," and "We just did it so no one else would steal our domain" were commonplace comments heard in boardrooms inside of a decade ago. These days, we're far beyond just asking your IT department to slap up your brochure on the Web. Now, the Internet is a place of action and engagement. It's where people do their research and find information and where transactions and lead generation takes place. When we build websites in today's business environment, before we even start thinking about colors or content, we define goals. Our goals are answers to one simple question:

What do I want someone to do when they reach this website that has value to me?

The answers to this question should be many, and defining them is something that should take a significant amount of time, thought, and planning. And beyond just the actions a user can take on your website, it's important to extend this even further. What could my audience do in the offline world as a response to my campaign? Do they pick up the phone and call me or walk into my brick-and-mortar store? And what could people do on other web properties that I don't necessarily own? From blogs to Twitter and social networks, how is my message getting spread and how is that adding (or taking away) value to (or from) my business? What influence can I have on my target audience's awareness and perception of my brand? In creating a marketing plan that includes display advertising, we need to be able to answer the same fundamental question when planning our campaigns:

What do I want someone to do as a result of my advertising campaigns that has value to me?

Once you've defined and assigned value to all of the answers to this question, you can begin to measure the impact your campaigns are having on your advertising objectives. And using a framework of defining goals and their values along with the advertising objectives to support those goals brings with it the notion of accountability. Understanding the costs of your advertising endeavors along with the value of the goals you're able to accomplish gives you everything you need to get a picture of the return you're getting back from your advertising investment.

Defining Your Goals

While goals can happen both online and offline, a good place to start when we're working with display ads is with the website question: If someone does click on that ad, what do I want them to do that has value to me? The most obvious answer is "buy my product or service," but in reality, most of us are not selling something online, and very few of us are deriving all of our top line revenues purely from online sales.

The fact is, most advertisers aren't expecting to make a sale on the first online touch point, and many more will never close their deals via the Web. One of our oldest clients sells industrial packaging and processing machinery and gets virtually all of its business from the Web. But it comes in the form of leads; there's no one putting million dollar industrial equipment lines on their PayPal account.

So how are you getting people to enter your sales funnel, no matter how long that buying cycle may be? Maybe it's a phone call; maybe it's a request for a quote. It might be the download of a PDF white paper or watching a video or listening to a podcast. Perhaps it's following your company on Twitter or +1ing or Liking your pages. The point is, there are *lots* of goals that you have and lots of valuable things that people can be doing on your website and on the Web. The following are a handful of goals that we see fairly often, and hopefully this list will get your juices flowing as you list all of *your* organization's goals.

Examples of Goals

This is by no means a to-do list, but as you read through it, think about which of these could apply to your own organization and its advertising goals. Understanding just what you want to get back for the advertising dollars you're spending in your display campaigns is the first step in being able to measure the profitability and effectiveness of your display advertising endeavors.

E-commerce For those that are trading product for money through a web transaction, e-commerce goals are the most rock-solid, easy-to-measure metrics out there. You know when they bought something, you know what was in their cart and what they paid, you know your costs, and you can calculate your margins. Done deal.

Lead generation When your potential customers arrive on your site or interact with your other online assets early on in the buying process, your goal might be to simply get them into your sales funnel. They might fill out a form requesting more information, perhaps they give you a call, maybe they schedule a demonstration of your product or service, or maybe they just fill out your contact form. Every one of these actions has value.

Phone calls Phone tracking has become extremely robust these days, and services like those mentioned earlier provide tracking that integrates with analytics packages, records calls, and ties them back to your ad campaigns at varying levels of granularity. Some services even offer things like on-the-fly voice-to-text transcription, conversation sentiment analysis, and even mining this data for certain words being said in the conversations!

Newsletter signups If a visitor isn't ready to buy yet but they're interested, offering them the ability to sign up for your email list to receive special offers, detailed information, or even just a once-in-a-while reminder that you exist is a fantastic way to build up your marketing lists. Providers like Exact Target, Campaign Monitor, Constant Contact, Vertical Response, AWeber, and more make it easy to get your message to potential customers that have actively shown interest in your products and services by opting in to your lists.

Social network/feed interaction Along the same lines, getting your visitors to follow you on Twitter; like you on Facebook; +1 you on Google Plus; Digg, Stumble, Tweet, and share your pages or email them to a friend; bookmark you on Del.icio.us; subscribe to your feed; add you to their reader; "check in" when they visit your physical location; or mark you down as a favorite can be extremely valuable to you. Spreading the word and building networks of potential customers provide you with an opportunity to get your messaging out on more familiar and informal mediums and capture prospects and sales.

Information dissemination Many companies and organizations publish white papers to display the more detailed advantages of their products and services as well as establish thought leadership in their industries. Getting those white papers downloaded, read, or even quoted by press and media can be fantastic goals of your marketing department. And what's a great way to let the media know you're available for interviews and expert quotes? Through your downloadable press kit, another goal you can track.

Downloads Beyond white papers, other types of downloads can have real value as well. Think of coupons redeemable at a brick-and-mortar store, free chapters of a book or previews of a video, podcasts to be listened to by a prospective customer in the car or on the treadmill, or even a software application that helps in the sales process. A great example is Crucial.com, a company that sells computer memory upgrades. It offers visitors a download that scans your computer and figures out exactly what memory configurations and sizes will fit your specific machine!

Customer service Sometimes it's not about making money, but saving it. We've seen our clients measure usage of FAQ or automated help solutions to reduce the need for call centers or customer service representatives. And don't forget things like allowing your visitors to get maps and driving directions to your physical storefront or providing how-to videos, instructions, and diagrams for the things your customers tend to have trouble with.

Page/ad impressions Many websites make money based on the number of ads shown on their pages, and this is particularly relevant for larger content publishers like news sources, informational article publishers, review sites, magazines, and even blogs and video sites. Each set of eyeballs that sees that recipe, reads that article, watches that video, or scours those reviews is worth money to the site serving up the ads being shown.

Audio/video/rich media consumption If you run podcasts or create video content or build interactive components on your web properties, then you'll definitely want to consider it valuable when your visitors interact with these items. When a prospective customer watches your sales demo or listens to a podcast of useful information that establishes your expertise in your market vertical, they're interacting with you and your brand and are one step closer to a possible sale. Think of the vehicle builders on all the automotive websites that let you construct your car with the colors, trim, and options you're after or the Pizza Tracker that lets you know how close your dinner is to your table when you order from Domino's.

Login/usage Many people have websites that require a login in order to actually use the service. One example might be a video training website like Lynda.com; there's only so much a visitor can preview on the site without a membership and signing in. Once they do, they have access to thousands of training video titles, and their usage of the service is extremely valuable. Online services ranging from Netflix to premium forums to streaming music sources derive value from logins and online usage of their products and services.

Leave reviews According to a June 2010 Harris Interactive poll, a full 71 percent of respondents say that reviews from family members or friends influence their decisions to use a particular brand, company, or product:

```
www.harrisinteractive.com/vault/HI-Harris-Poll-Opinions-In-Social-
Media-2010-06-03.pdf
```

Pointing your visitors toward third-party review sites like Yelp!, Google, Trip Advisor, Urban Spoon, Angie's List, and more can help your potential customers decide on you rather than your competition. And if you have an e-commerce component to your site, options like PowerReviews, Bazaarvoice, and even Amazon provide fantastic frameworks to get people reviewing your products and services.

Outbound clicks If you're an affiliate of another retailer, your main goal is to get someone off of your site and into the shopping cart of the product or service that you're marketing. Tracking these clicks from your site to the merchant you're an affiliate for is going to be an essential part of measuring the success or failure of your campaigns.

Mobile app download Many websites allow additional services or make access to their products and services easier through mobile applications that can be downloaded to and run from a smartphone or tablet device. Think about the burrito ordering app provided by Chipotle restaurants or the viewing application offered by the Economist that lets subscribers download and read their magazine on their tablet or mobile device. Downloading these apps gets customers one step closer to their first purchase, a repeat buy, or a renewal.

Company and internal goals You might also want to consider users of your website beyond your current and prospective customers. How about each time a potential investor downloads your prospectus or takes a look at your financials? How about each time a job applicant submits their resume to your human resources department to apply for an opening?

These are just a smattering of goals that we've seen our clients come up with over the years, and they may or may not apply to your company or your situation. But we encourage you to take a hard look at all the actions that can be taken on and off your websites to establish all the goals of *your* organization.

Assigning Value to Your Goals

Once you've gone through the exercise of listing all the actions you'd like your prospective customers to take, it's time to assign values to those actions. Understanding this value along with the cost of your advertising will give you everything you need to measure and improve upon ROI as you expand and optimize your marketing campaigns.

As we mentioned earlier, e-commerce goals are the easiest to define. Right down to the individual product level, you can figure out exactly how much a specific transaction is worth to you. E-commerce is one of the few hard metrics you can grab onto. Leads, however, are a bit of a softer metric. For those organizations that enjoy a well-planned and effectively utilized customer relationship management (CRM) or enterprise resource planning (ERP) system, this is often fairly easy to measure. If you know your average transaction value and you know how many of what kinds of leads it takes to close a transaction, you can calculate a cost-per-lead value against which you can measure your advertising campaigns. But even if you don't run a sophisticated back end to track your sales funnels, you can come up with ballpark numbers fairly easily, and this can apply to a number of the goals we listed earlier. Let's look at some examples.

Even without a phone tracking solution in place, you can simply get a separate phone line dedicated to your online campaigns. When you look at your books, figure out how many of those phone calls turned into how much revenue and how much of that was profit. Divide that number by the number of calls to your dedicated number that you find on your phone bill and you've got a value per phone call.

By keeping track of the coupons downloaded from your website and placing specific codes on them, you can start to understand how many of those downloaded coupons get redeemed and how much profit results from them. Divide that number by the total number of coupon downloads and you've got a value per downloaded coupon.

If you're doing email marketing, you can track how much profit resulted from each blast that you've sent. If you make $1,000 each time you blast to your list of 1,000 email addresses, then you know that getting one more email address on that list is worth at least $1 to you—and probably more over the life of that subscription to your newsletter.

When you're just starting out and don't have much data, it's okay to work with the numbers you've got in order to get yourself in the ballpark. With very few exceptions, it's better to have *some* idea of the value of your goals than no idea, and as you start to get more data and your processes become more sophisticated, you can run these calculations against monthly data, a rolling quarter's worth of data, or any other frequency that makes sense to your organization.

One more way you can value your goals is through measuring correlation between your goals and business performance. Tracking things like the number of new Twitter followers, Facebook likes, application downloads, video views, PDF downloads, or any other softer metric you're measuring allows you to correlate them with your monthly financials. While in many of these cases, you can actually track revenues that directly result from the action, in other cases you won't be able to say that a direct causal relationship exists. But by tracking these against the business numbers, you can start to infer at least some point of reference to value these activities.

Direct Response Advertising

With just about all of the goals we've just looked at, we've been assuming that the purpose of our advertising campaigns is to prompt some sort of an action, or get the person that saw our ad to *do something*. This is known as direct response advertising. Direct response marketing requires that we have a specific and measurable action that our advertising is attempting to solicit and we're interacting directly with our customers.

When someone sees our ad, we want that person to pick up the phone and call. We want them to click through and sign up for our newsletter or buy our products and services. Or we want them to click the Like button or watch a video or download a file or log in. Direct response to our advertisements and our marketing efforts is also the easiest to measure.

With enterprise level analytics, abundant tracking tools, and the widespread availability of reports and data from all kinds of sources, these days we're running out of excuses *not* to be measuring the impact made by our marketing dollars spent.

Introduction to Attribution

One of the most important aspects of measuring direct response is attribution, and a quick example from one of our e-commerce clients can illustrate the concept quite well.

Let's pretend that a nursing student is looking for advice on what kind of shoes to buy, and they go to Google to search for some help. They end up on the allnurses.com forum and see an ad like the one shown here.

Continues

Introduction to Attribution *(Continued)*

They click it, and they're taken to ScrubsAndBeyond.com, where they browse through the site, but they decide not to buy anything. A few days later, they head over to Bing and do a search on "medical scrubs" and then click on the first organic result and end up on ScrubsAndBeyond.com again.

This time, they still don't buy anything, but they're interested in making a purchase some day, and they decide to sign up for the newsletter so they'll be the first to know when sales or special events are happening.

Now here's the tough question: Who should get credit for this newsletter signup? The display ad that was clicked on that forum or the Bing search? You could easily argue this either way. If it weren't for the display ad, this person wouldn't have ever even known about Scrubs and Beyond. But it was the Bing result that actually drove the visit during which the newsletter signup occurred.

Let's make it even more interesting: Two weeks later, this visitor gets an email from Scrubs and Beyond like the one shown here, clicks on one of the offers, and buys a shopping cart full of products. Now, who gets credit for that purchase?

Continues

The answer is not cut and dried, and to help marketers attribute value to different touch points along the way to a final transaction, there are many attribution models in use these days. While attribution modeling can get extremely complex and sophisticated, and while there is much work going on in the industry to help solve these problems, there are a few simplistic ways to look at attribution.

Continues

Introduction to Attribution *(Continued)*

It's important to note that this isn't a question of right and wrong, it's just a question of perspective, and many advertisers choose to look at a few different attribution models when evaluating their campaigns.

First touch attribution   This is just what it sounds like: The first touch point gets all the credit. So in our example, all of the credit for that purchase would go to the display ad the user first clicked.

Last touch attribution   When we use last touch attribution, we assign the full credit to the last touch point before the conversion action occurred. In this case, the newsletter would receive all the credit for the purchase. Many client-side analytics solutions, like Google Analytics for example, use this attribution model as a default.

Multiple touch attribution   This starts to get a bit more complex, but the general premise is that the advertiser can split up the credit among the various touch points. In the simplest example, we might choose to divide the credit evenly among the touch points. So the display ad click would get one-third of the credit, the Bing search would get one-third, and the newsletter would get one-third. Many analytics solutions such as Coremetrics and Google Analytics Premium allow for various customized configurations to be modeled, and the Multi-Channel Funnels feature of Google Analytics also provides visibility into multiple touch points along the way to a conversion. Additionally, many enterprise-level organizations employ extremely complex and sophisticated methodologies across many integrated systems to effectively model attribution.

Any touch attribution   This model is typically used in the reporting features of the advertising platforms themselves, and it is also the one used with Conversion Tracking inside Google AdWords. Google AdWords takes credit for any conversion that happens within 30 days of a click on the ad, whether it's the first interaction, the last interaction, or any interaction between.

So which one is right for you? In the case of Scrubs and Beyond, when its display campaigns are analyzed and optimized, a number of different models are used along with the Multi-Channel Funnels reports of Google Analytics. Each of these models presents a slightly different perspective on the value of various marketing efforts and helps us determine where to most effectively spend marketing dollars.

Branding and Positioning Goals

When we bring it all back to our core marketing concepts, businesses need to compete based upon their competitive advantages. Those competitive advantages typically fall into one of three general categories:

- Cost or price differentiation
- Quality or feature differentiation
- Brand advantage differentiation

Differentiation and Competitive Advantage

We can think of some great examples of each of these. Companies like Southwest Airlines and Walmart became extremely successful by competing on price.

Southwest cut its costs everywhere it could, removing meal services, seat assignments, and fare classes and even standardized on one single plane to reduce turnaround times and allow for the most efficient maintenance divisions possible. As a result, travelers got a no-frills seat that got them from point A to point B for a discount.

Walmart invested so heavily in its supply chain and information technology platforms that it was able to cut out distributors completely and use a just-in-time approach to stocking its shelves with everything from groceries, electronics, and books to sporting goods, clothing, and housewares. This cost savings, along with the scale of its operations, allows Walmart to offer lower pricing than just about anyone else.

Quality or feature differentiation is extremely common as well. A Ferrari isn't competing on price;, it's positioned as one of the fastest, most luxurious, hand-crafted cars on the road. Rolex isn't selling a means to tell time; it's selling a combination of fine jewelry, status, and exquisite craftsmanship. Both of these are prime examples of competing on quality.

As far as feature differentiation, an example we commonly use is projectors. As frequent speakers and presenters, we live and die by the projector we use to put our slides up on the big screen, and the marketplace offers quite a few options. One of our favorite offline ads (seen in Figure 2.4) was one for InFocus that clearly differentiated on ease of use. "If your users have a problem with one of our projectors, you can be 99.9% sure it's not plugged in" is extremely effective messaging for us! While other manufacturers are competing on features like size, brightness, and the life span of lamps and bulbs, InFocus has chosen to target the fear of not being able to get a projector to work when standing in front of an audience.

We also find examples of feature differentiation just about anywhere we see a commoditized product. Think about the largest players in the beer industry. Over the past years, just in bottling alone we've seen everything from wide mouth openings and labels that change color with temperature to full pint aluminum packaging and "write on" labels so you can keep track of which one's yours. They all offer a mass-market light beer, and they're using the features of their bottling to differentiate.

Branding and Positioning Your Competitive Advantage

If we dig into each of the examples we just looked at, we can also see that these companies have done a pretty good job of associating their brands with certain ideals and concepts. When you think of Ferrari or Rolex, you think of quality. When you think of Walmart or Southwest, you think of low prices. What about some other good examples?

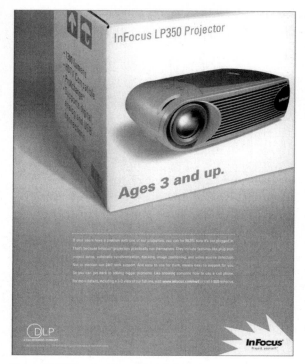

Figure 2.4 Offline advertisement for InFocus projector

What do you think of when you see the Volvo brand? Volvo has done a pretty good job of making its name synonymous with safety, which is the feature that it's competing on. The messaging that it's trying to drive home is that unless you happen to be sitting in the trunk, if someone rear-ends you at a stoplight, you and your family will be just fine.

What about something like JOHNSON's Baby Shampoo? We'll bet without even looking at Figure 2.5 you knew that the little red teardrop at the top is emblazoned with the "No More Tears" message. When you think of that bottle, you think about babies *not* crying and happy images of bathtub time.

Figure 2.5 JOHNSON's Baby Shampoo bottle

Now…how about *your* brand? What do your name and logo get people thinking? Is your brand strong enough or positioned in the right way to be an effective competitive advantage for you? Clearly, branding for awareness and positive sentiment along with the way your brand is positioned in the marketplace has value, but the problem is that the exact dollar value is difficult to pin down on a quarter-by-quarter or month-by-month basis.

Defining and Measuring Your Branding and Positioning Goals

When you attempt to measure the impact of your advertising initiatives on your branding and positioning goals, you don't have the luxury of direct-response-style metrics like purchases or leads or downloads. The metrics you need to look at are the "soft" ones—these don't necessarily directly put dollars on the top line of your income statements, but they do provide you with an indication of the impact your campaigns are having on educating and influencing your potential market.

First, you can't forget traditional marketing research methodologies, and a tried and true way to measure brand impact is through formal studies. Through a structured process of before-and-after surveying, advertisers can start to understand the impact of their campaigns on things like aided and unaided brand awareness, message and brand association, and even intent to take a desired marketing action.

On the online front, there are a host of metrics you can use to assess the impact your advertising has on branding and positioning goals. For example, Google AdWords tracks a metric called "view through conversions" as the number of conversions that occur within a certain number of days (30 is the default) of a visitor *seeing*, but *not clicking*, your ad. This can be a helpful metric in determining how your advertising campaign is exposing your brand early in the buying process.

Traffic that finds a website via a search on a branded keyword term is often tracked as an indication of the effectiveness of a branding campaign. If Toyota can influence a boost in traffic looking for a "Prius" rather than a "hybrid car," it has likely been doing a good job of branding its flagship hybrid automobile lately.

You can even use tools like Google's Insights for Search (www.google.com/insights/search) to monitor trends beyond your own websites and look at how often people are going to Google and searching on your branded keywords.

And there are a host of social media monitoring tools that can measure things like mentions and influence among social networks as well as identify virality, authority, shareability, and even positive, negative, or neutral sentiment in content posted about your brand around the Web.

Even tracking the number of Twitter followers, Facebook likes, Google +1's, LinkedIn shares, Pinterest pins, and other social media metrics can help you measure the impact of your branding campaigns.

Fundamental Display Advertising Concepts

3

Display advertising has radically transformed itself in the last 20 years from static magazine ads and billboards to sophisticated electronic auctions that allow placing thousands of bids and the ability to create custom ad creatives on the fly with no human intervention—all in just a few milliseconds. In this chapter we'll start with the fundamentals of display ads, outlining the networks, the terminology, and a basic process you can follow to get off to the right start in display advertising.

Chapter Contents

The Ecosystem: Advertisers and Publishers
Starting Out with the Google Network
Campaign Targeting Strategies
The Big Picture: The Process of Display Advertising

The Ecosystem: Advertisers and Publishers

There are two distinct groups in advertising: the advertisers who pay to advertise their products or services and the publishers who provide the space for the ads and charge the advertisers to utilize that space. In traditional, offline advertising such as magazines, newspapers, and even television and billboards, the advertiser-publisher relationship is well understood.

Online marketing shook things up in many ways. Although the traditional rectangular banner ad has been around via the *Prodigy* online service that predated the modern Internet in the 1980s, online advertising really took hold once cost-per-click ads tied to search engines hit the scene. Starting with GoTo.com (later Yahoo!) and subsequently Google, the value of online advertising soared due to the incredible inherent power of ads that appeal directly to customers actively searching for information.

While it's always been possible to advertise on sites other than search engines, the process was difficult and disjointed and thus the search engine–based ads dominated the landscape for the next decade. This caused the role of advertisers versus publishers to become less clear as the search engines and their ad networks disrupted the traditional model. With the advent of Google's AdSense Content Network, it was possible for advertisers to easily advertise on both independent websites and search engines through the same interface. So now a Google AdWords advertiser has the option of bidding not just on keyword phrases that users search on via search engines but also on websites that agree to offer space on their sites as inventory to AdWords customers. This brought the market back closer to the traditional model of advertiser versus publisher, where the advertisers buy ads via the AdWords system and publishers display those ads on their content via the AdSense system. In this case, Google.com and other search engines are simply additional publishers offering space for ads. However, despite this greatly expanded capability and number of sites to advertise on, ads on the search results page continued to be most popular with advertisers and accounted for the lion's share in revenue.

Besides the appeal of search advertising bringing your ads to a pool of potential buyers actively seeking solutions, the model in which the ads themselves were sold held some major advantages for advertisers. Instead of publishers offering a set price, the ad inventory was auctioned off in real time via a self-service web interface, allowing the market to set the prices for the each keyword or web page. Additionally, most advertisers opted for the cost-per-click (CPC) cost structure, where there was no charge for simply displaying an ad. Instead, an advertiser was only charged if someone actually *clicked* the ad. This automated auction was far more efficient and cost-effective for both advertisers and publishers and allowed the market to grow much more rapidly than would have been possible through the manual process that was prevalent in traditional newspaper, magazine, or phone book advertising.

However, two factors are turning the tide in many advertisers' minds, making them question any steadfast preferences of search over display advertising. The first is simply one of volume. The search market is somewhat saturated, and there are only so many searches performed each day. As more advertisers move more of their overall ad budget toward online media, they are fighting over the same limited inventory on search results pages. The second is that while searches may be flattening out, overall consumption of Internet content is growing rapidly. This includes not just traditional HTML-based web pages but also iPad/iPhone apps, YouTube videos, social media, mobile formatted websites, and more. This lack of competition and availability of supply can make display advertising more cost effective if done right.

Display Networks Come of Age

Some of the primary criticisms of early display networks have been mitigated by modern tools and technology. When the Google Display Network was first introduced, it was known as the Content Network and it garnered a bad reputation with advertisers who were accustomed to ads targeting search results pages. Usually these advertisers who came from the search side had the primary goal of direct response rather than overall branding initiatives. The search ads were a good fit because someone searching is looking to take action while someone browsing is in a much more passive state. So simply enabling the search-based campaigns to bid on ad space on the Content Network almost always produced poor results (and still does).

But over the years, best practices have evolved and Google and others have worked hard to create tools and technology that allow a much greater chance of success. With this overhaul, Google renamed its Content Network; it is now the Display Network, and many believe it was both a symbolic and pragmatic attempt to show that the new network is significantly different from the old. Throughout this chapter and the rest of the book, we walk through those best practices, tools, and technology so you can maximize your effectiveness in display advertising.

When publishers of sites and apps make their space available as ad inventory, they can do so directly or through an ad network or ad exchange. A large site may have enough interest that they can go to the advertisers directly. For example, you can place an ad directly with the *New York Times* online just as you might in its print newspaper edition. And as Facebook has grown, it has developed its own relationships with advertisers and they can place an ad directly. However, you can also reach both of those sites through the ad networks, such as the Google Display Network. This ability to reach millions of websites through a single interface represents a much more efficient path for the average advertiser and thus is the focus of the majority of this book.

Technological Advances Lead to Extreme Complexity

Since much of the recent performance improvement of display advertising is due to better tools and technology, there has been an all-out race in recent years to hone and perfect this technology to squeeze ever more profits from your display advertising dollar.

This has led to an explosion in the amount of investment and sheer number of companies working on technology to optimize the process.

Some of the more effective technology has enabled advertisers to target audiences far more precisely. By showing your ads only to those who have proven more likely to convert into paying customers, you can increase the profitability of your advertising. Previous online behavior, demographics, location, and many other factors allow algorithms to better target their audience.

Real-time bidding (RTB) is a technology that allows computer algorithms to optimize bids in real time. In a few milliseconds, the automated system can learn from the various publishers what inventory is available because a user is requesting some content, such as a web page or mobile app. The system can also learn information about the user who is going to load the ad, such as location, browser, device type, and potentially more detailed demographic information. The system then decides whether or not this ad is valuable to the advertiser and if it should place a bid. If it does, it must determine just *how* valuable it is so it knows how much to bid for maximum cost savings. If the bid is placed and the auction won, the system then has to serve the correct ad copy and creative. All of this, including the back and forth from the publisher to potential advertisers, must take place extremely fast. It starts when a user requests a page and has to finish while that page is loading so the ad can be loaded as a seamless part of that page—all of this takes place in less than one-third the time it takes a human to blink.

Some tools cater to large advertisers who spread their budget over multiple networks. Demand side platforms (DSPs) have emerged to take advantage of the latest technology while simplifying the process of bidding and buying. They incorporate real-time bidding as described previously but across multiple ad networks and exchanges. The DSPs also bring together and integrate with multiple systems that supply technology not just for bidding but for ad serving, analytics, and reporting—all in one user interface.

Those are just two examples among hundreds. On the advertiser side, there are companies and technologies that focus solely on serving dynamic ads and other ad creative optimization tools that generate the creative for the ad in real time. On the publisher side, there are specialized inventory tools to maximize yield, optimize ad serving, and more. There is also an entire industry of measurement tools that provide analytics and reporting to assist optimization and help advertisers analyze and optimize their ad spend. There are also hundreds of agencies that to varying degrees may try to use this technology on behalf of their clients while simultaneously interfacing with publishers. They often have their own proprietary interfaces and platforms, which add even more pieces to the puzzle. The number of middlemen who sit between advertiser and publisher has swelled so rapidly that even many industry experts are struggling to grasp how all the pieces work together (or don't work together in many cases!).

Terence Kawaja, CEO at LUMA Partners, attempted to piece together this framework and came up with a now-famous graphic (Figure 3.1) that identifies some (but not all) of the companies involved in display advertising optimization.

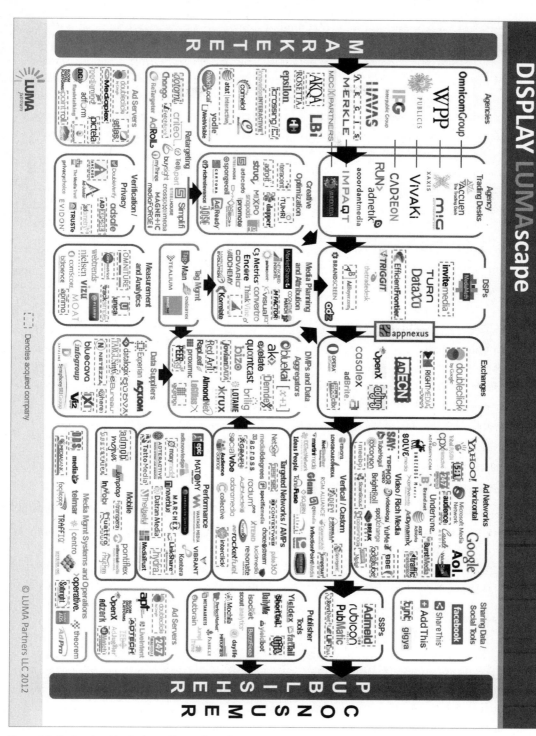

Figure 3.1 Display advertising landscape (Terence Kawaja)

The landscape is complex, and no one company provides access to all of the technologies available for optimization, nor would it be productive or cost effective to do so. However, Google provides by far the most extensive platform that encompasses more pieces of that puzzle than any other. It has either acquired or developed solutions that address many of those technologies to provide an end-to-end system that is as close to comprehensive as anything that exists today. The sheer reach of the Google Network in particular is unprecedented. It is currently estimated to reach 80 percent of the world's Internet users—a number many think is actually lower than reality.

The following is a partial list of Google acquisitions and web properties that help make up its display advertising platform:

Google AdWords The primary self-service interface for advertisers to advertise on both the Search Network and the Display Network.

Google AdSense The primary self-service interface for publishers to offer inventory on their content to Google AdWords advertisers.

DoubleClick A massive platform in itself that is a wholly owned subsidiary of Google and offers advertiser and publisher tools as well as a major ad exchange. Much of the platform is integrated with other Google tools, including AdWords, Analytics, and AdPlanner among others.

Invite Media A full demand side platform that offers RTB, behavioral targeting, and more.

AdMeld Sell-side platform that helps sellers manage different ad networks to increase the amount they receive for their inventory.

Teracent Display ad optimization technology that can modify graphical elements, images, messaging, and products automatically and in real time.

AdMob Leading display ad provider for mobile apps.

AdScape Provider of in-game ads for video games.

dMarc Broadcasting Radio advertising platform formerly integrated with Google AdWords.

Google Analytics (Urchin) A leading analytics package that is deeply integrated with Google AdWords, AdSense, and DoubleClick.

Android The fastest growing smartphone platform and a key component of Google's mobile advertising platform.

Motorola Mobility The largest Android smartphone handset provider.

The Google Network provides advertisers with an impressive array of tools within a single interface. While sophisticated or very large advertisers may have justification for taking a different approach, for the average or beginning advertiser, the Google Display Network (GDN) is a clear and logical starting place. The GDN, combined with other integrated (and free) tools such as Google Analytics and AdPlanner, is a compelling platform. And while this Google-based platform provides the majority of the examples in this book, the same principles can be applied on other networks and platforms as you expand your knowledge and capabilities.

Starting Out with the Google Network

In the preceding section, you saw that the wide reach and array of tools make the Google Network an appropriate place to start when beginning a discussion about display advertising. Here we'll look at some of the primary components and technology in more depth to understand how they all fit together.

What Is This Page Really About?

The secret to so much of Google's success comes from its ability to display highly relevant ads. For ads displayed next to search result, Google uses algorithms that take data from the keywords in the search query, the text in the ads, the landing pages, historical performance and more to determine the most relevant ads. But on the display side, successfully serving a relevant ad comes down to how well Google can target the user without the advantage of a keyword search. For the most popular method of targeting on the Google Display Network, contextual targeting, Google tries to determine the relevant topics and themes of the page itself in order to match relevant ads. Determining the topic and true meaning of a page of text is a reasonably simple thing for even a young child to do, but for computers it can actually be quite difficult. There are so many subtle but complex elements that we evaluate subconsciously when viewing a page. For example, does the word *Apple* refer to the fruit or the technology company? (Hint: The words surrounding it might serve as a clue, or even whether the word is capitalized in the middle of a sentence). Other challenges revolve around what is the important content of the page versus just boilerplate structure, such as disclaimers or even repetitious menus.

But true relevance goes much farther than this. Udi Manber, VP of engineering for Google, gives examples of the extent to which Google goes to understand the meaning of language:

Google understands that "GM" stands for "General Motors," while "GM foods" is actually "genetically modified." If you search for "B&B AB," Google knows that is "bed and breakfast in Alberta," while "Ramstein AB" is "Ramstein Airbase."

To accomplish this challenging task of getting computers to understand meaning, Google employs a small army of linguists and engineers who work together to study how to determine what a page means and what ads are relevant. This team was kick-started with the acquisition of Applied Semantics, which had developed this type of technology for a product called AdSense. Founded in 1998 as Oingo, it built an algorithm to detect meaning based on a lexicon called WordNet, which was developed at Princeton University and had been researched and improved for over 15 years. This technology underlying the AdSense platform gives Google one of its greatest strengths: to parse a page (on a Google site or otherwise) and determine which ads are relevant for readers of that page.

Google-Owned Properties

In addition to the familiar Google.com search results pages, a number of other sites serve ads for Google's huge search ad business. These include Google Shopping (product search), Google Maps, and even other search engines, such as Ask.com, AOL.com, and Netscape.

Google also operates other properties that offer display ad inventory based on the meaning of the page. When one of these pages is loaded, the text of the page is parsed by Google's algorithm to determine meaning. At this point, ads for AdWords advertisers who have opted in to the GDN can be shown if they are bidding on keywords that match the theme of the page or if they have specifically opted to advertise on this page. Note that while this keyword-based bidding is the traditional way of displaying your ads on these pages, it's not the only way. We discuss additional targeting options later in the chapter. Some of the additional Google properties available via the Google Network are:

Gmail `mail.google.com`

Gmail ads are based on the text of the emails in your account (Figure 3.2). As you accumulate more email, Google has a pretty good understanding of the types of conversations you have and thus a good idea of what types of ads are relevant to you. Here, an email about basketball is open, so the ads are about basketball-related items.

When Gmail launched with orders of magnitude more free storage than anyone else, it was presumably because the more email in your account, the more accurate its algorithms could target you with ads. This initially caused quite a stir because many people were uncomfortable with the idea that Google would be reading through their email to learn more about them. These concerns are understandable and predictable. If someone has access to your credit card bill and email, they can ascertain an incredible amount of information about your life—habits, interests, and personal correspondence are all laid bare in an easily analyzed fashion. So the idea of Google actively mining, interpreting, and evaluating the contents of your email may be unnerving. But as you can guess, no real humans read your mail at the Googleplex. Rather, they retarget and tweak the algorithms discussed earlier to determine which ads are relevant to your email discussions. Google has always maintained—any many agree—that this is actually a useful service because it removes ads that have no significance to you and replaces them with information that they hope you will find not just relevant but timely.

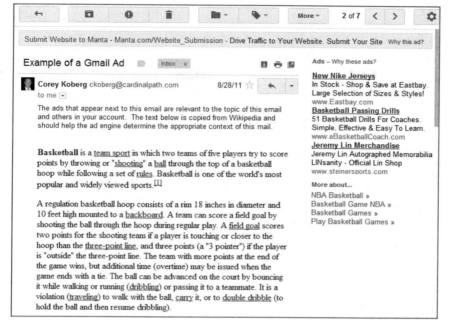

Figure 3.2 Gmail ads target the context of the message.

Google Finance `finance.google.com`

Google Finance is an informational site within the Google.com domain. Unlike search engines, which are designed such that the searcher leaves the site on the next click, this site is designed for the user to remain and consume information on the site itself. Google serves ads from these pages like the one in Figure 3.3 and makes this inventory available via the GDN.

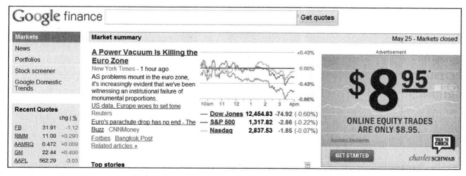

Figure 3.3 Google's popular finance portal offers several display ad inventory options.

Similar to Google Finance, Google Maps is another property where information is displayed directly to users rather than simply as a jumping-off point to other sites. In addition to the local business-specific advertising opportunities via Google Places, it provides display advertising (Figure 3.4).

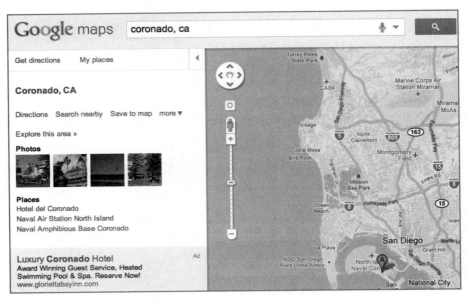

Figure 3.4 Google Maps serves location-specific and other ads.

Blogger `blogger.com`

Blogger, which Google acquired in 2003, hosts blogs at no charge for bloggers who don't want to deal with hosting or installing server software. Display advertisers can place ads on blogs that have content relevant to their target audience (Figure 3.5). This is our first example of a Google site where the content of the page is written and maintained by someone else.

AdSense for Content

While the previously mentioned Google properties receive a large amount of traffic, the largest opportunity to serve your display ads through Google actually comes from sites that are not owned by Google.

Site owners who want to earn revenue from advertising can put code on their site to allow ad networks to display ads on the site in exchange for a portion of the proceeds of the ad sales. Site owners participating in Google's AdSense program make their sites available to AdWords advertisers. Google scans the content of the page, senses what the page is about, and displays ads that target that content. The site owner can select which types of ads to allow, such as text ads or various sizes of image ads.

The display ad in Figure 3.6 is on a computer enthusiast site, so the firewall software ad is relevant to the audience reading that page.

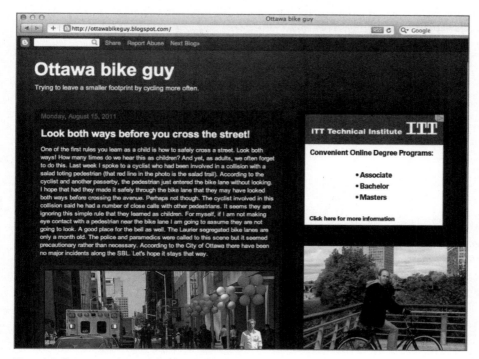

Figure 3.5 Blog contents determine the context of display ads.

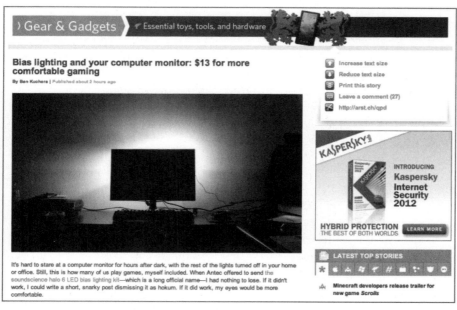

Figure 3.6 The computer related ad is targeted to the reader.

The text ads shown on Target.com (Figure 3.7) are also relevant, because visitors to Target are likely the right target market for JCPenney.com and Carters.com. However, this is likely an undesirable situation for Target. The only way it gets revenue from those ads is if someone clicks them and leaves Target.com. But sending your hard-earned traffic to a competitor's site may not be worth the revenue from the click or ad impression. All publishers must contemplate and manage this situation. Tools are available to enable publishers to exclude their competitors from showing.

Figure 3.7 Publishers may wish to block competitors' ads.

Mobile Sites and Apps

AdSense for mobile is similar to AdSense for content sites, but it's targeted and designed to fit mobile devices. The ads are targeted to the content of the page, just as on a standard desktop site. Mobile apps can serve display ads through technology Google acquired from AdMob. These ads are designed for the user interface of mobile apps and include some interesting formats, such as graphical interstitial ads that can interrupt the app experience and appear as a simulated browser (Figure 3.8).

Figure 3.8 An ad for a mobile optimized website appearing on a smartphone

There are also video interstitials that appear as full-screen video ads and auto-play until the user closes the window and returns to the app (Figure 3.9).

Figure 3.9 An in-game ad for a smartphone app

Feeds

Many site owners publish content not just through their website but also on RSS feeds that get pulled into all sorts of devices and readers. Site owners want to monetize their content no matter how it is consumed, so embedding display ads within the feed is a natural progression. Advertisers enjoy the same targeted audiences and relevant content and often have far fewer competing ads and other distractions than on an equivalent web page. Figure 3.10 and Figure 3.11 show how either a text ad or an image ad can be served from the feed.

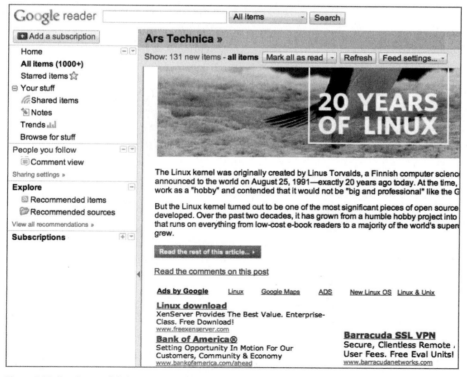

Figure 3.10 Text format ads help monetize an RSS feed.

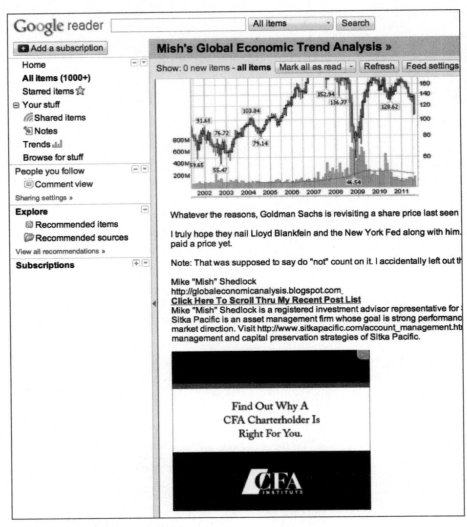

Figure 3.11 Image format ads help monetize an RSS feed.

YouTube and Video

YouTube is the second largest search engine in the world. Its users are highly engaged in the content, and it offers advertisers opportunities for ads narrowly targeted to content and audience. YouTube offers much more in terms of premium inventory than most sites in the GDN. For example, Homepage Takeover offers a 100 percent share of voice for 24 hours.

Google also offers opportunities for video advertising within the GDN outside of YouTube. These ads can take the form of text overlays; in-stream ads that appear in the beginning, middle, or end of videos; or even click-to-play ads. Click-to-play ads are embedded as a standard ad size in a web page where the user must click to see the video, making the video less intrusive or obnoxious than an autoplay might be.

This section introduces the topic of YouTube and video ads as options for your display ad arsenal, but given the importance and uniqueness of video ads, we devote Chapter 8 to them.

The DoubleClick Network

Google's acquisition of DoubleClick in 2007 for $3.1 billion was the first in a long line of investments aimed squarely at making a serious push into the display advertising market. DoubleClick brought with it unique technology but also an entrenched position in the display market that included relationships with a significant number of large ad agencies and the vast majority of online publishers.

Initially Google operated DoubleClick at arm's length from the rest of the AdWords/AdSense business, possibly because of the privacy concerns raised with the merger or because part of DoubleClick's appeal to customers was its independence from the ad networks it helped manage. Even today you can manage Bing campaigns from within the DoubleClick interface.

DoubleClick has sophisticated tools for site owners through its DoubleClick for Publishers (DFP) division, which helps owners manage and optimize their ad delivery. On the buy side, it has a suite that includes DoubleClick for Advertisers (DFA), which is an ad-serving and management platform used by many large ad buyers. DFA enables advertisers to serve their own ads and provides extensive targeting and reporting capability across multiple networks, exchanges, and publishers.

Ad Exchange

Over the past several years, much of the technology from both Google and DoubleClick has worked its way into both product lines. One of the most visible benefits to AdWords advertisers is the ability to access the DoubleClick Ad Exchange.

The Ad Exchange works much like a stock exchange, such as the NYSE or NASDAQ. It allows large buyers and brokers to come together and transact high volumes of business in a marketplace designed specifically to trade ads. It enables publishers to access multiple buyers and ad networks simultaneously. These potential advertisers can bid against each other for the right to display their ad for a particular impression opportunity (inventory) made available on the exchange. This allows publishers to maximize the value of their inventory by serving the ad of whoever is willing to pay the most. Advertisers can access a vast amount of inventory across multiple networks and use sophisticated real time bidding (RTB) and targeting options.

Sounds great, right? But just as at a real stock exchange, not anyone can walk in off the street and buy and sell; you must have a seat at the exchange. Luckily for users of the GDN, Google has a seat (it is Google's exchange after all) and thus AdWords advertisers can bid on inventory listed as available on the DoubleClick Ad Exchange. This allows them to bid on Google.com, the extended Google Search Partner network, the AdSense network, and Ad Exchange inventory all through one interface, which makes it the logical place to start your display advertising campaigns.

Campaign Targeting Strategies

The major shift in the effectiveness of display advertising comes from no longer casting a wide net across the Internet but instead targeting users where your ad will be effective. The GDN provides the following main targeting techniques: context (keywords), placements, audiences, and topics. Chapter 5, "Month 2: Targeting Your Audience," is devoted to the details and implementation of targeting strategies, but it's important to introduce the concepts here.

Targeting Campaigns with Keywords

Contextual targeting means that you target content in which to display your ads based on the context of the page, that is, what the page is about. Google uses AdSense technology to determine what a page is about via semantic analysis.

Often advertisers who are used to bidding on search ads find this bidding confusing because they still must select keywords to bid on but the ads are not being shown on search results pages. In this case, the keywords are not chosen to match search queries but rather to indicate to Google the *themes* of pages that the advertiser is targeting. Google looks at this group of keywords the same way it looks at the words on a page to extract a theme and overall meaning. When the theme of an ad's keywords matches the theme and meaning of a web page in the AdSense network, then the ad can be entered into the bidding for that space.

One example of this is the ads next to the email message in Figure 3.2. They advertise basketball passing drills, jerseys, and merchandise from popular NBA stars. While the content of the message doesn't specifically match the ads keyword for keyword, the ads are appropriate to the audience because the theme of the targeted keywords matches the theme of the content surrounding the ad.

Targeting Campaigns with Placements

When Google searches out relevant places for your ad to appear, it chooses those placements for you automatically. But you can also manually choose sites on which you want your content to appear via managed placements. In fact, you can even choose specific subsections of a site if you want to target specific content. For example, if you are the vendor of the Internet security software in Figure 3.6, you may be interested in the overall demographic of the readers of CNN.com but particularly those viewing articles in the technology section. On the other hand, basketball-oriented advertisers are more likely to be interested in the sports section.

Targeting via managed placements can also be useful if you determine that a particular site is performing very well for you and you want to increase your bids to occupy a greater percentage of the impressions available on that site. In this case you use keyword-based automatic placements to discover advertising opportunities but then tweak and optimize with managed placements. Note that strictly using managed placements does not require keywords because Google need not automatically match themes.

Targeting Campaigns with Audiences

Audience targeting, or behavioral targeting as it's often known, is an extremely powerful tool in the display advertiser's arsenal. Unlike the previous two options where you target based on the *content* being viewed, in this case you focus on the *person* doing the viewing. If a person displays a certain behavior, such as entering your shopping cart funnel or viewing a key piece of information, you can target that person with ads specific to that behavior.

When a Unique Individual Isn't Really a Person

It's important to note that when discussing audience targeting technology, we talk about targeting a person, but the technology doesn't personally identify an individual. It doesn't work via a name or email or anything identifiable but rather by placing a cookie on a user's browser. Cookies have been used since the early Web—around 1994—to recognize a browser that previously interacted with a site. These audience targeting technologies set a unique cookie on a browser to allow them to recognize that browser when they encounter it again on an ad network or website that employs that targeting technology. Because of this ability to uniquely distinguish individual browsers, advertisers should ensure that their privacy policy is up-to-date and states that they use these targeting tools.

One goal of audience targeting can be to increase your conversion rate. Retargeting, or remarketing as it's known in Google AdWords, is a great tool for this because it specifically targets the low-hanging fruit and is thus one of the most powerful tools at your disposal. Many argue that it is revolutionizing the way we approach display advertising. It allows you to target visitors who have already visited your site or shown an interest in your products/services. It is far easier to convince someone who has already shown this interest than it is to start from scratch with someone coming in cold, which is one of the reasons retargeting is so effective. We address the implementation and best practices in Chapter 11, "Month 8: Advanced Topics," but retargeting generally works by setting a special cookie when visitors visit a particular part of your website.

Two additional types of audience targeting technology have the goal of increasing your volume and reach. Known as demographic bidding and interest categories on the GDN, they help you expand your reach to your targeted audience. And unlike with remarketing, there is no need for the target audience to have already visited your site. Using cookies, Google tracks a user's behavior as they visit sites within the AdSense network and combines that with third-party data to understand what demographics and interests apply to this user. This information can be used to serve ads that target those groups. For example, the sport jersey manufacturer may decide to target males of a certain age group or those who have shown an interest in recreational sports.

The Big Picture: The Process of Display Advertising

In the remainder of this book we lay out everything you need to know to get started in display advertising as well as plenty of strategies and best practices. But before we get into the details, it's worth looking at the overall process.

The first step is to get an account where you can publish your ads. Although it's certainly an option to go directly to publishers and operate your own ad server, we believe most readers of this book are best served by taking advantage of the integrated interface and vast inventory of a large ad network such as the Google Display Network (GDN) via AdWords.

Once you've done that, it's time to think about whom you are marketing to and how to target them. As outlined in the previous section, you can choose to target by several criteria:

- Keywords
- Specific sites
- Demographics
- Audience interests
- Behavior/remarketing
- Topics

Before you begin sending traffic to your site, think ahead about two extremely important pieces: remarketing and measurement. By placing remarketing tags on your site, you begin to build lists of cookies from users who have exhibited certain behaviors on your site.

Over time, you'll build up enough of a list of cookied visitors that you can begin to effectively use remarketing campaigns. Common strategies are to target those who show a deeper interest or even to exclude those who are *unlikely* to convert, such as a visitor who just completed a purchase. After all, if someone just purchased a refrigerator for their home on your site, the chances that they will purchase another one soon are fairly low.

In the past, the GDN was harshly criticized by many advertisers who considered it a complete waste of money. We previously advised our clients to avoid it in most cases because the performance wasn't compelling. That sentiment is shifting as things have improved. Today Google is quick to point out that 99 percent of its top 1,000 advertisers are running display ads, and we've changed our advice to clients as well. The biggest reason for the change in how the GDN is regarded comes down to measurement. All of the targeting technologies and the ability to optimize your campaigns depend on solid data. We simply can't emphasize enough the importance of a robust measurement system. And given the quality of the free tools available, there is no excuse for not using them. Not only does Google provide an enterprise class tool for free in Google Analytics, but that tool has the ability to access the same backend databases AdWords uses. This, combined with the built-in reporting suite of the GDN, puts an amazing amount of information at your fingertips. This can give you a decided competitive advantage if you know how to capitalize on it.

Both remarketing tags and analytics tags should be in place *before* you unleash your advertising so that you can use the data from the visitors the ads generate to refine and optimize your campaigns. A basic optimization strategy may be as follows:

1. Determine which sites are performing for you and which aren't.

2. Consider managed placements to manually bid for more inventory on the good sites and specifically exclude sites that aren't performing.

3. Determine which behaviors on your site lead to high conversion or engagement rates and retarget those users.

4. Look at your most successful users and determine their demographics and interests.

5. Use that knowledge to have Google go out and find more of those types of users!

This last step of refinement is the secret to success on the Display Network and one that we focus on a great deal in this book.

Month 1: Planning Your Campaigns

The key to running successful campaigns lies in the planning stages, and successful advertisers spend plenty of time there. Before you start creating ads and setting up campaigns, you must clearly define the goals you're trying to accomplish and understand just who your customer is. Then it's time to plan your budget, messaging, and message positioning in the marketplace and take stock of the resources you need to create, maintain, and optimize your campaigns.

Chapter Contents:
Week 1: Define Your Display Advertising Goals
Week 2: Showcase What You Do Best
Week 3: Take Stock of Your Resources
Week 4: Plan Your Budget

Week 1: Define Your Display Advertising Goals

Perhaps the biggest mistake advertisers make is to ignore a basic rule of business: Define your *specific* advertising objectives and put strategies in place to measure them. If you're one of those who ignore that rule, don't get too down on yourself—you're not alone. The depth of measurement and sea of metrics that have recently become available have revolutionized the accountability of digital marketing activities. It takes time to get used to this new reality.

It used to be that we designed and implemented our marketing campaigns, and then, after a long time, we tried to identify and correlate any lift in the sales of our products and services with those campaigns. If we were disciplined and focused, we had specific measures in place to track where our sales came from: training call centers to ask callers "how did you find out about us," putting tracking codes on the bottom of every catalog page, printing different codes on coupons that went to different newspapers and magazines, or adding a "mention XYZ when you come in for a discount!" line at the end of our television and radio commercials.

Until recently, this was the best that most of us could do, but these strategies are all prone to human error: The call center operator forgets to ask where the customer heard about you, or the customer isn't motivated to say "I'm supposed to mention XYZ."

In the digital age, we can define a wide variety of goals for our advertising campaigns, and we can measure performance and attribute real value to our advertising efforts in a matter of minutes or hours. And we can do this without the constant risk of human error. Today's tools and measurement technologies give us an unprecedented ability to plan and execute our campaigns and get immediate feedback about how those campaigns resonate (or don't) with potential customers. Armed with that information, we can constantly optimize those campaigns, making them more effective every day.

Monday: Understand the Objectives of Display Advertising

Your first task is to ask yourself the toughest question of all: *What am I trying to accomplish with my display advertising campaigns?*

If you're like most organizations, display is just one component of your marketing mix, so you must define what you want to get out of it. Once you define general objectives, you can define specific goals to help you understand if and just how successful your campaigns are.

Attract More of the Right Kind of Traffic

Want to drive more traffic to your website? Run the ad shown in Figure 4.1 everywhere you can.

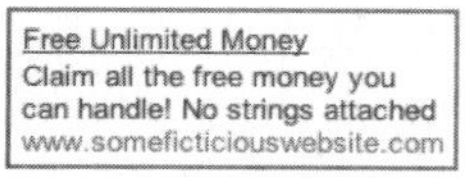

Figure 4.1 An ad that will drive lots of traffic

This might make website *visitor* reports look good, but your business model probably doesn't involve giving away money (if it does, please contact us directly!). The visitors who give you that click will be disappointed, and disappointed visitors rarely convert into revenue and profit.

This is an over-the-top example, but many advertisers spend time and effort attracting—and paying for—the wrong kind of visitors to their websites. Traffic alone is useless. You want visitors *who are interested in your products and services* and *likely to convert on your goals.* With the targeting capabilities and extensive reach of display advertising, you can accomplish that goal.

Increase Your Sales and Conversions

Once you spend time, money, energy and resources to attract that highly qualified, likely-to-convert traffic, you must convert that mere *visitor* into a monetized *customer* or *prospect.* Only then can you gain a positive return on this investment.

An obvious—and good—objective of your marketing campaigns is to increase sales, but don't forget all the other valuable things people can do when they visit your pages. Many business websites have no e-commerce component at all. Other businesses have long sales cycles and it can take months or years to close a deal. But actions of value (conversions) can still occur on your website. Filling out lead forms, downloading white papers, signing up for newsletters, watching videos, getting driving directions, sharing your pages with others, interacting with social media components, and even offline goals like picking up the phone and calling you can all be measured, and they all have value.

Find New Customers and New Markets

Leveraging the enormous reach that display advertising has around the globe and in the most specific pockets and niches of the online world, you can absolutely have as an objective finding new customers and new markets. You can reach people in far-away locations you couldn't before penetrate or didn't know how to reach, but this goes farther than crossing physical distances.

If you have a local business or local restrictions on your business, such as a lawyer licensed to practice in only a single state or a retailer that can ship only to a limited set of destinations, you can still use this medium to find a new group of customers in your physical target locations that are hanging out in virtual places you couldn't access before.

Opportunity Bounces

You may find that your potential customers face problems that you can help them solve with new products and services or a repositioning or offshoot of the products and services you currently have. In the 1940s, a General Electric engineer named James Wright worked on synthetic rubber for military vehicle tires and infantry boots. One of his compounds had interesting bouncy properties. It traveled around scientific circles looking for a useful application until it came under the nose of a Connecticut toy store owner who turned it into Silly Putty! Imagine how much faster ideas can spread today! Whether it's an example like this or something as simple as a men's and women's clothing retailer uncovering a market demand for children's sizes (or even canine and feline versions of the same styles), opportunities for new customers and markets abound.

Expand, Position, and Build Your Brand

Branding and positioning are two long-time goals of marketers and advertisers, and display advertising offers unique ways to accomplish both. You may have heard that with the Web, branding is dead. You may have been told that with e-commerce and real-time shopping comparisons, there's no more brand loyalty. Well, branding may be injured, but for many marketers, it still has a strong pulse. If branding didn't matter anymore, then no one would pay what we do for our iThings, we'd all drink generic cola, and any handbag would do.

As consumers making buying decisions, even in the age of the Internet, we often *do* care about a brand and its reputation, and one of the best definitions of a brand comes from author, entrepreneur, and marketer Seth Godin:

A brand is the set of expectations, memories, stories and relationships that, taken together, account for a consumer's decision to choose one product or service over another. If the consumer (whether it's a business, a buyer, a voter, or a donor) doesn't pay a premium, make a selection or spread the word, then no brand value exists for that consumer.

Source: http://sethgodin.typepad.com/seths_blog/2009/12/define-brand.html

You can use display advertising campaigns to help increase the awareness and position of your brand in the marketplace and help create the concepts and guide the perceptions that you want your brand to be associated with.

Tuesday: Define Your Direct Response Goals

Direct response goals are the specific actions we hope our visitors take after clicking our ads. For example, if we're selling products through e-commerce, we want a visitor who has clicked our ad to purchase something from our online store. In a lead generation scenario, we hope that visitors call us or fill out a form with their contact information.

Any clear *actions* that visitors can take on our websites can be defined as direct response goals, goals that are specific and whose value can be measured. A good way to identify direct response goals is to fill in the blank in the following sentence as many ways as you possibly can:

After clicking my ad, I want someone to _____ on my website.

Here are some common examples:

- Purchase something
- Put something in a shopping cart
- Download something
- Watch something
- Listen to something
- Read something
- Fill out some form
- Call some phone number
- Sign up for something
- Log into something
- Get directions to somewhere
- Search for something
- Find something
- Post something
- Click something
- Share something

When you replace the word *something* with your specific goals, you can come up with *a lot* of direct response advertising goals. Let's take a few specific examples in terms of both specificity and measurability.

A Purchase

Say we have an online store with a shopping cart, a buy now button, or some other way for users to check out online. In an e-commerce scenario, customers trade money for products or services right on our website. This is the easiest kind of direct response goal to measure.

A purchase is specific and measurable. For example, our firm, Cardinal Path, runs Google's Seminars for Success live trainings all over North America. We want visitors to our Seminars for Success website (Figure 4.2) to sign up to attend any or all of the five days of live training. They go through a shopping cart process to choose cities and dates.

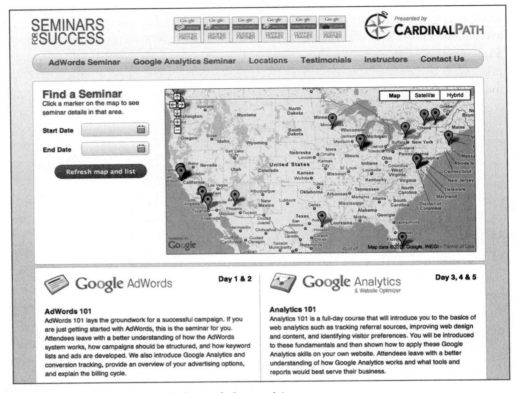

Figure 4.2 Choosing cities and dates on the Seminars for Success website

Our product types are line items like "Chicago, Jun 1-5, Days 1 and 2." Each has specific revenue and cost, so we can calculate the profit (or loss) associated with every seat sold for each day of each event.

A Lead

Leads are another likely direct response goal. Someone who reaches your site may not be ready to trade money for a product or service right now, but they're interested. They can enter your sales funnel as a prospect or a lead by calling you, filling out a form, requesting a product demonstration, or in some other specific way, giving you information that will help you reach out to this new prospective customer.

With a little effort we can get an accurate understanding of how much leads are worth. Let's go back to the Seminars for Success example.

We can track how many people click over to our website and look around. We know how many people contact us by phone or email to ask questions or get more information. We store their information and can maintain details about each time they contact us or interact with us both on- and offline. If they end up signing up for one of our events, we know exactly how much that transaction is worth to us.

With a little math, we can also figure out exactly how much that first phone call or email is worth to us! If it takes 10 incoming phone calls to get one signup and our average signup is worth $10.00, that means each phone call is worth approximately $1.00 to us. And we can differentiate between different types of leads as well. If it takes 20 email leads to get one signup, an email lead is worth only $0.50 to us, half as much as a phone call.

Tip: Looking at average value numbers for these types of goals over longer periods of time helps provide a more precise picture of the value of your leads. Revisiting this lead data along with sales closure rates on a monthly or rolling quarter basis can help you ensure that the values you place on your leads are as current and accurate as possible.

A Signup

Beyond a purchase or a lead, there are many other types of valuable actions visitors can take. One of the most common is a signup. This should be something specific like signing up for an email newsletter or a free webinar. It can even be following you on Twitter or liking or +1ing you on Facebook or Google Plus. The key here is that these people are actively registering an interest in you and your products or services, and that has value.

Lots of people click over to the Seminars for Success website but don't buy anything and don't call or email us. They may be interested, but they're not ready to pull out the credit card right now. Rather than call or email, they sign up for our newsletter so that they'll be contacted when we post new dates and locations. That way, next year when there's a new training budget or when we post an event that's geographically near them, we still have a chance to convert them into paying seminar attendees.

Each time we send out the newsletter, we can track how many seminar seats we sell. If we send email to 1,000 people and sell $1,000 worth of seats as a result, then we can value each signup for our email list at $1.00! And if we start to look at lifetime values of our customers, we can do more complex math and potentially assign an even higher value to this goal.

Wednesday: Define Success Metrics for Direct Response Goals

Once you have defined what you want people to do on your website and how much each action is worth to you, you need to look at how to measure the success— or failure—of your display advertising campaigns.

By using the features and metrics that Google AdWords provides and web analytics solutions like Google Analytics, you can determine whether your marketing dollars are making or losing money. The following are key metrics to help measure success against direct response goals:

Conversion A *conversion* occurs when a visitor takes a desired action. AdWords records a conversion and attributes it to your advertisement if someone clicks your ad and within the next 30 days converts on a goal you have defined.

View-through conversion A *view-through conversion* occurs if someone *sees, but does not click,* your ad and within a defined period of time converts on a goal you have defined. This is especially relevant to display advertising.

Conversion rate The *conversion rate* is the percentage of the time visitors perform a desired action. AdWords simply divides the number of conversions by the number of clicks.

Cost per conversion *Cost per conversion* is the average amount of money you spend for each conversion. It is important to compare it against the break-even point (or value per conversion) of your business goals. AdWords calculates this by dividing your advertising cost by the number of conversions.

We look at many additional metrics later in this book, but understanding these numbers provides a baseline for understanding how your campaigns are performing.

For the Seminars for Success website, let's assume we're looking at our goal of an email newsletter signup (remember, each email signup is worth at least $1.00 to us). Table 4.1 provides three hypothetical campaigns and numbers that we can use to start doing some analysis.

▶ **Table 4.1** Sample direct response conversion metrics

Campaign	Cost	Conversions	Conversion Rate	Cost Per Conversion
Campaign A	$150.00	75	1.0%	$2.00
Campaign B	$40.00	50	1.5%	$0.80
Campaign C	$1.00	2	100.0%	$0.50

Which was our best campaign? Campaign C has the highest conversion rate, but it nets us only $1.00:

1.00 value/conversion – 0.50 cost/conversion = 0.50 net/conversion

2 conversions × 0.50 net/conversion = $1.00 profit

Campaign A has the most new signups, but because of the low conversion rate, it actually *loses* us $75.00:

1.00 value/conversion – 2.00 cost/conversion = –1.00 net/conversion

75 conversions × (–1.00 net/conversion) = $75.00 loss

Campaign B has a small net profit per conversion and enough conversions to make it the most profitable:

1.00 value/conversion – 0.80 cost/conversion = 0.20 net/conversion

50 conversions × 0.20 net/conversion = $10.00 profit

Table 4.1 looks at an aggregate campaign level, but if we want, we can drill down to a specific ad version on a specific page of a specific website: We can get as granular as we like. Once we have the basic metrics and our direct response conversion actions defined, we can quickly and easily see which of our campaigns deserve what part of our marketing budget for a maximum return on investment.

Thursday: Define Branding and Positioning Goals

Branding and positioning goals are often tougher to define than direct response goals, and we often don't look for a direct, causal relationship between our advertising efforts and a specific action. Instead, we want customers to know and be influenced by us, so they think of us (and think of us positively) when they *do* have a need that we can fill.

In the online world, when we think about defining specific goals that we can measure, we look for data points that indicate things like how many people know about us and how we're viewed and positioned in the marketplace. To help us understand these things, we can do another fill-in-the blank exercise:

As a result of my branding and positioning display campaigns, I want someone to _____.

- Visit my website for the first time
- Come back to my website more often as a returning visitor
- Stay on my website and engage with my content
- Find my website through branded keyword searches
- Share information about my brand with others in a positive way
- Follow or endorse my brand through social media channels
- Be more likely to know or recognize my brand than they were before
- Have a more positive view of my brand than they did before
- Know where I have positioned my brand among my competitors
- Recommend my products and services to someone else
- Provide favorable feedback after interacting with my website
- Search for my brand name at some point in the future

Let's explore some of these branding and positioning goals.

Interact with My Website

These days, when people learn about a new brand, product, or service for the first time, they often check it out online. Web analytics tools like Google Analytics can provide a wealth of information about visitors to your pages and what they do—especially when they don't buy anything.

To find out if you're attracting new visitors, for example, you can look at a New vs. Returning visitor report and measure the percentage of traffic that's visiting for the first time. A Frequency and Recency report helps you understand how many times visitors come back and how many days since they last checked in. Engagement metrics and flow reports show you how people traverse and consume different kinds of content on your site. None of these metrics alone can define the success or failure of your marketing actions, but taken together with other data points, they give an idea of how visitors are engaging (or not engaging) with your content.

Google Analytics also has an entire set of social reports that can help you understand what visitors that come to your site from social channels are doing and provide insights into the conversations that mention and share your pages around the Web. For example, you can configure Google Analytics to track when people click the little social buttons you see all over the Internet (Figure 4.3).

Figure 4.3 Some popular social sharing buttons

Figure 4.4 shows a visualization of social value and a basic social engagement report, both available in Google Analytics.

Above all, you're after the conversions, and this is a great place to measure your display advertising campaigns' impact on any of those great direct response goals we defined earlier, *even if your display ads don't directly result in those conversions.*

The Multi-Channel Funnels (MCF) reports in Google Analytics provide a unique and useful way to understand the effect your display campaigns are having on conversion actions over time. Figure 4.5 shows an Assisted Conversions report, filtered for paid advertising sources.

Take a look at that second row. Our display ads (labeled Content in Google Analytics) generated only $44K in direct response revenue, but they *assisted* in generating 10 times as much! This terminology is borrowed from basketball, and with good reason. The player that puts the ball in the basket gets credit for the points, and the player that passed the ball to the shooter gets an assist. Without that pass, those points wouldn't have been scored.

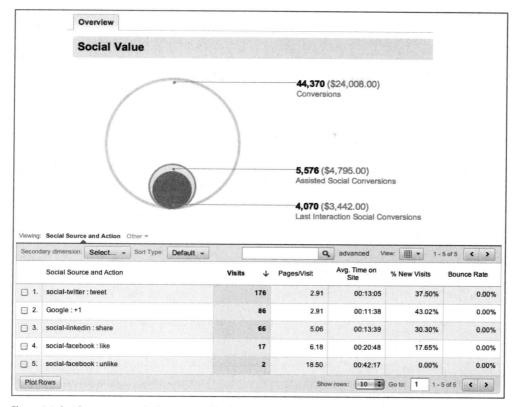

Figure 4.4 Social engagement and value reports in Google Analytics

	Basic Channel Grouping	Ad Distribution Network	Assisted Conversions ↓	Assisted Conversion Value	Last Interaction Conversions	Last Interaction Conversion Value	Assisted / Last Interaction Conversions
1.	Paid Advertising	Google Search	13,696	$2,418,608.27	11,162	$1,029,644.00	1.23
2.	Paid Advertising	Content	4,092	$440,076.00	3,659	$44,806.00	1.12
3.	Paid Advertising	Search partners	2,368	$334,536.00	2,019	$176,479.50	1.17
4.	Paid Advertising	Unknown	375	$142,583.00	175	$22,875.00	2.14

Figure 4.5 Tracking assisted conversions in Google Analytics

The Top Conversion Paths report (Figure 4.6) is another valuable MCF report that shows the different touch points along people's journey to convert on our goals. Our paid advertising campaigns may not directly result in the conversions, but they do have a real and measurable influence.

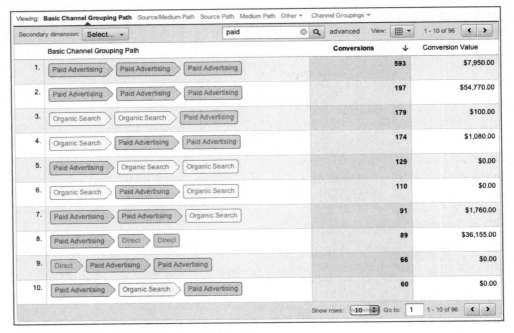

Figure 4.6 Tracking the top conversion paths in Google Analytics

Rows 5 and 8, for example, tell us that visitors found us through our paid advertising campaigns and then later came back by doing an organic search for us or going directly to our websites. Our ads didn't directly result in the conversions, but without them, the conversions may not have occurred!

Social Media's Impact on Brand

Social media has exploded in recent years. We cannot afford to ignore its effect on our brands and how they're perceived in the marketplace.

For example, a common response to "What do you think of United Airlines?" is "United breaks people's guitars and doesn't care about their customers." That's because a guy named Dave Carroll made a YouTube video complaining about the way United baggage handlers treated his guitar. More than *10 million people* watched it, and it got to #7 in *Time* magazine's 2009 Top Viral Videos.

By contrast, JetBlue started its search for a marketing agency by testing its online savvy with a tweet to see who would reply. Jet Blue has been a consistent positive example. Its main account, @JetBlue, has over 1.5 million followers, and another quarter million follow its @JetBlueCheeps account, which offers exclusive deals on last-minute flights. Even better, it uses Twitter to conduct business and keep customers happy, all squarely in the public's eye. Canceled flights get rebooked, baggage gets found, delays get communicated, and customers become happy. Those customers become advocates, spreading their positive experiences with the JetBlue brand across social circles faster than wildfire.

Friday: Create Strategies to Measure Branding and Positioning

Measuring the effectiveness of your advertising against branding and positioning goals can be tough.

Of course, we have many traditional means of measuring brand impact that can be done through formal marketing research. We can commission studies to help us understand the effects of our campaigns on aided and unaided brand awareness, intent to purchase, and brand association and favorability, but there are a number of online metrics, tools and resources that can help us as well.

Visits from Branded Keywords

This fantastic metric can help you see how people find you by your brand terms over time. Let's look at how to do this with the advanced segmentation feature of Google Analytics.

An advanced segment is a set of criteria you can define that when applied to your reports, limits the data you see to *only* visits that match those criteria. In our case, we want to look only at website visits that began as a result of someone searching on one of our branded keywords.

Figure 4.7 shows what the settings of this advanced segment might look like for our firm, Cardinal Path.

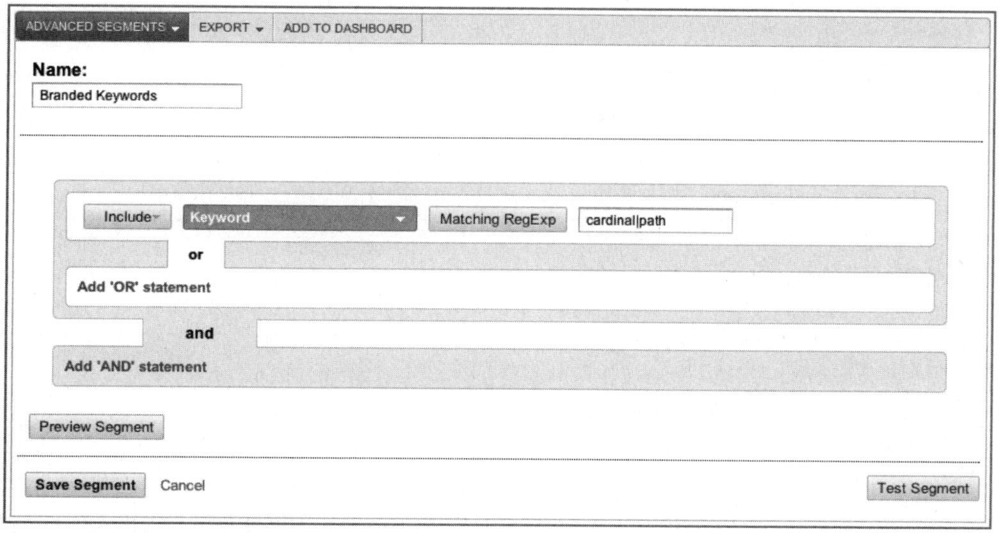

Figure 4.7 Specifying branded keywords

Here we used what's known as a regular expression to define our matching criteria. The regular expression "cardinal|path" simply means anything containing "cardinal" or "path," but keep in mind that you can choose different matching criteria from the dropdown menu and use the "Add statement" links to add logical AND or OR criteria to catch all the ways people use your brand names..

 Tip: For more information about regular expressions and the types of operators that are supported in Google Analytics, head over to this excellent help center post: http://support.google.com/googleanalytics/bin/answer.py?hl=en&answer=55582

Once we apply this advanced segment, we can navigate to any reports within Google Analytics and see *only* data that matches our segment. Figure 4.8 shows a Visitors Overview report with the Branded Keywords segment applied.

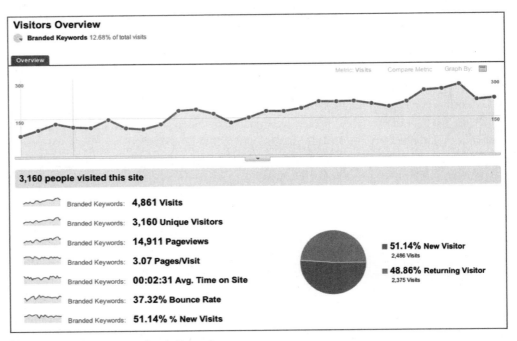

Figure 4.8 Tracking visitors versus branded keywords

We see good things happening at even a very basic level! The graph is moving up and to the right, indicating that people are getting to know our brand and visiting our websites by searching for *us* and our brand terms.

Social Media Interaction

Another great way to see how you're doing with getting your brand out there is to look at the ways you engage and are engaged with across social media channels. For example, you can look at the number of people liking you on Facebook over time through Facebook Insights.

On the Twitter side, tools like Twitalyzer, TweetReach, and TweetStats can help you get a feel for how many people you're reaching and influencing, and tools like Klout can extend well beyond just the Twittersphere.

Tools like the free SocialMention and the not-so-free Lithium and Radian6 allow you to dive even deeper to understand where your brands are part of conversations all over the Web.

These solutions help you find metrics about volume of activity across different social media platforms, sentiment (social mentions that are viewed in a positive, neutral, or negative light), and the qualitative aspects of brand perception found in the social content itself.

Examining Your Market Share

Google Insights for Search exposes information about the keywords people search on when they go to Google. This can be used as an indicator of branding reach and market share: The more people typing your brand into Google, the more people know about you.

Get started at www.google.com/insights/search by entering the search terms you're interested in exploring and comparing and refining settings of search type, location, dates, and categories.

Figure 4.9 shows search queries for the names of the top four browsers. As Microsoft's once dominant Internet Explorer and Apple's Safari meander along, Mozilla's Firefox enjoys a healthy lead. But over time, Google's Chrome is introduced and trends rapidly upward. You can start to watch your brand move in relation to others in your market and use this as a measure of your branding impact.

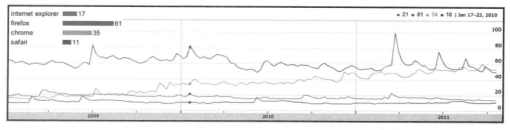

Figure 4.9 Tracking browser keywords in Google Insights for Search

Compete.com is another resource that can help you understand your competition and your market share, providing statistics and numbers for different domains around the Web. Figure 4.10 compares the three fastest-growing restaurant brands in the United States over the course of one year. While Five Guys stayed relatively constant throughout the year, Jimmy Johns experienced consistent growth. Chipotle seems to have had something going on in March through May, and this can be explained in part by Chipotle founder Steve Ells' appearance as a judge for NBC's reality show *America's Next Great Restaurant* during that time. But it wasn't all positive press; Chipotle faced a criminal probe into its hiring practices by the US Attorney's office.

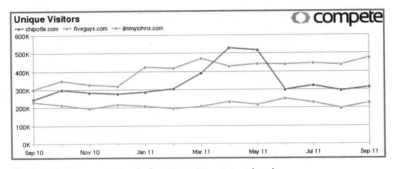

Figure 4.10 Compete.com data for fastest-growing restaurant brands

With paid versions of this and other tools (for example, Experian's Hitwise), you can start to understand your share of search results from specific keywords and even use demographic and lifestyle data to identify key groups of potential visitors and their behavior in order to target them with your display advertising campaigns.

Week 2: Showcase What You Do Best

Before you create ads and try to put them in front of the right kinds of eyeballs, it's important to take an inward look and understand who your customers are, what they're really looking for, what options they have in the market, and why they should choose you over those other options.

Monday: Solve Your Customers' Problems

As marketers, we're not trying to sell products and services. Yes, we make widgets and have line items on our menu of ways to help our customers, but that's all there to support one goal: *Solve the problems our potential customers are having right now.* What we sell are solutions to people's problems, not widgets or line items. This fundamental concept can help us identify where to run our ads, what audiences to target, and how to craft our ad creatives. Often, we the marketers are the worst people to figure out what's going through the minds of our prospects as they wander through the purchase cycle. Let's take a couple of examples.

Service Example: The Plumbing Professional

Let's imagine that we run a plumbing business that's open 24/7/365. There's a natural tendency to describe our products and services from our own perspective. For example, we might think we repair and maintain fill valve shank washers, detect and eradicate p-trap blockages, and ensure that overflow tubes and flappers are appropriately sealed and functional. But how many times has the average customer called up needing someone right away to address the fact that the atmospheric pressure being applied to the bowl apparatus is no longer pushing the "bad stuff" past the closet flange?

If we put ourselves in the shoes of this consumer, they might be searching on websites describing how toilets work with diagrams and step-by-step instructions on how to fix common problems. They might be looking at a series of blog posts about do-it-yourself plumbing, or maybe it's a YouTube video showing how to use a snake and a plunger on a backed-up toilet. These are exactly the kinds of places that we as advertisers want to be. Figure 4.11 shows two very different types of ads.

Figure 4.11 Two very different ads aimed at the same end customer

While the text ad probably makes sense to a plumbing professional, it has very little impact on the consumer who's experiencing the problem. The 300×250 pixel image ad is *exactly* what the customer is looking for. They connect with the broken toilet—theirs is broken too! And this place is open *right now*! And I can call them at *this phone number* and they're *local*, so they'll be here within 30 minutes! This is the kind of reaction we want from our potential customers—and one that has a much higher probability of producing more inbound phone calls to a plumbing company!

Product Example: Intel Inside®

A favorite example of the classroom and a wildly successful campaign, Intel Inside® was (and still is) a prime example of a company understanding how to talk to its end users.

Just as those with a plumbing problem aren't talking the technical jargon of the industry, the vast majority of those in the market for a computer aren't talking about what lithography process created the best dies cut out of what size of wafer. So how did Intel manage to convince the world that they should insist on something they cannot even describe, much less understand its most technical characteristics?

Intel's marketing efforts have successfully positioned the microprocessor as the brains of any computer we might be buying—its most important part. The message is clear: If we don't insist on having Intel inside, then we could be in trouble. An Intel Inside ad from the early 1990s has the tag line "How to spot the very best PCs," which speaks directly to the customer's problem: If I don't know what RAM stands for and haven't a clue how many megahertz I need, then *how do I know how to spot a good computer when I'm looking for them*?

Tuesday: Look at Your Competition

Now that you've identified the problems that your products and services solve for would-be buyers, let's find out who competes with you for that buyer's business.

Why We Evaluate Competition

One of the most common questions advertisers ask, regardless of whether they're the largest of enterprises or the smallest of new businesses, and regardless of whether they've been advertising online for an hour or a decade, is this:

How am I doing compared to my competitors?

Over the years, we've seen this question take many forms. What's a good click-through rate? How many visits does my competitor get every month? What's a good conversion rate? All of these questions are essentially asking how our ads, campaigns, and websites stack up to all the others, and our favored response goes as follows:

Q: What's a good [insert metric here]?

A: Better than *yours* was yesterday.

If you find that your click-through rate is better than the industry average, will you stop trying to get a better rate? If you learn that you have half the conversion rate of your top competitor, do you change your goal of continuously improving it? If you find that your competitor has less traffic than you, do you stop trying to get new, targeted, likely-to-convert visitors on your site?

Clearly not. We use these metrics not to compare ourselves to others but to compare today's performance with that of the past and strive for continuous improvement. We've seen websites with extremely high conversion and click-through rates go belly up, while some with low conversion rates or highly targeted traffic acquisition campaigns bringing in very few (but the *right* kind) of visitors thrive.

Competitive analysis is important, but it's also important to understand why we're doing it. Rather than looking for benchmarks and spending money on tools that estimate how others perform, how much they pay in what ad networks, and how many clicks they attract, it's often more important to understand your market's landscape.

Who plays in it, how do they position themselves, and what do they offer? With *that* information, you can segment your markets and tailor your ads to the right audiences with the right message that shapes your products and services as the best solutions to the problems your potential customers are looking to solve.

Where to Look and What to Look For

As you seek to understand the markets in which you compete, you can take some logical steps to gain enormous insight and perspective.

First, put yourself in the place of the end user. If you're the plumbing service we talked about, imagine that *you* have that problem in your bathroom. Go to your favorite search engine and start solving that problem—you might start with a search for "24 hour emergency toilet unclogging service."

The organic, or unpaid, search engine results probably reveal three types of competition: direct, inconsequential, and accidental. Direct competition is other plumbing companies willing and able to service this client. Follow those links and understand what they offer and why they think they're better. Are they cheaper? Of better quality? Do they guarantee their work? Do they respond quickly? Only use a certain brand of parts? All of this information helps you identify why *you* are a better choice than they are.

Inconsequential competition cannot serve your target market. If you live in California, a local plumber in Maine offers similar services but not in your geographic market. While you don't compete with them directly, following their links to understand their service offerings can be valuable. They may offer a competitive advantage that your market doesn't have yet.

Accidental competition shows up often on the Web and can help us avoid mistakes. For example, if you are trying to sell hotel rooms for the Hilton in Paris, France, imagine how much money you might waste by showing your ads on sites that are all about the famous heiress Paris Hilton. Take a look at what comes up when you start researching your own terms. Looking into the way ad-serving platforms determine relevance can provide valuable insight that you can use to your advantage as you get into later chapters.

In addition to competition, your search results probably contain informational articles, how-to videos, listing and review services, and more. These can be incredibly useful, especially if they carry advertising inventory! Figure 4.12 shows a site from the first page of Google results for emergency plumbing.

When doing this research, try to emulate your customer's process of solving the problem. If *you* saw a search result about how much it ought to cost to unclog a pipe or a toilet, would you click it? Someone with a plumbing problem wants to get a sense of how much this is going to cost before they give up and call. If you look at the page, you can see that it serves Ads by Google, which means you can advertise on this page through the GDN! You'll likely find many such pages, and it's a good idea to write them down. If *you* find them, odds are good your prospective customers might land there as well.

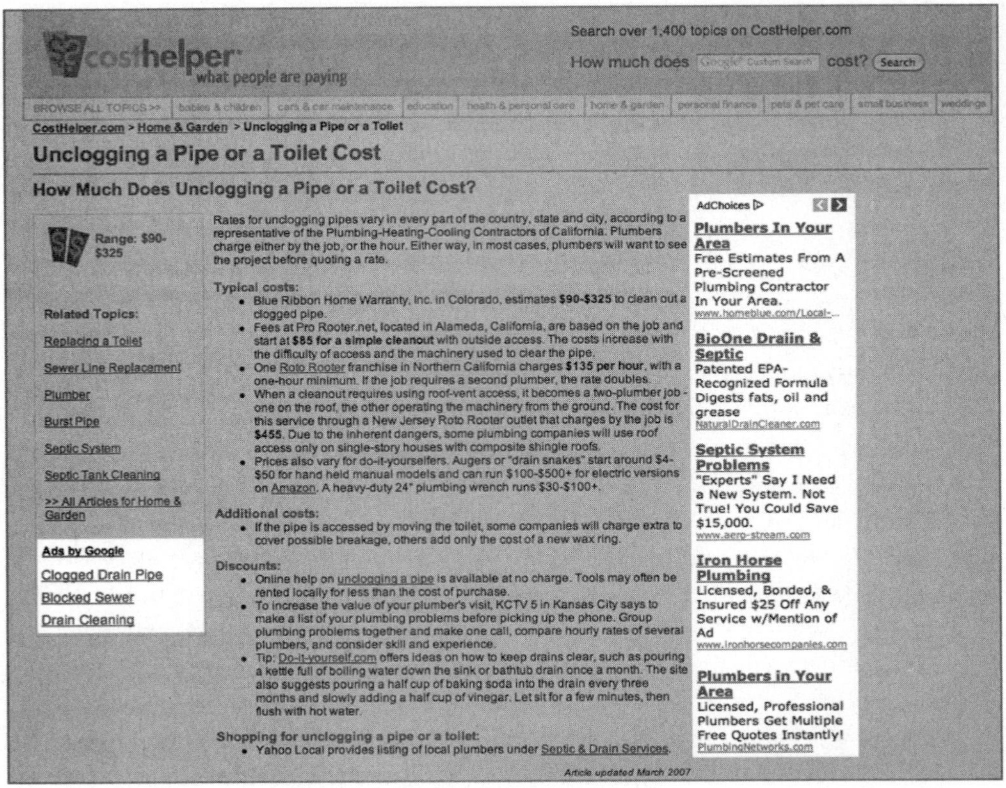

Figure 4.12 AdWords inventory available on an informational website

Another type of search result is a listing service—an online version of the Yellow Pages or something specific to plumbing services. Look through these listings as well and spend time on more of your competitors' websites.

You can also see who is spending money in search advertising simply by looking for their ads on search engine results pages. You can identify who you may need to compete with in the paid search markets and research their websites and their offerings just as you did the organic results. The plumbing service from Maine might still be bidding on California clicks, and whether that company can service your clients or not, you're still competing with them for ad space here, and you can use these lessons to appropriately target your campaigns later.

When you find informational sites where you'd like to run your display ads, make sure you know who's advertising there as well. Are there ads for other local plumbing services? Are there ads from e-commerce stores selling new toilets? Noticing these things is helpful as you create relevant ads and build your ad groups to target these sites later on.

Last, see if you end up being followed by an advertisement after all of this research. We talk more about audience targeting and *re*targeting later, but for now, it's good to know which (if any) of your competitors are doing this!

Wednesday: Identify Your Competitive Advantage

At this point, you understand your potential customers' problems, and you have a good feel for who competes in your market. Now it's time for the most important question of all:

Why should they choose us over anyone else?

This is not always easy to answer, but trying to do so helps you create, organize, and position your advertising campaigns for maximum success.

Competing on Price and Quality

The most common things to compete on are price and quality. While that may be where you want to focus, just about everyone else will be trying to compete here as well.

When consumers with plumbing problems are digging around for information, they're likely early in their search for a solution. They're trying to decide whether to keep trying to unclog their toilet or give up and call a professional. Both price and quality can certainly be factors in deciding to hire a professional. They might be thinking something like, "Well, that's cheaper than 5 hours of my time trying to figure it out, and there are good professionals who have fixed this problem a thousand times before." But once they decide to hire *someone*, you need to convince them to hire *you*, not your competition.

If you compete on price, your competitive research is crucial. If your competition offers to send someone for $50, can you be cheaper and still maintain a viable business? Can you make up a loss in margins by gaining volume? Let's assume that you can do it for $45. The point here is that if your ad is essentially the same as your competitors with a savings of $5, you might win the click, but it's not very hard for your competition to beat you—all they need to do is drop their price to $40. In this race to the bottom, whoever can keep the business running at the lowest cost spread over the largest volume wins, but it might be a race you don't want to enter.

On the other side of this spectrum, you can hold your price point higher, say at $60, but compete on the quality of your service. Of course, you need to do something better than the competition if you charge more. Maybe you tell potential customers that you use better parts, that your technicians have better training and qualifications and are better at resolving problems. The end customers must believe that they will get higher quality and better experience for those extra dollars.

Competing on Something Else

It's difficult to stand out as cheaper or better when everyone else is saying the same kinds of things, and display advertising helps us go well beyond cheaper and better. Chapter 2, "Overview of Display Advertising," talks about finding competitive differentiation on something other than price or quality, but now that you've done your homework and understand who else is playing in your markets and what their messages are, it's time to find *your* competitive advantage.

Note: One of the most powerful facets of advertising online is that we can easily test different ideas and concepts, so feel free to identify all kinds of options. What follows are just a few guidelines that we've found helpful in identifying messaging that goes beyond price and quality and positions your ads for success.

Remember Your Targeting

When you create an ad, it's important to keep in mind what you know about the eyeballs you've targeted. Perhaps you know the kind of web page your ad will show up on because you've used effective contextual or placement targeting. For example, if you target web pages about how to fix your own toilet, you can carefully craft a message catering to the do-it-yourselfer who is likely on the fence about whether to hire a plumber or try to fix the problem. Rather than being the cheapest or the best, maybe you push a message to appeal to this type of customer: "We show you how we did it so you can do it next time."

With ads targeting a very specific geolocation, you can position yourself as a local option offering personalized service: Sure, you can go with that national chain and have them send a truck from two counties away, *or* you can go with us. If you go with us, we'll be there faster. If we mess up, you know where to find us. And you have a neighborhood resource you can recognize and count on next time.

Sweeten the Deal

Another way to stand out from the competition is to offer something special or something different that comes along with selecting you over a competitor. You don't choose the Burger King Kids Club meal over the McDonald's Happy Meal because of price or quality. They compete on the toy. From Beanie Babies and Legos to action figures from the latest box office hits, ads for these meals promote anything *but* price or quality.

In the plumbing example, you might try offering a full 10-point inspection of the other toilets in the house while you're there. It might cost a little more, but the customer will know if there are any other toilets on the fritz before you leave.

Appeal to the Emotion

We are emotional beings. We make most of our decisions using the most basic and ancient part of our brain, and we use intellect and rationalization to justify the emotional decision to ourselves. If that were not the case, not a single candy bar would leave the shelves of a store. Candy bars do not help our bodies operate in a healthy manner: Intellectually and rationally, we should not eat them. And yet they elicit an emotional response that drives consumers to buy them in droves.

An excellent example of appealing to the emotion is the way Volvo positions its brand and its ads around safety. It no longer even sells cars—it sells the fact that if someone rear ends you at a stoplight, you (and your family too!) will be safe.

Odds are good that you can find emotional sentiment to appeal to in your ads. Nobody *wants* to dig around in a clogged toilet. Your plumbing service might compete on the message that you'll do the dirty work and leave your customer's bathroom as fresh as a spring day.

Thursday / Friday: Define and Find Your Customers

You've spent a lot of time putting yourself in the shoes of your potential customers and emulating their process in choosing a solution to their problem. Now it's time to define just whose shoes you've been walking in.

Creating and Using Personas

For nearly two decades, personas have had a role in marketing, software design, and user experience work. They boil down to creating fictional characters meant to represent different kinds of users or target audiences. Creating personas takes time and research. A great way to start is by talking to your existing customer base, because these are the people you've already convinced to convert on your marketing goals.

As an advertiser, you want to create and become familiar with a wide spectrum of personas representing your potential clients. Then you can use them to help identify client problems, walk through how they go about solving those problems, and figure out how you can stand out to them among all the other options. Let's look at two sample personas. We use a brief narrative format here for the sake of demonstration.

John is 22 years old and only two years out of school but happily in the early stages of his career with a great job that offers great growth opportunities. John has just bought his first home, and he's very mindful of his monthly expenses.

He's a pretty handy guy—he grew up fixing things in his parents' house and knows his way around a hardware store. But, John works a lot of hours and can't seem to find the time to do anything except meet with his friends on the weekends.

John is also very Internet savvy—he can find just what he's after very quickly on his laptop, his iPad, and his Android phone.

———

Jane is a grandmother of seven and lives alone in the same house she's lived in for the past 30 years. Jane knows the house inside and out and has boxes full of receipts for every service ever performed on any brick, shingle, or pipe.

Jane is particular about who services her home and is insistent that a good service will do what they say they'll do for a fair price and stand by their work.

Her children and grandchildren have successfully gotten her addicted to Facebook, and she religiously logs in to keep tabs on her friends and family, but email is a bit beyond her means. Jane knows how to go to "the Google" and type in what she wants, but she often ends up lost in the World Wide Web and has to click that house thing to get back to the Google.

Let's say both Jane and John find themselves with a toilet that won't flush. Is there a difference in the kinds of searches they do to find a solution? John likely does specific searches on how to fix his broken toilet and follows links to how-to sites until he realizes he doesn't have time to do it himself. Jane will go to Google and likely type in something like "reputable local plumber." She's not going to try to fix this herself.

Going down those paths yourself, you can see who you're competing with and identify great ad placements and networks to be on.

Following through with these personas, you can find the competitive advantages that are likely to resonate with Jane and John. While John might be looking for flexible service times and speedy repairs (remember, he works all the time), Jane might be more interested in a lifetime guarantee from a family-owned business in her town.

Understanding Market Segments

Remember as you build out and use personas that they are different from market segments and that both are quite useful to us as advertisers. While personas help you understand the *kinds* of people that could be buying your products and services, market segmentation can give you a structured look at who is likely to be your customer and how many of them are out there.

We typically segment markets by things like geography, demographics, psychographics, and behavioral traits. Segments identify subsets of a larger group that demonstrate a high probability of buying what we're selling.

If we sell snow blowers, then the Southern California geographic segment won't likely account for many of our sales. Demographics include things like age and gender, while psychographics include values and attitudes. Behavioral segments are defined by actions taken. In the online world that might be sites visited, forms filled out, or other browser-based activities.

For example, by conducting surveys or looking through customer relationship management (CRM) system data, a plumbing services company may find that many customers are 35- to 44-year-old males on the north side of town who have signed up for the e-newsletter to receive home improvement tips. That combination of characteristics constitutes a specific market segment, and a desirable one at that.

Finding Where They're Likely to Be

Spending time creating personas that accurately depict potential customers and maybe even getting some market segmentation data makes it easier to identify where potential customers are hanging out and how you might get the right kind of ad under their noses at just the right time.

You know Jane is on Facebook every day, so you might want to use Facebook display ads to plant the seed in Jane's head that you're the plumbing service that will stand by her side forever. You can target the do-it-yourself blogs and web pages that John is reading with messaging to help convince him that hiring professional help is a better idea than wasting his precious time trying to do it himself.

If you know you're going after 35- to 44-year-old males in a specific geography, you can target a campaign to a physical location and websites that attract a high concentration of 35- to 44-year-old males to show your ads. And since you know that people who sign up for your home improvement newsletter are likely to become your customers, you can target audiences of Internet users who have exhibited interest in home improvement websites.

In Chapter 5, "Month 2: Targeting Your Audience," we look at the tools and mechanics that allow you to do exactly what we've just laid out: Find these websites and set up your campaigns to target just the right kind of prospect. But before you can do this, you need to have the tools and processes to define the right kind of prospect, and personas and market segments are a great place to start.

Week 3: Take Stock of Your Resources

Before you dive into display advertising, spend some time understanding the skill sets and resources you need to create, maintain, and optimize your campaigns. Networks like the GDN are accessible to everyone from the small business owner to the most sophisticated of enterprise teams. Whether you wear all the hats in your organization or are putting together a team dedicated to your display efforts, this week offers insights and suggestions about bringing on resources or developing, nurturing, and continuing to build your own skills.

Monday: Understand the Process of Success

Figure 4.13 shows the cycle of creating and refining your campaigns. This week we look at the skills needed to accomplish each stage.

Figure 4.13 The cycle of creating and maintaining your campaigns

Research and planning A lot of research can go into planning an effective campaign. We use every piece of data we can get to understand our potential customers, our market, our offer, and any results we've achieved so far.

But launching a campaign is no time to stop! It's like a wedding: Hopefully it's the least happy day of the newlyweds' new life together. That might sound strange, but continually working on the relationship leads to even happier days going forward. Because we can always do better, we use performance reports, visual and clickstream analytics, voice of customer, user experience studies, and a host of other data and information sources to plan our next iterations. When we hit click-through rates of 100 percent with conversion rates of 100 percent and infinite ROI across every goal we can think of, we can stop. Until then, there's work to do and we can always learn and improve.

Implementation Only when you have a plan that's informed by research, analysis, and exploration is it time to start implementing. With a new campaign, this means everything from naming the campaign and defining targeting and budgets to structuring and building out the ad groups that turn your blueprints into reality. Planning serves as an instruction manual for building out your campaigns.

Ever bought an even mildly complicated piece of furniture from IKEA and tried to put it together without the instructions? Odds are it took a lot more time, generated a lot more frustration, and didn't end up looking quite like that floor model. As with anything else, having directions to follow leads to better results.

Creative and landing pages While you can't implement a campaign without finishing the research and planning stage, you can often save time by building out ad creatives and landing pages in parallel with the campaigns. Creating ads requires that you know who you're talking to, what message you want to convey, and how best to convey it. And once prospects click, you must take them to a place that is primed and ready to guide them gracefully to your conversion goals.

Installing tracking code There's no avoiding it: You need to install some code or have it installed for you. At the very least, you need conversion tracking code and a web analytics solution, complete with goal and possibly e-commerce tracking. At the very most, the sky is really the limit on what you can track, from the millisecond your ads appear somewhere in the world to what happens from that point forward.

Deploying the campaigns With campaigns built, creative in place, landing pages ready to go, and tracking installed, it's time to launch. With today's ad-serving platforms, this is often instantaneous—the second you say "go," you can participate in auctions and advertising across an almost inconceivable amount of available inventory on the Web. With the GDN, you immediately have access to over 80 percent of the Internet-using world.

Measuring and analyzing results Once you start serving your ads, you start to get information about where those ads are shown, what triggers them, how they are interacted with, and whether or not they get clicked. And that's just the beginning.

Once a visitor arrives on a web property you control, you can see what happens on that and subsequent visits. You can start to understand what actions your advertising efforts help to promote and what goals they help your potential customers accomplish.

Rinse and repeat Congratulations! If you've made it this far, you're just in time to start all over again. With the new data you collect and the new research you do, you're ready to make informed decisions about the next round of refinements and campaigns. As you get your campaigns tuned and optimized, remember that the world around us is constantly changing. What worked yesterday may not work tomorrow, and new competition pops up every day. Continual optimization and refinement positions you for success.

Tuesday: Identify the Campaign Implementer

The campaign implementer is a key role in any display advertising initiative—and for good reason. This person translates the vision into reality, putting the research and analysis into tactical practice. Often, the implementer is also the coordinator, rounding up and organizing the relevant data and research, collecting the ad creatives, and ensuring that landing pages and tracking mechanisms are in place. Plan to spend time, money, and resources here.

To be successful, the campaign implementer needs the skills described in the following sections. The list is not complete, but it should give you an idea of the kind of person you need to perform this task—or the skill set to develop if that person is you.

Platform Expertise

The campaign implementer works on one or more platforms and must know everything that can and cannot be done there. A campaign implementer using the GDN, for example, should know everything from AdWords account structure and hierarchy to what dials and knobs can be turned and tuned to target everything from day parts to custom-defined audiences.

Many implementers teach themselves and refine their skills through experience, but resources for formal education and training are appearing. Books like this one, blogs, instructional videos, live seminars and training programs, certification programs, and even university-level courses pop up every day.

In addition to taking advantage of continuous education, an implementer should know how to find help when it's needed. A network of professional contacts and familiarity with online help files and resources can save countless hours when it comes time to implement.

Project Management and Organizational Skills

As the ringleader, the campaign implementer must pull together deliverables and coordinate schedules. The ability to organize not just the resources and components of a successful campaign but also the very structure of that campaign is critical. How do you break down campaigns and ad groups and spread them across the account to reach the target audiences with the targeted messages within the budget? Is it better to create a brand-new campaign, build a new ad group inside an existing campaign, or simply make a change to something that's already in place? Being able to quickly group and categorize tasks and objectives from a functional perspective goes a long way here.

The campaign implementer herds all the cats. Ensuring that analysts and market researchers dig for and find insights to drive the campaigns, ensuring that designers have the background they need to deliver the most relevant ads with the right messaging and the landing pages necessary to seal the deal, and enabling programmers to build out pages and implement tracking solutions are all part of the master plan. Scheduling, task management, and constant communication are necessary whether your team is made up of 50 people or a single person wearing lots of hats.

Maintain the Broad Vision

Understanding the overall process and how all the pieces fit together —seeing both the forest and the trees—is a key component of implementing a clear and focused strategy. For example, knowing how the messaging garnered from persona development is targeted based on market segments and how anything can change over time is instrumental in designing campaigns and ad groups that not only accomplish goals but are also easily scaled, updated, and extended. Building infrastructure correctly to begin with repays the effort more and more, the longer the campaign goes on. A firm foundation is easier to build on and change.

Wednesday: Identify the Market Researcher

If you have a large marketing department, you likely have market researchers, and the overall objectives of this role haven't changed since before the Internet came around.

The goal of this role is to lead and execute on the research and planning phase. The job description includes finding and organizing sales and internal data, exploring new data sources, and running interviews, surveys, and focus groups to gather as much information as possible about the customer, the market, and the positioning of your products and services. This is not an exhaustive list, but these types of skills and traits can be extremely helpful to market researchers.

Quantitative and Analytical Skills

Market research teams often include Excel and data visualization experts. The amount of available data can be overwhelming, and the hardest thing about data is translating all those numbers, metrics, and dimensions into actionable information. Strong skills in mathematics, statistics, and analysis can help find patterns in the numbers and explain what the research is telling you.

Communicating insights is as important as finding them. The ability to summarize data sets or build effective visualizations of the message in the data makes the difference between recommendations that gather dust and those that get implemented.

Communication and Listening

Trained focus group leaders or surveyors can walk a subject or a group through a series of questions or activities without guiding them toward a desired response or introducing bias. They are a pleasure to watch, and it comes down to effective communication and listening skills.

Many marketers have a hard time listening to customers and hearing what they're really saying—especially if it differs from their preconceived notions. The ability to keep an open mind, probe for clarity, and pull the essence of meaning from the words being said are essential to making sense out of mountains of qualitative data.

Human Behavior and Psychology

A keen interest or formal training in human behavior and psychology coupled with a healthy curiosity of what makes people do what they do is almost a necessity in a market researcher. Lessons in cognitive psychology abound in marketing, and the more knowledge you gain about how the human mind wraps itself around and digests information in order to make decisions, the more you understand how to sway those decisions toward your own products and services.

Principles of psychology can help define branding and positioning, test ad copy or imagery, and build landing pages and a conversion funnel. They can help take visitors through a process that ends not just in a purchase but in a lifelong repeat customer who is also your biggest advocate.

Thursday: Identify the Graphic Designer and Developer

Graphic designers and developers often work together, especially on the landing pages and user experience on the website itself. Graphic designers create and refine ad creatives, wireframes and mockups of websites, landing pages, and other online assets. Developers implement the code behind rich media ads, integrate client-side analytics and conversion tracking code, and build and update landing pages and websites.

Graphic Designer Skills

The tools of today's graphic design trade extend well beyond pen and paper. Designers should use tools like those found in the Adobe Creative Suite as skillfully as a Jedi uses a light saber—both to provide a better finished product and be more efficient as well.

Beyond tools, the line that separates designers and programmers has blurred recently. Designers with expertise in XHTML, CSS, and JavaScript can not only mock up great designs, they can also implement front-end code. In fact, many designers use code for rapid prototyping, reducing the time to implement changes during the back and forth of design approvals. And with responsive design that takes advantage of the latest client-side browser technologies, a good designer can ensure that designs automatically look great on laptops and desktops, mobile phones, and tablets.

A good graphic designer must be artistic, and this contains elements of both nature and nurture. The former is, unfortunately for the rest of us, something that just cannot be taught. But it's often not enough on its own, and formal training can bring out the best in even the most incredible natural talent.

Graphic designers must have effective communication and interpersonal skills. Designers joke about how their clients tell them what they want: "It should be funky, but not over the top. We want to say we're professional, but we're hip and edgy too." The ability to carry out a constructive conversation and tease out ideas, thoughts, and requirements—whether as formal style guides or loose creative direction—is often the difference between missing the mark on the creative vision and effectively translating that vision to an incredible visual design.

Developer Skills

Programmers can typically be classified as either front-end or back-end. A front-end programmer must be an expert in XHTML markup, CSS, and JavaScript. They often work in frameworks like JQuery, MooTools, YUI, or Prototype. They may also use rich media formats like Flash or be on the cutting edge of HTML5.

Back-end programmers must know the tools that pertain to the type of website you have. Common server-side technologies include PHP, C# .NET, Java servlets, and more. They commonly use databases like Microsoft SQL (MS SQL) or MySQL. Code frameworks are common here, and often a database architect is a separate role from the back-end developer. These folks build and update all the code responsible for generating the front-end code the browser eventually shows to your users.

Regardless of languages and technologies, developers solve problems. Programming is logic, and implementing a design in code is like solving a puzzle. Good developers take the time to plan before they write code, mapping out the logical steps, then selecting the right technology, platform and approach to implement the solution. They stay abreast of industry developments. A new code framework or a new browser standard may be just what's needed to solve the puzzle in a more efficient manner.

Good developers also understand the application of whatever they're building and how it fits into online marketing objectives. Knowing how to code a landing page from a Photoshop file is important, but developers must also understand how to ensure that the code is friendly to search engines, how to install the JavaScript necessary for tracking, how to use caching and asynchronous server calls to improve the user experience and speed up page load times, and much more. Developers who understand the bigger picture can see what's coming—they let you know when it's time to implement a new feature of HTML5, gain efficiencies by taking advantage of a new application programming interface (API), or update a new plug-in in a content management system (CMS) you don't even know you're using!

Friday: Identify the Analyst

Online marketing is the most measurable form of advertising ever known. The amount of data generated from every ad impression, every click, and every action taken on the Web is astounding. Traditional marketing may have suffered from a lack of data (or at least accessibility of that data), but we now face the opposite problem.

Analysts take this data and turn it into the information we need to make decisions. We care less about counting hits than finding the lessons and stories that the data is telling us. The latter helps us refine our messaging, target and find more of the right consumers, and put our campaigns on a course toward continuous performance improvement.

Of course analysts need to crunch numbers, find the insights, and visualize them in a way that tells a story. But those are the obvious skills. The skills in the following sections might not be as obvious, but they can help make any analyst a more effective and valuable member of the team.

Ability to Question Authority

One of the best analysts we ever hired was a political science major who found a passion for analytics after reading Michael Lewis's *Moneyball: The Art of Winning an Unfair Game*—well before it became a movie.

The book's lesson is clear: Don't do what everyone else does just because it's the way it's done. Find the stories and opportunities in the data and dare to try something different. Find the opportunities, take the calculated risks, and then measure what happens.

Decision-Making Skills

Analysts usually provide the information necessary for *someone else* to make decisions, but analysts who think like decision makers do a better job. We rarely have clients who enjoy flipping through hundreds of pages of charts and graphs showing month-on-month comparisons. Free tools exist to track and keep track of numbers. Analysts *use* those numbers to build hypotheses and recommendations.

"Your campaign spend increased 4 percent this month" is not analysis. Good analysts provide informed decisions or recommendations on what you should do, given the numbers and what they mean. Analysis looks like this: "We should move 20 percent of our spend from Campaign A to Campaign B this month because we believe there are more clicks to buy at a more profitable rate in the area Campaign B is targeting, and this will improve our return on investment."

Persuasion and Negotiation

In addition to general communication skills, analysts should master the arts of persuasion and negotiation. Years ago, when pay per click meant nothing to the general public, we described our job to family and friends as translator between the marketing and IT departments.

Effectively communicating *why* a recommendation is being made or a mandate is coming down using reasons that make sense to the person receiving the information is extremely important. Politics and personalities regularly impede this process.

Ever had to tell someone from IT to do something "simple," like remove a few fields from a form? Sounds easy enough, but what if the IT person has personal pride in that form—the one that *they* designed, and it has been working just fine for years? Or maybe the change has technical implications that make it difficult to implement. Being able to receive pushback, convey the benefits of a solution, and negotiate to a solution that fits schedules and budgets makes an analyst more valuable.

Week 4: Plan Your Budget

One of the most important decisions with any type of advertising is the budget. How much should you spend and how should you spend it? Display advertising is likely to be just one element of your marketing mix. To determine how much of your spend should go here, you must understand how that budget will be spent and what options you have. We focus on the GDN, but many of the bid types, auctions, and billing methods function similarly on other platforms.

Monday: Choose between Bid Types

One of the first things to determine is how to bid for your ads to appear out there in the wild, and you have a few options. Each is covered in more detail in Chapter 6, "Month 3: Building Your First Display Campaign," but for now, we want to focus on the different ways you can choose to pay for your ads. The bidding options in AdWords fall into three categories: cost per click (CPC), cost per thousand impressions (CPM), and cost per acquisition (CPA).

Figure 4.14 shows the bidding and budget options you can choose from in a GDN campaign. In the following sections, we focus on how advertisers are charged in each case.

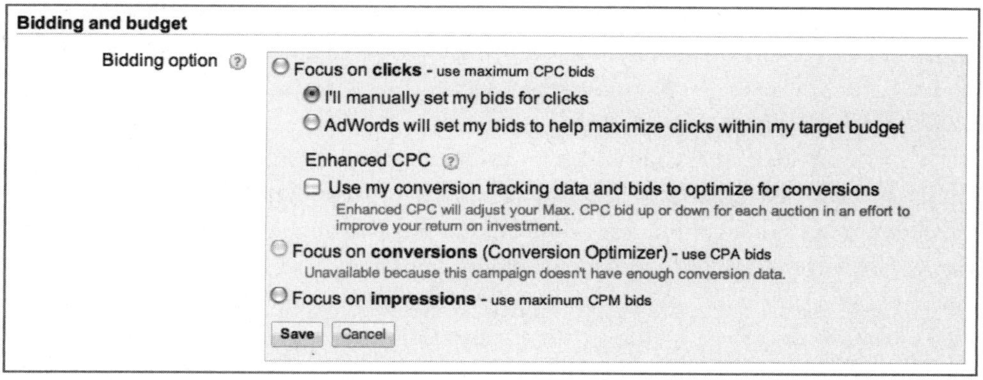

```
Bidding and budget

Bidding option  ⓘ    ◯ Focus on clicks - use maximum CPC bids
                         ⦿ I'll manually set my bids for clicks
                         ◯ AdWords will set my bids to help maximize clicks within my target budget

                      Enhanced CPC  ⓘ
                         ☐ Use my conversion tracking data and bids to optimize for conversions
                            Enhanced CPC will adjust your Max. CPC bid up or down for each auction in an effort to
                            improve your return on investment.
                      ◯ Focus on conversions (Conversion Optimizer) - use CPA bids
                         Unavailable because this campaign doesn't have enough conversion data.
                      ◯ Focus on impressions - use maximum CPM bids

                      [ Save ]  [ Cancel ]
```

Figure 4.14 Setting campaign bidding options

Focus on Clicks

Whether you bid manually or take advantage of automatic bidding options, when you choose any of the Focus on Clicks options, you use maximum CPC bids. This means that if your ad is shown to a user and they click it, AdWords charges you.

You tell Google the absolute maximum amount you're willing to spend on a click of your ad, and that bid is used (along with a host of other factors) in the auction that determines which ads go where. It's important to remember that a Max CPC bid is rarely what you'll actually pay. Because of the way the auction works, the AdWords system charges you only the minimum amount necessary to maintain the position you win in the auction.

If you opt into both display and search networks, you can use different maximum CPC bids on those networks. Search networks are tailored to the search queries people type into search engines—someone searches for a term, and you pop up your ads in response. On the display side, you likely have different goals and strategies, so it makes perfect sense that you have different bidding options. In fact, a best practice in AdWords campaign management is to create completely independent campaigns for display and search networks to keep them separate.

While you must specify a default maximum CPC bid price at the ad group level, you can override that default at any more granular level of targeting. If you use contextual targeting in your ad group, you can specify a different bid for each keyword. If you use placement targeting, you can make different bids on different placements. If you target audiences, you can bid specific amounts for each audience.

Focus on Conversions

When you focus on conversions, you still pay AdWords for clicks, but you let AdWords set your maximum CPC based on the probability of a conversion and how much that conversion is worth to you. AdWords looks at your historical data and builds a model that helps it understand which factors are likely to result in a conversion and which are not. Based on past data, AdWords assigns probabilities to future events and bases bids on those probabilities.

For example, if AdWords finds that users from a certain geographic location who see your ad on a certain website with a certain browser type have a high tendency to click that ad and convert on your goals, it automatically raises your bid for that situation, while it automatically lowers your bid for situations that are not likely to convert based on past performance.

AdWords does not *promise* to get you conversions at or below your target price. It *tries* to get you those conversions for the price you define. It uses your target or maximum CPA bids in its calculations, but if you change your ads, your website, your landing pages, or anything else that can affect conversion rates, the historical data is no longer applicable, and AdWords might send you clicks that you can no longer convert as well as you did before. Also, you need to be realistic. If you have a cost per conversion of $50 on your own, you can ask AdWords to get you conversions for $1, but it may well fail.

You must satisfy certain requirements to use this bidding option. First, you must have conversion tracking in place so that the AdWords system can connect the data with the clicks that convert. Second, you need historical data, and the more you have, the more accurate the model AdWords can build and use as a prediction engine. Currently, the system requires that you have at least 15 conversions over a 30-day period. We've found that the more conversions and data you have, the better the system gets. Last, the data should be stable. If you change your campaign to respond to a seasonal market, for example, the data on which AdWords makes its predictions is changed, so those predictions are no longer accurate.

Focus on Impressions

Focusing on impressions means cost per thousand impression (CPM) bidding, which is available only to campaigns that target *only* the GDN. The option disappears the moment you enable a search network for the campaign. Your primary goal with this type of bidding is no longer to draw a click, but to put your ad in front of eyeballs. Because you pay every 1,000 times your ad is shown, regardless of whether or not it is clicked, this bidding strategy is typically associated with branding and positioning goals, not direct response actions.

Given its huge ad inventory, there are lots of places for Google to show your ads, so you need to exert control over how often your ads show. While maximum daily budgets can help to limit overexposure, it's not your only tool. You can also use frequency capping, which lets you determine and set the number of times individual people will see your ad. We look at how to implement this setting in Chapter 6, but for now, just know that it can help control costs and exposure.

It's also important to remember that CPM bids and CPC bids are not comparable. In CPM bidding, you pay for the right to let your ad take up valuable virtual real estate for a given page view. With CPC bidding, because showing up doesn't make anyone any money, the bidding takes into account factors such as relevance and the probability of an ad being clicked.

Tuesday: Understand How the CPC Auction Works

One of the best things about networks like Google AdWords is the level playing field. The big guys who can use their big budgets and big sway with the big advertising agencies to buy up all the traditional media lose that ability in the auction: for much of the Internet's ad inventory, paying more doesn't necessarily win you auctions or get you better placements.

Calculating Ad Rank

To help decide which ads to show where, Google uses Ad Rank, which it calculates whenever a page with available advertising space is loaded. In the auction, the ad with the highest Ad Rank value wins the best placements. Although things have changed a bit (more on that soon), it wasn't that long ago that Ad Rank was simply calculated as follows:

Ad Rank = Maximum CPC × click-through rate

From Google's perspective, this makes perfect sense. The advertiser can offer $1000 per click for the ad in Figure 4.15, but Google won't make a penny on it because nobody will click it. If you can create a better-targeted ad, you're more likely to draw the click. Higher click-through rates are good for Google, and (assuming they lead to profitable conversion actions) they're good for you as well. So as an advertiser, you are rewarded handsomely for having high click-through rates because you pay less for those clicks.

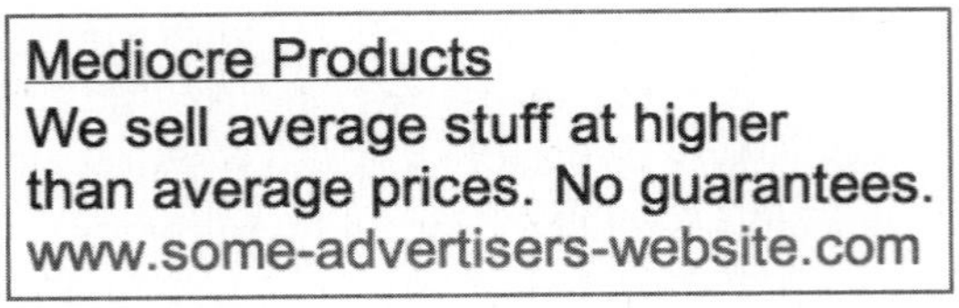

Mediocre Products
We sell average stuff at higher
than average prices. No guarantees.
www.some-advertisers-website.com

Figure 4.15 A really horrible ad

Google wants end users to have a positive experience and find what they want. Providing that positive experience is paramount for Google, and click-through rate is one measure of how happy a user is to see a particular ad. The more often the ad gets clicked, the more relevant it must be to the user who saw it.

Introducing Quality Score

In its quest for a positive user experience, Google soon realized that click-through rate alone is not enough to capture the happiness factor, and the formula changed to take other factors into account:

Ad Rank = Maximum CPC × Quality Score

Quality Score is a numeric representation of how relevant an ad is to the user who might see it on that page. While click-through rate is still very much a part of Quality Score, Google takes other factors into account when it calculates Quality Score, and those factors are different between search and display networks.

On the GDN, these factors are used in the Quality Score calculation:

- Historical performance of the ad on this site and similar sites
- How contextually relevant the ads and the keywords making up the ad group are to the content of this site
- The overall quality of the landing page a click on the ad takes users to, as determined by things like page load time and relevance

Google uses many other factors to determine Quality Score, and the factors can depend on the bid types and targeting options you use in your campaigns.

A Quality Score Example

To understand how this works, let's take an example of four different advertisers, all of whom are using CPC bidding and vying for advertising space on a page in the GDN in an auction. The Quality Score values, Maximum CPC bids, and Ad Rank values are all shown in Table 4.2.

Jill wins the best placement with her bid of $0.75, which is her reward for having such a great Quality Score. Jack must bid $0.25 more for every click to come in second place, and poor Clyde can't figure out how his competition can possibly be profitable here if he has to bid $6.00 a click just to come in last!

	Quality Score	Maximum CPC	Ad Rank
Jack	7	$1.00	7.00
Jill	10	$0.75	7.50
Clyde	1	$6.00	6.00
Bonnie	5	$1.25	6.25

It's common for bids that are far less than the competition to win auctions, and those cost savings across thousands and thousands of clicks make it worthwhile to focus on optimizing your Quality Score!

Now let's look at what advertisers *actually pay*. Table 4.3 orders our advertisers by Ad Rank and expands the table with an Actual CPC column.

▶ **Table 4.3** Calculating actual cost per click

	Quality Score	Maximum CPC	Ad Rank	Actual CPC
Jill	10	$0.75	7.50	$0.71
Jack	7	$1.00	7.00	$0.90
Bonnie	5	$1.25	6.25	$1.21
Clyde	1	$6.00	6.00	Minimum Bid

The AdWords Discounter calculates how much Google charges you. It uses the following formula to compute the minimum (in dollars) you need to pay to keep the position you won with your Ad Rank:

Actual CPC = [Ad Rank of advertiser below you] / [your Quality Score] + 0.01

Using this formula, even though Jill is *willing* to pay $0.75 for the click, she only *needs* to pay 7/10 + 0.01 = $0.71 to keep her top spot, so that's how much Google charges her for that click.

Meanwhile, Jack needs to pay $0.90 per click from a lower position, while Bonnie is paying $0.50 more than Jill for her lower position!

Update to Computing Ad Rank

Our examples assume the formula

Ad Rank = Quality Score × Maximum CPC

While this was once the case, Google now describes Ad Rank as a *function*, not otherwise specified, of Quality Score and Maximum CPC.

This provides Google with more flexibility in how it chooses to weight Quality Score and Max CPC bids, but it remains true that optimizing Quality Score leads to better ad placements and lower costs.

Wednesday: Understand How CPM Bids Compete in the Auction

You've now seen just how important maximum CPC bids, click-through rate, and other Quality Score factors can be in winning the best placements in the Google auction, but how do ads compete when you're defining Max *CPM* bids and you no longer care about clicks?

It's worthwhile to explore how CPC and CPM bids compete with one another for available ad space across the GDN.

CPC and CPM ads compete side by side in the same auctions for the same ad space. The basis of comparison is a metric called effective cost per thousand impressions, or eCPM. To simplify a little, eCPM is just how much the CPC ad would cost to run 1,000 times at its average cost per click and click-through rate:

eCPM = average CPC × click-through rate × 1,000 impressions

The last thing to consider before we walk through an example is that different ad units can be filled in different ways. Take, for example the 250×250 pixel ad unit in Figure 4.16.

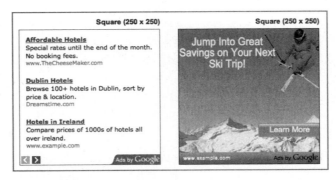

Figure 4.16 Two ways to fill the same ad unit

The same ad unit can serve three different text ads or one single 250×250 pixel image ad. This complicates things just a bit, and many of the various ad sizes and formats can be filled in different ways.

Let's assume that there are three different text ads competing for this ad unit, all using CPC bidding, and one image ad using CPM bidding. Table 4.4 shows the bids and eCPMs.

▶ **Table 4.4** A mixture of CPC and CPM bids

Advertiser	Ad Format	Bid Type	eCPM
A	Text	CPC	$1.00
B	Text	CPC	$2.00
C	Text	CPC	$3.00
D	Image	CPM	$5.00

If Google shows the one image ad in that ad unit, it can charge advertiser D $5.00 for the impression. But if it uses that ad unit to house the three text ads, it can charge $6.00 over time, based on the click-through rates and bids of advertisers A, B, and C. This is the logic Google uses when filling ad units.

To win an ad slot, a CPM bid must be higher than the combined eCPMs of all eligible CPC ads that can otherwise fill that ad unit. In this case, the text ads show rather than the image ad.

Thursday: Understand How Google Spends Your Budget

As you plan budgets and forecast your advertising spend, you need to know how to ensure that those budgets are adhered to, and the best way to do that is to understand just how Google handles and spends your money.

AdWords uses a hierarchical structure. At the top is your account, which contains multiple campaigns. Each campaign contains multiple ad groups, and each ad group contains the actual keywords, placements, topics, and audiences you target and the ads that you show.

AdWords Budgets Are Set at the Campaign Level

While your *bids* can be specified at the ad group, keyword, placement, topic, or audience level, your *budget* is aggregated at the campaign level and is set via your campaign settings (Figure 4.17).

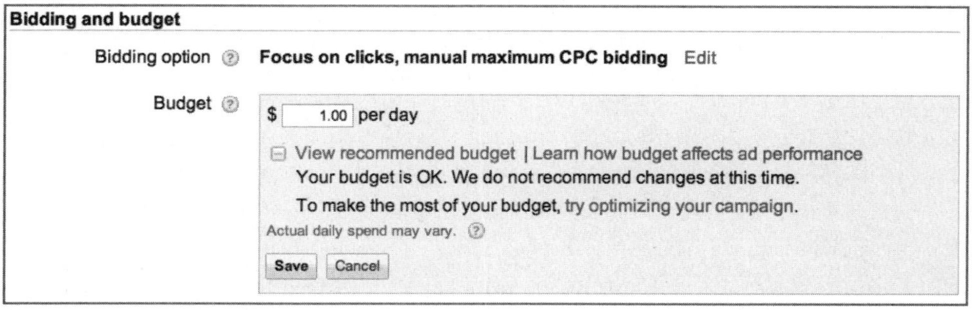

Bidding and budget

Bidding option ⑦   **Focus on clicks, manual maximum CPC bidding**   Edit

Budget ⑦ $ [1.00] per day

⊟ View recommended budget | Learn how budget affects ad performance
Your budget is OK. We do not recommend changes at this time.
To make the most of your budget, try optimizing your campaign.
Actual daily spend may vary. ⑦

[Save] [Cancel]

Figure 4.17 Setting the campaign budget in Google AdWords

We go through this and other campaign settings in Chapter 6, but for now it's important to understand what this means. First, you don't set a budget for your entire account, which as you'll soon see, is actually a good thing.

Let's say that your AdWords account contains four campaigns:

- Campaign A: Search Network – Branded Terms
- Campaign B: Search Network – Product Terms
- Campaign C: Display Network – Brand Awareness
- Campaign D: Display Network – Remarketing

Hopefully you have more campaigns than that, all taking advantage of various targeting techniques, but for this example we keep things simple. Let's assume that your organization has budgeted $1,000 per month to spend on Google AdWords. At the most basic level, you can allocate $250 to each of your four campaigns to get the whole account to $1,000, which might seem like a lot of work for the average advertiser when compared to just setting an account budget of $1,000.

But what happens when you realize that your remarketing campaign is outperforming anything else you've got? Or when you decide to add a new campaign but you just want to put your toe in the water to see how it does? By setting your budgets at the campaign level, you have much more control over how to spend your marketing dollars. You can take budget from underperforming campaigns and amp up spend on successful campaigns or try new things with a small part of your overall budget.

AdWords Budgets Are Defined Daily

The other thing to understand is that inside AdWords, you don't set your budgets on a monthly basis; you set them daily. This has important implications as you plan your spend, and they're worth discussing.

First, since most businesses and organizations think about budgeting on a monthly, quarterly, and annual basis, you need to be aware of how this translates to the AdWords per-day budget.

AdWords differentiates between an "actual daily spend" and a "monthly charging limit," and it breaks down as follows.

If you set a campaign with a daily budget of $10, then over the course of the month, you can rest assured that you won't be charged more than $304, which is your daily budget multiplied by 30.4 days per average month. But over the course of a single day, AdWords can overspend your account by up to 20 percent in order to "help your campaign reach its potential." What this means is that on a single day, AdWords might spend $12, but over the course of the month it will make sure your total spend averages out to the monthly charging limit or below.

This is actually not a bad thing, as you can imagine that not all days are equal over the course of a month. Weekends may not have the same levels of traffic as weekdays, and holidays can drive more or less advertising potential. Think about the US Thanksgiving holiday—people napping on a couch in front of the television after eating too much turkey aren't likely to see your ad, while the shopping frenzy that occurs from Black Friday through Cyber Monday keeps web servers operating at full capacity!

Friday: Understand AdWords Billing Options

Google is a business just like yours, and it is good at making money. If you advertise with Google AdWords, you have to pay the bill, and you have a few options. Remember that specific payment options vary slightly by currency and country, but for the following sections we assume the United States and the US dollar.

Automatic Payments

Automatic payments used to be known as a postpay option, and that's essentially how they work. You give Google a form of payment, which can be a credit or debit card or even a direct bank payment, and your ads start running. You get charged for your account's activity either after 30 days pass or you reach your billing threshold, whichever comes first.

The billing threshold starts at $50 for new advertisers and can be raised with each successful payment to a maximum of $500. If you are a new advertiser, the first time you accrue $50 worth of activity on your account, AdWords charges your credit card or other form of payment. If that happens in less than 30 days, your billing threshold is raised to $200 and you aren't charged again until you accrue another $200 worth of activity or another 30 days pass. If you hit your threshold before 30 days, your threshold is again raised until you hit the maximum of $500. To increase your threshold further, you must talk to AdWords Support.

Alternate Payment Options

Google lets advertisers add as many payment options as they like to their accounts with billing information that can differ from account information. This gives you the flexibility to move your AdWords spend across a number of payment sources. It also ensures that your ads keep running. Credit cards expire, debit cards get rejected, and bank payments don't always go through. If you define alternate payment methods, your ads keep showing while you update whatever needs updating.

Manual Payments

The manual payment option lets you prepay for your ads. You load your account with a balance, and as your ads run, the clicks, impressions, or actions you're paying for are debited from that balance. When the balance is gone, your ads stop running. Click the Make A Payment button in the Billing tab of your account to get them started again.

This can be helpful if you have very strict budgets in place and need to plan for future costs or if you want to get expenses on your books early! Just keep in mind that with this option, in order to keep advertising, you need to ensure that there are funds in your account.

Invoicing

For advertisers that spend enough money with Google AdWords, an invoicing option is also available. To see if you're eligible, contact AdWords Support from inside your account (or go through your AdWords sales representative if you have one) and apply.

If your application is approved, Google offers you a credit line and payment terms. If you accept, your account is converted to monthly invoicing. You get an invoice every month, and you can pay by check or wire transfer, depending on your country and your currency. If your balance goes over your credit line, or if you're outside your payment terms, your ads stop running.

Month 2: Targeting Your Audience

5

The Internet is a big place, and choosing among the millions and millions of places where we'd like our ads to show up can be a very daunting task. This month, we'll be focusing on how to find the audiences that you want to target through contextual, placement, and audience targeting options. Once we've identified the various options you can take advantage of to seek out exactly the kinds of eyeballs you want your ads in front of, we'll take a look at how to organize your various campaigns in ways that set you up for success.

Chapter Contents:

Week 5: Understand Targeting Options
Week 6: Find Good Keywords
Week 7: Find Good Placements
Week 8: Organize Campaigns and Ad Groups

Week 5: Understand Targeting Options

Among the most powerful features of online advertising is the ability to target your audiences. Within the GDN, you can show your ads to people based on the *kinds* of sites they're visiting, the *actual pages*, or things that you know about their past behavior.

This week, we look at the types of targeting supported by Google AdWords for display campaigns and discuss when to use them and how to use them together.

Monday: Using Contextual Targeting

Contextual targeting means choosing the websites you want your ads to show up on by using keywords. This is Google's bread and butter for search advertising, but it works differently in display. To understand the difference, let's take an example through both search and display scenarios.

Keywords from a Search Campaign Perspective

Say you're selling a line of autographed jerseys from professional sports teams. On the search network, you try to find the keywords that people type into a search engine when they're looking to buy an autographed jersey. You want to show your ad to anyone who searches for keywords like those in Figure 5.1.

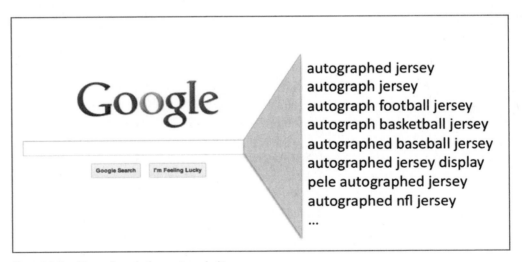

autographed jersey
autograph jersey
autograph football jersey
autograph basketball jersey
autographed baseball jersey
autographed jersey display
pele autographed jersey
autographed nfl jersey
...

Figure 5.1 Possible search queries for an autographed jersey

This is pure direct response advertising. They type a keyword that indicates they want to trade money for the product you sell. You want them to see your ad, click it, and close the deal. Here, you evaluate keywords with the following questions:

Which words are being searched for?   Look for all semantic and thematic variations of the keywords. Singulars and plurals are different, so you need both "jersey" and "jerseys."

You want synonyms like "uniforms" or "shirt," and you need to combine those with other words like "nfl" and "nba," actual player names and more! Fortunately, there are many tools that can help find all the different ways your prospective customers are searching for the products you sell.

How often are they being searched? A variation like "1986 new york mets world series home opener world series autographed jersey" probably gets little traffic, while "autographed jersey," according to the Google AdWords Keyword Tool, gets typed into Google over 40,000 times per month!

How relevant are those keywords? *Think of relevance* as the percentage of people who search for the keyword that are actually looking to buy something you sell.

By this logic, you might conclude that "jersey" is 0 percent relevant to your products. Surprised? Think of it this way: There are many reasons to type "jersey" into a search engine other than to buy what you're selling. For example, that searcher may be looking for *un*autographed jerseys for a local Little League team or even information about the *state* of New Jersey. Realistically, fewer than 1 of every 100 people that type "jersey" into a search engine are likely to be looking for an autographed sports collectible. On the other hand, "buy autographed nfl jersey" is extremely relevant.

How competitive are those keywords? There's likely to be a lot of competition on basic keywords like "autographed jersey," but by spending time on keyword research, you're likely to find keywords that your competition hasn't dug up yet and aren't competing on.

Once you've found all the keywords people are typing into search engines and evaluated them based on frequency, relevance, and competitiveness, you can build out your search-based campaigns using the keywords that give you the most benefit for the least cost.

Keywords from a Display Campaign Perspective

Display campaigns use keywords in a very different way. With display campaigns, you don't try to match what searchers type into search engines; you try to match the *context* of the kinds of *websites* your target audience is *visiting*.

On the display side, your potential customers are probably not actively looking to buy anything when you show your ad. Here, you try to figure out what kind of website someone who might be interested in buying an autographed jersey would hang out on. Your keywords need to describe *those kinds of websites*.

With display advertising, you'll use keywords to describe different kinds of websites a sports fan might frequent, such as those in Figure 5.2.

You want to target websites that have to do with autographed jerseys, but you'll likely find that there just aren't that many out there. So, you can broaden your scope to target websites that have to do with the larger category of sports memorabilia. Someone browsing such a page may well be interested in your autographed jerseys.

autographed jersey autograph jersey autograph football jersey autograph basketball jersey autographed baseball jersey autographed jersey display pele autographed jersey autographed nfl jersey	sports memorabilia sports memorabilia stores buy sports memorabilia unique sports memorabilia cheap sports memorabilia sports memorabilia gifts sports memorabilia display cases
fantasy football football fantasy 2010 fantasy college football fantasy playoff football fantasy football rankings fantasy football projections fantasy football cheat sheets	sports news breaking sports news sports news headlines football news basketball news baseball news hockey news soccer news

Figure 5.2 Keywords that describe potential websites for a jersey ad

This is a common strategy: To find more eyeballs, you can widen your net further and further to include websites dedicated to things like fantasy football or sports news or whatever people in your potential market spend time browsing. Visitors to these websites aren't actively looking to buy an autographed jersey, but if your target market is a group of fans who live and breathe sports, what better place to reach them than the places they frequent every day?

Contextual targeting allows you to take advantage of keywords to find the kinds of websites your target audiences are likely to visit rather than focusing on the keywords your target audience is typing into a search engine.

Tuesday: Using Placement Targeting

While contextual targeting places your ad on the right *kinds* of websites, you can also target specific pages, areas, and sections of specific websites explicitly. Later in this chapter we discuss a number of tools to help find specific websites and specific advertising opportunities on those websites, and each such potential spot is called a *placement*.

Depending on the advertising opportunities a given web property provides, you can specify an entire website, a page or group of pages on that website, or even a specific ad unit on a single page.

Not all websites on the GDN allow for all levels of placements, and different ad slots have different sizes and formats. But understanding where you can show your ads and how you can group and target those placements is fundamental to display advertising.

Using our autographed jersey example, let's look at the levels of placements you might choose to target. Remember, you're trying to get your ads in front of eyeballs that belong to sports fanatics that might be interested in buying what you've got to sell.

Sitewide Placement

Someone frequenting a site like the SportsCardForum.com website (Figure 5.3) might be interested in a collectible autographed jersey, and this website accepts ads through the GDN. Google AdWords enables you to target all ad slots on the website, and that makes sense for you. In the absence of specific data, there aren't any sections of this site where you wouldn't want your ad to show, and it doesn't appear that there are any specific pages or ad slots that you would want to target over others.

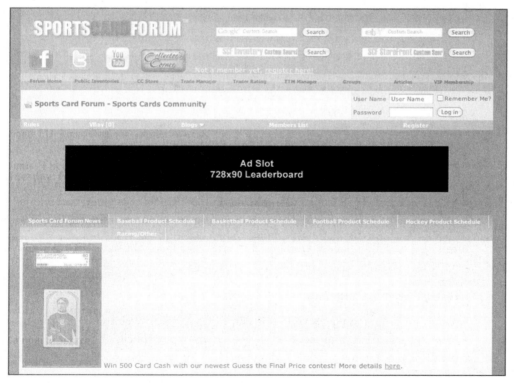

Figure 5.3 An advertising opportunity on SportsCardForum.com

The trick is to balance the specificity of the audience with the number of eyeballs you can get on your ads. With lots of topics and threads inside a forum about sports cards (all very relevant to your product), you can choose a sitewide placement that allows your ad to run anywhere across the entire site for maximum exposure to this fairly well-targeted audience.

Subsection Placement

Where else can you find those sports fanatics? They might be interested in reading sports news, so let's look at the *New York Times*. You likely don't want a sitewide placement in this case since this is an enormous website. To find those sports fanatics, you would rather place your ad in the *sports* section than in other sections.

The *New York Times* offers a placement on the GDN that targets all of the ad units of *just its sports section*, and this is exactly what you're looking for. Figure 5.4 shows the available placements on one of those sports pages.

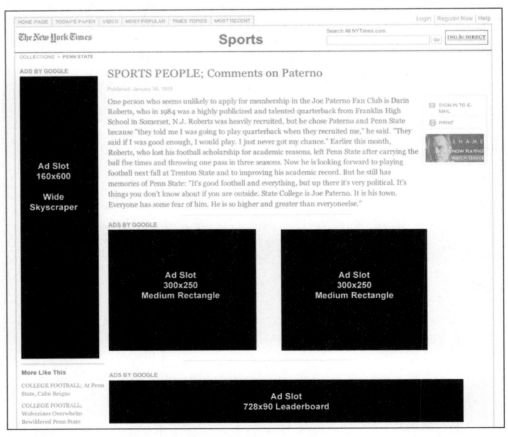

Figure 5.4 Advertising opportunities in the sports section of NYTimes.com

While a sectional placement can be as refined as a single page on the Web, it can also include thousands of pages and multiple ad slots on each one, which can put you in front of a lot of eyeballs with a single placement target.

Ad Slot Placement

You've seen that you can throw out a wide net and get in front of a lot of potential sports enthusiasts, but you can use placements to laser target as well.

In Figure 5.5, you target not a website or a section of a website but that one skyscraper ad slot on the right side of a specific page. The page, dedicated to the Green Bay Packers, attracts die-hard fans of a specific nature. You can take advantage of that specificity and what you know about this audience to run ads showcasing *Green Bay Packers* jerseys, autographed by famous Green Bay Packers players.

Figure 5.5 A highly targeted ad slot on JerseyAl.com

Wednesday: Using Audience Targeting

You can tell Google *what kinds* of websites to put your ads on with keywords, and you can tell them *exactly* where you'd like your ads to show up with placements, but as the Internet becomes more and more sophisticated, advertisers are shifting toward what is broadly termed *audience targeting*.

When you target audiences, you don't guess at the places your target audiences might be hanging out. Instead, you mark your audience members as they exhibit certain behaviors that flag them as an ideal set of eyeballs to put your ads in front of, and then you follow them around *no matter where they go*. In short, you target the *visitors*, not the *sites* they go to or the content they consume.

Targeting by Users' Interests

Google has tracking code on millions of websites around the world (and that number is constantly growing). Whenever a user visits one of those pages, Google sets and uses cookies in their browsers. A cookie simply stores information on the user's machine and can be accessed as the user browses the Web. These are extremely common, and they help make our online experience easier, doing everything from remembering that we're logged in to a site to prefilling forms we use on a regular basis.

From Google's perspective, every time a visitor goes to a page that is part of the Google Network, this cookie allows Google to associate that user with a pattern of web browsing that helps to identify their interests. For example, if that cookie is known to visit websites like sports blogs, sports forums and sports memorabilia auction sites three times a day seven days a week, then Google may infer that this particular cookie belongs to someone interested in sports memorabilia. As it happens, sports memorabilia is one of the 1,000+ interest categories that Google has defined, and this category includes somewhere between 500,000 and 1,000,000 unique users!

In addition to browsing patterns, Google can also use its extensive data sets along with third-party data to make assumptions about things like gender, age, and other demographics, but the important thing to remember is that you're now targeting *that cookie*, wherever it may roam.

In our autographed jersey example, once you decide to target people who have an interest in sports memorabilia, you don't care where they happen to be: You want your ad in front of them. So when they get hungry and visit a recipe website, you want your ad to show—even though that food site has nothing to do with the autographed jerseys you're selling. And keep in mind that in many cases, it can be cheaper to advertise on sites that are less desirable from a contextual perspective but that your target audience might be visiting!

Targeting by Specific Behaviors

You can define an audience by inferring their interests based on where they go and how often they go there, but one of the most powerful features of Google AdWords is the ability to define additional actions that users take and define custom audiences based on those actions. This is one aspect of what is known broadly as *retargeting*, and in the context of the GDN, these groups of people are known as *remarketing lists*.

We cover remarketing in greater detail in Chapter 11, "Month 8: Advanced Topics," but for now, we just want you to understand the concept. As people interact with your website (or any web page that you control), they may do things that are of interest to you. Let's continue with our autographed jersey example.

First, a user might click one of your ads and end up on your website. At this point, they might just be browsing, thinking of what to get for that special sports fan in their life for their next birthday. And even though they're not yet ready to buy, they decide to sign up for your email list so that they can get your newsletter and be the first to know about sales or new inventory. The moment they sign up for that email newsletter list, you can sign them up for a remarketing list that you've defined as newsletter subscribers.

A different visitor might come to your site and put one of those autographed jerseys in their shopping cart but then decide to wait and shop around a little more before actually checking out. You might want to add this person to your remarketing list called shopping cart abandoners.

Yet another visitor might come into your site, put that autographed jersey in the cart, and finish the transaction! You've now got the conversion you were after, and you can add them to the remarketing list called past customers.

Once you've started to identify these behaviors and you're adding visitors to your various lists, you can start to advertise to them no matter where they go around the Internet. For example, every time one of your newsletter subscribers is on a website offering advertising opportunities through the GDN, you can show them an ad highlighting a sale that's only available to your very special newsletter subscribers. "Hey, *I'm* a very special newsletter subscriber!" thinks the casual visitor. "Maybe I ought to go see what that's all about!"

For those that have abandoned their shopping carts, you can start showing ads that offer a coupon code for 10 percent off today only. "Lucky me!" thinks the user. "I was just about to buy that, and now I can save 10 percent!"

You can show your past customers ads for the wonderful display cases you sell to house the autographed jersey they just bought. "Wow, that's just what I need... And I just set up an account at that store, so it will be easy to buy!"

Targeting by Other Third-Party Data

Google is certainly not the only company collecting and using data from Internet users as they browse the Web, and more data is becoming available to advertisers by the second. A host of data aggregators associate web users with all the information they can get their hands on, including what they're searching on, what they're buying, and even what offline data can be gathered about those users from traditional consumer data providers.

Think of this as having access to those remarketing lists we just discussed, except those behaviors can be tracked and aggregated across many sites, not just the ones that you control.

Google's Stance on Privacy

If you find this whole thing a little creepy, you're not the first to be concerned. But it's important to note that when you target audiences, you're not actually targeting *individual people*. What you're really targeting is those *cookies* that live in someone's browser.

When we add audience members to a list, whether by the websites their browser visits or the actions they take on our own pages, we do not associate the audience members with personally identifiable information (PII) like a name, email address, Social Security number, address, credit card number, or anything else that could be used to identify them. From the perspective of the ad-serving platform, that cookie we're targeting is nothing more than a unique code that allows us to identify it as it moves from website to website. We don't care that it's John Smith or Sally Johnson clicking around the Internet. All we care about is the fact that a unique browser loaded a certain set of websites or performed certain actions we care about.

If you've been on the other side of audience targeting, now you know why you tend to see advertisements that have to do with your tastes and preferences, and you also know why certain ads have been following you around! But if you give that same computer to a friend or a family member, *they'll* see the same ads that have been targeted to *your* browsing patterns. When you delete the cookies, you're no longer part of anyone's list until you again exhibit behaviors that define you as part of an audience.

Last, on the Google platform, cookies—anonymous and not containing any PII—are never associated with interest categories that might be based on race, religion, sexual orientation, health status, or financial status.

Thursday: Using Additional Campaign Targeting Options

Chapter 11 discusses the final type of targeting, topic targeting. This is typically best used not as a primary targeting option but as a refinement.

In addition to keyword, placement, audience and topic targeting, however, the AdWords system also gives you a number of supplementary options you can use to target your optimal audience at the campaign level. We discuss how these are implemented when you create a campaign in Chapter 6, "Month 3: Building Your First Display Campaign," but it's important to provide an overview here because these features can be used in tandem with other targeting options to zero in on the kinds of people you want to be showing your ads to.

Inside a Google AdWords account, you have a number of different campaigns, and under each campaign you have a number of different ad groups. Every ad group that lives under a campaign inherits that campaign's settings, and a number of those settings have to do with targeting.

Location Targeting

Location targeting allows you to show your ads only to people who are located within certain geographic boundaries. Google can figure out where users are by looking at IP addresses, the user's location preferences inside their Google account, a GPS or cell tower signal, or a known WiFi network.

With this information, advertisers can target cities, countries, postal codes, or even a particular radius from any point on a map. Figure 5.6 shows an AdWords campaign targeting the city of San Francisco and anyone within a 20-mile radius of the Golden Gate Bridge!

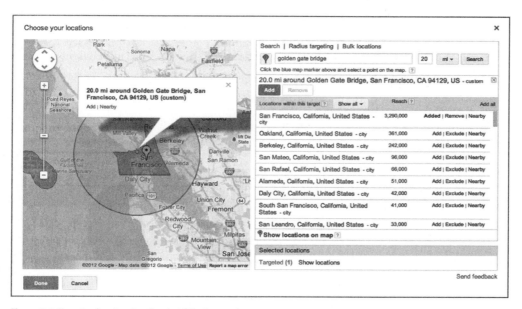

Figure 5.6 Targeting locations in a Google AdWords campaign

Language Targeting

You can target users whose Google interface language matches one of over 40 languages. This can be a powerful option when you decide to translate or localize your advertising campaigns, and with it you can create ads that speak to a target audience in their language.

For example, in the United States you might run both Spanish and English campaigns, while in Canada you might run English and French ads. Language targeting is often combined with geographic targeting. For example, English spoken in the United States can differ from dialects spoken in the United Kingdom or Australia. The Spanish language has more dialects than there are countries that speak it, and French speakers in Paris are quite different from those in Quebec City. By combining a geographic boundary with a language, you can use the right copy and message for the right audience.

Ad Scheduling

AdWords enables you to control your ads based on day of week and time of day in 15-minute increments. For example, if you sell sleep aids, you can choose to only run ads weekdays between 12:00 a.m. and 4:00 a.m., exactly the time insomniacs might be online, desperately seeking something to help them get some sleep! You can even choose to automatically increase or decrease your bids based on the time of day or day of the week, and we discuss these settings in Chapter 6.

Device Targeting

You can also target an audience based on the kind of device they use to access the Internet. You can choose between desktop or laptop computers, mobile devices, and even tablets. Within the mobile and tablet device settings, you can even target specific device manufacturers and models, a mobile operating system or the carrier providing the data connection!

Friday: Combining Targeting Types

One of the GDN's greatest assets is its enormous reach and the sheer number of people advertisers can access through it. But targeting is all about showing your ad to the *right* kind of web surfer and filtering out the others. Finding the balance between a relatively small number of highly targeted, highly likely to convert eyeballs and a much larger number of people in a more general audience is the key, and to do this, you need to know how targeting options interact with one another when used in tandem.

Targeting options set at the campaign level are restrictive. That is, whatever criteria you set for a campaign will either include or exclude your ads for every ad group under that campaign, whether those ad groups use contextual, placement, topic, or audience targeting.

For example, if you set a campaign to show only to English speakers using tablet devices located in the United States, then every ad group in the campaign is bound by the intersection where all three of these conditions are met. At the ad group level, you can then choose to target your ads within that intersection using keywords, topics, placements, audiences, or a combination of these.

Google AdWords gives you two options to use in the GDN when you have more than one type of targeting enabled at the ad group level: broad reach and specific reach (Figure 5.7). As the names imply, the broad reach allows your ads to show to a larger audience with fewer constraints, while the specific reach option more strictly limits where your ads can be seen and by whom.

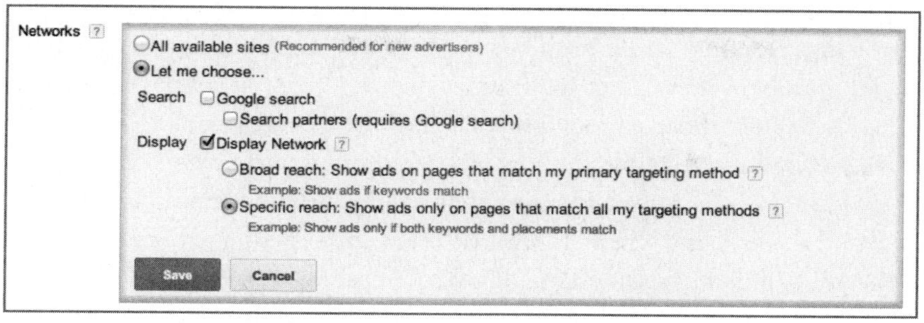

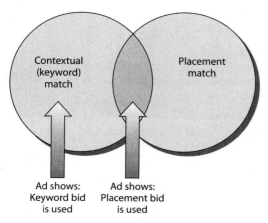

Figure 5.7 Specifying a campaign's reach

Broad Reach

The broad reach option tells AdWords to show your ad whenever your most general targeting matches but if you can get matches on more than one targeting type, to use an even more specific bid. Assume that you have an ad group that contains both keywords (contextual targeting) and placements. With the broad reach setting, your ad is eligible to show on any contextually relevant page or ad slot regardless of whether or not you had defined it explicitly in your placements.

But if that specific ad slot matches both your keywords *and* a placement, then you define and use a more specific bid to reflect the more specific match. Figure 5.8 shows this visually, and the important point is that only one of your match types is needed to trigger your ad being shown.

Figure 5.8 Broad reach with contextual and placement targeting together

Specific Reach

Specific reach is a more restrictive approach to reconciling multiple targeting types being used together: They *all* must match in order for the ad to be eligible to show. Following the previous example where both keywords and placements are used, with the specific reach option you show your ad on only contextually relevant pages where you have specifically defined those pages with your placement targeting as well. The only situation where your ad is eligible to show is where *both* criteria have been met.

Keep in mind that you can set different bids for your different types of targeting, and this can get a little confusing when all of those targeting types have to match in order to show the ad. Which bid should Google use?

If you *do* have different bids set for keywords and placements and audiences, Google will use whichever is present and of the highest priority: placement bid first, then audience, and then keyword (contextual).

Table 5.1 summarizes how Google AdWords treats different combinations of targeting types under each of the broad and specific reach scenarios.

▶ **Table 5.1** Targeting type combinations by campaign setting

Targeting Types	Broad Reach	Specific Reach
Keyword (contextual) only	Ad shows on contextually relevant pages.	Ad shows on contextually relevant pages.
Placement only	Ad shows only on defined placements.	Ad shows only on defined placements.
Audience only	Ad shows only to defined audience members.	Ad shows only to defined audience members.
Keyword plus placement	Ad shows on contextually relevant pages. Placement bid is used when both placement and keyword match.	Ad shows only on contextually relevant placements you've explicitly defined.
Keyword plus audience	Ad shows on contextually relevant pages. Audience bid is used when both keyword and audience match.	Ad shows only on contextually relevant pages viewed by explicitly defined audiences.
Placement plus audience	Ad shows to explicitly defined audiences. Placement bid is used when both placement and audience match.	Ad shows only on explicitly defined placements viewed by explicitly defined audiences.

Week 6: Find Good Keywords

Contextual targeting depends on keywords, and finding the best keywords to describe the kinds of sites you want your ads showing up on can be as much an art as it is a science.

Google provides two tools specifically that can help you efficiently build out your campaigns using contextual targeting: the Keyword Tool and the Contextual

Targeting Tool. This week we'll explore each of these tools and see how you can use them to ensure that your ads are being shown on the right websites across the GDN.

Monday: How Google Determines Relevance

Figuring out just what a web page is all about is the central and fundamental capability that Google has, and it does it extremely well, which is why we use *google* as a verb. Every minute of every day, Google has its bots and spiders crawling the Web looking at content and trying to figure out exactly what that content is all about. When returning search engine results, Google looks at a couple hundred different factors to find the most relevant pages.

From the perspective of a search engine, that's the single most important thing that needs to be done well. From the perspective of an advertising platform, that same information can be leveraged by Google AdWords to allow advertisers to use keywords to choose the websites on which they want their ads to show.

How Contextual Targeting Works

Google analyzes pages on the GDN by looking at language and linguistic factors, links, page structure, and a host of other items. In addition, it looks at the words that appear on the page in terms of thematic and semantic relationships, frequency, and more. From all of this analysis, Google can figure out what the page is about and match it to advertisers trying to show ads on pages like it.

For example, if you want to buy a GPS for your car, you might wind up at gps.about.com. Google examines this page and finds that its central theme is GPS devices and specifically how to buy a GPS device that you plan to use in your car. When advertisers use contextual targeting with keywords like "buy gps device" or "in-car gps" in their ad groups, Google can confidently show their ads on this page.

There are millions of pages that can potentially serve ads, each with varying degrees of relevance to the keywords defined in different advertisers' ad groups. Remember from Chapter 4, "Month 1: Planning Your Campaigns," that when your ad goes to auction, it competes for those spaces with other advertisers on both bid price *and* Quality Score and that Quality Score is in part made up of relevance.

Google knows that an advertiser bidding on "buy in-car gps device" is much more relevant to this particular page than a generic keyword like "electronics" or "gadgets," and this is reflected in the auction. For this reason, the more specific you are when building out your contextually targeted ad groups, the better your Quality Score and the less you need to pay to win the placements at auction.

Google's 2012 Contextual Targeting Update

In early 2012, Google released an update to its contextual targeting engine that it called its biggest enhancement ever: the ability to combine the reach of display with the precision of search using Next-Gen Keyword Contextual Targeting. As advertisers, this means that if you were used to building your ad groups by adding lots of different keywords to establish a certain type of theme, you can now optimize performance down to the individual keyword.

Essentially, Google can now go out and find potential ad placements for you based not on the general theme of a *group* of keywords but on *individual* keywords. As Google's director of product management Brad Bender described it, this update has "brought the science of search to the art of display."

Google now uses its expertise in understanding what a page on the Web is actually about to match it with the display keywords you bid on in a much more refined and direct way.

In the autographed jersey example, you may have an ad group containing keywords like "fantasy college football," "fantasy football," and "fantasy football draft." Using this group of keywords in an ad group establishes a central theme of websites having to do with fantasy football, and traditionally you would have optimized this *set* of keywords as an ad group.

With this update to the contextual targeting engine, you can now optimize bids based on the performance of *each* keyword separately. Google knows that the keyword "fantasy football draft" refers not to websites just about fantasy football but those that are dedicated specifically to drafting players. You may find that visitors to these sites are concentrating on statistics and deciding who they want on their team this season, so they can't be bothered to purchase autographed jerseys. Visitors on sites dealing specifically with "fantasy college football," however, may be in more of a perusal mode, and your products and services may attract them with better click-through and conversion rates.

Now you can confidently set and optimize different bids for each of these keywords and manage them based on the performance of each individually.

Topic Targeting

We discuss topic targeting in more detail in Chapter 11, but it's important to understand at this point as well. The basic premise is this: While you can define keywords to match to the context of web pages that can show your ads, you can also choose predefined topics that match the general theme of those web pages.

Inside a display campaign, instead of targeting keywords, placements, or audiences, you can select certain topics to broaden the range of potential locations that your ad can show across the GDN. But more important, you can *combine* a topic with another targeting type to *refine* the audience you're going after, and this is how topic targeting is often used.

Tuesday/Wednesday: Using the Google Keyword Tool

The Google Keyword Tool is something that search advertisers can't live without, but it can also be extremely useful for display campaigns. This tool not only gives us an enormous amount of data about lots of keywords that people are searching for, it also provides insight into how Google determines context and relationships between types of keywords.

Traditionally, search advertisers have used the Google Keyword Tool to look for ideas as to which keywords they should be bidding on based on things like relevance, volume, and competition. Typing a few words that describe your products and services or entering URLs from your website can provide hundreds or even thousands of possible keywords to which you as an advertiser might want to show an ad in response.

From the display side of things, we're not quite as interested in the raw numbers. Instead, we want to gain an understanding of what people's mindsets are when they use search engines. We can find new insights and opportunities, and we can even catch a glimpse of how Google figures out context and relevance.

Getting Started

To start using the tool, simply select it from the Tools and Analysis tab inside the AdWords interface. Once there, you see options for finding keywords, as shown in Figure 5.9.

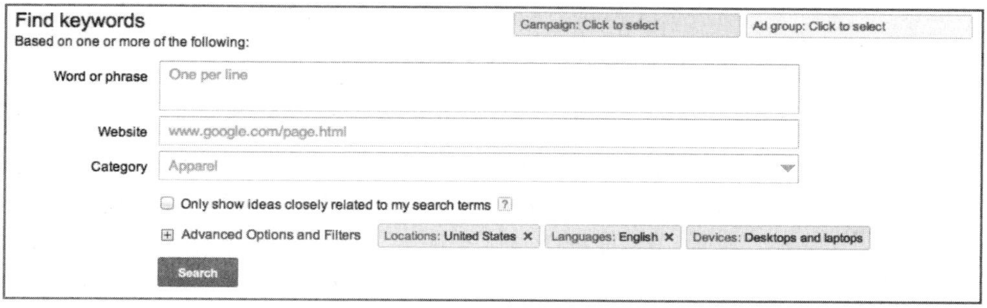

Figure 5.9 Entering keywords or a website into the tool

Say you're selling wintertime sports equipment, and you're looking for ideas to help build out some campaigns around your snowshoes. Assuming you have a page on your website dedicated to snowshoes, your first option is to simply enter the URL for that page and Google crawls the site, figures out what it's about, and returns a list of keywords relevant to that page. We talk a bit more about using this feature later, but for now, let's go with the keyword option instead.

To get started, you might want to keep things pretty general and just type in "snow shoe" to see what you find. As you continue your research, however, make sure to try typing additional words as well: This can really change the keyword suggestions that the tool gives back. If you enter more than one word, enter them one per line, and keep them as relevant to one another as you can. If you sell skis in addition to snowshoes, for example, you're better off saving your ski-related terms for another keyword research session and focusing this one on your snowshoes.

Advanced Options and Filters

Before you click the Search button, let's take a look at some of the other filters you can use, as shown in Figure 5.10.

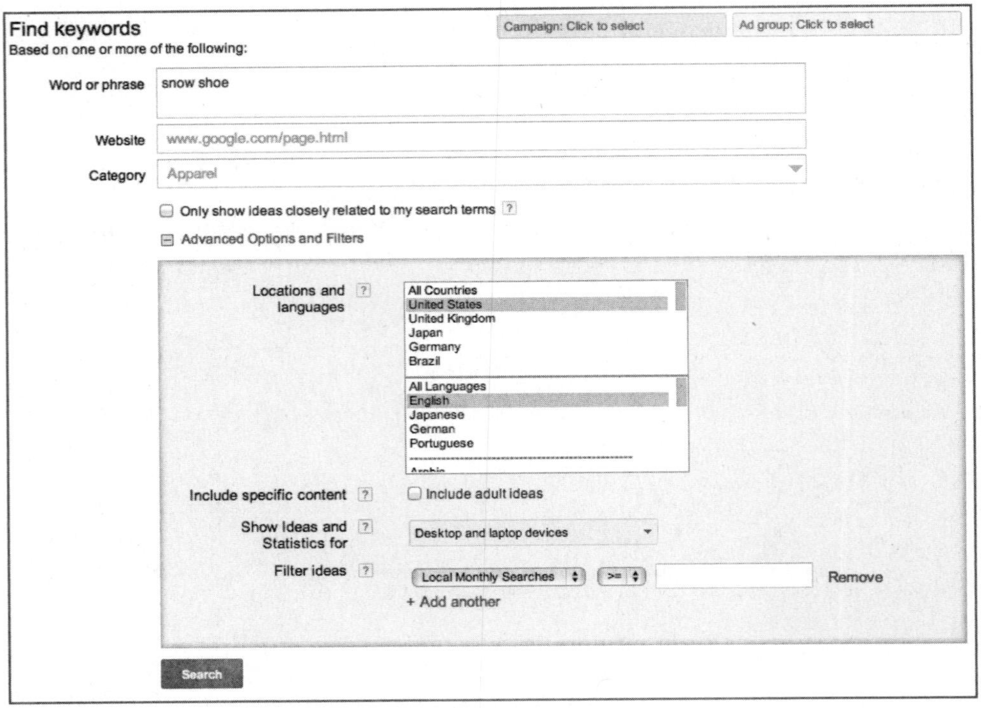

Figure 5.10 Advanced options and filters in the Google keyword tool

While many of these options are aimed much more at keyword research for search advertising, you should play with them to understand how they impact the results you see when researching for display advertising as well.

Locations and languages   You can specify a language, and if you use a specific location, you see regional data such as monthly searches, search trends, and competitive data for only the selected country.

Devices People type very different keywords on different devices. If you want to see only the search terms used on mobile devices, for example (which tend to be shorter), narrow the results to WAP or mobile devices capable of Internet browsing.

Filter ideas Here you can add additional filters to your result set based on the metrics that are reported back and simple less than / greater than logic. For example, if you want to see only keywords that are searched at least 1,000 times a month *and* have low competition, add two filters as shown in Figure 5.11.

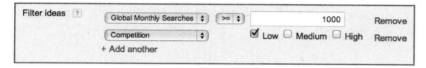

Figure 5.11 Using filter ideas in the Google keyword tool

Additional Refinements

There are a few other options for refinement to the left of the screen. You can use the Include and Exclude boxes to either include or exclude certain words in your result set: Simply enter the word or words and click the + button. Note that if you enter multiple words in either of these boxes, they are treated as one *or* the other, while if you enter those multiple words inside quotation marks, the phrase is treated as a single keyword.

The check boxes next to the three match types that search advertising supports can refine the reported metrics, although this is likely not as useful for display research.

Once all the filters and refinements are in place, click Search to see a result set like the one shown in Figure 5.12.

The search terms you entered explicitly are in the first block of results, and underneath that are rows of keyword ideas. These are the keywords that Google believes are relevant to either the keywords you typed into the tool or the URL that you entered, subject to any filters or refinements you have in place.

Understanding the Data

You can click the Columns drop-down at the top right of the result set to add or remove different metrics to your results, but let's take a look at a few that will be useful and are pictured in Figure 5.12.

Competition This is an indication of how many different AdWords advertisers are bidding on this term. While the AdWords interface provides you with only low, medium, or high values, exporting the data gives you numeric values from 0 to 1 that represent this in more granular detail. This can help you gauge how many other people you have to compete with for this keyword opportunity.

Keyword	Competition	Global Monthly Searches ?	Local Monthly Searches ?	Approximate CPC (Search) ?	Local Search Trends
☐ snow shoes ▾	High	135,000	74,000	$1.33	
☐ snow shoe mtn ▾	Low	18,100	18,100	$0.66	
☐ snow shoeing ▾	Low	8,100	4,400	$1.48	
☐ snow shoe resort ▾	Medium	9,900	8,100	$0.75	
☐ snow shoe rabbit ▾	Low	12,100	8,100	$0.99	
☐ kids snow shoes ▾	High	1,900	1,600	$1.21	
☐ snowshoe ▾	Low	301,000	246,000	$0.95	
☐ tubbs snow shoes ▾	High	5,400	4,400	$1.40	
☐ snow shoe siamese ▾	Low	2,400	1,900	$0.69	
☐ snow boot ▾	High	368,000	165,000	$1.52	
☐ snow shoe skiing ▾	Low	880	880	$0.84	
☐ snow shoe cat ▾	Low	3,600	1,900	$0.74	
☐ snow shoe hair ▾	Low	260	210	$0.91	
☐ snow shoe drink ▾	Low	91	73	$0.94	
☐ snow shoe shot ▾	Low	170	91	$1.04	
☐ toddler snow shoes ▾	High	260	210	$1.38	
☐ how to snow shoe ▾	Low	246,000	165,000	$0.95	
☐ best snow shoes ▾	High	2,400	1,600	$1.33	
☐ snow shoe sizing ▾	Low	880	720	$2.42	
☐ snow shoe mt ▾	Low	1,300	1,000	$0.70	
☐ snow shoe ski resort ▾	Low	2,900	2,900	$0.85	
☐ snow shoe poles ▾	High	720	590	$1.07	
☐ dog snow shoes ▾	High	390	260	$0.71	

Figure 5.12 Viewing results in the Google keyword tool

Monthly Searches (Global and Local)   An approximate 12-month average of how many times this particular search happens around the world (global) and in the country you've selected in the Advanced Options And Filters settings (local). The reported numbers are subject to the match type defined, so you may choose to check only the Exact or Phrase match type if you're interested in more specific search volume numbers. This can be a good indication of how much interest there is in a certain keyword.

Approximate CPC   Approximate cost per click that advertisers are paying for this keyword, averaged out across all the different ad positions. This metric can be used to evaluate the competitiveness of a particular keyword.

Local Search Trends   Bar graph showing seasonal trends for this keyword. The first month in the bar graph is the current month, and you can hover the mouse over a specific bar to see the month and year the bar represents. This is especially useful in understanding *when* people are searching on specific keywords so you can adjust your campaigns and expectations accordingly.

Evaluating Keywords

The first column of data in the Keyword Ideas section contains the list of keyword suggestions, and for display advertising, this can often be the most enlightening column of all to look at. Let's examine some of the results in Figure 5.12 and see what insights we can find.

Let's start with the fourth row: "snow shoe resort." This is already some incredibly valuable information, specifically *because* it has very little to do with what we're selling! As it turns out, there's a ski resort called Snowshoe Mountain in West Virginia, and an average of 9,900 people (8,100 of them in the United States) are looking for this resort on the Web every month. You can see that almost all of this searching happens during the winter months and that there are advertisers out there bidding on this term. Those advertisers might be travel agencies or event promoters or even the resort itself, and you probably *don't* want to be spending your snowshoe advertising dollars on people wanting to book a ski vacation!

The ninth row, "snow shoe siamese," is also interesting. There's actually a rare breed of cat called a Snowshoe that is a cross between Siamese and other shorthaired cats. Clearly, websites about this cat are not places you would want to be spending your advertising budget. And how about "snow shoe rabbit" in the fifth row? People looking for this are probably looking for the *Lepus americanus hare*, and again, although there are plenty of websites out there dedicated to this North American animal, they're not websites you want to be advertising on.

The point here is that some quick keyword research with this tool can give you enormous amounts of insight about the other kinds of things that Google might think are contextually relevant to the ads you want to show. When you're building out your ad groups, being able to exclude these kinds of sites (which we look at in Chapter 6) can save you countless dollars in wasted advertising.

And just as you can find themes you don't want to be advertising to, you can also find unique opportunities. Sure, you knew all about "men's snowshoes" and you probably even knew about all the brands that people are typing in, but take a look at the row "snow shoe sizing." As an advertiser, you may not have thought that people are interested in how to find the right fit for a snowshoe, but they are! And those kinds of people are *exactly* who you're looking for: people in the later stages of the snowshoe buying cycle. And how about "dog snow shoes"? Maybe you didn't know there was a market for a new product or at the very least a place where snowshoeing dog owners hang out online—and where you can show your ads.

The more you play with this tool, the more opportunities you'll find and the more problematic themes you can avoid, so carve out some time to really explore: You'll be glad you did.

Assessing Volume and Seasonality

Once you've got some themes nailed down, you can take a look at the monthly search data to understand the relative size of the advertising opportunity, but equally important is the impact of seasonality. In the snowshoe example, especially given that the results have been set to look at only the United States, you wouldn't expect a whole lot of people to be buying snowshoeing equipment in the middle of the summer, so you want to ensure that your advertising budget gets allocated over the year according to the potential to find interested consumers.

You can also use the Language and Location targets to find additional opportunities. Sticking with the English language, take a look at Figure 5.13. Maybe you want to get into the snowshoe business in New Zealand during the off-season in North America!

Figure 5.13 Seasonal trending in different countries

Using Competition Data

Using the Competition and Approximate CPC columns can help you understand just how many other advertisers know about the various themes and opportunities you're uncovering.

While all the other advertisers are fighting each other for the more obvious (and more competitive) terms like "buy snow shoes" and "men's snow shoes," you can find opportunities by digging through some of the lesser-known topics. You've already seen that there is quite a bit of interest in things like "snow shoe sizing," and a little more digging can find even more opportunities to show your ads where competition is not quite as fierce and prices are not quite as steep.

Validating Relevance with the Keyword Tool

The last thing to point out with the Google Keyword Tool is that it provides us with a unique opportunity to test the way Google is figuring out context. Remember that your Quality Score is largely made up of relevance factors, and the more relevant your keywords are to the kinds of placements in which you want your ad to show up and the landing page you take people to when they click, the better your Quality Score. And the higher the Quality Score, the more likely you are to win the auction and the lower the price you have to pay.

So because relevance is so important to you, you can use the keyword tool to see just what kinds of keywords Google believes are relevant to either your landing pages or placements.

While by no means a perfect approach, typing in the URL of the landing pages or placements you want to target can give you some ideas of keywords to include or themes you want to exclude, things you can use to build out your ad groups in a way that sets them up for the best chances at success.

Thursday/Friday: Using the Contextual Targeting Tool

An efficient way to build out contextually targeted ad groups is with the Contextual Targeting Tool. It takes a list of keywords and returns suggestions for other keywords all grouped together, and these groups can be a starting point for creating the ad groups in your campaigns.

This tool is not only useful for exploring opportunities from a research and planning perspective, it can also be used as a tactical tool for creating your ad groups. Let's continue with our outdoor winter sports theme, only this time we'll shift from snowshoes to snow skis.

Getting Started

The Contextual Targeting Tool can be found in the AdWords interface under the Tools and Analysis menu. To get started, enter up to 10 keywords, separated by commas, to describe some of the ski and ski accessory equipment websites that you might want to advertise on.

You can also specify language and location, which affect the keyword groups that the tool returns. Explore these settings if you have different markets or if you're advertising in different languages.

Click Search to see the results, as shown in Figure 5.14.

Working with the Results

There are only three columns of data to look at here, and along with them there are a few things that you can do. First, you'll see a list of suggested ad group names, which is essentially the theme that the tool has identified as one that might be of interest to you based on the keywords you've entered and the language and location settings you've used. In the first row in Figure 5.14, the tool has found the theme of snow skis, and in the Keywords column is a list of keywords the tool is suggesting that could be used inside a contextually targeted ad group.

The last column provides a suggested bid, which is meant to provide a starting point for you if you were to choose to create an ad group like this one using CPC bidding. To get this number, the tool examines a history of bids that have been used in the AdWords system to win placements that would be contextually relevant to the group of keywords. Choosing a bid price for a new ad group can be challenging, and while not the *only* data point for you to use, this is certainly a good one to look at when it comes time to choose your default bid.

Suggested ad group name	Keywords	Suggested bid ⑦
☐ Snow Skis	⊕ ⊖ snow skis, snow ski equipment, snow skis for sale, used snow skis, discount snow skis	$1.64
☐ Discount Snow Skis	⊕ ⊖ discount snow skis, discount snow ski gear, discount snow ski equipment, discount snow ski apparel	$1.61
☐ Snow Skis For Sale	⊕ ⊖ snow skis for sale, snow ski sale, snow skis on sale, used snow skis for sale, cheap snow skis for sale	$1.72
☐ Snow Ski Reviews	⊕ ⊖ snow ski reviews, on the snow ski reviews, 2011 snow ski reviews, snow ski reviews 2010, snow ski equipment reviews	$1.72
☐ Used Snow Skis	⊕ ⊖ used snow skis, used snow skis for sale, used snow ski equipment, used snow skis and boots, used kids snow skis	$1.65
☐ Snow Ski Sizing	⊕ ⊖ snow ski sizing, how to size snow skis, snow ski sizing chart, snow ski size calculator, snow ski size guide	$1.71
☐ Head Skis	⊕ ⊖ head skis, head ski boots, head skis 2011, indian head ski resort, head skis for sale	$1.80
☐ Atomic Snow Skis	⊕ ⊖ atomic snow skis	$1.69
☐ Snow Skis Boots	⊕ ⊖ snow skis boots, khombu snow ski boots, snow ski boots for sale, used snow ski boots, used snow skis and boots	-
☐ Skis	⊕ ⊖ skis, skis for sale, ski pants, ski helmets, k2 skis	$1.69
☐ Skis Sale	⊕ ⊖ skis sale, skis for sale, used skis for sale, water skis for sale, snow skis for sale	$1.69
☐ Ski Review	⊕ ⊖ ski review, ski reviews 2011, ski reviews 2010, volkl ski reviews, snow ski reviews	$1.77
☐ Line Skis	⊕ ⊖ line skis, line skis sale, line skis for sale, line skis 2011, cheap line skis	$1.78
☐ Rossignol Skis	⊕ ⊖ rossignol skis, rossignol ski boots, rossignol skis 2011, rossignol ski bindings, rossignol ski jackets	$1.80
☐ Roxy Skis	⊕ ⊖ roxy skis, roxy ski jackets, roxy ski boots, roxy ski goggles, roxy ski jacket ladies	$1.60

Add to campaign | Export to AdWords Editor | Remove | About this data ⑦

Go to page: 1   Show rows: 15 ◆ |◀ ◀ 1 - 15 of 34 ▶ ▶|

Figure 5.14 Contextual targeting results

Of course, each time you change the keywords and click Search, you see different suggestions and different data. As always, this is a great place to experiment, and you can try entering a variety of different words in different combinations to see what Google thinks might be contextually relevant for you.

Once you see an interesting grouping, there are several ways to refine the results and ultimately add them to an ad group or create a new one. You can add or remove any of the keywords in the list of suggestions by hovering the mouse over the list and clicking. For example, if you don't sell used skis at all, you can delete that term from the list. Once you do that, the data associated with the suggested grouping changes to reflect the new keyword group.

Expanding Keyword Groups

There are two green circle icons next to the suggested ad group name column: a + sign and an ellipsis. Clicking the + icon expands a suggested group into more specific groups. If the icon is disabled, that indicates that the suggested ad group cannot be expanded any further.

Let's expand the third row in Figure 5.14, Snow Skis For Sale, by clicking the + icon. The updated result set appears in Figure 5.15.

Add to campaign	Export to AdWords Editor	Remove		About this data ⑦
☐ **Suggested ad group name**		**Keywords**		**Suggested bid** ⑦
		8 ad groups were expanded Undo ad group expansion		
☐ Snow Skis	⊕ ⊖	snow skis, snow ski equipment, snow skis for sale, discount snow skis		$1.63
☐ Discount Snow Skis	⊕ ⊖	discount snow skis, discount snow ski gear, discount snow ski equipment, discount snow ski apparel		$1.61
☐ Snow Skis For Sale	⊕ ⊖	snow skis for sale, snow ski sale, snow skis on sale, used snow skis for sale, cheap snow skis for sale		$1.72
☐ Rossignol Snow Skis	⊕ ⊖	rossignol snow skis		$1.74
☐ Salomon Snow Skis	⊕ ⊖	salomon snow skis		$1.74
☐ Snow Skis Buying Guide	⊕ ⊖	snow skis buying guide		$1.66
☐ Snow Skis Clearance	⊕ ⊖	snow skis clearance		$1.61
☐ Snow Skis Reviews	⊕ ⊖	snow skis reviews, on the snow ski reviews, 2011 snow ski reviews, snow ski reviews 2010, snow ski equipment reviews		$1.73
☐ Used Snow Skis For Sale	⊕ ⊖	used snow skis for sale		$1.75
☐ Snow Skis Buy	⊕ ⊖	snow skis buy, how to buy snow skis, snow skis buying guide, buy snow skis online		$1.66
☐ Volkl Snow Skis	⊕ ⊖	volkl snow skis		$1.78
☐ Snow Ski Reviews	⊕ ⊖	snow ski reviews, on the snow ski reviews, 2011 snow ski reviews, snow ski reviews 2010, snow ski equipment reviews		$1.72
☐ Used Snow Skis	⊕ ⊖	used snow skis, used snow skis for sale, used snow ski equipment, used snow skis and boots, used kids snow skis		$1.65
☐ Snow Ski Sizing	⊕ ⊖	snow ski sizing, how to size snow skis, snow ski sizing chart, snow ski size calculator, snow ski size guide		$1.71

Figure 5.15 Expanding a list in the contextual targeting tool

At the top of the result set is a notification telling you how many new ad groups resulted from the expansion along with a link that lets you quickly undo these changes if needed.

You now see more specific ad groups around brands like Rossignol Snow Skis and Salomon Snow Skis as well as synonyms like Snow Skis Buy. There are even more related themes like Snow Skis Clearance. Exploring these group expansions can be a great way to identify themes that you may not even know exist.

Viewing Sample Placements

Clicking the ellipsis icon next to any of the suggested ad group names opens a new screen with a list of predicted placements. This can be a great way to get a feel for the kinds of websites and pages on the GDN where your ads might appear if you were to create a contextually targeted ad group using the keywords in the ad group.

You can expand the predicted placement domains to see actual examples of pages in the GDN that Google considers relevant to the theme of this group of keywords. If these are the kinds of sites you want your ads to show up on, then this might be a good ad group for you. If not, you might want to reconsider some of those keywords.

And if you find that while the majority of the predicted placements make sense for you but a few don't, then make note of those sites that you *don't* want your ads appearing on so you can exclude them, which is something we discuss in detail during week 7.

Adding Ad Groups to Campaigns

Once you have a list of keywords to turn into an ad group, you can do this right from the tool.

First, put a check in the box next to the suggested ad groups (Figure 5.15) you want to add and click the Add To Campaign button (the button becomes active once you've checked one or more rows).

Next, select a campaign you want the ad group to live under, and click the Create Ad Groups button. Note that when you do this, the new ad group remains in a paused state until you create some ads to run in it.

Tip: Another way to add new ad groups to your account is by way of the AdWords Editor, which is an offline tool you can download and use to manage your Google AdWords accounts. To add new ad groups, simply click Export To AdWords Editor to download a CSV that can be easily imported into the tool.

Week 7: Find Good Placements

Choosing the exact placements for your ads gives you enormous control over your advertising, but with millions of potential advertising opportunities across the GDN, finding the right ones can be a daunting task.

This week is dedicated to sorting through all the possibilities to find the placements that are best for you, and luckily, a number of tools can help you do just that. Specifically, we look at the DoubleClick Ad Planner and the AdWords Placement Tool, and by the end of this week you should feel more confident in your ability to seek out and target a host of placements that are right for you.

Monday/Tuesday: Use the DoubleClick Ad Planner

The DoubleClick Ad Planner is a free Google product that allows advertisers to find and research millions of websites, whether they're part of the GDN or not. It works by letting users filter through sites by many different criteria and generate lists of relevant websites to target in things like display campaigns.

This is a powerful tool containing many dials and knobs and bells and whistles, but in the following sections, we focus on some of the most useful features of Ad Planner in finding placements that you can then target in your AdWords campaigns.

To follow along as you read this section, you can find the DoubleClick Ad Planner at www.google.com/adplanner.

Where the Data Comes From

You're about to start looking through a *lot* of data, and any time you play with data, it's important to understand just where that data comes from. In the case of Ad Planner, you look at a website's usage statistics, demographic information around that website's visitor base, and even aggregated user information that can tell you what interests visitors of that website, what other sites they visit, and what keywords they tend to type into search engines.

A minimum threshold of data needs to be available for a website before Ad Planner displays it, and this data comes from a variety of sources:

- Google Toolbar, which many people have installed on their browsers. Google Toolbar adds an area to the browser's other controls and features and allows its users to do things like search Google directly from the toolbar, translate pages, and share content. Users can opt into anonymous data sharing, and Google aggregates this anonymized data and uses it to learn about different websites.

- Information that web publishers provide directly as well as anonymized and aggregated Google Analytics data from websites that have opted into that data sharing setting from their Google Analytics accounts.

- Traditional data sources, such as opt-in consumer panels and good old market research.

All of these data points are then aggregated over millions of users and run through a number of processes before they show up in the bar graphs and tables of numbers we see in Ad Planner.

To show how to use this tool to find placements, let's dive in with an example. As we go through this exercise, let's pretend that you're advertising for a website that offers 24-hour emergency dental services to patients that live in the Los Angeles area.

In defining your target audience, one of your personas could be someone suffering from a toothache trying to figure out what's wrong in the middle of the night. Let's use Ad Planner to find some websites you may want to target with your ads.

First, log into the Ad Planner tool using the same Google account you use for AdWords. Select the Search For Placements tab from the default Research section of the tool, leave Placements checked in the "What are you looking for?" area and leave Audience Match selected for the ranking choice. This brings you to a list of placements with many filtering options at the top (Figure 5.16).

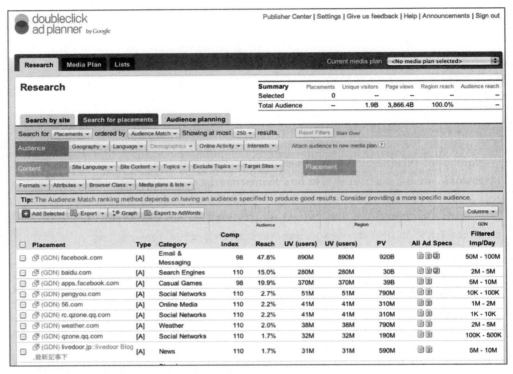

Figure 5.16 Initial unfiltered list of placements in Ad Planner

Under the Search For Placements subtab you can change the "What are you looking for?" and "How would you like them ranked?" options that got you here from the previous screen. Play around with these to see how they affect the list of placements.

Audience Filters

The first set of filters pertains to the audience. You can specify the geography and language of your target audience along with the kinds of keywords they type in, other websites they might visit, and their general interests.

The more restrictive you get with your filters, the fewer placements you'll see in your result set, so you want to make sure you strike a balance between a few laser-focused placements and a lot of more general placements.

In our example, the only restriction you really need is proximity to Los Angeles. No matter how bad someone's mouth hurts, you can't service their need unless they're within driving distance of one of your 24-hour dental clinics. Use the Geography dropdown to select the Los Angeles metro area as shown in Figure 5.17.

Figure 5.17 Selecting a target geography in Ad Planner

You can then target a specific language in your research. If you have a campaign dedicated to English speakers in the Los Angeles area and another campaign dedicated to Spanish speakers in the Los Angeles area, you can repeat your research for each of those language targets. For now though, leave the language setting unrestricted.

As far as the behavioral patterns—kinds of sites visited, keywords regularly used, or other interests—you probably don't care. Your service is targeting anyone who has a toothache when no other dentist is open.

Content Filters

Next, you'll want to look for the kind of pages where potential placements for your ads might live. If you put yourself in the shoes of someone suffering from middle-of-the-night dental pain, you get a good idea of the kinds of websites they might visit.

Ad Planner enables you to refine placements by a host of categories, but let's focus on the Site Content and Topics filters. When you click the Site Content dropdown, you can list websites and keywords to define the kinds of placements you're searching for. In Figure 5.18, we tell Ad Planner we're looking for self-diagnosis sites like webmd.com or directory listing sites like dentistdirectory.com as well as sites about toothaches or emergency dentistry.

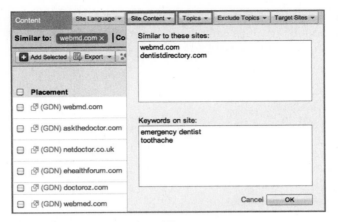

Figure 5.18 Content filter options in Ad Planner

Placement Filters

Your last filters refer to the placements themselves and include things like ad formats and attributes as well as the kinds of devices and browser types the placements support.

You might choose to connect with your target customer by using an image of someone in desperate pain, clutching their mouth in anguish in front of a window where you can see a lonely streetlight, making it clear that it's the middle of the night. When building out your ad creative, you need to know what size our image ads need to be, and Ad Planner lets you look for placements of specified sizes.

At this point, you might have a pretty long list of placements to investigate further, but make sure to play around with your filters to get to a *manageable* list so you can look at them one by one.

Researching Specific Placements

Suppose your list contains an entry for symptomchecker.about.com. To visit the actual site, click the pop-out arrow icon, or to find out more about it, click the name of the placement or the pop-out arrow icon and a new window opens giving you the site profile.

Although you might not be able to make out the details in Figure 5.19, you can see that the site profile page includes some great information about this subdomain of about.com that can help you decide whether to target it for your ads. The top section contains general information about the category of this placement, a description, and information about the advertising the site accepts. In this case, you can buy display inventory through the AdWords network.

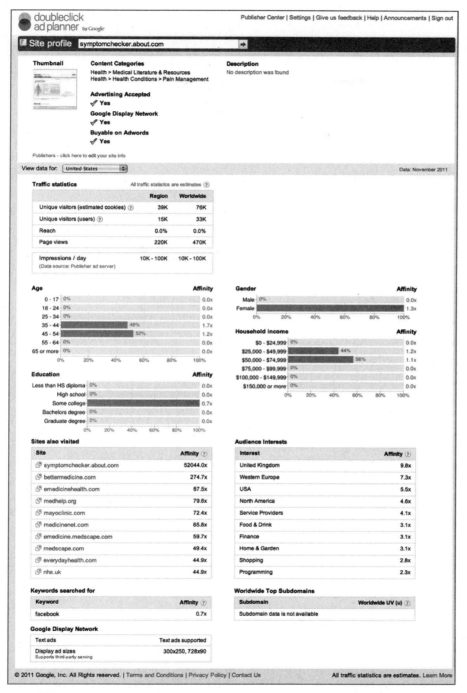

Figure 5.19   A site profile in Ad Planner

In the next section, you define a target region (in this case the United States) and see website statistics and demographic information about visitors to this site. The traffic statistics are for a typical month; they include things like unique visitors (defined by both users and cookies), page views, and approximate reach, expressed as a percentage of all Internet users. Below that is an estimated range of the number of ad impressions this website can serve up.

You also see demographic data about visitors to this site. These estimates can help you target specific audiences.

Moving down the page, you see a list of sites that visitors to symptomchecker. about.com also tend to visit and the kinds of interests they tend to exhibit. Looking at the Sites Also Visited section is an excellent way to find even more placement opportunities. In this case, people who were on this website also visited bettermedicine.com and mayoclinic.com. Clicking those links takes you to site profiles for each of those websites, and you can evaluate those potential placements as well!

For websites that accept advertising through the GDN, the last set of data gives details around the supported ad formats on that placement. Here, both text and display ads are supported, and there are two supported display ad sizes.

Last, when evaluating whether or not to target this placement, you should visit the site to see where your ads might show up. We talk more about this later in this chapter.

Media Plans and Lists

After evaluating placements, you can go back to the filtered list, select the placements you find interesting, and add them to either a media plan or a list. In Ad Planner, these are places where you can store a set of placements to help plan out your current and future campaigns as you're doing your research. A media plan is for a specific advertising initiative, while a list is for placements that can support future advertising campaigns.

If you're new to Ad Planner, when you click the Add Selected button, the first thing to do is create either your first list or your first media plan. To do this, give it a name, select a region, and enter an optional description. Save it, and all the selected placements are added to your media plan or list, which you can access and add to at any time from the top tabs.

Exporting to AdWords

Use the Export dropdown to export your list of placements in a number of different formats. You can even graph your results across four dimensions (click the Graph button and start playing!), but one of the most useful features in the Ad Planner tool is the Export To AdWords option.

Once you click the button, select one of your AdWords accounts (if you use the My Client Center, you may have access to more than one with your login), and then either add the selected placements to existing campaigns and ad groups or create new ones right there in the interface.

This will make more sense after we go through the mechanics of building campaigns and ad groups. For now, just know that it can be a real time-saver to export placements right from the Ad Planner tool.

Wednesday: Using the Placement Tool

Using the Google AdWords Placement Tool is another way to look for placements for your ads, and it lives right within the AdWords interface. To start using this tool, select Placement Tool from the Tools and Analysis menu and enter keywords or websites to define the kinds of placements you're looking for. Here, we enter "tooth pain" and see a set of placements (Figure 5.20).

Find placements
Based on one or more of the following:

Word or phrase	tooth pain
Website	www.google.com/page.html
Category	Apparel

⊞ Advanced Options and Filters   Locations: United States ✕   Languages: English ✕   Devices: All

Search

About this data ?

Add to account ▾   Download ▾   Sorted by Relevance ▾   Columns ▾

⊟ ✓ Save all   Results (174)   1 - 50 of 174 ▾   ‹   ›

	Placement	Placement Type	Ad Types	Impressions Per Day
☐	Mobile App: Hide Pictures in Vaulty (Android Market), by Squid Tooth LLC ▾	Mobile App	📄 📱	100,000 - 500,000
☐	Mobile App: Big Teeth Mole Lite (Android Market), by Gp Imports ▾	Mobile App	📄 📱	0 - 10,000
☐	Mobile App: Rooster Teeth Podcast (Android Market), by Pwnage Software ▾	Mobile App	📄 📱	10,000 - 100,000
☐	Mobile App: Ali's Teeth Out Free (iTunes App Store), by Game Fish ▾	Mobile App	📄 📱	0 - 10,000
☐	Mobile App: Share Apps (Android Market), by Squid Tooth LLC ▾	Mobile App	📄 📱	0 - 10,000
☐	Mobile App: iFangs Lite - Free monster teeth (iTunes App Store), by Show Pony Apps LLC ▾	Mobile App	📄 📱	0 - 10,000

Figure 5.20 Placement results

If you enter a URL, Google looks at the content of that page and tries to find placements that match the contextual theme of that page.

You can also narrow down results by a list of predefined categories. Take a look through the list of available categories and subcategories and experiment with applying these filters to your search: It can make your lists of potential placements a lot more manageable.

From here, you can look at the options you have for refining this list of placements and then dive into how you might do further evaluation and eventually add selected placements to your various ad groups.

In the Find Placements panel, expand Advanced Options And Filters to see the panel shown in Figure 5.21.

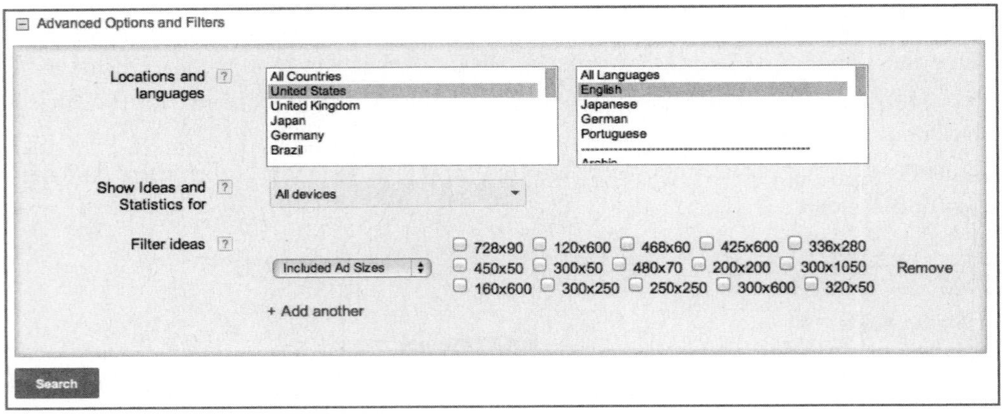

Figure 5.21 Setting languages and locations in the Placement Tool

Locations and Languages

By selecting an explicit language, you tell the Placement Tool to use the keywords that you entered earlier in the context of a specific language. Here, we select English.

When you choose a specific location, any numbers or statistics that appear in your result set are for the selected region. Here, we select the United States.

Device Filters

The next set of filters restricts placements to those compatible with certain types of devices, including laptops and desktops as well as mobile devices that support full Internet browsers or those limited to WAP (Wireless Application Protocol, which is a fancy way to say a non-smartphone). For example, changing this option to filter on mobile returns only placements eligible to show on mobile devices and adjusts the statistics in the result set accordingly.

Additional Filters

In the Additional Filters area, you can refine your results even further, by things like ad types and sizes and demographic information like age, gender, education, and household income.

Using the Add Another option, you can string together combinations of options to zero in on the placements you're after. So if you're looking for placements that support display ads in a few select sizes, you can set up the filters as shown in Figure 5.22.

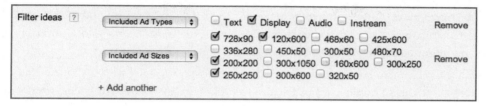

Figure 5.22 Setting additional filters on supported ad types and sizes

On the left side of the screen are the placement type options (Figure 5.23). You can play with each of these different placement types, but here, we want *websites* that accept our set of display ads, so we uncheck everything except Site.

Figure 5.23 Placement type filters

Working with the Results

After setting filters, you should have a result set that you can work with. By trying new keywords and websites and refining or opening up filter options, you can create a result set that is both manageable and representative of the kinds of placements you have in mind.

Columns The result set contains a row for each placement and columns that provide information about those placements (Figure 5.24).

Figure 5.24 A row of placement tool results

In the Placement column, you can click the magnifying glass icon to pop open a new window with the DoubleClick Ad Planner site profile information. The Placement

135

■

WEEK 7: FIND GOOD PLACEMENTS

Type column shows what kind of placement this is, and can be any of the types in Figure 5.23 (in this case, Site). The Ad Types column tells us what kinds of ads can run in this placement (in this case, both text and image). The Impressions Per Day column gives us the approximate number of impressions we might expect this placement to get in a 24-hour period. These numbers typically have a fairly wide range, and it's best to use them as relative comparators between placements, not exact numbers of impressions you might get.

Clicking the placement itself brings up additional information (Figure 5.25), including a link to where the ad might appear. Be sure to look there to ensure that it's an appropriate location for your ad!

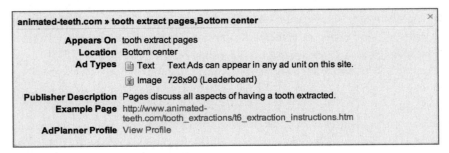

Figure 5.25 Researching a placement

Sorting options When working with large result sets, sorting options can help keep things organized. You can sort by relevance to your keywords or websites (default), but also alphabetically by placement name, by number of impressions per day, or by the relevance of the domain on which the placement appears rather than the placement itself.

Note that once you've sorted, you can switch the sort order from ascending to descending and back by clicking the column header.

Starring Starring enables you to keep a list of placements that you like as you do your research. When you find one that looks like it makes sense for your advertising objectives, click the star to the left of the placement name. You can expand the list of starred items at the bottom right of your screen at any time. This can be especially helpful as you continue to change your search and filter parameters to find more and more placements.

Adding Placements to Ad Groups

Once you find placements, you can add them to your ad groups. Check the boxes next to the placements you want to add and click Add Placements. In the dialog box that appears, select the campaign and ad group to add the selected placements to.

You can also use the Download drop-down to choose to download the entire result set, just the selected placements, or all of your starred placements in a number of different formats, including CSV, TSV, XML, or as a compressed file. With this data, you can continue to evaluate your potential placements in a tool like Microsoft Excel. Later, you can add the placements through the AdWords interface or the AdWords Editor tool (an offline tool you install on your computer to manage accounts from the desktop rather than from the AdWords online interface).

Thursday: Evaluating Placements

In the following sections we talk about what to look for when you're deciding whether to target potential placements with your ads or not. A good place to start is by looking for the right context and the best potential bang for your buck, and ultimately, a good placement will be judged by its actual performance against your predetermined advertising objectives.

Evaluating Context

You've spent considerable time and effort trying to understand and get into the minds of your target audience, and you've even developed personas for the kinds of people you want looking at your ads. You've thought long and hard about where they're likely to be hanging out online and what kind of messaging you can use to demonstrate your competitive advantage. And now it's time to imagine *your* ad in one of the available ad slots.

First you'll want to look at the placement itself. If it's a single page, you can focus on that page, and if it's a sitewide or multiple page placement, you can look for the general framework on which your ads would appear. You want to look at the different ad formats and sizes and their relation to the focal points of the page.

For example, suppose you see a long list of hundreds of search results and there are two ad slots that your ad might show up in: one skyscraper near the top just to the right of the beginning of the search results and one leaderboard at the very bottom of the page you see after considerable scrolling. Which one is more likely to get seen? Which one is more likely to draw the click if the ad were relevant to the website visitor? Depending on your goals, the answers may be different. But with the actual placement on your computer screen, you can get a good feel for how your ad might be shown.

You also want to understand the kind of content the website provides. For example, if Kmart advertises Radio Flyer wagons next to an article about a product recall on those wagons, the content is certainly contextually relevant to Radio Flyer wagons but probably not the context that Kmart is hoping for. An ad like this essentially says, "Looking for a wagon that can knock your kids teeth out and cause a trip to the hospital complete with stitches? Well you're in luck, because we've got it on sale!"

While this is an over-the-top example, it does demonstrate a few good points to look for when evaluating your placements. First, is this site going to attract people who are in the market for a Radio Flyer wagon? Of course not; these are people who already *have* one and are interested in learning more about a product recall, and that could be considered the exact *opposite* of being in the market for a product. Again, putting yourself in the shoes of someone who would be visiting the website you might be advertising on is often the easiest way to decide whether or not you'd like to choose that placement.

Getting the Most Bang for Your Buck

Another way to go about evaluating a placement is to understand the "bang for your buck" that it can provide. What this really means is striking a balance between volume and specificity in the audience that a placement is capable of attracting. On one hand, you want a highly focused, targeted group of people to avoid wasting advertising dollars on eyeballs that aren't likely to convert on your advertising goals. On the other, you have to get that message in front of at least some critical mass of eyeballs.

You might be able to find a placement that is *exactly* who you're looking for. In the Kmart example, maybe there's a blog out there dedicated to "the last things you need to do before buying your new Radio Flyer," and maybe the people who see your ad there convert at a rate of 100 percent. But if there are only two visitors to that blog each month, you'll have a hard time getting those wagons off your shelves.

But you don't want to open it up too much by putting your ad all over the place either. If you can get a million impressions a minute on irrelevant sites, that's not going to translate into profitable conversions.

For these reasons, we use tools like the DoubleClick Ad Planner and the AdWords Placement Tool to get an idea of the volume of traffic these placements have and balance that with relevance and likelihood of conversion on whatever advertising goals we've established. If you're going after pure brand awareness by the masses, then you'll likely lean much more heavily on highly trafficked websites that may not be as relevant to your products and services. If you're chasing after direct response goals, you may choose to target lots and lots of smaller websites, but sites that are extremely relevant to your products and services and attract visitors that have a high probability of becoming your customers.

Measuring Performance

We talk about this in greater detail in Chapter 9, "Month 6: Launch and Measure Your Campaign's Performance," but the way we evaluate *all* of our placements is by how they perform against our advertising goals. Do they get us more social network followers and fans? Do they lead to clicks that result in leads, purchases, or engaged visits? Do they make our telephone ring?

All the tools and all our research help us *guess* how our placements will perform. We don't actually *know* if they are successful until we try them and collect the data that tells us how many people we reached and how many of those we influenced to take a desired action. Research is an important beginning, but you have to actually try placements before you can evaluate their success.

Friday: Automatic and Managed Placement Strategies

Regardless of what kind of targeting you use, every ad ultimately runs in a placement. With other targeting types, Google AdWords automatically finds placements based on factors like the audiences, topics, or contextual targeting you define. Alternatively, you can explicitly define managed placements that you handle manually.

Many advertisers use a strategy that begins by allowing Google to find lots of placements automatically. Then they evaluate results and exclude placements that don't work well and add those that do to a list they manage manually. This strategy provides a lot more volume on many different placements that are being automatically found by AdWords, and most important, you get the data you need to decide which to keep and which to throw away. Don't think of this as wasting advertising dollars. Think of this technique as intelligently spending marketing research dollars. Here's how it works.

Using Automatic Placements

To set up a campaign to use automatic placements, adjust your campaign settings to use the broad reach option in the Networks setting (simply change the selection pictured in Figure 5.7 from specific to broad reach).

Next, set up your ad groups to use something other than placement targeting like contextual, topic, or audience targeting. With any targeting other than placements and a broad reach setting, Google AdWords automatically selects placements and starts showing your ads.

After these campaigns run for a little while, you have all kinds of great data about where your ads have shown, and it lives under the Placements subsection of the Display Network tab. Expanding the automatic placements link produces a list like that in Figure 5.26.

Here we've chosen to look at columns of data that include not just the number of impressions or clicks on our ads but also cost data, click-through rate, and most important, conversion data. These are the metrics we need to evaluate the performance of our placements and decide to keep them or throw them away.

To evaluate these placements, let's pretend that a conversion is defined as a lead form being submitted and that we know from our past sales data that these leads are worth $5.00 each. Ready to start analyzing?

Moving from Automatic to Managed

Look at the third row from the bottom, ehow.com. We spent $94.95 on this placement and it generated 72 clicks for us, of which 29 filled out our form. This equates to a conversion rate of over 40%, and at a cost per conversion of $3.27, we're making $1.73 on each of those conversions.

Sites	Ad group	Clicks	Impr.	CTR ?	Avg. CPC ?	Cost	Conv. (1-per-click) ?	Cost / conv. (1-per-click) ?	Conv. rate (1-per-click) ?	View-through Conv. ?
Total - Display Network		**10,223**	**10,451,538**	**0.10%**	**$1.19**	**$12,201.58**	**1,886**	**$6.47**	**18.45%**	**5,154**
about.com	Ad Group #1	214	134449	0.16%	$1.26	$270.22	61	$4.43	28.50%	562
cheapoair.com	Ad Group #1	154	56,897	0.27%	$1.32	$203.17	22	$9.24	14.29%	126
blogspot.com	Ad Group #1	17	265	6.42%	$1.07	$18.25	1	$18.25	5.88%	1
nytimes.com	Ad Group #1	9	101,637	0.01%	$1.33	$11.95	1	$11.95	11.11%	8
cnn.com	Ad Group #1	13	137,018	0.01%	$1.26	$16.44	2	$8.22	15.38%	0
dealcatcher.com	Ad Group #1	6	144	4.17%	$1.24	$7.47	1	$7.47	16.67%	0
accuweather.com	Ad Group #1	24	27,855	0.09%	$1.19	$28.60	4	$7.15	16.67%	12
mail.google.com	Ad Group #1	73	641,213	0.01%	$1.34	$97.80	19	$5.15	26.03%	0
wunderground.com	Ad Group #1	77	49,177	0.16%	$1.24	$95.61	3	$31.87	3.90%	34
ehow.com	Ad Group #1	72	8,722	0.83%	$1.32	$94.95	29	$3.27	40.28%	46
usatoday.com	Ad Group #1	73	10,293	0.71%	$1.29	$94.24	33	$2.86	45.21%	15
answers.com	Ad Group #1	7	4,065	0.17%	$0.87	$6.08	1	$6.08	14.29%	1

Figure 5.26 Examining results of automatic placements

This is clearly a placement that's working for us, so we add it to our managed placements. To do this, we check the box to the left of ehow.com, click the Manage Placement And Bid button at the top left of the screen, and enter a bid when prompted to do so. We can continue to monitor this one and make adjustments to our bids to get more profitable clicks and conversions from this placement.

You can also use sorting and filtering options in the interface to check off multiple placements and move them to the managed placements list all at once. For example, you can sort by the lowest cost per conversion and create a filter for a minimum threshold of conversions. Then you can check all the placements that match your criteria and click the Manage Placement And Bid button for a bulk edit.

Excluding Placements

Just as you can choose to focus on and manually manage your bids for certain placements, you can also isolate the placements that *aren't* working for you and exclude your ads from showing up on them. To do this, let's take a look at the row above the one we just looked at, wunderground.com. Here, there's lots of traffic and it's getting us some clicks, but the conversion rate is too low to be profitable for us. At a cost per conversion of $31.87, we're actually *losing* $26.87 on each filled-out form!

To exclude this placement and bar our ads from showing up there again, we place a check in the box to the left of this one and click the Exclude Placements button, located just to the right of the Manage Placement And Bid button.

See Details

Sometimes looking at the entire domain of the placement is too generic and you want to dig a little deeper to see how the actual *pages* or *sections* of the domain are performing. It's possible that some sections are profitable while others are losing you money, and rather than excluding or managing the whole domain, you can take action on a smaller subgroup of the domain to squeeze out even more performance from your campaigns.

Let's take a look at the first row, about.com, and figure out which placements on the about.com domain are performing for us and which aren't. To do this, put a check in the box to the left of about.com and choose the Selected option from the See Details drop-down.

The list expands considerably, and you can see which placements on the about.com domain are making money and which are not. Once again, you can use sorting and filtering to make bulk edits as you move placements into a managed state or exclude them altogether.

Week 8: Organize Campaigns and Ad Groups

At this point, you have a pretty good idea of the advertising goals you hope to accomplish, the type of websites and people you want to target, and the messaging you're trying to get in front of them. Now, it's time to put it all together into campaigns.

Many advertisers jump right in and just start building campaigns, and although that's tempting and can get your ads up and running quickly, it's also a recipe for disaster. Planning how your campaigns will reflect the audiences you're targeting, the messaging you're trying to get across, and the objectives you hope to accomplish may take a little more time up front, but it will pay big dividends in the long run.

Monday: Separating Your Display Campaigns

One of the most basic and important things you can do when advertising on the GDN is separate your display campaigns from your search campaigns. Most advertisers take their first foray into display either by accident or by casually just "adding that other network" in their campaign settings, and we strongly recommend that you not make this mistake.

If you're already an AdWords advertiser using search campaigns, you might want to go into the Settings tab for each of your campaigns and make sure that your existing search campaigns are targeting *only* search (and search partners) networks. Because the default settings inside AdWords are to target all networks on all devices, it's not uncommon to see the first radio button (All Available Sites) in Figure 5.27 selected.

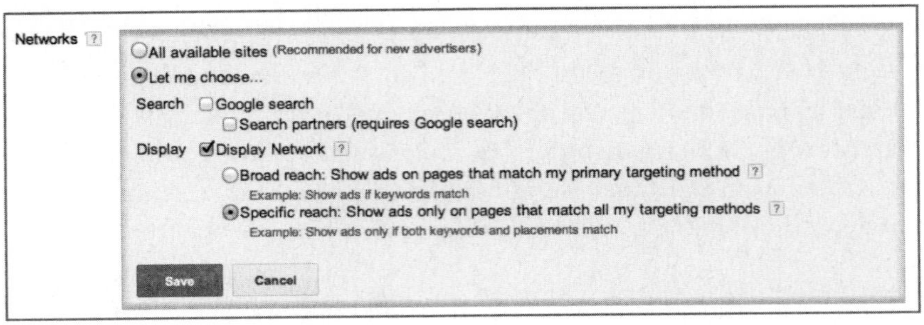

Figure 5.27 Choosing sites for the campaign

To ensure that your search campaigns target only search networks and your display campaigns target only display networks, select the Let Me Choose option to see all of the options, as shown in Figure 5.27. By default, all the search and display boxes will be checked. For your existing search campaigns, uncheck the Display Network box to ensure that you are targeting only Google search and Google search partners.

When you begin to build out your new display campaigns, do just the opposite: uncheck the Google Search box to ensure that you target only the Display Network, just like we've done in Figure 5.27. Then you can choose either broad or specific reach types, as discussed in week 5.

The benefits of keeping your search and display campaigns separate are many, and here we highlight just a few.

Budget

Your budgets are defined at the campaign level. You want to control how much is spent on search campaigns and how much on display separately. The *only* way to do this is to ensure that the campaigns are separate. Many advertisers find that poorly targeted or restricted display ads eat the majority of their daily budget, essentially cannibalizing and shutting down their search ads that live in the same campaign.

Search and display should work hand in hand toward your advertising objectives, but part of ensuring that both types of campaigns run optimally is controlling their budgets separately.

Targeting

Perhaps the best reason to separate your display and search campaigns is that they have different objectives and use different means to achieve them. Consider two campaigns dedicated to selling kayaks: one search and the other display.

In the search campaign, you target keywords that reflect a user's intent to buy a kayak—things like "buy kayak," "cheap kayaks," "deals on kayaks," or maybe "kayak prices." The keywords include specific brands, models, and lots of other things that people looking to buy a kayak might type into a search engine.

While these keywords may work wonderfully in a search campaign, they are probably *not* as effective in a display campaign. Remember how contextual targeting works: The keywords do not describe a searcher's intent; they describe the kinds of pages you want your ads to show up on. Many of the websites described by those kinds of keywords are the e-commerce sites of your competitors, and they're not likely to be accepting advertising from you! Sure, some will be relevant, especially those aimed at people early in the buying cycle (like "kayak reviews," for example).

Even more important, however, are all the websites you miss! What about sites that provide information about the best places to paddle your kayak and the best times of year to do it? How about all those blogs documenting past kayaking trips that are sure to be frequented by avid paddlers? And the myriad other websites that have nothing to do with "buy cheap kayaks" but are *exactly* where your target market is hanging out?

And the messaging to these different audiences is much different as well. While your search ads are likely to be promoting why it's better to buy a kayak from you than your competitors, the display campaigns could take a number of different angles in messaging different target audiences. For those that are on sites devoted to planning paddling trips, an image ad may promote kayak accessories that someone who already owns a kayak heading on a trip might need. For campaigns targeted toward review and informational sites, you know that the viewers are likely to be early in the stages of considering a purchase, and you might choose to promote a general buyer's guide in your ads.

This is in large part why advertisers typically achieve only limited success by trying to repurpose a search campaign for display. Display advertising lets you craft a variety of messages aimed directly at a variety of different audiences.

Ad Delivery

Yet another reason to separate search and display campaigns has to do with control over the way your ads are served.

You may choose to open up a geographic target for your display campaigns that you would rather keep tight in your search campaigns. For example, consider a brick-and-mortar Italian restaurant. You may have a group of search campaigns targeted at mobile devices within just a few miles of your front door, hoping to catch those hungry people looking for pizza within driving distance at just the right time.

But you may also have display campaigns intended to keep the restaurant in the minds of the general customer within a much larger geographic boundary. Here, you're looking to interact with the consumer, maybe get them to follow you on a social network or subscribe to a mailing list. When you push out a coupon, they can be incentivized to drive a little farther to get to you and plan their trip a little further in advance.

Ad scheduling is another thing that can be set at the campaign level. Going back to our example of selling sleep aids, you might choose to run your display ads during the middle of the night but let your search campaigns run all the time. When someone goes to a search engine and types in "something to help me sleep," you don't really care what time of the day it is—you know what they want! If they happen to be online at 4:00 a.m. just passing time as a result of their insomnia, you might be able to get your ad in front of them even if they weren't specifically looking for your solution.

Data Clarity

While the AdWords reporting interface is pretty good at letting you separate your data by search or display networks, as you'll see in Chapter 9, you'll very likely use an analytics package to help you manage and optimize your campaigns as well.

Figure 5.28 shows a Google Analytics account with different AdWords campaigns showing up as rows.

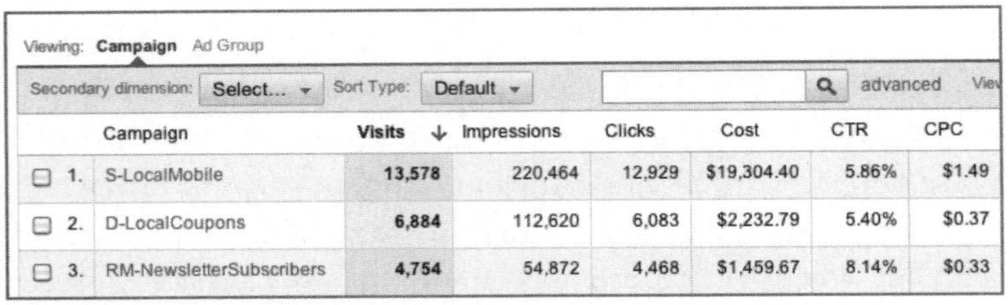

	Campaign	Visits ↓	Impressions	Clicks	Cost	CTR	CPC
☐ 1.	S-LocalMobile	13,578	220,464	12,929	$19,304.40	5.86%	$1.49
☐ 2.	D-LocalCoupons	6,884	112,620	6,083	$2,232.79	5.40%	$0.37
☐ 3.	RM-NewsletterSubscribers	4,754	54,872	4,468	$1,459.67	8.14%	$0.33

Figure 5.28 Tracking AdWords campaigns in Google Analytics

Here, we use prefixes in our campaign names to reflect what kind of network we're on, and it makes it extremely clear in the Google Analytics interface just what kind of a campaign we're dealing with. The *D* tells us that this is a display campaign, while the *S* says search campaign. We also have an *RM* campaign, telling us that this data comes from a campaign targeting a remarketing list.

If you target both search and display networks with one campaign, you can use the Ad Distribution Network secondary dimension to break out the search and display components in your Google Analytics reports, but other web analytics tools don't always have dimensions like that available.

And even if you do break out search and display and find opportunities for optimization in that single campaign, if it's targeting both search and display networks, it is nearly impossible to implement those changes on one network but not the other.

Regardless of which analytics and measurement tools you use, separate campaigns make it easier to evaluate performance metrics and implement changes for continual improvement.

Tuesday: Organizing by Campaign Settings

As you saw in week 5, AdWords campaigns contain targeting options that you can use to restrict where and how your ads are shown for every ad group that lives underneath a particular campaign. When you start to build out your AdWords accounts with multiple campaigns, a good way to start is by planning just which of these targeting options will be used in tandem with one another and then creating a campaign for each individual combination. These combinations allow you to create ad groups that you already know are focused on specific restrictions, and having that clarity from the outset is an important foundational step in building a well-structured account.

The Big Four

While there are lots of different settings at the campaign level, four are especially important for campaign organization:

Network Keeping search campaigns separate from display campaigns is a must.

Location If you have geographic restrictions, use them to ensure that only people in your target locations see your ads.

Language Different languages require different placements, keywords, and ads. And remember: AdWords does not translate any of your advertisements for you!

Device Users of mobile devices display different behaviors and intent from those on tablets or desktop/laptops. Your advertising strategy should change accordingly.

Of course, you can use other options at the campaign level, but the preceding four can help you create a structure that will get the right message in front of the right audience.

Examples of Different Campaigns

To tie this together in an example, let's say we have a chain of physical stores as well as an e-commerce site selling clothing and apparel into both US and Canadian markets. We know that in the United States, we have a strong English- and Spanish-speaking client base, and in Canada, our customers speak either English or French.

Our advertising strategy uses general campaigns around each of our product lines, and we also push promotions out to mobile phone users who are near any of our brick-and-mortar stores.

In this scenario, we have a minimum of eight different campaigns to focus on the various combinations of language, location, and device targeting, as shown in Table 5.2.

Campaign	Network	Location	Language	Device(s)
Campaign #1	Display	US store cities	English	Mobile
Campaign #2	Display	US store cities	Spanish	Mobile
Campaign #3	Display	All US	English	All
Campaign #4	Display	All US	Spanish	All
Campaign #5	Display	Canada store cities	English	Mobile
Campaign #6	Display	Canada store cities	French	Mobile
Campaign #7	Display	All Canada	English	All
Campaign #8	Display	All Canada	French	All

Campaign #1 contains ad groups that target on-the-go, mobile device users in cities in the United States where we have a physical store. It uses English language ads, which we can create to provide the message we want those people to see. We might use mobile QR code coupons that can be redeemed for immediate savings or promote closeout items in a today-only sale at "a location in [your town]."

We can use the same general messaging but translated and localized to the Spanish speakers in Spanish speaking locations in Campaign #2. In our Canadian campaigns, we can do the same, only this time we promote the product lines we sell in Canada in the right languages to people in the right places accessing the Web on the right platforms.

None of this would be possible with a single generic campaign targeting anyone in the United States or Canada who speaks any of three languages and is using any kind of device, and just think of the possible disaster scenarios. A Spanish speaker in the United States on the family desktop computer gets served an ad in French promoting a mobile QR code coupon that needs to be redeemed in Canada!

Wednesday: Organizing by Themes

Now that we've laid out the targeting structure of the campaigns that we're going to be building, it's time to start looking at the various products and services that we're advertising.

Let's continue with the example of an apparel scenario, where we might be advertising for a host of different kinds of clothing. There are many different ways that we might choose to organize our campaigns and ad groups, and hopefully this section will help get you started in thinking about the way that makes the most sense for you.

Campaign #3 in Table 5.2 targets all of the United States with English advertisements on any device, but this may be too generic to accomplish our goals. If so, we must break this into a set of more specific campaigns that share the same targeting options, and to illustrate how to do this, assume that we have product lines like pants, shirts, socks, and things of that nature. We start subdividing that third campaign with some of these product lines, as shown in Table 5.3.

▶ **Table 5.3** Campaign #3 broken out

Campaign	Network	Location	Language	Device(s)	Theme
Campaign #3a	Display	All US	English	All	Men's dress pants
Campaign #3b	Display	All US	English	All	Men's dress shirts
Campaign #3c	Display	All US	English	All	Women's dress pants
Campaign #3d	Display	All US	English	All	Women's blouses & shirts
Campaign #3e	Display	All US	English	All	Women's shoes
Campaign #3f	Display	All U.S.	English	All	Men's shoes

We can break these out to whatever detail is necessary, and this granularity helps us control budgets and evaluate the performance of our ads at whatever level we want. Again, we must balance specificity and control against a manageable number of campaigns and ad groups. To avoid getting *too* specific, start out broadly and break the campaigns down into more specific categories as you go.

Using Campaigns and Ad Groups Together

You can think of campaigns and ad groups as categories and subcategories. Every subcategory (ad group) should share targeting criteria with and fit nicely within its parent category (campaign), and there are lots of ways you can define these. In the example of men's pants, you can define a campaign, or category, as "brands of men's pants." In that category, you expect to see subcategories, or ad groups, like "dockers" or "haggar" or other popular brands of men's dress pants that your store sells (on the left in Figure 5.29).

Figure 5.29 Campaigns and ad groups as categories and subcategories

Alternatively, you might choose your category to be "types of men's pants" with subcategories like "wool" or "khaki" or "cargo." If all of these brands and types of pants share the same general campaign targeting options *and* you don't want to control how much budget is spent by either group, you can create a single campaign called Men's Dress Pants and put all of these ad groups under it (Figure 5.30).

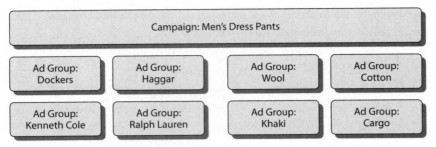

Figure 5.30 Single campaign with multiple ad groups

The key to creating categories and subcategories is to find what works for you. If your apparel business is more aligned with brands than product types, you can have an entire campaign dedicated to "dockers" with ad groups beneath it like "men's pants," "socks," and "dresses."

Spend some time at a whiteboard or with index cards to brainstorm all the ways to set up this structure, and be creative. In the end, you'll find a grouping that makes sense for your business objectives and is clean to manage and optimize.

Seasonal Campaigns

Another set of campaigns to consider deals with seasonal products and services. You can set when your ads are scheduled to run at the campaign level, and you can use this to your advantage.

Following our apparel example, you may have a special set of deals and discounts to promote when the retail sector explodes in the annual run-up to Christmas. You can group these together in a campaign dedicated to the period between Black Friday and Christmas Day, as shown on the left in Figure 5.31.

Figure 5.31 Campaigns organized by season

You can build this campaign and have it ready to go in a paused state, and every Thanksgiving you can flip the switch from paused to enabled and your special ads dedicated to all the Black Friday coupon and discount deal hunters are up and running.

You can also build more campaigns to highlight seasonal items, as shown in the campaign on the right in Figure 5.31. Here, there are spring and summer items that you may not want to spend much budget promoting in the dead of winter, but as soon as people start thinking about flip-flops and spring break, you are ready to get your ads in front of them.

Thursday: Organizing by Audiences

With your campaigns broken out by campaign-level targeting options and further built out by themes, you can start to add keywords and placements to your specific ad groups to start finding the websites you want your ads to show up on to reflect the messaging and the target of those ad groups.

But when you decide to target by audience—especially by remarketing lists— you can also benefit from completely separate campaigns. When you target *audiences* rather than the websites you hope those audiences frequent, it's important to understand the cases when you might benefit from keeping these campaigns separate.

Figuring out when you benefit from separate campaigns using audience targeting is, like everything else, a matter of understanding exactly who you're trying to target with what message. Your campaigns may of course be different, but as a general guideline, there are three instances to look at in deciding when to use separate campaigns.

Refining Existing Campaigns with Audience Targeting

Perhaps the most common way to start targeting audiences is within a campaign that is already using contextual or placement targeting. When you do this, you're essentially telling Google AdWords to show your ads on specific kinds of websites (or *specific* websites in the case of placement targeting) but also to take into consideration when the person is a member of a specific audience.

We talked about how the broad and specific reach settings work in the cases where we use multiple targeting options together in week 5, but the important point here is that in many cases, it's often fine to keep all of this in a single campaign. As a general rule, if your primary targeting option is either contextual or placement based and you use interest category audiences to either broaden your general reach or limit it to certain categories *on top of* your other targeting methods, you likely don't need to build out separate campaigns for your targeted audiences.

Separating Audience Targeted Campaigns

Sometimes, however, you want to ensure that you have a certain budget set aside to specifically target very defined audiences, and you truly don't care what site they happen to be on when they see your ads.

A good example of this is a pure branding campaign, say for a new movie release. If you want to get the word out to anyone and everyone that a new movie is about to hit the theatres, you might choose a separate campaign targeted at the more than 50 million people that Google has identified to have an interest in movies.

You have no contextual targeting and you do not define explicit placements in this ad group; your sole purpose is to get as many movie-loving eyeballs exposed to this message as possible as quickly as you can leading up to the box office opening day. With this advertising goal, it makes perfect sense to keep this as a separate campaign.

Within this standalone campaign, you can control your budget, you can use CPM bidding for maximum exposure, and you can turn on and turn off your campaign at specific times. You can even use things like frequency capping to limit how many times a specific user sees your ad; once they've seen it a number of times, they're aware of the movie and you can spend your money on others who have not hit that impression threshold.

Separating Campaigns for Remarketing Lists

We discuss remarketing lists in greater detail in Chapter 11. With rare exception, you'll want to break these out into their own campaigns because the specific actions that put them on your remarketing lists mean that you can market to them with very specific objectives.

For the remarketing list containing people who have begun the journey down one of your conversion paths but have at some point abandoned your process, you can incentivize them to jump back into your funnel. Think of someone that put a pair of pants in their shopping cart but then decided not to purchase. You might have a campaign dedicated to just those people offering a 10 percent off coupon code that expires today, and that might be enough to get them back to your site to finish their checkout process.

Keeping with our apparel example, you might have a host of lists containing people who have bought a certain product and can be cross sold or upsold depending on what that product is.

You might show those who have purchased shoes from your ads featuring socks or shoe polish kits that might go with their new pair of shoes. Once someone has bought a dress shirt, you can start showing them ads for ties. If they've purchased underwear, you might wait a year and then start showing them ads for new underwear with messaging focusing on the hygienic value of replacing undergarments after a year of use!

Friday: Using Exclusions

Just as important as telling Google where you want your ads to be showing up is telling them where you *don't* want your ads running. Lucky for us, AdWords gives us a few ways to explicitly tell it where and to whom we don't want to be showing ads.

Exclusions at the Campaign and Ad Group Level

We look at how to tactically do this in greater detail later in Chapter 6, but just as you can target specific keywords, placements, audiences, and topics that you want your ads to be eligible to show up for, you can define exclusions. With contextual targeting, you can define negative keywords and you can explicitly exclude specific placements, audiences, or topics from seeing your ads at either the campaign or the ad group level.

Campaign Placement Exclusions

Another way to manage exclusions is through the Campaign Placement Exclusions option under Shared Library, shown in Figure 5.32.

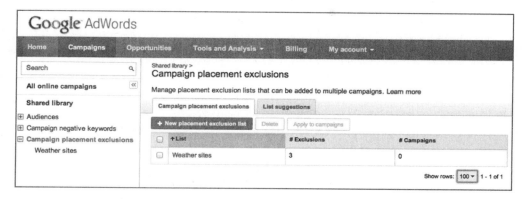

Figure 5.32 Campaign placement exclusions in the shared library

This feature allows you to create and maintain lists of exclusions that you can apply quickly and efficiently to the different campaigns in your account.

Creating a Placement Exclusion List

The first step is to create a campaign placement exclusion list, and you do that by clicking the New Placement Exclusion List button as shown in Figure 5.32. Next, provide a name for your list and enter the placements that you'd like excluded in it. When you're done, simply save it and it is added to the rest of the lists below.

Applying a List of Exclusions to a Campaign

Once you define various lists, you can choose the campaigns that use a list by selecting it and clicking the Add To More Campaigns button, as shown in Figure 5.33.

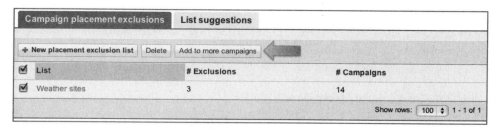

Figure 5.33 Selecting a placement exclusion list to apply to campaigns

Now use the Add and Remove links to have your different campaigns inherit the placement exclusions that have been defined in your lists. This is an efficient way to ensure that you exclude the right placements from the right campaigns across your account. You can edit the individual placements that make up your lists at any time. As soon as you save those updates, they are active across all campaigns that use your placement exclusion list.

Campaign Negative Keywords

Notice in Figure 5.32 the Campaign Negative Keywords menu item. This works in much the same way as Campaign Placement Exclusions, and you can use it to create lists of negative keywords that can be applied to campaigns throughout your account. Remember, keywords work very differently when being used for contextual targeting of display placements than for traditional search campaigns, so it is highly recommended that you create completely separate lists of negative keywords for your display campaigns.

Tip: Traditionally, many display advertisers have had trouble using negative keywords for contextually targeted display campaigns, but the recent updates to the contextual targeting engine have made these much more useful. This is discussed in further detail in Chapter 6.

Month 3: Building Your First Display Campaign

6

With planning complete and a strategy solidly in place, it's time to build out your first display campaign. This month, we focus on the ins and outs of creating a display campaign in the AdWords interface. We look at settings and features, bidding styles and budget options, and putting in place contextual, placement, and audience targeting parameters.

Chapter Contents:
Week 9: Choose Your Display Campaign Settings
Week 10: Choose Your Bidding Style and Budget
Week 11: Configure Advanced Campaign Settings
Week 12: Create Your First Ad Group

Week 9: Choose Your Display Campaign Settings

The first step in creating a campaign is to get the structure and settings right. You'll end up with lots of different campaigns in your account, and as you continue to manage and expand your display advertising efforts, ensuring that all the ad groups that live under the campaigns you build now share the same targeting and budgetary restrictions will pay off with a well-organized and efficient account structure.

This week we dive into the tactical execution of creating a campaign and choosing the proper settings. As you go through this process, refer to previous chapters and always remember the strategy you thought through and created. By the time you're clicking around in the AdWords interface, your planning should be done and you should simply be implementing your strategy.

Monday: Create a New Campaign

To create a display campaign, you must have an AdWords account, and to have an AdWords account, you must have a Google Account.

Creating Your Accounts

Step one is to create a Google account. To create a free Google account, go to www .google.com/accounts and provide your name, an email address, and some other basic information. Note that while creating a Gmail account automatically creates a Google account, they are not the same thing. A Google account is an umbrella under which all the other Google services live. Gmail, Google+, Apps, Picasa, Analytics, and of course, AdWords, are all Google services.

Many AdWords advertisers create a Gmail account just for their AdWords use (for example, MyOrgAdWords@gmail.com). A better idea is to create a Google account tied to your organization's email system. For example, adwords@ MyOrganizationsDomain.com is a good email address for the Google account you plan to use for AdWords for the following reasons:

- It associates and keeps the AdWords account with the organization, not with an individual who may leave someday.

- It allows your team to access your AdWords account regardless of whether they have their own AdWords accounts with their personal Google accounts.

- While it is better to grant access individually, it is often easier to let everyone use the same Google account to access the company AdWords account. When the list of people needing access changes, you can change one account password and disseminate it.

- If your organization needs to manage multiple AdWords accounts, you can use this account to create a My Client Center (more information is at www.google.com/ adwords/myclientcenter).

Once you have a Google Account, go to www.google.com/adwords and click the big blue Start Now button. Choose the option that uses the Google account you just created and follow the steps to set up your AdWords account.

Warning: Time zone and currency settings are permanent. They are used in every campaign in your account, and once you set them, you can't change them. If you advertise across different time zones and use features such as ad scheduling, the schedule is based on *the time zone you define here*, regardless of geographic targeting you may set in any campaign. If you need to pay Google in multiple currencies or if you need to see your metrics in multiple currencies, you need separate accounts. For example, if you operate in the United States and have your AdWords account in US dollars but want to run a campaign for a European subsidiary that does business in euros, consider having one account in US dollars and another in euros. Then you can see cost data in the correct currency.

Creating a New Campaign

After you create an AdWords account, Google prompts you to create your first campaign. If you're an active advertiser and you already have campaigns running, navigate to the Campaigns tab and click the New Campaign button (Figure 6.1).

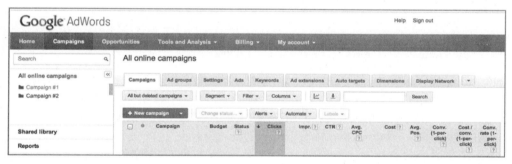

Figure 6.1 Starting a new campaign

Optionally, you can use the drop-down to pick a campaign type, and this creates a campaign with some options preset. If you don't pick a campaign type, AdWords sets those options to default values. In either case, you can change the options in subsequent steps, and we go through each of the settings in detail this week. Let's start with Display Network Only.

Overview of Campaign Parameters

Next you see the Select Campaign Settings screen, where you set all of the basic campaign configurations. We go through these settings individually in subsequent sections, but first let's take a high-level look at the decisions you have to make.

Campaign Name Give your campaign a name that expresses what you're trying to accomplish with it.

Locations And Languages This is the area where you define the locations to target with your ads and how you want that location determined.

Networks And Devices Here you specify which of the search and display networks to target and choose among types of devices such as smartphones, tablets, traditional desktops, and laptops.

Bidding And Budget These settings define how many of your advertising dollars you'll spend on this campaign and how you'll spend them.

Advanced Settings This is where you can define how and when your ads will be shown as well as additional features such as enabling Google+ annotations or frequency caps.

Tuesday/Wednesday: Target Locations and Languages

Showing ads to potential customers based on where they are is a powerful feature of online advertising, and the AdWords platform provides robust geotargeting options. Remember that these settings are at the campaign level and are applied to all ad groups in the campaign.

How Google Determines Location

Google uses a number of signals to figure out a user's location, and it's worth understanding exactly how the system works. When a device connects to the Internet, it does so through an Internet service provider (ISP), which assigns it a unique Internet Protocol (IP) address that can be associated with a physical location. Among other techniques, Google uses the IP address, which typically works quite well, but you should be aware of the following issues.

Not every ISP does a good job of providing the correct location data for IP addresses it assigns. AOL, for example, routes its millions of users through a single IP address. Regardless of actual location, every AOL subscriber seems to be standing in Virginia!

Users who connect to the Internet through a virtual private network (VPN) appear to be wherever that VPN is located. They might be in a European hotel room, but if they have connected to their corporate VPN, they might show up as being in the San Francisco corporate headquarters.

On the Search Network, Google has even more ways to identify where users physically are that unfortunately don't apply to display ads. For example, users on www.google.es who search for hotels might see ads targeted to Spain. However, users on www.google.es who search for Buenos Aires hotels can see ads targeted to Argentina, not Spain. Settings in AdWords allow Search Network advertisers to choose whether ads can be shown to people physically outside the geotargeted location if the keywords they use indicate intent in that location. But these methods and settings do not apply to the GDN because these ads are not shown in response to keyword searches on Google search properties.

If the app or the website on which an ad is eligible to be shown has permission to use the location of a user's mobile device, then cell towers, Wi-Fi connections, and even GPS can help geotarget a potential customer.

Notice the Locations And Languages section of the campaign settings (Figure 6.2). This defaults to wherever you happen to be (for example, United States and Canada), but the Let Me Choose option lets you be more specific (down to the zip code, for example). Figure 6.2 shows what happens if we specify Los Angeles.

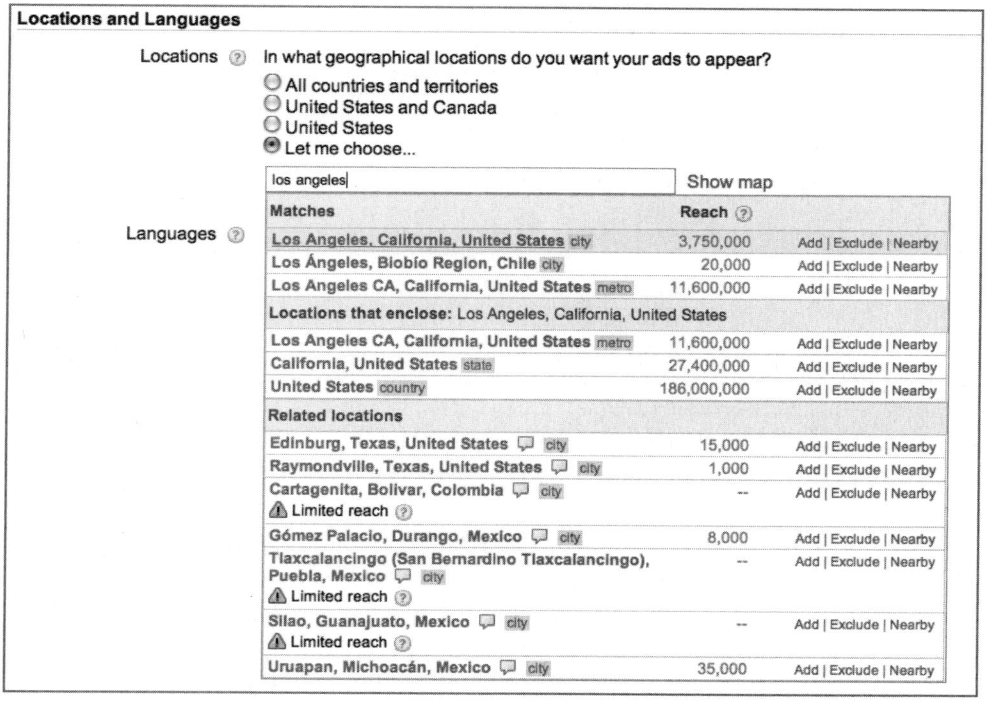

Figure 6.2 Geotargeting Los Angeles

The results are in three groups: matches to the search, enclosing areas around the search, and related locations. A label next to each listing designates it as a city, metro, state, region, or country. The next column provides an estimated reach for the specific location target, which is calculated based upon the estimated number of unique cookies seen on Google properties in that location. Los Angeles has an estimated reach of 3.75 million, but remember that it's an estimate. Use it as a general guideline or for comparing two potential location targets.

The Limited Reach warning identifies a target with either a very small number of users or poor mapping of IP addresses to physical locations. You can still select this location target, but keep in mind it might limit the exposure your ads achieve.

Hovering over a speech bubble icon in the Related Locations group brings up an explanation of how the location is related to the search. For example, the speech bubble for Raymondville, Texas, tells us that this location has a subdivision within its borders named Los Angeles.

Adding and Excluding Locations

The rightmost column contains actions you can take with each target location. Clicking Add or Exclude adds locations to the lists of those that you do and don't want your ads to show in (Figure 6.3). You can quickly build and manage your geographic targeting strategy without ever leaving this page.

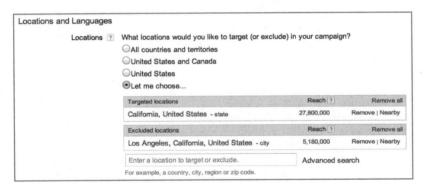

Figure 6.3 Targeted and excluded locations in the campaign settings

Using Nearby and Map View

Clicking Nearby for a target location brings up the mapping screen (Figure 6.4). On the right are nearby and enclosing locations, and adding or excluding one makes it show up as blue or red on the map. Clicking Nearby brings up yet another list of nearby and enclosing locations. Here we target the Los Angeles metropolitan area *without* a handful of cities, and the map shows us where our ads will and will not be shown.

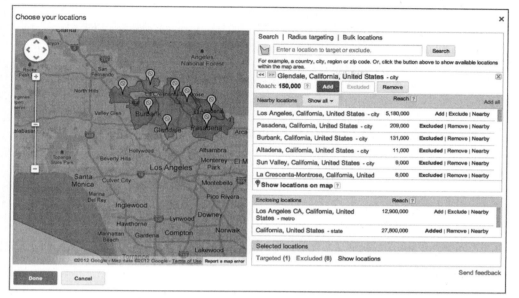

Figure 6.4 Targeting selected portions of the Los Angeles metro area

The Selected Locations area helps you visualize the areas you want to target or exclude. Selecting Show Locations in the Selected Locations section produces a list of targeted and excluded locations and resets the map to show them all in one view.

Targeting a Radius around a Specific Point

An especially useful option for certain types of campaigns is to pick a point on a map and define a radius of miles or kilometers around it. For example, a pizza place stuck in the restaurant district of a city with hundreds of other pizza places can run a campaign that targets only mobile devices within walking distance of the tables themselves. This might show an ad on a restaurant review site when someone nearby is deciding where to have lunch. Take that pizza place out to the suburbs and a campaign with ads touting free delivery within 15 miles can be targeted to a radius of 15 miles from the storefront.

To start, click Radius Targeting at the top right of a map view. Type an address, a landmark, or even latitude and longitude coordinates. The tool uses the same technology that drives Google Maps to find what you're looking for and draws a circle of the specified radius around it. You still see a list of other target locations within the boundaries of your defined radius, and you can use Add, Exclude, and Nearby just as in the normal map view. Also note that using a radius creates a custom area rather than something like city, state, or country, which means that estimated reach numbers may not be available.

Once you narrow down the locations in which you want your ads to show, click Done on the bottom left to return to the Campaign Settings screen, or click Cancel to discard your work and start fresh from the Campaign Settings screen.

Tip: AdWords also supports a bulk option for adding or excluding locations. To define up to 1,000 locations at once, click the Bulk Locations option from the top of the map view and enter one location per line. While these can be anything from city or country names to postal codes, note that they all must be within the same country. If you're targeting locations that span different countries, simply use one bulk update per country.

Selecting Language Targets

The lower part of the Locations And Languages screen deals with the languages that you want to target your ads to. For the GDN, Google looks at the pages that carry ad inventory to identify the primary language of the page on which the ad is eligible to show. If you set your language to target Spanish, all of the ads in this campaign are eligible to show on websites containing Spanish language pages.

When targeting languages, you can easily fall into traps that can cost you time and money. First, remember that AdWords does *not* translate your ads or your keywords. So if you are advertising in English and then decide to reach both French *and* English speakers across Canada, you might be tempted to check both the English and French boxes in the language settings. Don't do this. Instead, create a separate campaign targeted to the French language with French ads, landing pages, and targeting criteria. Showing English ads on French websites leads to less impact, lower click-through rates, lower Quality Scores, and wasted impressions.

Thursday: Set Target Networks

We've looked at Google's search and display networks for AdWords advertisers, and this is where you can distinguish which of these networks an individual campaign should target. There are two basic options: Search (and Search Partners) and Display.

The default option for a generic new campaign is to use all available sites, and if you don't proactively change this setting, you can be setting yourself up for failure.

Search and Search Partners Networks

This book is about display advertising, but it's important to understand what the Search Network is, and Chapter 1, "Online Advertising," explains this. Essentially, if you target Google Search, you bid on keywords that people are typing into Google as queries, and you create text ads to show on the search engine results page. If you include the Search Partners option, your ads can show in response to searches not only on Google's main search engine, but also on Google Maps, Google Product Search, and non-Google web properties like Virgin Media or AOL that serve Google search results. Note that you cannot target *only* the Search Partners: You'll need to also be targeting Google search.

And now that we're clear on just what the two Search Network options are, here's what you need to do for all of your display campaigns: uncheck them both!

Display Network Options

For a display campaign, the only network to target is the Display Network, as in Figure 5.7 in Chapter 5. This ensures that you use your contextual, placement, and audience targeting options not to respond to user queries on Google properties but to show your ads across potentially millions of websites that your prospective customers visit every day.

Chapter 5 (week 5) discussed broad and specific reach. The broad reach setting makes your ads eligible to show when *any* of your targeting criteria have been met, while the specific reach setting requires *all* of your targeting criteria to be satisfied. Once you decide which option works for the type of campaign you're building, select the appropriate radio button to finish this step.

Benefits of Targeting Only One Network per Campaign

Before we move on, it's worthwhile to remember why you should keep your Search and Display Network campaigns separate. While there are many good reasons to do this, the fundamental difference between the ways these types of advertising work is sufficient to justify separate campaigns.

Let's take the example of a successful Search Network campaign selling soccer shoes. Ad groups are neatly laid out in the campaign to focus on keywords like "men's soccer cleats" and "children's indoor soccer shoes." Campaigns in the United Kingdom make excellent use of regionalization with keywords like "women's football boot." The campaign even targets people searching on specific models with ad groups for each manufacturer containing model-related keywords like "adidas f10 trx" or "adidas predator."

Because of the campaign's success, you might want to go get *more* clicks on these ads to continue to grow your business, so you enable the Google Search Partners Network as well for this same campaign. And you notice that while there may be a decrease in performance, you have similar overall success and you're able to scale to even more clicks with minimal diminishing returns. After all, this is still a network of websites where people type search queries and get back these ads alongside their search results.

In an effort to scale even further, you add the Display Network to your targeted networks, but this time, you don't get positive results. In the Display Network, keywords are used to define *the kinds of pages* you want your display ads to show up on rather than user queries, but the keywords defined for a search campaign often don't do a good a job of defining those pages you want to target for display. If you want to show display ads on websites that soccer players might visit, keywords like "children's adidas f10 trx" aren't nearly as useful. Instead, you might have an ad group with keywords like "youth soccer forum" or "youth soccer league" or "soccer cleats reviews."

And not only do you want to build your display campaigns around contextual keywords that are different from search campaign keywords, you also want to take advantage of audience and placement targeting and bidding techniques that are exclusive to the Display Network.

Friday: Use Device Targeting

The next set of options you need to select are all about the actual types of devices that people use to access the Internet, and which of those devices you'd like your ads to show on.

Figure 6.5 shows a fully expanded view of US-based device targeting options. If this is the first time you're seeing this in your own account, the All Available Devices radio button is preselected for you. While you might want to show your ads across all devices used to browse the Web, here is where you can get more specific.

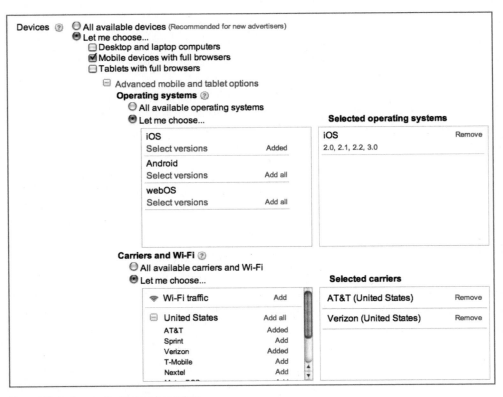

Figure 6.5 Device targeting in campaign settings

The three check boxes under the first Let Me Choose allow your ads to show on the following types of devices:

Desktop And Laptop Computers Leaving this box checked will allow your ads to show on "normal" computers such as laptops or desktops running fully functional web browsers. For example, this might be a Mac or PC running a browser like Internet Explorer, Firefox, Safari, or Chrome.

Mobile Devices With Full Browsers A full browser is defined as a browser that can show HTML, supports a full transaction, and accommodates analytics or tracking, which essentially means that the browser is capable of not only rendering a page, but also executing JavaScript and keeping cookies. Safari on an iPhone, Silk on a Kindle Fire, Dolphin on an Android device, or the native browsers in Palm webOS and Blackberry devices are just a few examples of places where your ads would be eligible to show.

Tablets With Full Browsers The most recent addition to device targeting is a response to the wild success of Apple's iPad and the slew of tablet offerings coming from manufacturers ranging from Amazon and Asus to Microsoft and Samsung. Targeting tablets with full browsers allows advertisers to target the space that's somewhere between your phone and your laptop.

Beyond these checkboxes, expanding the Advanced Mobile And Tablet Options section enables you to refine your targeting even further.

Operating Systems Here you can choose between iOS, Android, Blackberry and webOS operating systems. By clicking the Select Versions link, you can even select the versions of each operating system you'd like to target. For example, if you want to show ads to the early adopter crowd, you could target only the latest and greatest operating system versions.

Device Models By expanding the lists of operating systems, manufacturers, and device models, you can choose to target very specific models of the various mobile devices on the market. Since iOS does not support Flash, for example, you could create one campaign that targets every tablet *except* the iPad and includes Flash ads, and another campaign targeting *only* iPads that leaves Flash ads out.

Carriers And Wi-Fi You can also limit your ads to devices that access the Web through a specific carrier or through a Wi-Fi network.

Depending upon the countries you target, Google shows you the major carriers, and you can specify who you'd like to target based upon who they go through to access the Web.

If you choose to target Wi-Fi, your ads will show on devices using a wireless Internet connection rather than a mobile data plan, which can often indicate a user that's at home or in another relaxed setting. This is a very different user than one that's on the go, and can impact the kind of message you want to show them, the landing page you take them to and the conversion action you want them to take.

Week 10: Choose Your Bidding Style and Budget

At this point, you've created and named a new campaign, set the geographic locations and languages you'd like to target, and chosen the networks and devices you want your ads to be shown on. Now, we dive into the financials of how and how much you want to pay Google.

AdWords lets you set a budget and choose among different methods of bidding. There are no minimums or maximums; you can spend $1 a year or $1 million a day, and you can turn your campaigns on and off at any time. You can bid for clicks, conversions that result from clicks, or just eyeballs. This week focuses on bidding and budgeting options.

Monday: Learn Manual CPC Bidding

Manual CPC bidding is exactly what it sounds like. In a cost-per-click (CPC) auction, you bid manually for each click that you hope to acquire as a result of showing your ads in eligible placements on the GDN. This option gives you the most control over your bidding strategy, but it is also a lot of work. You need to consider this balance as you look at bidding options.

When you create a campaign, Google asks for a default bid, as shown in Figure 6.6. Whatever you enter here will be the default Max CPC for the ad groups you create in this campaign, but as you build them out, you can define a specific default Max CPC bid for each. Also, remember from Chapter 4, "Month 1: Planning Your Campaigns," that your *maximum* CPC bid is the most you *would be willing to pay* for a click, but you'll likely pay less. Google charges only the minimum amount needed to beat the next highest-ranking ad in the auction.

```
Bidding and budget

   Bidding option  [?]    Basic options | Advanced options
                          ⦿ Focus on clicks - use maximum CPC bids
                              ⦿ I'll manually set my bids for clicks
                              ○ AdWords will set my bids to help maximize clicks within my target budget

                              Enhanced CPC  [?]
                              ☐ Use my conversion tracking data and bids to optimize for conversions
                                  Enhanced CPC will adjust your Max. CPC bid up or down for each auction in an effort to improve your return on
                                  investment.
                          ○ Focus on conversions (Conversion Optimizer) - use CPA bids
                              Unavailable because this campaign doesn't yet have conversion data.
                          ○ Focus on conversions (percentage of sale) - use maximum CPA percentage bids  [?]
                          ○ Focus on impressions - use maximum CPM bids
                              Unavailable because this campaign is running on Google Search or the Search Network.

   Default bid  [?]      $ [        ]
                         This bid applies to the first ad group in this campaign, which you'll create in the next step.

   Budget  [?]           $ [        ]  per day
                         Actual daily spend may vary.  [?]
```

Figure 6.6 Setting bidding options

Setting a Manual Bid across an Ad Group

To set your campaign to manual CPC bidding, click the Focus On Clicks radio button, and then the "I'll manually set my bids for clicks" option. Enter a default bid, and that becomes the Max CPC bid for your contextual, placement, audience, or topic targeting options if no overriding bid is present.

Overriding Bids at More Granular Levels

As you build out your various ad groups, you can override the default bid for the contextual, placement, audience, and topic targets you've created. On the appropriate AdWords tabs, click the default value in the Max CPC column to override the default ad group bid. Figure 6.7 shows this for managed placements, and other targeting types are similar.

Figure 6.7 Overriding a managed placement bid

Finding a Good Starting Point for Your Bids

Successful advertisers base their bids on their own performance data and adjust these bids over time. Understanding the goals of your advertising campaigns, their value, and how much ad spend is required to convert on those goals is what determines your return on investment (ROI), and this requires good data and analysis. When you're starting out, however, you don't have data from your own campaigns to guide you, and many advertisers wonder how to find a good starting bid.

The tools covered in Chapter 5 can be a great place to get some ideas. If you plan to use contextual targeting, look at the suggested bids provided by the Contextual Targeting Tool. These may not be your optimal bid a few months from now when you have your own data to analyze, but they can be a good starting point. Google bases them on aggregated historical bidding information from advertisers bidding on similar sites.

We often tell our own clients to regard the first few month's AdWords spend not as part of a *marketing* budget but as a *market research* cost. In terms of learning, this is often the most cost-effective market research you ever do: Once you capture real data from your real campaigns, you'll have tested the waters with your own messaging and targeting and you'll have the numbers to predict how successful a campaign or ad group can be!

Tuesday: Learn Automatic & Enhanced CPC Bidding

If you're comfortable giving up the control of manual bidding and prefer to give Google the burden of setting your bids, then automatic bidding might be the right choice for you. While many new advertisers opt for this bidding style, remember that when you're using automatic bidding alone, Google maximizes the number of *clicks*—without regard to conversion data—while staying within an upper limit that you can set. Figure 6.8 shows how to select this option.

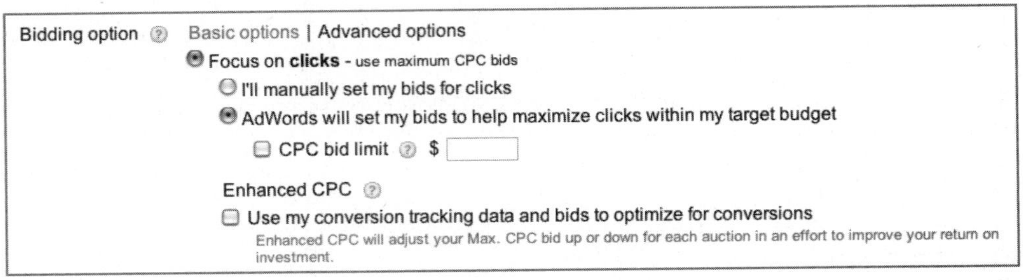

Figure 6.8 Using automatic bidding

How Automatic Bidding Works

When you select automatic bidding, Google automatically maximizes clicks for a given budget, and you do not get to choose a cost-per-click bid. Many advertisers notice that since higher or more desirable placements often result in a higher click-through rates, Google tends to use higher bids to gain those positions.

With no Max CPC bid defined, AdWords can theoretically spend your entire budget on a single click, so it's a good idea to set a CPC bid limit, which you can do on the same screen. Once this setting is enabled and a value is entered, the AdWords system never bids over your defined maximum. Keep in mind that setting this value too low can limit the number of clicks that AdWords is able to obtain, and because you can change these settings at any time, it's good to experiment and see what values work best.

Using Enhanced CPC Bidding

While the number of clicks is a metric to monitor, a click is often where advertisers *spend*—and not *make*—their money. Remember the goals of our campaigns: We're after *conversions*, not just clicks. If you use either manual or automatic bidding, the Enhanced CPC bidding option is a good way to make AdWords focus on conversions *as well as* clicks.

To opt into Enhanced CPC bidding, select "Use my conversion tracking data and bids to optimize for conversions." Then AdWords uses data around clicks and conversions in your campaign history to determine which auctions give the best chance of a conversion. If AdWords deems an auction highly likely to result in a conversion, it can raise your bid by up to 30 percent in that auction. Conversely, if AdWords deems an auction to have a low probability of conversion, it drops your bid price to reduce the chance of wasting money on a click that won't convert.

In practice, Google's system reserves a control group within your account on which it does not make adjustments. This allows it to monitor the effectiveness of the adjustments. The better the enhanced bids perform, the more often Google uses them. If they don't perform well, Google scales them back accordingly. The goal is that advertisers who use Enhanced CPC bidding do no worse than without it.

Conversion tracking must be enabled for this to work at all, and for it to work for your specific advertising goals, your conversion tracking must be installed and measuring the conversion actions you care about. Also, this algorithm is based on data. The more data you feed it, the better its predictions. It works best if you get lots of clicks and lots of conversions, but even if you have a lower budget, it's worth using because it is designed to minimize the chance of performing worse than without it.

Wednesday: Learn CPM Bidding

With manual CPM bidding, advertisers no longer bid for clicks but instead for every 1,000 times their ad is shown, or *impressed*. This is commonly known as cost per thousand impression bidding, and it can be effective when your advertising goals are more about getting your message to the masses for branding and positioning goals than looking for a direct response.

Enabling CPM Bidding

To set your campaign to use CPM bidding, select Focus On Impressions in the Bidding And Budget section (shown in Figure 6.6 earlier in this chapter). All ad groups in your campaigns change from Max CPC bids to Max CPM bids. You must set a default Max CPM bid at the ad group level, but as with CPC bidding, you can override the default for individual ad groups, contextual keywords, placements, audiences, and topics.

The Max CPM bid is the maximum amount you are willing to pay for 1,000 impressions of your ad. In the actual auction, the AdWords discounter charges you the minimum you need to keep the ad placement you earn, so advertisers often pay an *actual* CPM that's lower than their Max CPM bid.

Setting Your CPM Bids

When deciding on an initial CPM bid, remember that this is very different from a CPC bid. CPM bids have a minimum price of $0.25 (in US dollars, or the equivalent in your local currency) and tend to be higher than CPC bids for good reason. When you use image, video, or rich media formats, a single ad fills the entire ad space. A rectangular 300×250 pixel ad slot can accommodate four individual text ads but only a single image ad, as shown in Figure 6.9.

Figure 6.9 Filling an ad slot with text or image ads

CPM ads compete not only against other CPM ads in the auction but also against CPC ads. Chapter 4 (week 4) describes the way the auction works and presents a formula for the effective CPM of a CPC ad:

eCPM = average CPC × click-through rate × 1,000 impressions

One way to get a starting point for your ads is to look at the price you'd be willing to pay on a CPC basis and then use this formula to estimate the corresponding CPM bid. Remember that click-through rates for display ads are quite a bit lower than your average campaigns running on the Search Network: The average click-through rate for image, simple Flash, and rich media display advertising in the United States is 0.09 percent.

The estimate comes from DoubleClick benchmarks on these formats, and in our experience their estimates are a bit lower than what we actually see. Go to the following URL to explore rates for other countries:

www.google.com/adwords/watchthisspace/tools/click-through-rates/#graph-2

Say you have a similar ad group running under a CPC bidding model and you like the results you get with a bid of $0.50. For the sake of estimating your starting CPM bid, you might assume that you can achieve a click-through rate a bit higher than the average; say 0.15 percent. Using the equation shown previously, you have an effective CPM of ($0.50) × (0.15%) × 1,000 = $0.75, which can be used as a starting point for your CPM bid. Once you have actual data from *your* ads running with *your* targeting options and pointing back to *your* landing pages, you can adjust your CPM bids to accomplish your unique set of objectives.

Thursday: Learn the Conversion Optimizer

For advertisers with well-defined and measurable direct response goals, the Conversion Optimizer is a *very* exciting tool. It lets you bid for actual conversions, and this is known as cost-per-acquisition, or CPA, bidding.

When you define a maximum or a target CPA, the AdWords system uses a number of factors to generate a cost-per-click bid on your behalf to maximize the probability of a conversion at a target cost-per-conversion price. This is what direct response advertisers try to do in their day-to-day management of campaigns, and having the system do it automatically can be a powerful tool in your advertising arsenal.

When we use this bidding model at Cardinal Path, we commonly see double-digit improvements in conversions at lower costs per conversion, and we highly recommend it as long as you have well-defined conversion actions.

Understanding How the Conversion Optimizer Works

The Conversion Optimizer has an unfair advantage over those of us trying to optimize our campaigns manually for conversions: it has access to data that we as advertisers don't. The Conversion Optimizer uses many of those data points to build a predictive model that generates CPC bids that are likely to result in placements that attract both clicks *and* conversions.

Google uses your historical conversion and performance data to build this model, but it also uses factors such as the placement, the user's location and language settings, their browser and operating system, and even the time of day to decide whether or not this is a good auction for you to win. And Google knows the aggregate performance of *all* ads that have been shown on a given site or to a given audience, and it can weigh those factors along with the relevance of competing ads, the context, and the web page itself. Putting all these factors into a single, automated model can outperform hundreds of hours of building and optimizing specific campaigns and managing all of their different components.

Conversion Optimizer Requirements

The more data the Conversion Optimizer has access to, the better it can predict performance. To use it, your campaign must meet the following minimum requirements:

- Conversion Tracking enabled, or Google Analytics goals imported into your AdWords account
- At least 15 conversions in the campaign in the last 30 days
- A consistent rate of receiving conversions over the past few days

Beyond these minimum requirements, here are ways to improve your chance of success with the Conversion Optimizer.

Have clear goals. This feature works best for advertisers with clear goals, such as an e-commerce purchase or a specific lead generation action to which you can assign a specific value. When you bid using a CPA model, you need to know what each conversion is worth to you.

Collect a lot of data. The more data, the better the model, so this works well with mature campaigns that are obtaining lots of impressions, clicks and conversions. You might also consider not turning this on until your campaigns have collected a good, consistent history of data points to help the Conversion Optimizer make better predictions.

Abstract your goals if it makes sense. If you don't get very many sales but you *do* get lots of people putting things in their shopping cart, you might consider using a shopping cart addition as the conversion that AdWords optimizes toward. This assumes that if an ad is more likely to get someone to step X of your conversion process (the cart), then it's also more likely to get them to step X+1 (the sale), but it provides more data to the Conversion Optimizer which results in better predictions.

Don't use this for seasonal campaigns. The Campaign Optimizer relies on historical data to predict the future. If you collect data in December from a holiday-themed campaign, what the system learns about holiday shoppers probably does not apply to shoppers at any other time of year. For this reason, Conversion Optimizer is not recommended for campaigns affected by seasonality.

Enabling the Conversion Optimizer

If you meet the requirements for the Conversion Optimizer, then you'll be able to select the Focus On Conversions radio button in your campaign settings, as shown in Figure 6.10.

Until you meet the requirements, this option is disabled (grayed out), with a message telling you that you can't use it yet.

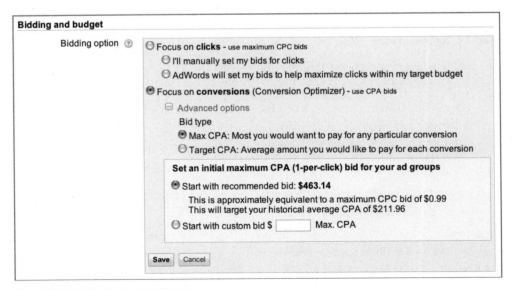

Figure 6.10 Selecting the Conversion Optimizer

When you first select this option, the system defaults to a Max CPA bid type and provides you with a recommended bid based on your own cost-per-click bids and conversion data. As with other maximum bids, the Max CPA bid represents an absolute maximum value and not what you're likely to end up paying. AdWords displays the approximate equivalent CPC bid and the historical CPA that your campaign has achieved. You can also enter your own custom bid by clicking the Start With Custom Bid radio button and entering a value.

When you start out with the Conversion Optimizer, it's a good idea to use the recommended bids. These are based on how your campaign is currently performing and so will ensure a smooth transition from CPC to CPA bidding. A typical result is more conversions at about the same cost per conversion.

Once the Conversion Optimizer has been running for a while, you can go after more conversions by increasing your CPA bid, or you can lower your CPA bid, which typically results in a lower CPA but fewer conversions. Setting CPA bids unrealistically low can have a very negative effect: If you have a CPA of $211.96 as in Figure 6.10 but you set a Max CPA of $1.00, you probably won't get any conversions!

Using a Target CPA Bid Type

Setting a Max CPA can be scary and confusing given how much higher it can be than your target CPA. The Target CPA radio button in Figure 6.10 lets you enter an *average* CPA value for the Conversion Optimizer to target. The system recommends a bid based on your historical data, but you can also enter your own Target CPA value.

Also note that using the Conversion Optimizer is no guarantee of how your campaign will perform. If the future does not live up to what the past has predicted, all bets are off. For example, if your market tanks or you change your landing pages, ads, targeting, or other campaign parameters in a negative way, your actual CPA can exceed your CPA bid.

> **Tip:** Note that there is also a conversion optimization setting dedicated solely to the Display Network called the Display Campaign Optimizer (DCO), which can find you even more placements that exhibit a high probability of conversion. This option is covered in full in Chapter 10, "Month 7: Optimizing the Performance of Your Campaigns."

Friday: Set Your Budget

Perhaps the most important financial consideration in your AdWords campaign settings is your budget, which determines how much money you spend. In the Bidding And Budget section of your campaign settings, enter the amount of money you're comfortable spending daily into the Budget box.

How AdWords Allocates Budgets

You set budgets at the campaign level, and you probably have multiple campaigns in your account. Assume that you are running two campaigns and want to spend $100/month. You must divide that $100 between your campaigns explicitly. You don't need to split it evenly; you can put $90 in one campaign and $10 in the other, for example.

Even though we set *daily* budgets, AdWords spends according to a *monthly* calculation. A given day's spending can be up to 20 percent more than your daily budget. Thus, if you set a daily budget of $100, AdWords may spend less than $100 some days and up to $120 on others. Over the course of a month, the system never charges you more than 30.4 (the average number of days in a month) times your daily budget, or in this case, $3,040.

Over the course of the year, some days get lots of traffic and others (like weekends or holidays) get less. Letting AdWords compensate for slow days by spending more on days when more traffic is available lets it react to demand while staying within your monthly budget targets.

Managing Ongoing Budgets

As you continue to manage and refine your campaigns, hopefully you'll find that every dollar you put into AdWords creates more than a dollar of value for you. With a measured, positive ROI, you can begin to allocate your marketing budget across campaigns to maximize your profitability.

You may find that spending up to $100 per day on Campaign A is extremely profitable, but then diminishing returns set in. In Campaign B, you can spend $1,000 a minute if you want, but you don't get the same ROI from these clicks. As you get a feel for how many clicks, impressions, or conversions you can buy in each campaign at what levels of profitability, you can adjust your budget targets to maximize ROI across your entire account.

To find out how many ad impressions you are missing because of your budget limits, enable the Impression Share and Lost Impression Share (Budget) columns in the Competitive Metrics section of the Customize Columns part of the Campaigns tab. These columns provide insight into how many impressions are out there and what percentage of them you're missing. In Figure 6.11, Campaign #1, with nearly 12 million impressions, is still missing 8 percent of what it *could* be doing.

		Campaign	Budget	Status ?	↓ Clicks ?	Impr. ?	Impr. share ?	Lost IS (budget) ?
☐	●	Total - all campaigns	$5,000.00/day		1,669,777	110,298,275	< 10%	41.30%
☐	●	⛶ Campaign #1	$1,000.00/day	Limited by budget ? ☑	306,530	11,886,532	38.26%	8.01%
☐	●	⛶ Campaign #2	$22.00/day	Eligible	207,203	2,858,624	35.89%	0.11%

Figure 6.11 Reviewing impression and lost impression share

Clicking the graph icon next to the Limited By Budget status item brings up a Budget Idea window (Figure 6.12) showing, based on the last two weeks of your data, how many extra clicks and impressions you might achieve by raising your budget to different levels. Of course, the reality of your business and budget constraints ultimately determines how much you allocate to Display Network advertising, but access to the profitability numbers and impression share data can help you plan campaigns and set budgets.

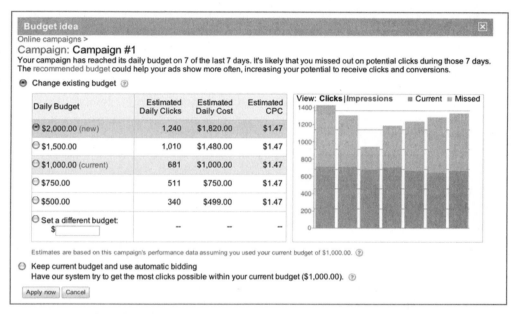

Figure 6.12 Budget idea window for a sample campaign

Week 11: Configure Advanced Campaign Settings

The AdWords system provides advanced campaign settings that can help you further target the audience you want to reach, and this week, we dive into some of the most useful of these features.

You can choose days of the week and times of day to show your ads, you can increase or decrease bids based on the day and time an auction is taking place, and you can even integrate your ads into the social fabric of the Google+ system. You can limit the number of times an individual sees your ads and change how you serve and rotate different ads into the mix as they're shown around the Web. These settings give advertisers finer control of display advertising efforts.

Monday/Tuesday: Learn the Ad Scheduler

Dayparting, a concept from offline advertising, is targeting different parts of the day to find specific target demographics. The differences in audiences between daytime, primetime, and late night television programming, for example, can be immense. The targeting options in the online world are radically more advanced, and controlling the days and times that your ads run can be very important to your targeting.

Why Ad Scheduling Is Important

Let's say that you're trying to sell natural sleeping aids through an e-commerce store on the Web. People who are sound asleep during the night are probably not your target customer: What you want are the late night web surfers, plagued with insomnia. Because they can't sleep, they pass the minutes and hours watching YouTube videos, catching up on news, reading blogs, and otherwise consuming online content. And every single one of their page views is an opportunity to reach them with display advertising. In this case, it's pretty obvious that there are *times of day* that you might want to run your ads.

Another example is an advertiser selling bartending books, drink mixes, shot glasses, and cocktail shakers. Figure 6.13 shows a screen shot from Google Insights for Search, where the solid line represents the volume of search queries Google sees for drink recipes versus time. Every weekend, search volume increases dramatically, peaking regularly on Saturdays. For this advertiser, not only is there more traffic on Saturdays, these visitors are also probably more likely to convert.

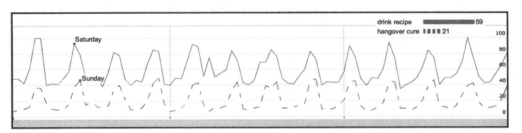

Figure 6.13 Google Insights for Search data

For the advertiser bidding on hangover cures, Sunday is the best day to run ads! You can find Google Insights for Search, a wonderful tool for understanding what people are searching for over time, at the following location:

`www.google.com/insights/search`

In the preceding examples, both day of the week and time of day clearly influence the targeted audience, but often there are differences in campaign performance that you *wouldn't* necessarily expect. Figure 6.14 is a Google Analytics Day Part report (from the AdWords subcategory of the Advertising reports). It shows how a campaign of one of our clients was performing at different times of day.

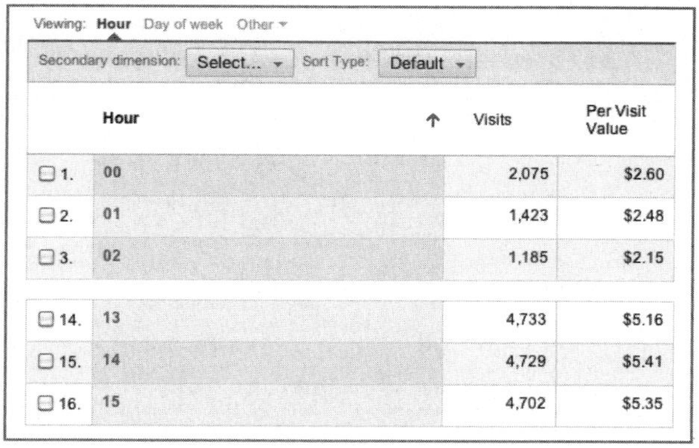

	Hour	Visits	Per Visit Value
1.	00	2,075	$2.60
2.	01	1,423	$2.48
3.	02	1,185	$2.15
14.	13	4,733	$5.16
15.	14	4,729	$5.41
16.	15	4,702	$5.35

Figure 6.14 Google Analytics

This particular website sells clothing and apparel; a product that you might think wouldn't be influenced that much by time of day. As you might expect, visits between midnight and 3:00 a.m. are significantly fewer than between 1:00 and 4:00 in the afternoon. But the interesting part is the per-visit value metric, which tells us how much the average click is *worth* to us against our defined advertising goals. Visits during the middle of the night are only worth half as much as the afternoon visits!

What makes this example even more interesting is that the average cost per click was hovering around $3, so ads running during the middle of the night were actually *losing money* while the profits during the day were compensating for the losses! By stopping ads from running at unprofitable hours, we can spend more on the clicks that provide a higher ROI.

Note at the top of the screen in Figure 6.14 that you can also look at the report by day of the week. Your campaigns might perform differently on different days as well as different hours of the day!

Automatically Adjusting Bids Based on Day and Time

While the Basic mode of the Ad Schedule page allows advertisers to either show ads or not based on the time of day or day of week, there is also another option. The Bid Adjustment mode lets you specify different bids for different days and times. Recall the example of our client for whom the per-visit value was $2 late at night and $5 in the afternoon. With a cost per click below $2 at night, we can still obtain profitable conversions, but during the day, we can afford a higher bid to get even more conversions since they're worth more. Figure 6.15 shows the Bid Adjustment mode settings that can help us achieve this.

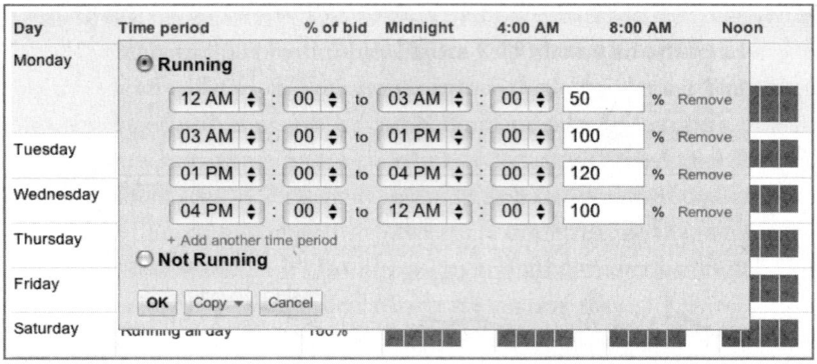

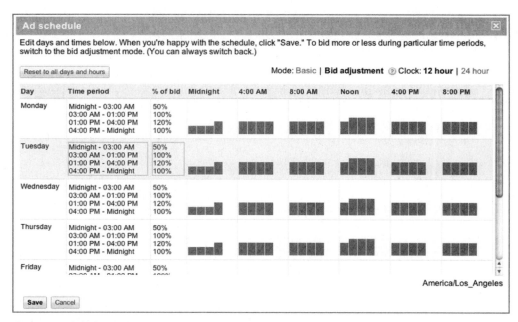

Figure 6.15 Adjusting bids for custom run times

We scale back our bid by 50 percent during the times of day when per-visit value is low, and we increase our bid by 20 percent during the most profitable times. Copying these settings across all days results in an ad schedule that looks like Figure 6.16. The different bar sizes represent the different bid levels. And you can still exclude ads from running on a specific day by setting that row to Not Running.

Figure 6.16 A bid-adjusted ad schedule

Limitations of Ad Scheduling

There are a few things to watch out for when using this feature. First, if you use the Conversion Optimizer, you can't schedule your ads because time of day and day of week are factors it uses to build a model to predict the probability of a conversion from a certain auction. To build this model correctly, it collects sample data across different times of day and days of week.

Also note that time is based upon the time zone set in your account, *not* the time zones of any geographic targets you may have set for the campaign. The time zone is displayed at the lower-right corner of the ad scheduler interface, and you'll need to calculate and account for the time differences. If, for example, your campaign targets New York and your account is set to the Los Angeles time zone, you'll need to make the adjustments here.

Wednesday: Understand Rotation and Frequency Capping

Advanced campaign settings allow you to control how different ads are rotated if there are multiple ads in an ad group as well as how often your ads can be shown to the same person. The "Ad delivery: Ad rotation, frequency capping" section of the advanced settings is where you specify these options.

Setting the Proper Ad Rotation

When multiple ads within a single ad group are eligible to fill an ad slot, AdWords chooses which one to send to an auction. By default, it selects the one most likely to draw a click because the ad with the highest probability of getting clicked is the one that's most likely to make Google money! From the advertiser's perspective, however, this can also be a good thing. Remember that Quality Score is largely influenced by click-through rates, and the ad that gets clicked more (all other things held equal) gets better placements and/or lower costs per click.

That said, money is *spent* on the click but *made* on the conversion. If you tell AdWords to optimize for conversions, it selects the ad with the highest probability of obtaining a conversion. Many advertisers choose this option because it focuses on actual advertising objectives. You might get fewer clicks, but the clicks you get are much more likely to result in conversions.

In either case, the system uses historical data to predict ad performance. It continues to serve all of your ads, but some ads begin to be served more frequently than others. If you optimize your ad rotation by conversion rate but you don't have enough conversion data to build a confident model, AdWords optimizes for clicks until it obtains sufficient data.

The last option is to show your ads evenly, where each ad is served approximately the same number of times. Use this option to gather data on all of your ads if you plan to run your own split tests.

> **Warning:** If you choose to rotate your ads evenly, the AdWords system will automatically revert you to an optimize-for-clicks model after 90 days. If you would prefer to let your ads rotate evenly indefinitely, you'll need to fill out the form at the following URL to opt out of this behavior:
>
> http://services.google.com/fb/forms/rotateoptout/

Using Frequency Caps

Frequency capping allows advertisers to limit the exposure any one person will have to a certain ad, ad group, or campaign over a specified time period. Essentially, this allows you to avoid overexposing your target audience to your messaging: If they didn't want what you had to offer the first 50 times (or whatever value you choose), then at the very least, backing off is probably the polite thing to do. Over and above brand perception and messaging issues, frequency capping can help improve your Quality Score because every impression that doesn't result in a click hurts your click-through rate.

Implementing frequency caps is straightforward. In the frequency capping section, specify the cap and the time period and scope to which it applies. You can limit daily, weekly, or monthly exposure at the ad, ad group, or campaign level.

Understanding How Frequency Capping Works

When AdWords shows your ad to a user, it uses cookies to keep track of which ads have been shown to whom. Since these cookies live inside the browser, in actuality, you don't really limit the number of times a *person* sees ads, you limit how many times AdWords serves it to a given *browser* on a given machine.

If you use both Internet Explorer and Chrome browsers and hit a cap on one browser, for example, you might continue to see those ads on the other browser. Or, if a father hits a frequency cap while using the family computer, it's possible that no one else in the family will ever be exposed to that ad. Lastly, if a user clears their cookies or uses a different machine altogether, the frequency count starts all over again.

Thursday/Friday: Integrate with Google+

The newest kid on the social networking block is Google+, and while it certainly has some nice features and differences compared to Facebook and other well-established networks, it's not the network itself that makes it such a powerful force. It's the integration with all the other Google products that people—your potential customers—are using on a day-to-day basis.

Google+ is what allows users to +1, or give a personal endorsement to, everything from organic search results and ads to websites and specific pieces of content. It's a lot like the ingenious Facebook Like button, only it can extend much further. If you're on Google+ and logged in, as you search the Web on Google, you see pictures of people in your social circles next to certain results, indicating that people *you know and trust* have endorsed this page. And if you use Search Plus Your World, you get results specifically tailored to you, with faces of your personal connections all over the page. Let's look at how this affects the ads you see across the Google networks. Figure 6.17 shows +1 annotations on both text and display ads.

Figure 6.17 Google ads with embedded +1 data

There are those faces again! People *you know personally* who have at one point or another said, "Hey, I like this!" People tend to trust their family, friends, and colleagues a lot more than they trust the average faceless corporate advertiser, and this, combined with the unique presence of Google in just about everything we do online, is why Google+ is such a powerful tool. As people check their email, get the news, search, and otherwise browse the Web, they see their friends' faces and recommendations on search results, web pages, and even in the ads across the Search and Display Networks. And people are more inclined to pay attention to—and click—an ad for something that is clearly endorsed by someone they know and trust.

Google has already released figures describing click-through rate increases of 5 to 10 percent for ads with +1 annotations, and although social integrations do not have a direct impact on quality score, the increase they can provide in click-through rate does. This can lead to better placements and lower costs per click, but more important, those clicks lead people to a landing page where someone inside their social circles has gone before and had a positive experience. That can boost conversions.

For your display ads to show +1 annotations, select that option in the Social Settings section of advanced settings. Your ads can then show +1 counts and faces of your potential customers' connections within the Google+ social graph.

Measuring the Impact of +1 Annotations

To monitor how often your ads show with +1 annotations and how their performance stacks up, use the +1 Annotations segment on the tab you wish to analyze. You can use this segment when analyzing campaigns, ad groups, ads, or any of your contextual, placement, audience, or topic targets, and it splits each row of data into Personal, Basic, and None, referring to the annotations that were (or were not) shown in the ad, as in Figure 6.18.

Personal annotations explicitly show a count of +1s and names and faces of people inside the user's social circles who have done the +1'ing. A Basic annotation shows a *total* count of the number of +1s received when none of those +1s have been given by anyone in the user's own social circles. As the number of people using Google+ increases, this feature will become increasingly useful, and while low percentages of your ads may show +1 annotations now, we expect the percentage to rise with time.

		Campaign	Budget	Status ?	↓	Clicks ?
		Total - all campaigns	$5,110.00/day			1,678,540
☐	●	Campaign #1	$350.00/day	Eligible		120,096
		Personal ?				780
		Basic ?				432
		None				118,884
☐	●	Campaign #2	$145.00/day	Eligible		85,890
		Personal ?				562
		Basic ?				319
		None				85,009

Figure 6.18 Data for personal and basic annotations

Social Ad Extensions

By default, +1 annotations are limited to +1s of the landing page of the specific ad on which the annotation is present. While this is a great starting point, the count of +1s is restricted considering that there are *lots* of pages and content out there that have to do with your brand, your products, and your services that could be +1'd along with that one landing page.

Social extensions allow you to link an ad to a Google+ page and take advantage of *all* the +1s that are tallied up on that Google+ page. A Google+ page is simply a page on the Google+ social network that is created not for an individual but instead for a business, product, brand, or organization. It acts much like a regular Google+ profile page: You can +1 it, you can add it to your social circles by following it, and it allows businesses and organizations a channel to share, host, and engage in a social conversation around brands, products, and entities. A Google+ page can also collect an *overall total* of +1s from web pages and other content around the Web that is associated with that Google+ page, not just +1s of the page itself.

Using social extensions lets you link a Google+ page to one or more AdWords campaigns. The ads then draw their +1 counts and personal annotations not from +1s of a single landing page but from the much larger aggregate pool of the Google+ page, extending the social reach of that ad. Enabling this extension is easy to do: On the Ad Extensions tab, select Social Extensions from the View drop-down. Click New Extension. Choose a campaign from the drop-down and enter the URL of the Google+ page you want to associate with that campaign. If you offer different lines of products or services, you can link different campaigns to different Google+ pages.

The extension also requires you to link your website to the Google+ page, and this must be done by an administrator of your Google+ page.

> **Note:** Google can use data from users who have +1'd your ads in its targeting. If you use broad reach contextual targeting, Google can show your ad to people who are in the social circles of anyone who has +1'd your ad based on that social association alone! If you use placement or audience targeting, however, your ads are restricted to showing only when placement or audience targeting criteria are met, and ads never show on placements or categories that you exclude.

Week 12: Create Your First Ad Group

By this point, you've created a campaign and you've enabled all the features and set all the settings in accordance with your strategy. You've set the languages, networks, devices and locations you want to target; you've chosen your bidding style and set your budgets; and you've leveraged the advanced settings for ad scheduling, frequency capping, and even social integrations.

Now it's time to build out the ad groups that will use those campaign settings. This week we focus on the tactical aspects of adding keywords, placements, and audiences to your ad groups as well as how to upload your display ads and how to manage your exclusions.

Monday: Add Keywords for Contextual Targeting

If your campaign strategy calls for contextual targeting in your ad groups, this is where you'll add keywords to your ad group.

Adding Keywords to a New Ad Group

Whether you build a new campaign or add an ad group to an existing campaign, you'll see the Create Ad Group screen, and you'll start by giving your ad group a name that reflects its specific advertising goal. For example, an ad group named Discounted Ski Vacations inside a campaign named RM-CA-FR Winter Vacations lets you know very quickly that these ads are in a remarketing campaign targeted to French-speaking Canadians and promote discounts on ski vacations during the winter.

Friday, we cover creating or uploading the first ad for this ad group, but for now we skip that and move to the Keywords section. Expand the Select Keywords area and enter the keywords you developed for your contextual targeting strategy (Chapter 5, week 6), one per line. By clicking Add Keywords By Spreadsheet, you can enter the keywords into a spreadsheet with Max CPC values and landing pages (destination URLs) for each of those keywords. If you leave these columns blank, the keyword inherits the default bid of the ad group and the default destination URL of the ad being shown, but note that you can always go back and change it later.

Adding Keywords to an Existing Ad Group

As you analyze performance, you might want to add or make changes to keywords within ad groups that are already running. To do this, drill down to the campaign and ad group you want to work with, and on the Display Network tab, click the Change Display Targeting button. This brings up the Change Display Targeting window (Figure 6.19).

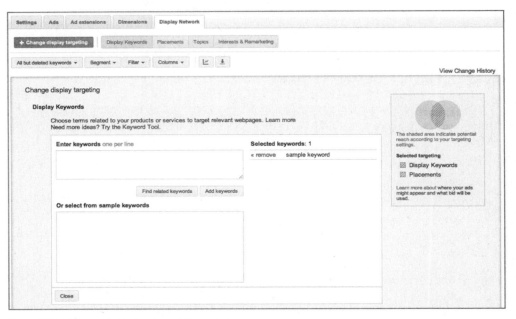

Figure 6.19 Add keywords interface from within an ad group

Notice the targeting diagram to the right. This changes with the various targeting options you enable for the ad group, and here you can see that both contextual keyword targeting and placements are being used. As you change your display targeting options, this diagram updates to help you picture who is eligible to see your ads. Once you update the keywords, click Close.

As you manage and optimize your ad groups, you'll also find cases where you want to pause, delete, or otherwise manage your keywords. To do this, simply navigate to the Display Keywords subsection of the Display Network tab, check the box next to the keywords whose status you wish to change, and then select Enable, Pause, or Delete from the Change Status drop-down.

You can also manage keywords and their attributes by clicking Edit to the right of the Change Status drop-down.

Keeping Things Relevant

As you build out your ad groups, remember that the system rewards relevance through Quality Score. And ads that are more relevant tend to get clicked more often, which also improves Quality Score. So a good best practice is to keep your ad groups as tightly themed as you can. If an ad in your ad group is not *specifically* applicable to the context of each and every keyword you target in that ad group, it's time for a new ad group with a new, more specific ad. Remember, you can have up to 20,000 ad groups for each of the up to 10,000 campaigns you can create, so the system is unlikely to limit you.

For example, you probably don't want a single ad group to target all aspects of a general theme like vacations. You are more relevant and better served with ad groups for different types of vacations, different destinations, and other different attributes. If you have one ad group for family Florida vacations, another for couples' cruises, and another for winter ski vacations, you can serve more relevant ads on pages that are more relevant to the keywords you target. Someone interested in a ski vacation is much more likely to be wooed by imagery of smiling people on a ski lift and fresh powder on the mountain than a generic ad of an airplane going somewhere.

Tuesday: Add Placements for Placement Targeting

Chapter 5 (week 7) focuses on how to find and evaluate placements using tools and techniques for identifying the kinds of websites, pages, and locations on those pages where you want your ads to show. Having that list of placements is a prerequisite for adding them.

The following sections discuss *managed* placements. *Automatic* placements don't need to be entered or specified: Those are the placements that the AdWords system identifies and targets based on contextual, audience, or topic targeting.

Adding Placements to a New Ad Group

As you build a new ad group, expand the Select Managed Placements area of the Placements section to see the screen in Figure 6.20. Use the text box on the left to specify the URLs of domains or pages to add as managed placements (one per line), and you can use the search box on the right to get a rudimentary list of suggested placements with some limited data. In the example pictured in Figure 6.20, we use scuba diving as the search term, but remember: While this can be a timesaving way to get started, we highly recommend spending the time and going through the processes and tools discussed in Chapter 5 (week 7) to put together a more complete list of well-thought-out and researched placements to start with.

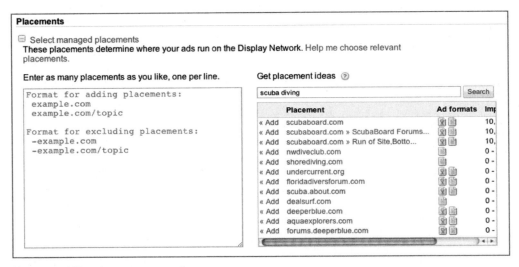

Figure 6.20 Adding placements to a new ad group

Adding Placements to an Existing Ad Group

To add managed placements to an existing ad group, drill down to the ad group and click the Display Network tab. Click the Change Display Targeting button, and expand the Placements section right under the Display Keywords section we just looked at. You can search for, add, and remove placements right there or click the Add Multiple Placements At Once link to open a separate window. There you can enter multiple placements, one per line.

Don't forget that typing them in is not the only way to add managed placements! You can review the performance of *automatic* placements and select those you wish to manage explicitly. This process is covered in Chapter 5 (week 7).

Editing Managed Placements

Just as you edit keywords, you likely want to edit, pause, or delete managed placements as you administer and optimize your account. From the Placements subsection of the Display Network tab, put a check next to the placements you wish to work with and use the Change Status drop-down to pause, delete, or enable them. The Edit button allows you to edit the checked placements right there in the interface.

Wednesday: Add Audiences for Audience Targeting

Targeting advertising by audience can be extremely powerful. If you like the idea of using interest categories or building remarketing lists, the Interests & Remarketing subsection of the Display Network tab is where you choose these settings and target your lists. You can use audience targeting in conjunction with contextual or placement targeting, and in general, targeting types for display campaigns are not mutually exclusive but can work together to find the right eyeballs to put your ads in front of.

You don't get the option of adding audience targeting while creating a new ad group, so you'll need to add it once the ad group has been created. We devote an entire week to the AdWords remarketing lists and custom combinations in Chapter 11, "Month 8: Advanced Topics," so this section focuses on the Interest Category options.

Adding Interest Category Audiences

To add an audience, drill down to the ad group you'd like to work with and navigate to the Display Network tab. Click the Change Display Targeting button and expand the Interests & Remarketing section. The Interest Categories tab contains a list of over 1,000 topics that potential viewers of your ads may have expressed interest in as determined by the websites they visit. You can use the search box, but it is also useful to browse the list, expanding the subcategories to get a feel for the types of interest categories that exist. Think about your target customers as you look through the lists, and look for opportunities that have less to do with the products and services you offer and more to do with the people you're marketing to.

For example, if you market summer travel getaways for US-based consumers, you might start to target the 10 to 20 million members of the Teaching and Classroom Resources audience because you know that teachers in the United States are likely to have the summer off and might take an extended vacation.

Editing Audiences

The interface for editing or updating the status of any of your audience targets is the familiar Change Status drop-down that lets you pause, delete, or enable. You can also use the familiar Edit button. A useful feature of the Audience tab, however, is the Copy button. Once you've established audiences to target, those audiences might apply to many of your campaigns and ad groups. Using this feature, you can copy audiences and optionally their bids and destination URLs from any other ad group in your account. From the Copy Audiences pop-up, use the Choose drop-down to select the ad group whose audiences you want to copy to the current ad group.

Thursday: Exclude Placements, Audiences, and Keywords

After you have set up all of your campaign targeting settings and then added keywords, placements, audiences, or combinations of these, AdWords knows exactly where and to whom to show your ads across the Display Network.

But it's also important to tell AdWords where you *don't* want your ads showing up, and this is done through exclusions. You can add exclusions at the ad group, campaign, and in certain cases even the account level, and Display Network campaigns allow for placement-, audience-, topic-, and even keyword-level exclusions.

Excluding Placements

Placement exclusions can be accessed from the Placements subsection of the Display Network tab by expanding the Exclusions area. Here, you see the exclusions you add to either the ad group or the parent campaign, with some straightforward actions that you can take. Figure 6.21 shows an example where ads do not show on cnn.com or sitipark.com for any ad group in the entire campaign, and do not show on usatoday.com or about.com for this specific ad group.

Figure 6.21 Exclusions at the ad group and campaign levels

To add a new placement exclusion at either level, click the Add Exclusions button to open a window into which you can enter domains or more specific URLs. You can also easily edit, delete, and download a list of your placement exclusions from this area. Remember from Chapter 5 (week 7) that as you manage your automatic placements or specific URL lists of placements, you can exclude placements directly from the list simply by clicking a button (note that this button is not present for manual placements). To use this feature for manually managed placements, use either of the See URL List drop-down options in Figure 6.22.

Figure 6.22 See URL List feature from managed placements

This brings up the URL list of the appropriate placements with all the performance metrics you need to decide whether or not you want to exclude them. You can check the box next to placements you want to exclude and click the Exclude From Targeting button to add them to your list of excluded placements.

Excluding Audiences

Excluding audiences works in much the same way as other exclusions. Navigate to the campaign and ad group you're working with and expand the Exclusions area at the bottom of the screen, this time selecting the Interests & Remarketing subsection (Figure 6.23).

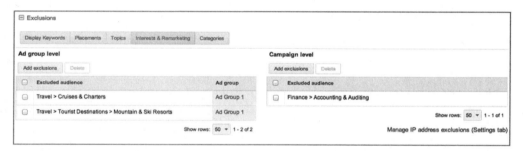

Figure 6.23 Audience exclusions at the ad group and campaign levels

Here, at the ad group level, people who like cruises or mountain and ski resorts are excluded, and the entire campaign excludes people who have shown an interest in accounting and audits. The advertiser has decided that accountants and auditors that ski and go on cruises are not at all the target audience. By excluding these audiences, the advertiser hopes to avoid impressions that aren't likely to get clicked or turn into conversions.

The process of excluding an audience is similar to that of adding one. Click Add Exclusions to see a list of categories.

The drop-down defaults to Interest Categories, but this is also where you manage your remarketing list and custom combination exclusions (see Chapter 11). To add interest categories to your audience exclusion list, browse or search for the interest you want to exclude and click the Add link.

Negative Keywords in Display Campaigns

If you're used to defining negative keywords in your search campaigns, then it's important to note that while the theory still applies to display campaigns, in practice, negative keywords don't behave quite the same.

Chapter 4 discusses the example of using "Paris Hilton" as a search term. If you are managing *search* campaigns for the hotel, you can add negative keywords to avoid showing ads with search results for "perfume" or "pics" or "tattoo" in order to avoid showing your ads in response to queries about Paris Hilton the person. This is easy to do with search campaigns.

On the Display Network, however, there are no search queries. The keywords in your contextually targeted ad groups describe the *kinds* of pages you want your ads placed on. For this reason, there is no longer a simple rule for the system to follow. In fact, if you define negative keywords in your display campaigns, your ads might even show up on pages that explicitly *contain those exact negative keywords* if Google deems the content as a whole contextually relevant.

AdWords allows negative keywords, and with the recent contextual targeting engine updates, they work better than they used to. Nonetheless, as a best practice, placement and audience exclusions are the most straightforward way to avoid irrelevant placements: If you exclude a placement or an audience, the ad simply does not show on that placement or to members of that audience.

Friday: Add Ads to Your Ad Groups

The next chapter is dedicated to creating ads for display advertising, and in it, we cover all the rules, best practices, tips, and tricks for building ads that conform to the AdWords requirements, convey the right message, and position themselves for clicks and conversions. In this section, you finish creating an ad group by adding one or more of those ad creatives.

When you build a new ad group, either as part of creating a new campaign or as an addition to an existing campaign, you see the Create An Ad screen (Figure 6.24).

The default selection is a text ad, which is a valid form of display advertising. If you want to use text ads in this campaign, you can create your first one right here. As you enter your headline, description lines, display URL, and destination URL, AdWords limits you to the proper number of characters and shows you a preview of your text ad.

To use another ad format, select the appropriate radio button. Note that if you select anything other than a text ad here, you must add your ad creatives to your new ad group manually once the ad group has been created.

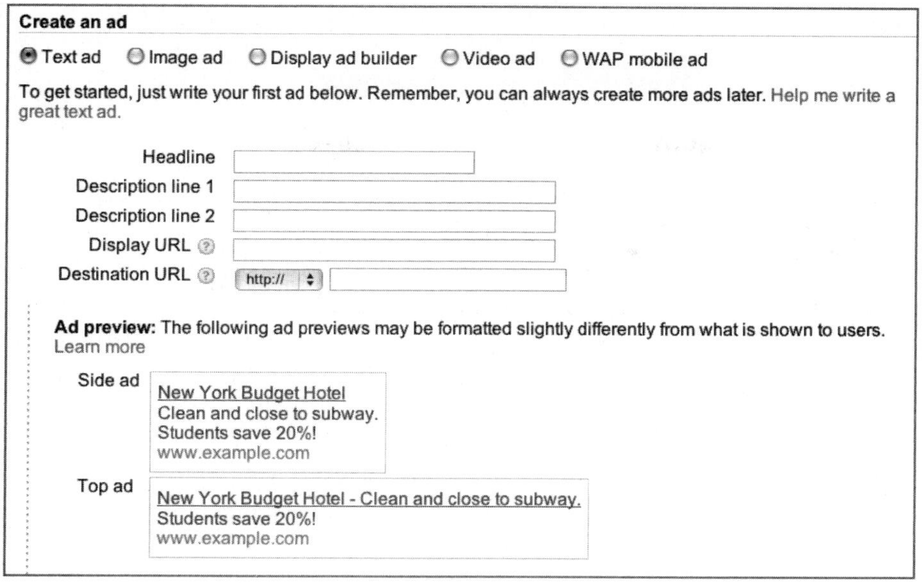

Figure 6.24 Selecting an ad for a new ad group

Once an ad group exists, you can always add and manage your ads through the Ads tab. To create a new ad, navigate to the campaign and ad group you want to work with, click the Ads tab, and use the New Ad drop-down. You can choose from various ad formats or access the Display Ad Builder tool (see Chapter 7, "Month 4: Creating Image Ads"). Choosing Image Ad, for example, brings up the New Image Ad screen (Figure 6.25).

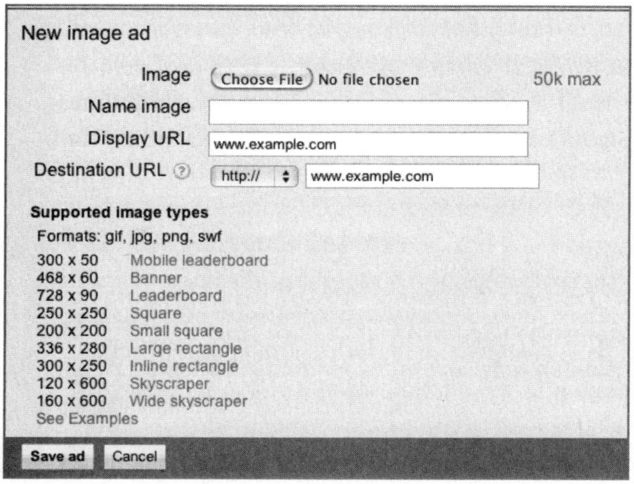

Figure 6.25 Uploading an image ad

To upload an image ad, select it for upload from your computer and give it a name, display URL, and destination URL. Then click the Save Ad button. The file must match one of the supported sizes, be less than 50 kilobytes, and be in GIF, JPG, PNG, or SWF (Flash) format. A very good practice is to upload ads in all supported sizes as this gives you maximum exposure across the Display Network: Regardless of the size and shape of the available inventory, you'll have an ad that fits.

Remember, you can always edit and manage ads as you do other components of an AdWords campaign. As you create and upload ads, you see them all listed in the Ads tab, and a pencil icon appears to the right of the thumbnail when you hover over an ad. Clicking it allows you to edit any aspect of the ad at any time. And just as in other areas of the AdWords interface, you can pause, delete, or enable ads by checking the box next to them and using the Change Status drop-down.

Month 4: Creating Image Ads

Image ads are the most common form of display advertising, so it's important that we spend time discussing how to create them effectively and efficiently.

Image ads are also inherently more challenging than the text ads commonly found in search marketing. Anyone can type text, so the bulk of work in creating text ads lies in linguistic creativity, not in physically creating the ads. Image ads require the same level of marketing skills, but the visual medium requires more creative and technical skills. In this chapter we look at tools and techniques to reduce the technical burden and maximize your marketing impact by taking advantage of the unique features of this medium.

7

Chapter Contents:

Week 13: Study the Science behind Great Image Ads
Week 14: Understand the Rules
Week 15: Dig Deeper on Image Ads
Week 16: Build Ads with Display Ad Builder

Week 13: Study the Science behind Great Image Ads

Just as there is a process for creating effective text ads for search or display advertising, there are techniques and processes for creating compelling image ads. In many ways, our freedom as marketers in the image-based world is much broader than in text. Text ads are constrained to just a few lines that must be carefully written to address not only user appeal, but Quality Score concerns as well. While we get only 95 characters in a text ad, a picture, as the old saying goes, can be worth a thousand words.

The image-based medium itself is inherently more flexible because we have a blank canvas that can take on an infinite number of forms. There are also more options—static images, animated images, interactive Flash-based ads, and even video.

Before we discuss graphics and formats, we start by looking at cognitive science research that can help you write ads that have greater appeal and invoke a stronger response from your audience.

Monday: Maintaining the Scent

One of the first cognitive concepts to keep in mind when designing ads is the fundamentally important idea of *maintaining scent*. The origins of this come from research done by Dr. Ed Chi, Stuart Card, and Peter Pirolli while at Xerox. Their research discovered that the way humans forage for information on the Web is actually based on the techniques our brains developed over time to search for food. Chi explains, "Evolutionarily, the optimization strategies that are innate in each one of us in looking for food in the natural environment occur extremely often in just about everything that we do."

Their research shows that we tend to use a hub and spoke pattern when surfing the Web. We start a central hub—a search engine, for example—and begin down a trail, following it as long as the scent stays strong. If the scent grows faint or disappears, the surfer will abort and return to the center. According to Chi, "People repeat this process until they're satisfied."

This has two immediate impacts on us as advertisers. First, we must go to great lengths to ensure that we maintain the scent at each step. Every click, every ad, and every landing page must reinforce the idea that the user is on the right path such that they unconsciously know it's correct without having to stop and question it. We can provide that reinforcement in our visuals and the language we use on both the ad creative and the subsequent landing page.

While we can incorporate subtle clues, most of the time it's the basics that are overlooked. For example, if we have an ad offering 60″ TVs, then the ad should lead visitors directly to the page about the 60″ TVs. Most marketers by now know to avoid sending folks to the home page in all cases (although a few offenders persevere), but far too many are still guilty of sending visitors to the overall TV landing page or even the Electronics section page.

It's also helpful to repeat imagery that supports the products or themes. For example, in both the ad and landing page for Target (Figure 7.1 and Figure 7.2), we see the common themes that ease the transition and let us know we're in the right place. These include consistent text fonts and colors, consistent background images, and perhaps most important, the repeated image of the Target RED card in both places. The consistent use of children in an educational setting (backpacks and a desk) reinforces both the scent and theme of the image-landing page pair. This idea of pairing is an excellent way to think of your ad and associated landing page—they are simply two parts of a set. This way you will avoid the temptation to use a generic version of either and it will be easier to remember to use a consistent look and feel in both.

Figure 7.1 Target ad creative

Figure 7.2 Corresponding Target landing page

The Verizon Wireless ad and landing page pair (Figure 7.3 and Figure 7.4) takes the scent reinforcement one step further by not only repeating the primary imagery of the mobile device but immediately letting users know they are in the right place by repeating the key phrase *Mobile Hotspot* in the headline of both places.

The second reality is that while it's true that our ad creative begins with a blank canvas, the pairing of the ad to the landing page means that whichever is created first may constrain the second. In many cases, the landing page being advertised already exists and likely even follows a corporate style guide. This means that our choices of patterns, textures, color palettes, and even fonts may be restricted if our desire is to match what is already in use.

Figure 7.3 Verizon Wireless ad creative

Figure 7.4 Corresponding Verizon Wireless landing page

However, this is simply a guideline and not a hard-and-fast rule. The most important rule is to do whatever will make the ad most effective. So while you usually want to maintain the scent, sometimes the most important design objective of the ad is to distract the user from the current page. Thus, a far brighter color palette and bold fonts could be in order. It's still important to maintain scent with text or iconography, but in this case you can discard the website's fonts, colors, and size for something more eye catching.

Tuesday: Creating Strong Calls to Action

The one universal best practice for display ads is to have a strong *call to action*. And while much of what we already knew about human behavior still applies online, in this case the rules of etiquette are different.

To illustrate, imagine you are walking through a mall department store, bags in hand, on your way back to your car when a salesperson steps in front of you pointing a loaded cologne bottle in your face and says in a loud and abrupt voice, "WEAR THIS COLOGNE!" This is highly unlikely to leave a positive impression, but online when an ad grabs your attention with bold imagery and implores to you in all capital, bolded letters to download a white paper, it's not generally perceived as offensive. The ad for *WIRED* magazine in Figure 7.5 engages us in large, bold caps and commands us to SUBSCRIBE NOW. It even includes an exclamation mark but doesn't seem belligerent. So while obnoxious behavior isn't recommended in any setting, what passes for obnoxious depends on the medium.

Figure 7.5 WIRED magazine ad shouts without offending

A good ad interrupts our primary task (reading the content of the web page), refocuses our attention on itself, and delivers a strong call to action that results in a click to the landing page and an action on that page as well.

Even ads that are primarily for branding should include a call to action. Having won the battle for your momentary attention, the advertiser should make the most of that brief moment. We can surmise that the main purpose of the Delta Air Lines ads (Figure 7.6 and Figure 7.7) is to raise awareness about its first class cabin on regional jets. The ads are shown simultaneously, the first at the top of the page and the other in the text of the article. The copy "Introducing First Class on Regional Jets" in Figure 7.6 is explicitly about awareness. Figure 7.7 goes beyond simple awareness to espouse the benefits—in this case more legroom. But with the primary branding and awareness goal accomplished, the ads still employ calls to action. Figure 7.6 encourages us to like the Facebook page. Figure 7.7 asks us to see all the perks, that is, to continue engaging with the brand via the website.

Figure 7.6 Delta ad at the top of the page

Figure 7.7 Delta ad on the side of the page

The mere *presence* of a call to action, however, is not enough. For example, the IBM ad in Figure 7.8 has a prominent headline followed by a tiny call to action that resembles a standard disclaimer, which our eyes have been trained to ignore.

Figure 7.8 The call to action is weak at best.

Wednesday: Using Enticing Imagery

To have any effect, your ads must entice users to break their concentration from the other content on the page and then hold their attention.

Some of the ways imagery is used depend on content. For example, if you advertise automobiles, it helps to understand what drives car-buying decisions. Certainly price is a factor, and fuel economy has become a major factor recently. But studies have shown that in the luxury and sports car markets, the number one factor is styling. Consumers may eventually evaluate other factors, but if a car's styling doesn't appeal to the buyer, it won't usually make it to the second round.

This was evident for Mazda in 2000 when its existing TV ads failed to perform. The company switched to the entirely new Zoom Zoom campaign, which focused less on technical details and comparative statements and instead was dominated by imagery of the cars zooming down the road. Sales skyrocketed, and much of the credit was attributed to the shift in advertising tactics. The ailing company saw a turnaround and the campaign has been in use ever since.

This lesson is evident in the online market as well. The four ads in Figure 7.9 are typical of the automotive segment, which should come as no surprise based on what we know about the importance of styling. If the primary question on the mind of a prospective buyer is what the car looks like, the imagery in the ad should address that question first and foremost! There are calls to action and supporting info, but the element that entices viewers to stop and linger is the shots of the cars.

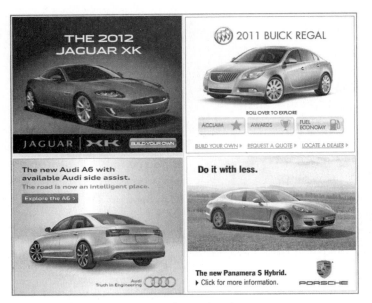

Figure 7.9 In this market, the imagery is all about the styling.

While the parallels of TV and online display (particularly video) are obvious, it's worth pointing out one major advantage of online advertising: to *fail faster*. This means there is more room for experimentation, but it can also act as the bellwether for other media. Because experimentation is cheap and fast online, you can vet and analyze a new strategy online before deciding to roll it out to the more expensive media such as TV.

Mazda had an underperforming campaign in 2000 and began the expensive and arduous process of creating an entirely new global ad campaign. If this campaign had failed, it's likely that the company would not have survived long enough to devise and launch yet another campaign, given the time and cost involved. Mazda was forced to bet its future on an unproven campaign strategy. Online experimentation reduces the need for such risks.

Experimentation is critical to understanding changing consumer patterns and understanding how different market segments react. Perhaps the sports car market segment is more sensitive to styling, but for other segments, factors such as warranty and brand strength play a bigger role. The ad in Figure 7.10, for example, breaks from the standard format and focuses on brand. Even within the same market segment certain geographies may respond differently. Ads that work in Detroit may fail miserably in Los Angeles. We devote much of Chapter 10, "Month 7: Optimizing the Performance of Your Campaigns," and Chapter 11, "Month 8: Advanced Topics," to the ideas behind testing and performance measurement.

Figure 7.10 The preeminence of brand elements is a departure from standard automotive ads.

Using Graphical Elements in Display Ads

Finding the right combination of images, style, fonts, colors, and other supportive graphics to use in display ads can be challenging. Through proper planning and execution, all of these elements can work together to create intriguing ads that users will acknowledge, clearly understand, and click! Here are some graphical element types to look out for when planning display ads:

Images What makes for a good image? Ultimately it depends on what the ad is about, the tone or emotional aspect of the image, and the natural lines an object or a person make that can draw a user's attention to other elements within the ad.

The images in Figure 7.11 show how you can use natural lines and white space within an image to your advantage. This is a highly successful method for creating a solid compositional setup for other ad elements.

ISTOCKPHOTO/SANDOCLR/YURI _ ARCURS

Figure 7.11 Natural lines and white space guide the eye.

Notice the man doing the push-ups? (Of course you did, but we'll cover that reason on Friday!) His body angle creates a nice setup for messaging and a call-to-action area. In the chocolate cupcake image, the cupcake is sitting on white and burgundy. This background color overlap creates natural lines that direct users' eyes up and out to the white space around the top of the cupcake.

The risk of not using an image with a display ad is not getting users' attention. More often than not, a user notices an image (or person) within the ad, reads the messaging/call to action, and acts (clicks or ignores the ad). This flow makes images extremely important in ads. No matter how clear and readable a text ad is, without imagery there is nothing interesting to entice our eye away from the article or other content that we are primarily there to see.

Figure 7.12 shows just how tight the competition for our gaze can be. This ad has images, but they are tiny and every remaining piece of white space has been filled by text in a small font. These issues and the lack of a prominent call to action make this ad difficult to read and easy to bypass when competing with the rest of the visually demanding elements on the page.

Figure 7.12 White space is not wasted space!

Style and color The visual tone of a display ad can affect a user's emotional reaction to the product/service being advertised. Style is often derived from the company's brand and personality.

For example, a resort might do display ads showing a beach with a young couple have messaging that speaks to getting away and relaxation. The visual tone of those aspects would be elegant and might naturally involve earth tones of blues (from the ocean or sky) and light browns (from the sand). To contrast those natural colors, the messaging could be in burgundy.

All of these elements would work together because it's elegant, and if that's portrayed in every ad element, it will connect with users. Because the image is used to portray so much of the mood, feeling, and emotion, the ad doesn't have to include as many words to convey the same meaning. For example, in Figure 7.13 the picture of the resort speaks for itself. The user can see the seaside location, the sandy beach, the thatch-covered cabanas and imagine themselves relaxing in one of the chairs. One of the few things that image doesn't suggest is how affordable this locale may (or may not!) be, so what little text the ad does contain addresses that potential concern of affordability.

Figure 7.13 A compelling image requires few words.

Fonts There are hundreds of thousands of fonts. Choosing the right combinations greatly improves readability and communicates the intended message. Fonts can set the tone and imply everything from urgency to elegance. The perfect font improves the user's understanding and allows us to say more with less.

Figure 7.14 contains a simple call to action: Request a quote now! Each of these fonts alone depicts a different tone within an ad. Sample A might be a common, more generic route, whereas sample C might be for something a little more hip and edgy.

Figure 7.14 The right font can change the feel without saying a word.

Thursday: Writing Good Copy for Display Ads

Today we listen to advice from Michael Straker of Cardinal Path. Michael is well known for the quality of his copy.

Ten Tips for Creating Great Display Ads

By Michael Straker, Cardinal Path

Do your research, understand your audience. To communicate effectively with your intended audience, you have to understand their deeply held feelings and beliefs. What drives and motivates them? What makes them pause or scares the hell out of them?

In an ideal world, you would interview actual users. But we rarely have that luxury. So find out what makes them tick. Read their blogs and tweets. Look at their Facebook and/or LinkedIn pages. Write in their style; make offers that will appeal to them; add interaction that will engage them.

Highlight a benefit. In developing and communicating promotional offers, consider what will be appealing to your users. Don't talk about features—focus on benefits. Solve a problem! Clearly explain the payoff: What's in it for them if they respond?

Talk about your customers, not yourself. Watch your *we* count. Your copy should be full of *you* and *your*, not *we* and *our*.

Add interaction. The best display ads involve users. Interaction not only makes ads more appealing and entertaining, it makes them much more salient, memorable, and shareable. Customization is great too, such as, for example, providing content relevant to the user when they enter a zip code.

Figure out how to delight your users: If possible, create an ad that's useful and/or fun.

Write a great headline. A compelling headline is vital. Highlight the wonderful benefit or payoff you're promising. Being clever is okay. . . but being clear is much more important.

Ten Tips for Creating Great Display Ads *(Continued)*

Try the following:

- Rouse curiosity by asking a question—for example, Are You Killing Sales with the World's Most Common Marketing Blunder? Users can't help but answer the question in their minds, and of course you're implying in the question that you have the answer.

- Promise that you'll help readers solve a problem or get some kind of advantage. How-to headlines are wonderful for this—for example, How to Increase Conversions 10% Overnight.

- Offer a helpful checklist or Top 10. Headlines that promise a solution (or a good laugh) are hard to resist—for example, Three Magic Words That Women Can't Resist.

- Make a surprising statement. Bold promises or guarantees can work well: If you don't agree my granola bar tastes great, I'll buy you three of the competing brand's. Also good are statements apparently against self-interest, such as, for example, Why You Should Never Shop at My Store.

Use attention-grabbing visuals. A great visual not only catches the eye, it excites and motivates. If appropriate, include images related to sex, food, or danger. Also, consider using faces. (Just make sure you use them right, as we'll discuss later in this chapter.)

For best results, your headline, visual, and call to action should reinforce each other.

Add a clear call to action *Tell* the visitor what to do, and make it obvious where and how to do it. Remove distractions. Make it clear *why* they should act: What's the payoff?

Blend with the site…to a point. People tend to ignore ads. So try not to look like an ad. Where possible, blend with the site.

But don't go too far. If you don't stand out, you'll risk blending in with the background noise. And if you deceive users and trick them into clicking, you will only succeed in angering them, and you'll pay for the click on top of it. Admittedly, this is a fine line to walk. Where to draw it will depend on things like the nature of your business and your target audience.

Don't lie…but remember the power of Might Be True. Avoid cheesy, clichéd promises like "You're a winner! Click here to claim your prize!" Blatant lies only serve to make you look like a scammer.

On the other hand, offers that might be true can invoke curiosity and therefore be very powerful—for example, Increase Sales By 25% Overnight, Or You Don't Pay. Again, it's a delicate balancing act, and the answer will depend on the situation.

Context: Ensure that your ad aligns with its destination. A great display ad is useless if the page it leads to appears disconnected or irrelevant. Make sure the destination page reflects the offer and content on your banner ad—and vice versa. Users need to know they've arrived in the right place… and what to do once they get there.

Try lots of implementations—test and test some more. Even for experts, it's hard to predict what will work well. So test lots of different messages and designs. Track the performance of each. And spend your marketing dollars based on actual performance.

Friday: Visual and Cognitive Psychology Concepts

Earlier we discussed some of the cognitive psychology research that you can learn from in the sections on maintaining scent and strong calls to action, but we've just scratched the surface. You can take advantage of discoveries by some of the greatest minds of the last century when designing your ads. There are entire volumes dedicated to these subjects, so we'll just address several highlights here, some of which we've adapted for the medium.

We all have different backgrounds, come from different cultures, hold our own views on the world, and have our own likes and dislikes. We focus on these differences because they are what make us unique and interesting. But that focus can exaggerate the level to which we are really unique. Research shows that much (in fact most) of the way our brains react and function is almost exactly alike and quite predictable. In fact, like it or not, we even share many of these traits with our more primitive relatives in the animal kingdom! In the following sections, we'll give some examples of these concepts and how we can utilize this knowledge.

Contrast

Contrast is one of the most important signals to our brains. Al Gore popularized Heinzmann's 1872 research that shows a frog immediately jumps out if placed in a pot of boiling water, but if the water temperature is raised slowly enough, the frog fatally overheats because it can't perceive the dangerous temperature shift.

Contrast is also important to our senses of sight and sound—both of which are important in display advertising. For example, if you look at Figure 7.15, you almost certainly see the white stone before you see the stone that is about three-quarters of the way up the page on the right hand side. For all our unique traits as individuals, our eyes are all drawn to the high-contrast object like moths to a fire!

ISTOCKPHOTO/WRAGG

Figure 7.15 One of these stones is not like the others.

This has obvious implications to us as image ad designers. The two most important may be how we are able to entice users to view our ad (that is, distract them from the other content) and then control what they see first in our ad. The contrast can influence what we see first, second, and so forth, even if the elements aren't in a traditional top-down, left-to-right layout.

The Beginning and the End

Another thing we humans tend to do is think of things in a bookended format. To illustrate this, think of the first car you ever drove. For Corey, it was a 1978 Mercury Zephyr that was known as the Hephyr.

Next, think of the most recent car that you have driven. For some of you, that may have only been a few hours ago.

Last, think of the fourth car that you ever drove. For most people, the first two are easy to recall and take you almost no time at all (Corey has tried to forget the Hephyr many times to no avail). But the fourth one, well.....that gets lost in the shuffle. Our brain tends to remember things in terms of the beginning and the end, and the middle details can get a little fuzzy.

So what does that have to do with image ads? Plenty. You see it's not just our memory that works that way but the way we process things visually as well. You may be familiar with a popular meme that includes this paragraph:

Note: Aoccdrnig to a rscheearch at Cmabrigde Uinervtisy, it deosn't mttaer in waht oredr the ltteers in a wrod are, the olny iprmoetnt tihng is taht the frist and lsat ltteer be at the rghit pclae. The rset can be a toatl mses and you can sitll raed it wouthit porbelm. Tihs is bcuseae the huamn mnid deos not raed ervey lteter by istlef, but the wrod as a wlohe.

There's little evidence this study ever happened at Cambridge, and the science behind it has been debated, but there is little doubt that you can read that nearly as fast as if it were spelled correctly. But if you removed the anchor points—the first and last letters—it would be much more difficult.

Order matters when it comes to how we see and process things, including ads and landing pages. At this point we can start to put several of these concepts together. The first thing we see sets the tone and determines if we'll continue down this scent trail. The last thing we see is how we'll remember the experience and the point where we decide whether to keep following this scent to the next hop or return to the hub. This is why the call to action is important at the end. We can influence the order in which things are viewed by carefully selecting the imagery, contrast, and white space.

The ideal process is as follows:

- To be visually enticed to the ad
- Be interested enough to read it
- Be intrigued/impressed enough to want to learn more
- Be motivated enough to heed the call to action

People Will Look at People (for Better or for Worse)

Just as we are hardwired to notice contrast changes, we humans have a built-in reaction to look at people, particularly at faces. If an ad or page contains a face, the majority of us will look at that first.

Advertisers can take advantage of this in a few ways. First and foremost is to get your ad noticed. Compare the simple creatives in Figure 7.16 and Figure 7.17. The implication of the imagery in both is clear: a phone call. But on a crowded page, the one with the face may be more likely to grab your attention and steer your eyes to the ad long enough to see that a free quote is just a phone call away.

Figure 7.16 The concept of the imagery is clear but may not attract the initial attention needed.

Figure 7.17 This operator suggests the same as the phone but is more likely to get noticed.

An attractive face may be desirable from a brand association point of view, but simple logic tells us that we must first look at it to make that judgment. So in that respect the mere presence of a face of any kind accomplishes the simplistic goal of attracting the user's initial focus.

In fact, in some cases including a graphical element that is too mesmerizing can actually work against our overall goals. The first goal of an ad is to distract the user from the other content on the page long enough for them to notice our ad. But we can't stop there because it's also important for the user to absorb the content of our ad and potentially follow through with our call to action. We're all probably familiar with the phenomenon of the Super Bowl ad that was highly entertaining, but no one remembers what the *product* was or even what *company* sponsored the commercial. In that case, the advertiser's goal of brand lift (let alone any type of direct response) is unachieved because the viewer, while entertained, has no association of the ad with the advertiser.

The example in Figure 7.18 is based on research done by James Breeze.

Source: http://usableworld.com.au/2009/03/16/you-look-where-they-look/

He tracked people's eye movements as they viewed an ad. The target demographic is clearly a new parent, and more likely a mom. There is almost zero chance that when viewing that creative, the cute baby isn't one of the first things seen. But now that the baby has our attention, do we ever look at anything else? The deep coloration on the face indicates long, lingering looks at the baby's face, but the product, headline, and company logo get far less attention.

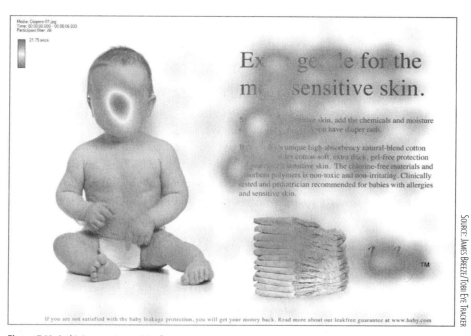

Media: Diapers-01.jpg
Time: 00:00:00.000 - 00:00:06.033
Participant filter: All

21.75 secs

Ex ge le for the m sensitive skin.

Figure 7.18 Is this imagery too enticing?

But all is not lost. There is another cognitive technique we can take advantage of to drastically change the performance: You look where I look. Magicians have known for centuries that humans naturally focus their attention where the performer is focusing theirs. So while we may lock ourselves in a staring contest with the baby looking directly at us, we have an entirely different reaction when the advertiser simply turns the baby. At that point, we ourselves become interested in what the baby is interested in, to the delight of the advertiser. Look at the amazing difference in the eye tracking heat map of Figure 7.19. Everything is exactly the same except that the baby has been turned to look directly at the text that tells us what the product is and what differentiates it. We still look at the baby of course, but then we move on to the other elements in the ad and overall spend more time in total looking at the ad. Notice that the baby is not looking down at the logo or product, but there is still a dramatic increase in the amount of eye focus sustained there, ostensibly because the copy has intrigued us enough to keep reading and taking in what the advertiser has to say.

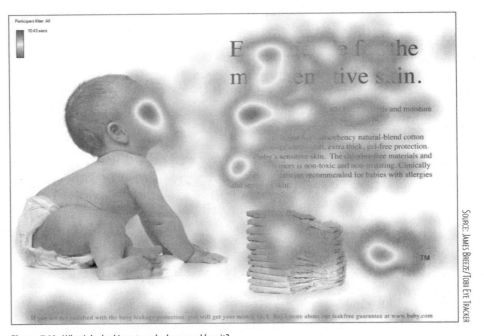

Figure 7.19 What's he looking at, and where can I buy it?

There are many well-known examples of this research spread across different industries. In the cosmetics industry, it's rare to see an ad of any type without an attractive model, so the image in Figure 7.20 isn't unusual. But the researchers at Bunnyfoot show in Figure 7.21 that by modifying the pose of the model to look toward the product, there is a vast improvement of the creative:

- Increased focus on the product

- Increased focus on the tagline/value proposition
- Increased focus on the brand logo at the bottom
- Longer overall time spent looking at the ad

(SOURCE: www.bunnyfoot.com/blog/2006/11/focusgroup_alternative)

Figure 7.20 A common cosmetics ad format

(SOURCE: www.bunnyfoot.com/blog/2006/11/focusgroup_alternative)

Figure 7.21 A simple change with a dramatic impact

Because rich media ads allow for more than a single static image, advertisers can actually combine these two concepts. Figure 7.22 first grabs and holds the viewer's attention with an attractive model. However, they don't want the viewer to be so mesmerized by the model that they forget about the product being advertised. So using the animation features of Flash, while the model has the viewer's attention she actually turns and points at the product headlines and call to action, ending with the scene in Figure 7.23.

Figure 7.22   Get the viewer's attention.

Figure 7.23   Then direct their attention to the call to action!

Tangibility

In online advertising, we often stress the need to make the benefits and value proposition clear in our ads. Consumers want to understand exactly what tangible benefits they'll receive if they do business with us. Image ads are a visual medium, and thus the creative lends itself to visual demonstrations of those tangible benefits.

Famous pitch man Billy Mays knew this was a key component of success. One of his first questions for any prospective product was not just whether the product worked, but whether it is demonstrable. Many of us recall the OxyClean ads showing the before-and-after pictures. The water was black and dirty prior to the product being used and clean and white after—a clear and tangible result.

But it's possible to have successful creatives with more subtle methods of showing tangibility than before-and-after tests. For example, there are three different versions of online ad creatives for wooden pet crates shown in Figure 7.24.

Figure 7.24 Good, better, and best

The first one, on the left, gives almost no indication of what the item is, so someone perusing a pet enthusiast website would have little reason to be interested. Is it a bank vault? Mausoleum? Who knows.

The picture in the middle makes it more clear what the basic function of the object is, but it doesn't satisfy all tangibility requirements that we need as a consumer. This crate sells for several hundred dollars, but I can get a plastic one from the local retailer for $20, so why would I pay so much more for this one?

The last photo makes that clear as well. Because this is more than just a pet crate—it's a piece of fine furniture. After all, you've spent thousands on your living room furnishings, why would you want a cheap, plastic crate to ruin the room when you can have this mahogany end table. The image that you choose in an ad can deliver your marketing message on many levels—make sure it's as effective as possible at demonstrating both what the item does for your potential customer and why they should choose it over the competition.

The Kindle is Amazon's most successful product ever, which is no small feat. And as you can imagine, a great deal of thought has gone into how to effectively market this product, which is only sold online. Its initial marketing was toward heavy readers who were comfortable with the traditional paperback book format. Previous interactions with digital screens most often came in the form of a laptop computer, which was awkward and unwieldy compared to a book. Amazon successfully addressed this concern in a subtle way by showing the device held in the same casual manner as a paperback. The imagery in the four creatives in Figure 7.25 simultaneously gives a sense of scale that can be difficult to achieve in online product photos and also provides a sense of familiarity for an active reader.

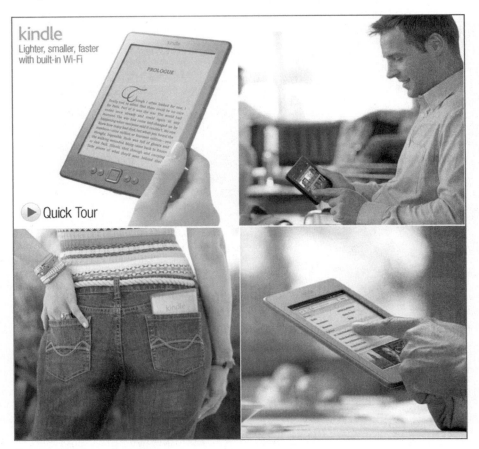

Figure 7.25 Subtle yet effective imagery

Ultimately, you want the imagery and supporting text in your creative to effectively communicate your value proposition and be the link from your marketing to the consumer's need. While your product or service may have several aspects, it's best to focus on one at a time in your creative to avoid clutter and effectively communicate the idea. For example, in the video projector market, there are lots of features you can compare, but the ad creative in Figure 7.26 with the taglines "If you have a problem, you can be 99.9% sure it's not plugged in" and the tongue-in-cheek warning that it must only be operated by persons aged 3 and up is very clear. Techno gadgets like projectors can be complicated and hard to use, but this one is apparently easy. That means when you've got an important presentation to give, you can focus on your ideas and not be scrambling around trying to figure out which input matches which resolution setting and so on. Ease of use is a tangible benefit indeed.

Figure 7.26 If ease of use is important, this ad hits home.

The ad in 7.27 for a competing project says nothing of ease of use but rather addresses another benefit entirely. The issue this projector was designed to address is weight. There is market demand for lightweight projectors, and this creative speaks directly to why this is such a problem. If you are a business traveler who can't stand the thought of adding even more weight to the litany of baggage you drag from meeting to meeting, city to city, then this image and tagline may speak volumes to you.

Sometimes the marketing department identifies a need in the marketplace and the engineers do a great job on the product. But it can all be for naught if the imagery and creative in the ad fail to communicate that value. You've already seen the example where a projector ad touted ease of use and the imagery suggested you didn't have to be a genius just to use it. So what does the imagery in Figure 7.28 say to you? Maybe you *do* have to be a genius to use it? Maybe smart people use it? Maybe it's that geniuses designed it? Actually, it's none of the above. The small print tells us that the imagery was trying to suggest that Einstein was bright…and so is the projector. No question that the brightness, measured in lumens, is an important differentiator among projectors. But does this ad really communicate that tangible benefit clearly?

Figure 7.27 If weight is the issue, this ad addresses it.

Figure 7.28 What does the genius in this ad say to you?

Week 14: Understand the Rules

Ground rules are never the fun part of the game, but because they can have a dramatic effect on the outcome, it's always worth devoting some time to them. Just as there are rules for text ads, such as how many characters a headline can have, there are rules for the images we can display. Each ad network and publisher has its own set of rules, although many are similar. The Interactive Advertising Bureau (IAB) has made progress toward industry standards that aim to achieve consistent terminology and even sizes and formats from one publisher to the next.

We don't try to provide an exhaustive list of publishers and networks here but focus on the IAB standards and the GDN because those are the standards and network most of you will start with. These rules also change extremely frequently, so it's worth checking from time to time to see if the rules for any particular set of available inventory have changed.

Monday: Supported Formats, Sizes, and File Sizes

Image ads can really mean a few different things—static images, animated images, and Flash animations (often with interactive elements). Flash in particular is interesting because it can easily bring sight, sound, and motion, which can blur the lines between an animated image ad and full-blown video. For the sake of categorization we stick to Flash ads in this chapter and devote Chapter 8 to true video-based ads and the ad formats traditionally associated with that format (pre-roll, post-roll, and so forth). But by no means do you have to adhere to rigid categories. In fact, some of the most effective ads integrate animation, video, and interactive elements all in one.

When a publisher decides to make inventory available, either through an ad network or directly to advertisers, it has to determine what formats it supports. The first decision here is about what sizes of ads fit in the layout of the publisher's pages. But it also has to determine whether to accept rich media and what file sizes to accept and make decisions about the other technical aspects pertaining to display ads. Generally speaking, advertisers don't want to have to recreate a new ad size for every possible placement, so there have been attempts to standardize the formats so that an ad can be created once and used multiple places. This is especially important on ad networks that may place an ad on any number of given sites. To attempt to put some standards around these sizes, the IAB's Ad Sizes Working Group has issued guidelines for marketers, agencies, and publishers to help streamline this process of creating, buying, and selling online media ads. These guidelines are voluntary; no one is legally or otherwise bound to use them. But because advertisers who target them will find a larger pool of inventory and publishers who offer them will find a larger pool of advertisers, it can be advantageous to abide by them. These guidelines, which define standardized Interactive Marketing Units (IMUs), are reviewed and updated twice per year as needed. The

GDN supports most, but not all, of these formats and a few more as well. Table 7.1 gives an overview of the currently supported formats for both the IAB and Google.

▶ **Table 7.1** Common ad units

Name	Size (W×H in pixels)	Supported standards and networks/publishers
Leaderboard	728×90	IAB/IMU, GDN
(Full) Banner	468×60	GDN (Retired from IAB)
Large Rectangle	336×280	GDN (Retired from IAB)
Half Page Ad	300×600	IAB/IMU
Medium Rectangle	300×250	IAB/IMU, GDN
Mobile Leaderboard	300×50	GDN
Square	250×250	GDN (Retired from IAB)
Small Square	200×200	GDN
Rectangle	180×150	IAB/IMU
Wide Skyscraper	160×600	IAB/IMU, GDN
Skyscraper	120×600	GDN (Retired from IAB)
Button 2	120×60	IAB/IMU
Micro Bar	88×31	IAB/IMU

The IAB specifies a maximum initial download file weight of 40 KB for all ads except for the Button 2, which is 20 KB, and the Micro Bar, which is 10 KB. Google is more generous at 50 KB for all sizes

For animated ads, the maximum animation time specified by the IAB is 15 seconds, but Google allows 30 seconds. Animated GIF ads on the GDN must have a frame rate of no faster than 5 frames per second (fps).

IAB Creative Specs Database

Keeping track of which publishers and networks support which formats can be tedious and time consuming. To combat this, the IAB has created the Creative Specs Database:

> www.iab.net/sites/creativespecs/

Here you can find detailed specs that include not just sizes, times, and file weights, but also maximum FPS, expandable size specs, whether third-party tags and tracking are accepted, how early the creative needs to be delivered, whether sound is allowed, and more.

Unfortunately this data is only good if it's up to date, and despite a mandate to update the database within 72 hours of a change, some publishers are better than others about keeping to that promise, so *caveat emptor*!

Future IAB formats: Rising Stars

This industry changes rapidly and it's not realistic to expect ad formats to remain stagnant. To address this, the IAB also has a list of ad formats known as Rising Stars, which are ad units that are designed specifically to push the envelope and spur creativity with large canvas, brand-friendly units. Gone are the days where display advertising is restricted to small, simple, or meek banner ads that politely sit alongside the primary content. These Rising Stars are interactive and are generally much larger than a normal display ad. They have dynamic content that often will even shift the other content on the page away in favor of the ad.

This normally would be considered quite invasive and unpleasant for the user, but these ads are designed to be very media rich so that they become a source of content themselves, not just the ad that sits beside the real content. One analogy is that of a movie trailer, which in some ways is just another commercial but is actually different. Despite their commercial nature, they are also entertaining and captivating so that people often actively seek them out.

The video at the following location introduces the formats with examples. It does a good job of showing why an advertiser might be interested and the extent to which the new formats transform the page and provide novel levels of interactivity:

```
http://bit.ly/iabrisingstars
```

The current crop of Rising Stars is outlined in Table 7.2 with official IAB descriptions. These formats are transitioned to the IAB Standard Ad Units list following six months of testing.

▶ **Table 7.2** IAB Rising Stars

IAB Name	Description	Why they were selected
IAB Portrait	300×1050 canvas format with state-of-the-art plug-and-play functionality.	Large, creative friendly canvas that balances well with page content.
IAB Slider	Overlay unit on the bottom of a page mirrors touch screen habit, prompting users to slide the entire page over, unveiling a full branded experience.	Optimal creative space keeping viewer fully in control of ad experience.
IAB Billboard	Large billboard running the full width of the page with full close-ability.	Love It or Leave It value exchange with viewer. If they don't love the large creative, they can close it.
IAB Filmstrip	A 300×3000 canvas, viewable through a 300×600 window and fully controlled by viewer.	Richly engaging experience with tons of content possibilities delivered in page with users fully in control.

IAB Name	Description	Why they were selected
IAB Pushdown	A push-down unit with broad functionality via visual toolbar.	Super rich functionality, elegant layout, and intuitive visual toolbar.
IAB Sidekick	Expandable format that launches from IAB standard ad, pushing page content leftward, revealing large, functional canvas.	Large canvas with myriad creative possibilities delivered without affecting page content and leaving viewer in charge.

Tuesday: Flash Ad Requirements

Flash ads allow far greater possibilities than simple static images or even animated GIFs. They can combine animations, interactivity, dynamically generated content, and more. But with these extra capabilities comes a more comprehensive and technical set of rules, which generally require a greater level of technical sophistication.

Each network has its own requirements and features it allows, but networks generally fall in the same categories, so we use the GDN as the example here.

All image dimensions indicated previously are accepted in Flash format, with the exception of the 300×50 Mobile Leaderboard. The 50 KB file weight still applies for Flash-based ads, except for on YouTube, which we discuss in Chapter 8, "Month 5: Video Ads."

The Flash ads must be designed and published for Flash Player versions 4 through 10 and ActionScript versions 1 through 3.

Some of the more complex rules are about the code that must be implemented for click tracking. Flash ads must support the clickTAG code, which was originally created by Adobe. This has become the de facto standard and is supported by every major ad network. The clickTAG is the tracking code assigned by the network (Google in this case) to the individual ad. This allows the network to track where the ad was displayed and when it was clicked, which is reported back to the advertisers to provide data on the effectiveness of their ads.

Fortunately, for someone with the technical ability to design Flash ads, this is relatively simple to implement. The code cannot be modified and varies slightly depending on which version of Flash you are targeting. The code will redirect any click to the URL specified in the clickTAG argument. It's important to note that you should *not* replace the "http:" in the script with an actual link because this is merely to specify the HTTP protocol and is correct as written. It's also important that you maintain the proper case (TAG is uppercase while the rest is lowercase) and don't input any extra spaces.

For ActionScript 2 it is as follows:

```
on (release) {
  if (clickTAG.substr(0,5) == "http:") {
```

```
      getURL(clickTAG, "_blank");
      }
   }
```

For ActionScript 3, use the following:

```
import flash.events.MouseEvent;
import flash.net.URLRequest;
// ......
someButton_or_displayObject_to_receive_mouseClick.addEventListener(
   MouseEvent.CLICK,
   function(event: MouseEvent) : void {
   flash.net.navigateToURL(new URLRequest( root.loaderInfo.parameters.
clickTAG), "_blank");
   }
   );
```

In the ActionScript 3 code, replace `SomeButton_or_displayObject_to_receive_` `mouseClick` with the actual name of the button that receives the click.

Once your ad is complete, you should upload it into your campaigns and verify that it's working as expected before going live. Some ads may require additional tweaking, such as prepending `_level0.` or `_root.` to `clickTAG`, to work properly, which is another reason to test first.

Implementing clickTAG

You can find more implementation details for clickTAG on the official Adobe Rich Media Tracking page:

http://www.adobe.com/resources/richmedia/tracking/designers_guide/

Google also has additional rules about what you cannot do and inspects each ad to ensure compliance with the following restrictions:

- The tracking of certain user behavior that does not specifically involve clicks, such as tracking view-throughs, key-modifiers, and mouse location, is not permitted.

- No extra server calls are permitted because all functionality for the ad must be localized to the code uploaded with the ad.

- You cannot implement tracking bypasses to change the behavior of the ad or bypass the AdWords redirect URL.

- Destination changes that would open the destination URL within the iFrame of the ad itself are also not permitted.

- Only audio that is user initiated may be played.

- Any cursor changes must be kept within the ad and either be auto-disabled after 5 seconds or revertible by the user.

- No code that randomly generates numbers may be used.

- No disruptive behaviors, which Google defines as being "designed or coded to circumvent the basic and usual AdWords flow. This includes (but is not limited to) the ad being displayed normally to users, Google registering the impression, and a click directing the user to the destination URL indicated by the advertiser in their AdWords account."

Wednesday: Editorial and Graphical Requirements

With many people ads have a reputation of being a necessary evil. People often tolerate commercial ads to support the real content. But Google believes strongly that ads are information and that if the right ads are delivered to the right user at the right time, they will actually be considered valuable. So relevance is obviously key to that notion, but Google also wants to make sure the overall experience is one that will keep users coming back and, above all, keep trusting Google. To protect this trust, Google has fairly strict editorial guidelines that go far beyond the image dimensions and file sizes, and it actually evaluates the message and claims of the ads it will allow.

These policies fall into the broad bucket of user experience. The primary goal is to remove the negative connotation around the interaction users have with commercial advertising and turning it into something that is effective, engaging, and useful.

Correct grammar, spelling, and text must be used while following standard form for phrases and sentences. We normally think of such rules in the context of text ads, which are often more strictly enforced in that format, but all of these rules apply to text in images as well. Even things like verb tense and subject-verb agreement can be enforced, although there are exceptions for commonly accepted misspellings, abbreviations, idiomatic phrases, and phrases with obvious puns. All u txt'rs m@y B upset 2 find that gimmicky punctuation as well as unnecessary or excessive numbers, letters, and symbols are disallowed. In fact, entire words can't be repeated unnecessarily, so the claim that your tax software is easy, easy, easy may run afoul of the guidelines.

Spacing and capitalization are also regulated, so attempts to M A K E   Y O U R   A D   S T A N D   O U T with irregular spacing or excessive capitalization will be disallowed. Exceptions are made for trademarks, such as its very own camel-case letter *w* in *AdWords* as well as acronyms like MADD, phone numbers, coupon codes, and currencies.

Click-to-play video ads (not instream/InVideo) are limited to 4 minutes and cannot loop or replay. The initial image and video must be considered relevant to the site the ad is advertising, and all images and text must be clear and legible (no blurry, unclear, or unrecognizable images or video can be used). Some advertisers have tried to use strange effects to draw attention, such as not occupying the entire frame, making the ad appear sideways or upside down, or even containing multiple copies of itself, but all of these are banned.

Thursday: Content Guidelines and Family Status

Google believes that maintaining its users' trust by delivering a safe and secure experience is paramount. As such, it takes an aggressive stance against any ads or advertisers it feels are not contributing to a safe user experiences.

User Deception

First and foremost, advertisers must not use the ads as a way to deceive the user into doing something they wouldn't want to do. Phishing attempts to steal users' personal information by disguising a site to look like another (legit) site. If Google detects this, a number of measures will be taken, including everything from disabling the ads to preventing new accounts from being created.

That is pretty black and white, and hopefully none of our readers would ever engage in such tactics! But one that's a shade of gray for some advertisers is the rule against inaccurate claims. For example, you may believe that your product allows your clients to lose lots of weight in a very short time without exercising. But Google may feel your ads don't accurately convey realistic expectations to users and disable them, especially if you don't have a disclaimer clearly visible on the page that indicates these results are not typical and may vary. Google isn't shy about its editorial voice, and it indicates that if you want to use its network to reach your audience, you must play by its rules. Currently that means for the weight loss category, it will accept only ads that claim weight loss over a period of time through a combination of healthy dieting and exercise. These rules also cover claims that you can fall in love or get married outrageously quickly, ads for cars that run on water, false celebrity endorsements, and ads for anything that is scientifically impossible.

User Safety

In addition to the claims just mentioned, there are several categories of prohibited claims around user safety. Miracle cures, uncertified online pharmacies, and other products or services that claim benefits beyond the realm of modern medicine are not permitted.

Sites must not contain illegal content or even contain content on products identified to be illegal. This is one of several rules that address both the ads themselves and the landing pages, which we will discuss in the next section.

Also disallowed are ads that sell free items, such as government forms that are offered for free to the public. This also applies to sites charging fees for otherwise free software as well sites that offer to sell AdWords coupons. Misleading claims about government affiliation or endorsement and false groups created to solicit donations are also not allowed.

Information harvesting that captures personally identifiable information must clearly state how it will be used. Billing practices must also be clear and not deceptive. Google goes beyond just its own editorial staff's opinion; if the advertiser has a low online reputation according to user reviews, it can be disabled based on that as well.

Financial services and income generation campaigns are heavily scrutinized. Get-rich-quick schemes and multilevel marketing programs that offer promises of large financial gain in exchange for low amounts of effort are not allowed. Work-from-home positions must clearly state the job description and not exaggerate the opportunity. Standard disclaimers required by local laws to protect and inform consumers about financial services must be in place.

Accurate Ads

If ads are to truly be considered valuable information by the user, then truth in advertising is important and Google takes ad accuracy seriously. Any ads deemed to be misleading, inaccurate, or deceitful will be disabled. Ads and keywords must directly relate to the product or service being advertised and advertisers.

Superlatives are where most marketers run into trouble. We all believe our services to be the best, but that claim has to be backed up. Claims like #1 must all be verified by a third party unrelated to your organization and clearly displayed on the landing page. And no, user reviews don't count! An example of an acceptable third-party verification of best be could *Consumer Reports* or the Best of the Web list from *Forbes*.

A close cousin of the superlatives is a competitive claim that states or implies that your product is superior to your competitor's. Any of these types of claims in the ad text must be easily located on your landing page or the ads could be disabled. The need for third-party verification is less stringent here, and a clear analysis comparing your product to the competition or even a chart outlining features or prices may qualify.

Free and discounted offers must be clearly and accurately displayed as soon as the user reaches your site (no more than 1 to 2 clicks). Prices quoted must be accurate and guarantees and warranties must clearly state any major limitations.

Ads that try to trick or prey on less-savvy users are not allowed. An example of this is ad text that tries to simulate an email inbox or social media notification. Generally speaking, your ad and landing page must make it clear what it is you are offering. Even ads that aren't intending to be misleading may be blocked for poor grammar or sentence construction. Google gives a humorous example of an ad that would be blocked for simply being confusing:

Ad Words, Word Ads
We are the words that
ad the world. Advertise!
adwords.google.com

Call-to-action phrases designed to inflate the clicks or that could apply generically to any ad (regardless of content) are not allowed. This specifically covers phrases such as *click here* or even *See this site*. Google also specifically prohibits ads that attempt to influence its social search program called Google+. Advertisers cannot encourage users to *Click +1* or *+1 our site*. Incentives to +1 the site, such as free items or discounts in exchange for these social interactions, are also prohibited.

Ads that imply affiliation, partnership, or relationships must have explicit authorization, particularly if that affiliation is used to gain credibility. For example, a Google Certified Partner can claim that status, but someone cannot promote a video as recommended by Google just because it's hosted on YouTube. Along these lines, any URL displayed must match the actual URL the ad sends the user to, so you don't get to display a link to Amazon.com and then send them to SuzysDiscountSuperStore.com!

Legal Concerns

Trademark laws vary from country to country, and Google puts the responsibility of complying with these trademark laws on the advertiser. However, that doesn't mean it has no policies or editorial guidelines about the subject. As a courtesy, it investigates trademark claims on behalf of the trademark owner for ads (but not for organic search). The owner must provide proof of ownership for the terms in question and subsequently the advertiser will need to provide proof of its authorization to use those terms.

And Now A Word From Our Attorney...

We are not lawyers, and this is not intended to be legal advice. While we can give some general guidelines, if you have any questions about the law as it relates to your area and your business, you are advised to consult an attorney with knowledge of your local laws.

Google has relaxed the trademark policy for ad content in recent years. In some cases, the advertisers may not be the trademark owner but still have a legitimate reason to display the trademark. For example, if you are authorized to sell Nike shoes, then you have a legitimate reason to use the word *Nike* and show the Nike shoes that you sell in your ad, even though you are not actually the Nike Corporation or trademark holder.

Bidding on a Competitor's Trademark

Most questions from marketers regarding trademarks come up when they are attempting to bid on a competitor or they are upset that a competitor is bidding on them. It's important to note that the rules regarding trademarks, generally speaking, cover ad content but do not cover bid terms. So while a competitor cannot represent themselves as your business, there is nothing stopping them from bidding on your trademarks as keywords. Their ad would then be displayed when someone searches on your trademarked terms. This is generally allowed as long as it's clear their ad is for their business and not yours. Publishers concerned about showing ads for their competitors on their sites can specifically choose to block advertisements for those sites of concern.

Just as with trademarks, Google makes the advertiser responsible for complying with local laws regarding the advertisement and sale of restricted items. However, there are some guidelines and rules. Drugs, weapons, alcohol, gambling, tobacco, fireworks, and endangered species have various restrictions associated with them. Counterfeit goods are not eligible for ads. For a full and current list of restricted products, see this page:

```
http://adwords.google.com/support/aw/bin/static.py?hl=en&topic=1310883&guide
=1308252&page=guide.cs
```

Values and the Google Brand

There is also a bit of a catch-all that covers campaigns that Google deems not to be in the interest of users and considers spam. This rule simply states, "Advertisers cannot exploit the system for financial gain." Some would argue that vague language could cover the majority of advertising, but Google specifically uses it to combat things like automated ad clicking, auto-created template sites, arbitrage systems, and other programs it decides are not beneficial to the user.

Some policies aren't created to combat illegal products or even misleading ads but simply goods or services that Google or its business partners don't like or want to be associated with. Sites that help to cheat on an academic test or groups that promote violence or use gruesome imagery are not consistent with Google's brand values and cannot be advertised on its network.

More information on these brand values and other restrictions based on technical limitations may be found here:

```
http://adwords.google.com/support/aw/bin/static.py?hl=en&topic=1310885&guide
=1308259&page=guide.cs&answer=175902
```

Family Status

Some ads are not banned outright but can still be restricted from certain audiences due to the family status that it carries. When an ad is reviewed, it is categorized into one of three family statuses based on the ad and website content:

Approved

Approved (non-family)

Approved (adult)

Ads that are marked as *Approved* have the potential to be shown to any audience and syndicated across any partner networks.

Approved (non-family) and *Approved (adult)* are similar but slightly different. The former has adult-themed content about, for example, strip clubs, sexual enhancers, plastic surgery, abortion, and gambling, but the content isn't sexually explicit or doesn't include nudity. Neither type of content can be shown on partner sites that don't accept it, for users who have activated their Safe Search filter on Google, or in countries where it is prohibited by law. Note that general dating sites and contraception- and STD-related information is still theoretically considered family safe by Google, but in practice our clients have often had them categorized as non-family, so it pays to keep a close eye on ads with those topics.

Friday: Site-Level Guidelines

Many of the guidelines put forth for the Google Network don't apply to just the ad content but the site the ad links to as well.

Malware

Your ad content can be 100 percent valid, but if your site is infected with viruses, worms, Trojan horses, or any other malicious software (malware) or—worse yet—sells it, then your campaigns will be disabled. Many of you may be thinking, "Okay, but I'm an upstanding business and I would never infect my users with viruses or malware!" Of course you wouldn't. But those that profit from such nefarious activities don't use their own sites to transmit the malware—they use yours. They hack vulnerable sites and the owners never even realize it. Google doesn't want to be party to this unwitting spread of infections. Thus, it scans its advertisers' sites to look for the illicit code and prevent those sites from appearing in its ads or organic listings. The best information on how to protect yourself, or what to do if your site has been compromised, is to register with Google Webmaster Tools (www.google.com/webmasters/). That site has great information, and more important, you can request a diagnostic scan that will tell you if your site is hosting malware, which you may have been unaware of.

Transparency and Privacy

Beyond not infecting users with malware, transparency and privacy are the next rules site owners must consider. Google believes that users should be able to clearly understand who is advertising, what they are offering, and how their personal information will be treated.

If you're collecting a user's information for the purposes of bulk mailing or text messaging, such as for a newsletter, it must be in an opt-in format. This means the user must actively solicit to be included on the list and not opted in passively or by default.

Google also prohibits sites that actively seek user information when it's not clear how that personal info will be used or a clear privacy policy is not in place. Sites that solicit this info in exchange for a free gift, survey results, quiz results, or to access the primary site content are prohibited.

Billing practices must be clearly explained to users (beyond just a link) and provided *before* the checkout. Additionally, any site that collects sensitive information such as Social Security number, banking information, or credit card numbers must do so on a secure sever enabled with the Secure Sockets Layer (SSL) protocol.

Just as Google scrutinizes financial services claims in ad content, it requires your landing page and linked site to be free of practices that could be perceived as preying on the financially vulnerable. The website itself must also be free of get-rich-quick schemes and other exaggerated claims for obtaining a large income with low risk or minimal effort. Genuine job opportunities are accepted, including work-from-home positions, but the role and compensation structure must be realistic and clearly laid out.

Software Downloads

First and foremost, the user must not be tricked into installing any software. Any applications being installed must be accompanied by clear and upfront information about its primary function as well as any other major functionality. If the software changes the user's environment or experience, the user must be advised and the reasons for the change must be explained. If the software transmits personal information of any kind, it should be made clear to the user prior to transmission. The application must be easily removed or deleted and should not be bundled with other applications that don't meet these guidelines. Any violation will result in the domain being disabled or the account suspended.

Dubious Practices

Sites that utilize the Google Network to advertise must also follow the Google Webmaster Guidelines, which apply to all sites that wish to be listed on Google. These guidelines cover issues like stuffing pages with long lists of keywords to attract search engines but delivering a poor user experience. Cloaking is another prohibited practice; it's generally defined as delivering different content to users than to search engines.

Usually this is done for the purpose of tricking the search engines into displaying for popular searches results that otherwise wouldn't have a chance of ranking. Doorway pages, deceitful redirects, and hidden text are some other practices that will earn your domain an expulsion from Google. A full list of these guidelines can be found here:

www.google.com/support/webmasters/bin/answer.py?answer=35769

Resubmission Guidelines

If your ad has been disapproved, the first thing to do is check the stated reason by hovering over the dialog bubble icon. The reason will be a hyperlink that you can click to learn more about that particular policy.

Once you have corrected the problem, simply editing and saving the ad will be enough to have it submitted for reapproval. If the problem wasn't with the ad content but rather because your landing page violated one of the site guidelines, you can manually request a review via this link after the problem has been corrected:

http://adwords.google.com/support/aw/bin/request.py?contact_type=site_policy

If the violation was covered by one of the Webmaster Guidelines (malware, keyword stuffing, etc.), you will also want to submit a request for reconsideration via this link:

https://www.google.com/webmasters/tools/reconsideration

Week 15: Dig Deeper on Image Ads

There is a lot to consider when launching an image ad based campaign. Now we'll turn our attention on how to tailor our ad for specific audiences and consider the various mediums available in the format.

Monday: What You're Trying to Accomplish

It's tempting for those familiar with search marketing to think of display advertising as a generic broadcast where the advertiser casts a wide net and tries to create mass awareness and appeal. But as you saw in the previous chapter, well-optimized display campaigns can be extremely targeted and should always have specific audiences in mind. Furthermore the campaigns should have well-articulated and measurable goals, even in cases where the goal is branding and awareness.

> **Key Message**
>
> Ultimately, your only real goal is to deliver the right ad to the right person at precisely the right time to maximize your goals as advertisers.

For example, when you are remarketing to a specific user whom you've targeted because they abandoned your cart halfway through the checkout process, a generic ad creative isn't the best choice. A more effective ad would include a picture of the exact item they left in the cart along with a free shipping coupon to get them over the hump.

A person who is looking at hotels in Paris shouldn't be shown a generic stock travel photo of Hawaii. You want to take advantage of the mindset of that traveler and supplement their travel daydream with images of the Eiffel tower and quaint cafes. Beyond the imagery, your ad content addresses your goal. Is it to get them to come back and book a flight? If so, offer an incentive based on that purchase. Or perhaps they are still in the research stage, so a softer sell, such as a *Top 10 Can't Miss Cafes in Paris* list, will be more effective.

You can incorporate this same goal in other types of targeting as well. For example, you can assume that a user on ESPN has an interest in sports, which can inform your contextual as well as audience targeting strategy. A travel company can target a user who is geolocated to the East Coast but is viewing the San Diego Chargers game summary page on *Yahoo Sports* with a travel package that includes a hotel near the stadium.

In general, you always want to keep in mind the following questions:

Who is the audience?

What is their mindset?

Where are they in the buying funnel?

What do I want them to know?

What do I want them to do?

Tuesday: Image ads for E-Com, Lead Gen, B2B, and Non-Profit Scenarios

In Chapter 4, "Month 1: Planning Your Campaigns," we looked at how to determine goals and values for different types of organizations. Each goal should be paired with an ad creative that specifically addresses it. The imagery, the call to action, and targeting should all work together to achieve the individual advertising goals of those organizations.

E-Commerce

E-commerce transactions are the most intuitive examples because they are a natural fit for advertising and goal measurement. Figure 7.29 shows an ad that is appropriate for targeting a user who has an interest in outdoor equipment. The goal is clear from the SHOP NOW call to action, and while the imagery is all about outdoor gear, the messaging of the ad is about the transaction. A good candidate for this would be someone who had been browsing gear like this on the site but had not actually made the purchase. They have already shown themselves to be considering the purchase, and by offering the incentives and discounts, you may be able to convince them to come back and complete the sale. This type of remarketing is discussed further in Chapter 11.

Figure 7.29 A clear example of an ad designed to lead directly to a transaction.

Lead Generation

The websites of most businesses are not actually e-commerce stores that collect credit card payments over the internet. By far the most common type of site is one where the business is looking to begin a relationship with a potential new customer. In that case, the image ads should reflect that goal. Figure 7.30 shows an ad that is not looking to *sell* life insurance but merely to provide the service of a quote. Placing this ad on an article about the basics of life insurance would mean that many of the people who see the question "Looking for a life insurance quote?" would subconsciously answer affirmatively in their mind as they begin to read the rest of the ad. Someone looking for a life insurance quote is showing a clear interest in protecting their loved ones, and the imagery of a mother holding her daughter close on a park swing suggests just that. It has a clear call to action and reinforces it with the brand strength and credibility of New York Life.

Figure 7.30 The goal of the company is to sell life insurance, but the goal of this ad is to issue a quote.

Figure 7.30 was forthright about wanting to make contact with you, and issuing a quote would certainly require your information. Some ads for lead generation are more subtle. In Figure 7.31, you see an ad for an educational institution that simply invites you to LEARN MORE. When you click the ad, you see a landing page with some basic information, but the real focus of the page is a form to fill out so the company can send you more information and, of course, market to you much more aggressively.

Figure 7.31 The overt quote request in Figure 7.30 and this ad's more subtle invitation to learn have the same goal: to source a lead.

B2B

Business-to-business (B2B) advertising can be tougher when it comes to precision measurement of goals, but it's definitely not impossible. It just means more thought has to be given to identifying key milestones in the sales cycle.

Figure 7.32 shows a traditional goal of a B2B ad—a free trial. This is an important step in the process, and the ad clearly calls the user to that action. In case the user isn't quite ready for that step in the sales funnel and is still gathering basic research, the ad also provides links to further resources such as white papers, seminars, and newsletters. For those familiar with JMP but an older version, it also reinforces that the next iteration of the product is what's being advertised by prominent positioning and repetition of the number 9. There are even nine links!

Figure 7.32 A classic B2B ad

In Figure 7.33, Medscape is targeting medical professionals with a clear goal and call to action of downloading its iPhone app. Obviously it hopes the free app leads to purchases down the road, but right now the goal of the ad and the company is to get people to use their app.

Figure 7.33 An intermediate step in the sales cycle, but a clear goal and call to action

Corning has an interesting campaign related to demand generation in Figure 7.34. It sells plastic that is used to manufacture cell phones—a B2B transaction if there ever was one. But as like Intel did with its famous Intel Inside campaign, Corning is hoping to make consumers aware of this component that ultimately does have an effect on their lives (scratched screens are a drag!). The imagery is eye catching and far more interesting than a manufacturing component would suggest. And the goal isn't merely awareness but an actual app that will let you determine if your phone has this special glass.

Figure 7.34 The 800-pound gorilla of cell phone screens pulls off a challenging ad very well.

Wednesday: Choosing Static or Rich Media Ads

Static image banner ads have been the standby since the dawn of display advertising and have near universal acceptance. But as the technology and sophistication of the format have grown, there has been a definite shift to rich media ads for many advertisers.

First and foremost, the click-through rate (CTR) is significantly higher for rich media. One of the challenges of display advertising is to distract the user's attention from the primary content and toward your ad. Rich media does this very well. The sight, sound, and motion capabilities are more enticing than the aptly named static image. Those capabilities give the advertiser the ability to tell complex stories and provide an immersive user experience through the animation, words, sounds, and interactivity all within the ad itself.

In addition to better CTR, rich media ads have higher conversion rates and view-through rates as well. In fact, a study showed that not only are the CTRs about 500 percent higher, but those consumers are also more likely to take action after viewing rich media ads versus viewing static image ads.

Rich mobile ads tend to have a significantly higher interaction rate. This can create higher brand awareness and also capture inputs directly from users. They can also measure subtle interactions, such as percentage of impressions where users didn't click but hovered the cursor over an image for more than 1 second. Some studies find around 80 percent correlation between where the cursor is and where a user's eyes are, which can be a great indicator of whether users are focusing on an ad. Thus, it's no surprise that studies find rich media ads more effective at increasing brand awareness.

The interactivity also means that users can remain on the site and still experience the content. That's better for the publisher, but also the desire not to leave the site has been shown to be a major reason users hesitate to click a traditional ad.

However, static images are far from gone and do have a few advantages. They have smaller file sizes, which can be important on content where download speeds matter, such as mobile phones. Speaking of mobile devices, the predominant rich media format, Adobe Flash, does not run on any mobile device made by Apple, including the iPhone and iPad.

The rules for Flash-based rich media ads are more complex, as was covered earlier in the chapter. There are also significant technical barriers to entry to creating Flash based ads. While nearly any business can create a JPG image, a Flash programmer may be harder to come by. However, in week 16 later in this chapter, we show you a way to create a rich media ad with no Flash knowledge whatsoever!

Thursday: Importing Your Image Ads into AdWords

Importing existing ads into the AdWords interface is a relatively painless procedure once you have all of the creatives. When you have different sized images, each image must be uploaded individually and already sized exactly to fit the available dimensions as outlined earlier in this chapter. You must also ensure that Display Network is selected on the Networks And Devices screen for your campaign.

After you create an ad group, select Image Ad from the New Ad drop-down on the Ads tab. A screen similar to Figure 7.35 appears. Choose a file in one of the supported formats and sizes on the right side of the screen. Rich media ads in the Flash format (SWF) are uploaded through this same interface and procedure.

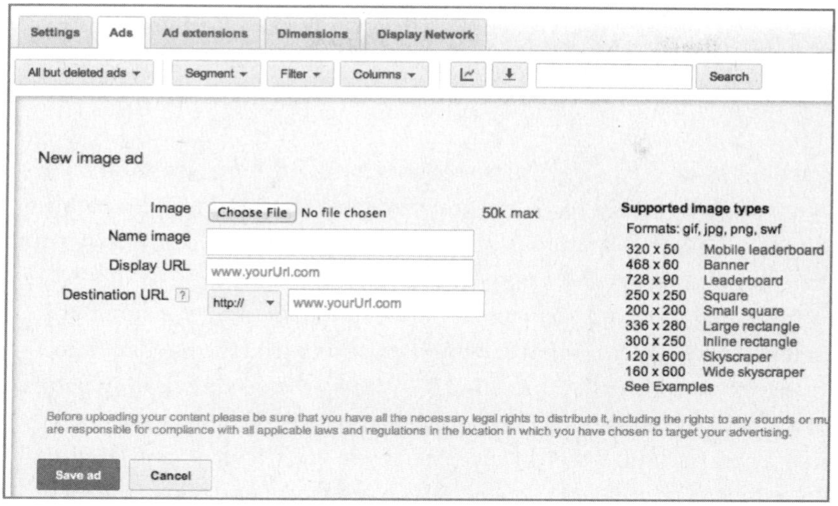

Figure 7.35 Uploading an image ad

Although a thumbnail appears when the upload is complete (except for an SWF file), provide a full description of the ad in the Name Image field because after you populate several ads, it's easy to get them confused. Google allows up to 50 characters for ad names. Indicate the image being used and what is different about the ad from the others, and even include the campaign and/or ad group in the name. It's important to think about not just managing ad inventory but also reading reports of how each ad creative performs. After you successfully upload the image, a line for the ad appears in the table of ads. You can click the preview link to ensure accuracy.

If the dimensions are incorrect or the file size is over 50 KB, the ad fails and returns an error. The system also checks to ensure that the guidelines outlined earlier in the chapter are adhered to. If you upload SWFs, this means you must support the clickTAG, as discussed in the Flash tracking requirements.

Friday: The Approval Process

As noted earlier in the chapter, Google has a fairly extensive set of editorial rules and policies. Each ad is reviewed for compliance with these policies and won't fully run on the Google Network until this evaluation is complete. Each time an ad is submitted or even edited, it is automatically added into the review queue.

The process takes about one to three business days, not including weekends and holidays. Image ads, video ads, and ads that target either Search Partners or the GDN can often take longer to get approved than pure text ads that target only Google Search. This happens because those formats cannot take advantage of the automated tools as easily and Google needs to be extra certain they are not distributing content to third-party sites in violation of the policies. Google makes money running your ads, so it does have a vested interest in getting your ads up and running as soon as possible.

Google reviews for not only the content and structure of the ads but also the account structure and linked website and landing page.

Statuses

As soon as you submit or edit an ad, it starts with an Under Review status and maintains it until it has been fully reviewed. It may also receive a temporary Eligible status that allows it to run on Google Search for users with SafeSearch turned off but not run on the Search Network or Display Network until further review.

An ad marked Disapproved has been reviewed and found to have issues that must be addressed before it can run again. You will be notified via the web interface and email when ads are disapproved. Since late 2011, Google started reviewing paused campaigns as well. The purpose is to enable campaigns to be turned on at a moment's notice and avoid approval delays. Keep this in mind if you create campaigns purely for testing purposes. Also, a notification on an old, abandoned campaign can be a bit surprising.

Ads can also be approved only for certain scenarios, such as adult, non-family, and limited.

Filters

By applying a filter to your account, you can see which ads are currently in which of the previously mentioned states. First select a campaign and choose the Ads tab (Figure 7.36). Choose Create Filter from the Filter drop-down and select Approval Status. Check the desired check boxes and click Apply to display a table of ads that match those statuses.

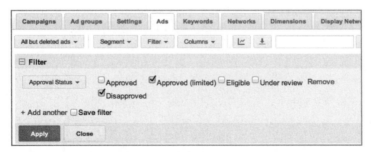

Figure 7.36 Filtering for a specific ad status

Because the rules can be somewhat vague at times, aggressive advertisers may be willing to test several ads that push the boundaries to see what they can get away with. This is generally not recommended for a couple of reasons, the first of which is that accounts that habitually incur ad rejections can be penalized, including a permanent suspension.

In addition, account users (not just the person who created the ad) will be notified of the disapproval. If your manager or your clients are on the account, they'll get a sternly worded email about the disapproval, which contains sentences such as *Repeated violations of our policies might result in your AdWords account getting permanently suspended.* An infrequent disapproval is nothing to be alarmed about, but receiving this email directly from Google multiple times has been known to cause clients or managers to doubt the competence of the staff managing the account.

Week 16: Build Ads with Display Ad Builder

Many advertisers who would normally use display advertising are discouraged because of the time and expense required to build the actual ad creative. The Display Ad Builder is a valuable template-based tool available from Google that allows you to easily create images or rich media for use within the Google Display Network.

Much of the time spent this week will not be in reading the text here but actually using the tool to experiment with new templates, apply different backgrounds, test new formats, and generally learn to maximize the tool.

Monday: Benefits and Drawbacks of the Display Ad Builder

One of the strengths of Google is making the difficult simple. As you saw earlier in the chapter, the technical skills and requirements for creating images and rich media ads far exceed those for text ads, where you simply have to be able to type. But with the Display Ad Builder, Google makes display ads almost as simple as just selecting a layout and typing. Even sophisticated interactive rich media built in Flash is created for you with no programming required.

Google provides templates that can be customized to varying degrees to allow you to make an attractive ad that is highly relevant to your specific business and website. These templates are optimized for the type of ad and include everything from direct response to embedded videos. Seasonal templates allow you to create ads that take advantage of the time of year.

Another major advantage of these templates is that by customizing a single creative, you can simultaneously generate several different sizes and formats. Normally, one of the most time-consuming parts of creating an ad is creating all the variations. Even skilled graphic artists have to manually adjust the imagery and text for each ad individually. This becomes even more of an issue when you move into interactive ads where the placement and movement of individual elements can vary. The ability to create this automatically for all formats is a major benefit of this tool.

There are, of course, limits to how far any template-based solution can take you. The interactive nature of rich media ads allows for nearly limitless possibilities and creativity beyond the relatively pedestrian options within the Display Ad Builder. Take, for example, the Prius ad in Figure 7.37, which allows you to draw your own picture of the sun right inside the ad. It then uses that user-drawn image within the ad as the source of solar rays streaming toward the car. An ad like this is simply impossible to create with a template-based gallery.

Figure 7.37 An interactive ad that contains a paintbrush program and incorporates the user drawing into the ad itself

However, the biggest drawback of using the tool is its popularity. Because there are a finite number of templates and a large demand for easy-to-build display ads, you have to work harder to make your ad unique. While many do, not all of the templates allow for full customizations. In the case where a background image is permanent, the look and feel of your ad may be so similar to others that it detracts from your brand identity. Later this week we show how to avoid these problems so you can take advantage of the tool and yet remain unique.

Tuesday: Browsing Your Options—Themes and Filters

The true power of the Display Ad Builder is in the over 200 templates and themes it offers. From eye catching to polished, seasonal to timeless, there are lots of options to use as a base on which to build your own ad. The base templates often include stock imagery and outlines where the headlines, text, and even product images can appear.

Templates are initially sorted by the featured sets, which include the following categories:

- Recently added
- Highest performing
- Frequently used
- Related to upcoming holidays

But their sheer popularity may lead to ubiquity. A second option is to sort by the highest click-through rate. This can be helpful for direct response ads that are specifically optimized for the included call to action, such as the one in Figure 7.38.

Figure 7.38 A base template designed around a call to action

Not all templates allow the background imagery to be changed, so in that scenario the theme may be predetermined. In that case, you'll want to filter by these themes to get the appropriate look and feel for your topic. Categories by industry include Entertainment, Financial, Retail, Technology, Travel, and Education.

Seasonality is another common way to view templates. You can sort by seasons, holidays, and even sports. And it's not just limited to Christmas, Mother's Day, and other common Western holidays; it also includes Chinese Double Ninth Festival, Respect for the Aged Day, and Raksha Bandhan. Keep in mind that new themes are launched all the time, particularly when it comes to seasonal ads.

Wednesday: Creating and Previewing an Ad

Begin building a display ad as you would any other ad by selecting the appropriate campaign and ad group. Select the Ads tab, click the New Ad button, and select Display Ad Builder from the menu.

The templates are listed, and clicking the headline of an individual template launches the customization wizard (Figure 7.39).

The build process is slightly different for each style of template, but one first step that is common across all is to assign a name. This name will not be shown to the user and should clearly distinguish this particular ad from any others in this ad group, campaign, and even account. The example in Figure 7.39 identifies the subject, the imagery, and the call to action. Keep in mind that you may need to distinguish these ads from others across the entire account because some reports combine different ad groups.

When specifying text, such as the headline or description, you can modify both the font and the color. In the case of templates with a button call to action, you can change the font and color for the button text as well as the background color of the button. Be careful with the length of lines of text because anything more than a few words overruns the allotted space and is not visible. Pay extra attention to this when checking previews of each ad format, particularly the tall thin ones where even three words may be too long.

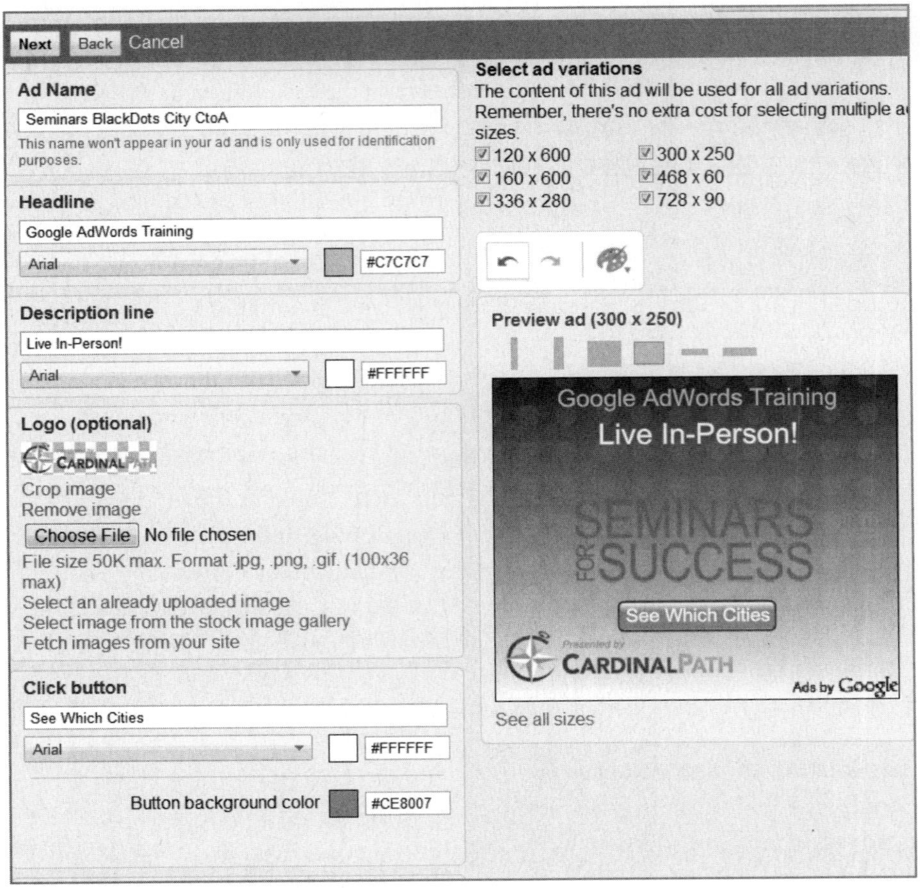

Figure 7.39 The Display Ad Builder wizard

This example has two images that can be applied—the mainstage image (Seminars for Success) and the logo in the bottom-left corner. These images can be uploaded from your computer or you can select an already uploaded image, select one from the gallery of stock photos, or even fetch one from your site. If you enter the main URL of the page on your site that hosts the image, the tool goes to that address and automatically pulls down all the images it finds. Alternatively, you can specify the exact URL of an image on your site.

It's important to set background colors and palettes that make your text stand out and fit your aesthetic and brand goals for the creative. In the case of Figure 7.39, the original background was too light, so the text across the top wasn't visible. When the background for the top half of the gradient is darkened, the light-colored text pops and is more legible due to the higher contrast.

The display URL and destination URL come next. They must follow the same basic rules as text ads for things such as tracking script redirects.

Note that changes can be undone by pressing Ctrl+Z or Command+Z, just as in a word processor or image editor. You can also use the undo/redo buttons above the image preview. Each of the six ad formats can be toggled by selecting the outlines above the ad preview.

Refreshing the Ad Preview

To preview the animation after changes, *do not* click the Refresh button on your browser! If you do so, you'll lose your edits thus far. Instead, hover the cursor over the top-left portion of the preview and click the small refresh icon that appears to see the animation from the beginning.

Clicking Next saves the ad, checks for initial editorial guideline issues, and moves you to the next step. The page that appears shows the final version of each ad format to preview in full size (Figure 7.40). You can select the check box for each of the sizes you wish to keep for this ad group and then click the Save Ad button.

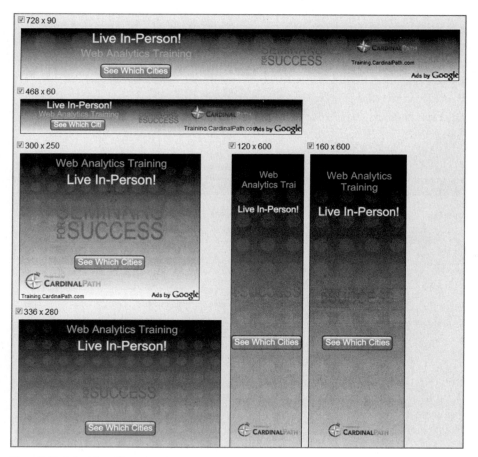

Figure 7.40 Each ad format is previewed.

At this point, each of the ads is created and it looks as if you uploaded the ads individually. The table of ads for the ad group gets an entry for each selected ad format. However, the system still treats them as a single ad based on that original source. In other words, if you edit an individual ad (for example, modify a headline), the edit applies to all of the ads in the set simultaneously.

Thursday: Advanced Ad Types

The Display Ad Builder is not limited to simple static image ads, but using the same simple process outlined in the previous section, you can also create sophisticated interactive ads. Because these ads would otherwise require far greater programming skills, the ability to create advanced ad types such as expandable ads, rotating product showcases, and mobile ads is a huge benefit of the tool. Video ads are also possible and are addressed in further detail in the next chapter.

Product Showcase

Several rich media templates that are designed to interactively display product photos and info are available. The one in Figure 7.41 has a rotating carousel of products that appear to float in space. To customize one of these templates, choose the Product Showcase link on the left-hand navigation and choose an appropriate template. Choose a photo and fill in the description and link; do the same for each photo. Because these images will overlap, it's strongly recommended that you use a transparent PNG image whenever possible. If that's not possible, set the background of the ad to match the background color of the images.

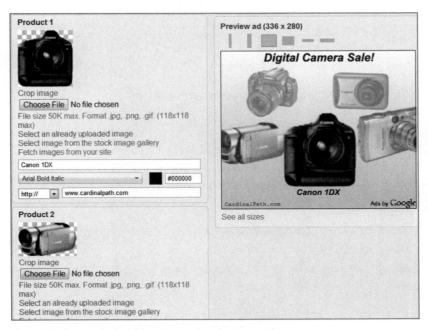

Figure 7.41 An example of an ad based on a product showcase template

Expandable Ads

Expandable ads are formats used across the GDN that allow the user to expand the ads to occupy a larger space and display more information without leaving the current page. Clicks to expand the ads do not count as clicks, and the advertiser is not charged unless the user actually continues on to the landing page by further clicking the expanded ad. An example of such an ad built via the Display Ad Builder is shown in both original and expanded form in Figure 7.42. Note that the button text changes in the expanded version as a click there will take you to the advertiser's site. To build an expandable ad, click the Expandables link on the left of the Display Ad Builder and choose one of the available templates. Because the different formats all change shape differently, it's especially important to preview these final ad formats before adding them to your account.

Figure 7.42 An ad prior to expansion and the same ad after expansion

Mobile

Mobile ads for Tier 1 phones, such as the iPhone and Android, can be created via the Display Ad Builder. For example, you can create a 300×50-pixel rich media mobile banner ad that cross-fades between two or more images that are uploaded by the advertiser. Because of the limited availability of Flash on mobile devices, avoid Flash ads when targeting mobile devices.

Friday: Tips For Creating Unique Ads

One downside of the popularity and ease of use of the Display Ad Builder is that a lot of advertisers are using the same templates. If you don't take the time to customize and make yours unique, your brand could suffer. Fortunately, there are some simple ways to take advantage of the power of the tool while still creating an ad that's one of a kind.

When choosing templates, you can sort the list by Most Popular. One quick suggestion is to continue to sort by Most Popular but click the right-most arrow, which will take you to the end of the list. These are the ads used least frequently by other AdWords users building their ads with this tool and therefore least likely to cause your ad to be a duplicate of another advertiser's ad. Make sure you like these templates because they may be unpopular for good reasons! However, many of these are actually very similar to the most popular templates. They often simply get overlooked because they don't appear near the front of the list and therefore don't get caught up in the self-fulfilling first page of the Most Popular list.

Some templates are more customizable than others. Some have background images or designs that cannot be changed. These are more likely to look the same regardless of the text each advertiser uses and should be avoided if that's a concern. Instead, choose one of the templates labeled as All Purpose, which are highly customizable.

The first place to begin is the often-overlooked box that is opened by clicking the painter's palette icon above the image preview (Figure 7.43). This will allow you to select an entirely different base color palette that can radically change the look and feel of your ad and match your own branding goals. Beyond the overall palette, each individual font style and color can be changed as well as the background color, right down to a specific RGB value.

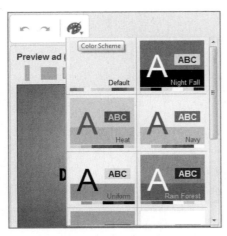

Figure 7.43 Using color schemes is an easy way to change your ad's look.

Your own images can and should be used to make your ad unique. Initial positions of the text and images are also not static, and these elements can move around the frame for a unique look. Figure 7.44 shows a base template on the left and a highly customized version of that same template on the right. The finished ad could never be recognized as coming from the original and is sure to look unique when compared to other ads based on that template.

Figure 7.44 Images, layout, fonts, and colors all combine to make your ads unique, even when they are based on a template.

Month 5: Video Ads

8

Television ads have long captivated audiences, but it's not so much the medium of television as it is the sight, sound, and motion of video. Video has moved beyond TV and is now being viewed online millions of times per day in innovative ways. In this chapter we discuss a few of the ways you can maximize the effectiveness of video for your business.

Chapter Contents:
Week 17: Understand AdWords Video Ads
Week 18: Create Video Ads
Week 19: Advertise on YouTube
Week 20: Advertise on Television with AdWords

Week 17: Understand AdWords Video Ads

While there are lots of avenues for video advertising on the Web, many of the larger sites require large ad buys or lack self-serve web interfaces for advertisers to place ads directly. However, through the Google Network, you can reach many of those destinations, including the world's largest video site (and second largest search engine of any kind)—YouTube.

The broad reach and easy self-serve interface make the Google AdWords Network a logical platform to begin our discussion of video ads. As you gain experience and hone your ads, the techniques and formats can be applied to other networks as well.

Monday: What They Are, Where They Show and When to Use Them

Video ads take several forms throughout the Internet, and even within Google there are a number of options that can be somewhat confusing at first. Some ads appear as standard static display ads and simply play video when clicked. Others are coupled with video content such as movies or online television episodes, such as the familiar pre-roll ads. Other video options allow us to overlay more traditional text and banners on top of video content. Google AdWords has recently consolidated its interface so that all of these options (including YouTube options) are available in one place and can be configured and managed alongside your traditional text and display ads.

Because of the rapid explosion in the use of video content and video-enabled devices, and the relatively high barrier of creating video ads (compared to text or image), there tend to be fewer ads competing for the inventory than with other media. Think of the level of customization of the ad creative in a search campaign or the display campaigns discussed throughout this book. The creatives are tailored to the audience, context, and landing pages. And in many cases multiple versions of the creative are tested for each of those combinations. Compare that to traditional television ads where a single spot is recorded and then used over and over—regardless of the audience, context, or call to action. The result is that viewers often get deluged with video ads that are not effective because they don't fit the wants and needs of the audience, resulting in wasted ad spend and viewer dissatisfaction.

Although video has traditionally been entirely focused on impressions, recently there is a distinct trend toward performance, interaction, and whether a visitor actively chose to view an ad or simply passively viewed it. For example, Hulu will charge only for ads that are viewed to 100 percent completion.

Google takes a similar approach via its TrueView format, which charges viewers only when they either actively choose to view the ad or watch the ad longer than 30 seconds (or to completion if less than 30 seconds). In addition, it not only takes advantage of a combination of higher precision targeting, it also provides the viewer with easy ways to choose to view the content they like and skip ads they don't. For this reason, direct response advertisers shouldn't necessarily shy away from video ads, but video ads do work best when some element of brand awareness is desired.

Video ads on the Google AdWords network show up on Google Display Network sites, YouTube search results, and within the videos, channels, and watch pages of YouTube Partners. YouTube Partners are content producers that enter a revenue-sharing deal with YouTube to monetize the content they post on YouTube via the ads Google displays.

Google has combined its older interface (known as AdWords Video Ads) with its newer YouTube-based section (known as AdWords for Video) for a one-stop shop. The traditional AdWords interface provides access to the rich-media-style video ads and the display ad builder, while the newer section hosts the TrueView ads and integrates YouTube fully into the AdWords interface. This new interface makes it much more convenient to manage these campaigns. Previously you had to do anything YouTube related directly within YouTube, but now both interfaces are hosted within the AdWords website. However, as you'll see throughout this chapter, some things are hosted within AdWords but aren't 100 percent integrated into the interface yet. We refer to features of both sections so you can manage both effectively.

Tuesday: Click-to-Play Video Ads

These are the more traditional video-based rich media ads that appear beside page content, as discussed in the previous Chapter 7, "Month 4: Creating Image Ads." Upon loading, they display a static image (known as a poster) and indicate to the user that there is video content available with the standard triangle Play button icon and progress bar along the bottom.

Similar to the new TrueView ads where advertisers only pay when users choose to view the ads, traditional click-to-play videos are also performance based. However, in this case advertisers aren't charged on the view itself, but only if the user clicks through from the ad to the final (offsite) landing page via a cost-per-click (CPC) model. In the cost-per-thousand-impressions (CPM) model, costs are based on impressions of the initial static image.

Google provides some templates that allow advertisers to create custom click-to-play ads via the display ad builder.

Wednesday: In-Stream and In-Slate Video Ads

In-stream and in-slate video ads are similar in format. They are not video ads that start as static images beside content but rather exist in the main window when someone is watching an online video. They generally either play before the content (pre-roll), play after the content (post-roll), or interrupt the content (commercial break) in the middle. This timing is generally up to the publisher.

In-Stream Ads

In-stream ads are the most common form and loaded automatically by the publisher before, during, or after video content. Google offers two variations of the in-stream format. The first is the older style (non-TrueView) that is available in the standard AdWords interface via the display ad builder as seen in Figure 8.1. It is available in a 15- or 30-second format and can utilize existing videos uploaded from your hard drive, existing YouTube videos, or ads created with SpotMixer.

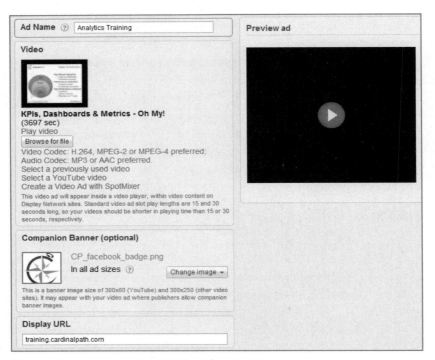

Figure 8.1 Creating an in-stream video ad in the display ad builder

The videos can also be accompanied on some GDN sites with a companion banner. This banner can be Flash or a static image, but the animation is limited to 15 seconds. For the publishers that show these, they are free and don't count as additional impressions.

Users cannot skip this form of ad, and if the viewer clicks the ad while it plays, their browser will automatically launch the ad's destination URL in a new browser window.

The newer TrueView in-stream ads are similar, but they offer users the option to skip the ad if it's not relevant to them. Advertisers are charged when a user views the video ad for 30 seconds (or ad completion if shorter than 30 seconds).

In-Slate Ads

Have you ever watched an online show on a site such as Hulu and been given the option of which ad you'd prefer to watch? The requirement to watch an ad may not be optional, but the viewer does get some choice in which ads they prefer to see. Other variations exist, such as the ability to swap out one ad for the other or to ask the user if they would rather watch a single (usually extended) ad upfront and then see the content uninterrupted or see shorter ads dispersed throughout the content in the form of commercial breaks.

Google's version of this technology is called the TrueView in-slate video ad format. These ads show before online video content that is 10 minutes or longer. Viewers can choose to watch one of three ads or see regular commercial breaks instead. The ads can appear only on YouTube video watch pages or on pages of video publishers who belong to the GDN. Because the ads are in the TrueView family, advertisers are charged only when the users choose to watch them. However, unlike some other ads in the TrueView family, in this format the choice is determined when users click to watch the ad, and the duration of time they watch the ad is not considered for billing purposes.

Thursday: InVideo Ads

Google's InVideo ads are different in that they are ads embedded in video content that streams from sites like YouTube, but they are not necessarily sourced from videos themselves. They are static images or Flash-based overlays that appear across the bottom 20 percent of the video window (Figure 8.2). The timing of their appearance is up to the publisher, and they are collapsible so viewers can hide or show them while they watch the video.

Figure 8.2 An ad for Visual Revenue overlays a streaming music video on YouTube.

When clicking on the ad, the viewer can be directed to an external landing page in a new browser window, a video ad within the video player, or in some cases an interactive Flash ad within the video player.

Friday: Evaluating Video Ads

Evaluating video ads follows a process that is similar to evaluating other rich media ads, except that you have to consider additional metrics and often additional branding goals as well. One approach is to evaluate how well each video is performing at each step of the interaction chain.

Impressions Are you targeting the right audiences and setting the proper budgets and bids to generate enough impressions to meet your goals?

Plays Are the impressions leading to plays? The exact metrics for this depend on the type of ad format chosen. However, the metrics provided for each format should give you an idea of how successful the ad is at piquing the user's interest enough to begin playing your content.

Completions Your ad may be successful at compelling a user to begin playing it, but then do they like what they see enough to continue watching? Do they complete the ad? At what point do they drop off? Later we'll discuss ways to evaluate how much of a video is viewed.

Generating awareness Even a performance-oriented video often provides some brand awareness benefit. Campaigns such as the Orabrush YouTube ads are the easiest to measure because their brand awareness is almost entirely due to their video ad presence. Are there increased searches noted on Google's Insights for Search? Are you seeing increased activity on social media channels, especially with respect to sharing of your video content?

Compelling call to action The exact call to action varies by format, but is the ad successful in that regard? For example, is the InVideo overlay driving visits to the landing page?

Bounce rate For those visitors who do visit the site after viewing your ads, are they staying or do they immediately leave? See Chapter 10, "Month 7: Optimizing the Performance of Your Campaigns," for more landing page optimization techniques.

Conversions For those who visit, do they convert? Note that conversions here may not happen immediately, and it's useful to track direct/immediate conversions as well as view-through conversions that occur within 30 days of viewing your video because some folks may choose to come back to the site at a later time. In some ways view-through conversions are even more interesting because they speak to the ability of your creative to leave a lasting impression on the viewer.

Reporting within AdWords

For video ads created within the older video ads interface (display ad builder), you use the same reporting interface as you did for other types of display ads. Figure 8.3 shows the Ads tab with the standard metrics of impressions, clicks, CTR, cost, conversions, view-through conversions, and so forth.

Keep in mind that the Free Clicks reports (Figure 8.4) can provide further insight into your video ads. Because video plays are not charged (only clicks to the landing page), these are considered free interactions by Google. You can also view how much of the ad was shown. Note that the website clicks metric applies only in the case of CPM-based bids. These are considered free because the cost is based on impressions and any clicks to the landing page resulting from those paid impressions are at no additional cost.

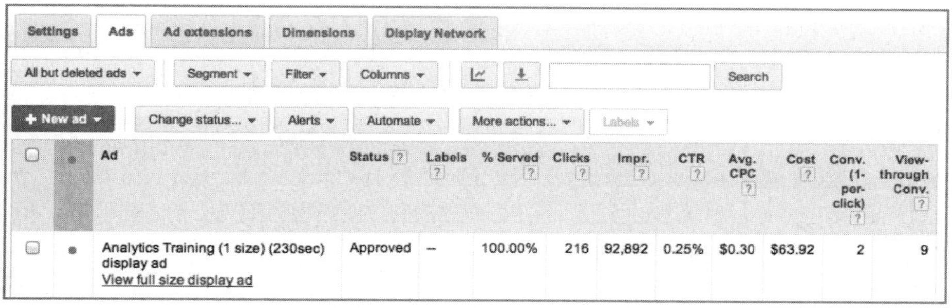

Figure 8.3 Evaluating video ads in the standard display ad interface

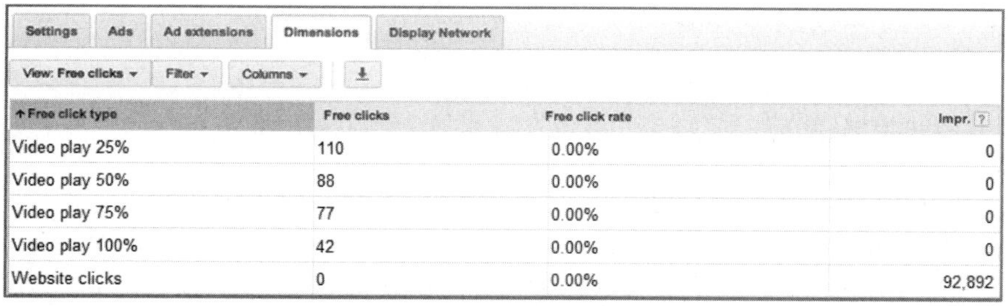

Figure 8.4 The Free Clicks report provides additional interaction information about your video ads.

Ads placed through the newer YouTube-based AdWords for Video interface provide richer metrics for the TrueView video ads. Get to these reports by clicking the All Video Campaigns link on the left-hand navigation, as in Figure 8.5.

In addition to the quartiles (similar to Figure 8.4), you can see views, view rates, sharing, and endorsement activity. You can also use the Ads tab to segment out your video by format (TrueView in-display, in-stream, in-search, and in-slate) as well as by network and by targeting group.

The Videos tab shows the combined stats from all your videos so you can see the total reach and performance in aggregate. The Targets tab allows you to view the performance of individual target groups. The View Rate metric here in these reports is synonymous with Play Rate from the display ads campaign section shown earlier.

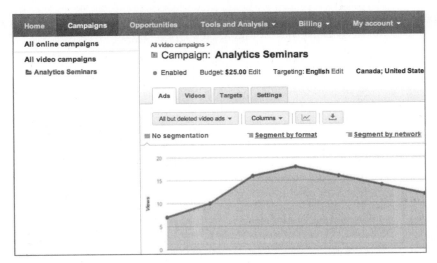

Figure 8.5 The newer YouTube-based AdWords for Video section

It's important to note that costs for your AdWords for Video (YouTube) campaigns does not appear within your campaign reports in the other display-ad-based interface. Campaign costs for these are visible here only within the All Video Campaigns section, but what you see in the Billing tab is the combined charges from both sections.

Week 18: Create Video Ads

There's no doubt that creating the video for this type of display ad is one of the biggest barriers. Just as image ads are more difficult than text ads and rich media ads are more difficult than image ads, video ads are often looked at as being the hardest of all to create. But that reputation may be overstated because the tools for both creation and distribution have come a long way. Consumer video cameras have enabled inexpensive HD video and YouTube plus AdWords makes distribution on a global scale easy enough that any business can get in the game.

Monday: Best Practices for Video Ads

Video used to mean one thing: TV. It was a purely mass market medium, but now with the explosion of user-generated content, social media, and interactive ads, the video-based advertising best practices have changed tremendously. The lure of viral campaigns has changed how we think about shareability, and better targeting means we need to think much more about engagement and personalization to encourage participation in our media. The passive model and a one-size-fits-all spray-and-pray approach is gone as users are no longer a captive audience. We now must ensure that our videos are interesting enough for them to *want* to watch. Google accurately points out that an effective ad has the right creative and hits the right audience at the right time.

Social

Is your content shareable? Does it inspire people to not only view it but want to make sure their friends view it as well? Ads can trigger this response in several ways. The most obvious is entertainment. Your ads should tell a story while appealing to the target user. This doesn't mean your videos have to follow the Super Bowl ad tendency of providing entertainment above all else. Some of the most effective ads are effective because they provide exactly the information the user is looking for, but they do so in an entertaining way, such as the ad for the Dollar Shave Club (`http://j.mp/ InfoAndHumor`).

Engagement

Is your ad enticing? With most of the modern available video formats, it's critical that you engage users immediately. Click-to-play ads don't autoplay, so they need an intriguing image or the user will never notice or care to click and watch the video in the first place. The poster image should be intriguing enough that the user will be curious to play the video and see what's on the other side.

Similarly, TrueView in-slate ads must be interesting enough that the user chooses your ad among the three to play before the primary content. Pre-roll in-stream ads must grab the user's attention in the first 5 seconds or they can be skipped, so don't bury the lead! This is not a captive audience, and advertisers are no longer allowed to force their videos on users. You must immediately convince them that your ad is worth continuing to watch. Engaging the user will increase participation, retention, and the emotional response to your product and brand.

Involvement

Historically, video has a tendency to be passive, but to fully optimize this digital channel you need to encourage your users to get involved in your brand and your business. A strong call to action is as important in video as it is in other display ads. Beyond the ad itself, things like blogs, contests, and newsletters all have the ability to continue the dialogue with the client. Make sure any interactive elements are simple and easy to use so you don't overwhelm or annoy users.

Targeting

The amazing thing about online video is that you can precisely target your audience. To the extent possible, you want to tailor your message to the audience for maximum effect. Just as in any other form of display advertising, you need to measure the performance of your creative with various audiences and optimize them continuously. Even if you can't easily modify your creative, you can increase your targeting of high-performing audiences, find look-alikes and expand your reach to similar audiences, and cut back or modify those that underperform.

Tuesday: The AdWords for Video Interface

It may seem intuitive that those wanting to buy video-based ads of all types on Google would do so through the AdWords interface, but that wasn't always the case. The AdWords for Video interface allows you to consolidate your video-based marketing in one place and greatly simplifies what used to be a cumbersome process. The new interface houses the TrueView ad formats, brings video-specific metrics, and links your YouTube account to your AdWords account.

However, the interface is actually a bit hidden. You must make it available by first creating a video ad campaign by selecting Online Video from the New Campaign drop-down, as seen in Figure 8.6.

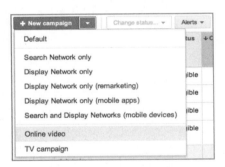

Figure 8.6 You have to hunt for the new AdWords for Video interface.

This will take you to the All Video Campaigns section on the left navigation panel and open the new campaign creation screen, which we discuss in detail in the next section. Next, on the bottom of the left navigation panel is the Linked YouTube Accounts link. Clicking this brings up the screen that lets you link your YouTube source files with the AdWords account. These are the video files hosted in the YouTube account you use when creating your ads.

You only have to go through these initial steps once to enable the interface. On subsequent visits, you use the left hand navigation to get back to the AdWords for Video interface. When logging into AdWords, you see the standard navigation panel but with the All Video Campaigns link appearing in the bottom on the left side. Clicking that link causes the All Online Campaigns section to collapse and the All Video Campaigns section to open, as on the right side of Figure 8.7.

Figure 8.7 Switching to the new All Video Campaigns interface via the left-hand navigation menu

Wednesday/Thursday: Creating a Campaign, Ad, and Targeting Group

When first enabling the interface you are prompted with forms that walk you through the process of creating a new campaign, ad, and targeting group all in one series of steps. On the first screen (Figure 8.8), provide a campaign name and daily budget. You can also set location and language targeting options for the campaign here. The estimated reach is shown next to each selection. Although targeted locations are originally countries, you can add cities, regions, or even zip codes. Use the Nearby link to help select custom regions. You can target by radius and easily add geographies that border the initial location. To make campaign management even easier, you can import settings to new campaigns from previous campaigns via the Load Settings button at the top of the screen.

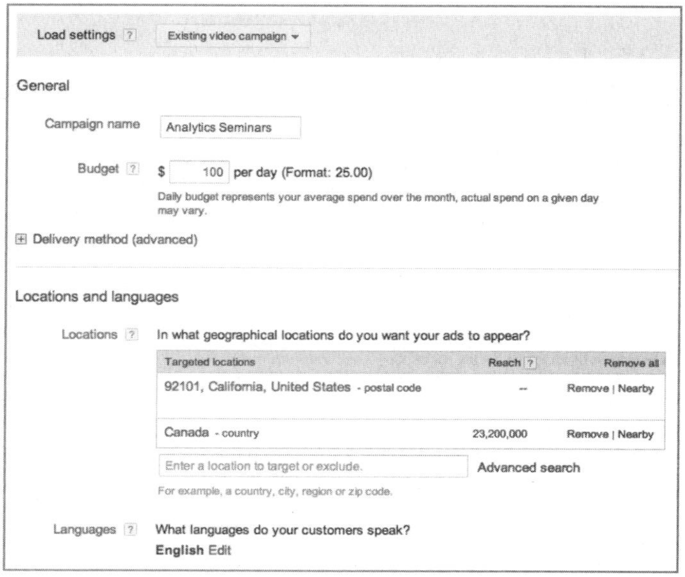

Figure 8.8 Setting up a new campaign

The next step is to create the ad itself. Begin by clicking the Select A Video button, which in turn brings up videos in the linked YouTube account. After selecting a video, you can let Google populate your video in all the available ad formats and networks or choose specific ones. In either case, preview each format to make sure it looks as intended (Figure 8.9).

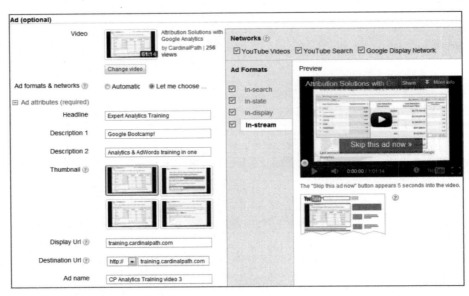

Figure 8.9 Selecting a video

The next step is to fill in the ad attributes, such as the headline, description, thumbnail, and URLs. If you have questions about how each of these elements is displayed in the various formats, click the question marks next to the fields. Advanced options are available, such as selecting a channel page or watch page as the YouTube destination (In-display and In-search ads) or choosing an image as a companion banner for In-stream ads. You can also select start and end dates, frequency capping, and ad rotation settings.

Click Continue to move to the bidding and targeting options. You can select either an overall max cost per view or different bids per format, which we recommend. Targeting options are fairly robust:

- Gender
- Age
- Topic targeting
- Interest targeting
- Manual placements: options for entire sites, portions of a site, specific YouTube channels, and specific YouTube videos

- Content keywords
- Search keywords

As you select targeting options, the Who Sees My Ad graphic on the right side of the screen updates to show the audience in real time. Each option narrows the audience, so if you select too many, your audience will be so small you won't achieve many impressions. Save your targeting group to complete the process for that ad.

Friday: Guest Lecture by Charlie Stone

Today we step aside and let you hear the perspective of a recognized expert. Charlie Stone is an award-winning producer and director. He is the founder of The Owned Agency. His tips on how to produce high-quality videos for your business appear in the sidebar "Slap Me for Good Videos."

Slap Me for Good Videos

BY CHARLIE STONE

As my granddaddy used to complain about the local newspaper, "...just cuz they own typewriters, don't make them Bill Shakespeares." Similarly, just because you own a fancy new video camera doesn't mean your videos will inspire Frank Coppola—or win new customers.

But if you want to create your own business videos, here are six quick tips to keep your audience awake, prevent them from feeling nauseated, and hopefully, inspire them to love you and buy your product.

Are you ready Lucaswan? Remember the following phrase: Slap Me. It stands for Steady, Lighting, Answer, People, Mics, Edit.

Steady Shaky video is the number one cause of vertigo, emesis, and dementia. Most people don't realize how fast they move the camera. Even small camera movements can cause big shakes. If you need to film handheld, stay frozen as a dead mouse. Literally. If you need to track motion, go super slow and pick a point on the subject and track it. But most important, invest in a tripod or unipod. Nothing expensive—just enough stability to prevent audience seizures.

Lighting Illuminate your subjects from the front—just enough light to highlight their faces. If you don't have a light kit, unscrew the lampshade of your wife's favorite lamp, turn it on its side, and direct the light to the subject using the shade. When filming outside, try to avoid direct sunlight by placing your subject in some shade but facing the direction of the sunlight. Remember, shadows on faces scare people—they will think you are selling derivative mortgages.

Answer Your video needs to finish the following sentence: "You must purchase our product or service because…" You have to fill in the "because." If you don't know the "because," you have bigger problems than learning how to shoot a video.

Continues

> ### Slap Me for Good Videos *(Continued)*
>
> **People** What people will you put in the video? Generally, articulate, attractive people will help sell your product. Don't be afraid to cast the genuine, sincere, attractive intern over the CEO who loves to say "at the end of the day" while putting insomniacs to sleep. The best company spokesperson is usually the person that everyone likes.
>
> **By the way, at the end of day, it's night.**
>
> **Mics** Sound is critical; bad sound implies bad content. Don't rely on camera mics to capture your sound. Invest in an external lavalier mic (the type local news anchors attach to their lovely ties) and plug it into your camera. Such a purchase may cost around $50, but the return will be immense—crisp, clear sound that is free of interference, unless there are jackhammers in the background.
>
> **Edit** Use iMovie or other simple editing software to select the best takes, add music, create simple titles and output to a variety of formats. Just remember: Avoid cheesy transitions like jaws wipes, cube spins, and page peels. They scream, "I have no impulse control." Also, keep your videos under 92 seconds. Fade in, provide "the answer," fade out, and leave them wanting more. Long videos are like overcaffeinated car salesmen—they won't stop talking, nor will they let you leave.
>
> If you follow the Slap Me tips, "God willing, and the creek don't rise" (another classic from my grand-daddy), your videos will inspire customers to clamor for your products and services.

Week 19: Advertise on YouTube

As always, the techniques and concepts here apply to the myriad of online video publishers. But our focus on YouTube isn't merely one of convenience: The video giant is nearly synonymous with self-serve online video. YouTube is the world's second largest search engine (Google is #1). It's also the third largest website in the world of any kind. It serves 3 billion videos a day to 800 million unique viewers per month. It hosts millions of publishers and reaches almost 90 percent of the online population. It has become a powerful business platform where existing brands can connect with their audience and many new companies have built their entire brands.

Monday: Advertising on YouTube

TV has long been known as an effective brand awareness builder, and online video is no different. A recent study found an average of a 20 percent increase in traffic to advertisers' websites based on online video ads.

YouTube is popular with businesses for several reasons, the first of which is that it offers tremendous reach. YouTube First Watch and home page ads can reach more than 20 million US viewers in a single day. But it also offers targeted options, and TrueView ads mean you pay only for engaged views rather than impressions. With this, Google is attempting to do with video what it has successfully done with web page ads—move the industry from an impression focus to a performance focus.

The first step to a successful YouTube campaign is to define your goals. One way is to evaluate the purpose of your ads based on the following categories:

Brand awareness YouTube is littered with examples of businesses that were simply unknown before their videos found a niche. One such example, Orabrush, has risen from the obscurity of a classroom marketing project to achieving over 48 million views of its brand channel. It has almost 190,000 people who have not only viewed its videos but actually subscribed to be notified when new videos launch. This ability for a video ad to personally connect with engaged users over an extended time is a brand manager's dream and unheard of in the TV model.

Product launch Even brands that are well known need to drive awareness when a new product launches. In the previous example we discussed how Orabrush became a known brand via YouTube. It then utilized its brand strength to launch a new product (tongue foam). Launching a new product can be risky for any entity, but with 190,000 subscribers to its brand channel, it becomes infinitely easier and has a higher likelihood of reaching Orabrush's target market.

Nissan is a well-known brand, but its Leaf is an entirely new product. It has uploaded several videos about the Leaf to YouTube, just two of which have received almost 4 million views. This kind of exposure helps this known brand bring awareness to its new product.

Direct response The online and interactive nature of YouTube ads means video is not just about awareness. A well-designed video can compel users to action. Whether this is to spur donations or sell products, YouTube has been shown to be an effective platform. One example, Rokenbok toys, was a pure brick-and-mortar company and now attributes a full 50 percent of its sales to its videos.

Reputation management Politicians and other organizations were some of the first to harness the power of YouTube to help shape public perception. These videos provide a fantastic vehicle to make sure your perspective is heard by your target market.

Audience Engagement One of the overlooked abilities of online video and the YouTube platform compared to passive formats like TV is the ability of users to comment, rate, subscribe, and share. Users can even record their own videos in response to yours, which further encourages community engagement. But it's worth noting that as with all social media, this carries a risk. If you enable these options, make sure you have thought through both the pros and cons of features such as user comments.

Once you have a goal in mind, it's time to focus on the creative. YouTube ads and videos for business can take many forms. The creative approach you take can vary widely and may include the following:

Informational videos These videos take many forms but ultimately serve the purpose of helping users understand your product or service. Product manuals for items that require assembly are notoriously hard to read and cause untold frustration with products and brands. Putting a video online of how to assemble your product can minimize returns, ease frustrations, increase product/brand satisfaction, and encourage social sharing.

Educational videos These are informational but not necessarily about your product specifically. Helping users understand a broader topic can lead them to inextricably tie your brand to that topic and lead to future business.

Sales videos Promotions and infomercial-style videos can be effective, particularly for users who are searching for information and are ready to buy.

Purely entertainment Some brands simply enjoy the goodwill associated with entertaining videos. On TV this approach is usually reserved for only the brands with the biggest ad budgets, but given the free video distribution of YouTube, many smaller brands have begun adopting this approach as well.

Tuesday: Channel and Call-to-Action Overlays

Savvy marketers can use free features beyond just video ads to maximize their brand's presence on YouTube.

Channels

While many YouTube pages have a familiar template feel to them, there are actually different kinds of channels that businesses can take advantage of. The user channels are the default. They are free and fairly basic.

Brand channels are also free, but they allow some customization of the images and the look and feel. They allow channel banners, a background image, and a branding box. You can also moderate (approve) comments left on your brand channel to encourage engagement without risking brand safety.

Brand channels also offer users the ability to subscribe, and videos played from within the channel will remain within the branded box. Metrics are available on the videos and also on the brand channel itself.

But you are not necessarily tied to a template at all. YouTube engineers can actually modify customized brand channels to have nearly unlimited modifications. However, large levels of engineering time usually accompany (and require) large ad spends to qualify. Custom brand channels also provide live streaming, user-generated submissions, gadgets, and other custom client services.

Call-to-Action Overlays

If you have AdWords for Video TrueView ads, you can now create overlays that apply to all video plays across YouTube. There is no extra cost and these are not dependent on the video being triggered by an ad, but they exist only as long as your ad campaign is running and are not a permanent part of your video as an annotation or caption would be.

They look similar to InVideo ads, but they start right away and are under your control. They can relay more information about the video itself or about your brand, your channel, or your website. When clicked, they can direct users to an external website. These are added by editing the video in the video manager.

Wednesday: TrueView In-Search and In-Display

These are video ad options that are available within AdWords for Video but were previously available only directly from YouTube.

TrueView In-Search Video Ads

In-search ads are similar to paid search ads, but they are in video results instead of web search results, as seen in Figure 8.10. Just like paid search, they can appear atop the other results or on the right-hand side. Advertisers are charged only when users click to watch their video.

Figure 8.10 In-search TrueView ads show up with video search results.

TrueView In-Display Video Ads

In-display ads are a combination of formats, including some legacy ones such as YouTube Promoted Videos, Promoted Video suggestions/related videos, and Google click-to-play video ads. They appear alongside other YouTube videos as they play in the watch page, such as in Figure 8.11. They can also appear on non-Google pages on GDN partners sites but still follow your targeting rules.

Thursday: Additional Tools

Earlier we looked at the targeting tools, which can tremendously improve the performance of your videos, but there are other tools that can help you target even more efficiently.

Figure 8.11 The top-right ad on this YouTube watch page is an in-display ad.

YouTube Keyword Tool

The keyword tool (`https://ads.youtube.com/keyword_tool`) can help you generate new keyword ideas and is similar to other keyword tools except it's specifically designed to work with the YouTube interface. It can accept base keywords and even derive its own related keywords from a video you supply.

You can add the keywords you select from the overall list to a running list that accumulates on the right-hand side. When you finish researching and are satisfied with your list, you can export to a number of formats and optionally include search volume metrics to assist in your targeting strategy. This is a great tool for in-search TrueView ads.

Placement Tool & Ad Planner

The Placement Tool helps to find relevant placements on YouTube. You can get this functionality by clicking Placements in the Display Ad tab and then clicking Change Display Targeting. Alternatively, you can use the Placement Tool (Figure 8.12) to find specific video placements on YouTube.

We also suggest that you use the Ad Planner because it has additional information on various placements, including TrueView formats and interesting information such as the duration of the target videos (Figure 8.13).

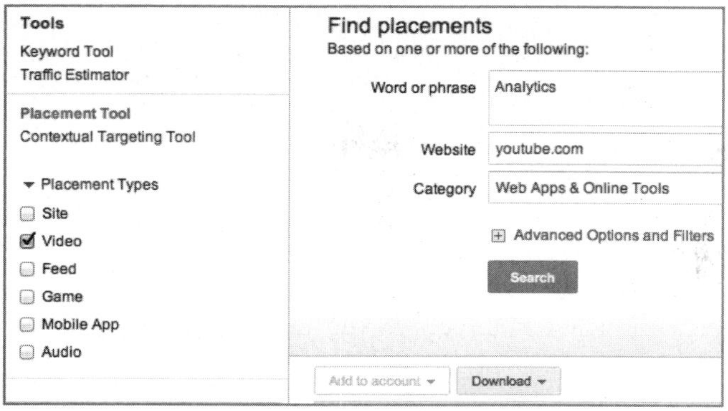

Figure 8.12 Finding placements in AdWords

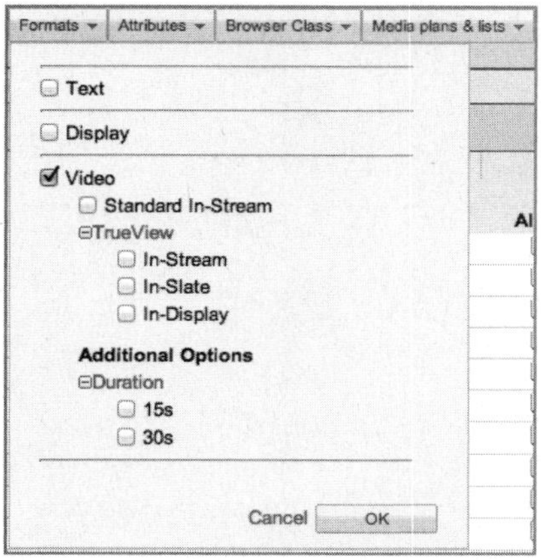

Figure 8.13 Ad Planner has advanced targeting options designed for YouTube placements.

Friday: YouTube Analytics

YouTube Analytics replaces the YouTube Insight reports with an improved and expanded interface. It provides unprecedented levels of reporting that can help you improve both your videos and the ads based upon them.

The reports are divided into two major sections: Views reports and Engagement reports (Figure 8.14). The Views reports provide insights on the following:

Views The most basic of metrics, but important nonetheless. Views are broken down over time as well as by geography. Did your video generate initial interest and then wane or did it slowly build up a following as word got out? Do different types of videos tend to follow different patterns of viewership?

Demographics Demographics are broken down by both gender and age. This can be very useful when determining your targeting options in AdWords. If you can determine that your video naturally appeals to a certain demographic, it can be an effective target for Video Ads. This info is also useful to measure whether your intended demographic responded as you originally hoped.

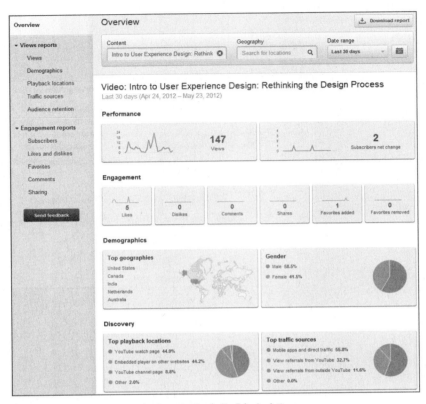

Figure 8.14 Overview reports and main navigation for YouTube Analytics

Playback Locations These reports are often overlooked but can shed critical insight on where your video was actually consumed. Did visitors come to your channel page first and then find the video, or was it the other way around? Do your users tend to view on their desktop computers or mobile devices? Was it via the standard watch page or did website authors decide to embed it on their pages to supplement their content? The individual pages that hosted your content can be found by clicking the Embedded Player On Other Websites link; it is some of the most important data of all.

Traffic Sources Marketers must spend time on these reports because they are some of the most information rich. They provide a wealth of targeting information because they show how people found your video. Clicking the YouTube Search link shows what the actual search terms were that resulted in your video, which helps optimize search targeting. Clicking the External Website link reveals which sites are linking into your video, and clicking Suggested Video reveals which video view preceded your video being viewed.

Audience Retention Unlike image or text ads, videos are consumed over a long period of time and users are notorious for not watching videos to completion. This slick report plays your video and shows second-by-second when people dropped out so you can understand how your pacing and scripting affected user retention.

The Engagement reports are as follows:

Subscribers Gaining subscribers is a major goal of YouTube marketers because it gives you the ability to get new content in front of users that have displayed an interest in your brand. These reports give you valuable insights into when, where, and how you gained subscribers.

Likes And Dislikes, Favorites You'd be hard-pressed to find a more clear visualization of how your users reacted to your content. Views are only part of the story—just because they viewed it doesn't mean they were satisfied. Analyze which videos generated likes, which geographies liked, disliked, or favorited your videos, and when they occurred.

Comments and Sharing Were users engaged enough to comment or share with their friends? If so, via which social media channels? Which videos?

Make sure you go beyond just casually viewing the overview graphs. The first step in any analysis is to segment in order to get past the aggregate numbers and into something you can actually use. Look for the unusual, such as a spike in views or engagement. Understand the trends—why do some videos spike and die in a viral fashion while others get consistent search traffic. Utilize days-of-the-week trends to determine a release schedule.

Use these reports to maximize your video ads. An interesting approach is to calculate the ratio of comments+sharing to views to understand which videos compelled a higher percentage of users to action. These often make for great ads because each view you drive is more likely to result in an engaged user. Obviously the same logic can be applied to subscribes, likes, and favorites. Understanding how the "free" (organic) traffic reacts to your videos is a great way to maximize your ad budget by understanding what works and doesn't work before you turn on the paid traffic.

Week 20: Advertise on Television with AdWords

YouTube and its brethren have caused many a pundit to predict the demise of TV advertising as we know it, but there is still a role for the broad reach of TV ads in many businesses. And Google is quietly changing TV ads in a way that is less obvious than the disruptive force of YouTube by doing the same thing it did with web advertising—making it more accessible to the masses.

In olden days, the only way to advertise globally in any medium was through a large agency's media buyers. Today we all know AdWords allows you to post text and display ads globally in less than 15 minutes with no external involvement. But Google has brought its direct-to-advertisers approach to TV as well, so national TV commercials are no longer out of reach for businesses with small ad budgets. These TV spots go right from your YouTube account and broadcast directly to the TV channels, and often for far less than you might think.

Monday: Is TV Advertising Right for You?

Television ads offer unique advantages, but make sure they match your needs before diving in.

Reach

The first question to ask before selecting an advertising medium is what are your goals? If maximum reach is a goal, TV can provide impressive reach and can allow your videos to reach people who may not watch them online.

Even for those that do see the videos online, two recent studies suggest that this overlap may be highly beneficial. CBS Media Labs found that when viewers saw video ads on multiple screens (for example, TV, computer, and mobile), they had more positive opinions about the brand. Another study, by Ipsos, found that viewers who watched ads on YouTube and TV had twice the recall of viewers who watched them on a single screen. The impact on the single-screen viewers was the same, whether the single screen was TV or YouTube.

Targeting

Google TV ads offer targeting tools that can select appropriate inventory based on demographics, psychographics, or interest targeting. Either Google automatically chooses the programs using set-top box data to determine which shows and networks are mostly likely to fit your targeting goals or you manually select networks, shows, and times.

One major limitation of targeting that stops many would-be TV advertisers is the inability to target by geography. Because the primary providers of the ads are national satellite providers instead of localized cable companies or over-the-air broadcasters, they are really only suited for brands or products with a national appeal. We have many clients who would love to have Google facilitate localized spots for their franchises, but there is not yet a simple way to do so effectively.

Measurement

We discuss measurement in greater detail on Friday, but Google carries its reputation for measurement and attribution to a medium that is normally considered very hard for both. Impression counts, audience composition, call attribution, and web attribution are all built in.

Cost, Control, Flexibility

Just as with TrueView ads on the Web, you pay only for ads that are watched for more than 5 seconds. If someone fast-forwards or changes the channel during your ads, you aren't charged. This performance-based pricing is in stark contrast to the usual potential/theoretical reach numbers used to sell TV spots.

You can also adjust your campaigns to optimize through the self-service interface, just as you would any other Google ad campaign. You can even tie your ad frequency to Google.com searches so that it senses when search volume increases and automatically starts showing your ads to take advantage of the trend.

Tuesday: Networks and Targeting

Google works with more than 100 TV networks, including ESPN, Bloomberg, CBS Sports, TNT, and CNN, to reach over 42 million US households. The ads are delivered via Dish Network, DIRECTV, Verizon FiOS, and ViaMedia and use those companies' set-top boxes for targeting, metrics, and impression data (since billing is per actual 5+ second impression). Each network, show, and even episode can be targeted with no minimum contract or bundling.

To choose the networks and other targeting options, create a new campaign and select TV Campaign from the drop-down. Click the Add Targets tab to select targets and build your campaign. Google offers the following three targeting options: Audience Search, Program Targeting, and Manual Network and Day Parting. You can select these options manually or automate with the campaign builder.

Audience Search

Figure 8.15 shows how to have Google find targets that match an audience, in this case those interested in technology and between the ages of 45 to 49. You can search by audience demographics such as gender, age, household income, and a list of predefined hobby and interest categories. The results are shown below along with some historical bids to give you an idea of relative cost. Select the programs of interest and click the Add button.

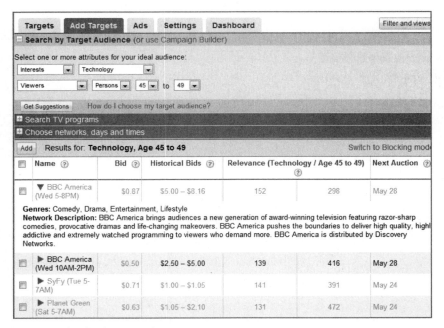

Figure 8.15 Searching by target audience

Program Targeting

This allows you to search for shows that are relevant to the keywords that represent your business, products, or audience interests. In the example in Figure 8.16, Google displays not only programs that match the keyword "horse racing" in the title, but also contextually related programs.

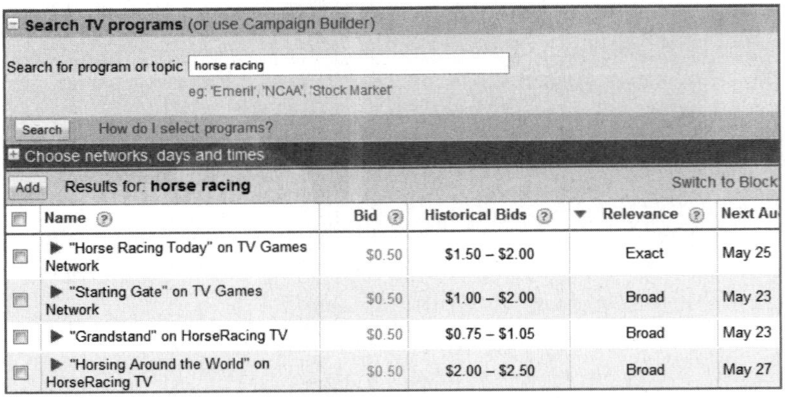

Name ⑦	Bid ⑦	Historical Bids ⑦	▼ Relevance ⑦	Next Au
▶ "Horse Racing Today" on TV Games Network	$0.50	$1.50 – $2.00	Exact	May 25
▶ "Starting Gate" on TV Games Network	$0.50	$1.00 – $2.00	Broad	May 23
▶ "Grandstand" on HorseRacing TV	$0.50	$0.75 – $1.05	Broad	May 23
▶ "Horsing Around the World" on HorseRacing TV	$0.50	$2.00 – $2.50	Broad	May 27

Figure 8.16 Targeting programs by keyword

Manual Network and Day Parting

If you already know which networks or programs are relevant to your business, you can simply select the networks, days, and times you want your ad to air through the intuitive scheduling interface. Figure 8.17 shows an example of a technology-focused network selection that will run on weekday evenings.

Wednesday: Creating Your Own Ads

Could it really be that easy (and cheap) to turn your video into an ad on national TV? Journalist Seth Stevenson simply didn't believe that for $100 he could put his homemade ad on TV and reach 100,000 people via Fox News (albeit in the early morning hours). But with a budget of $1,300, his quirky ad was shown 54 times on four national networks, reaching an actual audience of 1.3 million viewers. But beyond that, 1,000 of those people visited a website URL mentioned in the ad that was designed just for this experiment. You can read the humorous but illustrative article here:

www.slatev.com/video/how-i-ran-ad-fox-news/

As the article mentions, the toughest part of running a TV campaign used to be distribution. But as you saw yesterday in the YouTube section, distribution can now be made relatively easy. The toughest part now for many businesses is actually creating the ad. There is little doubt that a polished video does better in any medium, but the production quality on TV is generally very high, so in order to not compare unfavorably, it's worth putting some effort into planning your video.

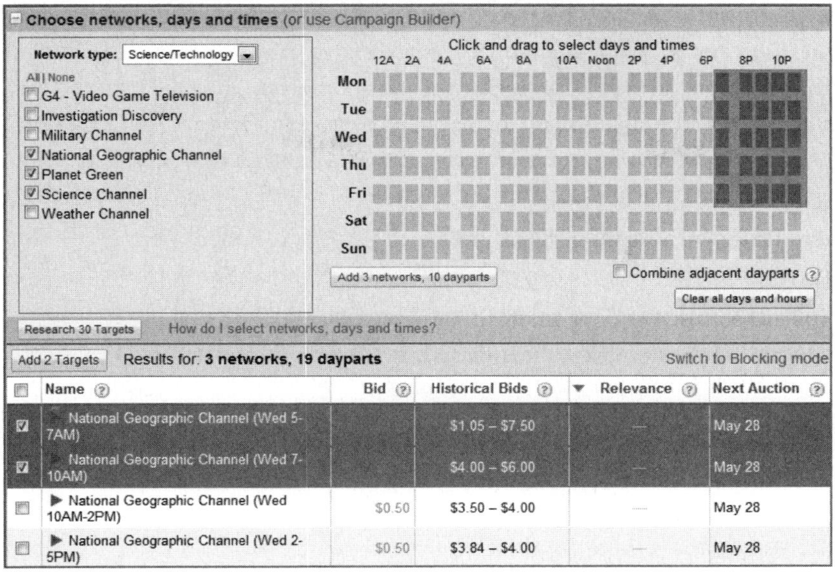

Figure 8.17 Manually selecting networks and times

Step 1: Plan: Set Goals and Strategy

Keeping the best practices discussed earlier in mind, you must plan your creative strategy. We suggest you don't just think about these things but actually write them out on paper.

Begin by defining your target audience in terms of age, gender, interests, and so on. Write out a product description of what it is you're advertising, including your value proposition to the audience. List all the reasons a member of your target audience should care about your business/product/service. You may find through this process that your target audience can be split into more segments because certain aspects of the product/service speak differently to different groups. For example, aviation enthusiasts may appreciate a product for its ease of use and low cost, while commercial pilots may appreciate that it has been certified by the FAA. Value propositions that speak to different groups may require their own specific videos targeted to that group, and by going through this process up front you can determine that before you begin.

Based on the creative strategy, pick one of the styles we discussed earlier (informative, sales, educational, etc.) and begin to develop the script. Due to the skippable formats and general lack of a captive audience, you *must* start the movie out with something that catches the audience's attention. Try to make your script memorable and differentiated. Don't forget to include a call to action at the end, either in script or overlay. Take the time to create an actual story board of the scenes, script, and editing.

Step 2: Action! Shoot and Edit

Review the tips from Charlie Stone earlier in the chapter on how to shoot successfully. In our experience, the two biggest things that amateur video shoots neglect is sound and lighting, and both are dead giveaways. A tripod and background that is free from distraction are also critical to success.

Consumers now have access to professional-quality editing tools that were once available only to high-end studios at great cost. Consumer-level software like iMovie and Adobe Premiere Elements can achieve great results, and even the next step up to the pro versions are still quite reasonably priced. Google also offers some basic editing for free inside the YouTube Editor (www.youtube.com/editor). One of the best things about this tool is the ability to choose a background soundtrack from YouTube's library of creative commons music. You can also add your own audio files, but be sure to never use copyrighted film or soundtracks in your videos because they can get rejected or even subject you to legal liability.

Step 3: Publish and Distribute

The first step is to ensure that your videos have been uploaded to your YouTube account library if you haven't already during the editing step. From there you can add annotations, descriptions, and other metadata.

Decide which distribution channels to use—YouTube brand channels and watch pages, video ads, TV ads, or some combination thereof. Follow the steps outlined earlier in this chapter to activate each of those options using your YouTube library as the storage and hosting for each.

Thursday: Outsourcing Ad Production

Cheap HD camcorders and editing software place video within the reach of many businesses, but this doesn't necessarily mean it's a good idea. Scripts, lighting, editing, and even makeup all have their own science, and the professionals make it look easy, but that doesn't mean it is. If your goal is to produce a video that projects a professional image or if you simply don't have the time or the desire, there are a number of options to outsource video production.

Ad Creation Marketplace

Google offers a way for people who need video production to obtain services from professionals who offer such services. You can browse through samples of their work to find a style that fits your needs as well as get an idea of what the services would cost and lead times. Visit the following website for an idea of how the marketplace works:

www.google.com/adwords/acm/

Freelance and Students

Portfolios are important for visual arts professionals, and many budding filmmakers are willing to create innovative, high-quality videos for a fraction of a what a full-scale production house would charge. Contact the film school at your local college or university to see if there is anyone who would be willing to take on the project. The now-famous Orabrush video was the result of a school project that launched both a successful brand and the careers of the students.

Friday: Measuring the Success of a Television Campaign

Television campaigns are notoriously hard to measure, especially compared to the high degree of precision we've come to expect from online campaigns. However, the integration with Google Analytics and the data from the millions of individual set-top boxes means that we do have more precise measurement options than you might expect.

Within 24 hours of your ads airing, you can log in and see reports that detail their performance, as shown in Figure 8.18. This includes data detailing the following metrics:

- Airings
- Billable impressions
- Average CPM
- Cost
- Overdelivery (delivered but not charged for)
- Calls attributed to the ads
- Website visits from URLs in the ads or searches resulting from them
- Networks, programs, and times that the spot aired
- Reach and frequency

Google Analytics can also integrate and overlay your TV ads data to help you understand how the ads are affecting your website visits. This can be particularly helpful if you use shortened/vanity URLs and campaign tagging as discussed in Chapter 9, "Month 6: Launch and Measure Your Campaign's Performance."

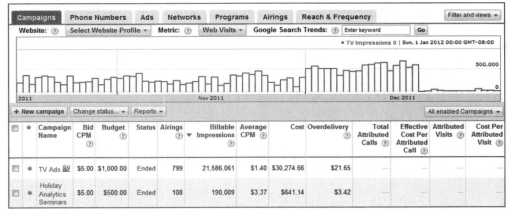

Figure 8.18 The amount of data available from the Google TV ads interface is one of its best features.

It can be important to make sure you are tracking and analyzing the most appropriate metrics. For example, Figure 8.19 shows an analytics report that overlays the TV ad impressions on website visits in Google Analytics. The client was trying to evaluate the effectiveness of the campaigns in driving site traffic.

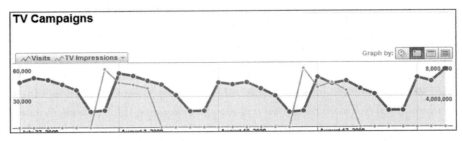

Figure 8.19 Google TV ad data overlaid on Google Analytics

As you can see, when the TV ad impressions (thin line) went up, there was a slight increase in site traffic. However, this was a very large, highly trafficked site, so the ability to "move the needle" on the overall site traffic was a tall order. Upon further inspection, we found that the TV ad was specifically advertising a new, important product on their site. When we compared TV impressions compared to conversions from that particular product, there was a very clear correlation: When the TV ads ran, conversion happened, and when they stopped running, the conversions went down (Figure 8.20). Google provides great data and tools for free, including web and call attribution, but it's critical that you plan your spots with this in mind and perform analysis that takes context into account.

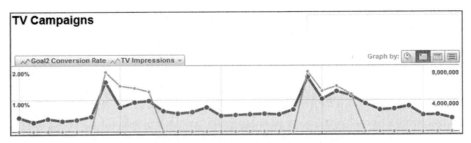

Figure 8.20 The thick line shows conversions from the specific product being advertised, while the thin line is TV ad impressions.

Month 6: Launch and Measure Your Campaign's Performance

The moment of truth has arrived. You've launched your campaigns and now the real work can begin! This month we look at how to measure campaign performance and set the stage for continuous optimization.

We examine best practices for using the built-in reporting tools of the advertising platform along with dedicated web analytics tools to understand exactly how your campaigns are performing and inform future advertising.

9

Chapter Contents:
Week 21: Launch the Campaign
Week 22: Use AdWords Reports
Week 23: Use Google Analytics
Week 24: Measure Branding and Positioning Goals

Week 21: Launch the Campaign

Hopefully, the day you launch your campaigns will be the worst ever in terms of how they perform. Through continuous refinement and optimization, you will constantly strive to improve the efficiency and effectiveness of your ads and get more value for your budget. However, most of the refinements and optimizations that we discuss in Chapter 10, "Month 7: Optimizing The Performance of Your Campaigns," rely on accurate data about the performance of the current campaigns. In this chapter, we look at what to measure and how to do it.

We use examples from the most common (and often free) platforms, such as Google AdWords and Google Analytics, but nearly all of the concepts apply to other platforms or measurement tools as well. The key is to understand the metrics, collect the data accurately, and be comfortable with how to use the reports and tools.

Monday: Setting a Benchmark by Taking Stock of Where You Currently Stand

The first thing you should do after you launch your campaigns is...nothing. Seriously. Although you are tempted to repeatedly hit Refresh waiting for the first results to come in, it's actually a great time to work through that backlog of email, catch up on industry news, or just catch a breather and take in a movie! Resist the urge to adjust your campaigns, because it takes time to get enough data into the account. However, this does assume that you already have data collection mechanisms such as a web analytics tool in place before you launch your campaigns. Even the data collection systems built into your ad network need additional configuration to be effective. Later in this chapter, we examine how to configure those tools and some specific reports to guide your analysis.

Before you launch your campaigns, you want an accurate understanding of your current site performance as a benchmark to evaluate the effects of your advertising. You should be familiar with basic, high-level site metrics such as these:

- Visitors: How many unique visitors does your site get each month? This is essentially attempting to count the reach or eyeballs. It's especially important for many display advertisers because the goal is often to expand reach and awareness.

- Visits: Similar to visitors, but instead of attempting to identify unique individuals, it counts every visit. So if 5 different people come to the site twice each, the visit count is 10.

- New versus returning visits: What percentage of visits over a given date range is by individuals that previously visited your site?

- Conversions/conversion rate: Visits and visitors are great, but it's critical to understand how well your current site and campaigns convert.

- Page views: Regardless of visits or unique visitors, how many total pages are loaded?

- Pages per visit: How many pages an average visitor views.

- Time on site: How much time an average visitor spends browsing your site.

- Bounce rate: What percentage of visits load the landing page but don't visit another page or click another link?

Tuesday: What to Expect and Do in Your First Week

The most important thing to do in the first week is to ensure that your measurement systems are working properly so you collect usable data. Because the first several weeks (and in some cases, months) are about amassing the data you need to optimize your campaigns, many savvy advertisers don't even consider the ad spend as part of the advertising budget. Instead, many of them consider it to be *market research*. And in some ways, it is the cheapest, most accurate market research you can get because it's *your* customers being shown *your* exact ads and sent to *your* site. It's not what people in a focus group might hypothetically do but rather what they *actually* do when shown your ads. This is invaluable data as you continue to build out and refine your campaigns, and the fact that you may get some paying customers out of it can be considered a bonus.

Of course, if you see huge red flags that are too big to ignore, you may need to correct them. While it's advisable to wait as long as possible and collect as much data as possible, you may have to stop the bleeding if it's particularly bad. But assuming it wasn't due to a typo or other genuine error, even drastically poorly performing ads shouldn't be considered a failure. Your hypothesis that they would work proved wrong, which is valuable marketing information.

How long to let the ads run and collect data depends on your account, and each is different. Accounts with more impressions and clicks obviously accumulate data faster. But it also depends on the number of ads and placements those clicks are spread across because each element has to generate enough impressions, clicks, and other data to be properly evaluated on an individual level.

So how much data is enough to determine performance? The answer depends on how *confident* you need to be in the accuracy. For example, an ad (Version A) that is shown to just two users and gets a single click has a CTR of 50 percent. But another version of the ad (Version B) shown to three users and clicked once has a CTR of just 33.3 percent. Can you conclude that Version A is vastly superior to Version B for CTR? Of course not. With one fewer click, Version A would have been at 0 percent CTR instead of 50 percent. There are not enough impressions or clicks to provide a reasonable level of confidence in the computed CTR. In the very beginning, the numbers fluctuate wildly (such as from 0 to 50 percent with one click), but you narrow in on the accurate result over time.

We address the idea of confidence intervals and levels in greater detail in Chapter 10, "Month 7: Optimizing the Performance of Your Campaigns," but for now, the more impressions, clicks, and conversions you accumulate, the more confidence you can have in the accuracy of your data. But you don't really need to know the underlying math in order to be confident in your data. To determine the exact confidence interval, you can use a simple online split testing calculator to do the math for you. We provide one here:

`www.cardinalpath.com/tools/ppc-ad-testing-tool/`

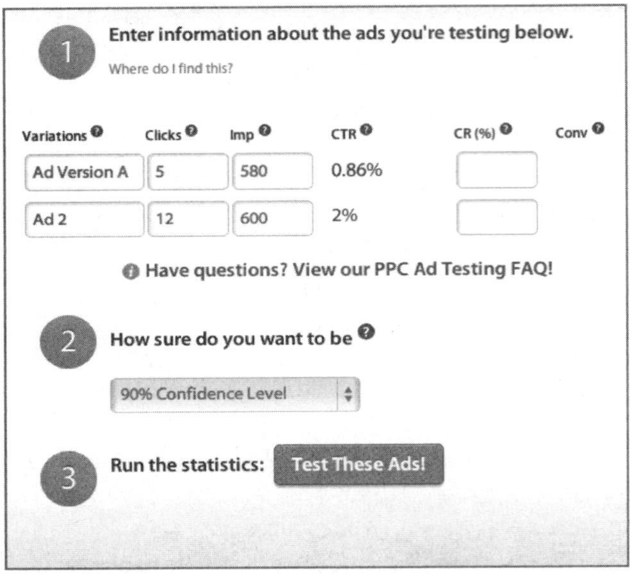

Figure 9.1 Using an online calculator to compare ads

Figure 9.1 shows two ads compared in that calculator. Version B has over twice as many clicks, but there isn't enough data to say with a 90 percent confidence level that Version B has a better CTR. But even if you get a massive number of impressions, clicks, and conversions in a short time, you still have to let it run for a while. A large number of impressions collected on Sunday evening still only represent the Sunday evening audience. The Monday morning, back-to-work audience may react completely differently, as might those interacting with your ads at 3 a.m. instead of 7 p.m. or on a holiday. Each day of the week is different, as is the last day of the month versus the middle of the month. To get the true picture of an ad, you need a true sample of the audience you're targeting, and that can take time to collect.

Wednesday: Getting Familiar with Reported Metrics

As you begin to evaluate your campaigns and the associated data, it's worth a quick discussion of the primary metrics that are reported via the ad network. The basic ad life-cycle progression is as follows. Display an ad impression to raise a user's interest and awareness. If successful, the ad gets a click, which results in a visit to the website and potentially a conversion event for direct-response-oriented sites. Each of these steps can be measured to help you understand any bottlenecks in the process. For this example, we use Google AdWords and start on the Campaigns tab. The table shows the campaigns and the metrics for each (Figure 9.2).

Campaign	Budget	Clicks ⑦	Impr.	CTR ⑦	Avg. CPC ⑦	Cost	Avg. Pos.	Conv. (1-per-click) ⑦	Cost / conv. (1-per-click) ⑦	Conv. rate (1-per-click) ⑦	View-through Conv. ⑦
Total - all campaigns	$3,376.00/day	1,564,133	105,152,444	1.49%	$0.62	$966,542.85	3.4	392,914	$2.46	25.16%	65,208
Caribbean Condos	$105.00/day	5,002	3,024,050	0.17%	$1.19	$5,961.11	1.3	1,498	$3.98	29.95%	18,638
Bahamas GDN	$150.00/day	18,087	12,465,962	0.15%	$1.16	$20,949.50	2.9	3,679	$5.69	20.34%	14,526
Caribbean Condos-Remrktng	$105.00/day	3,342	1,800,890	0.19%	$1.18	$3,933.74	1.2	1,158	$3.40	34.65%	14,096
Caribbean Cruises	$105.00/day	2,275	1,339,511	0.17%	$1.19	$2,711.33	1.2	750	$3.62	32.97%	12,514

Figure 9.2 Looking at campaign metrics in Google AdWords

To measure the first step, we look at *impressions*, which is how many times the ad was displayed to a user. Every impression is an opportunity for increased awareness of your organization and may generate a click. Measuring impressions helps us understand if we are targeting too broadly or narrowly and which ads are getting the heaviest rotation. Impression metrics are especially important for campaigns with a CPM model of payment.

The next metric of interest is how many *clicks* came from the ads in each campaign. The idea of a click is simple: an ad is displayed and a user clicks it, incrementing the count of clicks for that ad and its campaign. But the technical process of distributing, displaying, and processing clicks has several steps and can vary between networks. To provide uniformity of metrics, the Interactive Advertising Bureau (IAB) has defined a standard, which Google and many others follow, for when an ad network can count a click. When a user clicks the ad, the browser is sent to the ad network's servers, which redirect the user to the landing page. The ad network records the click when it issues the redirect. This means that if your ad contains an incorrect URL for the landing page and the user receives a 404/Not Found, the click is counted anyway. Visit http://j.mp/DisplayBook1 for more about this metric.

Every impression can generate a click, and the percentage of those that do is the *click-through rate* (CTR). An ad with 100 impressions that lead to five clicks has a 5 percent CTR.

Cost is the current running total cost for a given campaign or ad group. While important for budgeting, it's not terribly useful for analysis. For campaigns using the cost per click (CPC) model, *average CPC* indicates how much the average click costs. It is the total cost of all clicks divided by the total number of clicks in the campaign or ad group. This is important because while you control Max CPC, the Google AdWords auction model almost always leads to a different CPC. Avg CPC helps you understand the real costs, and thus performance, of your ad campaigns.

Conversions are of course a tremendously important metric. AdWords uses a conversion script to track every conversion that happens in a 30-day window after an ad is clicked. The default reported metric is conversions (1-per-click), which means that even if multiple conversions happen, AdWords counts only the first. There is an option to view many-per-click as well.

Cost per conversion (Cost/Conv) is the total cost divided by the total number of conversions. It is a critical metric that tells how much advertising money that conversion cost. It also accounts for all the misses where someone clicked and cost money but didn't convert.

Standard conversions tied to a click are relatively intuitive, but they don't tell the whole story and tend to undervalue the advertising. Especially display ads can raise awareness of your brand, product, or site. A user may not click immediately but may visit the site later through a direct visit or an organic search, and convert. This scenario, where a user views your ad but does *not* click and then later converts (for example, makes a purchase or fills out a lead form) is called a view-through conversion. Note that if the searcher later does an organic search and clicks a search ad, both ads are credited with the conversion, although you can prevent this through the de-duplication option in the Settings tab.

The overall Campaigns tab includes all of your campaigns across all networks. To see just the Display Network metrics click the Networks tab and select the campaign or ad group from the left navigation pane. Then click the Show Details link for each placement type (managed or automatic). The table expands to show the metrics for the selected segment.

Thursday: Calculating ROI

AdWords and paid search in general revolutionized the advertising world in a lot of ways. Just 15 years ago it was unheard of that any form of advertising could go from ad copy in someone's head to an ad being delivered to millions of people all over the world in less than 15 minutes. The delivery costs and efficiency have caused massive disruption in the advertising industry.

But the biggest change by far has been the accountability. Certain Google folks like to say that advertising in the past was a faith-based initiative. You paid your money for the magazine, billboard, or TV ad and just had to have faith that it was going to work. That is a huge leap of faith indeed. Online advertising brings infinitely greater ability to track the performance of the ads right down to who saw what ad, what they did, or even how much they spent.

You can tell exactly which campaigns are working, which creatives are working, which placements are working and, just as important, which aren't. One of the most enlightening and actionable things you can do is to examine the return on investment (ROI) of your campaigns. When you know the ROI, you can confidently manage your bids and even compare your online networks to your offline spend to make sure you're getting the most effective channel/media mix possible for your marketing dollar. Let's first talk about what we mean when we talk about measuring the ROI.

The first step is to understand your goal conversion rate. We talked earlier about defining goals and conversions, so let's start with a common direct response example, such as a product purchase. In this example, we have a shop that markets and sells handmade, organic knitted hats. If each hat sells for $50 and the total cost (except advertising) for the shop to get the hat into the customer's hands is $20, then the shop makes $30 profit on each sale.

price – cost = profit

$50 – $20 = $30

So when it comes to advertising, we can spend up to $30 to get a hat sold and still break even. So if the shop advertises via a cost per action (CPA) model, it can bid up to $30 and never lose money. However, most businesses don't just want to break even; they want to make money. So the CPA target needs some margin built in. In this example the goal is to make at least $10 profit on every hat, so the CPA target is up to $20 rather than $30.

total budget – minimum profit desired = available ad budget

$30 – $10 = $20

But many advertisers don't bid via the CPA model. The most popular model for direct response is where we set the maximum cost we're willing to pay for each click (max CPC). So to understand how that CPA translates into max CPC, we have to dig further. In AdWords or by using a web analytics tool, we find that for 100 clicks, 10 convert for a 10-percent conversion rate.

$$conversion\ rate = \frac{conversions}{clicks}$$

$$conversion\ rate = \frac{10}{100} = 10\%$$

This gives us one of the most important numbers for any bidding strategy, the value per click (VPC), which is the upper bound of the profitable CPA multiplied by the conversion rate, resulting in value per click.

$$value\ per\ click = max\ profitable\ cpa\ \times\ conversion\ rate$$

$$value\ per\ click = \$30 \times 10\% = \$3$$

In other words, because 1 of every 10 people who click our ads gives us $30, each of those clicks is worth $3. Therefore, if we pay $3 for every click, we just break even, and so it is the absolute max we can afford to pay for a click. Note that if you want to guarantee profit margin, you can adjust the Max Profitable CPA value.

Here are some things to keep in mind. People sometimes come back later, so when calculating conversion rates, make sure you use a large enough date range to cover your sales cycle. With Google AdWords it's 30 days by default.

Bake the best estimate you can into your cost. If you include only your wholesale costs (gross margin) and don't consider the other costs associated with your business, you don't represent the true cost of goods sold.

The max CPC is an upper bound. Usually you pay less. If you set your max per click at the VPC, it lets your ads compete in the auction at the highest price you can, but you still make money because the auction often doesn't reach that limit. That is a popular strategy but not without risk. Another strategy is to build a minimum margin into your bid price, so if you need a 20 percent margin, you adjust your bid to include that 20 percent.

Determining VPC helps ensure that you have a profitable bidding strategy, but after the campaign runs you want to calculate your actual return on investment (ROI) so you can see how your strategy played out and how much money you're making, if any!

$$roi = \frac{return - investment}{investment}$$

In other words:

$$roi = \frac{profit - cost}{cost}$$

We already calculated profit per hat earlier, so now we need to calculate the money we spent on advertising.

We can get everything we need from the Google AdWords or Google Analytics reports, so let's take a look at how our campaigns are performing from an ROI point of view.

Table 9.1 shows our campaigns and the number of times our ad has been shown for each one.

▶ **Table 9.1** Impressions Per Campaign

Campaign	Impressions
Unique gifts	1,330
Handmade	2,850
Ski gear	4,750
Baby shower	950
Organic hat	16,720
Newborn hat	12,350
Stocking stuffer	8,550

As you can see, the organic hat campaign is very popular and the newborn and stocking stuffer campaigns held their own. But of course this doesn't tell us much—it's just impressions. Maybe those popular ads didn't actually get users to take the next step. Let's look further at the data in Table 9.2.

▶ **Table 9.2** Clicks Per Campaign

Campaign	Impressions	Clicks	Clicks
Unique gifts	1,330	38	2.9%
Handmade	2,850	285	10.0%
Ski gear	4,750	380	8.0%
Baby shower	950	143	15.0%
Organic hat	16,720	665	4.0%
Newborn hat	12,350	570	4.6%
Stocking stuffer	8,550	190	2.2%

This changes things a bit. We can see that while handmade only got 2,850 impressions, it did generate a decent number of clicks. And while stocking stuffer got many more impressions, its CTR was poor, so those ads didn't convince many viewers to click.

CTR is clicks divided by impressions. You can see how useful this value is because it provides a quality context to the pure volume of the impressions. We can now see not only where the campaigns are shown, but also which of those attracts an audience intrigued enough to click.

The next item of interest to us is how much we paid for that traffic and how much each click cost. Remember, cost is a major component of our ROI calculation. Table 9.3 shows our cost for each campaign.

Campaign	Impressions	Clicks	CTR	Total Cost	Avg CPC
Unique gifts	1,330	38	2.9%	$ 13.60	$ 0.36
Handmade	2,850	285	10.0%	$ 501.50	$ 1.76
Ski gear	4,750	380	8.0%	$ 688.50	$ 1.81
Baby shower	950	143	15.0%	$ 357.00	$ 2.51
Organic hat	16,720	665	4.0%	$ 520.20	$ 0.78
Newborn hat	12,350	570	4.6%	$ 608.60	$ 1.07
Stocking stuffer	8,550	190	2.2%	$ 763.30	$ 4.02

To get an idea of how much each click costs, we look at average CPC, which is the cost divided by how many clicks make up that cost.

$$average\ cost\ per\ click\ (cpc) = \frac{total\ cost}{clicks}$$

AdWords does this for us right in the interface, as you can see in the last column of the table. Here we see a large variance in how much our clicks cost. Some are at $0.36, while some are up to $4.00! We can only hope those stocking stuffers are making a lot of money because they certainly cost a lot. To answer that question, we need to know how many of those clicks turned into conversions. If you have conversion tracking enabled either via the AdWords script or through a web analytics tool such as Google Analytics, that data is readily available (Table 9.4).

▶ **Table 9.4** Campaign Conversion Data

Campaign	Impressions	Clicks	CTR	Total Cost	Avg CPC	Conv's	Conv Rate
Unique gifts	1,330	38	2.9%	$ 13.60	$ 0.36	4	4%
Handmade	2,850	285	10.0%	$ 501.50	$ 1.76	57	10%
Ski gear	4,750	380	8.0%	$ 688.50	$ 1.81	40	7%
Baby shower	950	143	15.0%	$ 357.00	$ 2.51	10	4%
Organic hat	16,720	665	4.0%	$ 520.20	$ 0.78	134	12%
Newborn hat	12,350	570	4.6%	$ 608.60	$ 1.07	105	10%
Stocking stuffer	8,550	190	2.2%	$ 763.30	$ 4.02	15	4%

While stocking stuffers triggered a ton of ad impressions and brought in 190 clicks, only 15 of them turned into actual paying customers! Conversion rate gives us a good idea of the relative power of a given campaign to turn clicks into impressions. We're now close to what we need to calculate ROI.

We know that each hat sold makes us $30 in profit before ad spend, so what we need to know now is the ad spend. That metric is the cost per conversion, one of the most important metrics in all of AdWords. Now we have all the pieces in place to calculate ROI:

$$roi = \frac{(profit - AdWords\ cost)}{AdWords\ cost}$$

$$roi = \frac{(profit\ per\ conv - cost\ per\ conv)}{cost\ per\ conv}$$

The Cost/Conversion column in Table 9.5 shows that campaigns vary hugely in the advertising spend needed to move hats out the door, which leads to very different ROIs. Although some campaigns have a high ROI, some actually cost the shop money for every hat sold!

▶ **Table 9.5** Campaign ROI

Campaign	Impressions	Clicks	CTR	Total Cost	Avg CPC	Conv's	Conv Rate	Cost/ Conv	Profit per Conv	ROI
Unique gifts	1,330	38	2.9%	$ 13.60	$ 0.36	4	4%	$ 3.40	$ 30	782%
Handmade	2,850	285	10.0%	$ 501.50	$ 1.76	57	10%	$ 8.80	$ 30	241%
Ski gear	4,750	380	8.0%	$ 688.50	$ 1.81	40	7%	$ 17.21	$ 30	74%
Baby shower	950	143	15.0%	$ 357.00	$ 2.51	10	4%	$ 35.70	$ 30	−16%
Organic hat	16,720	665	4.0%	$ 520.20	$ 0.78	134	12%	$ 3.88	$ 30	673%
Newborn hat	12,350	570	4.6%	$ 608.60	$ 1.07	105	10%	$ 5.80	$ 30	418%
Stocking stuffer	8,550	190	2.2%	$ 763.30	$ 4.02	15	4%	$ 50.89	$ 30	−41%

So how much money is being lost? Well, it turns out even ROI doesn't tell us the whole story because it's only measured on a percentage basis. For example, if we go purely by ROI, the unique gifts campaign is doing phenomenally well at 782 percent. The problem is, that's 782 percent on only four hats ever sold. And though that margin is great, four hats can't pay many salaries or even keep the lights on. The final metric we need takes that volume into account and gives us net profit—or loss as the case certainly is with the stocking stuffer campaign! We calculate net profit as follows:

$$net\ profit = (conversion \times profit\ per\ conversion) - total\ cost$$

Or said another way:

$$net\ profit = total\ profit - total\ cost$$

Table 9.6 shows that although the handmade, organic, and newborn campaigns are very successful, the baby shower and stocking stuffer campaigns need to be addressed ASAP. And the unique gifts campaign is highly profitable, but it's a niche at best.

▶ **Table 9.6** Campaign Net Profit

Campaign	Impressions	Clicks	CTR	Total Cost	Avg CPC	Conv's	Conv Rate	Cost/ Conv	Profit per Conv	ROI	Net Profit
Unique gifts	1,330	38	2.9%	$ 13.60	$ 0.36	4	4%	$ 3.40	$ 30	782%	$ 106.40
Handmade	2,850	285	10.0%	$ 501.50	$ 1.76	57	10%	$ 8.80	$ 30	241%	$ 1,208.50
Ski gear	4,750	380	8.0%	$ 688.50	$ 1.81	40	7%	$ 17.21	$ 30	74%	$ 511.50
Baby shower	950	143	15.0%	$ 357.00	$ 2.51	10	4%	$ 35.70	$ 30	−16%	$ (57.00)
Organic hat	16,720	665	4.0%	$ 520.20	$ 0.78	134	12%	$ 3.88	$ 30	673%	$ 3,499.80
Newborn hat	12,350	570	4.6%	$ 608.60	$ 1.07	105	10%	$ 5.80	$ 30	418%	$ 2,541.40
Stocking stuffer	8,550	190	2.2%	$ 763.30	$ 4.02	15	4%	$ 50.89	$ 30	−41%	$ (313.30)

Friday: Linking Google Analytics and Google AdWords Accounts

You just saw how to use the AdWords reports and conversion tracking to analyze conversions and even ROI. But while that is certainly better than relying on just impressions or clicks, it's still a limited view of the interactions on your site. By combining your data provided by the advertising network with web analytics, you gain a deeper understanding of the visit, including engagement metrics like bounce rate, time on site, pages viewed, and even subsequent visits and path analysis.

Google Analytics is a powerful (and free) web analytics tool, but for those using Google AdWords, it's even better. In addition to special reports tightly integrated with

AdWords, it shares the same backend databases to get even more data than would be otherwise possible.

Even if they use another analytics package as their primary analysis tool, we often recommend to our clients that use AdWords to use Google Analytics in addition because of these extra AdWords capabilities. And it's free, so there is little downside.

But before you can take advantage of this integration, you have to link the two accounts to allow data sharing. By far the easiest way to do this is via the AdWords interface. Begin by making sure the Google account you use to access AdWords is also an administrator on the Google Analytics account you intend to link.

From within the AdWords interface, select Google Analytics from the Tools And Analysis drop-down. The Google Analytics account list opens. Click the gear icon in the upper-right corner and select the account you wish to link. Its Account Administration screen opens. On the Data Sources tab, click the Link Accounts button. The dialog box in Figure 9.3 appears.

Figure 9.3 Providing tracking details

Unless you have a specific reason not to, leave auto-tagging enabled. You can select multiple profiles via the drop-down. Click Continue to complete the process. You can link multiple AdWords accounts to a single Google Analytics profile by repeating these steps.

Week 22: Use AdWords Reports

You can't manage what you can't measure. The next two weeks we examine how to use the available reporting tools to measure the performance of your advertising. Google provides a tremendous amount of information to advertisers savvy enough to use it and turn it into a competitive advantage.

Monday: Understanding AdWords Conversion Tracking

Last week we discussed how savvy marketers can employ Google AdWords integrated conversion tracking and supplement it with the more comprehensive Google Analytics data. While these systems both convey performance data, they work in different ways and measure different things.

A practical difference is in implementation. In the AdWords system, the site owner places a special snippet of code on a special page to record a specific conversion whenever it runs. For example, if the conversion goal is a checkout, the site owner places that code on the receipt page at the end of the checkout process. The code itself doesn't care what page it's on and neither does AdWords, which knows only that when the code fires, it must increment the specific conversion metric (shopping cart transactions in this case) by one. You can also create specific conversion tracking code to place on a key page, such as the Contact Us page or a page with a comparison between you and your competitors, newsletter signups, lead form completions, video views, and so forth.

Google Analytics goals work in a very different way. Unlike AdWords, which has a specific piece of code pasted on a page to identify a particular goal, in Google Analytics you put an identical piece of code on every page of the site. Then, within the interface you select which page URL or engagement behavior you want to qualify as a goal. The only exception is the Google Analytics e-commerce conversion data, which does have a special tag to collect more information.

Collecting more information is a key difference between AdWords tracking and web analytics. AdWords tracking is very narrow and often the data is of a binary nature—did you convert or not? AdWords doesn't track things like how long you spent on the site, the bounce rate, how many pages you viewed, or how many visits it took before you pulled the trigger and converted. Simply did you convert and, if it was a commerce conversion, what was the goal value? Web Analytics provides a much richer data set full of indiscrete information, such as how engaged the user was and what path they took through the site before either abandoning or converting.

If you prefer the great flexibility of Google Analytics to do things like record a goal if a user views over five pages but still want to see the conversions reflected in AdWords reports, you have the option of actually importing Google Analytics goals into AdWords. We explain how to enable this in the next section.

Tuesday: Installing Conversion Tracking Code

Google AdWords tracks conversions via JavaScript that must be installed on your site. But you don't need to be technically proficient because Google does all the heavy lifting and creates this script for you via a simple wizard. All you have to do is paste the code on the appropriate page on your site.

Before installing the conversion code, clearly define which pages on your site you want to track as conversions and thus which pages will host the conversion tracking script. Creating a simple matrix like the one in Table 9.7 will keep you organized and ensure that you've thought through the process.

▶ **Table 9.7** Conversion Pages

Name	Location	Category
S4S Mailing List	`/ListSubmit.php`	Signup
S4S checkout	`/thankyou.php`	Purchase/Sale
Newsletter	`/list2.php`	Signup
Form Complete	`/success.php`	Signup
Mobile Call	`/m/index.html`	Lead

Once you have your plan in place, follow these steps for each conversion page to generate the code:

1. Log in to AdWords, click the Tools And Analysis tab, and select Conversions. Click the New Conversion button.

   The New Conversion screen appears.

2. Copy and paste the name from the matrix you create (like the one in Table 9.7). The name should be meaningful and describe the conversion.

3. Select whether the conversion you are tracking is a standard web page or click-to-call action button on a website designed for mobile phones.

   This tells AdWords what type of code to generate in the final step. The conversion tracking script wizard appears (Figure 9.4).

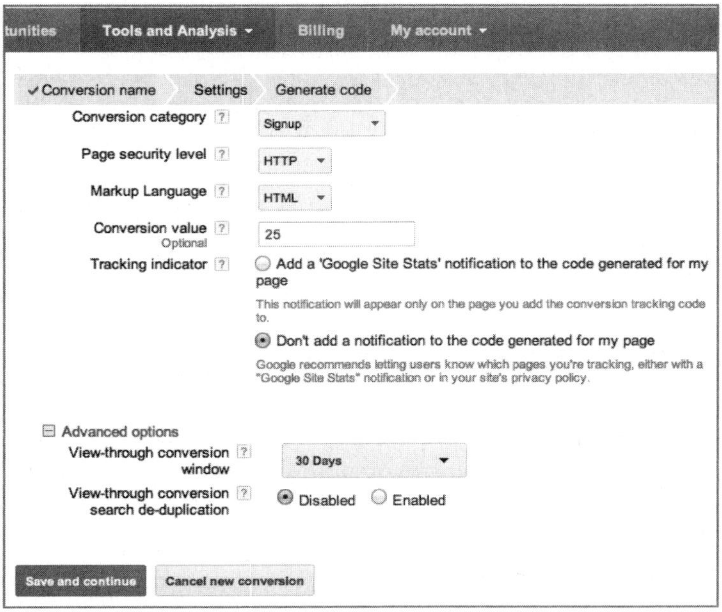

Figure 9.4 Conversion tracking script wizard

4. Select the type of conversion from the Conversion Category list.

Choices include Purchase/Sale, Signup, Lead, View of a Key Page, and Other.

5. Select whether your page is a secure/SSL page or standard HTTP.

If you have a secure cart or any other reason to use HTTPS, make sure you select that option to avoid giving your users a scary browser warning that will negatively impact your conversion rate and brand trust.

6. Choose a markup language.

For almost all standard desktop sites, even ones that run on dynamic code such as ASP and PHP, leave this as HTML. The other choices are for mobile sites.

7. Optionally, enter a conversion value.

If you can calculate or estimate a conversion value, you can put it here. Note that you can also insert a server-side variable here if you have dynamic conversion values. For example, if you have a shopping cart checkout as your conversion goal, you can't prepopulate the value here because you don't know how much each person will put in their cart and each will be different. So instead, you specify the variable that holds the final cart total, and it will automatically send the correct value back when it runs. For more information on specific languages and code example, see `http://bit.ly/vbdF1Y`.

8. Optionally, click the radio button that causes Google to add a Google Site Stats tracking notification on the page.

The default setting is not to add notification. Note that this will appear only on the page that is being tracked and after tracking has already occurred.

9. Expand Advanced Options and select any you wish to use.

The first view-through option allows you to select a time window in which conversions are attributed back to the ad impression.

Enabling de-duplication prevents double-counting a single conversion toward both click-through and view-through metrics. Only click-throughs are counted if both exist.

10. Click Save And Continue.

The code generation page appears. Specify whether to email it (for example, to your developer) or display it onscreen where you can copy it to paste elsewhere.

Regardless of whether your developer handles the code or you do it yourself, insert the generated code between the `<BODY>` and `</BODY>` tags on the desired page of your site.

To import goals you created in Google Analytics, click the Import From Google Analytics button on the main Conversions screen and select the desired goals from the list.

Wednesday and Thursday: AdWords Display Network Reports

Google offers two distinct divisions of its advertising platform, the Search Network and the Display Network. This book focuses on display, but we know that many advertisers have both networks in a single account. However, because the strategies and behaviors are so different, we treat them completely independently. The old Networks, Audiences, and Topics tabs are consolidated under the Display Network tab, which makes it much easier to manage display ads (Figure 9.5).

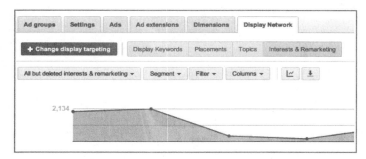

Figure 9.5   The Display Network tab consolidates several older tabs and reports

Clicking the Display Network tab brings up reports. Initially the data is for all online campaigns, but you can drill down into campaigns and ad groups via the left-hand navigation pane. As you step through the campaigns, double-check that you don't have both search and display running simultaneously (indicated by the presence of both Keywords and Display Network tabs). In Figure 9.5, there is no Keywords tab, so this campaign is exclusive to the GDN. It has both managed and automatic placements.

By expanding the Exclusions link, you see the ad group and campaign level exclusions. In this case several domains are excluded on the ad group level.

Clicking to expand each placement type shows the individual placements and their associated performance metrics (Figure 9.6). One common use of this report is to determine which of Google's automatic placements to promote to managed placements and which poor performers to exclude. You can see several examples of sites that generated impressions, clicks (and their associated costs) but no conversions and so were added to the exclusion list. We delve into optimization strategies in the next chapter.

To promote an automatic placement to a managed placement, select the check box and click the Manage Placement And Bid button. One advantage of moving placements from automatic to managed is to control the bid prices per placement. You can do this when moving the placement, or you can adjust the bid prices afterward from inside the managed placement report of the Display Network tab.

Domain	Clicks ⓘ	Impr. ⓘ	CTR ⓘ	Avg. CPC ⓘ	Cost	Conv. (1-per-click) ⓘ	Cost / conv. (1-per-click) ⓘ	Conv. rate (1-per-click) ⓘ	View-through Conv. ⓘ
Total - all automatic placements	16,925	19,594,723	0.09%	$0.26	$4,348.64	1,125	$3.87	6.65%	0
3dwindows7.com Excluded	434	13,339	3.25%	$0.24	$102.14	0	$0.00	0.00%	0
about.com	253	27,706	0.91%	$0.27	$68.78	87	$0.79	34.39%	0
mail.google.com	204	855,511	0.02%	$0.32	$65.31	20	$3.27	9.80%	0
ulinkmobile.com Excluded	222	2,128	10.43%	$0.23	$52.02	0	$0.00	0.00%	0
3dwindows7.com Excluded	221	8,744	2.53%	$0.21	$46.33	0	$0.00	0.00%	0
about.com	140	17,102	0.82%	$0.27	$37.60	20	$1.88	14.29%	0
ibilihin.com Excluded	192	1,616	11.88%	$0.19	$37.39	0	$0.00	0.00%	0
aitcheye.com Excluded	150	28,246	0.53%	$0.24	$36.26	1	$36.26	0.67%	0
mail.google.com	86	561,179	0.02%	$0.33	$28.17	7	$4.02	8.14%	0

Figure 9.6 Automatic placement details on the Display Network tab

By default, placement reports show the domain or section of the site, but advertisers can click the See URL List button to drill deeper to see which URL hosted the impression. In Figure 9.7, we see where on the About.com site our ads were shown and the performance metrics of each. From there we can manage the placement by adjusting bids or excluding it altogether.

URL	Clicks ⓘ	Impr. ⓘ	CTR ⓘ	Avg. CPC ⓘ	Cost	Conv. (1-per-click) ⓘ	Cost / conv. (1-per-click) ⓘ	Conv. rate (1-per-click) ⓘ	View-through Conv. ⓘ
gocaribbean.about.com/od/7/tp/bahamasinclusive.htm	19	522	3.64%	$1.14	$21.63	13	$1.66	68.42%	12
travelwithkids.about.com/gi/dynamic/zoffsitetopad.htm	13	377	3.45%	$1.21	$15.78	2	$7.89	15.38%	19
honeymoons.about.com/od/allinclusives/u/all-inclusives.htm	9	240	3.75%	$1.36	$12.25	5	$2.45	55.56%	14

Figure 9.7 Drilling down in the URL list to see exactly which page displayed our ads

There is much more to the Display Network tab than just a report of activity on each network. You can optimize display ads from within the reporting interface, which allows you to take immediate action while examining the performance metrics of the individual placements. Because so much of the success of a display campaign can hinge on weeding out poor performers and adjusting bids on the others, we highly recommend you get acquainted with this powerful set of reports.

Friday: Using the Dimensions Tab

One advantage of the GDN, and a major reason we use it as the primary example for this book, is the transparency of exactly where, when, and how your ads are shown. Beyond just sharing the data, Google provides excellent tools to analyze that data.

A relatively new addition, the Dimensions tab of the Campaigns section is one of the most powerful tools in the arsenal of the advertiser because of the visibility it provides into the performance of your campaigns and ad groups. It not only allows you to slice and dice your data to draw conclusions about when and where your ads are performing but also to visualize those trends over time for an ad group or campaign or even across the entire account. Advanced users can customize the metrics and apply filters to extract the exact data required for analysis. The different dimensions available in these reports are shown in the drop-down in Figure 9.8.

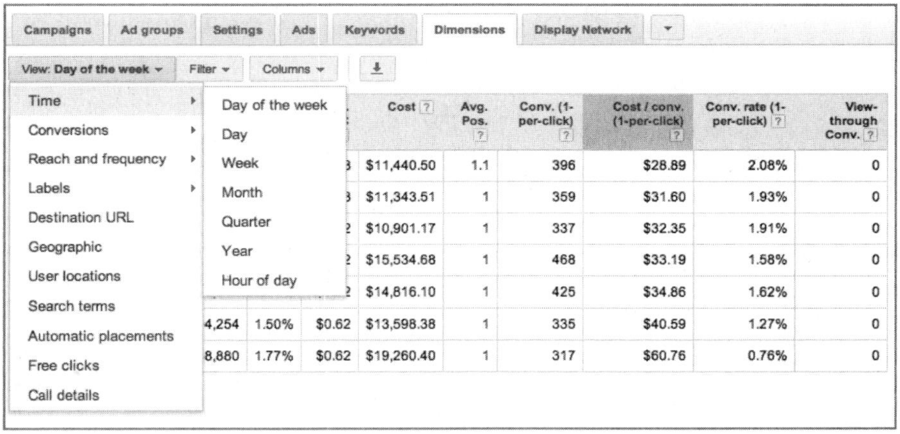

Figure 9.8 The Dimensions tab offers options for dimensions, filters, and metrics.

Time

The first dimension option is time. You can analyze how your campaigns perform at different times of day, days of the week, months, or seasons. In Figure 9.9 you can see that while Tuesday is the best day of the week in terms of conversions, Monday is the worst. Monday also has the worst conversion rate and cost per conversion. And although Sunday gets the least number of impressions, it holds its own at third place in terms of number of conversions and cost/conversion.

In a similar analysis using time-of-day rather than day-of-the-week, you see in Figure 9.10 that for this campaign the best conversion rate (and cost per conversion) comes in the early morning hours from 5 a.m. to 7 a.m. So if you're purely concerned with profitability, that's great to know. But if you're more interested in volume/revenue, the highest conversion volume comes at the other end of the day, from 4 p.m. to 8p.m., as seen in Figure 9.11. It's interesting to note that this higher volume comes with a heavy price tag because the cost per conversion essentially triples.

Figure 9.9 Day of the week analysis via the Dimensions tab

Day of the week	Clicks	Impr.	CTR	Avg. CPC	Cost	Avg. Pos.	Conv. (1-per-click)	Cost / conv. (1-per-click)	Conv. rate (1-per-click)	View-through Conv.
Tuesday	2,506	202,246	1.24%	$1.30	$3,253.09	4.9	382	$8.51	15.25%	0
Thursday	2,450	199,315	1.23%	$1.28	$3,147.16	4.8	357	$8.82	14.57%	0
Sunday	2,375	162,453	1.46%	$1.27	$3,004.66	5.1	341	$8.81	14.36%	0
Friday	2,437	189,728	1.28%	$1.25	$3,058.38	4.8	341	$8.97	13.99%	0
Saturday	2,396	164,988	1.45%	$1.28	$3,073.56	4.9	333	$9.23	13.90%	0
Wednesday	2,531	202,854	1.25%	$1.27	$3,205.20	4.8	332	$9.65	13.12%	0
Monday	2,475	192,361	1.29%	$1.29	$3,193.16	4.8	303	$10.54	12.25%	0

Figure 9.10 Hour of the day analysis by conversion rate

Hour of day	Clicks	Impr.	CTR	Avg. CPC	Cost	Avg. Pos.	Conv. (1-per-click)	Cost / conv. (1-per-click)	Conv. rate (1-per-click)	View-through Conv.
6	777	190,521	0.41%	$1.17	$908.22	1.1	59	$15.39	7.59%	0
5	459	119,254	0.38%	$1.14	$521.25	1.1	29	$17.97	6.32%	0
7	1,421	321,160	0.44%	$1.01	$1,439.91	1.1	74	$19.46	5.21%	0

Figure 9.11 Hour of the day analysis by conversion volume

Hour of day	Clicks	Impr.	CTR	Avg. CPC	Cost	Avg. Pos.	Conv. (1-per-click)	Cost / conv. (1-per-click)	Conv. rate (1-per-click)	View-through Conv.
20	29,551	2,323,187	1.27%	$0.42	$12,476.80	1	242	$51.56	0.82%	0
19	26,643	2,091,047	1.27%	$0.44	$11,758.09	1	241	$48.79	0.90%	0
18	22,655	1,889,160	1.20%	$0.45	$10,243.33	1	205	$49.97	0.90%	0
17	19,397	1,712,877	1.13%	$0.47	$9,182.45	1	187	$49.10	0.96%	0
16	14,738	1,518,978	0.97%	$0.51	$7,508.77	1	176	$42.66	1.19%	0

Conversions

Rather than seeing conversions as a monolithic event, you can segment them down to their individual components. During the conversion tracking configuration we examined earlier in this chapter, you saw that you give conversions a name and a category related to the purpose of the conversion, such as a purchase, sign-up, lead, or view of a key page. The first option in these reports is to segment your conversions into those purpose buckets. In this way you can analyze your purchase versus your lead forms. You can also segment them via the name you gave the action.

Because of the nature of how AdWords tracks these conversions, you likely want to enable the many-per-click columns within the reports. Although these reports give you finer, more accurate data than the aggregate reports, for this type of conversion analysis Google Analytics offers a more robust conversion analysis platform, as you'll see later in this chapter.

Reach and Frequency

One of the options display advertisers have to consider is how often to show an individual person the same ad. Some strategies call for repetition and high frequencies, especially for a group that is known to convert well. Other strategies call for spreading your budget to reach as many different people with your ads as possible and limit the number of times any given person is shown your ad. These reports can help analyze how performance varies when an ad is shown to a given person X times. Armed with this data, you can construct an optimal frequency capping strategy.

Reach is the number of unique users, and frequency is the average number of times a user is exposed to an ad. These metrics are available from September 2011 to present for advertisers using frequency capping or interest-based ads.

Destination URL

These reports help you analyze the performance of landing pages. Poorly performing landing pages hurt overall advertising performance—a great ad that leads to a bad landing page doesn't achieve the end goal. Landing page usability along with how well the ads and other scent factors are matched to the landing pages all affect performance, as discussed in Chapter 7, "Month 4: Creating Image Ads." Google Analytics, which can present a much more comprehensive data set, handles this critically important topic better than AdWords.

Demographics

For publishers such as social networks, dating sites, and video sites, which provide demographic information about visitors, AdWords shows the ad performance according to user demographics. This data includes age ranges and gender categories for the corresponding publishers. Since the GDN offers demographic bidding, it can be useful to understand which demographics are performing well for your site.

Geographic

Understanding how different geographies are performing can be highly illuminating, especially for businesses that have a local presence or are geographic in nature, such as cold weather clothing. But even in national campaigns, different areas can have outliers both positive and negative, which savvy advertisers can use to their advantage. Geographic analysis is best done in concert with a web analytics tool, but AdWords can provide some interesting metrics too.

One of these is the ability to distinguish what triggered the ad. Google can trigger a local ad based on physical location or location of interest. In other words, even if a user is physically located in Georgia, if they are browsing a map of San Francisco, the content displays an interest in that locale. The reports also provide the metro area, which is something Google Analytics doesn't support by default. There is also an interesting metric that provides the most specific location the system can determine. Note that to view all of these metrics you may have to customize the columns shown because they may not be included in the default view.

Automatic Placements

Similar to the Networks tab you saw earlier, this report shows the correlation between the domain and the exact URL of automatic placements as well as performance data.

Free Clicks

This is one of the more interesting (and somewhat misleading) reports available for display advertisers, particularly those using rich media or video ads. This report provides information about how people interacted with your ads in ways that didn't result in the advertiser being charged for a click. For example, clicking the plus sign to expand the ad or video plays that don't result in a site visit are captured here. Even some things that are technically not clicks, such as hovering the cursor over an ad for at least 1 second, are included (Figure 9.12).

Although they are not all clicks, they are interactions for which Google does not (yet) charge, so they are listed here as free clicks to distinguish from interactions that do cost the advertiser. However, despite not qualifying for a click charge, they can still be valuable interactions to an advertiser. This finer granularity can help advertisers understand how engaging their ads are and how successful they are at capturing the user's initial attention.

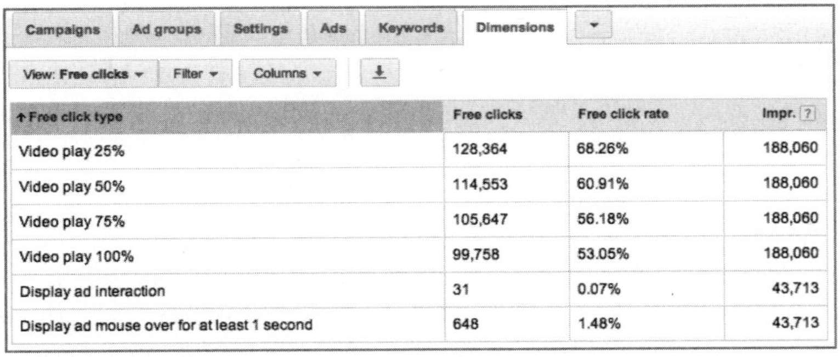

↑ Free click type	Free clicks	Free click rate	Impr. [?]
Video play 25%	128,364	68.26%	188,060
Video play 50%	114,553	60.91%	188,060
Video play 75%	105,647	56.18%	188,060
Video play 100%	99,758	53.05%	188,060
Display ad interaction	31	0.07%	43,713
Display ad mouse over for at least 1 second	648	1.48%	43,713

Figure 9.12 Free Clicks data via the Dimensions tab

Call Details

Advertisers using the call extensions with Google forwarding numbers can get data about those calls via the Call Details report (Figure 9.13). The following metrics are available:

- Call start time
- Call end time
- Missed versus received (call status)
- Duration
- Caller area code
- Cost
- Call type (manual dial versus click-to-call)
- Campaign
- Ad group

Note that the data is provided for general Google Voice calls as well as the click-to-call extensions. The missed calls info can be illuminating because it helps you to understand *why* an ad interaction didn't convert (because you didn't pick up the phone!) and can act as an additional data point to inform your day parting strategy.

View: Call details ▾	Filter ▾	Columns ▾	⬇				
↓ Start time ?	End time ?	Status ?	Duration (seconds) ?	Caller area code ?	Phone cost ?	Call type ?
Dec 31, 2011 2:33:42 PM	Dec 31, 2011 2:36:35 PM	Received	173	919	$0.00	Manually dialed
Dec 31, 2011 1:14:34 PM	Dec 31, 2011 1:17:56 PM	Received	202	707	$1.00	Manually dialed
Dec 31, 2011 1:06:56 PM	Dec 31, 2011 1:08:48 PM	Received	112	919	$1.00	Manually dialed
Dec 31, 2011 11:03:33 AM	Dec 31, 2011 11:05:03 AM	Received	90	720	$0.00	Mobile click-to-call
Dec 31, 2011 9:44:51 AM	Dec 31, 2011 9:51:42 AM	Received	411	912	$1.00	Manually dialed
Dec 30, 2011 6:47:44 PM	Dec 30, 2011 6:48:55 PM	Received	71	313	$1.00	Manually dialed

Figure 9.13 Call details report

Week 23: Use Google Analytics

The holy grail of ad analysis is to have a complete picture of the entire life cycle of an ad and its effect on user behavior. This starts with understanding the very first awareness of our ads, which is tracked as impressions and ad interactions. It continues with the user's first visit to the site (including view-throughs that don't receive a click) and subsequent visits that can help us calculate the lifetime value of a visitor.

With recent developments linking Google AdWords, Google Analytics (particularly the Premium Edition), and DoubleClick for Advertisers (DFA), we are closer than ever to that level of end-to-end visibility to truly inform our campaigns and strategy.

Google Analytics exists for the sole purpose of measuring and reporting. And Google provides this enterprise-class analytics tool, for free, for one reason—to help AdWords users maximize their online presence. The low barrier to entry (standard edition is free) ensures that nearly all your competitors are taking advantage of a web analytics tool. But just installing the tool isn't enough; you must be able to use it. Some of the best web analysts we know are actually advertisers who understand that web analytics skills are as important to their craft as familiarity with ad networks, if not more.

This chapter cannot replace an in-depth course on Google Analytics. What follows is a high-level overview to get you started in the right direction. We highly suggest that serious advertisers get serious about analytics and take a Google Seminars for Success course (discount voucher available in the back of this book), pick up one of the many books available on the subject, or contact a certified partner if you need additional assistance.

Monday: Campaign Level Report and Clicks Tab

AdWords has its own dedicated section in the Google Analytics reports. Navigate to it via the Standard Reporting tab and click Advertising, then AdWords, and then Campaigns. Data in the AdWords section is pulled from two different data sources and combined into a single report. To view this report, select the Clicks tab in the secondary horizontal navigation bar (under Explorer).

The Campaigns report shows AdWords campaigns and their associated metrics (Figure 9.14). Visits are counted when Google Analytics detects a visit that originated from the AdWords campaign. The next five columns (Impressions, Clicks, Cost, CTR, and CPC) are imported directly from the AdWords database, not actually calculated by Google Analytics. In fact, Google Analytics cannot detect impressions because the analytics script executes for the first time when a user lands on the landing page. The remaining columns are the mashup of this data. Google Analytics calculates the amount of revenue it's aware of via e-commerce transactions and goal values and compares that to the clicks and cost imported from AdWords to compute ROI and margin.

Campaign	Visits ↓	Impressions	Clicks	Cost	CTR	CPC	RPC	ROI	Margin
googlestore-general-ps	15,319	110,168	13,616	$4,658.77	12.36%	$0.34	$14.65	4,181.77%	97.66%
California	7,434	395,178	7,313	$4,670.26	1.85%	$0.64	$2.00	212.89%	68.04%
Other Brands	5,764	109,908	6,367	$9,862.13	5.79%	$1.55	$5.68	266.77%	72.73%
Product Listing Ads	5,008	254,740	4,721	$2,840.88	1.85%	$0.60	$4.22	600.62%	85.73%
Industry Terms	3,998	147,122	3,665	$5,219.98	2.49%	$1.42	$2.51	76.00%	43.18%
Remarketing	3,367	1,165,110	3,242	$3,722.04	0.28%	$1.15	$3.23	181.69%	64.50%
Vendors	2,146	47,098	1,883	$2,689.80	4.00%	$1.43	$5.34	274.00%	73.26%
Scrubs & Beyond Tablets	1,206	3,239	1,116	$126.53	34.46%	$0.11	$8.51	7,407.27%	98.67%
Dickies Scrubs	1,031	19,176	994	$1,399.70	5.18%	$1.41	$2.44	73.37%	42.32%

Figure 9.14 The AdWords Campaigns report in Google AdWords

Shouldn't Clicks Match Visits?

Many users are confused about why the Clicks and Visits columns don't match. After all, it's logical to assume a 1:1 ratio because an ad click recorded by AdWords should be immediately followed by a website visit recorded by Google Analytics (and both with the same campaign name). However, that almost never happens. The following are some of the most common reasons that clicks and visits don't match:

Landing page isn't tagged properly.   If the Google Analytics code isn't properly implemented on the landing page, the visit isn't recorded (but the ad click is).

Redirects strip the URL tags/parameters.   Google Analytics relies on the query string parameters being left intact when the landing page loads. So in this case, the visit is still recorded but Google Analytics has no idea it belongs to that campaign, so it isn't recorded in the right place.

Incomplete page load.   If the analytics code doesn't load right away (common when pushed to the bottom of the page), it's possible for users to navigate away, click the Back button, or close the browser before the visit can be recorded.

Cookies/JavaScript not enabled.   Google Analytics generally requires both to run, but ad clicks can be recorded regardless.

Filters have modified the data stream.   Be sure to understand the consequences of any profile filters you have applied in Google Analytics, particularly those that contain campaign variables.

Invalid clicks removed.   The previous are reasons why clicks exceed visits, but in some cases the visits are greater. One reason may be that suspicious clicks are removed from the AdWords account. However, if those clicks result in recorded visits, Google does not remove the associated analytics visits, so they remain in your data set even though the ad clicks do not.

Long date ranges.   These may include periods when the data sources were not linked.

Tuesday: Campaign Tagging for Non-Google Networks

Google Analytics has all kinds of tools and visualizations for slicing and dicing your data into segments and comparisons that can be highly illuminating and actionable. You saw a couple of those in the previous section, but there are far more to come in the rest of this chapter. The trick is that you have to get the right data *into* Google Analytics in order to take advantage of these features. When it comes to the different campaign variable buckets that Google Analytics understands, there are four that we worry about for display advertising.

Campaign Source

This is *who* is sending the traffic. If you place ads on engadget.com, then the source is engadget.com. If you place ads on Facebook, the source is facebook.com. Although you can put whatever value you want in this field, we recommend that you stick to the domain name whenever possible.

Campaign Medium

This is *how* the traffic was sent. It's used to compare different media to determine the value of a particular channel. It's possible that a single source may have multiple media, such as when you advertise on Google ads and also get traffic from Google organic listings. The source is always Google, but the media vary. Common (nondisplay) media are email, CPC, social media, magazine, newspaper, offline, and so forth. For display ads, we suggest just display. In general, keep media as broad as possible so they can easily be compared with other channels. Absolutely resist the urge to stuff other variables—for example, ad sizes (like 728×90), time stamps, or even ad formats (like rich media)—into the medium field.

Campaign Name

This has less to do with logistics (who and how) and more to do with the organization of your business and the advertising initiatives you have in place. For example, if you have a seasonal business and have marketing initiatives around Christmas shopping, you can have a campaign named Christmas2012 with multiple sources of traffic and multiple media.

When you choose a campaign name, it is listed in the Campaigns reports alongside your Google AdWords campaigns and any other campaigns you have running (such as email, social media). Each of these fields can be evaluated independently, so you can analyze within a given campaign to determine which medium or source is performing the best, or you can analyze that source and medium across your entire account, which may span multiple campaigns.

Campaign Ad Content

This is the field where you have the most latitude and granularity to describe exactly which ad triggered the visit and under what circumstances. This is the field where you can include sizes and time stamps and calls-to-action that describe a particular ad. For example, in Chapter 7, "Month 4: Creating Image Ads," Figure 7.6 and Figure 7.7 show two different ad creatives that actually appear simultaneously on the same webpage, just in two different places.

We want to know which of those ads generates the click. If we analyze the campaign source, they are the same (they were on the same page at the same time). The campaign medium is the same (display). Campaign name is the same (both ads support the new regional jet first class campaign). But the actual *content* of the ads is different and that's where we can see the difference. In fact, because all the others are the same, we can easily see which ad creative is more effective at generating visits (and conversions) very easily by drilling into the campaign/source/medium and simply comparing content.

The most popular naming convention describes the size, creative, and call to action in one field separated by underscores to allow for maximum analysis. This generally follows the format {ad format}_{size}_{call to action}_{optional creative variation}. You should customize this to meet your business needs, such as by dropping the ad format description if it's not needed. So continuing the example of the airline ads, we can set the content fields to `728×90_fblike_jet` and `300×250_seeperks_seat`.

Tagging the Links

Not surprisingly, Google understands how to get the data into Google Analytics and the importance of the data, so for the most part those campaigns are automatically tagged. You can check your settings under My Account › Preferences › Tracking and ensure that auto-tagging is set to yes. Note that if you prefer to manually control the campaign parameters, such as by setting GDN ads to display, you can turn off auto-tagging and manually tag Google campaigns just as you do other sources, as explained later.

While Google auto-tags by default, for most other ads and networks you are responsible for getting that data into Google Analytics. To see how to do this, let's say that we are advertising an upcoming webinar about Google Analytics Premium Edition on an industry news site with the goal of getting people to register on our site. When visitors click our ad and we send them to the landing page, we attach variables, called query string parameters, to the URL. Google Analytics knows how to match the parameters to the variables. Table 9.8 shows the tags Google Analytics uses.

▶ **Table 9.8** Campaign variables

Campaign Variable	URL Tag	Example
Campaign Source	utm_source	online-behavior.com
Campaign Medium	utm_medium	display
Campaign Name	utm_campaign	ga_premium
Campaign Ad Content	utm_content	300x250_webinar_chart

So if the URL of our landing page is `http://AnalyticsPremium.com`, we use a URL like the following to send a clicking user there:

```
http://AnalyticsPremium.com/
    ?utm_source=online-behavior.com
    &utm_medium=display
    &utm_content=300x250_webinar_chart
    &utm_campaign=ga_premium
```

Note that this affects only the underlying destination URL. This long, ugly URL isn't printed anywhere or visible to users before they click.

> **Note:** If you don't manually tag your non-Google ads, Google Analytics tags the ads from most non-Google networks as a `Source = Direct` and `Medium = None`. This is not only useless for analysis of those campaigns, it pollutes the true direct visits data source as well. If those campaigns do very well, you will mistakenly believe that the direct visitors were numerous and converted well when in fact it was the traffic from the ads. Or worse, the ads do poorly and are wasting money, but you have no way to know that because they aren't trackable.

The syntax for that query string parameter can get a little messy, so use an available tool to translate your variables into the URL complete with properly formatted query string parameters. The first such tool is Google's URL builder, which has a nasty URL and is thus most easily found by just doing a Google search for "URL builder." Perhaps this is a plot by Google to force the habit of searching versus typing in URLs! This simple wizard generates the URL for you (Figure 9.15). Note that Campaign Term is not used for display ads.

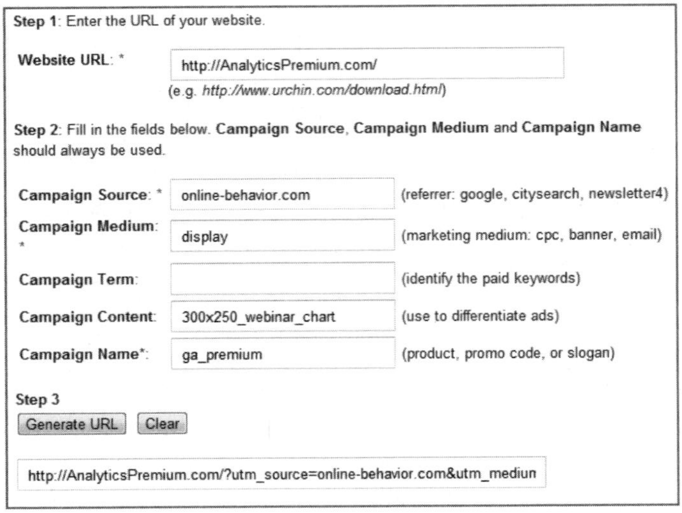

Step 1: Enter the URL of your website.
Website URL: *
http://AnalyticsPremium.com/
(e.g. http://www.urchin.com/download.html)
Step 2: Fill in the fields below. Campaign Source, Campaign Medium and Campaign Name should always be used.
Campaign Source: *
online-behavior.com
(referrer: google, citysearch, newsletter4)
Campaign Medium: *
display
(marketing medium: cpc, banner, email)
Campaign Term:
(identify the paid keywords)
Campaign Content:
300x250_webinar_chart
(use to differentiate ads)
Campaign Name*:
ga_premium
(product, promo code, or slogan)
Step 3
Generate URL
Clear
http://AnalyticsPremium.com/?utm_source=online-behavior.com&utm_mediun

Figure 9.15 The Google URL builder tool

However, if you are building out lots of URLs, the tool can get tedious. The extremely repeatable pattern lends itself well to spreadsheet formulas. With a spreadsheet you can not only create lots of variation extremely quickly, but you have a record of your past URLs. We provide such a spreadsheet at `http://j.mp/tracksheet`.

It's worth highlighting that consistency is incredibly important. If you call your medium "display" one day, "banner" the next, and "displayads" in another campaign, accurate segmentation is nearly impossible. In fact, even case matters, so display and Display are tracked separately.

After you have tagged the ads, you can test them by simply clicking them and noting the resulting URL in the address bar of the browser. First ensure that all the campaign variables are present and then wait a few hours to verify that the visit registered in Google Analytics as well.

Wednesday: Drilling Down to Ad Groups and Using Secondary Dimensions

In Google Analytics, when you first enter the AdWords reports, you see campaigns, and if you click one, you see its ad groups and associated performance metrics.

You can also see the ad groups all in one table (regardless of campaign) by selecting the ad groups link above the table. This can be useful when you have similar ad groups that happen to be in different campaigns not due to major differences but logistical settings such as geographic targeting.

However, these reports contain only traffic originating from AdWords, that is, source = google and medium = cpc. To view all campaigns—including the ones defined earlier—you can switch to the more general Campaigns report under Traffic Sources › Sources › Campaigns, which includes *all* campaigns, AdWords or otherwise.

From here you can do your full campaign analysis. If you drill down into a campaign, it shows the sources and media that contribute to that campaign. You can also click the Medium link across the top to show how all the media compare to one another across your campaigns, as seen in Figure 9.16.

Because campaign data is a matrix, it can be analyzed independently, as you just saw. But often you want to see how a combination of two related variables performs. For example, if you want to determine your top campaigns and landing pages but don't want to drill into each campaign separately and keep track, you can select a primary dimension of Campaign and a secondary dimension of Landing Page (Figure 9.17). In this case, you see that the googlestore-general-ps campaign dominates but does give up the first and sixth positions. There are infinite scenarios where you would want to associate two "buckets" of data. Perhaps you want to determine which landing pages are the best in which campaigns, the top geographic areas for the campaigns, or the best-performing combination of ad creative and landing pages.

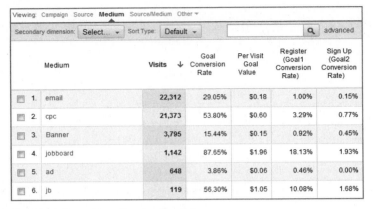

Figure 9.16 Comparing media across all campaigns

	Medium	Visits ↓	Goal Conversion Rate	Per Visit Goal Value	Register (Goal1 Conversion Rate)	Sign Up (Goal2 Conversion Rate)
☐ 1.	email	22,312	29.05%	$0.18	1.00%	0.15%
☐ 2.	cpc	21,373	53.80%	$0.60	3.29%	0.77%
☐ 3.	Banner	3,795	15.44%	$0.15	0.92%	0.45%
☐ 4.	jobboard	1,142	87.65%	$1.96	18.13%	1.93%
☐ 5.	ad	648	3.86%	$0.06	0.46%	0.00%
☐ 6.	jb	119	56.30%	$1.05	10.08%	1.68%

Campaign	Landing Page ⊗	Visits	Pages/Visit	Avg. Time on Site	% New Visits ↓
googlestore GA by Kathy	/googlesearch.aspx	29	3.21	00:00:59	100.00%
googlestore-general-ps	/Accessories/Rubber+Magnet.axd	32	1.11	00:00:02	96.30%
googlestore-general-ps	/You+Tube/Accessories/14+oz+YouTube+Tumbler.a	92	1.20	00:00:04	94.74%
googlestore-general-ps	/Eco/Hercules+Grocery+Tote.axd	144	1.75	00:00:17	94.12%
googlestore-general-ps	/Fun/Clear+Bouncy+Ball.axd	38	1.22	00:00:08	93.75%
Google Store: English - Americas - Display Only	/shop.axd/Home?catid=1	172	1.74	00:00:22	92.96%

Figure 9.17 Secondary dimensions show the performance of a combination of dimensions.

Thursday and Friday: Very Useful Reports for Display

How you approach your analysis in a web analytics tool like Google Analytics depends greatly on how well you have implemented campaign tracking to provide clean, accurate, and well-tagged data. It also depends on whether your goals are mostly for direct response (a purchase or other action), mostly branding and awareness, or somewhere in between.

One of the simplest reports to start with is the Direct Traffic report found at Traffic Sources › Sources › Direct (Figure 9.18). It provides information about visitors who come to the site by typing the URL directly into the browser without following a link, organic search result, or other online ad. Because one of the goals of display advertising is to improve awareness of your site and brand for later recall, display ad campaigns can directly lead to a rise in direct visits. Many analysts ignore this report because the information is not as precise or irrefutable as other campaign data, but these customers tend to be some of the most loyal and often convert the highest. Consider the scenario where you are reading an online article discussing the best lenses for a new digital SLR camera you bought. If you see an ad for a tripod, you may not visit at that time, but two weeks later when looking for a tripod you may recall the brand and visit the site.

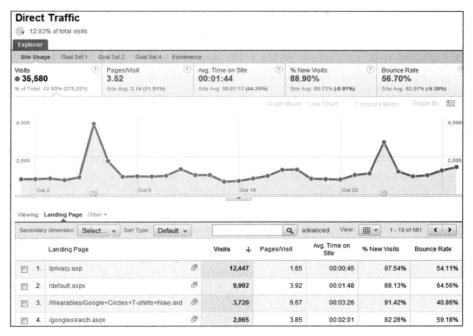

Figure 9.18 Direct Traffic report

The two large spikes in direct traffic are particularly interesting, and you want to tie those to events, promotions, or other activities on those days. The annotation below the first spike includes a note from the PR team that a major news outlet showcased your site that day, which likely led to the increase in direct traffic. Another clue is in the bottom half of the report where it indicates the landing pages that direct visitors landed on. Unless you specifically and overtly advertise a vanity URL such as CardinalPath.com/Careers, you can expect most of your visits from general awareness campaigns to hit the home page. However, if you see long URLs like the ones here, then it could be a bookmark, but it's more likely that the traffic is improperly tagged and not true direct traffic. It's highly suspicious that 3,700 people typed in a long page name such as the one shown in row 3 in Figure 9.18. They more likely clicked an external ad, paid link, or shortened URL that wasn't tagged with analytics parameters and thus shows up as direct traffic. By segmenting out these other non-display sources of direct traffic, you are left with a more accurate picture of the branding and awareness campaigns that eventually result in increased traffic to your site.

It's also common that the tripod shopper may not remember the exact URL but instead remembers the product name or brand name and does a search. Segmenting out just your branded keywords in the organic search reports can give you an idea of how successful your brand awareness efforts have been. There are lots of ways to focus on branded keywords in Google Analytics, such as advanced segments, but one of the simplest ways is to configure an inline filter. Navigate to the organic search reports via Traffic Sources › Sources › Organic and select the Advanced Filter option to display the filter options seen in Figure 9.19. Here the Manfrotto tripod company uses the regular expressions feature to filter the report to include only the specified branded keywords. They include the keywords in the Matching RegExp field, separated by vertical pipe (|) characters.

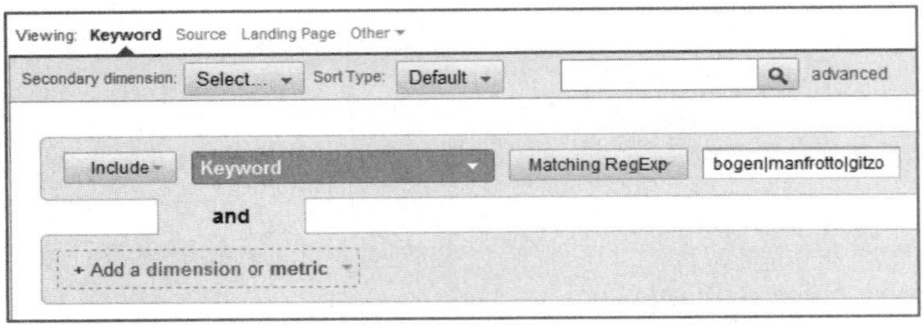

Figure 9.19 Advanced inline keyword filter for branded terms

These are all indirect reports where you have to make some assumptions about how your display campaigns lead to overall awareness that ultimately results in site traffic. But if you've properly tagged your campaigns as discussed in the previous section, you can also measure the direct results of your ads with no need to make assumptions or inferences.

Advanced segments are an analyst's best friend. They are easily one of the most important features of Google Analytics, and every advertiser needs to understand them well. They allow you to create segments that meet criteria that you specify and juxtapose them in report graphs. For example, if you want to see how your display ads are doing, you can create a segment that includes only traffic where the medium is display.

Now you can decide which segments to compare in your reports. You can focus only on display traffic or include additional segments and compare them to your display traffic. You can also compare display to other media such as search. In Figure 9.20, we select the custom segment for display ads (here we call that medium Banner), the default segment of Direct Traffic, and all visits to the site.

Figure 9.21 shows these segments in the Ecommerce Overview report, which shows that while the e-commerce conversion rate of our direct traffic remains similar to the site average, our display ad traffic (square points on the graph) has improved significantly and maintained the higher rate.

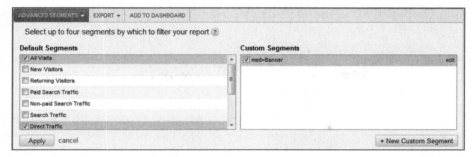

Figure 9.20 Specifying segments to report

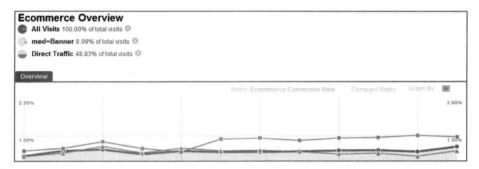

Figure 9.21 Comparing e-commerce rates of our segments.

The New vs Returning report (Figure 9.22) indicates whether we are successfully reaching out to a new audience. The top line (circular points) represents display
traffic, while the lower line (square points) is direct traffic, which represents users
who are familiar with our brand. These two segments can include long-time users
or users who have recently become aware of our brand/product/sites and are making their first visit. The % New Visits column tells us which. We can also understand
how our display ads are being consumed. Are they first-time visitors or are our ads
keeping our site top of mind with those who have already checked it out, such as with
remarketing?

Once you isolate the traffic from display ads, you want to focus on which ads
work well and which sources perform so you can optimize your ad spend. The report
in Figure 9.23 shows the different ads and the number of visits that resulted from
them as well as the relative bounce rate of the individual ads. This is a critical report
because the worst thing that can happen is for a customer to get just past the point of
making you pay for an ad and then leave, which is what a bounce represents. The bars
to the left (green) and right (red) of the vertical line represent winners and losers from
a bounce rate perspective. You configure this by selecting the performance view and
choosing bounce rate as the metric.

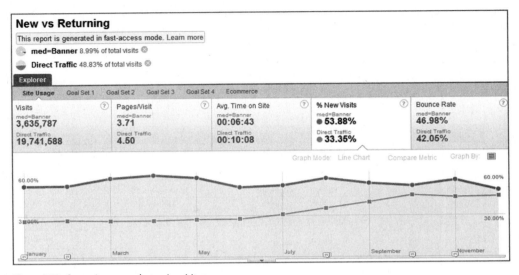

Figure 9.22 Comparing new and returning visitors

Ad Content	Visits	Bounce Rate (compared to site average)
Shop The Google Store	11,339	-38.51%
Google Notebooks	332	22.77%
Google T Shirts	4,809	-42.68%
Chrome Notebooks	1,330	6.33%
Android Notebooks	703	28.58%
Ceramic Coffee Mugs	551	27.01%
Google Shopping Totes	446	-41.23%
Neoprene Laptop Sleeves	370	33.79%
Official Google Clothing	370	2.31%

Figure 9.23 Evaluating ads based on visits and relative bounce rate

This type of analysis is similar to what AdWords provides, but it represents *all* networks and traffic sources, not just Google. With a complete web analytics tool, you can also see engagement metrics beyond just visits and conversions.

On that note, another segment to consider is not just the display traffic, but the display traffic that was *engaged*. Figure 9.24 shows an advanced segment configured to show visits from display that also saw four or more page views. This allows you not only to determine where your display ads connect with audiences but also to compare it against overall display ad traffic. A segment with low engagement ads is also informative. Analysts have plenty of digging to do in these reports, and segmenting the traffic types is the first step.

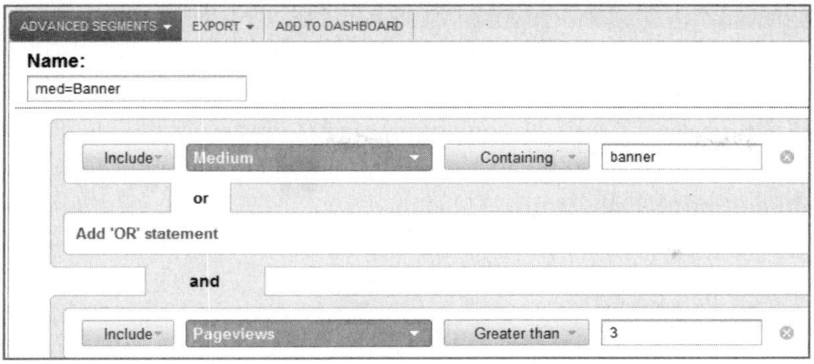

Figure 9.24 Creating a segment with engaged display ad viewers

Advanced segments provide a wealth of information, but you can also customize the metrics and dimensions that you see. The report in Figure 9.16 earlier in the chapter shows how different media perform against each other. You can take this further with custom reports to see exactly the metrics you need. The report in Figure 9.25 shows metrics that are relevant to display advertisers—the quantity (visits and unique visitors), type (new visits), engagement (bounce rate and pages/visit), and conversion outcomes (revenue and goal completions)—all on one screen.

	Medium	Visits	Unique Visitors	New Visits	Bounce Rate	Pages/Visit	Revenue	Goal Completions
1.	(none)	1,526,805	798,949	695,474	36.31%	4.49	$629,100.35	3,333
2.	organic	756,498	354,954	251,996	25.09%	4.57	$303,355.18	2,204
3.	Banner	243,615	148,712	120,328	34.91%	4.17	$140,211.19	1,448
4.	referral	189,984	105,340	80,806	28.45%	3.86	$39,770.14	270
5.	email	164,774	41,253	14,686	27.93%	4.59	$70,974.25	165
6.	webinar	59,519	26,536	17,596	15.22%	3.87	$12,268.88	282
7.	affiliate	39,448	22,913	17,031	23.50%	4.12	$11,197.73	159

Figure 9.25 Comparing media on selected metrics

This report was configured via the custom report builder (Figure 9.26).

Note that you can customize drill-down options, not just metrics. When you click a medium, you see all the campaigns associated with that medium. This allows you to create hierarchical relationships that aren't natively included in Google Analytics. Figure 9.27 shows the same custom report but with the campaign dimension after we've drilled down into the medium of *banner*, which represents our display ads.

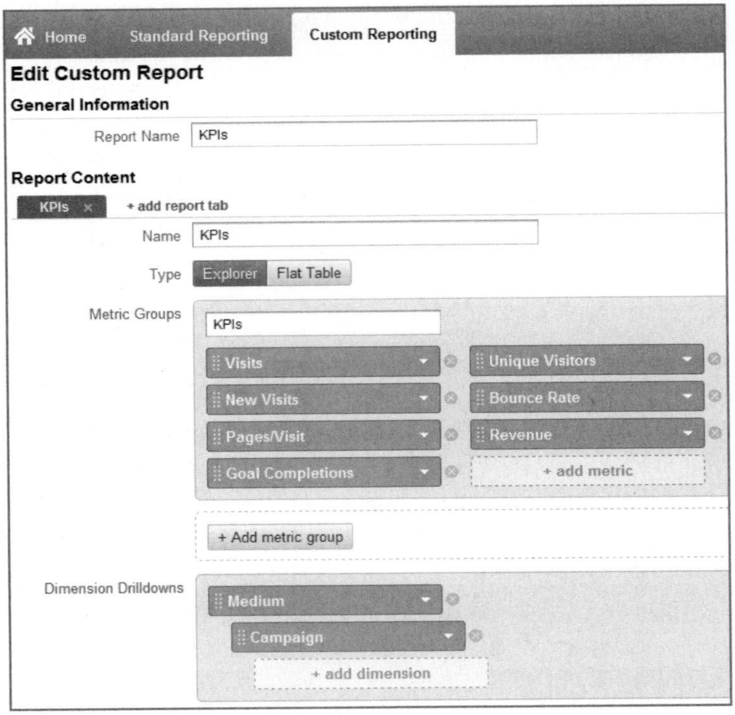

Figure 9.26 Custom report configuration

Campaign	Visits ↓	Unique Visitors	New Visits	Bounce Rate	Pages/Visit	Revenue	Goal Completions
googlestore-general-ps	10,766	9,823	8,898	55.25%	4.02	$5,796.45	4,514
Google Store: English - Americas - Display Only	171	159	157	71.93%	1.67	$0.00	16
(not set)	151	144	143	78.81%	1.36	$0.00	7
googlestore GA by Kathy	31	30	30	48.39%	2.90	$0.00	6
Google Store: English - Americas	19	18	17	63.16%	2.00	$0.00	2

Figure 9.27 Drilling down to display campaigns in the custom report

The reports are highly interactive. Clicking a metric in the scorecard above the graph adjusts the graph to show that metric's trend over time. You can see how bounce rate, new versus returning visits, and so forth change over time for the given data.

Marketers with direct response goals are highly interested in outcome-based metrics, such as conversions and ROI. Per-visit value is extremely important for pay-per-click bidders because it tells you exactly how much value you get from each click. Since you pay per click, this is a relevant comparison and immediately actionable.

Branding- and awareness-focused advertisers want to pay attention to bounce rate, time on site, pages/visits, video views, and so forth. But goal conversions matter here as well. You can set up engagement goals that flag a visit as a conversion when a certain threshold is crossed, such as a certain number of pages per visit or time on site. Chapter 4, "Month 1: Planning Your Campaigns," describes additional soft metrics, including some outside Google Analytics, such as Compete.com and Insights for Search metrics.

Landing page and exit/abandonment analysis is also critical for any advertiser. Google Analytics has an incredibly intuitive and actionable report to visualize visitor paths through the site, including landing and exit pages (Figure 9.28).

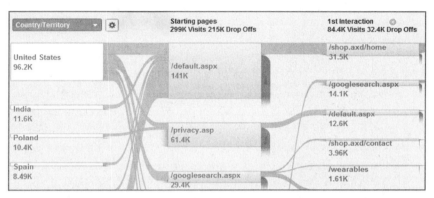

Figure 9.28 Landing page, path, and funnel analysis via flow visualizations

Week 24: Measure Branding and Positioning Goals

This week we continue examining how to measure and optimize campaigns. We can't attain the precision of analytics in branding and awareness goals that we can in direct-response-oriented goals, so some advertisers don't bother to analyze and optimize these softer metrics. But there are plenty of ways to improve the accuracy of our measurements, and it's precisely the lack of exact data that makes it important to use best practices and extract all the value we can from our analytics to gain a competitive advantage in this overlooked area.

Monday: Dealing with Soft Metrics

You can argue that we've become spoiled. The ease and accuracy of accountable advertising that we've become accustomed to online is relatively new. What we call soft metrics are what advertisers and marketers have been relying on for centuries. All we have to do is adapt them for a new medium.

Trends

If web analysts want a catch phrase, a good candidate is "up and to the right." In conferences and classes we often get asked, "What is a good bounce rate?" The tongue-in-cheek answer is "one that is better than last month." And it's true because for most of our metrics, they are what they are and all we can do is try to make them better. It doesn't matter if another site has a 40 percent bounce rate and you have 60 percent. They have a different market, different product, different visitors, different traffic sources, different ad budgets, and so on.

On a similar note, individual user path analysis is an almost entirely useless endeavor because you should never change your site based on something that *one person* does (even if it's the boss' mother). We're interested in identifying trends among segments of users. If we find that new users consistently behave in one pattern while returning visitors behave in another pattern, that's something we can take advantage of as advertisers and site owners.

Goal Values When There Are No Transactions

We like to focus on the examples where we can nail down an exact e-commerce transaction that resulted from a click an ad. We then know down to the penny how much value that click generated and can manage our bids with extreme precision. But that's not realistic for most of us. Most businesses are not e-commerce shops that accept credit cards online. The most common type of business online is one that uses the Web to initiate a relationship of some kind with a potential customer or client. This type of lead generation scenario takes several forms, from contact form submissions to test drive appointments. What they have in common is that they don't generate funds directly, but they all lead to revenue at some point in the future.

Our goal is to assign a monetary value to that action as effectively as the data allows. We know it isn't as precise as e-commerce data, but it's no less important. Doing this has two primary benefits: First, we can evaluate our traffic sources against each other. If certain publishers send traffic to our site that is well qualified and results in premium leads, we want to be able to distinguish that from sites that send high volumes of poorly qualified traffic. Second, we can put value on the action to inform our advertising. If we have some idea of how much a visitor is worth, we know roughly how much we can afford to spend to acquire that visitor.

To arrive at this number, we can look at offline or historical values. If we know that it generally takes five leads to get one eventual sale (20 percent close rate) and the average sale is worth $250, then each lead is worth $50. There's no reason for you to not be confident in this method as long as your historical values are reasonably accurate. Armed with this data, you can set a goal value in Google Analytics for each lead and then run reports that incorporate actual dollar values, which are some of the most actionable by far.

The value of this cannot be overstated, and as consultants we see it every day. Figure 9.29 shows data from a real client who was adamant that its budget should go almost entirely toward its network of referral affiliates because it brings in over twice as much traffic as all of its other sources *combined*. The display ads are a particularly lost cause because they only bring in about 5 percent of the traffic yet must be managed by staff that could be dedicated to the affiliate program.

	Medium	Visits
1.	organic	140,685
2.	referral	953,454
3.	banner	58,861
4.	CPC	198,396

Figure 9.29 Traffic broken down by medium is not the whole story.

Given the data available, it is hard to argue with that. But an experienced analyst knows that volume data without good metrics is often worse than no data at all. Once we implemented the lead valuation project, the rest of the story revealed itself. Figure 9.30 shows that the 5 percent of traffic from display ads leads to a significant portion of the revenue and the organic traffic that is only about 15 percent of traffic has almost double the revenue of the referral channel. For all its traffic, the referral channel sucked up the company's resources and sent largely junk traffic. The site owner had no way to value the visits, so he put all his eggs in the wrong basket.

	Medium	Visits	Revenue	Transactions ↓	Average Value	Ecommerce Conversion Rate	Per Visit Value
1.	organic	140,685	$28,915.32	591	$48.93	0.42%	$0.21
2.	referral	953,454	$15,840.72	362	$43.76	0.04%	$0.02
3.	banner	58,861	$11,293.46	198	$57.04	0.34%	$0.19
4.	CPC	198,396	$7,906.20	178	$44.42	0.09%	$0.04

Figure 9.30 The rest of the story reveals the benefit of putting a value on visitor behavior.

Sadly, that situation is far from unique. And even if you can't put an actual monetary value on goals, there are still ways to take advantage of the built-in commerce metrics. Let's say, for example, that you have a car dealership website and you have three different contact forms:

- Schedule a test drive
- Inquire about financing
- General questions/comments

The first represents someone fairly far along in the buying cycle who is often ready to buy, so this is a valuable lead. The second is still a solid lead, but not as valuable as the first, and the last is the least qualified of all. The problem is that if three ads send visitors to the site and each converts on a lead, they each show the same conversion rate and are valued equally when they clearly don't deliver the same level of value to the advertiser. A useful strategy is to assign a dollar value to each lead—not based on eventual revenue but rather as a relative weight. If the first lead is twice as valuable as the second and 10 times as the third, we can assign a lead value of 10 to the first, 5 to the second, and 1 to the third. Then when the three visitors arrive from the ads, they are given the proper credit and the advertiser has no trouble optimizing ad spends based on measured outcomes.

Engagement and Micro-Conversions

Many advertisers struggle with what to do when the conversion happens offline or many months from the initial interaction, both of which make tracking conversions back to their source difficult. In the previous section we discussed leads that we know ultimately lead to a conversion (even if offline). We are really talking about the funnel steps that indicate progression toward a conversion. Each step along the way shows that the visitor is getting ever closer to converting. For example, in a long-lead-cycle purchase such as enterprise server software, the chance that the ad convinces someone to purchase on the first impression is almost zero. That's why our ads target each phase of the buying process, including early research, vendor selection, price and feature comparison, and so forth. So it's important that we measure the steps—sometimes called micro-conversions—that show the visitor taking actions that will someday lead to a conversion.

Micro-conversions take many forms. Some are actual funnel steps such as registering for an account. Some are more research oriented, such as reading a white paper or watching a video. Some are simply secondary goals of your website that still have business benefit, such as submitting a job application or applying to become an affiliate. The important thing is that you gather as much information as possible about beneficial activities and behavior on your site. This way you are well informed when it comes to evaluating the performance and value of the traffic that your ads deliver.

Tuesday: Multiple Touch Point Analysis

In the preceding section, we alluded to the difficulty of proper analysis when the sales cycle is long and may cover multiple visits. Advertisers who are tasked with upper-funnel phases have long decried the lack of credit given to their work by last-click attribution model analytics programs such as Google Analytics—and many display ad campaigns fit that description.

Let's take the example of a novel product a prospective buyer may not even know exists, such as the Eye-Fi memory card that also serves as a Wi-Fi enabled network card to allow you to instantly download pictures from your digital camera. If users don't know the product exists, they don't search for it. The folks at Eye-Fi hope that upon learning of this neat device via a compelling display ad, you will visit the site and instantly buy one, but that's not always the case. Perhaps first you need to discuss it with your neighbor the photo-buff, who knows all about the gear. Or perhaps you need to check reviews to see if these really work and then peruse the competition. While searching for the competition via the search "network memory card," you ultimately end up back at www.eye.fi again. This time you sign up for the newsletter. When the photo buff stops by the house, you show him the site and he's impressed. The next morning when you get an email with a 10 percent off coupon, you click the link and make the purchase.

The path to your purchase is convoluted but not unusual and looks something like this:

1. Display ad
2. Referral link from review site
3. Organic search
4. Direct
5. Email
6. Conversion

The email gets all the credit, but the display ad sparked the initial interest and deserves at least some of the credit. This is difficult to track via traditional analytics, so Google Analytics introduced multi-channel funnels to shed some light on the process.

The Multi-Channel Funnels report (Figure 9.31) is in the Conversions section and starts off with a Venn diagram that shows our overlapped conversion path. Hovering the cursor over it shows the interactions between various channels and their associated metrics.

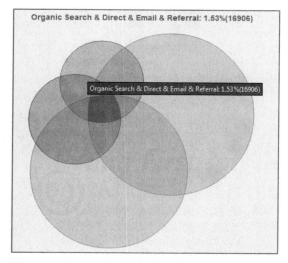

Figure 9.31 Diagram of multi-channel funnels

The Top Conversion Paths report (Figure 9.32) highlights the overlaps that lead to the most conversions. Part of the power of the tool comes in the ability to edit and create your own channel grouping. You can specify the criteria that qualify a visit to be grouped in with another. This example shows some default groupings, such as Social Network. Advertisers often create a group called Branded Search to distinguish an organic search where the user is already familiar with your brand from a generic search. This allows you to test whether generic searches are usually how users find your site as opposed to the Eye-Fi scenario, where the generic search was actually the third visit to the site.

	Channel Grouping Path	Conversions ↓	Conversion Value
1.	Social Network › Direct	5,022	$244,782.99
2.	Social Network › Direct › Direct	2,290	$104,025.89
3.	Display Ad › Direct	1,203	$42,443.63
4.	Organic Search › Organic Search	1,176	$61,802.76
5.	Display Ad › Display Ad	893	$28,221.34
6.	Direct › Organic Search	847	$27,975.65
7.	Social Network › Social Network	643	$14,363.71
8.	Social Network › Social Network › Social Network › Direct	620	$19,527.59
9.	Display Ad › Social Network	581	$31,977.17

Figure 9.32 The Top Conversion Paths report shows the most common paths to a conversion.

With an understanding of the common paths, it helps to look at the Assisted Conversions report (Figure 9.33) to determine which channels tend to appear at the top or bottom of the funnel. An assist indicates that the channel is involved in a conversion path but is not the last interaction prior to the conversion, so in the last click model it doesn't get credit. You can think of this like an assist in basketball. The channel makes an assist that leads to the eventual conversion. One of the most useful things to do is to sort on the last column, the assists ratio. The higher the ratio, the more likely the channel is involved in an assist rather than a last click. We see that social networks are more likely to be an initial step in the path and that paths almost always end with direct visits, which take the lion's share of the conversions.

The reports get us ever closer to our stated goal of understanding everything from the initial awareness all the way through subsequent visits and conversion and everything in between. As Google continues to integrate more DoubleClick/DFA features into its main product lines, we can start measuring before the first visit (view-throughs) and continue all the way through to the final conversion.

	Channel Grouping	Assisted Conversions	Assisted Conversion Value	Last Interaction Conversions	Last Interaction Conversion Value	Assisted / Last Interaction Conversions ↓
1.	Social Network	99	$2,049.32	42	$1,550.00	2.36
2.	Email	1,571	$92,366.49	881	$49,328.03	1.78
3.	Referral	1,751	$60,968.81	1,041	$38,881.67	1.68
4.	Display Ad	6,079	$183,398.67	5,595	$164,211.49	1.09
5.	(Other)	3,032	$88,219.35	2,845	$72,463.27	1.07
6.	Organic Search	8,862	$301,286.83	9,205	$309,448.98	0.96
7.	Direct	21,822	$930,423.44	36,124	$1,690,415.94	0.60

Figure 9.33 The Assisted Conversions report is great for uncovering hidden value in upper-funnel channels.

Attribution Modeling

Google Analytics offers a custom attribution modeling tool for its Premium Edition that can assign different weights to each touch point in the funnel based on the model you choose. For example, rather than the default of last-click attribution, you can choose to weigh the first click more heavily, weigh all evenly, decay the credit based on time, or even create a custom model of your own.

Wednesday: Social Media Metrics—Traffic on Your Site

Entire books have been written about how to measure social media. Our goal is to help organize your approach and highlight a few common strategies. Measuring social media presents a tremendous challenge for advertisers and analysts because the activity is distributed across several sites and media rather than concentrated on your site. On top of this, the social media ecosystem is advancing so incredibly rapidly that the tools and measurement industry are struggling to keep up.

Today we focus on social media activity (including social media advertising) that specifically drives traffic to your site and the social interactions that take place on your site. Although we don't focus much on code in this book, data collection is a major challenge of social media measurement, so we point you in the direction of code that you or your developer can use.

Social Media as a Source

We start with the most basic case: links to your site promoted via social media. This is one of the few scenarios in social media where we control the process end to end, so there's little excuse for not getting it right, but many folks still don't. The reason is that a little data is often worse than no data. It's easy to look at the analytics report in Figure 9.34 and see data from Twitter and assume it's tracking correctly.

Source/Medium	Visits ↓	Revenue	Transactions	Average Value	Ecommerce Conversion Rate	Per Visit Value
twitter.com / referral	1,811	$375.00	2	$187.50	0.11%	$0.21

Figure 9.34 Traffic referred to your site from Twitter

The problem is that there are many ways to view and consume tweets, and most them are not on the actual Twitter.com website. If you click a link in a tweet via Tweetdeck or other application, it does not show up as a link from Twitter.com (because it's not). If you got no visits with Twitter as a source, you would suspect a tracking error. But because *some* of the clicks come from Twitter.com, you may have the false sense that you're collecting data properly and that your tweets don't generate many visits.

Fortunately, the fix is incredibly simple: use campaign tracking tags in your links. For example, if you click the link in the tweet in Figure 9.35, it expands from http://j.mp/xg0DXz to the following:

```
http://www.cardinalpath.com/extracting-value-out-of-google-analytics-multi-
channel-funnel-keyword-reports/
?utm_source=twitter
&utm_medium=social
&utm_content=tweet_010412
&utm_campaign=book
```

Figure 9.35 A standard tweet with a shortened URL that expands to a fully campaign-tagged link

To do this, construct the long URL, then use a URL shortening service like bitly.com to produce the short version you include in the tweet. The real beauty of this solution is that it captures the true marketing reach of a tweet because no matter how many times it gets retweeted, emailed, or posted on CNN's iReport crowdsourced news, as long as the shortened URL is intact, it always expands to the fully tagged link that forces Google Analytics to attribute this visit to a source of twitter and a medium of social. And we even capture the fact that this is used in this book in the utm_content field, so we know if any of you actually type it in and can distinguish that from traffic based on the original tweet.

Because we tag the link properly, viewing the impact of the tweet is easy. We open the All Traffic report in Google Analytics and look for the source/medium of twitter/social. And because we've tagged the medium as social, we can also easily account for the total value of all social media versus other media to evaluate ROI in that area (Figure 9.36). This example uses Twitter, but the same principles apply to any link posted on a social media site, including (and especially) advertising.

Medium	Visits	Revenue ↓	Transactions	Average Value	Ecommerce Conversion Rate	Per Visit Value
cpc	5,090,529	$1,845,842.16	26,999	$68.37	0.53%	$0.36
organic	2,446,461	$811,889.42	16,128	$50.34	0.66%	$0.33
direct	895,789	$424,458.50	8,567	$49.55	0.96%	$0.47
social	567,728	$231,968.07	3,222	$72.00	0.57%	$0.41
referral	671,207	$135,207.09	2,495	$54.19	0.37%	$0.20
affiliate	131,806	$54,111.67	1,711	$31.63	1.30%	$0.41

Figure 9.36 Comparing ROI of social and other media

Social Interaction on Your Site

But social media doesn't end when the visitor arrives on your site. There are plenty of social signals, such as likes, +1s, tweets, emails, and a plethora of other ways to interact socially with the content on your site. Capturing the data on these interactions can give you great insight into which content and which visitors are actively engaged, and since it's on your site, you can capture it via web analytics.

> **Note:** It's possible that the code samples in this section are out of date. For the latest Google Analytics social tracking code check http://j.mp/DisplayBook3.

The Google Analytics _trackSocial method can track those interactions across your site and compare them against each other to evaluate your content and the various networks, the number of which seems to grow daily!

The standard procedure is to fire this special event whenever something that you want to track happens. Usually this comes in the form of a JavaScript onclick event, such as a link or button press. The general format of this method is as follows:

```
_gaq.push(['_trackSocial', 'network', 'socialAction', 'optional-target', 'optional-pagePath']);
```

Here's an example:

```
_gaq.push(['_trackSocial', 'Facebook', 'Like']);
```

If not specified, *optional-target* defaults to the URL of whatever page the visitor was on when they clicked the link. If not specified, *optional-pagePath* defaults to the URI (the URL minus the hostname), including whatever query variables (values following ? or &) are in that URI.

It's easy enough to add code to fire this event on an action within your HTML. Tracking shares and tweets is a bit more difficult because there is no way to listen for these events without somehow having access to the inner workings of Facebook and Twitter. Thankfully, the folks at Facebook and Twitter have created APIs that help you listen for successful events specific to their platforms, such as Like, Share, or Tweet. You can then append the Google Analytics _trackSocial tag to the listening code in order to have _trackSocial set off by a social event. For Facebook that looks similar to this:

```
<script
 src="http://connect.face book.net/en_US/all.js#xfbml=1">
</script>

<fb:like> </fb:like>

<script>
 FB.Event.subscribe('edge.create', function(targetUrl){_gaq.
 push(['_trackSocial', 'social-facebook', 'share', targetUrl]);});
</script>
```

For Twitter, a sample implementation looks like this:

```
<script
 src="http://platform.twitter.com/widgets.js"
 type= "text/javascript">
</script>

<a href="http://code.google.com/apis/analytics"
   data-url="http://code.google.com/apis/analytics"
   class="twitter-share-button">Tweet</a>

<script>
 twttr.events.bind('tweet', function(event) {
  if (event) {var targetUrl;
    if (event.target && event.target.nodeName == 'IFRAME') {
      targetUrl = extractParamFromUri(event.target.src, 'url');}
    _gaq.push(['_trackSocial', 'social-twitter', 'tweet', targetUrl]);}});
</script>
```

One major benefit is that because you're listening for success events via their APIs, you only track the social event on a successful like, unlike, tweet, or other action. Thus the report won't contain failed attempts where the user didn't complete the login process (or perhaps never had an account to begin with).

Reporting & Segmentation

Google Analytics reports social media interactions on your site. Figure 9.37 shows networks plus actions taken from those networks, such as like and unlikes.

Viewing: **Social Source and Action** Social Source			
Secondary dimension: Select... ▾	Sort Type: Default ▾		
Social Source and Action	Social Actions ▾ ↓		Social Actions
1. ■ social-twitter : tweet		247	48.34%
2. ■ social-linkedin : share		142	27.79%
3. ■ Google : +1		80	15.66%
4. ☐ social-facebook : like		31	6.07%
5. ■ social-facebook : unlike		11	2.15%

Figure 9.37 Social interactions including network and action

You can get a sense of the shareability of the content as a whole in the Engagement report, but perhaps a more actionable report is the Pages report (Figure 9.38), which shows which actions were taken on individual pages. This makes it easy to see which blog post or page generated the most social activity.

Viewing: **Social Entity** Page			
Secondary dimension: Select... ▾			
Pivot by: Social Source and Action ▾	Pivot metrics: Social Actions ▾ Select... ▾		
	Total	1. social-twitter : tweet	2. social-linkedin : share
Social Entity	Social Actions ↓	Social Actions	Social Actions
1. blog | Web Analytics | javascript-libraries-that-conflict-with-google-analytics]);	18	16	2
2. blog | Cardinal Path | using-googles-new-social-analytics-reports]);	14	14	6

Figure 9.38 Pages report shows the amount of social interaction on each page.

So far we've been content-focused. But a powerful way to use this functionality is to focus on users. We want to segment users and understand who uses these buttons, who are engaged, who share the content. We can then compare those segments against our email, CPC, and other types of traffic to understand the relative value and get a better understanding of how our visitors behave.

This is especially important because in social more than other types, the disparity between quantity and quality of traffic can be high. Your organic traffic may have sought you out specifically and been highly qualified, but that video that went viral may have brought thousands of visitors, none of whom had any interest in buying anything.

The first step is simply to segment by network (Figure 9.39), using a simple source-based advanced segment. The Average Value column shows that traffic from Facebook had an average value of $17.20 per transaction and brought the site nearly $1,000, while the next nearest was only $134.56. Once you create those segments, you can evaluate them against any criteria for any report in all of Google Analytics, from bounce rate to top landing pages.

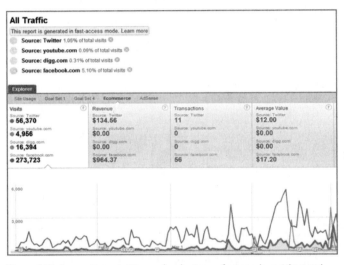

Figure 9.39 Segmenting out visitors and evaluating performance by social network.

Demographics

Marketers have been trying to infer and deduce demographics for years, and still do. But one of the best things about social media and analytics integration is that users willingly give up that information and we can extract it into our analytics reports. Wouldn't it be great to see how male users interact with your content versus female users? Or to evaluate the ad targeting platforms to see how accurate their statistics are. We look at one way to do just that.

This is possible because you connect your site to Facebook's API, and any users that visit your site and connect to Facebook (to simplify a registration process for example) make their profile details available to that page. Folks like Mat Clayton of

Mixcloud and others have shown how easy it is to pull demographic data from these profiles with code like this:

```
function fbdemos()
{
    FB.getLoginStatus (function (res)
    {
        window.console.log(res);
        if(res.status === 'connected')
        {
            window.console.log("user connected");
            getFBDemos();
            window.console.log("returned demographics: ");
        } else if (res.status === 'notConnected')
        {
            window.console.log("user logged in");
        } else if(res.status === 'unknown')
        {
            window.console.log("No Facebook Session detected");
        }
    });
}
```

Once you extract the data, you can set a custom variable in Google Analytics to tag that visitor with the extracted data. With a simple advanced segment (Figure 9.40), you can do amazing demographic analysis on your user base with highly accurate data supplied by the users themselves. And because you can set custom variables to be persistent, the demographic information persists from visit to visit, as long as they don't delete their cookies.

Figure 9.40 Advanced segments based on gender supplied by Facebook and stored via custom variables in Google Analytics

Thursday: Social Media Metrics—Activity Outside Your Site

The challenging part of social media measurement is that so much of the conversation happens on sites we don't control and thus don't have direct analytics access to. But some tools are available, and more are on the horizon.

Network-Based Analytics

The various social media sites often have their own proprietary analytics data they provide to users. One of the most well known of these is Facebook's Insights. Although not nearly as extensive as a true analytics package, it does provide data about how users have interacted with your Facebook presence. Facebook also provides some more granular data about individual posts, such as the Reach, Engaged Users, Talking About This, and Virality metrics. But as you saw, some of the most valuable data on Facebook is in the form of demographics (Figure 9.41).

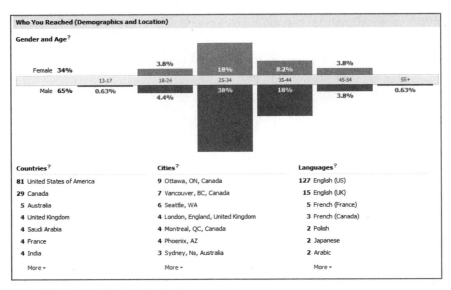

Figure 9.41 Demographic data on Facebook

Another popular social media site is YouTube, which provides its own analytics. Although Google allows brand channel users to gather page-view data within Google Analytics, the primary reporting interface is still within YouTube itself (Figure 9.42) and includes YouTube-specific information about how your channel was discovered and embedded and mobile info, likes and dislikes, subscribers, favorites, and comments. Advertisers looking to take advantage of data gleaned from social media can find some great data, such as the audience retention graphs.

Twitter's API has spawned an entire industry of tools. Many of them, such as Klout.com, provide a proprietary measure of influence for individual Twitter accounts to benchmark themselves against others. Recently Twitter has launched its own analytics package as well (Figure 9.43).

Channel: CardinalPath

Top 10 videos Browse all videos

	Video	Views ↓	Likes	Comments
1.	Presenting Google Analytics Premium	917	25	0
2.	Google Analytics Premium in 5 Minutes	722	17	0
3.	KPIs, Dashboards & Metrics - Oh My!	380	4	0
4.	Understanding Google Analytics: The V5 Interface	313	4	0
5.	Analyze & Optimize: Measuring your SEO performance	215	1	0
6.	Reciprocation... and Revenge	182	0	0
7.	Online Persuasion The Power of Social Proof	170	0	1
8.	Back to Basics: Google Analytics Setup and Best Pra...	149	1	0
9.	Online Persuasion - Loss Aversion and Scarcity	144	0	0
10.	Taking your Website Worldwide	79	0	0

Demographics

Top geographies

United States
Canada
France
United Kingdom
India

Gender
● Male 83.9%
● Female 16.1%

Figure 9.42 YouTube Analytics

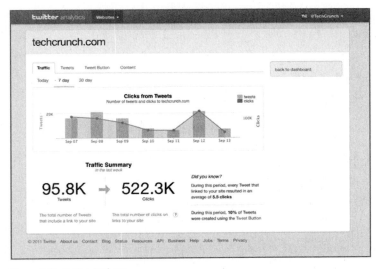

Figure 9.43 Twitter Analytics

Social Metrics Aggregators

Trying to collect all this data from the different networks in a meaningful way can be a monumental task. And even if we can collect the data, it's difficult to combine so many disparate sets of data, often with no common element to tie them together.

This was why Google bought PostRank and launched the Social Data Hub. Still developing rapidly, it tries to be a single point of aggregation for users to pool their data from the various networks. Google has defined a generic framework to gather the various posts, votes, shares, comments, bookmarks, and other activities involved in social media. Although this offers great promise to account owners (and Google), it's not yet clear if large established social media networks will voluntarily give up the valuable data on the activities of their users.

But while Google's approach of warehousing data submitted via APIs is new, it is hardly the first to try to aggregate this data. Tools such as Salesforce's Radian6, Sysomos's Heartbeat, Autonomy, and Viralheat scrape and collect massive amounts of data to help companies monitor their social media presence. One of the primary advantages of these tools is to monitor sentiment and determine whether your brand is being discussed in a positive or negative light.

Friday: Correlation and Causation

The goal of measuring our advertising and our site is to improve it and optimize it. We want this process to be data driven, and we use analytics with the intent of finding actionable data to inform and drive our decisions. To do this we pore over the data, trying to understand what our visitors want, what motivates them, and how we can incentivize and encourage them to visit our site and convert.

As we analyze this data, we can see *what* they did, but not *why*. We can make inferences and look for connections between behaviors and events, but we really can't say for sure if what someone did was what they intended to do or what their motivation for doing it was. As we try to connect the dots, we can apply some calculations and examine correlation.

The math behind the statistics is beyond the scope of this book, but essentially we can say X and Y are correlated if as X increases, Y increases, and as X drops, so does Y. The problem is that even if we know two things are correlated, we still can't say for sure that one caused the other. This fallacy is known by the Latin *cum hoc, ergo propter hoc*, which means "with this, therefore because of this." The error pointed out here is that just because there is a relationship between two things, it doesn't mean one caused the other. The most famous example is the rise in shark attacks that is correlated with increased sales of ice cream. There is indeed a relationship, but one doesn't cause the other. Increases in ocean swimming and ice cream consumption are both caused by warmer weather, not each other.

Assuming a causal relationship is an easy trap to fall into, and on occasion there are assumptions we are willing to make, but we have to do so with caution. But this doesn't mean there is no reason to examine correlation. The fact that we don't understand the relationship doesn't mean there isn't one. And it could well be causal. Correlation is also beneficial when we can easily measure one aspect but not the other. If we are interested in X but can't easily measure it, then a correlation to easily measured Y becomes interesting. For example, studies have shown there is an 80 percent correlation between where you move your mouse on the page and where your eyes are looking on the page. This intuitively makes sense because we move our mouse to click things we're looking at and our mouse tends to move to our point of focus. As we analyze layouts, we're interested in how people perceive our page, where they look, and in what order. But true eye-tracking systems are prohibitively expensive and time consuming for most businesses. However, tracking mouse movement is extremely easy, and software solutions are available that are easily installed for a very low cost.

Speaking of sharks, one of our clients for whom we run online marketing and advertising runs an island vacation destination. A few years ago, the client's site had a sizable spike in traffic. We did the analysis to trace it back to the source and found it was essentially all direct traffic, but even more intriguing was that it converted at an extremely high rate. Keen to capture more of this valuable traffic we tried all the tricks in our toolbox—isolating it to a specific geography, examining landing pages—but were unable to find evidence linking any other aspect to the spike. We couldn't even find correlation, let alone causation! Weeks later a visitor to the resort mentioned that she saw a show on the Discovery Channel's *Shark Week* that featured the resort. We researched the airings and found that within an hour of the show, the traffic spike began, and in this case, we found the assumption of causation acceptable!

Sometimes the question isn't just about causation, but which metrics to look at for correlation. We once consulted on a television campaign for a major multinational with a well-known website. The analytics team was trying to determine whether the TV ads had been successful, but the problem was that the site and company were already well known, so it was impossible to isolate variables, and naked eye correlation was difficult. The metrics (Figure 9.44) showed a thin line when the TV ads ran Sunday through Wednesday, but there was already a trend of a big jump of traffic (thick line) on Monday morning. Did the ads perform? We ran the numbers and it turns out there was a statistically significant improvement correlated to the ad spots that could be mathematically proven, and even the naked eye could see that the rise appeared to follow the ads.

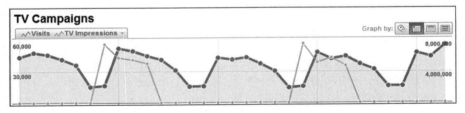

Figure 9.44 Traffic increases correlated with TV ad impressions

But we were looking at the wrong metrics. The purpose of the ad was to drive traffic to a particular tool on the site. This tool had proven to be extremely effective at converting customers to sign up for the client's service, so the goal was to get as many people through this tool as possible. So the measure of performance of the ad was not simply did it cause a bump in raw traffic to the site but did it increase use of the tool. When we examined tool completions against the ad spots (Figure 9.45), the correlation was clear to the naked eye. The math proved with a 97 percent certainty the correlation between running the ad and an immediate sharp spike in tool conversions. And when the ad stopped, the conversions fell.

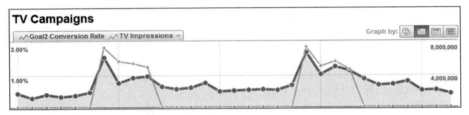

Figure 9.45 Conversions correlated with TV ad impressions

This correlation satisfied the team placing the ads enough to continue with no hesitation, and the assumption that the ad *caused* the usage was perfectly acceptable. But to remove any doubt, we examined the numbers for the months that followed and the pattern continued.

Another way that correlation can useful is examining the effect of overall branding and awareness campaigns to drive searches on the Web and corresponding traffic to your site. For example, let's say that you're the online brand manager for a just-released action movie with a blockbuster budget and plenty of marketing resources behind it. The question is, Have your awareness campaigns been working?

Figure 9.46 shows the overall amount of searches for the name of your movie via Google's Insights for Search tool. This gives you an idea of whether or not people are motivated to hit the Web and start searching for information related to the movie and a great indicator of interest and pent-up demand. You see a small spike when the movie was announced and then a big spike once your flood of advertising was released.

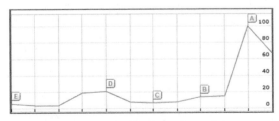

Figure 9.46 Internet search volume for your keywords

But you also want to see if those searches result in searches to your site. Figure 9.47 shows organic traffic to the site, which is publicly launched two-thirds of the way through the graph. You definitely see those same searches resulting not just in general buzz but in traffic to your site as well. You want to see not just the fact that the brand awareness is on the Internet but that it's correlated to traffic to your site.

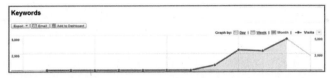

Figure 9.47 Organic search volume to your site from those keywords

Month 7: Optimizing the Performance of Your Campaigns

10

One of the primary benefits of online display advertising compared to other media is the ability to hone, tweak, and optimize your campaigns to maximum effect. Initially in this chapter we focus on the ads themselves, but the real improvements are realized when the entire life cycle of the customer's journey is optimized, including your landing pages.

The perfect ad has the right message directed to the right audience at the right time. This chapter is about optimizing those elements to create high-performing campaigns for your business.

Chapter Contents:
Week 25: Refine Your Campaigns and Ad Groups
Week 26: Expand Your Reach
Week 27: Test Your Ads
Week 28: Create Effective Landing Pages

Week 25: Refine Your Campaigns and Ad Groups

Chapter 5, "Month 2: Targeting Your Audience," showed how to evaluate different advertising inventory and ad formats to match your campaign goals and maximize your chance of success. But no matter how much research you do before buying, you don't know the true performance until you put the plan into action and evaluate the results. What you do to optimize from here largely depends on the results you see from your initial campaigns.

Monday: Evaluating Performance

As advertisers used to working in Google search-based campaigns, one important difference in display ads is the metrics we optimize for. Search campaigns focus heavily on Quality Score, of which click-through rate (CTR) is a major factor. Quality Score is also important on the Google Display Network (GDN), but CTR much less so. Initially we concentrate on optimizing for impressions, so we can gather enough data to optimize our placements, ads, and landing pages.

Drilling Down

As you make your evaluations and determine an optimization strategy, remember the basic hierarchy of Google AdWords: Account › Campaigns › Ad Groups. Choosing the right level to change is critical. Sometimes you must adjust an entire campaign, sometimes an ad group or individual ad. You must decide whether the placement site is hopeless or whether you haven't targeted that site's audience with an ad that speaks specifically to them. As you evaluate an account, follow the account structure and hierarchy. First, ensure there are no account-wide issues, such as billing problems. Second, drill down to campaigns and finally to ad groups, where you can consider more granular adjustments to placements and the ad creatives.

With any new account or campaigns, keep an eye out for alerts, announcements, and notifications that may indicate that your account is not performing to its full potential. Alerts may pertain to disapproved ads, new or discontinued features, billing issues, and even automatically generated optimization suggestions from Google based on things it notices about your account. You can adjust how to receive these notifications by navigating to My Account › Notification Settings.

Further optimization begins with examining the decisions you made in Chapter 5 and looking for potential high or low performers. Click All Online Campaigns in the left-hand navigation bar and scroll through the high-level metrics on the Campaigns subtab to see all campaigns, search and display.

Click to select each campaign of interest and sort by impressions, then clicks, conversions, cost, cost per conversion, and view through conversions to understand at a high level how each campaign is performing. Are there any surprises? Are your top impression campaigns also your top clicks? Are there ad groups with high cost per conversion or low view-through metrics? Poor performers on any of these metrics need to be examined but can often be salvaged. Just as important are high-performing ad groups that provide successful benchmarks of ads, placements, and audiences. These can provide insights into how to improve the low performers and find similar opportunities.

The place to start evaluating display campaigns is the Display Networks tab, which consolidates the former Networks, Audiences, and Topics tabs. Begin by double-checking that no search impressions snuck into your display campaigns. Google provides visibility into the performance of individual keywords in contextually targeted display ads, but best practice is still to manage search and display ads in separate campaigns. The easiest way to check for a search campaign is to look for a Keywords tab. Similarly, the Display Network tab indicates a display campaign (Figure 10.1). This can be confusing because you can contextually target keywords in a display campaign. But those display keywords appear on the Display Network tab.

Figure 10.1 The top row shows a display-only campaign, the center row a search-only campaign, and the bottom row shows a campaign with both.

On the Display Network tab, click Placements and initially sort the top-level domains by cost to identify placements that dominate the budget. Do this for both automatic and managed placements. Do these sites appear to be relevant? Are they performing well in terms of clicks? Conversions? View-through conversions? You might see a wide discrepancy in cost per conversion.

Identify a few placements to examine further. In Figure 10.2, for example, shows that the checked domains severely underperform the rest. The first, a dating site, is particularly concerning because it consumes a large part of the budget. Despite many impressions, which isn't a bad thing at this point, it has no conversions, which is a concern.

Click See URL to see the URLs of pages on which your ad appeared (Figure 10.3). Are there individual pages that vary significantly in performance or budget used? As before, sort on various metrics such as view-throughs, conversion rate, clicks, cost, and impressions.

You're just evaluating at this stage. Avoid taking action until you understand more about *why* the placements don't perform. But if you see domains or pages that are obviously irrelevant or non-brand-safe placements, you may want to exclude them immediately by selecting the row and clicking Exclude Placements. From here you can exclude placements from either an ad group or an entire campaign.

	Domain	Clicks	Impr.	CTR	Avg. CPC	Cost	Conv. (1-per-click)	Cost / conv. (1-per-click)	Conv. rate (1-per-click)	View-through Conv.
	Total - all automatic	7,927	14,227,989	0.06%	$1.36	$10,789.79	298	$36.20	3.76%	2
☐	anonymous.google	386	1,487,927	0.03%	$2.16	$833.21	47	$17.73	12.18%	0
☑	okcimg.com	173	877,510	0.02%	$1.93	$333.29	0	$0.00	0.00%	0
☐	anonymous.google	193	720,876	0.03%	$1.14	$220.34	10	$21.84	5.24%	1
☐	youtube.com	503	534,433	0.09%	$0.97	$487.69	9	$54.19	1.79%	0
☐	zillow.com	754	459,464	0.16%	$1.24	$934.50	4	$233.62	0.53%	0
☑	bearinsider.com	38	213,396	0.02%	$1.89	$71.66	0	$0.00	0.00%	0
☐	seniorpeoplemeet.com	63	174,740	0.04%	$2.15	$135.37	1	$135.37	1.59%	0

Figure 10.2 Two underperforming domains that merit further investigation

	URL	Clicks	Impr.	CTR ⑦	Avg. CPC ⑦	Cost
☐	www.seniorpeoplemeet.com/v3/profile	20	40,842	0.05%	$2.33	$46.59
☐	www.seniorpeoplemeet.com/community/media/photo.cfm	8	30,613	0.03%	$1.97	$15.78
☐	www.seniorpeoplemeet.com/v3/whoviewedme	6	15,227	0.04%	$2.14	$12.86
☐	www.seniorpeoplemeet.com/community/search/search-my-match-results.cfm	3	1,036	0.29%	$2.25	$6.74
☐	www.seniorpeoplemeet.com/v3/profile/todaysmatches	4	8,839	0.05%	$1.66	$6.63

Figure 10.3 Individual URLs

After you examine the high-level metrics of each placement, the Dimensions tab can help you dig deeper and understand the behavior of your audience. Review Chapter 9, "Month 6: Launch and Measure Your Campaign's Performance," for the options available in the Dimensions tab, and incorporate those elements into your evaluation. Is there a time of day that your ads do particularly well or poorly? For example, in Figure 10.4, you can see that the late afternoon/evening hours (5:00 p.m. to 7:00 p.m. Eastern US time, 2:00 p.m. to 4:00 p.m. Pacific US time) do very well with over 13,000 conversions and a cost per conversion of around $16, while the hours after midnight have just a few conversions with a cost/conversion as high as $24.

Hour of day	Clicks ⑦	Impr. ⑦	CTR ⑦	Avg. CPC ⑦	Cost	Avg. Pos.	Conv. (1-per-click) ⑦	Cost / conv. (1-per-click) ⑦
18	623,724	13,418,970	4.65%	$0.39	$245,093.71	2.4	14,121	$16.00
17	597,216	12,297,552	4.86%	$0.39	$233,131.23	2.4	13,825	$15.53
19	594,396	13,628,206	4.36%	$0.40	$235,605.19	2.4	13,115	$16.52
0	91,153	4,858,738	1.88%	$0.42	$38,060.83	2.3	1,425	$24.37
1	51,616	2,530,637	2.04%	$0.41	$21,350.13	2.4	856	$22.71
3	35,144	1,935,313	1.82%	$0.41	$14,493.49	2.4	829	$16.20
2	34,369	2,031,772	1.69%	$0.41	$14,207.13	2.4	617	$21.04

Figure 10.4 Dimensions reports provide details about how your ads perform.

Are there additional insights to gain from the Geography reports and User Location reports? What about the Reach and Frequency reports? Do your placements offer any demographics insights? Continue through the available reports, paying special attention to dimensions that apply to your specific business or website, such as Call Details if you use call metrics.

The Tools and Analysis › Conversion › Search Funnels report can provide insight into ads, clicks, and impressions that happen in the earlier stages of the buying cycle. They aren't counted as delivering the final conversion (last click), but they're nonetheless important as the initial contact with the potential customer (first click). Examine these assists to see if your display campaigns aid your search campaigns. Specifically, look for clicks and impressions with a high assist number and, if you track them, high view-through conversions.

Google AdWords offers many ways to evaluate traffic but provides a limited view of how that traffic performs—usually just whether or not a conversion script executes. But a web analytics tool such as Adobe SiteCatalyst, Coremetrics, or Google Analytics provides more comprehensive information about what happens after the click (post-click). For AdWords users, Google Analytics is a great tool because it can be configured to automatically pull in data from AdWords campaigns (see Chapter 9). Analytics packages have two main advantages over AdWords conversion tracking.

First, AdWords provides only the most basic conversion information. Web analytics tools can go much deeper into the type of conversion, how many, what categories, which stock-keeping units (SKUs), and so forth. They also provide more complex conversion analysis, such as multi-channel funnels and multi-session analytics to show what happens when AdWords campaigns are mixed with other media over the course of several visits where only the final visit results in a conversion.

Second, not all campaigns can be measured strictly on a conversion event. Display campaigns often drive awareness and engagement, which are much better measured via a web analytics package than the simple conversion tracking code of AdWords. An illuminating metric for a display campaign is the bounce rate, which tells us whether someone clicked the ad to visit the landing page and then left immediately without taking any further actions. A non-bounce doesn't indicate a conversion per se but rather gives an idea of whether they were engaged enough by the landing page to consider further exploration of the site. Metrics like pages/visit, time on site, and even revenue/impression give a glimpse into how far the user goes beyond the landing page. To evaluate specifically where the traffic from particular campaigns or ad groups went on your site, you can use a Flow Visualization report (similar to the one in Figure 9.28 in Chapter 9), segmented by ad group.

Pay extra attention to campaigns that receive a lot of clicks—is the traffic qualified? In addition to segmenting by entire campaigns and ad groups, you want to pay particular attention to the landing pages themselves (destination URLs of the AdWords reports). Are there particular landing pages that are over- or underperforming?

The analysis possibilities to evaluate ad performance are nearly endless. Ultimately your goal is not just analysis, but action. So as you progress through your evaluation, be sure to note areas where you can optimize your campaigns based on the data you collect and insights you derive.

Tuesday: Optimizing Ads

One critical determination is whether poor performance is due to an audience that's not relevant to your business or an ad that's not relevant to your audience (even if your business is relevant to that audience).

Overcome the temptation to shut off placements that are dragging down your ad groups. Instead, take a hard look at the underperforming campaign or ad group and ask why. This is especially true for sites that are well targeted to your niche. By shutting those sites off prematurely, you miss what can be some of your most valuable traffic while leaving less-relevant sites active.

If overall performance does not meet expectations, it's not likely your placements that need the most work—it's your conversion funnel. The first step at improving that funnel is making sure the fundamentals of imagery, persuasion, and scent, discussed in Chapter 7, "Month 4: Creating Image Ads," are properly applied to your audience selection, ad creative, and landing page.

One of the most important things to do is put yourself in the mind of the person viewing your ad. Now that you have more information about what pages the person is viewing, how they interact with your site, and potentially even demographic data, your chances of portraying an accurate picture of the viewer are better than ever. For example, if you sell bicycles, the mindset of someone viewing your ad on a page on About.com that discusses how to start training for a triathlon may be very different than someone reading a post on a social network about their friend's finish in a triathlon. The former is very likely to be making (relatively expensive) purchases in the near future, while the latter may just be killing time. The mindset of the first person makes them a fantastic audience, for whom you may be willing to bid a high amount. Your ad creative here can contain an offer to sway someone who is lower in the buying funnel.

But the person viewing the social network may not be a lost cause. Before you exclude such social networks, consider whether the ad needs to be adjusted. Someone viewing their friend's triathlon experience may be contemplating trying it themselves, as peer involvement can be a strong motivator. The person contemplating a triathlon may respond to an ad that appeals to their curious but uncommitted mindset. Or your ad may speak to a concern they have, such as the costs involved with triathlons or how physically fit someone has to be to participate.

Even websites or pages in a similar category may attract users with very different mindsets. For example, someone browsing a news site that is focused on news from their industry or profession, such as AviationNews.net, may be focused on work. Alternatively, someone perusing a news site focused on last night's Oscar winners may have anything but work on their mind and thus respond very differently to ads. In both of these situations the person viewing the ad may be an ideal candidate for your product or service and the site can potentially convert well for you, but how you approach advertising to them may vary considerably.

If you're unsure of why a site is performing the way it is, use Networks › Placements › See URL List to see exactly which pages were showing your ad and how it performed on each. Actually visit the page and understand where your ad would appear and think about the visitors consuming that content.

You can also use the Google Ad Planner techniques shown in Chapter 5 in reverse—instead of using it to find a potential page to advertise on, use that information to give you more information about a site you're evaluating. Using Ad Planner to research AllFreeSewing.com, you can see that the site has an extreme skew to the female demographic (Figure 10.5). Ad Planner provides this and other demographic data that will likely affect how you market triathlon bikes. While women are not the majority of triathlon competitors, they are the fastest-growing demographic. So a marketer who takes a tailored approach may find great success over those who use traditional imagery, ad copy, and landing pages. However, the data for AllFreeSewing.com also shows that by far the largest age demographic is 55 to 64, and (not shown) the interests suggest that these people may prefer to spend their free time on not particularly athletic hobbies. Here your best option may be to exclude this site and forego its audience.

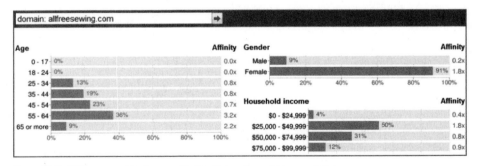

Figure 10.5 Ad Planner provides demographic data that can be useful to your strategy.

Note: If you want to show your customized ad to a demographic that you have specifically targeted (such as women over 55 years old), you need an ad group with only that ad, and its placements must match your demographic. You must exclude those placements from your other campaigns.

As you optimize your ads, one useful metric is relative CTR. In search campaigns, standard CTR (nonrelative) gives you information about how relevant your ads are to the user's query based on how often they click your ad when doing that search. However, in display campaigns there are many more factors involved, and the page displaying the ad is not a standardized search results page that gives a level playing field to all. On the GDN, your ad may perform differently from one placement to the next. Similarly, the *same* ad on the *same* placement may perform differently if it appears in different ad blocks on the same page, particularly if one is low on the page (below the fold) and requires users to scroll to see it.

Relative CTR considers only the CTRs of other ads shown in that exact placement:

relative CTR = (your CTR) / (average CTR of the other ads)

You can compute relative CTR for an ad group or an entire campaign. If your ad has a CTR of 0.1 percent and the other ads in those placements have an average CTR of 0.02 percent, then your relative CTR is 5 and your ad is doing five times as well as your competitors. A relative CTR greater than 1 indicates that you are outperforming other ads in that space, while a value less than 1 says you have work to do! Note that an ad group with text ads is compared only against other text ads, and similarly display is compared to display. An ad group with both uses an average of the two. This metric is not available for CPM bidding and is not shown by default. To enable it, customize the columns (Figure 10.6).

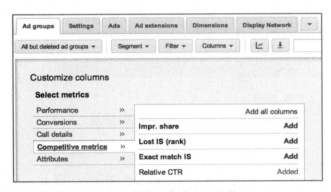

Figure 10.6 Enabling relative CTR from the Competitive Metrics screen

Remember that when it comes to evaluating ads against engagement metrics, a web analytics tool such as Google Analytics can tell you much more about the performance of an ad creative and its placement than AdWords. Using metrics such as bounce rate with the Ad Content dimension and a secondary dimension of Placement Domain (or Placement URL) can provide deep insights into ad performance.

Wednesday: Optimizing Placements

Once you have some confidence in the ability of your ads and landing pages to convert relevant traffic, it's time to start evaluating the quality of that traffic so you can adjust and optimize your placements as needed. Remember that we initially optimize for impressions to gain enough data to make valid conclusions. Much of the evaluation can take place right in the Display Ads tab (see Chapter 9).

As noted earlier, it's important to have a well-functioning ad creative and landing page that address the audience. You also need a strategy before you start changing things. One strategy that many employ successfully is to create different types of campaigns and ad groups for performance tiers of traffic. Normally you would think about separating campaigns for technical or logistical reasons, such as targeting different geographies or different audiences. In this case, the idea is to segregate your solid, known performers from placements that may justify lower bids or need customized ads and landing pages to correctly address the audience.

Figure 10.7 shows a typical scenario for display advertisers. On the bottom left there is a highly targeted group that makes up the core audience of your product or services. Ads in this group tend to be highly effective, which leads to a low cost per action (CPA). But these sites have less traffic volume than general-interest sites, such as CNN.com. Likewise, the number of people in your highly targeted audience is small compared to the general population. By moving placements that have proven themselves to be part of this core group into their own campaigns, you can target them more aggressively.

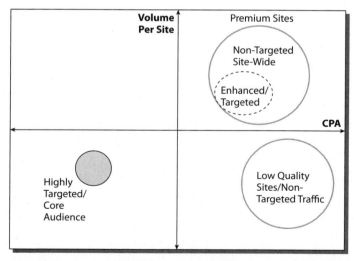

Figure 10.7 A common categorization of placement performance that can organize your optimization strategy

The premium sites are NYTimes.com, CNN.com, economist.com, and so forth. They have high traffic volumes but also higher-quality traffic. However, the traffic is less targeted by default and therefore can have high CPA. In the next section, we show how to limit your ads to the relevant parts of those sites to lower the CPA to something closer to your core audience.

The low-quality sites provide highly irrelevant traffic without the high traffic volume of the premium sites. Make these your lowest priority sites, and in most cases, exclude them entirely.

Often you find that one particular URL is blowing through your budget but is highly profitable. Because budgets can be set only at the campaign level, you want to pull this URL into its own campaign, which includes only placements known to be highly profitable. Then you can feel comfortable setting high budget caps and allowing the campaigns to accrue a high ad spend.

Once you've identified the high performers and pulled them into their own ad groups or even campaigns, you can continue to maximize the opportunity with other techniques. These include testing highly relevant ads, varying bids and budget, and testing landing page variations, as discussed later in the chapter.

Thursday: Optimizing with Contextual Keywords

Occasionally an ad that you know to be relevant to your audience, displayed on a high-quality site where you know relevant content exists, can receive plenty of impressions and still underperform. For example, traffic to the page on About.com that discusses how to begin training for a triathlon is extremely relevant to an advertiser selling starter packages for triathlons. That's likely to be a great placement. However, there are over 10,000,000 pages on About.com, and most of them have nothing to do with triathlons!

Here you can take advantage of the enhanced online campaigns discussed in Chapter 5 to simultaneously target a placement and keywords. We know there is relevant, quality traffic on About.com, but it's masked by the nonrelevant traffic. Figure 10.7 on the top-right quadrant are the premium sites, but the dotted line represents the subsection of those sites with content directly relevant to your ad and likely to have a higher CTR and lower CPA.

Of the two ads on the About.com page in Figure 10.8, the top is relevant to the content, while the one on the right side may find better performance on the site's pages that have to do with saving on your utility bills, green living, or even disaster planning!

As you evaluate your placements, before you exclude a high-quality, high-traffic site entirely, it's worth investigating whether you can narrow the traffic to only the relevant parts of the site by pulling it into a separate ad group that uses keywords to refine where on that site the ad can show. This reduces the overall impressions for that site and works best for news and other large informational sites.

Figure 10.8 Generally, the more relevant the ad is to the content, the better performance it's likely to have.

If you have exhausted opportunities to optimize the traffic through the techniques discussed here, it may be time to exclude the placement for good. As shown on Monday, this can be done from the interface and can be done for ad groups or the entire campaign. It's also possible to create exclusion lists that are stored as shared libraries and can be used on multiple campaigns. This is useful if you have lots of campaigns, so you don't have to update the exclusions manually for each campaign.

When filtering websites to be excluded, you have several options that can allow more granular filtering. You can block the entire domain, just a subdomain, or even a single directory on that domain. For example, if you exclude About.com, it blocks the entire domain, but blocking `powerboat.about.com` allows everywhere else on the site, such as:

    http://powerboat.about.com/od/safetyandeducation

Similarly, if you block `powerboat.about.com/od/safetyandeducation`, then your ads don't appear on safety pages, but they can appear on:

    http://powerboat.about.com/od/buyingsellingaboat

Friday: Optimizing Audiences

So far, you maximize the performance of your campaigns by optimizing your ads, optimizing your placements, and narrowing in on relevant content within those placements. Now that you have a good benchmark for what your campaigns are capable of delivering, we turn our attention to optimizing the targeted audiences.

While the fundamental techniques are unchanged, the interface is rapidly evolving (as always), but as this book goes to press, the Audiences tab is under the Display Ads tab in the Interests & Remarketing section.

Much of the optimization for audiences follows the same patterns as you've followed thus far—identifying and then isolating high and low performers. The performance of the audiences in Figure 10.9 is wildly different. The top row (vacation offers) is earning the second highest number of conversions and maintaining the second best cost/conversion. The second row (weather news) is performing terribly relative to the others, with the highest spend and a paltry number of conversions at enormous cost per conversion. The bottom row (team sports) is highly profitable with more than double the next highest number of conversions and by far the lowest cost/conversion. Continue to evaluate, isolate, and optimize audiences as you did for placements.

Audience	Clicks	Impr.	Cost	Conv. (1-per-click) ⑦	Cost / conv. (1-per-click) ⑦
Display Network	**757,607**	**96,681,234**	**$345,438.93**	**6,943**	**$49.75**
Travel > Travel Agencies & Services > Vacation Offers	4,068	9,228,417	$7,086.66	218	$32.51
News > Weather	9,710	7,389,791	$14,123.61	28	$504.41
News > Sports News	3,232	4,107,770	$2,849.68	60	$47.49
Sports > Team Sports	2,580	3,336,193	$4,562.55	546	$8.36

Figure 10.9 Examining the performance of audiences in display campaigns

After the initial examination, you'll have a better understanding of how various audiences perform. You can use that to further refine the lists to improve targeting. Remarketing lists are high performing, so they are often some of the first and largest display campaigns. By using placement, contextual, or topic targeting to layer on top of remarketing lists, you can further refine the targeted audience.

Another successful way to optimize audiences is by diversifying the lists to become more granular. If you started remarketing to all visitors who visited your site but didn't convert, try adding lists for specific products or promotions. Because remarketing gives you the ability to reach out to site visitors via ads at a later date, you might think of remarketing as naturally continuing a conversation with potential customers—they just didn't realize they were having the conversation! Since you know specifically what they were looking at when they abandoned the funnel, marketing to those users with specific products, promotions, and messaging that ties directly to past behavior can lift conversions rates.

As you grow your remarketing lists, you can employ more-sophisticated and -targeted strategies such as message stacking. This is an effective technique where you stack campaigns one after the other based on the performance of the previous campaign. For example, if you have a promotion or event—such as a steeply discounted anniversary sale—that drives a significant amount of traffic to a landing page, you can set a remarketing cookie on that page for up to 540 days. You remarket the sale to the audience for the duration of that event but then return to that same audience and market a new sale with specialized messaging that builds on what they have seen, such as a private sale available only to clients who participated in the anniversary event. Or if you had printers as a loss leader during that sale, ink, photo paper, and toner a few months later can be effective (with bonus points if you set a specific remarketing audience cookie on those that checked out with the printer!). Begin creating a conversation with the audience by continually adjusting your message to build on what you already know. Stacking ad copy romances customers into buying—and buying again.

Week 26: Expand Your Reach

A phrase commonly used in display advertising is "Nail it, then scale it." You spend much of this chapter honing, optimizing, and tweaking your entire flow. What you have done so far gives you the confidence to hit the gas and expand the reach of your campaigns to deliver even more conversions.

Monday: Expanding Reach with Ad Group Bids

When you are optimizing toward impressions, it's important to make sure you aren't missing potential opportunities because your campaign is limited by budget. The campaigns in Figure 10.10 are very profitable but are being held back by a budget set too low. Google obviously wants to avoid this situation, so it notifies us in a brightly colored font!

☐	●	Campaign	Budget	Status ⑦		Clicks ↓ ⑦	Impr.
☐	●	industry terms	$7,000.00/day	Limited by budget ⑦	☒	143,472	9,348,873
☐	●	Industry Terms - C	$500.00/day	Limited by budget ⑦	☒	116	9,793
☐	●	Statistics	$500.00/day	Limited by budget ⑦	☒	109	6,801

Figure 10.10 Campaigns limited by budget

Once you identified an audience or placement that is highly profitable, you want to maximize the opportunity and take every chance you can to show your ad to those users. Once you determined that a niche is a high performer, you want to own as much of that niche as possible.

Impression share is calculated as the percentage of impressions you achieve divided by the number of impressions you are *eligible* to receive. Eligibility takes into account all of the factors that determine ad placement—your ad targeting settings, approval statuses, bids, quality scores, and so forth. The report in Figure 10.11 gives reasons why the opportunities were missed, including lack of budget (campaign level) and poor ad rank. To enable this report, click the Campaigns tab, open the Columns customization drop-down, and select the competitive metrics.

One of the campaigns in Figure 10.11 is performing very well with a large number of conversions that cost just $17.16 each, compared to $304.94 for another campaign. Unfortunately, while we are receiving a reasonably high impression share on the poorly performing campaign, the majority of possible impressions are missed in the high-performing campaign. The next columns give an indication of what we can do to fix that. The first tells us that 25.73 percent of the time we simply ran out of budget and another 26.23 percent of the time we had a low ad rank, which is a combination of Quality Score and bid price.

Clicks (?)	↓ Impr.	Cost	Conv. (1-per-click) (?)	Cost / conv. (1-per-click) (?)	Conv. rate (1-per-click) (?)	Impr. share (?)	Exact match IS (?)	Lost IS (budget) (?)	Lost IS (rank) (?)
37,739	12,360,344	$116,808.16	1,388	$84.16	3.68%	10.21%	70.28%	14.00%	75.79%
1,113	6,590,233	$1,718.11	3	$572.70	0.27%	10.02%	–	22.16%	67.82%
3,301	3,635,745	$5,889.25	2	$2,944.62	0.06%	< 10%	–	3.81%	88.76%
16,518	499,344	$15,751.88	918	$17.16	5.56%	48.04%	57.45%	25.73%	26.23%
8,842	495,751	$61,598.15	202	$304.94	2.28%	74.45%	85.89%	5.59%	19.96%

Figure 10.11 Impression share metrics

We can increase our budget for the overall campaign by editing the settings for that campaign and increasing the value in Bidding and Budget. We can also increase the default bid settings for the ad group and specifically the Display Network (Figure 10.12).

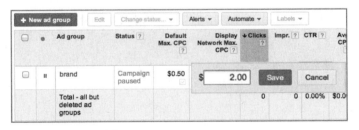

Figure 10.12 Ad group bids

A common strategy (Figure 10.13) is to start with a tightly constrained campaign with broad targeting options. Proven winners are then promoted to campaigns with higher budgets and bids. You halt less-successful placements, ad groups, and audiences or move them into separate campaigns and ad groups. By isolating them, you can target a specific subsection of the site or massage the message in hopes of turning them around. If those more granular ad groups underperform, then you block them as well.

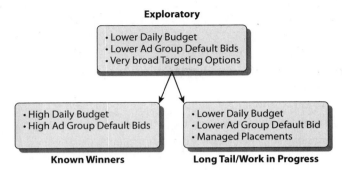

Exploratory
- Lower Daily Budget
- Lower Ad Group Default Bids
- Very broad Targeting Options

- High Daily Budget
- High Ad Group Default Bids

Known Winners

- Lower Daily Budget
- Lower Ad Group Default Bid
- Managed Placements

Long Tail/Work in Progress

Figure 10.13 Strategically using budgets, bids, and targeting options to maximize our reach while maintaining high performance

Note: When you move a placement from a more general ad group to a more specifically managed ad group, remember to block the placement from showing in the former to avoid having multiple ad groups trying to target the same placement.

Tuesday: Adjusting Keyword and Placement Level Bids

Because impression share is reported only on the campaign and ad group levels, another advantage of having relatively isolated placements within ad groups is that you can use ad group level controls on a smaller group. But often adjustments to entire ad groups are too broad and you want to either increase your exposure in a particular placement or implement cost controls compared to the others in the ad group.

While you can't get impression share values, you can get the information you need to make adjustments to the bid price by checking the status of the placement. As you can see in Figure 10.14, hovering over the speech bubble icon in the Status column shows us that the *Los Angeles Times* placement does not show because the ad rank is too low. We should address Quality Score first, but we can also increase bids on that placement to increase our chance to show ads there. To increase the bid for an individual placement, edit the bid price on that row of the managed placements list. You can get impression share for a single placement by isolating it in an ad group where it's the only placement. The figures are from that point forward, not retroactive.

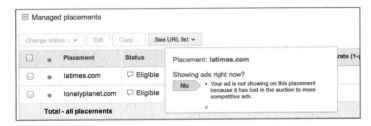

Figure 10.14 Checking to see if a placement is ad rank constrained

When promoting an automatic placement to a managed placement, you can set the bid at the same time (Figure 10.15).

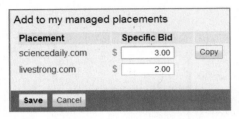

Figure 10.15 Moving a placement from automatic to managed and setting the bid all in one step

For automatic placements, you can adjust bids for an individual keyword under the Display Ads tab (Figure 10.16). This is useful for work in progress and exploratory campaigns.

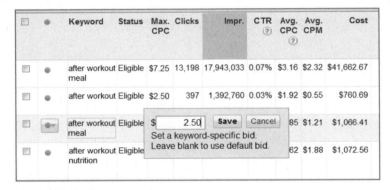

Figure 10.16 Editing bids for display keywords

Wednesday: Adjusting Audience Bids

Figure 10.13 shows how you use the exploratory campaign to find new placements and audiences that perform well for you. As you adjusted bids for individual placements in the previous section, you can do the same for audiences. Some audiences shown in Figure 10.9 are performing extremely well. We want to capture as much of that audience as possible and likely move it to a more specific ad group so we can tailor our message to that audience. You can adjust individual bids by clicking in the Mac CPC field and entering a new value.

The process of exploring new audiences, tailoring messages with specific ad groups, and adjusting individual bids to find the sweet spot of reach versus profitability is not overly complex, but it takes effort and analysis to do correctly. Far from being tedious, however, this process helps you innately understand how particular audiences interact with your ads and website and will ultimately provide the insights to help you create subsequent campaigns.

Thursday: Using Ad Planner to Find More Placements

In Chapter 5, you used Ad Planner to find some initial sites to advertise on. Today you'll use the data in Ad Planner to improve and expand the campaigns. Earlier in the chapter we looked at the data from the initial placements and determined which are performing well and which are not. We discussed ways to optimize those placements, such as removing irrelevant placements, using keywords to narrow the scope, and increasing bids on top performers. While those actions may increase profitability and impression share, they don't do much to expand your reach. We are interested in not just removing irrelevant traffic, but reaching more of the valuable traffic.

Look-Alike Modeling

One way to gain a greater reach without compromising performance is to use look-alike modeling. Google (Ad Planner), ComScore, Quantcast, Compete, and other similar data sources provide information you can use to target more effectively. These databases are used in the look-alike modeling approach, using cookies to keep track of which sites users visit. If two websites have similar people visiting but you advertise on only one, it stands to reason that you will find similar performance on the other site as well. The correlation between the sites is referred to as affinity, and this data can be defined by demographic, psychographic, and behavioral aspects.

We use Ad Planner in this example because it's free and uses Google's large dataset. Let's say, for example, that your placements on EpicSki.com perform very well and you want to expand your reach with this audience. By visiting www.google.com/adplanner, clicking the Research › Search By Site, and entering "domain: EpicSki.com," you can return the dataset for that site.

Although you can use the demographic information supplied in this data, such as age, gender, education, and household income, for your current goal, the real value comes in the reports that show the sites also visited and audience interests. Figure 10.17 shows the 10 sites most like EpicSki.com. It shows that visitors to EpicSki.com are 533 times as likely to visit skinet.com as the average Internet user. By advertising on skinet.com, you have additional opportunities to show impressions to those valuable EpikSki.com users and can also reach new audiences that have similar tastes and behavior.

To view more information about a particular site, including whether it accepts various forms of advertising, click the site name to see the full details of that domain. Note that Ad Planner isn't limited to just the Google Ad Network sites. It indicates whether the site accepts GDN advertisers as well as additional networks or direct advertising. Figure 10.18 shows a site that is in the GDN (skinet.com) and one that accepts advertising but is not part of the GDN (tetongravity.com).

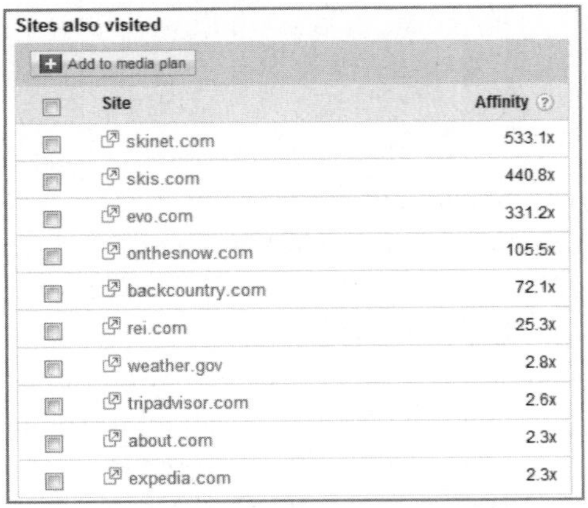

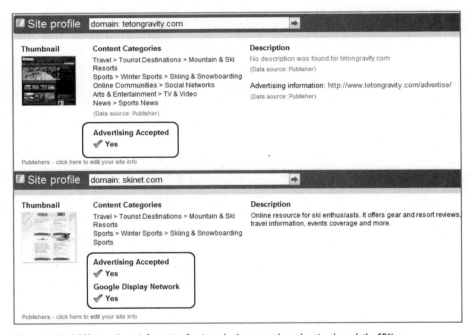

Figure 10.17 Sites with a high affinity indicate similar user bases.

Figure 10.18 Ad Planner shows information for sites whether or not they advertise through the GDN.

If you want to advertise on a site in the Sites Also Visited list, click the check box and then Add To Media Plan. This keeps a running list of the sites you add to the plan throughout your research, and it can be exported for easy import into an ad network via AdWords- or MediaVisor-compatible CSV files. If you know you are interested in high-affinity sites but are advertising only with Google AdWords, go ahead and add the others to the media plan anyway. There is no need to check each individually because the final list in the Media Plan tab also indicates which of your chosen placements are in the GDN and which of the various ad formats (text, image, and rich media) are accepted. It's easy to scrub that list once at the end before export.

Another type of look-alike modeling is to target users with interests similar to the interests of those who have performed well. Because you know that visitors to this site are high converters, you can look at the audience interests list to see what interests those users have and target those specifically. For example, users who come to EpicSki.com have the interest affinities shown in Figure 10.19. Users who are interested in skiing and snowboarding are 140 times as likely to visit as the average Internet user, and those interested in winter sports, mountain and ski resorts, and sporting goods also have high affinities. Expanding your ad group reach by adding these interests is straightforward via Display Network › Interests & Remarketing.

Audience Interests	
Interest	Affinity ⑦
Skiing & Snowboarding	140.6x
Winter Sports	87.3x
Mountain & Ski Resorts	65.5x
Sporting Goods	15.7x
Tourist Destinations	8.1x
Sports	4.1x
Travel	3.8x
North America	2.1x
USA	1.9x
Hobbies & Leisure	1.6x

Figure 10.19 Ad Planner can help expand your reach by identifying interest affinities of your high-performing placements.

Audience Planning

In addition to searching directly by site, you can use the Audience Planning tab to take advantage of remarketing lists and interest lists similar to those discussed in the previous section.

In the previous section we identified a behavior known to convert well—visiting EpicSki.com. But with remarketing lists (explained in detail in Chapter 11, "Month 8: Advanced Topics"), you have another type of behavior that you know to be high converting. Select your AdWords account and then select Remarketing in the drop-down, as shown in Figure 10.20.

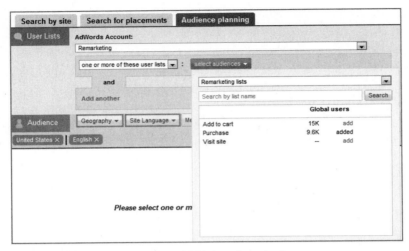

Figure 10.20 Including remarketing lists in Ad Planner audience planning

You can also create an audience plan based on the interest categories, such as those identified in the previous section. In addition, you can directly specify conditions, such as the requirement that the audience belong to multiple lists, as well as demographic data like geography. For example, in Figure 10.21 you see an audience condition set that is very specific. Users must be interested in winter sports (subcategory of sports) and either off-road vehicles or boats and watercraft, and the site language must be English. Here's another way to view this relationship:

```
(English) AND (Winter Sports AND (Off-Road Vehicles OR Boats/Watercraft)
```

Research

Search by site   Search for placements   Audience planning

User Lists   **AdWords Account:**

Select recently viewed account...

one or more of these user lists ▼ : select audiences ▼

Sports
Winter Sports   Remove

and

one or more of these user lists ▼ : select audiences ▼   ⊗

Autos & Vehicles
Off-Road Vehicles   Remove

Autos & Vehicles
Boats & Watercraft   Remove

and

Add another

Audience   Geography ▼   Site Language ▼   Media plans & lists ▼

No audience specified

Figure 10.21 Specifying audience interest conditions in Ad Planner

This audience search generates affinity-based lists of sites and placements visited, as seen in Figure 10.22 and Figure 10.23. As you can see, some of them have extremely high affinity metrics, such as vintagesleds.com, msasnow.org, and fishweb.com, which are all over 2000! The placements are even more specific with certain parts of the fishweb site, achieving an affinity of almost 3500.

	Sites also visited	
	☐ Add to media plan	
☐	Site	Affinity ⑦
☐	🗗 vintagesleds.com	2626.8x
☐	🗗 trails.msasnow.org	2385.0x
☐	🗗 fishweb.com	2170.8x
☐	🗗 msasnow.org	2168.8x
☐	🗗 cs.amsnow.com	1971.9x
☐	🗗 snowest.com	1630.0x
☐	🗗 amsnow.com	1481.3x
☐	🗗 forum.snowmobile.se	1223.0x
☐	🗗 en-us.ski-doo.com	1112.7x
☐	🗗 snowmobilefanatics.com	1112.6x

Figure 10.22 Sites visited by audiences with the conditions specified in Figure 10.21

	Placements also visited	
	☐ Add to media plan	
☐	Site	Affinity ⑦
☐	🗗 (GDN) fishweb.com::Sub Pages,Middle left	3496.4x
☐	🗗 (GDN) vintagesleds.com	3178.7x
☐	🗗 (GDN) fishweb.com	2626.9x
☐	🗗 (GDN) snowmobilefanatics.com	1972.3x
☐	🗗 (GDN) snowmobilefanatics.com:: All pages on the site,Middle left	1972.2x
☐	🗗 (GDN) snowmobilefanatics.com:: All pages on the site,Top center	1629.6x
☐	🗗 (GDN) sledswap.com	1481.3x
☐	(GDN) snowmobileforum.com::All pages, Middle right	1346.9x
☐	🗗 (GDN) dootalk.com	1224.9x
☐	🗗 (GDN) snowmobileforum.com	1224.4x

Figure 10.23 Placements visited by audiences with the conditions specified in Figure 10.21

Look-Alike and Retargeting

We talk about retargeting in the next chapter, but it's worth pointing out how these fit together. Both retargeting and look-alike modeling are types of behavioral targeting that focus on performance by targeting groups known to convert well. Many marketers consider retargeting to be the more effective of the two, but most retargeting requires that users have already visited your site, while look-alike is a way to reach out to new audiences that have yet to visit your site.

Because look-alike audiences are targeted for their likelihood to convert, they can be very effective in building your retargeting lists. The new users attracted to the site are more likely to do the things that get them placed on a retargeting list and are generally more likely to convert as well, so an already targeted audience combined with effective site retargeting can work for both the upper and lower funnel, resulting in a very effective acquisition strategy.

Conversion Data Is the Key

Note that all of the audience targeting discussed today hinges on the fact that you can properly identify a high-performing audience based on the techniques discussed earlier in the chapter. If your account is one of the millions that have no form of conversion data (either from the conversion tracking script or imported from Google Analytics), then it can't distinguish your high performers from your low performers. In short, you can't do anything discussed earlier!

Audience targeting through look-alike modeling can be complex, and what we've described so far is just a start. But when done properly, it can be a great way to expand your reach without sacrificing quality. The techniques described in this chapter will get you started on the right path.

Friday: Using Display Campaign Optimizer

So far in this chapter we've discussed techniques to use the data collected in various places to evaluate the performance of the campaigns. From there, poor performers are modified or shut down and you try to replicate your success with the high performers by identifying and locating similar audiences and placements.

However, this is a fairly manual process that can be time consuming and tedious. Even with ample time, there is a limit to how many variables you can realistically analyze by hand. Thus the process outlined earlier can be effective, but some may find it limited and simplistic.

In fact, while much of this book focuses on the creative marketing you need to create persuasive display campaigns, this data-driven optimization process is one place where an intelligent algorithm has an advantage. Google's Display Campaign

Optimizer (DCO) is one such algorithm that savvy advertisers can employ because it attempts to automate a process similar to that just described.

DCO starts with an initial campaign. It evaluates conversion performance, optimizing toward a cost per acquisition (CPA) target. It utilizes Google's servers to continually monitor performance. It then eliminates placements that aren't working and finds additional ones that are similar to high performers. Sound familiar?

The algorithm is fairly sophisticated. It uses predictive models that examine where and what types of placements, times of day, geography, and even how likely an individual is to buy. The algorithm takes thousands of variables into account as it tries to maximize conversions for the CPA you've targeted.

Sound too good to be true? There are some catches. Just as your campaigns start as educated guesses, DCO starts with assumptions. The CPAs may initially be high and the performance less than stellar, but it adjusts and hones in on your target CPA. Resist the urge to adjust and instead take a hands-off approach in the beginning. The tool needs a minimum of about 15 display-based conversions per month to have enough data to begin its calculations.

To run the DCO, set up an entirely separate campaign. Make sure it's set for display only with no keywords, managed placements, topics, or audiences targeted. Navigate to the bidding options (Figure 10.24) and focus on conversions with a target CPA. In the campaign settings, select automatic campaign optimization and a targeting mode of auto-optimized. Beyond that, you provide only the budget, a target CPA, the ad creative, and time and patience! The DCO is not for everyone, but it can be a highly effective way to put Google's servers to work on your behalf.

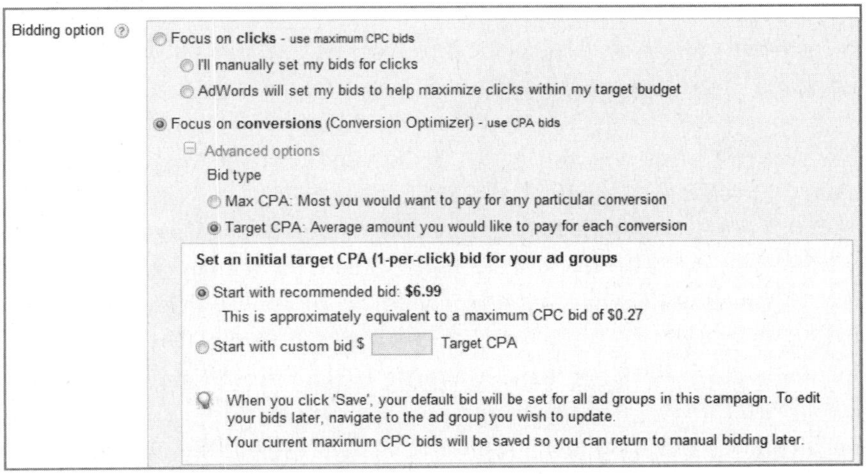

Figure 10.24 The DCO runs in a campaign set to focus on a target CPA.

Week 27: Test Your Ads

Placements and audiences aren't the only components of campaigns that need to be aggressively optimized. Split testing ads is one of the most effective but all-too-often overlooked ways to dramatically improve your campaign performance.

Monday: Understanding Ad Split Testing

Testing different creatives is one of the oldest and most common activities for advertisers. While the advertisers and often the audiences remain the same, the creatives used to reach those audiences are constantly tested and refined. Even highly successful ads are subject to creative wear-out because ads that once connected with audiences can lose their effectiveness after repeated viewings.

Savvy advertisers never run just one version of an ad, and modern display advertising networks make it incredibly easy to split test different ad creatives. The same audience, keywords, and placements can be targeted, and the ad network serves different versions of the ad.

Often beginner advertisers make the mistake of believing that only radically different ads show measurable improvements in performance, which is not true. The exact same joke delivered by a professional standup comedian likely elicits more laughter than when we try it over a cocktail. Slight variations in delivery make all the difference. Similarly, ad variations with the most subtle changes to phrasing or even text placement can often have a large impact on how the ad connects with your audience.

For example, the Hilton hotel chain made only basic changes in the first three variations of the ads in Figure 10.25. They use the same background, the same colors, the same imagery, the same layout and even the same button text. The fourth Hilton ad is different in almost every way. We include it to contrast the others. Even though it is the same advertiser targeting the same audience, it probably belongs to a different ad group because it targets an entirely different activity and purpose. Split testing generally tries to find different ways of getting a user to the same end goal and thus the last creative is a poor ad to split test against the first three.

However, this doesn't mean that split test creatives must all look or sound alike. Even the three ads that have the same end goal of entering the Olympics sweepstakes appeal to different motivations to do so. The first copy appeals to someone who likes games of chance, the second appeals to the aspirational dream of reaching the Olympics (albeit as a spectator rather than a competitor!), and the last appeals to a sense of national pride for your Olympic team.

Advertisers may choose to take this even further. One ad for a getaway vacation package may appeal to someone looking for the chance to enjoy dancing, dining, and social activities as a break from the daily grind. Another variation for that same resort may show a desolate beach and appeal to someone who is feeling decidedly *anti*social and wants to relax in peaceful solitude. Another common tactic is to show men in one variation and women in another because it's often easier to identify with a person of your own gender.

Figure 10.25 Split testing often involves variations on a theme.

Behavioral and audience targeting may allow you to target the most receptive audience, but most often you don't have that level of granularity. You need to run both ideas to see which connects with your audience and drives the desired response. Also don't be afraid to test commonly held assumptions. A well-known technology company had ad variations with a famous man and woman. They assumed the female demographic would respond to the woman but found that the variation with the handsome man did much better, and likewise for the men. The beauty of split testing is that you don't have to assume, so test those assumptions!

Tuesday: Understanding Statistical Significance and Sample Size

Statistical significance and sample size calculations can scare some marketers off as they conjure up complicated statistics concepts. But actually, we all already intuitively understand. While we don't go into the details of the math, it's essential that every online advertiser understand the basics to avoid making costly mistakes. Chapter 9 touches this important concept, but we explore it further in this section because it's essential for testing ads and landing pages.

We can illustrate the concept with this simple scenario. Moving objects here on Earth are affected by the Earth's rotation. This *Coriolis effect* is best known for causing storms and ocean currents to swirl in different directions in the northern and southern hemispheres and must be accounted for in long-distance marksmanship. But there are other claims that are a bit more suspect, such as the ability to influence the direction of water swirling down a drain or even the chance that a flipped coin lands heads or tails.

Any true scientist believes in testing and experiments. We can investigate the idea that a coin flipped in the northern hemisphere is more likely to land on tails with a simple test: we call a friend in the southern hemisphere (in Australia) and have him flip a coin while we flip a coin in the northern hemisphere. We record the results in Table 10.1.

▶ **Table 10.1** Coin flip test results

	Flip #1	Flip #2	Flip #3	Chance of Getting Tails
Northern hemisphere	Heads	Tails	Tails	⅔
Southern hemisphere	Heads	Tails	Heads	⅓

Proof! The statement "You are more likely to flip tails in the Northern hemisphere" has been scientifically proven to be true! In fact, you are *twice* as likely to get tails in the Northern hemisphere!

Not buying it? Well certainly the math looks correct. The reason this test is faulty is something we all intuitively understand—we didn't flip the coin enough times. The true chance of getting tails (the conversion rate of this example) should be about 50 percent and that's what we would expect over time.

But how do we really *know* it should be 50 percent? Probably because our teacher told us it was! We can't ever *really* know the true conversion rate; we can only know what we observe. And therein lies the rub—we don't believe our observed result because the sample size was too small. We believe that over time if we flipped that coin 100,000,000 times, the observed conversion rate would be very, very close to 50 percent (maybe 49.99999 percent) and our *observed* conversion rate would converge on what we believe to be the *true* conversion rate of 50 percent.

So the real question is, how many times is enough? Do we need to do it 100,000,000 times to be sure our observed conversion rate is close enough to the true answer to call the test complete? We all suspect we don't need that many. But how many *is* enough? 10? 100? 1,000? 100,000?

That question gets to the heart of the issue of statistical significance: at what point do we have enough data to draw a valid conclusion, and how sure are we of that answer? Fortunately, statisticians have simple formulas that we can use to shed some light on that question.

These formulas produce confidence intervals (ranges) and confidence levels that tell us the range in which we expect to find the true conversion rate as well as how certain we are that the range contains the correct answer. In the preceding example, we got a result (twice as likely to land on tails), but we have extremely low confidence that the answer is correct!

There are two questions advertisers seek to answer. The first is how many samples we need (impressions, visitors, etc.), which helps us decide how long we have to collect data. The second related question is how confident we are, given the data collected thus far, and whether we can conclude that one variation is better than the other.

Estimating Sample Size

As with the coin flips, the number of samples needed depends on how certain you want to be that the observed conversion rate reflects the "true" conversion rate. The more samples, the more certain you can be. Note that we're defining conversion loosely here and it doesn't necessarily mean a website goal conversion. In the coin flip, a conversion was simply landing on tails. For ads, a conversion may be defined as a click, but it can also be a more traditional goal like an email signup, white paper download, a non-bounce, and e-commerce checkout, and so forth.

To estimate sample size, you follow a known formula, fill in the variables, and solve for the unknown. This same formula applies whether you are testing ads or landing pages or any two variables. At our company, we developed an internal tool to automate these calculations. As a benefit to our readers and clients, we've released this tool to the public for free. Just click Sample Size Calculator Tool on the Web Analytics and Statistical Analysis Tools page:

```
http://j.mp/Display10-1
```

Fill in the requested information, some of which you have to estimate for now. Keep in mind that this is just an estimate. The real number of samples and length of time required depends on how accurate your estimation of performance turns out to be. If you overestimate your new ad's performance, the calculator underestimates the amount of time it will take.

Fill in the fields as follows:

Expected Conversion Rate All things being equal, you expect your current ad or landing page to convert as it has in the past, so this is essentially just your current/historical conversion rate as determined by your analytics package or ad network. We say expected because we recognize that things may change and past behavior is no guarantee of identical future performance. However, for the purpose of this estimation, we *expect* that the conversion rate of the ad tomorrow will be similar to the conversion rate up until now. So grab your current conversion rate and use it to populate the field. In our example, we use 5 percent.

Improvement Also known as lift or relative improvement, this is your biggest assumption because if you *know* what the lift will be for the new variation, you don't need the test in the first place! The tool presents a number of different scenarios, so unless you have a good estimate, put it at 5 percent for now.

Time Estimation Set this to the estimated number of unique visits to your test page per 24-hour period. This lets the calculator translate the required number of samples into a time period. So if you do A/B testing on a landing page that receives 1,000 unique visitors per day and the tool calculates that you need 30,000 samples, it estimates that you need 30 days to complete the test. The tool assumes a landing page testing scenario, but it can be used for ad impressions as well. In our example, we use 1,000 per day.

How Sure Do You Want To Be? This is your confidence level. Often, people are tempted to select a high value because no one wants to be wrong. However, this can dramatically increase the number of samples needed, potentially to a point that prevents the test from reaching a valid conclusion. For life and death scenarios, such as testing a new pharmaceutical, you want to be very sure and thus require a very high confidence level. In that scenario, the USFDA requires 98 percent confidence, but for your ad testing, we advise you to use 90 percent or even 85 percent if necessary. Your specific scenario dictates your risk tolerance, but we prefer many tests completed with a 20 percent chance of being wrong to a small number that are highly certain. The chance of getting the optimal result on the first ad or landing page you create is small, so for every ad or landing page you don't or can't test, you are almost always suboptimal. For this reason, the more tests the better, even if they are at a lower confidence level. To show the effect of a high confidence level, we use 95 percent in this example.

Click the Find My Sample Size button to compute the result (which for our example is shown in Figure 10.26). For the numbers given previously, the tool indicates it will take almost 3 months to complete the simplest A/B test and require 84,228 samples! Note that this assumes only two variations (simple A/B). For tests that may have more than two (A/B/n), you have to multiply the number of variations by 42,114 to get the total number, so a four-variation test needs 168,000 samples and takes 5.6 months to finish, which is completely unreasonable. Not only does that prevent you from completing a useful number of tests, but the test is likely to be invalid because how your audience reacts to an ad or a landing page may change substantially over that time, and the product or service is likely to change as well. Waiting almost six months to complete a test for the landing page related to the Olympics ad earlier in the chapter is pointless, because the games will be over before you decide! This is why estimating sample size is so important; it helps you design tests that have a chance to be successful.

If you look at the table, you'll see that all is not lost. If we reduce our confidence level to 90 percent and achieve a 10 percent lift, our minimum required samples drops to just 6,537. This means a four-variable test (A/B/C/D) can complete in just 26 days instead of 5.6 months and a simple A/B test can be done in a couple of weeks.

TEST RESULTS

SAMPLE SIZE ESTIMATION ANALYSIS:

Q: How large of a sample size do I need?

A: In order to show a **5%** relative improvement in your test, and assuming that the original version maintains a conversion rate of **5%**, you will need a sample size of 42,114 per test group, or a **total sample size of 84,228** at the **95%** confidence level.

If you can collect **1000 samples per day**, then you would need to run your test for approximately **84 days**.

The table below shows you the various sample sizes you would need at different confidence levels to show different relative improvements.

RELATIVE IMPROVEMENT:

Conf Level	1%	2%	5%	10%	20%	30%	50%
80%	270,333	67,902	11,017	2,818	736	341	133
85%	410,125	103,014	16,714	4,275	1,117	517	201
90%	627,231	157,546	25,561	6,537	1,707	791	308
95%	1,033,424	259,572	42,114	10,771	2,813	1,303	507
98%	1,611,074	404,665	65,655	16,791	4,385	2,031	790

Figure 10.26 Results of the sample size estimation

One important thing to note is that even if the sample size calculator says you have enough traffic to finish the test in two days, you shouldn't. You might exceed the minimum sample requirement, but the samples may not be representative of your population. Those two days may be during a weekend, in which the traffic is different from weekday traffic. They may be too near the end of the month, when buying habits change. Or during a storm. Or a holiday. Or any number of reasons that would cause that short time period to be anomalous. We recommend a minimum of two weeks and ideally three weeks before concluding any test to ensure enough time to get a representative sample audience through the test.

Statistical Significance

Other tools on the Web Analytics and Statistical Analysis Tools page approach the problem from different angles. Instead of estimating the performance and solving for the required number of samples, we look at the data from variations (ads or landing pages) that are already running. We don't solve for sample size (we already know that), but instead we solve for the conversion rate by calculating confidence intervals. As briefly explained in Chapter 9, the goal is to determine whether our data includes enough samples to support a statistically valid conclusion that an apparent difference between two variations represents an actual difference.

Though designed for different scenarios, two other tools on that page can help. The first is the A/B testing tool, which we cover later in the chapter. The second is the Ad Split testing tool, which you saw in Chapter 9; we'll take another look at it on Thursday of this week.

Testing is a critical part of optimization, but to do it right you need to understand whether you are drawing statically valid conclusions. With these tools, you can quickly determine the sample sizes, confidence intervals, and confidence levels you need to improve your bottom line.

Wednesday: Setting Up a Split Test

Now that we've discussed some of the theory, it's time to implement a test. One important thing to keep in mind is that unlike text ads on search results, where the only thing likely to change is the text, with display ads you test both message and visuals. On top of this, you also have additional variables of placements and ad format. There is more opportunity for creativity, but also more to manage and control.

First run a sample size calculation as we did yesterday to see approximately what size test you can support. Can you support lots of variations at once and still complete them in a reasonable time frame? If not, a simple A/B test with just two creatives is a safer way to start.

To add creatives on the GDN, navigate to the individual ad group, select the Ads tab, and click New Ad. Google can automatically change the delivery of your ads to favor and show more impressions for the ones it predicts will perform better. Usually this is good, but not during split testing because lower-performing ads may not receive enough impressions to support a valid result. To avoid this problem, set ad rotation to Rotate (Figure 10.27).

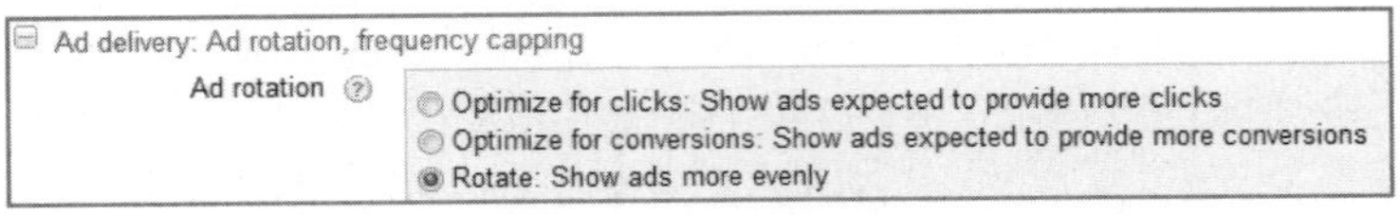

Figure 10.27 Changing the ad rotation settings to ensure all ads receive enough impressions

If you use AdWords to supply the performance data and add a new ad to an existing ad, you have conflicting data sets. The old ad has impressions/clicks/conversions data, but the new ad is starting from scratch, and you don't want the old ad data to confound the calculations. You can make note of the date range and compare metrics for only the dates when both ads are running, or you can reset the historical data for the existing ad. To reset the metrics, upload the ad again or make a minor modification to the ad and change it back immediately. Any such change restarts the counters and metrics for the ad.

Campaign Experiments

AdWords provides the campaign experiments for testing optimizations to your account beyond additional creatives. For example, say you are the advertiser we saw earlier with a promotion tied to the Olympics. You are interested in testing higher bids to get more traffic, but even if you see a rise in traffic, you can't be sure if it is due to the bid changes. It might reflect heightened interest in your subject matter as the event draws closer. Unlike with ads where you can run two creatives simultaneously and serve them equally, bids affect everything at once.

Campaign experiments allow you to test changes like bid increases against a control and see if it the modification made the difference. With campaign experiments you can test the following elements:

- Bids on managed placements
- New placements
- New keywords for contextually targeted ad groups
- Ad group default bids, including max CPC and max CPM
- Max CPA if campaign is using Conversion Optimizer
- Additional ad groups
- New display ads
- Different remarketing options
- Site exclusions

However, modifications to settings for that campaign while the experiment is underway affect both the test and control. Unfortunately, this means you cannot test some interesting elements, such as these:

- Ad extensions
- Daily budgets
- Ad scheduling
- Frequency capping
- Targeting of any sort (geographic, language, network, or device)
- Bidding features
- Campaign-level negative keywords

You can also run only one experiment at a time.

To begin an experiment, use the web interface to navigate to Campaign Settings › Advanced Settings. Click Specify Experiment Settings to see the specifications screen (Figure 10.28).

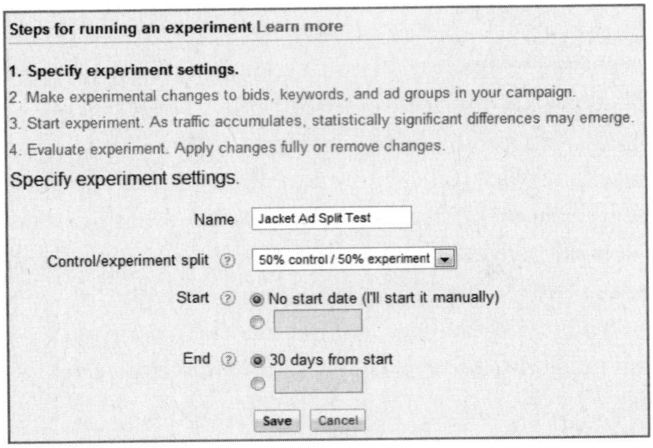

Steps for running an experiment Learn more

1. **Specify experiment settings.**
2. Make experimental changes to bids, keywords, and ad groups in your campaign.
3. Start experiment. As traffic accumulates, statistically significant differences may emerge.
4. Evaluate experiment. Apply changes fully or remove changes.

Specify experiment settings.

Name	Jacket Ad Split Test
Control/experiment split ⑦	50% control / 50% experiment ▾
Start ⑦	⦿ No start date (I'll start it manually)
	○ [ ]
End ⑦	⦿ 30 days from start
	○ [ ]

Save Cancel

Figure 10.28 Configuring a campaign experiment

Enter a meaningful, descriptive name. Then specify how you want traffic split between the control and experiment and enter the start date and the end date. You can make up to 1,000 changes as part of each experiment. As you make a change, use the check box to add the change as an experiment (Figure 10.29).

Figure 10.29 Adding changes to a campaign experiment

To view the reports and evaluate the experiment, run an experiment report from the Campaigns tab. Click the download icon and select Experiment in the Segment field (Figure 10.30). The report shows how the control varies from the experiment. It also indicates statistical significance via arrow icons. A gray up and down arrow icon indicates a change that is not statistically significant. A single arrow indicates a 95 percent chance the change (good or bad) is significant and not simply a chance event. In other words, there is only a 5 percent chance that if you apply that change across all auctions (instead of just the experiment), the metric will not move in the direction indicated by the arrow. Two and three arrows represent the 99 percent and 99.9 percent confidence levels.

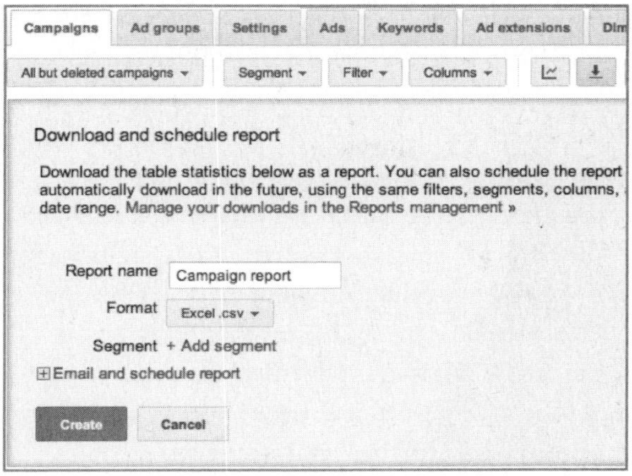

Figure 10.30 Evaluating a campaign experiment

Thursday: Interpreting the Results and Tools

On Wednesday you set up and ran the split test, so now it's time to interpret the results. Hopefully you let at least a couple weeks go by to ensure that you have a representative sample of your audience and at least one of your variations performed well. But as pointed out earlier in this chapter, you still need to check that the apparent improvements are statistically significant and tested on a large enough sample size. Returning to the Cardinal Path Web Analytics and Statistical Analysis Tools page, take the data from analytics or the ad network and populate the Ad testing tool (Figure 10.31).

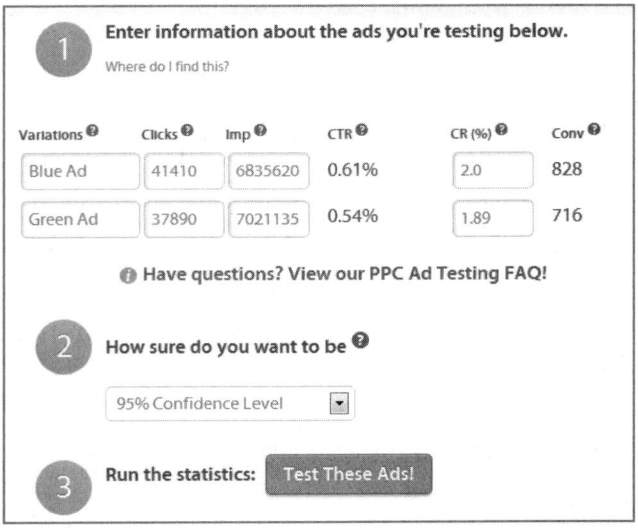

Figure 10.31 Calculating statistical significance for two ad variations

The blue ad appears to be a superior. It has a better CTR and a better conversion rate. When we click the Test These Ads button to run the analysis, the tool tells us that that the CTR advantage is statistically significant, but while the conversion rates appear to be different, they are actually not statistically different. We still choose the blue ad as the winner because we get more clicks with no drop-off in conversion rate.

Often, however, a changed ad is better at getting clicks (and therefore incurring costs) but has a lower conversion rate. The choice then comes down to how significant the conversion drop is and whether your priorities for the campaign favor volume or profitability. In either case, the testing gives you the data to inform that decision.

Don't worry too much about the statistical details provided by the tool. The important part is whether or not the tool found a significant difference in CTR or conversion rate. The rest is there in case you want to do further analysis or see just how much longer the test would have to run.

Further Splitting Ad Groups

After you determine the results from your tests, it's time to take stock and draw conclusions. Optimizing campaigns means separating winners from losers, but it also likely requires you to split ad groups into further specialized themes. This is particularly true when you test ads that appeal to different motivations.

For example, in the vacation resort ad test from earlier in the chapter there was an ad appealing to users interested in dancing and dining and another for users looking for isolation. While they are both in the getaway ad group, they are decidedly different mentalities—one is social and the other antisocial. If the dancing ad performs significantly better on the placements for that ad group, you may not want to halt the tranquility ad entirely. Instead, form an ad group with placements or keywords that relate to the themes of that ad, which is reducing stress and stress-free vacations. This is especially true if one variation is superior but they both attract enough clicks or conversions to warrant further optimization, even if it isn't the high performer of the ad group.

This is where the art of advertising comes in. You must determine whether the ads are similar enough to cut the loser or if other forces are at play. Using these techniques and incorporating what you learn from the test, you can create or modify ad groups to turn the underperformer into a profitable one. A savvy and creative marketer backed up by statistically valid data is a powerful force.

Friday: What Should I Test?

No doubt about it: determining what to test is one of the most important decisions you have to make. As you saw earlier in the chapter, the amount of lift (relative improvement) from one variation to the next can make a huge difference in the number of samples required and how many tests you can complete. Figure 10.26, earlier in this chapter, shows that moving from a 1 percent improvement to a 10 percent improvement reduces the number of samples required from over a million to just 10 thousand!

That said, the biggest hurdle advertisers have is not that they are struggling to achieve significant lift. Rather, it's that they don't test in the first place. You do not have to be sure that a variation is going to win. All you need is a hypothesis of why it *might* win, preferably one based on data. You need to be able to verbalize a statement such as "Our market research shows that price is the largest motivating factor and differentiator for us, so showing our discount in red on the ad will attract more clicks and conversions." Requiring a hypothesis means this isn't random testing; requiring a sure thing means no testing will ever happen. As Dan Weiden of Wieden + Kennedy famously said to Nike in 1988, "Just do it."

Often the hypothesis forms itself as you sift through the data and try to draw conclusions. As one creative outperforms another, possible explanations form in your mind. These lead to another set of variations to test that theory. Patterns in user behavior lead to ideas for how to further capitalize on successes and niches.

For example, you may find that your audience tends to move quickly and spend a short time on individual pages, so an ad that takes a long time to reach its call to action may not perform as well. Figure 10.32 shows panels from a single media rich ad that is full of high-resolution images and motion. The ad downloads for several seconds before it begins and then takes 17 seconds before the screen with the call-to-action button appears. This ad was placed on a sports news home page. Unlike visitors to pages that host articles, people on home pages and index pages tend to click to the next screen relatively quickly because these pages simply host links that point to content within the site. In other words, the purpose of this page is often to get people to the *next page*. So a reasonable hypothesis to test is that a variation of the ad that reaches the call to action faster will perform better. Perhaps make it load faster or give it a consistent call-to-action button on the bottom that allows users to immediately recognize what the ad is offering and click as soon as they are ready. Can we guarantee it will perform better? Of course not. But we have a good reason to believe it can because it addresses a potential shortcoming of the first ad.

It's nearly impossible to generate the perfect combination of message, layout, color, imagery, sound, sight, and motion on the first try, so there are nearly infinite opportunities for variation there. Chapter 7 described elements of successful ads, such as scent and visual elements, and it's well worth reviewing that chapter for more in-depth discussions of the effects of various elements, such as adding faces to an ad.

Figure 10.32 Taking too long to reach the call to action

Some ideas to consider:

Calls to action These often have a drastic effect on ad interaction. A button that says "sign up now" instead of "learn more" suggests very different levels of commitment, and which is better depends on where the user is in the sales cycle—are they researching or ready to pull the trigger?

Button messages, color, text styling, and so forth can all make a difference. The button in Figure 10.32 is barely differentiated from the background, buried in the middle of the text, and extremely small. Buttons versus text links also make for interesting tests.

Tone Is your ad casual or professional, serious or lighthearted? Are you attempting humor/entertainment or addressing an important concern? Are you making an emotional appeal, or is your value proposition more pragmatic? Would another approach work better?

Layout Possibilities here are endless, particularly with rich media formats. Everything from contrast and eye movement to story development for rich media.

Format The Hilton example earlier in the chapter is not just a test of different messaging. Some of those ads are dynamic, rich media ads while others are static. Even within rich media, there are myriad options for using sight, sound, motion, and interactivity. The design options of interactive ads are endless and could be the subject of an entire book themselves—ample room for testing there.

Imagery of people Variations with women versus men. Looking at the camera versus looking at the product or the call to action. Do you include beautiful models or every-man models that users may more easily relate to?

Message What are the motivations of the different groups who see the ad? Testing different messages within the creatives that appeal to each one tells you which are strongest and most numerous. You can then use that data to build dedicated ad groups.

Think about a model such as Maslow's hierarchy of needs. Where do your different creatives fit in that model? Where should they? Are you appealing to needs that are highly motivating?

Credibility can be incorporated into your message, either from an authority (Ranked #1 by *Consumer Reports*) or peer groups (More moms choose us than any other brand).

Different value exchanges can be built into the message. What do users get if they proceed? Why would it be a good idea for them? Your marketing generates a list of multiple features and benefits—test messaging for each.

Time or quantity limits (Offer ends on September 1st) can drive action.

Generating hypotheses and associated variations becomes easier over time, which is ironic since the beginning is when there are the most possibilities to try. Start out based on different marketing ideas and over time move to ideas that flow from the data generated by these test-and-learn efforts.

Week 28: Create Effective Landing Pages

Often we get so focused on the ads themselves that we forget about the other half of the equation—the site to which the ads link. Many of the breakthroughs in display advertising that have enabled the medium to improve so rapidly are around what's known as performance display. The goal here is not just awareness, but *outcomes*. Whatever the purpose of your site is, whether it's leads or information dissemination or e-commerce, you want to optimize toward those goals. This means that it's not enough just to dump the traffic off at the front door of the website and walk away. You need to optimize the entire process. Far too often there is a disconnect between the advertisers whose responsibility it is to generate traffic and the site operators who maintain the code.

Our definition for landing pages is fairly broad—it is the first page on the site you reach after clicking a link. That means it could be the home page or literally any page on the site that has an inbound link pointing to it. It's often very effective to have purpose-built landing pages that are specially designed for specific ads, but there are legitimate occasions to send traffic to the home page as well. So for this book we use the broader definition of simply the first page you land on.

Monday: Understanding What Makes a Good Landing Page to Google

In the very early days of Google, it and the other ad networks were concerned only with the ads themselves. Once the user clicked past the ad, their fee was collected and it was no longer their concern what happened to that traffic.

However, this was quickly regarded as short-term thinking and has changed drastically in recent years. Google wants to earn and keep its users' trust, but it also believes that ads should be information. This means that landing pages have become part of the evaluation process for the quality of the ads and that editorial guidelines extend to the landing page as well, as discussed in Chapter 7.

Quality Score on the Display Network

Google calculates a Quality Score (QS) for both the ads and the landing pages. The higher your QS, the higher your ad rank, which can mean a higher position. In many cases for display, only the ad with the highest rank is shown at all. Because ad rank is a combination of QS and bid, a low QS requires a higher bid. If you have too few impressions on the GDN, it may indicate that your QS isn't high enough for your current Max CPM or CPC bid price. In some cases, low QS means that the ad won't be shown at all regardless of bid price.

How to Check Landing Page Quality Score

First view the keywords table and hover over the speech bubble in the Status column. This launches an information box that indicates the current state of your quality score, including that of your landing page (Figure 10.33).

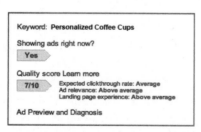

Figure 10.33 Landing page Quality Score diagnosis

Landing page QS is divided into three main tiers:

No Problems This is what you want to see! Your landing page is not reducing the effectiveness of your ads.

Poor In Google's opinion, the landing page does not provide a good experience to users, so your ad is likely to perform poorly.

Not Applicable Your landing page violates Google's editorial policies as outlined in Chapter 7. Your keywords pointing to this site show a site suspended status. You should address this immediately.

Improving Quality Score

Although raising bids can improve the rank of low QS ads, we recommend against it. Google weighs the algorithm to punish low quality advertisers, so your efforts are better spent improving QS.

Quality Score in display is a little different from Quality Score in search, in part because the ads run on other sites beyond just Google.com search results pages. Different sites mean your CTR can vary greatly, so it's calculated differently. For CPC bids, the QS is judged by the following factors:

Relevance How well do your ad and keywords align to the target placement?

Historical performance On this and similar placements, what is your historical CTR? Relative CTR (discussed earlier in this chapter) is a great indicator of how Google thinks your ad stacks up to the competition.

Landing page quality This is evaluated against the editorial policies and suggestions outlined in Chapter 7, which are primarily as follows:

Relevant and original content

Transparent and open business practices

Ease of navigation

Absence of prohibited items and activities

Tuesday: Understanding What Makes a Good Landing Page to Your Visitor

Designing effective landing pages is the subject of entire books, and there is an entire industry devoted to it. We can't cover all of the elements here. We highly encourage you to study this subject further because even the greatest ads can't overcome a substandard landing page.

In the following sections, we just touch on a few ideas to get you to think about elements of your landing pages you can test. There are some best practices but few absolute rules. What works for some audiences may not for others, which is why we test!

Forms

Bad forms have wasted more advertiser money than any other page element since the dawn of the Web. We work hard to get visitors to notice and click our ads. We employ well-designed landing pages customized to the user with clear calls to action.

Users decide to become our customers and open their wallets. The only thing standing between them and our bank account is a web form. Unfortunately, poorly designed forms are everywhere, and many site owners have no idea how poorly they perform and how many customers they lose.

Site owners often refuse to acknowledge the damage that forms do. They think that customers who want it badly enough will find a way to make it work. Double-digit gains can go unrealized because advertisers don't realize the magnitude of the problem. That's why Cardinal Path's optimization and analytics consultants try hard to show site owners just how much their forms are costing them.

First and foremost, focus on reducing the friction of submitting the form. Our research shows that the majority of people who encounter an error on the form do not ultimately submit it correctly. Think about that—most people who want to be your clients but get an error never convert. Do everything you can to point out (or reduce) required fields.

Make sure it's extremely clear how to correct errors or people will simply walk away. Take additional steps to correct common errors. For example, don't require a special format for phone numbers. You know the 10 most common ways to write a phone number, so correct it on the server backend. Don't force customers to conform to your arbitrary format choice.

Similarly, if you detect an error, keep the data that's already entered. Nothing is more frustrating than having to reenter correct data. While some may want your product enough to fill out form after form, most do not.

Reduce the number of fields on the form. There is an inverse correlation between form length and willingness to submit it. Ask yourself how many clients you are willing to give up to get that fax number. In many cases the phone number itself is not required, and people are often hesitant to give up their home phone number.

Consider testing a multistep form instead of a large, intimidating one. Gather the critical information first, then put the nice-to-have background or demographic information on subsequent pages. That way if they abandon the form halfway, they aren't lost entirely. On the other hand, it's been shown that every additional click and screen causes some loss, so if your end goal is to get all the data filled out, you may be better off with a single large form. Test it!

Many of these issues are so damaging that if they exist on your site, the fixes arguably don't even need to be tested! For those looking to improve their campaign and website conversions with quick and impactful improvements, forms are a great first step.

Clear Call to Action

A clear call to action is often the most important element of a landing page. The user has arrived and stayed long enough to absorb your content, so now it's important to provide a clear next step.

Just as in ads, the text of the call to action can have a dramatic impact because just a few words can imply so much. For example, tests show that a subtle change from a noun phrase (Online Ordering) to an imperative verb phrase (Order Online) can make a significant difference.

Sometimes a call to action variation can be very simple. Make a clear call to action even *clearer*. Just as in ads, this can be done by layout, color, font styling, size, or even motion elements. The only difference between the landing pages in Figure 10.34 is the button size. Simple variations like this require little effort and may be especially effective on ads like the one in Figure 10.32 earlier in the chapter.

Figure 10.34 A call-to-action test that simply changes the size of the button

Landing pages like the e-commerce product detail page in Figure 10.35 have a more severe problem. If you were persuaded to purchase this dog shampoo, how would you? Is the site just informational? Most users won't ponder that long before moving on.

Similarly, after you select a model of the car in Figure 10.36, what do you do? Whoever created the site probably knows what the next steps are, but to someone who's never seen the site before, it needs to be obvious, which it isn't.

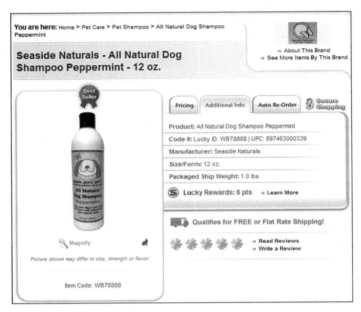

Figure 10.35 A call to action that is anything but clear

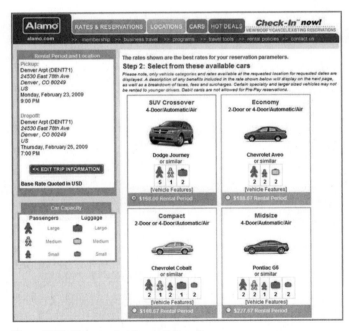

Figure 10.36 After you select the car, what next?

We can't come right out and say what button text is most effective, because it's highly dependent on your website and your audience. For example, the landing page in Figure 10.37 is designed to match people who want to volunteer their time with organizations that need volunteers. People come to this page because they want to help. So a button that says "I want to help!" is entirely purpose aligned with users and may test better than more generic phrases.

Figure 10.37 Aligning a call-to-action button with the visitor's intent

Copy

The amount of testing you can do with copy rivals that of imagery. Just as tone is important for ads, it's also important for landing pages. And usually it works best if the tone of the landing page matches the tone of the ad.

People often skim pages, so write copy that is skim friendly. There are tools that can evaluate ease of reading and complexity of words and sentence structure to arrive at a grade level. Your readers aren't stupid, but they are in a hurry, so copy written with that in mind may test better. You want them to absorb the information, not admire your eloquence.

Saying the same thing in different ways can have an effect. Ninety Percent, 90%, 9/10, Nine out of Ten, and 9 of 10 all say the same thing, but 90% is easiest to skim.

The words you choose in the copy are ripe for testing. The landing page for a car insurance company might offer a free quote. The irony here is that insurance quotes are essentially always free, but you have to test it.

Emphasizing free offers can be useful when you are appealing to value, but it can also associate your site with being cheap, gimmicky, or discount. So if you're a Bentley dealer, a landing page whose value proposition and text are around the word "free" is not likely to test successfully.

Reduced Checkout Friction

An interesting Forrester study shows that of customers faced with a registration screen during checkout, 30 percent did not purchase and 23 percent of them left the site immediately. As marketers, we want as much data and client information as possible, but not at that cost.

Perhaps your primary goal is to register users, so offering a guest checkout is a non-starter. But if your primary goal is selling, then not losing 30 percent of your customers might be worth testing a guest checkout. After all, if you don't have to register for a frequent flyer account just to buy an airline ticket, why should you have to register to buy a pair of shoes?

In general, try to prefill information whenever possible to make moving through the form as easy and quick as possible. Amazon took this to the extreme with its One-Click patent, but even standard forms can avoid repetitive entries. Figure 10.38 shows Macy's Express Checkout option, which remembers information already entered.

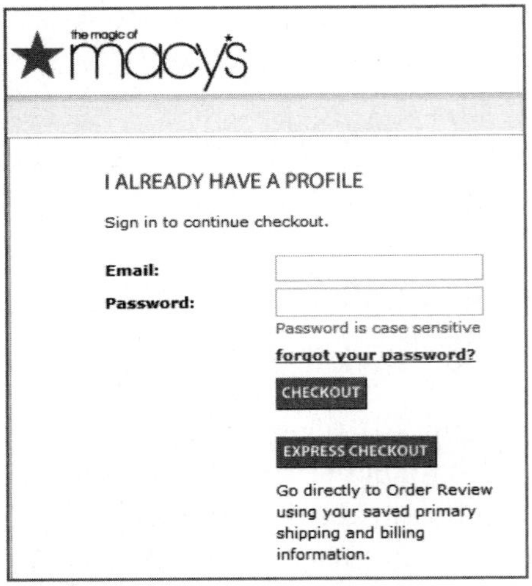

Figure 10.38 Macy's Express Checkout

What else can you test to make the checkout process easier?

Point-of-Action Assurances

The general idea of a point-of-action assurance is objection handling. You put yourself in the shoes of potential customers and imagine what might keep them from taking the next step. The variations you test are digital forms of what you might say if you were standing next to that person. If they are worried about giving you their email, you might put notice that indicates how seriously you take their privacy. Or at a checkout you might indicate that you use banking-grade encryption if you think they are concerned about security. Figure 10.39 shows how Banana Republic places its return policy and security information right next to the checkout button so users with those common concerns can get them addressed immediately.

Figure 10.39 Banana Republic addressing two major objections right at its point of action

However, not all point-of-action messages have a positive effect, so testing is important. Perhaps the message introduces a concern that was never there ("Hmmm... maybe I should be concerned about security?"), or perhaps users click the link to read the message, get distracted, and never make it back to the page to complete the purchase.

The text above the call-to-action button in Figure 10.40 is particularly dangerous. It clearly states that this product "cannot be gift wrapped"! Unless that little girl in the picture is buying a $300 map for herself, this is definitely a gift. A gift that cannot be wrapped is a problem for many buyers.

Figure 10.40 Sorry, this product cannot be gift wrapped.

Savvy readers of this book understand the order fulfillment process and realize that they mean that it will be drop shipped and can't be gift wrapped at the warehouse—not that it is literally impossible to gift wrap this item yourself. But many parents and grandparents shopping for such presents may not realize or think that through. Putting this ominous message next to the Add to Cart button is risky. They should test another way to deliver that message!

Reduce Clutter

As you ponder adding point-of-action assurances and call-to-action buttons to your landing page, one of the most successful improvements you can make (and then test) is to *remove* things from your landing page. Reducing clutter and simplifying your message and funnel very often have a positive effect. For many businesses, extra items and clutter happen because various groups within the organization want their project or group represented.

Even in smaller organizations there is the tendency to try to get all the marketing messages, features, and benefits out once, hoping one of them will resonate with the visitor enough to move them to the next step. But by testing variations with various parts removed, you can learn which marketing messages do *not* resonate with customers, which is incredibly valuable information.

It stands to reason that photographers love looking at pictures. So when Google created a landing page for the (then new) Picasa photography software, it included a pleasant picture in the design. But it also created a simplified version with no photos and a very simple Download Now button. The page with no photo won in a landslide. When creating reduced clutter variations, examine every element of the page and ask yourself if it's essential or if it can be presented at a later step in the funnel.

Wednesday: The Importance of Dedicated Landing Pages

Dedicated landing pages usually outperform generic landing pages and are highly recommended. This does *not* imply that you should use squeeze pages or other very specific formats. It simply means that the landing page is a logical next step from the ad.

Landing pages should maintain the scent, which often includes look and feel. GEICO recently had six completely different ad campaigns running: The GEICO Gecko, Cavemen, Pile-of-Money (Kash), Rhetorical Questions, Talking Objects, and Motorcycles and Toys. Clearly it makes no sense to send someone who's laughing at the latest comical Cavemen escapade to the Gecko home page. And the much more practical motorcycle ads appeal to users who are serious about protecting their investment, so sending them to a silly pile-of-cash-with-googly-eyes-themed landing page isn't likely to perform well.

Each of those ad campaigns is designed to target a specific audience and fulfill a specific purpose. It's only logical that each also has a corresponding landing page designed with that purpose and audience in mind.

The extent to which you segment the audience can go much deeper than simply matching the ad. If a set of placements has demographic data that skews heavily toward women, you might test a landing page designed to appeal to women, just as you would the ad creative. Political campaigns are well known for microtargeting very specific groups, so obviously they want the landing page to address the specific issues and appeal to the audience targeted. A generic landing page squanders the effort of targeting in the first place.

This can be tedious, and you may be tempted to cut corners. Obviously a cost/benefit analysis must be done to determine the extent to which you customize, but the more tailored you can make the customer journey, the more successful you are likely to be. The time spent here is not necessarily about learning new techniques or concepts but rather the effort of mapping out and creating the appropriate landing pages for each audience.

Thursday: A/B Split Testing

With dedicated landing pages to match your different creatives, the last thing you may feel like doing is creating even *more* landing pages, but creating landing pages that perfectly capture the purpose, tone, and mix of elements discussed on Tuesday on the first attempt is nearly impossible. So for all the same reasons that it is critical to test multiple ads (and even more because there are even more opportunities for variation and design decisions), you want to test multiple landing page variations.

Just as you followed a mathematical process for split testing ads, you can apply those same concepts to determining the optimal landing pages. The underlying math of the formulas is the same, but because landing pages have a slightly different set of metrics, we updated the tool to reflect that. The A/B testing tool can be found on the same tools page: www.cardinalpath.com/tools/.

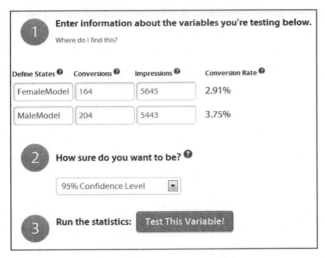

Figure 10.41 Using the free Cardinal Path A/B testing tool is a simple way to ensure a statistically valid result.

Figure 10.41 compares two landing pages. For ads, we use CTR and conversions as success metrics, but at this stage of the funnel we care only about final outcomes. Compared to sample size calculation and ad split testing, this is a simpler set of requirements. We really need to know only two things about a landing page: visits and conversions. To populate the tool, fill in the state (the variation name), impressions (unique visitors to the page), and unique conversions. Most people leave the confidence level at the default of 95 percent. Using lower values lets you accomplish more tests at higher risk. In the example in the figure, when we click Test This Variable, the analysis tells us that we have a statistically significant difference between the two and thus our test can be concluded.

This tool is useful for evaluating performance and interpreting results *after* the variations have all been served to visitors. To automate the process of serving different versions of a landing page to different visitors in a statistically random manner, there are plenty of tools we recommend. Our simple, free tool allows analysis of only two states (A/B), but more sophisticated tools such as JMP and Minitab offer much more in-depth analysis. More sophisticated testing techniques are discussed further in Chapter 11.

Friday: Multivariate Testing

A/B testing allows you to determine which of two landing pages is superior. Multivariate testing (MVT) is a slightly different kind of testing that can dive much deeper into optimizing elements of the pages themselves. These tools often make your testing much more efficient.

Often our hypothesis about how to improve a page doesn't involve a radically different design but rather changing an element such as the color or text of a button. MVT allows the site owner to test lots of different variations by simply modifying these elements rather than re-creating entirely new pages.

But beyond just convenience, MVT also measures interaction effects between the elements, which can be extremely important. For example, if you are testing buttons, your A/B/n testing may tell you that red buttons work best. Another test may tell you the color scheme with the orange backgrounds tests best. Individually both may be true. But because you are designing an entire page, you need to make sure all of your elements work together for the best complete page possible. An orange background with a red button may perform poorly because the combination of the two similar colors makes the low-contrast button more difficult to see.

MVT tests each of those elements (background color and button color) individually but is ultimately looking for the complete page combination that performs best. Because both the page rendering and the analysis can get fairly complex, we highly recommend you use one of the tools discussed in Chapter 11 to accomplish this type of powerful testing.

When to Use A/B vs. Multivariate?

Both tests aim to find the optimal result in an efficient manner, but they should be employed in different scenarios. It may be helpful to think of A/B/n tests as you would a first responder to an accident, such as an ambulance or fire truck. Their focus is to treat the major problems first, such as putting a splint on a limb or stopping the bleeding. Once they transport the patient to the hospital, the staff there can worry about the intermediate concerns such as putting casts on broken bones and then smaller issues such as bandages on superficial wounds.

With your websites as the patient, you want to triage in a similar manner. The A/B tests help you understand which of two completely different concepts is better. Should the page for the getaway ad use the dancing/dining motif or the isolation/solitude theme? Should you use a page centered around a form or around a video and interactive elements? A/B tests allow you to compare entirely different page concepts.

Once you determined that Page A is better than Page B, you still don't know that A is optimal. You only know that it is better than B. MVT can test and optimize every element of Page A to ensure it has the best headline, the best background image, the best button text, and so on. Every element on the page can be tweaked and tested until you have not only the best concept but also the best combination of elements for that concept. The combination of A/B/n and MVT can be a powerful way to optimize from the large changes down to the minute.

Further Reading

Landing page testing is a skill and technique that separates good marketers from great, and we encourage you to learn more about this important activity. We recommend books such as Tim Ash's *Landing Page Optimization: The Definitive Guide to Testing and Tuning for Conversions* (Sybex, 2012).

Month 8: Advanced Topics

11

With a solid display advertising strategy and campaigns built out to fulfill your strategic goals, you've prepared and launched. By putting in place a robust measurement and optimization plan, you're improving performance day in and day out. And there's still more you can do! This month, we focus on some of the advanced and less used strategies that can bring your display advertising to yet another level.

Chapter Contents:
Week 29: Retarget and Remarket
Week 30: Learn Tools for Testing Landing Pages
Week 31: Go Beyond Clickstream Analytics
Week 32: Target Topics

Week 29: Retarget and Remarket

Right now is an exciting time for display advertisers, and it's primarily because focus is shifting from targeting the *content* of a page toward the *people* consuming that content. While contextual targeting defines the kind of page we think a certain kind of user might go to, and a placement target explicitly focuses on one or more of those identified pages, audience targeting goes after *that certain kind of user*, no matter what pages they happen to browse.

When we combine technology with the vast inventory of advertising opportunities available across the Web, once a user has exhibited a behavior that we as advertisers would like to target, we can show that user our ads, even on sites that have nothing to do with our products and services. Retargeting makes all of this possible, and more.

Monday: Understanding Retargeting

Retargeting is not new—companies offering this service date back to the mid 2000s—and a good way to think of retargeting is as a sort of natural progression of online marketing. If you search for basketball shoes, you see ads for basketball shoes beside the search results. This is traditional search marketing, which revolutionized advertising.

But if you click on one of those ads, you'll be taken away and every other advertiser on the page that didn't garner the click will have lost the opportunity. You're gone, and since you didn't click on their ads, you may never be exposed to those advertisers again! If only there were some way to *mark* you as interested in basketball shoes *even if you didn't click on an ad* so those unfortunate advertisers can catch up with you later.

Search Retargeting

What search retargeting allows advertisers to do is just that. When users enter search queries on search engines or do searches on an array of websites around the Internet, they are labeled as part of certain groups or as interested in certain topics. Advertisers can still use text ads and search marketing to target people who search for basketball shoes on the search engine results pages, but now they can also use display ads to *retarget* those searchers wherever they go. By using search retargeting, advertisers who don't get a click on the search results page have another opportunity to target a user who is clearly interested in the products and services they offer.

Types of Retargeting

Search retargeting is only one of many types of retargeting, and the following section summarizes a few of the more popular ones that are being offered by a host of third-party solutions.

Contextual retargeting This is what AdWords Interest Categories do, but it's also available from other sources. Users are categorized by the context of the websites they visit. For example, a user who spends time on recipe sites, cooking show forums, and food critics' blogs is labeled as interested in food and cooking.

Product retargeting If you see product retargeting in action, you think that either you're extremely lucky or someone is watching you. You go to a website, put a product in your shopping cart, then leave without buying it. As you visit other sites, you start to see ads for a discount on *that same exact product* from *the exact same site* you left.

Email retargeting If you sign up for an email newsletter, you might become part of a retargeting campaign. Advertisers show display ads around the Web to their email subscribers to solidify a consistent cross-channel message or target a certain segment of an email list with specific and relevant messaging.

Social retargeting This lets you target not just your prospective customers but also those in their social networks. A friend of your target customer is likely to share many of the qualities that made your customer a target in the first place.

Just about any action that can be taken on the Web can also be used to build a targeting list, and there are many more retargeting types than those listed here. But one of the most controllable types of retargeting is one that can be triggered by any action you care to track on any website that you control.

Site Retargeting

Site retargeting is perhaps the most common type of retargeting. You add a bit of code to your website to detect when a user has taken a certain action, known as the *qualifying action*, and put that user on an associated retargeting list, which you can then use to show your ads in display inventory all over the Web to only those users.

For example, many automobile manufacturer websites let users choose a model and then add features and preferences to build their perfect car online. They can choose trim, pick interior and exterior colors, add options, upgrade to available packages, and finally get a quote for the car they just built. However, very few people whip out a credit card and buy it on the spot!

But now, the auto manufacturer *knows* that this user is interested in a certain model of car at a certain price. Let's say it was a high-end, two-door sports coupe. This user is likely to do some research, and go to buyer's guide websites and blogs and forums and even valuation pages. All of these are potentially good targets for contextual or placement targeted campaigns.

But after doing all that research on sports cars, they go on with the rest of their lives. They might head to a news site to catch up on current events, they might watch some videos on YouTube for entertainment, they might check out sports scores, and they might even get hungry and look up a recipe on a food site. Through site retargeting, the car company can advertise to this user, based on a demonstrated interest in this car, *everywhere that user goes*. And the ads can be specific: The advertiser can show them messaging touting the special offers and benefits of owning *that* two-door sports coupe.

When users exhibit behavior that indicates their intent, we're much less interested in what kind of website they happen to be looking at. We now target the *user*, not the *sites* that we believe will attract our generic target audience. And we know exactly what this user wants. We don't show minivans or sports utility vehicles; we show a two-door sports coupe speeding around a highway curve.

Third-Party Retargeting Solutions

Many retargeting vendors provide unique sets of retargeting options, reach, and service offerings. The following list is by no means complete, but you may want to explore these vendors as you grow your retargeting strategy.

- AdRoll: Robust site retargeting platform; no setup fees or contracts (www.adroll.com)
- Buysight: Product retargeting and dynamic ads based on a trademarked Buyer Intent Map (www.buysight.com)
- Chango: Well-established search retargeting platform supporting dynamic ads (www.chango.com)
- Criteo: E-commerce product retargeting focus with dynamic ads featuring product recommendations (www.criteo.com)
- Fetchback: Solution owned by eBay and GSI Commerce that offers product retargeting using patent pending FIDO technology (www.fetchback.com)
- Magnetic: Site with strong focus on search retargeting and keyword lists on an open technology platform (www.magnetic.is)
- ReTargeter: Site retargeting platform with contextual, social, and email retargeting options (www.retargeter.com)
- Simpli.fi: Single platform offering search and site retargeting as well as contextual and geotargeting solutions (www.simpli.fi)

Tuesday: Using AdWords Remarketing

Google was not the first on the retargeting scene, but the AdWords system makes site retargeting available across its large network of ad inventory in a very powerful and extremely accessible way. In the world of AdWords, this is known as *remarketing*.

Remarketing with Google AdWords

While there are many third-party vendors and ad networks that offer a wide variety of retargeting capabilities, for advertisers already running Google AdWords display campaigns, targeting audiences through the remarketing lists they build is perhaps the easiest way to get started. We encourage display advertisers to explore all platforms and solutions on the market today, but for many, the first experience with retargeting will be through AdWords remarketing, and here are a few reasons why.

First, the Google Display Network is immense, and it allows you to run your remarketing campaigns across an extremely large set of inventory. While there certainly are a lot of other ad networks and a lot more inventory out there, using AdWords remarketing gives you enormous reach from a single platform that many advertisers are already working with.

Next, Google's network is extremely fast. Third-party retargeting solutions can leverage real-time bidding platforms, piggyback on lots of different cookies, and provide access to all the inventory you could ever want, and they can do this within hours or in some cases minutes of an event occurring on the pages of your site. That's impressive, but by having the code, the cookies, and the inventory on one platform, the AdWords system allows remarketing ads to start on the very next click!

Another reason you might find yourself starting with AdWords remarketing is that it lives within an interface you already use, it's completely self-serve, and remarketing is not subject to minimum spends or budgetary commitments. For small and mid-sized businesses and organizations, this offers the simplicity of using a single platform and complete financial control.

Last, if you use AdWords conversion tracking, the code you need to generate and add to your website is familiar. The same concepts apply to defining a list qualification event as defining a conversion event. To build a remarketing list for newsletter subscribers, for example, you place the remarketing code on the page that says, "Thanks for signing up for our newsletter," where you know the list qualification behavior has just occurred.

How It Works

Inside the Google AdWords interface, advertisers can define various remarketing lists, generate the code that uses cookies to mark the user as a part of that remarketing list, and then uses those remarketing lists to define audiences for an ad group to target.

This is accomplished through the DoubleClick cookie, which is present on just about everyone's browser. This cookie assigns each specific web browser on a specific computer a unique 18-digit ID. It's important to note that this cookie contains nothing to identify an actual *person* (like a name or an email address). It's simply a unique random set of characters.

As that browser loads pages across the Web, code on those pages uses the DoubleClick cookie to track things like interest categories, control how often a user sees a certain set of ads (this is how frequency capping is achieved), and keep track of which ads have been shown to which DoubleClick cookies. Without these cookies, things like impression counts and view-through conversions can't be tracked.

AdWords also uses these cookies to manage remarketing lists. The code you put on your pages associates the cookie's ID with the remarketing list whenever the qualifying event occurs. When you decide to target that list with your ads, as a browser loads a page, code on that page reads the DoubleClick cookie. If its unique ID is on your list, it becomes eligible to show the targeted ad.

TravelNevada.com Case Study: Capitalizing on Visits That Don't Convert

When the Nevada Commission on Tourism wants to get people making travel plans that include the state of Nevada, one of the best tools they have at their disposal is the TravelNevada.com website. While just about anyone can conjure up an image of the Vegas strip, far fewer people associate the state with its vast range of activities, which include everything from ghost town tours to whitewater kayaking and world-class skiing to year-round golf. And while visitors to the website can explore and discover all of the various activities as they browse around, odds are good that they won't uncover *everything* before they've left.

What happens when someone leaves without finding those key areas of content? What if they never come back? Has the chance to expose them to a marketing message been lost forever?

Through AdWords remarketing, JoLyn and David of the Nevada Commission on Tourism have found an incredibly effective way to get tempting imagery and tantalizing messaging in front of those lost visitors and bring them back once again. Take, for example, all the visitors that leave TravelNevada.com without being exposed to the winter vacation opportunities across the state. By creating and maintaining remarketing lists around what content visitors *have* seen, custom combinations can be used to target and show ads that highlight the things people are still unaware of, like the one shown here.

Not only are "lost" visitors exposed to opportunities they may not have known existed, they're also lured by the chance to win the experience! Enticing? Well, as it turns out, we've had the pleasure of working with TravelNevada.com, and we can tell you that remarketing has led to conversion rates of *three and a half times* those of other campaigns!

Wednesday: Creating Remarketing Lists

Creating a remarketing list inside Google AdWords is straightforward, and once you decide on a target audience, you can get started.

Creating a New Remarketing List

Use the left-hand navigation bar in the AdWords interface to select Audiences under Shared Library. The right-hand pane shows the audiences defined in your account, and this is where you can manage existing audiences and add new ones. To add a new remarketing list, select Remarketing List from the New Audience drop-down, and the New Remarketing List window appears (Figure 11.1).

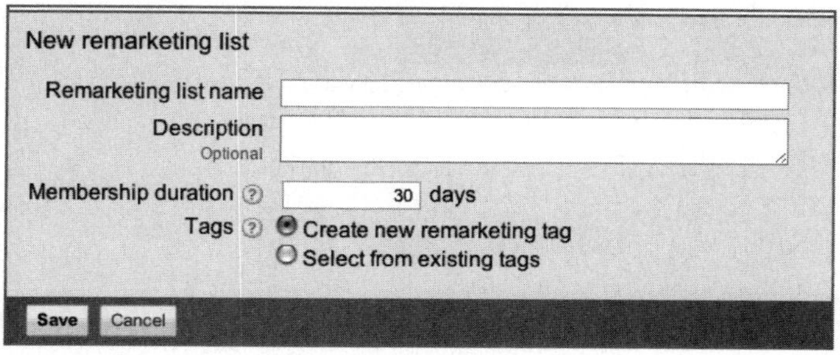

Figure 11.1 Creating a new remarketing list

As you do when naming campaigns or ad groups, give the remarketing list a name that succinctly describes exactly what someone has done to become a part of this list. A name like Added to Shopping Cart clearly identifies a list of visitors who have added something to their shopping cart. Converted - Purchased is a list of visitors who have purchased something. Use the description field to describe the qualifying event.

In the Membership Duration field, enter the number of days a qualifying person should stay on the list. Say you send a coupon valid for 7 days to people signing up for your email newsletter and you put them on a remarketing list. If you set the membership duration to 7 days on this list, then those subscribers see your ads only until their coupons expire. On day 8, they are no longer eligible to see the ads. The default duration is 30 days, but you can set it as high as 540 days. That's a full year and a half after the qualifying event, and we discuss creative ways to use this upper limit a bit later! Each time a user completes that event again, the clock restarts at zero.

Next, you need to choose between creating a new remarketing tag or using tags that already exist within the account.

A good case for using existing tags is to create a remarketing list from conversion actions you've already configured through the AdWords Conversion Tracking feature. By adding conversion tracking code to the page on your website that signifies the conversion action has occurred, you also define an event that can now be used to build a remarketing list. If you want to create a remarketing list based on an existing conversion event, choose the Select From Existing Tags radio button (Figure 11.1) and choose the action that you wish to use to qualify a user for a remarketing list. For example, if you've already configured and added the code for a conversion like Purchase, you select that tag to create a remarketing list called Past Purchasers.

For qualifying actions that you've not yet defined as conversions, you'll need to create a new tag, and you can do this simply by leaving the Create New Remarketing Tag option selected and saving the new remarketing list. To get the code you need to add to your website, click the Tag link in the Tags / Rules column of the audience list to see a pop-up that looks like Figure 11.2.

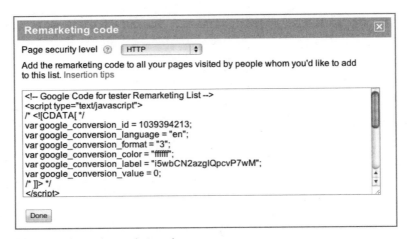

Figure 11.2 Getting the remarketing code

In the Page Security Level field, select HTTP or HTTPS. If you're not sure which to use, navigate to the page on which you plan to put this code. If the URL in the browser address bar starts with `https://`, use HTTPS. Otherwise use HTTP.

Finally, copy the code and paste it onto the page where users complete the qualifying event. For example, in building a remarketing list to target email newsletter subscribers, put this code on the page a user sees after successfully signing up.

Tip: Remarketing code is just JavaScript, so if you know what you're doing, you can manipulate it to fire just about anywhere. Code-savvy readers can see that the remarketing code includes a simple image request, and if you create a function to execute that image request, you can call that function on any event you can track on your web pages or in your web application. That includes Flash, AJAX, or anywhere else that a browser can execute JavaScript. You can also use server-side code to evaluate criteria for sending the remarketing code back to the browser. For example, to create a remarketing list of people who have logged into your site more than five times, you can check a user's login history in your database and render the remarketing code if the criteria has been met.

Targeting a Remarketing List in an Ad Group

Once you create a remarketing list and add the code to your website, that list starts to grow as users complete your qualification actions. Once you have a minimum of 100 users, you can start to target them as an audience in campaigns and ad groups.

To target your remarketing lists, it's a best practice to create a brand-new campaign dedicated to remarketing. This way, you can control the campaign-level targeting and budgets for your remarketing efforts, which will likely perform quite differently from your other display campaigns. Once you create your new campaign, navigate to the ad group focused on these list members (or create a new one). On the Display Network tab, click Change Display Targeting, and you see the Change Display Targeting panel. Scroll down to the Interests & Remarketing section and click the Remarketing Lists tab (Figure 11.3).

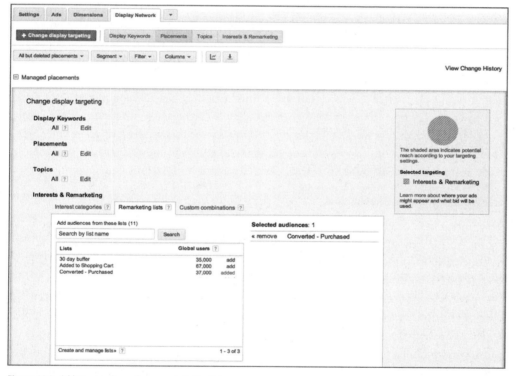

Figure 11.3 Adding an audience from a remarketing list

Here you see all your remarketing lists with the (approximate) number of users on each. In Figure 11.3, the word *added* next to our Converted - Purchased list indicates that we identify this group as a target audience. After we save our targeting settings, this ad group lets us show certain ads only to the 37,000 people who have already purchased from us. We can show them ads featuring repeat customer discounts, cross sells, membership benefits, or anything else we can dream up!

Of course, you need to set campaign targeting options and create ads specifically for this audience. And make sure your ads are available in all supported sizes to maximize the placement opportunities!

Thursday: Using Custom Combinations

Custom combinations allow you to mix and match different interest categories, remarketing lists, and even other custom combinations through a series of logical combinations. Today we discuss the details of how this works and how to do it, but let's start with an example.

When to Use Custom Combinations

Let's say we want to create a remarketing list for people who put something in their shopping cart, but do not check out with it. If we simply target everyone who puts something in their shopping cart, what happens when someone actually *does* check out? They have still completed the qualifying action of putting something in their cart, and therefore they're *still* on our list. To our horror, we're still showing them ads encouraging them to come back to finish a purchase they already completed! Not good. We don't really want to target the list of people who have put something in their shopping carts; instead, we want to target a *combination* of this remarketing list and something else. We want to target everyone on the Added to Shopping Cart list combined with *nobody* on our Bought Something list. Custom combinations can accomplish this.

Creating a New Custom Combination

To create a new custom combination, you start out the same way you would start if you were creating a new remarketing list. Go to Shared Library › Audiences and select Custom Combination from the New audience drop-down. That brings up the New Custom Combination screen (Figure 11.4).

This custom combination targets users who have put something in a shopping cart but not purchased anything. The user *must be* a member of the Added to Shopping Cart list and *must not be* a member of the Converted - Purchased list. When visitors put something into their shopping cart, they can see our remarketing ads; they match our criteria. But once they purchase something, they no longer meet the targeting criteria and no longer see our ads.

You can define matching criteria as all, none, or "one or more of" the audiences that you define (Figure 11.5).

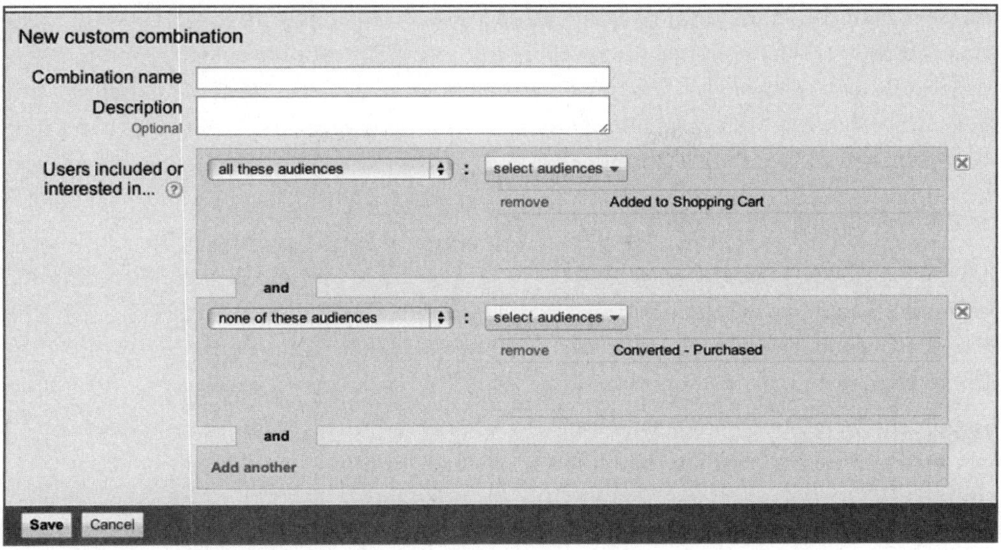

Figure 11.4 Adding a custom combination audience target

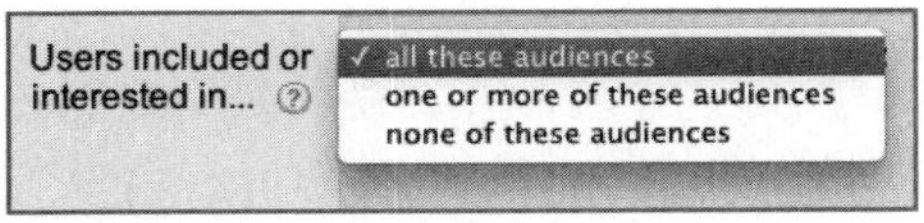

Figure 11.5 Defining matching criteria

Clicking the Add Another link at the bottom of the custom combination interface allows you to build more and more elements of your custom combination, and for each element, you use the Select Audiences drop-down to add one or more interest categories, remarketing lists, or other custom combinations to the matching criteria (Figure 11.6).

Figure 11.6 Selecting audiences

Targeting a Custom Combination in an Ad Group

Once you define and save your custom combination, you can use it as an audience target the same way you use interest categories or remarketing lists. Navigate to the campaign and ad group you wish to set the audience target for, click the Display

Network tab, and click Change Display Targeting. In the Interests & Remarketing section (Figure 11.3), select the Custom Combinations tab to see the custom combinations defined in the account. Use Add and Remove to define which custom combinations this ad group targets, and once you apply these new targeting settings, your ad group targets your new custom combination!

Friday: Leveraging Remarketing Best Practices

Hopefully you're excited about the power and flexibility of remarketing, and you have ideas you'd like to start implementing. Here are some of the best practices and tips and tricks that we've used to help our remarketing campaigns perform for our clients over the years.

Start with a Strategy

The number one mistake that advertisers make with remarketing is not using it in the first place. But after that, the biggest mistake people make is not having a strategy. We've seen countless AdWords accounts that are creating remarketing lists based on the fact that someone has been to *any* page of your site, and unfortunately, just because someone visited your home page and left after half a second does not typically qualify them for a list that can be targeted with any kind of a specific message.

Think about what actions people take on the pages of your website, what kind of intent those actions indicate, and make sure you're thinking about it in the context of the products and services you offer. Then, spend some time brainstorming the kind of messaging you could put in front of those groups of people to entice them back so they continue further and further down your sales funnel.

Write these things on a whiteboard or put them in a spreadsheet and talk through your ideas, asking yourself the following questions:

- What action does the user take?
- What is their intent?
- What messaging would resonate with them at that point?
- For how long?
- What is the next step I want them to take?

Let's take an example of a lead generation website that has a very long sales cycle. Reading a white paper on the site is an action we can use to qualify users for this list. They are likely in research mode and very early in the sales cycle. They're looking at a technology or process and investigating their options. They're very likely evaluating competitors as well, so our messaging might be intended to keep us top-of-mind during the research phase and showcase why we're better than our competitors.

Assume that our internal sales data tells us the average purchase cycle lasts for a year, during which the first six months are typically just research and requirements gathering. This helps us set our membership duration for this list.

Last, we want to graduate users from this list to the next step of our sales cycle, which might be talking to one of our salespeople or signing up for a demonstration. So we can tailor the experience accordingly, creating ads and landing pages that funnel these users toward scheduling demonstrations or a call with a salesperson.

And then, we start again and add new lists to our overall remarketing strategy called Scheduled Demo and Scheduled Sales Call!

Start Out Generic and Refine Lists over Time

Many advertisers start down the path of remarketing and are overwhelmed quickly because there are so many opportunities to create and market to lists but not enough hours in the day to create or manage them. The best thing to do is start out with large groups and get more granular over time.

For example, if you've got an e-commerce store that sells all kinds of clothing, start out with a single remarketing list that includes anyone that has put *anything* in your shopping cart. The ads you build for this campaign must be generic—you don't know *what* they put in their cart, but you know they put *something* there.

Next month, break out your remarketing lists and create ad groups that target overall product categories. At this point, you might have one remarketing list and ad group targeting people who have put *shirts* in their shopping carts and another list and ad group targeting people who have put *pants* in their shopping cart. Your ads can now be even more specific, showing the *type* of product you know this person was looking at.

Eventually, you can explore dynamic ads and product retargeting vendors, and you can show people who put size 32×30 semi-washed relaxed fit blue jeans in their cart an ad promoting a special on that exact size, brand, color, and style! But don't feel that you need to get to this level of granularity tomorrow: You can evolve your campaigns over time and balance the benefits of specificity with the time and effort it takes to obtain it.

Know When to Stop

Perhaps the worst thing you can do is try to sell someone something they've just bought from you for less than they just paid! There are three ways to stop remarketing to someone once they qualify for your lists.

List expiration Membership durations are a last-resort, catchall way of stopping your remarketing ads from showing up for someone who isn't interested. In many cases, you either know your business well enough or have the analytics and sales data to understand at what point a potential customer is lost.

For example, recreational travel typically takes just under 30 days to book from the time an average user starts research online. If you sell vacation packages and target people who have not booked but are looking through your photo galleries, you can set a membership duration in the 45- to 60-day range. By day 60, they're at twice the average and they've probably booked somewhere else, so there's a good chance that at this point your ad impressions are being wasted.

As always, make sure to experiment with membership durations and let the data be your guide.

Frequency caps Frequency capping (Chapter 6, "Month 3: Building Your First Display Campaign") is another way to control your messaging. By limiting the exposure any user can have to a specific ad group or campaign, you avoid overwhelming them, leaving them with a negative view of you and your brand, and wasting money on excess impressions.

If you show someone an ad 1,000 times in a week, they're probably not going to change their mind and finally click on it the 1,001st time. In fact, you might even be doing brand damage, leaving the user desperate for you to leave them alone!

Custom combinations and exclusions Perhaps the most effective way to stop showing a certain message or start showing a *different* message is through custom combinations. You can use different remarketing lists in logical combinations to target just about anyone at any stage of a buying cycle.

Let's take the shopping cart abandonment example one step further. Once they *have* completed the transaction, you can graduate them to a new list where you can cross sell other products and services they might need, like accessories or a warranty.

But what if the conversion happens offline? For an automobile purchase, there's no web page associated with coming into the dealership and signing all the papers! But you *can* drive recent new car buyers to a special, owners-only website where they can download coupons for oil changes or register their vehicles or sign up for email notifications of scheduled maintenance. On any of these pages, you can put code that qualifies someone to be part of a Purchased a Car list.

Last, don't forget that AdWords lets you set exclusions at the audience level, as discussed in Chapter 6.

Use Buffer Lists to Delay Delivery

Notice the remarketing list called 30 day buffer in Figure 11.3. Buffer lists can be extremely powerful for remarketing campaigns, and they work like this: Let's say that you're selling diapers on the Web. You know that if someone buys a pack of 100 diapers, they probably won't be in the market for diapers for another month or two, so targeting them with repeat-purchase discounts isn't likely to be relevant right after the purchase. But 30 days from now, they'll be running low on those diapers and starting to think about getting some more. *That's* when you want your remarketing ads to start showing up around the Web for that user.

To accomplish this, create a new remarketing list called 30 Day Buffer, and set it to expire in 30 days. Now, when a user checks out with a 100 pack of diapers, you include the code for *both* this buffer list tag (with a 30-day expiration) *and* the conversion tag with an expiration of somewhere in the 60- to 90-day range.

Finally, create a custom combination that that includes everyone who *is* a member of the Bought 100 Pack of Diapers list and who is *not* a member of the 30 Day Buffer list. As soon as users check out, they are active on both remarketing lists, and they do not meet the second part of the criteria for the custom combination. On day 31, however, they are no longer a member of the buffer list, but they *are* still a member of the Bought 100 Pack of Diapers list, so they qualify for the custom combination, and they start seeing your ads!

Don't Be Creepy

Nobody likes to be watched or monitored, and you probably don't want to give your target users the impression that you have cameras installed in their houses. That said, remarketing isn't quite the secret it was a few years ago, and many savvy consumers are aware of what's going on when they start seeing those ads that hit a little too close to home.

A good rule of thumb is to be just relevant enough that it's *almost* believable that this is sheer coincidence. The reaction you're looking for is something like, "Wow, I almost bought that for $10.00 yesterday, and now it's on sale for $5.00! How lucky I am!" What you don't want is your users thinking, "How did this company hack their way into my computer and why are they following me???" Experiment with different ads and different levels of creepiness to see what works best for you.

Get Creative

Finally, be creative. You can integrate remarketing strategies with just about any marketing campaign or advertising initiative. We end this week with a couple more examples to get your creative juices flowing.

CRM integration You might have access to demographic, behavioral, or historical data around users as they log into and use your site or interact with your organization, and developing remarketing lists that take advantage of this information can help you refine your targeting even more. For example, females start shopping for Valentine's Day weeks earlier than their male counterparts. By using customer relationship management (CRM) data of logged-in, opted-in users, when Sally is on your site, you can fire a remarketing list tag that signs her up for the Females remarketing list.

This is still anonymous—remember that Sally's cookie is still a unique, random number tied to a browser and contains no personally identifiable information, but you can start showing Sally's browser ads for a certain line of products in a campaign that launches two weeks earlier than the one that targets members of the Males remarketing list.

Cross-channel integration Many of our clients advertise not just on the Web but offline as well with television, radio, print, outdoor, and direct mail. Remarketing can be a fantastic way to tie together imagery and messaging to keep the scent of a cross-channel marketing campaign regardless of that channel.

One of our clients runs television ads that point users to a specific microsite that lives at a URL mentioned only in that television ad campaign. The microsite matches the look, feel, and messaging of the TV commercial, and when users arrive, they're added to the Seen TV Spot remarketing list. Display campaigns continue the messaging with image and video ads that continue to tell the story that the 30-second TV spot began with the same look and feel across the Web. And if a user signs up for an email newsletter, purchases something, or otherwise makes it into a CRM system, the same campaigns can be extended through email or direct mail.

These are just a few examples of how advertisers are leveraging the use of remarketing to provide the right audience with the right message at just the right time, and hopefully you're now ready to get creative with *your* audience targeting!

Week 30: Learn Tools for Testing Landing Pages

The importance of landing page and website testing to the effectiveness of your advertising campaigns cannot be overstated, and when it comes time to actually implement a test, you're going to need to select a tool. There are many fantastic testing tools on the market today, and we certainly encourage you to evaluate each one and choose what works best for your situation.

From server-side to client-side and proxied solutions, many vendors offer a range of services and technologies to help in your testing strategy. There are many more, but here are a few important ones:

- Adobe/Omniture Test & Target (www.omniture.com/en/products/conversion/test-and-target)
- Autonomy Optimost (promote.autonomy.com/promote/products/optimost.page)
- HiConversion (www.hiconversion.com)
- Maxymiser (www.maxymiser.com)
- Monetate (www.monetate.com)
- Optimizely (www.optimizely.com)
- SiteSpect (www.sitespect.com)
- Vertster (www.vertster.com)
- Visual Website Optimizer (www.visualwebsiteoptimizer.com)

A fantastic resource for researching and learning about different testing solutions is the highly recommended online comparative guide to landing page testing platforms at www.whichmvt.com, curated by our friends at Conversion Rate Experts.

Unfortunately, we don't have room to zoom in on each of these tools, so this week, we focus on just the basics of two solutions that are both easy to use and financially easy to handle for many advertisers: Google Analytics Content Experiments (www.google.com/analytics) and Optimizely (www.optimizely.com).

Monday: Understanding Google Analytics Content Experiments

For those who have grown accustomed to using Google's Website Optimizer testing tool over the past few years, the bad news is that as of August 1, 2012, Website Optimizer is a thing of the past. The good news is that by deprecating this product, Google has not abandoned testing but instead brought it inside the Google Analytics product with a feature called Content Experiments.

Google Analytics Content Experiments

Google Analytics Content Experiments launched publicly in Q2 of 2012 and provides users with an integrated A/B testing tool. This tool allows you to test alternative versions of key pages on your website and measure their impact on any goals you have configured inside your Google Analytics account.

To get started, head over to the Content section of a standard Google Analytics interface, and click Experiments to see the overview screen (Figure 11.7). Once you launch your first experiment, that overview screen is replaced with a list of your current and past experiments, and it's from there that you dive into individual experiment reports.

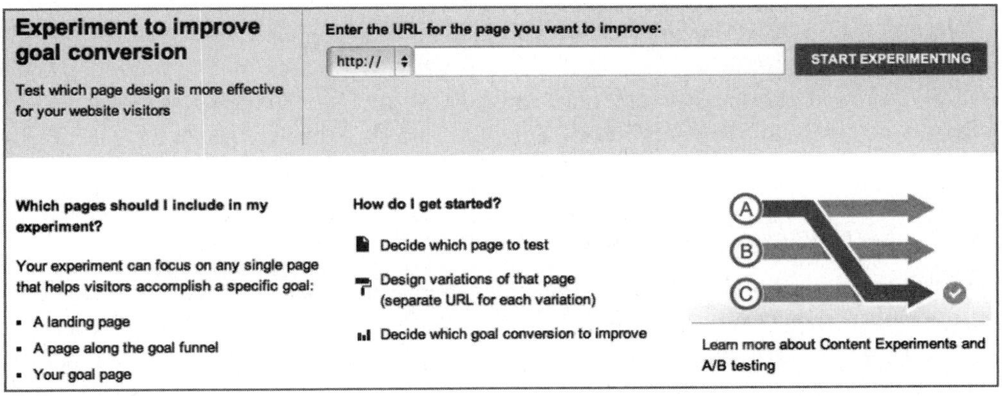

Figure 11.7 Google Analytics Content Experiments

Differences from Google Website Optimizer

Because the transition from Google Website Optimizer to Content Experiments is a recent development, it's important to note some of the differences between the two solutions:

Multivariate and advanced tests If you run advanced implementations of multivariate experiments with dynamic code hacks and custom variable integrations, you'll probably be a bit disappointed in the simplicity of Content Experiments. At launch, there is no support for multivariate testing (MVT) and users are limited to testing 5 variations of a page versus the 10,000 that Website Optimizer was able to support.

Ease of use Content Experiments are clearly targeted at the masses, and for this reason, they're likely to get a lot more use than Website Optimizer ever did. Experiment code now requires only one control script, and the interface follows a straightforward four-step process that allows even the most casual of Internet marketers to quickly and easily set up and run tests.

User segments Since Content Experiments lives within the Google Analytics interface and uses the same data, you can take advantage of other Google Analytics features when evaluating an experiment. Understanding how your variations perform across all visitors is one thing, but using Advanced Segments allows you to evaluate your page variations with respect to any subgroup of traffic you wish to isolate.

Adaptive model While Website Optimizer contained a crude auto-pruning feature to limit the risk of users seeing a page variation that performs poorly, Content Experiments uses an adaptive model to adjust the percentage of traffic each test variation is shown during an experiment. This allows you to confidently try new things without worrying as much about losing business from variations that do not perform well.

Straightforward results Website Optimizer provided a wealth of data around the variables and combinations of variables that make up a test, but you needed to understand statistics to truly *use* that data. Content Experiments uses a different statistical model than Website Optimizer and protects users from coming to false conclusions too soon by not declaring winners until at least two weeks have passed to ensure that a representative sample has been collected. By contrast, while a Website Optimizer experiment could run for eternity, with Content Experiments, tests are shut down after 90 days if there is no winner.

Tuesday: Set up a Google Analytics Content Experiment

The first step in using Content Experiments is to identify a page to optimize. Using the data and reports in Google Analytics can be a fantastic way to isolate the pages that are causing problems, so focus on optimizing the following:

- Weak points in a defined conversion funnel
- Pages that you're spending a lot of money on
- Pages that attract a lot of traffic
- Pages that feed high-value conversions

By following these guidelines, you give yourself the best chance for success because you improve pages that have a lot of potential gain, a lot of potential value, and a lot of potential eyeballs!

Setting Up Your Experiment

Once you decide on a test page, it's time to create the variations you want to test. Content Experiments supports up to five variations per test, so you can try out a few different hypotheses. Every good test begins with hypotheses, and it's important to think through *why* you believe that changing a picture or a layout or text will improve the conversion rate.

Figure 11.8 shows the versions of the Cardinal Path home page that we tested with Content Experiments and that will serve as an example as we walk through the process of setting up a test.

Figure 11.8 Two versions of the Cardinal Path home page

As you can see, the test is between two versions of a call to action on a button. To run this test, we simply keep our control (our existing homepage) at http://www.cardinalpath.com/, and we create our test page (the one with the alternate call to action) on a different URL, in this case, http://www.cardinalpath.com/homepage/.

To begin, if you're a first-time tester, just enter the URL of the page you want to test in the interface shown in Figure 11.7 and click the Start Experimenting button, or if you're looking at your list of previous experiments, click Create Experiment (not shown) to be taken to step 1 (Figure 11.9).

Give your experiment a name that's descriptive of what you're testing, and enter the URLs of the original and variation pages. Also provide a name for the variation, to be used in reports. It's helpful to name this something that reminds you of what the variation is testing. Here, we use the calls to action as the variation names.

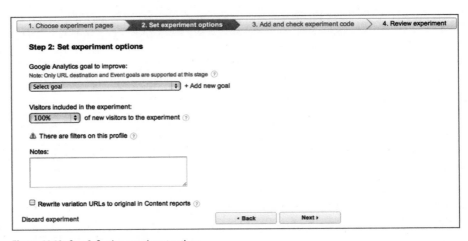

Figure 11.9 Step 1: Choosing experiment pages

Note also that clicking Add Variation at the bottom allows you to add more variations to your experiment up to the maximum of five.

Tip: If you're using virtual page views in your Google Analytics implementation, enter your *actual* page location into step 1. For example, if your actual page is `http://www.domain.com/index.php?id=12345`, but you're using a virtual page view so that Google Analytics reports this page as `http://www.domain.com/blue-socks-product-page.html`, enter the actual page URL (the one ending in `?id=12345` above) into the Content Experiments tool.

Figure 11.10 Step 2: Setting experiment options

Click Next to go to step 2 (Figure 11.10), where you have a number of options:

Select a goal   Start by selecting the goal that you wish to improve. For our example, it's clicks of the button we're testing, but you can use any goal configured in the profile. Clicking Add New Goal takes you to the goal configuration settings in Google Analytics. It's also important to note that at launch, Content Experiments does not support using transaction data. Instead of relying on e-commerce data, you must create a goal in the profile to track a purchase.

Traffic to test with   Next, select what percentage of traffic to test with. You can choose values up to 100 percent and as little as 1 percent. If you're not sure how your variations are going to perform, you might choose to start out with a small percentage of your traffic and then increase that percentage if your variations perform well.

Filter warnings   If you have filters enabled on the profile, you see a warning. In Google Analytics, you can filter in or out data based on certain criteria, and these filters impact your experiment. For example, if you configure Google Analytics to filter out traffic that comes from your organization's IP address, everyone in your organization may continue to see test pages, but their data is not included in the Content Experiment reports.

Notes   You can write notes about what you're testing. This can be useful in the future when you come back to see what you tested and how the experiment turned out.

URL rewrites   If you don't check this box, Google Analytics treats your experiment page like any other. What this means in our example is that the day we start our experiment, our Google Analytics reports show roughly half the number of page views to our home page as we would expect. The other half show up as views of our variation page. Checking this box tells Google Analytics to count all views of the variation page as views of the home page so as not to introduce this confusion into our data.

> **Tip:**   If you're comfortable using Advanced Segments and you're testing landing pages, you may want to leave the URL rewrite option unchecked. By creating a custom segment for each of your variations where the landing page metric is equal to the URL of those pages, you can compare your original and test versions against any metric in nearly any report in Google Analytics!

Wednesday: Run a Content Experiment

The final steps to running a test with Content Experiments are to add the experiment code, validate your installation, preview your test, and finally launch your experiment.

Adding and Validating Experiment Code

Your next step is to add the experiment code, and you have two options, as shown in Figure 11.11.

| 1. Choose experiment pages | 2. Set experiment options | 3. Add and check experiment code | 4. Review experiment |

Step 3: Add and check experiment code

To set up your experiment, your original page will need a small amount of code added to it.

○ I'll add the experiment code myself ⑦

○ I'll send the experiment code and instructions to my webmaster ⑦

After you have updated your pages with the experiment code, click **Next** to validate the code, review your configuration, and run the experiment.

Figure 11.11 Step 3: Adding experiment code

If you're comfortable with code and you have access to your web server, select the first radio button and copy the resulting block of JavaScript code to your clipboard. Paste this code into the <head> section of your *original* page.

Although not mentioned in the interface, it's a good idea to add the following code to your experiment pages:

```
<link rel="canonical" href="[ORIGINAL PAGE URL]" />
```

Simply replace `[ORIGINAL PAGE URL]` with the URL of your original page; this tells search engines to look at the content of the original page, not your test pages, for SEO purposes.

If you have a webmaster or IT department making code changes to your website, simply select the second radio button and send an email containing the instructions directly from the interface.

Tip: If your Google Analytics implementation crosses domains, you need to add a bit of JavaScript above the experiment code to make Content Experiments work. To match the _setDomainName() method used by Google Analytics, you need to set the _udn variable in its own script block *above* the experiment code. If you use other methods, you also need to set their equivalents before the experiment code.

Validating, Previewing, and Launching Your Experiment

Once the experiment pages are live and the experiment code is installed, you need to validate the code. Google goes to each page you define and looks for both a valid Google Analytics implementation and the experiment code. If it finds both, you see the message in Figure 11.12.

Figure 11.12 Validating experiment code

If you see errors here, fix them. Sometimes, however, you see errors even though the implementation is correct. For example, if the page sits behind a login, Google's crawlers can't find it and so return an error. If you use an advanced or nonstandard implementation of Google Analytics, you might see errors reported as well. If these or other similar situations apply to you, you'll see the error messages, but there will also be a Skip Validation and Continue link at the bottom. To bypass the automated validation check, simply click that link (not shown). The next step is to review the experiment one last time before launch (Figure 11.13).

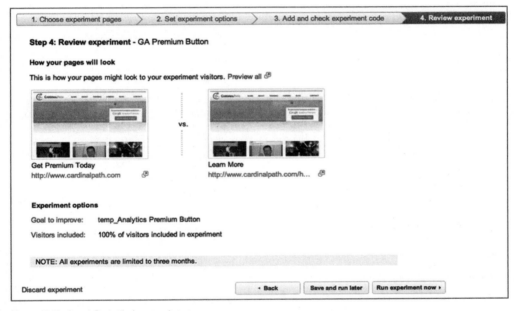

Figure 11.13 Step 4: Reviewing an experiment

Here you find a recap of your experiment settings and a preview functionality that allows you to cycle through your variations in a preview pane before you launch. Once everything looks good, you can either launch the experiment immediately or save the experiment to launch later. Once you click Run Experiment Now, your test is live!

> **Tip:** Before launching your test, make sure to preview each page variation in all browsers that your visitors use. It may look good in Firefox version 231.8 beta on your development machine but not on Internet Explorer version 7!

Thursday: Reading Content Experiment Reports

Once your experiment has launched, you can see reports by navigating to the Content › Experiments section of Google Analytics and selecting the experiment from the list (Figure 11.14).

Working with Experiments While They're Running

You can do a number of things with a running experiment. First, you can see visit and conversion data for the experiment (Figure 11.15), complete with a graph that defaults to daily granularity. Here there is no winner yet, despite 6,058 visits over 69 days.

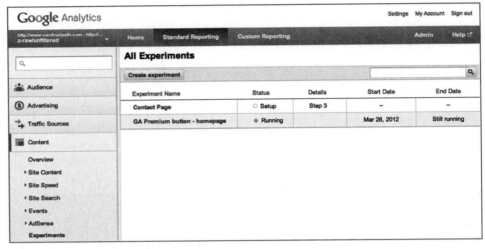

Figure 11.14 Experiment list in Google Analytics

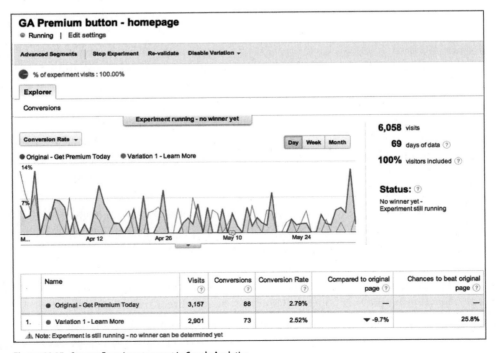

Figure 11.15 Content Experiments report in Google Analytics

By clicking the Edit Settings link at the top, you can change the name of your experiment and variations, vary the percentage of traffic that's being tested on, and add to or edit the notes for the experiment. Across the top bar you see additional options. If one of your variations is performing poorly after a week or two (and you have more than one alternate variation in the experiment), you can disable it. Perhaps most useful, however, is the Advanced Segments feature, which brings up the interface shown in Figure 11.16.

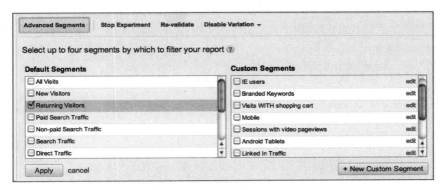

Figure 11.16 Applying an advanced segment to a Content Experiments report

Here, you can apply any of the default or custom segments, which automatically updates the report to include *only* data from that segment. Want to see how your variations perform for *only* mobile or tablet traffic? How about comparing first-time visitors with repeat visitors or people from Chicago with people from Los Angeles? Or see how your variations impact newsletter subscribers or past customers? You can analyze just about any segment of traffic you can dream up!

Completing an Experiment

When Content Experiments finds a winner, the experiment ends and everyone starts seeing the original page again, even if an alternative wins (Figure 11.17).

You then have some decisions to make. First, evaluate your key segments to decide whether or not to replace the original version with the winning variation. If you do so, evaluate the impact to your SEO strategy: When you replace your original with a new page, the search engines will start to crawl it and analyze its content.

Next, you'll need to do something with the variation pages that are no longer being tested. Someone may have found those variation pages and bookmarked your test URLs, and if they come back, you don't want to serve them a 404 – Page Not Found error. As a best practice, place a 301 permanent redirect from the variation pages to your original page once the experiment is over. This automatically redirects users trying to access the other variations to the original URL, and it tells search engines not to index those variation pages.

Your last step is to launch another experiment! Every test you run is an opportunity to learn something, and you can take that knowledge and apply it to more hypotheses. You can stop this cycle of testing as soon as you have a conversion rate of 100 percent!

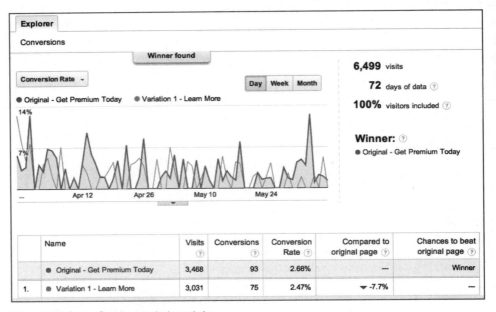

Figure 11.17 Content Experiments winning variation

Friday: Running a Test with Optimizely

While there are many testing tools and platforms on the market today, one cost-effective and easy-to-use platform is Optimizely. With Google Website Optimizer now retired and Content Experiments not supporting multivariate testing, this tool is an inexpensive and intuitive solution with a host of features, options, and capabilities. While we don't cover all the bells and whistles of the tool, we close out this week by walking through the basics of how to create and run an experiment using Optimizely.

Creating an Experiment in Optimizely

Your Optimizely account is organized by projects. Within each project, you can have draft, active, and archived experiments. To create a new experiment, click Create Experiment in the Drafts section of a project. In the window that opens, supply a name and URL. Optimizely shows you the live page you're testing with, only now you can interact with all the elements on the page and change whatever you'd like to test.

In this example, we run a test on a signup page from the Google Seminars for Success program. The goal of this site is to entice visitors to sign up for live, in-person training on Google Analytics and Google AdWords, and in order to get people registering, we might want to test a different design for the Register Now button (below the

Google map). Hovering over that section of the page highlights it, and right-clicking brings up a number of options (Figure 11.18). We can resize it, move it, or even do more advanced things. If we choose Edit HTML, for example, an edit window opens, displaying the relevant portion of the page's source HTML. Whatever changes we make define a variation we can test against the original, and as we edit and make changes, the interface updates to show us exactly what our new variation looks like! To create more variations, click Add Variation at the top of the page. You can move things around and alter just about any aspect of the page by clicking elements and selecting appropriate actions.

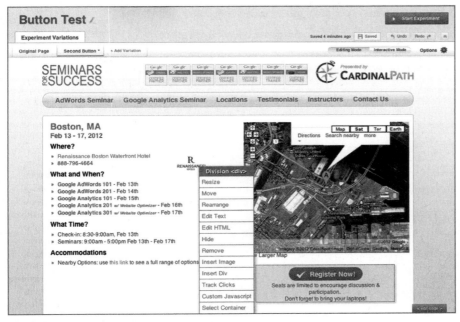

Figure 11.18 Creating variations in the Optimizely interface

Using Optimizely Options

After you create variations of the page you'd like to test, Optimizely provides a number of options, available by clicking on the Options gear icon at the top right of the page shown in Figure 11.18. We encourage you to explore this tool and all of its capabilities, but for now, let's look at just two of the useful features built into Optimizely.

Traffic Allocation is an especially useful option (Figure 11.19). It allows you to choose how much traffic to run through your experiment.

Just as with Content Experiments, controlling the percentage of visitors included in your experiment can limit the cost of a poorly performing test variation during your test and gives you control over the exposure of different variations to your website visitors.

The Analytics Integration option (Figure 11.20) lets you integrate Optimizely with other analytics tools.

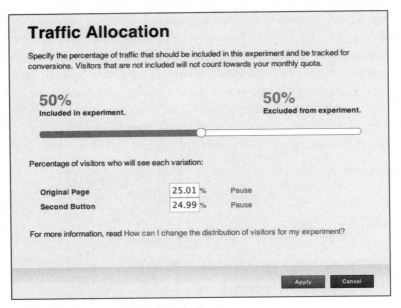

Figure 11.19 Changing an experiment's traffic allocation

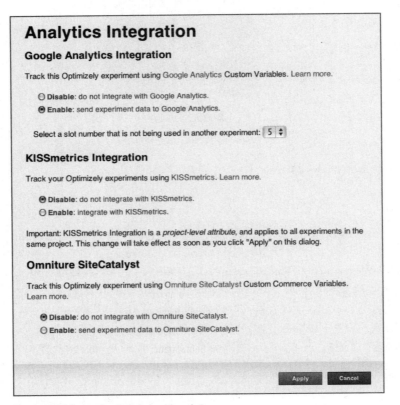

Figure 11.20 Integrating Optimizely with analytics

Here, you can very easily integrate with Adobe/Omniture SiteCatalyst, KISSmetrics, and Google Analytics. In the case of Google Analytics, for example, the tool automatically sends back a custom variable containing the variation that has been served in the slot that you select right here in the interface, saving you from having to introduce additional code to the pages of your website.

Catalogs.com Case Study: Integrating Testing with Google Analytics

To truly understand an experiment, it's important to look at all the relevant aspects of how the test variations impact website performance. Over at Catalogs.com, customers can browse through hundreds of their favorite merchants and retailers across a wide range of categories. When they find one they like, they can order a print catalog or click over to the merchant's online store, both of which are considered conversion activities for the website.

We helped Catalogs.com run an experiment to test three different page layouts of their merchant pages: Alpha, Beta, and Gamma. The experiment was run for over 70,000 unique visitors, and the Google Analytics data was extracted and analyzed through a statistical program called JMP (www.jmp.com). The first thing we looked at was bounce rate, and you can see the results pictured here.

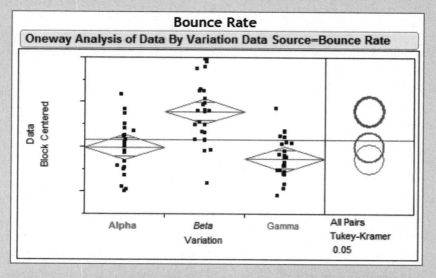

The Beta variation has the highest bounce rate, meaning visitors landing on Beta pages are leaving the website! If we pick just this one single metric to look at, we conclude that Beta is the worst variation. But there are other metrics, including time on site, conversion rates of individual conversion goals, and average per-session values of all of those goals together. While the Beta variation doesn't perform as well in a number of user engagement metrics, it *does* provide the most revenue of any variation.

Catalogs.com Case Study: Integrating Testing with Google Analytics *(Continued)*

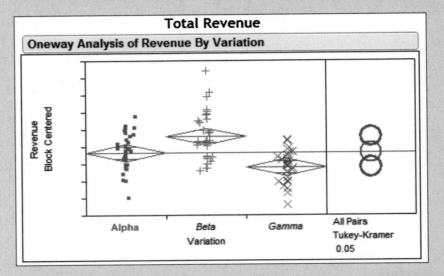

By looking at the complete picture and evaluating more than a single conversion action, we can see that the Beta version allows visitors to recognize quickly whether or not what they are looking for is available to them. If it isn't, they leave, and we see shorter times spent on the site and higher bounce rates. But if those visitors *do* find what they are looking for, the Beta variation increases catalog orders by over 10 percent and aggregate site conversion rate by 7.4 percent.

Thanks to the additional data provided by the Google Analytics integration, Catalogs.com saw the full picture, made an informed decision, and reaped the rewards of the experiment!

Installing Optimizely on a Test Page

Installing Optimizely on your website is easy. For every experiment you run within a single project, one line of code is all you need to install on your website. This snippet of code is unique to each project and looks like the code in Figure 11.21. You need it only on test and conversion pages, but installing it one time in the <HEAD> section of every page allows you to run many experiments without ever bothering your IT department again! Once this is done and your variations are created, click Start Experiment (in the upper right in the screen shown in Figure 11.18).

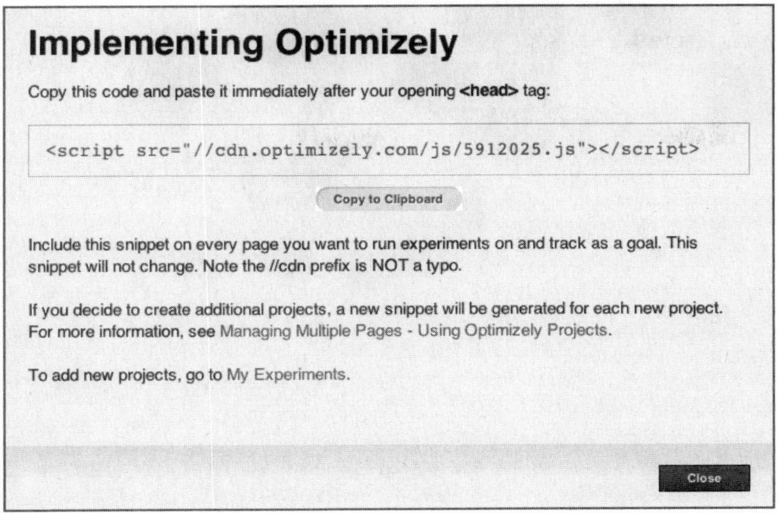

Implementing Optimizely

Copy this code and paste it immediately after your opening **<head>** tag:

```
<script src="//cdn.optimizely.com/js/5912025.js"></script>
```

Copy to Clipboard

Include this snippet on every page you want to run **experiments** on and track as a goal. This snippet will not change. Note the //cdn prefix is NOT a typo.

If you decide to create additional projects, a new snippet will be generated for each new project. For more information, see Managing Multiple Pages - Using Optimizely Projects.

To add new projects, go to My Experiments.

Close

Figure 11.21 Implementing Optimizely with JavaScript code

Reading Optimizely Results

As your test collects data, you start to see results. As with any test, let the experiment run long enough to get a good sample; a couple of weeks is typically a good guideline but a month is even better. To see your test results, select View All Experiments from the My Experiments drop-down (found in the blue bar at the very top of your Optimizely account, not pictured) and click Results next to the experiment name. Figure 11.22 shows basic information from your experiment, such as how many test participants have been recorded and their distribution across your variations.

Links at the top allow you to edit or reset the experiment and share either by downloading a CSV of the data or sending out a shareable link. Last, you can set the ranges of the dates for which you want to display data from this experiment.

By default, the Conversion Goals section contains a goal called Engagement, defined as the percentage of visitors that click anything that's clickable on the test page. While this can certainly be interesting to look at, scrolling down a bit allows you to create additional conversion goals. Figure 11.23 shows the different types of goals you can define for an experiment. Select the type of goal to track, and Optimizely creates a corresponding results module.

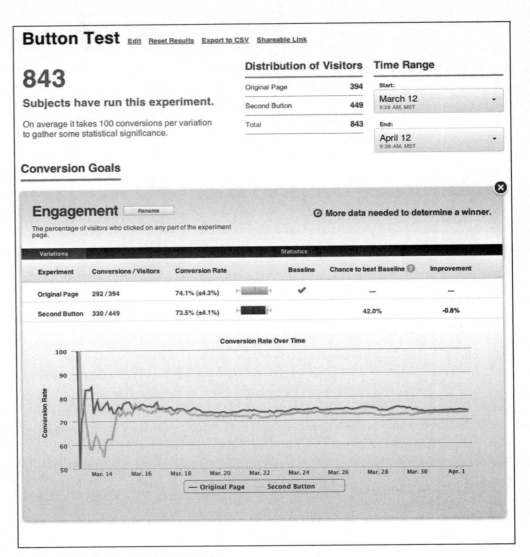

Figure 11.22 Reading Optimizely experiment results

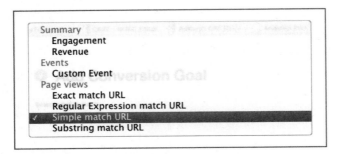

Figure 11.23 Different conversion goal types

While the Page Views grouping of goals does not require additional code or configuration (because it is based solely on page URLs), it does require some additional code to be added to your website in order to report back options like Custom Events and Revenue . For those with a technical inclination, the implementation is very well documented and extremely straightforward, offering enormous flexibility in defining the conversion actions that make sense for your organization.

Figure 11.24 shows an example of a results module for a custom event defined for this experiment. The second button is statistically worse than the original, to the tune of almost 40 percent! In this experiment, while our hypothesis turned out to be wrong, we learned a valuable lesson about our visitors and what they do and do not like to click when it comes time to sign up for a seminar.

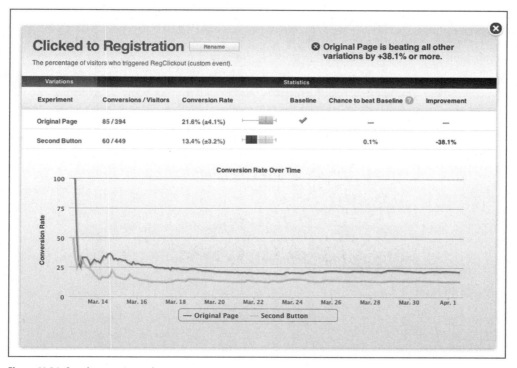

Figure 11.24 Sample conversion goal report

Week 31: Go beyond Clickstream Analytics

Tracking everything that happens after a click, especially a click you've explicitly paid for, is essential in measuring the performance of and optimizing your display campaigns. To this end, good web analytics is not an optional luxury; it's a necessary tool that you can't live without. And *clickstream* analytics—or the measurement of all the things users do as they click around your pages—using tools like Google Analytics,

Adobe/Omniture SiteCatalyst, WebTrends, Coremetrics, and others is a core component of your digital measurement strategy.

But beyond this, there are many other ways to understand just how your users interact with your pages that can help you take actions to improve the user experience on everything from your landing pages to your final confirmation emails. This week, we explore some of the additional tools and concepts you can use to squeeze even more performance from your display campaigns.

Monday: Using Qualitative Feedback

While there's no shortage of data generated by advertising platforms, analytics tools, and backend systems, sometimes the most impactful insights come the old-fashioned way: asking for them.

User feedback can be obtained in a variety of ways, ranging from free-form conversations with customers to sophisticated surveys. But regardless of the method employed to gather the feedback, the most important point is that qualitative user feedback lets you listen to real customers, understand their likes and dislikes, and ultimately remove the pain points that they identify as roadblocks to improving your bottom line.

A good example of really understanding the people on your website comes from ReadWriteWeb, who in early 2010 published an article announcing a partnership between Facebook and AOL (Figure 11.25).

Figure 11.25 ReadWriteWeb article published in 2010

The article ranked well in the organic search engines, and as users searched for Facebook, they ended up on this page, many of them actually believing that this was some kind of new redesign of Facebook! There was so much feedback and so many comments from confused readers that ReadWriteWeb added a section to this page explaining to visitors that this was *not* some kind of new Facebook page and provided a link to the real Facebook site. While all the metrics and data point to a phenomenal success at driving traffic, the qualitative feedback tells quite a different story!

Getting Feedback from User Interactions

First and foremost, many organizations have actual contact points between them and their customers. This can take the form of interactions at a brick-and-mortar physical location, a conversation with a service representative in a call center, or even online chats and email-based support. Each of these channels is capable of providing incredibly useful insights, and training members of your organization to record user feedback and probe for issues that could have made an individual's experience a bit better can be an excellent investment.

As an example, a travel client that we work with hosts a large call center to provide personal attention to website visitors having trouble or needing advice when booking flights and hotels on its website. By focusing on the problem the customer is calling in to solve, and through regular reviews of all issues encountered in the call center, a number of strategic improvements have been made to the website. Customers can walk call center agents through exact sets of steps necessary to re-create obscure website errors that can later be fixed, user interface and account management processes have been streamlined, and even backend control panels have been improved to reduce the amount of time an agent needs to address common user issues.

Using Online Feedback Tools

Without an actual point of person-to-person interaction, there are a number of tools that can be used to collect user feedback right on the pages of your website. Figure 11.26 shows some common examples that you've likely seen as you surf the Web, and we encourage you to look into solutions from providers like the following (and a host of others):

- ForeSee (www.foreseeresults.com)
- iPerceptions 4Q (www.4qsurvey.com)
- Kampyle (www.kampyle.com)
- KISSinsights (www.kissinsights.com)
- OpinionLab (www.opinionlab.com)

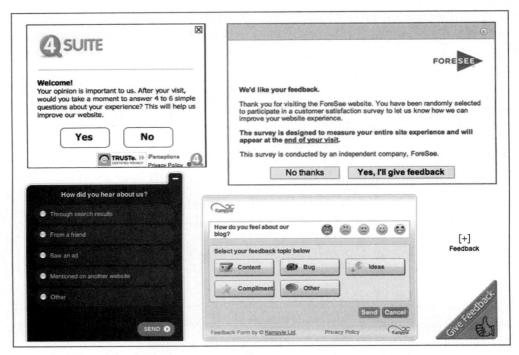

Figure 11.26 Online feedback tools from 4Q, ForeSee, Kampyle, OpinionLab, and KISSinsights

While statistically very few people actually fill these out, those that do often provide interesting and useful comments. For example, a user filling out a survey with feedback stating that they would have loved to buy something from your store but they couldn't find a button to add an item to your cart is not something you should ignore. You might find that the visitor was using a certain type of browser or configuration that rendered it impossible for them to check out in your shopping cart, and that single comment could unlock sales you may have been missing from all the other visitors using that same configuration! Many of these tools allow you to control what kinds of questions you can ask, when to trigger the survey to appear, and ultimately report on how your users think you can be doing a better job.

Using Survey Tools

Surveys can also be a very good mechanism for collecting qualitative feedback, and there are many different ways they can be used. Online surveying tools abound in the marketplace, and here are a few that you may want to look into:

* eSurveysPro (www.esurveyspro.com)

* FluidSurveys (www.fluidsurveys.com)

* FreeOnlineSurveys (www.freeonlinesurveys.com)

- SurveyGizmo (`www.surveygizmo.com`)
- SurveyMonkey—recently purchased Zoomerang (`www.surveymonkey.com`)

Each of these tools allows you to design and conduct an online survey, and they allow for different types of questions like free-form response, multiple choice, and rating scales. Many also support advanced features like conditional branching. They also collect responses and provide reports that help you make sense of your results.

Aside from good survey design, you also want to focus your efforts on planning exactly when, how, and to whom to distribute your survey in order to provide you with the right kinds of insights. For example, if you want to understand a purchase process, you can send a survey invitation to visitors that have already made a purchase a set number of days after they've completed the transaction. Another example might have nothing to do with a conversion action but could be meant to provide you with a better understanding of the visitors on your site. This survey might be promoted to a dedicated percentage of traffic right from the home page or key landing pages on the site for a period of time.

Case Study: Leveraging Voice of Customer Data

We've been working with Twiddy & Company Realtors for a number of years, and there's no one we've come across that understands the value of customer feedback quite like marketing director Ross Twiddy. The Twiddy.com website showcases over 900 vacation rental homes in the Outer Banks of North Carolina, offering potential vacationers the opportunity to browse and ultimately book a beach vacation.

Using tools like Kampyle as well as conversations with the reservationists available to advise and talk guests through their questions, Ross and his team found that many website visitors want to get a feel for how they would sleep a large family or a large group in a particular rental home. They also wanted to know *where* the home was in relation to things like the beach, grocery stores and other attractions. This led to the development of website features like virtual tours and actual floor plans of the homes on the website, allowing visitors to visualize exactly where to put grandma and the kids.

Aerial view photography and map views were also added to the site, allowing family vacation planners to see exactly where a home is located and explore the areas around it with their mouse.

These website features have virtually eliminated the most common questions that guests tend to ask when planning their trips, and it has allowed Twiddy reservationists to focus on more hospitable questions about a family or group's needs and provide even more value to the customer experience.

"If there is one thing we've learned in marketing, it's to throw your pride out the door and open up your big ears," says Ross Twiddy. "Listening to guests is like smelling good food; it just doesn't get old."

Tuesday: Using Visual Analytics

We've all heard that a picture is worth a thousand words. In the case of visual analytics, a picture can be worth more than that! While there are many different tools and solutions to help us understand how visitors look at, move around, and click elements of a page, visual attention maps and click maps can give us insights to help us understand and improve the user experience.

Let's take the example of the Google Seminars for Success program, which offers live, in-person training seminars led by a select group of Google Authorized Seminar Leaders. At Cardinal Path, we've been teaching Google AdWords, Google Analytics, and Google Website Optimizer through these seminars since 2008. We've learned an enormous amount about our target Seminars for Success audience over the years, and much of that understanding has come from visual analytics. Figure 11.27 shows an example of an early version of the website that we used to promote these seminars.

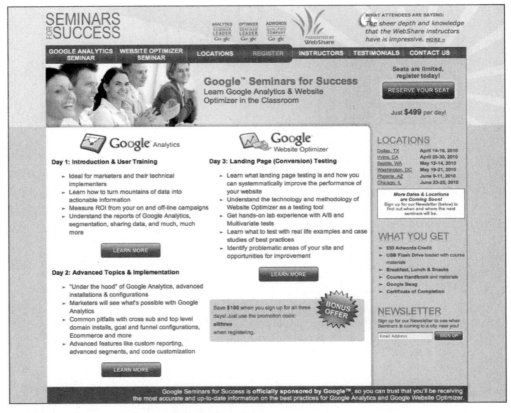

Figure 11.27 An early version of Seminars for Success microsite home page

Using ClickTale's Visual Attention Maps

A tool called ClickTale (www.clicktale.com) can be used to help understand how users experience the pages of your website through a variety of features ranging from video capture of individual sessions to scroll mapping and click mapping as well as one of our favorites: visual attention maps.

Figure 11.28 shows a visual attention map of the same Seminars for Success microsite page.

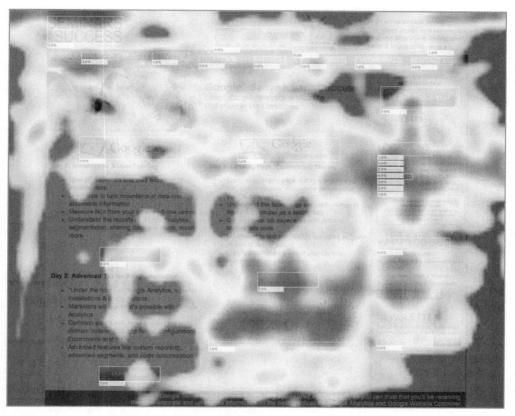

Figure 11.28 ClickTale visual attention map of Seminars for Success microsite home page

While a bit difficult to see in grayscale, this tool provides a heat map that shows how long users spend looking at certain elements of the page; the hotter the color (closer to red), the longer users spend looking. The technology works by collecting the X and Y pixel coordinates of users' mouse movements during their visits. There's a strong correlation between where people's mice go and where their eyes go, and this technology allows us to put together a very good proxy for a true eye-tracking study, where a larger budget can buy you a controlled experiment using an array of expensive equipment and sophisticated technology.

Looking at Figure 11.28, we quickly see that visitors to this page are most interested in the bonus offer, the section about what they receive at the seminar, and of course, where and when the seminars will be. It's also interesting to see that page elements placed near focal points also command attention. Notice that the Learn More button for the Website Optimizer training gets more attention than any of the others. This is very likely because it is located right next to the bonus offer, which is something our visitors are paying attention to.

Another important point we can take from this attention map is what visitors are *not* paying attention to. The email newsletter signup form at the bottom right gets very little attention, even though it is considered a high-value conversion action. This is the way people can sign up for a mailing list that announces new dates and locations, and this visualization indicates that it might be a good idea to move this somewhere else on the page where it *will* get noticed (maybe by that bonus offer!). It also seems that people don't really care what they're going to learn at these seminars; they're much more interested in the swag they'll get and what cities they might be going to than reading the bullet points describing the curriculum!

Click Mapping with Crazy Egg

Another way to look at a page visually is to take stock not of where people are *looking*, but where they're *clicking*, and this can tell a whole different story. Figure 11.29 is a screen capture from a tool called Crazy Egg (www.crazyegg.com), a pioneer of click-mapping technology.

This tool helps to tell the rest of the story. Remember how the attention map made it seem like people didn't care what they were going to learn? Well here, we can see that although visitors don't spend a lot of time reading the bullet points for each of the seminar topics, they *are* clicking on those Learn More buttons to read the complete agendas and curriculums. So as it turns out, this is important information, but all of the space on the page that was used for those bullet points might be better utilized by something people really *do* care about.

One good solution could be to dedicate that space to listing more dates and locations. We saw on the attention map that people are spending time looking at dates and locations, and the click map confirms that they're also clicking them. And remember the email signup form we thought no one was looking at? Well it turns out that they actually *are* clicking there to sign up; they just don't spend a lot of time hovering their mouse around it before they make that decision.

In addition to providing more context around the user experience, from this single click map we can also discern some other interesting insights that lead to actions we can take. For example, in the top navigation bar, we can see that there are quite a few visitors clicking Instructors. This tells us that people want to know who they'll be spending their days with and make sure that those seminar leaders know their stuff! This has led us to build out content complete with instructor biographies.

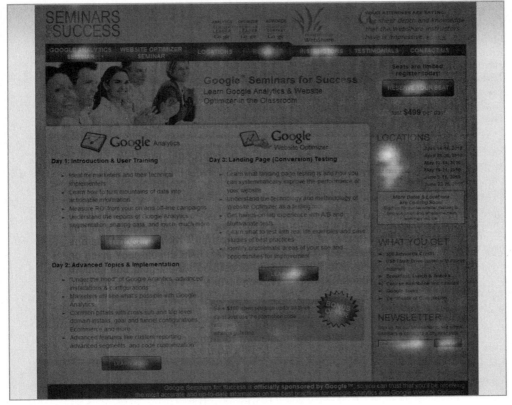

Figure 11.29 Crazy Egg click map of Seminars for Success microsite home page

Wednesday: Using Form Analytics

For many conversion actions that can be accomplished on a web page, a form needs to be filled out in order to accomplish the objective, and while funnel reports in web analytics tools can help you understand where users drop off during a page-to-page conversion process, they often stop short of telling you where *inside a particular page* those users abandon you.

Form analytics can help you understand how users are navigating, filling out, and either completing or abandoning those forms, and this can lead to some very actionable insights.

Optimizing Forms for Performance

Let's take an example of a typical kind of form you might find on the Web (Figure 11.30). The goal is to get someone to trade their contact information for a free gift of some kind, to be mailed out to the postal address they fill out here. That free gift will of course include some promotional materials, a catalog of products, and a host of other components with branding and marketing value.

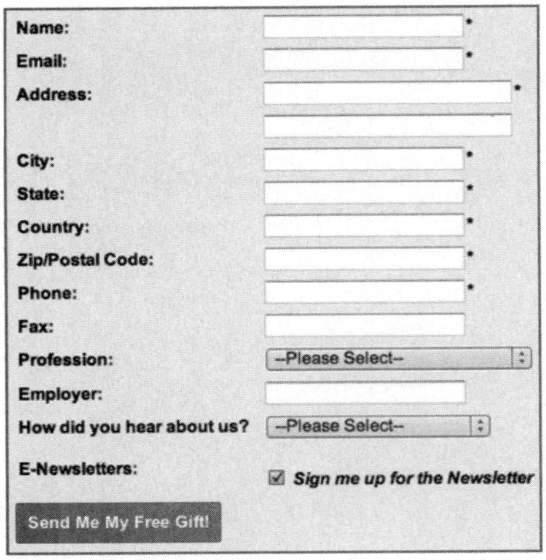

Figure 11.30 A typical website form

Suppose that our analytics reports tell us that we have no problem driving people to the page that contains this form but that very few people ever get to the "thank you" page that follows a successful submission of this form. The conversion rate on this particular goal is in desperate need of improvement. While we know that people aren't submitting the form, what we don't know is *where* on this particular form we're losing people, so let's dive into this analysis.

Unfortunately, a form like this is often the product of a marketing department talking to an IT department about just what kind of data they want about their website visitors, and the visitor experience is often forgotten. What results is a long and intimidating form that combines all the elements of the marketing department's wish list along with all the database fields the IT department has access to in the backend of the website. The form ends up asking for way too much information, terrifies website visitors, and more often than not has a very negative impact on conversion rate.

Before we even get into the form analytics, let's take a look at that form again. What information do we *absolutely need* in order to collect the lead from this web page? Really, to send them their free gift, all we need is their mailing address. That's it, nothing more. Anything else is really just icing on the cake. One thing we might experiment with is a multistep form, where the first step asks for nothing more than the address. A very simple form that is inviting and unintimidating, and once the user submits this, the information is captured, the free gift is sent, and the "Step 2" form is presented to the user to collect additional information. This could be an excellent experiment to run, and we can find out just how many steps are optimal for our conversion process and even what fields to put inside each of those steps!

Using ClickTale's Form Analytics Reports

To help us understand what's happening on the form we're working with in its original state, however, one option for us to turn to is the form analytics feature of ClickTale. Figure 11.31 shows one of those reports, called the Drop report.

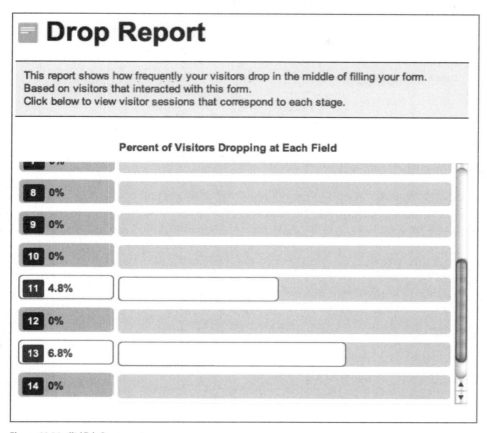

Figure 11.31 ClickTale Drop report

Each form element is numbered and labeled, and this report gives us an idea of the fields from which people are dropping. Field 11 corresponds to the Profession field of the example form, and field 13 is the "How did you hear about us" question.

We see these kinds of marketing questions asked fairly frequently, and they're very often points of failure on a web form. Not only are they not necessary to accomplish the goal in this instance, they're also very likely to provide false information because the user is selecting something from the list quickly to get past that step. In one case, a client of ours was asking the profession question on a form and found that the overwhelming majority of their users were academics. Yep, you guessed it: That was the first option of an alphabetical list!

So not only are questions like these leading to people abandoning the form process, they're also prone to providing bad data. Let's move on to the Blank Field report, pictured in Figure 11.32.

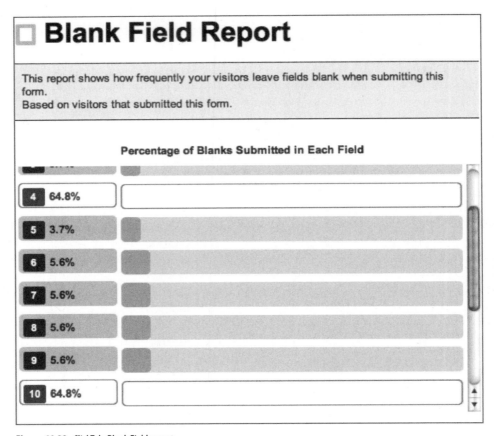

Figure 11.32 ClickTale Blank Field report

Field 4 corresponds to the second address line, and field 10 is the field asking for a fax number. Many addresses don't need a second line, but office suites, apartments, and things of that nature often require this, and users are used to seeing two lines for addresses. This is probably okay, and we certainly don't want to exclude people with apartment numbers from being able to convert on our goal!

Now, let's take a look at the fax number. First of all, it's probably worth asking ourselves what we're really going to do with that number. If we have a business case for keeping a fax number on file, that's one thing, but if we're asking for it because our IT department told us there's a field for it in the database, that's not a very good reason to make our form look bigger and more intimidating. And what would we lose by removing a field that everyone is leaving blank anyway? Nothing.

Another interesting way to look at a form is by how long it takes people to fill out each of the form elements, and this can be seen in the Time report shown in Figure 11.33.

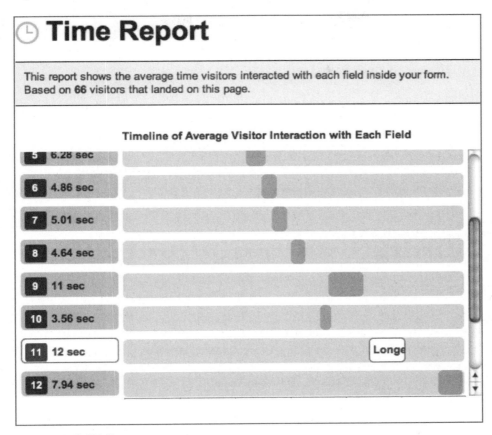

Figure 11.33 ClickTale Time report

Let's take a look at form element number 9, which is the phone number. It's actually quite common that people tend to type numbers a little slower than they do other information, and we can see that on this form; it takes an average user about 11 seconds to fill this out. That coupled with the pause that most of us have before deciding whether or not to divulge this sensitive information is reflected in the time it takes us to get past this step.

Now let's examine field 11, which is that Profession drop-down list again. Not only are people leaving the form because of this field, it takes them 12 full seconds to try to figure out which list item describes what they do for a living. In the world of text messaging, TiVo, and YouTube, 12 seconds is a veritable *eternity*, and this provides us with even more data to support removing this field or placing it in a step further down the conversion funnel once we've already received more pertinent information. One thing is sure; we don't want to lose this conversion just because someone doesn't want to describe their job!

There are certainly many other reports and tools that can help you understand how your users are working with the forms that lead to your conversions, and form analytics can be a very powerful tool as you optimize your campaigns, landing pages, and conversion funnels.

Thursday / Friday: Evaluating the User Experience

When all is said and done, the only thing that matters is whether and how you can transform mere website visitors into monetized customers, and to do this, you need to understand the user experience. Usability work focuses on understanding and improving upon the user experience (often referred to as UX), and while concepts of usability are vast, the topic is important enough that we'll end this week talking about at least the very basics that can help you achieve continual improvement in your online marketing strategy.

Making Usability Part of Your Process

Unfortunately, many organizations consider usability as an afterthought. They assume that they understand the typical website visitor and they design a process, a website, and ultimately an advertising campaign to achieve the goals of the organization instead of solving the problems of the customers that the organization is trying to serve.

In Chapter 4, "Month 1: Planning Your Campaigns," we looked at the importance of putting yourself in the shoes of your would-be customers, and we even went through the process of creating personas. This planning is actually very much about the user experience, and it can be a great step to take before a single website layout is ever drawn on a whiteboard.

The point is that usability work is best done early in any process, when revisions are easy to make and time and resources have not already been spent going down a path that has not been informed by user experience testing and feedback. Making an investment in usability early in the process is a lot like buying an insurance policy: It costs you a little bit more during the process, but at the end of the day, you save yourself from the consequences of a catastrophic event.

Conducting User Testing

User testing will always be the usability practitioner's most powerful tool. There are many different ways to conduct tests, but the core concept behind all of the tools, processes, and procedures is to observe real users as they attempt to complete tasks that have been assigned to them.

Before conducting any user testing, it's important to identify a range of test subjects that are representative of the type of visitor you might have on your website. If you're selling products that help make dealing with the day-to-day challenges of old age easier, you likely won't learn much from a test group of 12-year-old MySpace music fans. But you also aren't likely to learn much from setting up a computer at the old folks home: It's very likely that it's the *children* of the old folks that are buying these products. Know your audience and make sure to test with subjects that share the same characteristics.

Tests can span a wide range, from quick and cheap to extremely structured and expensive, and to give you some ideas of different types of user testing, let's walk through a few different examples.

On the more involved side of things, identify a panel of somewhere in the range of three to eight users and compensate them to come into a central location to take part in a user test. A paid and qualified moderator explains to the participants that they will use a certain website and that their goal is to perform a certain set of tasks. If this were, say, a retail clothing website, a task might be "buy a red sweater in your size" or "share an interesting sale item with five of your friends." The moderator also explains that the sessions are recorded. Each participant has their voice and face recorded along with a screencast of what's happening on their screen. Finally, they are told to talk their way through what they're doing and provide any verbal feedback as they go. Common tools for this type of testing include Morae (www.techsmith.com) and a less expensive alternative for Mac users called SilverBack (www.silverbackapp.com).

Here, the user's session is fully captured, and in reviewing the audio and video, it becomes extremely apparent where visitors to your site are having trouble or getting caught. We've seen visitors struggle to locate products or search functionality and fail to find lead forms, and we've seen visitors state that even after clicking through the pages of a site and reading all the content, they still have no idea what the website is about! It's often a very humbling exercise, but it's always a very valuable one!

Formal studies can also be done remotely, saving the costs, equipment, and effort required to perform an onsite user test. While you're not likely to get the same depth of feedback, you *are* still likely to find valuable insights. Services like UserTesting.com (www.usertesting.com) and Feedback Army (www.feedbackarmy.com) can match website owners up with reviewers for a nominal fee, and the entire process is managed over the Web. Platforms like Usabilla (www.usabilla.com) and OpenHallway (www.openhallway.com) allow researchers to create and run remote tests with users of their choice.

Finally, a usability test does not need to be formal at all. Having people from your social circles review a site and provide verbal feedback can offer insights and perspectives that you would never find in a thousand years. Those of us who spend every day on the websites that *we* design know how they work and often don't get caught in the same traps as those farther away from our businesses do!

Using Heuristic Evaluations

Heuristic evaluations are really just expert reviews performed by a UX professional, and they can often be relatively quick and inexpensive to implement. This is like a physical examination to make sure a person is in good health.

In the medical world, it starts out by visiting a medical professional, and a comprehensive series of tests and checks are run, each one either passing or failing with scores and notes indicating where issues may exist.

In the world of usability, this checklist is a number of well-established best practices, and the doctor simply approaches the patient website as a normal website user would. The UX professional then goes through the checklist of best practices and checks for compliance, making notes and indicating where users are likely to get confused or frustrated.

A typical heuristic evaluation examines a number of different website components, and it might start with site layout and design. This is where you find issues with the visual aspects of color palettes and contrast, lines and edges, fonts, imagery, layout grids, form elements, buttons, and more. Next might come a set of heuristics around overall ease of use, and this might include navigation and menus, search functionality, user-generated actions like popping up windows, filling out and submitting forms, clicking buttons, playing videos, and navigating from page to page.

Information architecture is also a typical category of a heuristic evaluation, and this will expose problems with how the various pages of your site are grouped together, how they relate to one another, and how users can navigate between pages and groupings. You might find that your site's organization is too deep or too flat or that once users drill deep into a subsection of your website it becomes very difficult to find their way back.

Another common focal point of an evaluation is copywriting. While users generally focus on headlines and images to scan for keywords during the first few seconds of their visit, as they become more and more invested in the site, they'll spend more time reading the copy. This is an area where it is extremely important to know your audience. Are you writing technical guides for rocket scientists and engineers or do you have a light-hearted entertainment blog that people are taking in while having a conversation, texting their friends, and ordering a coffee? You'll want to make sure the reading level, tone, and construction fit the bill.

And last, it's quite common for technical implementation elements to be evaluated. This may include things like cross-browser testing or reporting on site elements that require plug-ins or additional technologies. For example, while your Flash website may look just fine on a desktop, laptop, or Android device, it will never show up on a iPhone, iPad, or i*Anything* because Flash is not supported. And if you've chosen to use something like Microsoft Silverlight to develop aspects of your site, those components will not work in a browser in which the plug-in has not been installed.

Running Focus Groups

Where user testing can expose holes and problems in specific procedures and heuristic evaluations can identify areas for improvement based on existing designs, focus groups can often be very helpful in getting a feel for how users might react to new ideas you might have.

Creating a series of mockups for new website designs or building a very simple demonstration of what a new process might look like takes very little time and resources compared to building, testing, and pushing changes to a live website, and running a focus group can give you feedback on the direction you're moving in very early in the process.

Many firms and vendors can run formal focus groups for you, and there are even more resources out there that can help you run these on your own.

An experienced focus group leader is needed to moderate these sessions, and they can revolve around a number of different topics. For example, a series of different page layouts are mocked up and shown to users. The discussions are videotaped and later edited after review for the key comments and points of interest. In the same focus group, users are walked through a new feature, and even though the feature is not yet functional, they can see exactly how it *would* work and what benefit it *would* provide.

Controls and moderation skills are critical to ensuring that participants are not biased toward ("hey, look at this awesome new feature and tell me how much you love it!") or away ("the programmers made me show you this one too, so tell me how bad it is and I won't be offended") from any particular item on which you're getting feedback, and a good moderator facilitates a conversation and encourages each of the participants to share their unique views.

Focus groups can provide a wealth of knowledge and can include all kinds of exercises, activities, and topics. We've found that exercises like card sorting can be helpful in grouping website or page elements into logical layouts and orders, and open-ended survey questions can be helpful as catalysts for some great conversations!

Week 32: Target Topics

We've discussed using contextual keyword targeting, placement targeting, and audience targeting at length, and there exists one more form of targeting inside the GDN: topic targeting.

While contextual keyword targeting allows advertisers to specify keywords that define a certain type of page, topic targeting allows advertisers to choose from a predefined list of website content categories. With a handful of exceptions, it is not typically recommended to use this kind of targeting by itself, and this week we'll look at what topic targeting is and when and how to use it.

Monday: Understanding Topic Targeting and When to Use It

Topic targeting is very similar to targeting by interest categories; in both cases you can select from a wide range of categories and subcategories. The difference is that when you choose interest categories, you're trying to find categories that describe the behaviors of the *people* you'd like to target, wherever they may be, and when you choose topics, you're describing the types of *web pages* you'd like your ads to show up on. By targeting one or more specific topics, advertisers can very quickly place their ads on many web pages that include content deemed relevant to those topics, and in this respect you might think of this as a very broad way to contextually target without keywords.

Using Topic Targeting to Broadly Increase Reach

For advertisers that simply want to get their ads in front of a maximum number of eye-balls very quickly and have large budgets, the use of topic targeting can attract a very broad audience with minimal management at the expense of performance and the control and specificity offered by other targeting types.

If you fit this description and you're looking to build a campaign with very broad coverage around a certain kind of content, you likely want to build out your topic-targeted campaigns separately. This lets you at least control things like geography and language settings along with a budget that you can control on this type of campaign.

You also want to find a balance between maximum exposure and relevance. Each of the nearly 30 top-level topics can produce tens of millions of daily impressions, while some subtopics can be much more limited in their reach. You can narrow down the number of placements on which your ads will be eligible to show by targeting subtopics rather than top-level topics, but keep in mind that when you get below the one million impression mark, you may be limiting yourself to a very small set of eligible inventory.

Last, if you do want to target an entire top-level topic, it's a good practice to go through each of the subtopics in that grouping. You may find some subtopics that just don't apply to you, and explicitly targeting lots of subtopics gives you more granular reporting so that you can see which subtopics attract traffic and how that traffic performs. For example, at first glance, you may think that you want to target every website that has anything to do with food and drink to get the word out about your new steak house. But you can quickly see that you really don't want to target sites about culinary schools or coffees and teas, both of which are subtopics of the food and drink topic!

Complementing Other Targeting with Topics

For most advertisers, topic targeting is used in conjunction with another type of targeting to narrow down your potential audience. Topic targeting can be used with keywords, placements, and audiences and allows you yet another way to refine your target audience.

In the case of contextual keyword targets, you can refine the list of sites that are contextually relevant to your keywords *and* limit those sites further by the topics of those pages. We've looked at the example of trying to market the Hilton hotel in Paris, France, and the targeting challenge presented by the heiress of the same name. Adding a topic target of "Travel › Hotels & Accommodations" using the specific reach setting can filter out many of the sites that have nothing to do with Paris Hilton the hotel and everything to do with Paris Hilton the person.

Using placement targets along with topic targeting allows advertisers to choose broader placements and allow the topic targets to find the most relevant inventory. For example, the Paris Hilton hotel might also want to target a placement on CNN.com, but choosing travel-related topics could limit advertisements to showing up only on travel-related CNN placements.

Finally, audience targeting can be combined with topic targeting to limit the context of the pages your target *people* happen to be browsing. For example, if you've qualified for my remarketing list by getting a quote on a hotel room at my website, I may want to remarket to you only when you're on websites that have to do with travel. While I still know that you have an interest in my hotel no matter what website you happen to be on, you might not be in "travel booking" mode when you're looking up a recipe to cook for dinner tonight.

In all of these cases, you'll want to experiment with the targeting combinations that make sense to your specific scenario and advertising goals and, as always, let the performance data guide your optimization strategy.

Tuesday: Adding and Editing Topic Targets

To add and edit topic targets within your ad groups, you use the same interface and do it in the same basic way you would add or edit keywords, placements, or audiences. Just as with audience targeting, this is something you need to do once an ad group is created, and if you choose to run an ad group that is solely using topic targeting, you need to create one without adding keywords or placements.

If you've already got keyword, placement, or audience targets defined, then adding topic targets will simply complement your other targeting according to the type of reach you've defined in the Network preferences of your campaign settings (broad or specific).

Adding Topics to an Ad Group

To add a topic target to an ad group, start out by navigating to the campaign and the ad group to which you'd like the topic target to apply. Then, select the Topics subsection of the Display Network tab and click Change Display Targeting. This brings up the familiar Change Display Targeting interface, and expanding the Topics section brings you to a screen like the one in Figure 11.34. You can create a list of topics and subtopics to target using the Add and Remove links. Once you settle on your list and apply your changes, your topics show up as rows in the Topics section of the Display Network tab interface and you start seeing data as your ads begin to run.

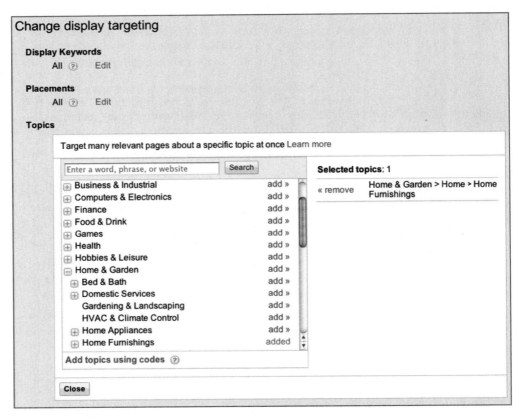

Figure 11.34 Selecting topic targets

Editing Topic Targets

You edit topic targets in much the same way you would edit other targeting options. Figure 11.35 shows the Change Status drop-down that allows you to enable, pause, or delete targets you have selected with a check box in the interface, and you see the familiar Edit button that allows inline editing of topic-level bids and status.

Figure 11.35 Editing selected topics

It's also worth noting that the Copy button is available for topic targeting, and this feature allows you to select topics and quickly apply them to other campaigns and ad groups in your account. Different ad groups often share the same topic targets, and this feature can save you quite a bit of time as you replicate topic targets across different areas of your account. As with copying audience targets, you can also copy bids and destination URLs that you may have specified for a given target.

Wednesday: Working with Ad Planner Codes

The DoubleClick Ad Planner is a powerful tool in the display advertiser's arsenal, and we've looked at various ways to use it in planning out display campaigns. It's worth noting that the topics you can define as you research potential audiences for a media plan can also be imported into AdWords as topic targets.

Identifying Topics in Ad Planner

As you research different potential placements and websites in which you might want to advertise, you'll notice that one of your content refinement criteria is called Topics. You can use this list as one of your many filters to isolate a set of placements that you want to target, and exploring different restrictions and filters as well as the resulting placements and their reach can be an excellent way to start planning a campaign.

You can also use the Ad Planner to search not just for placements but for topics themselves, as shown in Figure 11.36, and this can be a great way to see the number of impressions you might expect to see with pure topic targeting campaigns restricted to different languages or other campaign parameters.

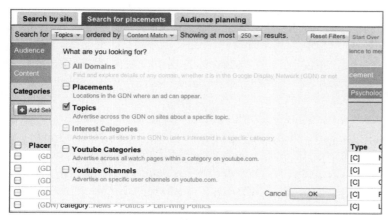

Figure 11.36 Searching for topics in DoubleClick Ad Planner

Once you've done your research, you can export a selected set of topics or placements directly into AdWords, or you can export your list into a CSV format. From here, you can work with your list until you're satisfied, and then you can head over to the AdWords interface.

Importing Topic Codes

The topic codes you see in Ad Planner are the same ones you can use in the AdWords interface, and in addition to checking the box next to all the topics you'd like to target, you have the option of adding topics using codes. Using this option brings up the interface shown in Figure 11.37, and you can copy and paste your list of Ad Planner codes into the text area and click Add.

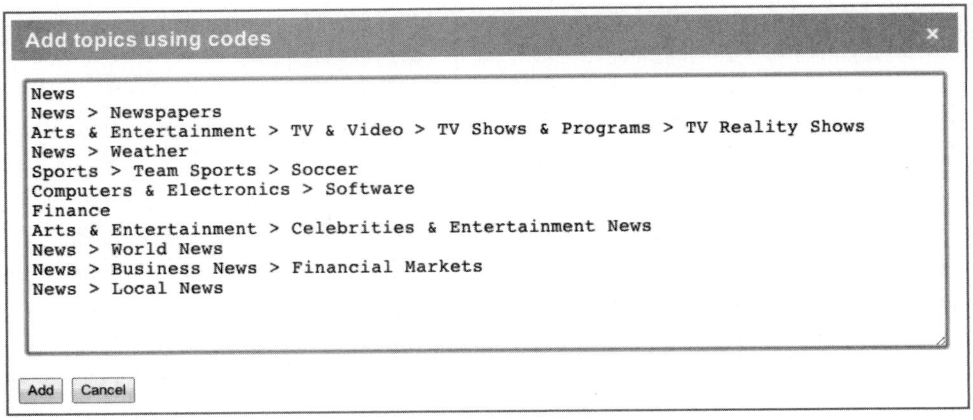

```
Add topics using codes                                                    ✕

News
News > Newspapers
Arts & Entertainment > TV & Video > TV Shows & Programs > TV Reality Shows
News > Weather
Sports > Team Sports > Soccer
Computers & Electronics > Software
Finance
Arts & Entertainment > Celebrities & Entertainment News
News > World News
News > Business News > Financial Markets
News > Local News




 Add   Cancel
```

Figure 11.37 Pasting topic codes into the interface

As you use Ad Planner more and more to build out your audiences, the ease of transferring your media plans into AdWords can save you time and frustration while providing insights into who you'll be reaching and what you can expect from your campaigns.

Thursday: Managing Topic Exclusions

As with other targeting types, AdWords gives advertisers the opportunity to define what topics they *don't* want their ads showing up for, and these are managed through topic exclusions.

These work in much the same way as other exclusions, and they can be extremely useful in controlling what kinds of websites your ads are eligible to show up for. Continuing with the Paris Hilton example, to avoid showing hotel ads on celebrity websites, an advertiser can choose to explicitly exclude a topic like Arts & Entertainment › Celebrities & Entertainment News and add topic targets in the travel sector.

And remember, these work in combination with other targeting methods as well, so you can enhance or refine placement, keyword, or audience targets to *not* show on sites of a certain topic just as easily as you can define preferable topics.

Adding a topic exclusion is straightforward, and to get started, simply navigate to the Display Network tab and expand the Exclusions area at the bottom of the page, making sure to click the Topics subsection as shown in Figure 11.38. From here, you can add and delete excluded topics from both the campaign and ad group levels.

Figure 11.38 Exclusions at the ad group and campaign level

To add a topic exclusion, simply click the Add Exclusions button from either the campaign or ad group level areas and select the campaign (campaign level) or campaign and ad group (ad group level) you want the exclusion to apply to, and then you see the familiar topic list.

Once again, you can search or browse the list and expand subtopics, using the Add and Remove links to select the topic exclusions you want to apply. If you're using Ad Planner to research topics that you would prefer your ads not show up for, you can use the Add Topics Using Codes option when defining topic exclusions, just as when you're adding topic targets.

And just as with other targeting types, it's good to let the data be your guide in identifying which topics to exclude. Look at the performance metrics from topics and subtopics that you've been targeting, and if you find topics that are spending your money without a positive return on investment, add them to your list of exclusions to allow your budget to be spent on better-performing targets.

Friday: Using Topic and Audience Targeting Reports

Topic targeting is no different from any other setting we configure, knob we turn, or dial we set inside AdWords: Its purpose is to support accomplishing our advertising goals and achieve a positive return on our advertising investment. To this end, we end this week by looking at some of the nuances of topic and audience targeting reports that make them a bit different from other AdWords reports.

Finding Topic Target Data for Broad Reach

If you have defined a broad reach in the network preferences of your campaign settings, then you're essentially telling AdWords to find potential placements for you across *any* of your targeting criteria, and you'll have a situation where primary bids can be adjusted based on secondary targeting criteria.

To illustrate what happens in this situation, let's take an example where both placement and topic targeting methods are being used and the ad group garners 1,000 impressions. Let's say that 250 of those impressions are based on a managed placement bid and the other 750 come from a match on the topic targeting that was specified. In the AdWords interface, navigating to the Display Network tab, you see the full 1,000 impressions in the Placements subsection: 250 of them are in the managed placements section with the other 750 in the automatic placements section.

Over on the "Topics" subsection, however, you would see only 750 of the 1,000 impressions, and they would be associated with the topics that triggered the ad to show. Figure 11.39 shows an example of what this might look like with some larger numbers. Only a small percentage of the almost 19 million impressions are accounted for here.

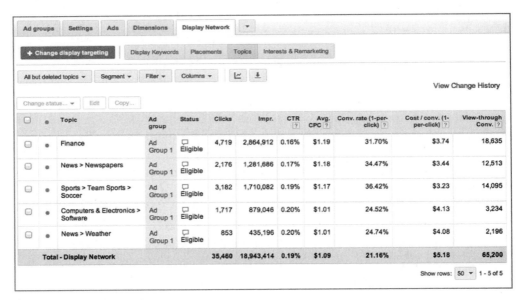

Figure 11.39 Reviewing topics data

In this case, topic targeting has been used as a secondary targeting criterion, and the Total - Display Network row is *not* a sum of the topic-matched clicks reported here. The Topics subsection displays only the data for the impressions that are not triggered by the primary matching criteria.

While Google is working to include all data in the Topics and Interests & Remarketing subsections, it is important to know that at the time of this publication, only selected data is available here under the broad reach scenario.

Topic and Audience Target Data Limitation for Specific Reach

If you've chosen to use a specific reach in the network preferences of your campaign settings, you've told Google that *all* of your targeting criteria must match in order for your ads to be eligible to show. For the sake of reporting, what this means is that there will *always* be a primary targeting method that has matched, and as a result, even though the secondary targeting criteria have also been met, there is no data available in the Topics or Interests & Remarketing subsection reports (Figure 11.40).

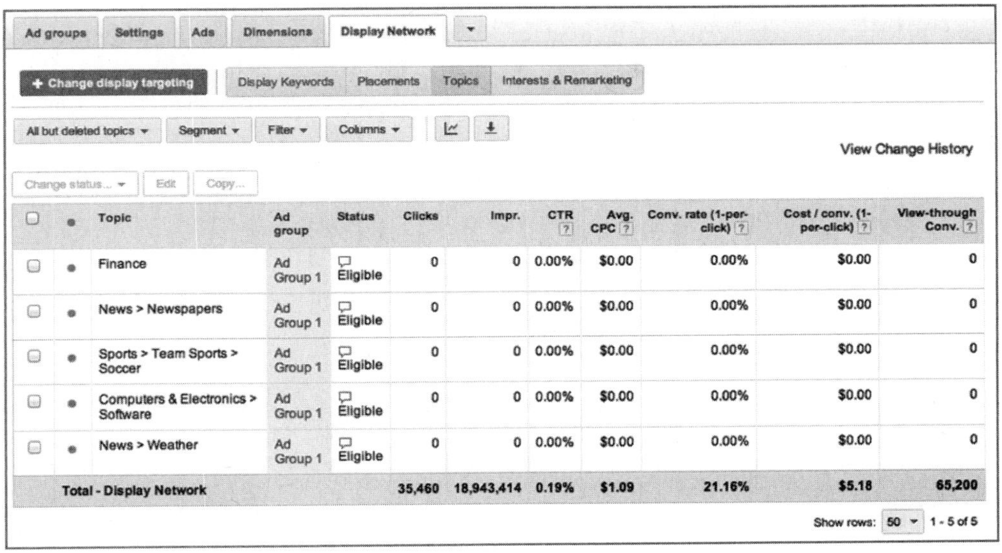

Topic	Ad group	Status	Clicks	Impr.	CTR	Avg. CPC	Conv. rate (1-per-click)	Cost / conv. (1-per-click)	View-through Conv.
Finance	Ad Group 1	Eligible	0	0	0.00%	$0.00	0.00%	$0.00	0
News > Newspapers	Ad Group 1	Eligible	0	0	0.00%	$0.00	0.00%	$0.00	0
Sports > Team Sports > Soccer	Ad Group 1	Eligible	0	0	0.00%	$0.00	0.00%	$0.00	0
Computers & Electronics > Software	Ad Group 1	Eligible	0	0	0.00%	$0.00	0.00%	$0.00	0
News > Weather	Ad Group 1	Eligible	0	0	0.00%	$0.00	0.00%	$0.00	0
Total - Display Network			35,460	18,943,414	0.19%	$1.09	21.16%	$5.18	65,200

Figure 11.40 Sample empty data set in the Topics tab

While you still have a row for each targeted topic, all of the values are zero. The actual values are in the Placements and Display Keywords subsections, where you can look at the performance metrics in terms of the primary targeting criteria. Of course, you can always look at ad group or campaign level reports. These contain the aggregate metrics regardless of your targeting types.

Month 9: Using LinkedIn and Facebook Display Ads

12

While the Google Display Network lends itself to examples and serves as a great starting place for those new to display advertising, it's far from your only option. Both LinkedIn and Facebook provide unique ways to target additional audiences and extend your reach. LinkedIn provides unprecedented professional demographics, while Facebook offers advertising opportunities based on social interaction that is unrivaled in the history of mankind.

Chapter Contents:

Week 33: Advertise on LinkedIn
Week 34: Launch and Measure LinkedIn Campaigns
Week 35: Advertise on Facebook
Week 36: Launch and Measure Facebook Campaigns

Week 33: Advertise on LinkedIn

Since its launch in 2003, LinkedIn has seen its membership grow from 4,500 users the first month to over 150 million members across more than 200 countries. Simply stated, this is *the* network to be a part of for students, professionals, companies, and organizations.

The success of LinkedIn lies in its large and active user base, and like many social sites, it has opened access to this group of potential customers to advertisers, offering the ability to target by information available on the platform.

Especially from a business-to-business (B2B) perspective, LinkedIn can often be a very valuable addition to your media mix, and if you've ever wanted to target prospective customers of your products and services by combinations of things like job titles, industries, and company names along with your standard demographics, then this might be just what you're looking for.

While not nearly as expansive or complex as the options you've seen in the GDN, LinkedIn advertising is still powerful. This week and next are dedicated to the basics of advertising with LinkedIn.

Monday: Understanding LinkedIn Advertising

LinkedIn is the professional's social network of choice, and people all across the world regularly log in to update their profiles (read "the only resume that matters these days"), maintain and grow their professional networks, establish and collaborate with specialty groups, troll for potential hires and contacts, learn about other companies and organizations, and keep up with the movement and happenings of other professional connections.

As with other social networks, users of LinkedIn regularly update their information, and this information is stored in the platform. This lets advertisers target an audience by some unique options.

LinkedIn Advertising

As you traverse a LinkedIn account and click around, you probably notice that LinkedIn serves ads from its premium inventory slots and other ad networks as well. You see video and rich media ads in rectangle and skyscraper formats all over the site. You see social recommendations and even home page takeovers. This is *not* the kind of advertising we're talking about here. As do other large and highly trafficked web properties, LinkedIn offers premium advertising options, and the first step in running these ads is to contact LinkedIn directly (and get ready to disclose what better be a fairly high budget).

What we're talking about is the LinkedIn Ads program, which is first and foremost a self-serve platform, much like Google AdWords. You don't need an agency or an account manager to place these ads, and you can create, manage, and optimize your campaigns all through the online interface.

Ads in LinkedIn can be purchased through a cost-per-click or cost-per-impression model, you can direct your clicks to other LinkedIn pages or to your own web properties, and you can define and manage your ad spend with no minimums or contracts.

When you create campaigns, you choose who you want to see your ads, how much to bid for a click or an impression, and how much you want to spend. Use a combination of an image and text to build your ad, enter your payment details, and you're up and running!

Where Ads Show Up

The LinkedIn Ads program promotes a specific format that combines an image and text, and this format can be shown in a couple of different ways.

Figure 12.1 shows just the textual component of an ad displayed across the top of a user home page. Here, one of the authors is targeted to get a new credit card when he logs into his account.

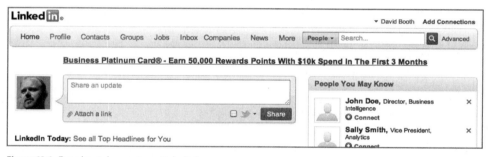

Figure 12.1 Top ad text placement on a LinkedIn home page

The combination of image and text can appear in sidebars as well, and in Figure 12.2, we see two ads on the right side of a company search results page. LinkedIn says in a note at the bottom of the column that the ads are from LinkedIn members.

Additional bottom and right column formats, supporting both text only and image and text formats, can show across many different pages throughout the LinkedIn interface:

User home page The page a user is taken to upon logging in or opening the site after having already logged in.

Profile pages The pages that act as the online resume of the twenty-first century. You can see ads on your own profile page or on others.

Search results pages When you search for things like individual members or companies, you may see ads with the search results.

Groups pages LinkedIn Groups pages are dedicated to specific interest groups created and maintained by LinkedIn members.

Inbox When you check your messages and connection invitations, you can also see ads.

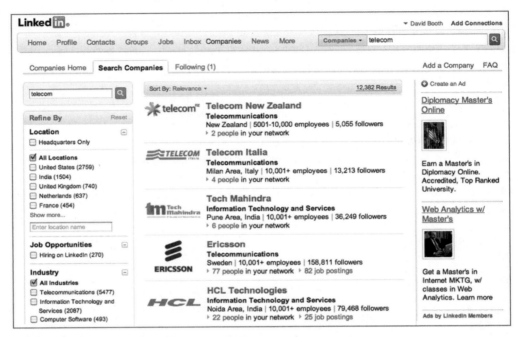

Figure 12.2 Right column placement ad unit on a LinkedIn company search page

Tuesday: Knowing When to Use LinkedIn Advertising

There are obvious reasons to use LinkedIn's advertising platform—the enormous user base, the specific targeting criteria, and the business-to-business nature of a social network for professionals—but there are also guidelines to help you find success when expanding your advertising reach into the LinkedIn space.

Have a Specific Goal

Most important, this is still advertising, and it must be accountable. Accountability starts with defining goals, and the LinkedIn platform is no different in that respect.

These ads cost money whether you pay for clicks or impressions, and to determine the return on this marketing spend, you need to spend some time defining what actions you want users to take or what objectives you want this advertising to accomplish for you. It's good to revisit the direct response and branding and positioning goals you've defined for your other online advertising, and you might be able to extend your reach into this network with the same kinds of campaigns.

But it's also important to remember that with LinkedIn, you have an opportunity to refine your targeting criteria to a level you don't get in many other places. Here, you can target specific job roles from specific companies in specific locations and even specific groups. As a result, you might end up with more specific goals.

As an example, one of our clients operates exclusively in the B2B space as a vendor to many of the world's largest companies. These companies pay for access to and use of a specific set of services, and those services are then freely available to employees of those large companies. Our client makes money when those employees use the services, and a significant challenge of a model like this is that companies with tens of thousands of employees can have a hard time making sure that everyone knows these services are available.

The marketing goal is easily defined as getting as many people as possible to use the services, and in this situation, LinkedIn advertising offers a way to run ads to employees of every company that our client serves. We can be extremely specific with the offers and landing pages we take visitors to, and our messaging can be very clear: *You, the person who just saw this ad, already have access to these services for free, so go ahead and start using them!*

Understand the LinkedIn Audience

Once again, targeting is an important factor in finding success with LinkedIn advertising. As you define your audience, the interface provides an estimated target audience, which is a numeric value of LinkedIn members that match certain targeting criteria. As you'll see later, the more you refine your targeting, the smaller (and more precise) this number gets.

You can use those numbers, however, to get a feel for just what kinds of audiences use LinkedIn, and it's important to know who's on LinkedIn so you know the audience for your advertising. The following list includes some quick and dirty insights you can take from the estimated target audience numbers as of the second quarter of 2012:

- Just under 60 percent of LinkedIn users are male.
- Nearly half of LinkedIn members are in the United States.
- Europe and Asia contain just under 20 percent of LinkedIn users each.
- Just over 20 percent of users are C-level executives (CEO, CMO, etc.), owners, or directors.
- Almost half of LinkedIn members are senior or management level.
- The 25-to-34 and 35-to-54 age groups account for roughly 35 percent of users (each).
- Top industries of LinkedIn members include high tech, finance, manufacturing, and education.
- Top job functions include entrepreneurs, sales, operations, IT, finance, consultants, and educators.

Be Relevant

With the level of targeting you have access to, it's more important than ever to ensure that your ads take advantage of what you know about your target audience to ensure that your ads are as relevant as they can possibly be. If you know, for example, that the person seeing your ad is an engineer at a top high-tech company, then don't be afraid to get technical. If you know they own their small business, appeal to the emotions and traits that only small business owners possess. Well beyond the demographic and geographic targets, the more you can use your targeting to create ads that speak directly to your potential customers, the better.

It's also good to be aware that visitors have not come to LinkedIn to be sold something: they are not shopping. They're making and maintaining professional connections, updating their profiles, requesting recommendations, and doing a host of other things that they will more than likely deem much more important than clicking your ads. The art of distraction that we discussed early in this book is more important here than ever, and you need to make your ads stand out enough to get noticed and have something worthy of a click.

Finally, you might consider experimenting with softer sells. While strong calls to action often include phrases like "buy now" and "download today," you may have more success appealing to someone who is much earlier in the sales cycle. Remember, they didn't come here to buy what you're selling, and it's likely they've never heard of you. Learning about your company, trying a demo, comparing with the competition, or just learning about how you solved someone else's problems can be less intimidating offers for a consumer to take advantage of.

Wednesday: Working with LinkedIn Ad Formats

The LinkedIn ad format is unique to this advertising platform and consists of both textual and image components. It's important also to note that while you can use an image in your ad, some placements show only your text, such as the top placement (Platinum Card) shown in Figure 12.1.

Figure 12.3 illustrates some sample ads provided from within the LinkedIn advertising interface, and there are rules to follow when writing your ads.

First, the only supported language for LinkedIn ads is English. While you can target non-English-speaking geographies, LinkedIn will not translate your ads, and you can't do it yourself either.

The first line of text is known as the headline and may contain up to 25 characters, including spaces. There's not much you can say in 25 characters, so craft your copy carefully to appeal to your target audience.

The next two lines of text can include up to 75 characters worth of text. There is not a limit for each line individually as there is in AdWords; your text wraps when appropriate.

Figure 12.3 Sample LinkedIn ads

Your image can be a PNG, JPEG, or GIF file of up to 2 MB, but whatever you upload is always resized to a 50×50-pixel square.

Figure 12.4 shows the interface to use to create your ads, and there are two additional parameters that you'll need to define.

Ad Variation 1

Ad Destination:
- ◉ Your web page

  `http://www.example.com`

- ○ A page on LinkedIn

Add Image	Headline
	Click to enter a description of up to 75 characters to span 2 lines
	From: Cardinal Path

Duplicate | Delete

Figure 12.4 Interface for creating a new LinkedIn ad

First, tell LinkedIn where to send a visitor who clicks your ad. You can enter the URL of a landing page appropriate to the content and messaging of the ad. You have up to 500 characters, so include any necessary tracking parameters (we discuss this later specific to Google Analytics).

You can also send them to a specific LinkedIn page by clicking a Page on LinkedIn and then using the drop-down to choose an appropriate LinkedIn page that you have control of.

In practice, you have more control over landing pages on your own website, and just as with any other type of advertising, the more specific and relevant you can make the landing page to the ad and the visitor that clicked it, the higher the probability of a conversion.

Finally, specify the profile link, to link to either your or your company's profile directly from the ad. This link establishes that this ad is coming not from some nameless, faceless corporate advertiser but from you, a fellow LinkedIn member.

Editorial Guidelines

To ensure that your ads are eligible to be shown, follow LinkedIn's common-sense rules, which say what we all already know:

Don't lie. Being deceptive in your competitive claims, pretending to be someone (or affiliated with someone) you're not, or offering something you can't actually provide isn't just bad for ad networks, it's bad for business as well.

Don't curse. This is a professional network visited by people who don't appreciate inappropriate language or offensive content. If you use it, your ads are removed.

Don't steal. Trademarks can be used only if you own them or have express permission to use them. If your trademarks are used inappropriately, report the violation to LinkedIn Customer Service.

Don't stalk. Do not use LinkedIn advertising to collect personally identifiable information (PII). This includes usernames, usage data, or any data from the LinkedIn users you're advertising to.

Don't cheat. Use text only in a grammatically correct way, and use characters only for their intended purpose. That means spell out "at" instead of using the @ sign, don't add 20 exclamation points to the end of your text, and don't yell at your audience by using all capital letters.

In addition, the following areas of content are prohibited from being promoted on the LinkedIn advertising system:

- Affiliate marketing
- Illegal products or services
- Alcohol, tobacco, or cigarettes
- Drug or drug-related products or services
- Pharmaceuticals, prescription or otherwise
- Weapons, ammunition, explosives, or other violent products and services
- Sexual or adult content
- Dating sites
- Downloads of copyrighted content
- Gambling
- Ringtones
- Hate or violent text against any individual, group, or organization
- Bulk or multilevel marketing products
- Inflammatory political or religious content

Using Images Effectively

It's worth taking a moment to consider the kind of image that you choose for your ad. A 50×50-pixel image is very small, so keep that in mind when you create it. Images of complex themes or detailed product shots are not an option; you're limited in what you can show with such a small format. There are a few best practices to make the most of this tiny image, and you can see some examples of modified images in Figure 12.5.

Figure 12.5 Examples of image treatments for LinkedIn thumbnails

You probably cannot fit your entire company name and logo in 50 pixels, so if you're trying to appeal to brand, use just your logo. Pictures of people, and in particular, pictures of women's faces, tend to draw attention. Don't be afraid to crop the tops and bottoms of faces or focus on a specific part of a product for clarity. It is better to see a small part of something we can identify than a full picture that's too small to recognize.

Thursday: Setting LinkedIn Targeting Options

The true power of LinkedIn advertising comes in its targeting. Each user faithfully enters and maintains a profile that contains information about where they work, what industry they're in, what job title they hold, and what groups they belong to over and above the general demographic data that's captured.

When you create a LinkedIn campaign, you select certain targeting criteria. LinkedIn dynamically updates an estimate of current LinkedIn members that match those criteria (Figure 12.6), and this can give you a good idea of the reach you might expect from your campaigns.

> **Estimated Target Audience*:**
> **130,327,757**
> **LinkedIn Members**

Figure 12.6 Dynamic estimated target audience display

Targeting Types

The following are your targeting options with LinkedIn advertising:

Geographic targeting Through a hierarchy including continents, countries, states, provinces and territories, and even city regions, you can choose up to 10 different geotargets per campaign. While the list is extensive, many countries are missing, and some countries have no subdivisions. You need to target at the level of specificity LinkedIn provides.

Company targeting Figure 12.7 shows LinkedIn's company targeting options. You can target specific companies by name, or you can select up to 10 industry targets from a list including nearly 150 choices. Take time to explore the industry listings because it's likely you'll find something quite specific.

You can also target companies of specific sizes, selecting from groups that range from a single sole proprietor to 10,000+ employees. Note also that industry and company size targeting can be used together to refine one another.

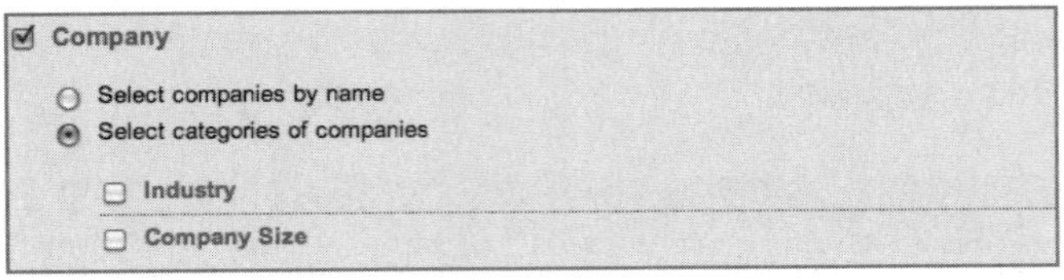

Figure 12.7 LinkedIn company targeting options

Targeting by job title You can target by specific job titles or a combination of predefined job functions and levels of seniority (Figure 12.8).

If you choose Select Specific Job Titles, you search for what you're looking for and choose from the search results. The Select Categories Of Job Titles option lets you choose up to 10 combinations of job function and seniority. You can pick from more than 25 job functions and 10 levels of seniority ranging from C-level executive to unpaid positions.

Figure 12.8 LinkedIn job title targeting options

Group targeting LinkedIn users can form, join, and participate in groups that cover just about any professional interest or skill set. As an advertiser, you can target members of these groups. Search and you see a list of search results appear as you type. Select the ones you're interested in to add members of those groups to your targeting criteria.

Demographic targeting LinkedIn allows advertisers to target by age range and gender. Don't forget to check the estimated target audience metric as you refine your target audience. Make sure you have the right balance between total reach and the specificity of targets that's appropriate for your advertising objectives.

Friday: Selecting LinkedIn Bidding and Budget Options

Just as on other advertising platforms, you need to choose how and how much to pay for your ads on LinkedIn. For each campaign, choose your cost model, set your bids, and determine a daily budget.

Choosing Your Bid Type

LinkedIn allows advertisers two cost models: you can pay for clicks (CPC) or you can pay for impressions (CPM). As with other advertising platforms, the choice comes down to your advertising objectives. If you want someone to take an action that you can define and value as an advertising goal, then you likely want to choose CPC (Figure 12.9). If your branding and positioning goals can be reached by getting your ads in front of as many eyeballs as possible, consider choosing the CPM option shown in Figure 12.9.

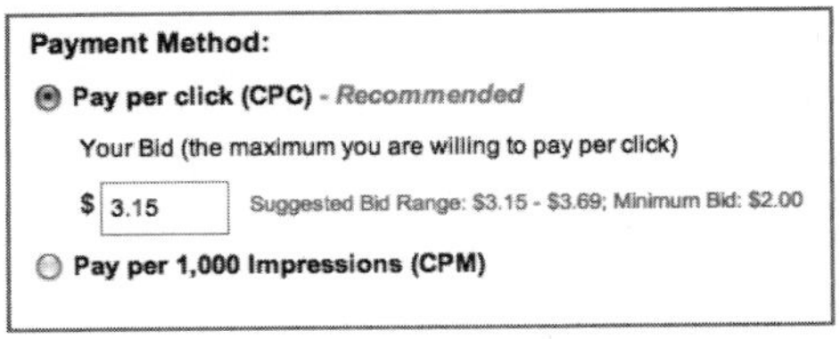

Payment Method:

◉ **Pay per click (CPC)** - *Recommended*

Your Bid (the maximum you are willing to pay per click)

$ 3.15   Suggested Bid Range: $3.15 - $3.69; Minimum Bid: $2.00

○ **Pay per 1,000 Impressions (CPM)**

Figure 12.9 LinkedIn pay-per-click (CPC) bid setting

Whichever way you go, you need to define a maximum bid. LinkedIn provides a suggested bid range based on your targeting criteria. The suggested bid range is actually an estimate of competing bids by other advertisers currently in the system, so while it can be a good guideline for getting started, let measurement and performance ultimately dictate a bid price that provides you with a positive return on your investment.

The minimum bid for CPC or CPM bidding is $2.00. Depending upon the kind of business that you're in, LinkedIn advertising may be on the expensive side when compared to other advertising platforms, but in many cases this cost is offset by the level of targeting available.

And just as in AdWords, your maximum bid is the *absolute maximum* you would consider paying for a click. The actual amount you are charged is often less, based on the demand for that ad impression. As your campaigns run and you begin to collect data, you can refine your bids as you optimize your advertising.

Setting Your Budget

Once you set your bids, tell LinkedIn how much money (minimum $10.00) you'd like to spend every day. Your ads are eligible to be shown until you reach your daily budget, but they're not shut off immediately. In the fine print, LinkedIn reserves the right to charge you up to 20 percent in excess of your daily budget should your ads get shown or clicked in the short period of time it takes for the system to stop displaying them.

On the other hand, you may find that given your targeting, your ad's performance, and your bids, it might be difficult to spend your budget every day. By setting your daily budget to a certain amount, you are not guaranteed that LinkedIn will spend that amount.

Last, LinkedIn ads are billed as charges accrue. You need to provide a credit card, and there is not a pre-pay option. Depending upon how large your budget is and how much of it you spend, your credit card is charged for ad impressions or clicks on either a daily or weekly basis.

Week 34: Launch and Measure LinkedIn Campaigns

Now that you've seen the basics of LinkedIn advertising, hopefully you can decide if it's something you'd like to try. This week we cover the more tactical side of launching, managing, and optimizing your LinkedIn campaigns. The same general rules and strategies used in any online advertising efforts apply to LinkedIn campaigns as well. Defining a tight campaign structure, targeting the right audience, and showing them the right ads are key factors to success. And once the ads are running, your real job begins: measuring performance and using that data to optimize.

Monday: Launching Your LinkedIn Campaign

Before you even log into your LinkedIn account, take some time to define your strategy and plan your campaigns. As in any other form of advertising, success starts by structuring your campaigns to support your marketing objectives.

Campaign Structure

LinkedIn is one level of hierarchy simpler than Google AdWords. There are no ad groups, only campaigns, and you may need quite a few to hone in on your specific goals.

Perhaps the easiest way to separate your campaigns is by a combination of message, desired action, target audience, and budget. For each group of people you want to target, you need a separate campaign. For each action you want them to take, you need ads specifically designed to persuade the targeted visitors to make the first click toward that action. And for each set of financial restrictions you have in place, you need to define campaign budgets accordingly.

Let's say that you work in the B2B space, and you have two distinct goals for your LinkedIn advertising: you want to sell your existing clients on your new complementary products and services, and you want to attract new customers in a number of specific industries.

At the very least, you need two campaigns. The first is targeted to the companies on your current client list. You show them ads that demonstrate the value of purchasing more products and services to enhance what they've already got. You point these ads to a landing page dedicated to this concept, and every word of your messaging speaks to customers who already know you and already use at least some of your products and services.

Your second campaign targets people of a certain job function working in a certain industry, and the ads focus on introducing the value of a product or service the user has presumably never heard of before. The messaging and imagery in these ads and their dedicated landing pages are devoted to new customer messaging that reflects higher, broader levels of the sales funnel.

Launching a Campaign

After you define your goals and sketch campaigns to accomplish those goals, you're ready to get started, and the first step is to log into your LinkedIn account. If you've never advertised on LinkedIn before, click Advertising at the bottom of the screen. If you're an existing advertiser, you can click Go To LinkedIn Ads at the top left of the screen. Click New Ad Campaign to start a brand-new campaign or begin with the settings of an existing campaign. The wizard shown in Figure 12.10 appears.

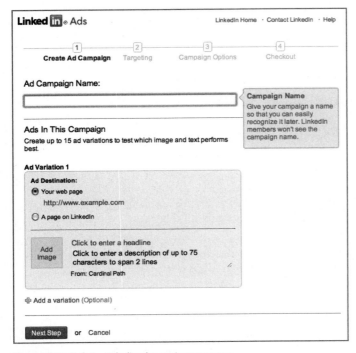

Figure 12.10 Defining LinkedIn ad campaign parameters

The first step is to name your campaign, and as with other online marketing platforms, a best practice is to name the campaign to reflect its targeting and objectives. Something like Existing Customers - Product X Cross Sell is much better than Campaign 1 when it comes time to evaluate performance metrics.

The next step is to create your ad. The interface is quite intuitive—just click on what you want to edit and it turns into either an input field or a drop-down with contextual help appearing to the right. Begin either by specifying a destination URL or selecting from a drop-down list of LinkedIn pages that you control. Next, enter your ad's headline (25 characters) and a description line (75 characters). Then enter a profile in the From field. Finally, add an image by clicking Add Image and uploading a file from your computer. Remember, this image is only 50×50 pixels in size, so make sure you make the best use of this small thumbnail.

To creating additional ads to test against one another, click Add A Variation to build up to 15 different ads per campaign. You can always come back and edit existing ads or build more after you create your campaign. Click Next Step to proceed to the targeting options screen (Figure 12.11).

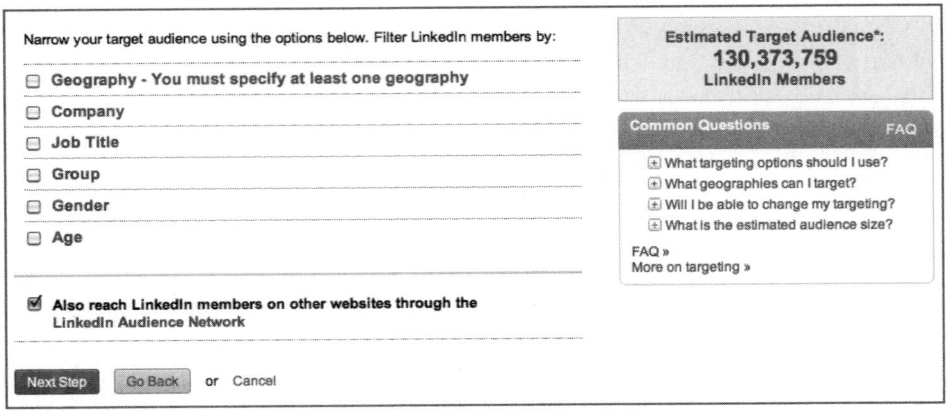

Narrow your target audience using the options below. Filter LinkedIn members by:

☐ **Geography - You must specify at least one geography**

☐ **Company**

☐ **Job Title**

☐ **Group**

☐ **Gender**

☐ **Age**

☑ **Also reach LinkedIn members on other websites through the LinkedIn Audience Network**

Next Step   Go Back   or   Cancel

Estimated Target Audience*:
130,373,759
LinkedIn Members

Common Questions   FAQ

⊞ What targeting options should I use?
⊞ What geographies can I target?
⊞ Will I be able to change my targeting?
⊞ What is the estimated audience size?

FAQ »
More on targeting »

Figure 12.11 Selecting LinkedIn ad campaign targeting settings

As discussed last week, this is where you select the geographic, company, job title, group, gender, and age targets for this campaign. Note the estimated target audience at the top right. It changes dynamically as you add targeting criteria. The check box at the bottom enables you to expand your reach to partner websites outside of LinkedIn through the Audience Network, which we discuss later this week.

Once your targeting options are set, click Next Step to proceed to the Payment Method screen (Figure 12.12).

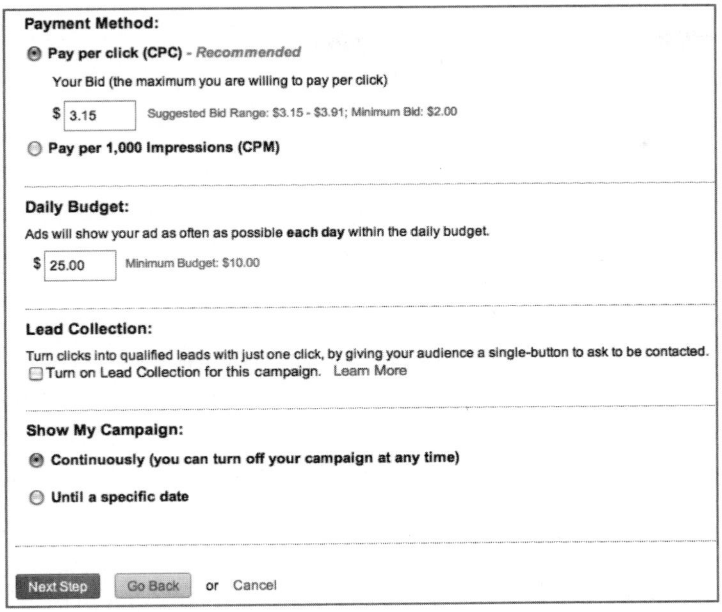

Payment Method:

⊙ **Pay per click (CPC)** - *Recommended*

Your Bid (the maximum you are willing to pay per click)

$ `3.15`   Suggested Bid Range: $3.15 - $3.91; Minimum Bid: $2.00

○ **Pay per 1,000 Impressions (CPM)**

Daily Budget:

Ads will show your ad as often as possible **each day** within the daily budget.

$ `25.00`   Minimum Budget: $10.00

Lead Collection:

Turn clicks into qualified leads with just one click, by giving your audience a single-button to ask to be contacted.
☐ Turn on Lead Collection for this campaign.   Learn More

Show My Campaign:

⊙ **Continuously (you can turn off your campaign at any time)**

○ **Until a specific date**

[Next Step] [Go Back]   or   Cancel

Figure 12.12 Choosing LinkedIn campaign and payment options

Choose between CPC and CPM bidding models, enter your bid, and set your daily budget. We discuss lead collection later. If you wish to enable this feature, click the check box. Last, you can set a date on which you'd like your campaign to automatically stop. All of these settings can be edited at any point after the campaign is created. Click Next Step again to come to the checkout screen, where you can provide billing information and review and place the order.

You are charged a one-time $5.00 activation fee, and you can apply any advertising coupons you may have. Coupons apply only to advertising spend—you'll still need to pay the activation fee.

At this point, you've defined your campaign, you've built an ad, and you've told LinkedIn how it can charge you. Congratulations! You're now advertising on LinkedIn! From this point forward, when you log into your LinkedIn Ads account, you see the Ad Campaigns tab, where you can see the overall performance of your campaigns (Figure 12.13).

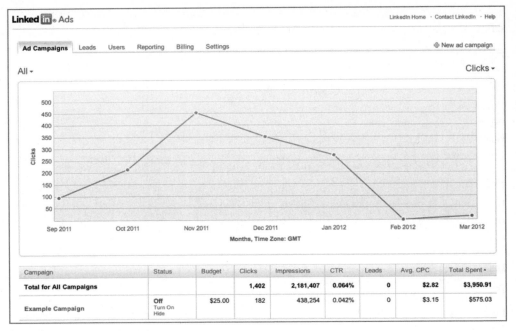

Figure 12.13 Reviewing LinkedIn ad campaigns

Tuesday: Using the LinkedIn Interface

The LinkedIn Ads interface is straightforward, and everything you need to adjust, update, create, or maintain can be accessed through the tabs shown in Figure 12.13.

Ad Campaigns Tab

The default view is the Ad Campaigns tab, and the first thing you notice on this tab is the top graph. From the left side drop-down, you can choose a date range or create your own with the Custom option as shown in Figure 14. The drop-down on the right lets you select what to see on the graph. You can choose from cost, impression, and performance metrics to help you to manage and optimize your campaigns.

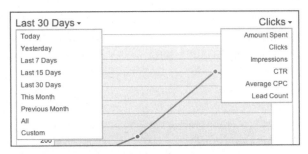

Figure 12.14 LinkedIn Ad Campaigns tab top graph options

Below the graph is a list of your campaigns along with data for each of those campaigns for the date range you selected (pictured in Figure 12.15).

Campaign	Status	Budget	Clicks	Impressions	CTR	Leads	Avg. CPC	Total Spent ▴
Total for All Campaigns			1,402	2,181,407	0.064%	0	$2.82	$3,950.91
Example Campaign	Off Turn On Hide	$25.00	182	438,254	0.042%	0	$3.15	$575.03

Figure 12.15 LinkedIn Ad Campaigns tab data set

To edit any aspects of a campaign, click its name in the first column and make the changes. You can also see these metrics at the ad level as well as edit and create new ads from this screen. The Status column allows you to quickly turn a campaign on or off, and the remaining columns show you some familiar metrics for each of your campaigns.

Leads Tab

If you enabled lead collection in Figure 12.12, the Leads tab shows the leads your campaign has collected. You can use refinement options (Figure 12.16) to manage this list, and note that you can go back only 90 days.

Figure 12.16 LinkedIn Leads tab options

As this book went to press, LinkedIn provided no way to export a list of collected leads, so consider grabbing this information while it's displayed here.

Users Tab

If you use a business account, the Users tab lets you manage who has what types of access to your LinkedIn Ads. The list of users (Figure 12.17) shows their role and a check next to the billing and campaign contacts.

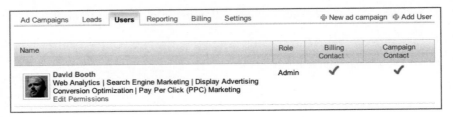

Figure 12.17 Managing LinkedIn users

Each user is assigned a role of Standard, Viewer, or Admin, and these roles have the following attributes:

- Standard—Can create, edit, and view campaigns and ads and has access to the Ad Campaigns and Reporting tabs.
- Viewer—Can view campaign data and reports through the Ad Campaigns and Reporting tabs.
- Admin—Can manage users; create, edit, and view campaigns; and access the Users, Reporting, Settings, and Billing tabs.

Additionally, you can define a billing and campaign contact, and this user (regardless of role) can manage either billing or campaign settings.

To add a new user, click Add User at the top right and assign the proper roles.

Reporting Tab

The Reporting tab allows you to download a comma-separated (CSV) file of your campaign or ad performance metrics. Select either the Campaign Performance or Ad Performance report type and select a date range. You can choose from a set of pre-defined ranges or enter a custom range. Select the granularity of the data set (daily, monthly, or yearly), and click Download CSV for a file that you can easily open and manipulate in a program like Microsoft Excel.

Billing Tab

Administrators and billing contacts have access to the Billing tab (Figure 12.18). You can edit your billing and credit card information, see how you're being charged, and see your receipts. You can see a line-by-line accounting of daily charges accrued over a given month and payments billed to your credit card in your account.

If you've received promotional coupons, you can enter and redeem them here for credit against your advertising costs at any time.

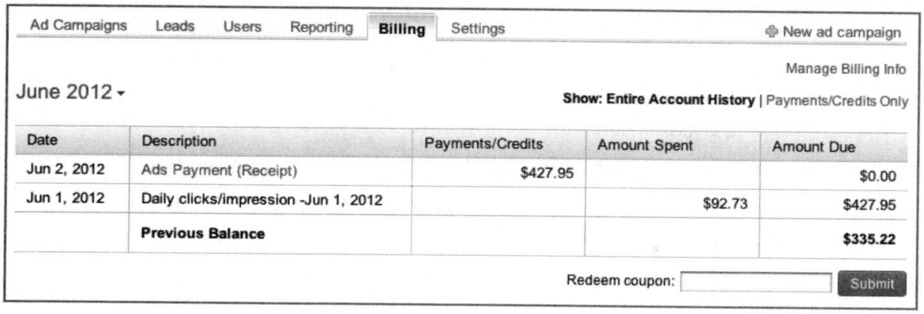

Figure 12.18 LinkedIn Billing tab

Settings Tab

The Settings tab, accessible to Admin users and the campaign contact, allows you to define which events you want LinkedIn to notify you of. If you actively manage your LinkedIn advertising, you likely want to leave all items checked. Knowing when your ads are approved or rejected and receiving suggestions for how to optimize your campaigns can be very helpful in the day-to-day management of your LinkedIn advertising.

You can also set whether or not to send a network update throughout the LinkedIn system to those connected to you or your company each time you launch a new campaign. If LinkedIn users in your network click this notification, you aren't charged for the click, so in many cases you want to check this option. If, however, you don't want to advertise that you've just started advertising, uncheck this box.

Wednesday: Integrating with Google Analytics

As with any form of advertising, performance measurement is crucial, and you should use some form of analytics above and beyond the limited LinkedIn data to analyze the impact of your campaigns. While any enterprise analytics tool can be configured to measure LinkedIn ad clicks, today we look at using one of the most popular tools in the world today: Google Analytics.

Campaign Tagging

Campaign tagging allows you to tell Google Analytics where a specific visitor comes from based upon the link they follow. If you use campaign tags in the destination URLs that you define, Google Analytics ignores any referral data it may have access to and overwrites the source of the website visit with what you define it to be.

Being a Google product closely tied in with Google Analytics, Google AdWords can autotag each link it sends users to on your site, so we have not had to worry about this so far. But LinkedIn is a different company and a different website, so each time we create an ad for a LinkedIn campaign, we tag it appropriately so that we can see exactly what happens on our websites after the click.

Google Analytics allows us to define up to five campaign dimensions that describe the source of a website visit: Campaign, Source, Medium, Content, and Term. The last dimension, Term, is reserved for visits that result from a search query, and because this does not apply to LinkedIn ads, we don't use it. The others, however, are fairly self-explanatory. Table 12.1 shows a list of these dimensions, the query string variables you use to define them, and recommended values to give them.

▶ **Table 12.1** Campaign Tagging Parameters for LinkedIn Ads

Parameter	Query String Variable	Recommended Value
Campaign	utm_campaign	LinkedIn campaign name
Source	utm_source	linkedin
Medium	utm_medium	social
Content (optional)	utm_content	Variation number

In order to tag a destination URL so that Google Analytics sources the visit to these dimensions, include these query string parameters in the destination URLs.

You can use these query string parameters with other query string variables. They don't change or alter the landing page in any way from the user's perspective. So, if you send someone who clicks one of your ads to a URL like http://www.yoursite.com/landingPage.html, change the URL to the following (a single URL appearing on multiple lines to clarify its structure and make it fit the width of the page):

```
http://www.yoursite.com/landingPage.html?utm_source=linkedin&
utm_medium=social&utm_campaign=new-customers-productname&
utm_content=advariation1
```

Then you can use Google Analytics to evaluate your return from users who click those ads and cost you marketing dollars.

Finding Tagged Campaigns in Reports

We've spent quite a bit of time looking at how to use Google Analytics to measure and report on activity generated by Google AdWords, and the same concepts and strategies apply here. The only difference is that with LinkedIn, you don't have a set of reports dedicated to this advertising medium as you do with AdWords.

With your campaigns tagged properly, you can navigate to the Traffic Sources reports, and the first one to look at is All Traffic Sources. Just under the graph, you see some options (Figure 12.19).

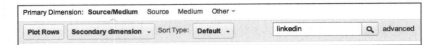

Figure 12.19 Setting Google Analytics report filter options

To narrow this list of traffic sources to just those coming from LinkedIn, type **linkedin** into the search filter and click the magnifying glass icon. Use a secondary dimension to distinguish among LinkedIn ad campaigns by choosing Secondary Dimension › Traffic Sources › Campaign. With these two settings in place, you see a list of traffic sources (Figure 12.20).

Primary Dimension: Source/Medium Source Medium Other

Plot Rows | Secondary dimension: Campaign | Sort Type: Default | Advanced Filter ON | edit

	Source/Medium	Campaign	Visits	Pages/Visit	Avg. Visit Duration	% New Visits	Bounce Rate
1.	linkedin.com / referral	(not set)	160	2.58	00:02:06	60.62%	36.88%
2.	linkedin / social	NewCust_ProductX	11	1.82	00:00:25	90.91%	72.73%
3.	linkedin / social	NewCust_ProductY	11	2.64	00:00:14	36.36%	9.09%
4.	linkedin / social	RepeatCust_CrossSell	11	7.45	00:08:25	18.18%	9.09%

Show rows: 10 Go to: 1 1 - 4 of 4

Figure 12.20 Filtered All Traffic Sources report with secondary dimension in Google Analytics

Each LinkedIn campaign has a row with user engagement metrics like pages per visit, time on site, and bounce rate. These metrics can help you understand how users react to and engage with your contact after the click. Also look at the impact your campaigns have on your goals and e-commerce. To do this, you need to have configured Goals (or installed and configured the Ecommerce module) within your Google Analytics account. Then you can simply toggle between these metrics using the options under the Explorer tab.

Another report you may find helpful, especially if you run and test multiple ads in each campaign, is at Traffic Sources › Campaigns. Here, you filter on whatever campaign you wish to analyze and enable a secondary dimension of Ad Content (Figure 12.21).

	Campaign	Ad Content	Visits	Pages/Visit	Avg. Visit Duration	% New Visits	Bounce Rate
1.	NewCust_ProductX	advariation1	345	2.34	00:02:09	58.02%	58.40%
2.	NewCust_ProductX	advariation2	340	1.33	00:00:27	49.18%	86.89%
3.	NewCust_ProductX	advariation3	352	2.55	00:11:34	1.67%	43.33%

Figure 12.21 Google Analytics Campaigns report filtered with secondary dimension

By defining the optional Content parameter in your campaign tagging, you can see a separate row for each ad variation within a campaign, and you can use this data to evaluate which of your ads are most effective. Again, Figure 12.21 shows only site usage metrics, but you're only one click away from looking at goal and e-commerce conversion data as well.

Social Reports

In the first half of 2012, Google Analytics announced a set of reports called Social Reports that we'll examine a few times in this chapter. They help advertisers and web content owners understand the impact of social media on their business goals. Google Analytics understands that LinkedIn is a social source.

Google Reports has two components. First, Google Analytics can automatically detect and source traffic from hundreds of different social media outlets around the world. Keep in mind that in addition to your paid LinkedIn advertising, you likely get free referral traffic from LinkedIn, so make sure to use campaign tagging to differentiate between paid ads and free traffic from LinkedIn.

The second part of this feature is the Social Data Hub, where social networks can share activity with Google Analytics. The benefit of this is that much social activity happens *off* your website, where Google Analytics cannot track it. However, if the social networks that are part of the Social Data Hub report shared links and mentions of you to Google Analytics, you can evaluate the impact of offsite social activity against your business goals.

The new reports are in the Traffic Sources section. They include data about social sources, specific pages being shared, conversion reports, and even a flow report to show you how visitors from social sources traverse and drop off the pages on your site.

Thursday: Optimizing LinkedIn Campaigns

The day you launch your campaign should be the worst that it ever performs, because the moment you start collecting data, you can optimize your campaigns for performance. By understanding how the LinkedIn ad auction works and using performance metrics from both LinkedIn and an analytics package like Google Analytics, you are well on your way to tuning your campaigns for a positive return on investment.

The LinkedIn Auction

The first step toward a successful response to your ads is to get your ads shown in the first place, so let's take a quick look at how LinkedIn determines which ads to show in which spots.

This works like other ad networks: each time an ad slot is available, LinkedIn holds an auction to fill it. Your ranking is purely a function of your bid and your ad's click-through rate (CTR). This makes perfect sense. With a predominantly pay-per-click model, LinkedIn collects only when a click occurs, so it wants to maximize the product of how much it makes from the click multiplied by the probability of that click occurring.

From our perspective as advertisers, this is a good thing too: if we create ads that are more likely to draw clicks than our competition's ads, we're rewarded by better placements at lower prices.

Optimizing LinkedIn ads is in large part improving CTR. LinkedIn's documentation cites 0.025 percent as a good CTR, though many practitioners agree that this should be a floor, not a ceiling. In fact, many advertisers have trouble getting their ads to show at all if they exhibit CTRs of less than that number.

Since CTR is such an important metric, you can use a couple of different strategies to improve it. First, you can up your bids to the higher end or even above the recommended bid range provided by LinkedIn. This results in more exposure and more opportunities to draw clicks from better ad positions and placements. Once you establish a solid history of good CTR, you have the luxury of dropping your bids to take advantage of the position you have in the auction.

But getting your ads shown is only half the battle. The other component of your optimization strategy is testing your ads against one another to compare their CTRs.

Testing Your Ads

Each of your LinkedIn campaigns can support up to 15 ad variations, and while that may be a large number for most small and medium-sized advertisers, for formal split testing you should always run at least 2 ads per campaign. LinkedIn recommends that you have at least 3 different ads in each campaign, and the majority of advertisers should be able to accommodate testing those ads, even with relatively small budgets.

With LinkedIn ads you can use the same strategies, tools, and techniques discussed in Chapter 10, "Month 7: Optimizing the Performance of Your Campaigns," to create and execute statistically valid ad split tests against metrics like CTR and conversion rate, and in order to collect this data evenly, you need to adjust one campaign setting. Click the specific campaign on the Ad Campaigns tab and set Rotate Ad Variations (Figure 12.22). Select Rotate Variations Evenly to tell LinkedIn to serve your ads in equal proportions so you can collect the same number of samples of each of your ad variations for analysis.

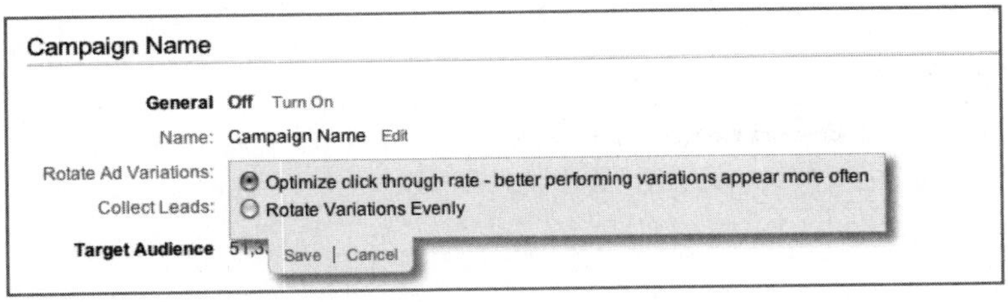

Figure 12.22 Changing ad rotation settings for LinkedIn Ads campaigns

If you don't want to do the formal statistical analysis of your ad variations, you can let LinkedIn automatically optimize for click-through rate by showing ads that have higher CTR more often. While you can put this option on autopilot and not do any more work, remember that this takes *only* CTR into consideration and that the value of your advertising efforts is in *conversions*, not clicks.

Testing Your Landing Pages

Optimizing your ads for better placements and more clicks helps you drive traffic to your website, and this is where the real work begins. The millisecond a user clicks your ad they've cost you real money, and it's up to you to extract as much value as possible from the resulting website visit.

We've devoted quite a bit of time in this book to landing page optimization, and it all applies to LinkedIn traffic as well. First, make sure to use the most relevant landing pages you can. If you don't have a page on your site that speaks specifically to the audience you're targeting and the offer you're promoting, consider creating one. The more relevant the ad to the page it takes a user to, the smoother the user experience and the higher the likelihood of a conversion.

Just as we try new ads and test them against one another, we test landing pages as well. You can alter the destination URL between ad versions, or you can use any of the testing tools discussed in Chapter 11, "Month 8: Advanced Topics." In either case, don't stop optimizing until you have a conversion rate of 100 percent!

Measuring Against Performance Goals

Ultimately, you want to use the same analysis tactics for LinkedIn ads as you do with other campaigns, and that means digging into your analytics reports. You've seen how to get LinkedIn ad data into a tool like Google Analytics, and you can use its myriad reports and data segments to refine your targeting, understand how users consume and engage with your content, and continually optimize the experience for this specific traffic source and its different campaigns.

You may find insights that pertain specifically to LinkedIn visitors that you can take advantage of in your advertising strategy. For example, the majority of LinkedIn visits occur during the week and not on weekends. You might find that a higher concentration of conversions from certain campaigns occurs on specific days of the week, and this can affect how you set and spend your budget.

Friday: Taking LinkedIn to the Next Level

As you create campaigns in LinkedIn and continue to optimize them against your advertising goals, there are just a few more things to note when working with this advertising platform.

The LinkedIn Audience Network

You can keep your reach within the pages of LinkedIn by using the LinkedIn Audience Network. This network consists of other partner websites on the DoubleClick Ad Exchange and leverages the targeting power of LinkedIn and the inventory size of DoubleClick.

This is a specific case of the retargeting concept we talked about in Chapter 11. Essentially, if you have a LinkedIn Ads campaign targeting marketing managers, then those marketing managers see your ad on the pages of LinkedIn. But their cookies are signed up for a list you'd like to market to across the entire DoubleClick ad network so that once they leave LinkedIn, you can still show them ads on other partner websites.

You can opt into or out of this distribution option at any time, and it works the same way other LinkedIn ads do. Either select the box at the targeting step of a new campaign (Figure 12.11, earlier in this chapter), or go back and change this setting from the campaign details screen of an existing campaign.

Collecting Leads

The Lead Collection option lets you leverage the power of the LinkedIn networking features not only to gain clicks and visitors to your website but to give visitors a quick way to request a follow-up contact. When you enable this option from your campaign and payment options (Figure 12.12, earlier in this chapter), a user who clicks your ad sees a bar at the top of your website that looks like the one in Figure 12.23.

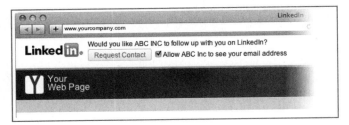

Figure 12.23 Collecting leads on LinkedIn

With one click, the user can request to be contacted via LinkedIn or optionally check the box to share their email address if they would prefer to be contacted by email. As an advertiser, you are notified by email whenever this happens, and you can review this person's LinkedIn profile and respond to them either within the LinkedIn interface or by email if they share their email address. From the Leads tab you can review the leads your campaigns collect and filter them by how recently they were collected or whether or not you've contacted them back.

Learning More

Finally, it's worth noting that the LinkedIn Ads program is relatively new, and as it continues to grow in both raw numbers and sophistication, we can expect new features and new options. The LinkedIn Help Center (http://help.linkedin.com) is a well-curated and easy-to-use set of FAQs, articles, and documentation that includes sections specifically for LinkedIn Ads: a quick search on "linkedin ads" gets you started, and more specific queries can find answers to more specific questions.

Week 35: Advertise on Facebook

Although Google is rising fast and set to the take the top spot in display advertising market share, last year the most display dollars went to Facebook. With one of every seven minutes online spent on Facebook, there are lots of impressions to be had and unique characteristics that advertisers can take advantage of, including stated interests and highly accurate demographics.

There are entire books written on Facebook marketing, such as the one from this series, *Facebook Marketing: An Hour a Day* by Chris Treadaway and Mari Smith (Sybex, 2010). With just half a chapter here we don't attempt to touch on every aspect or nuance but rather give a broad overview. We focus more on Facebook's display ad inventory and less on its conversation marketing aspects. The standard techniques of successful display ads discussed earlier in the book apply to this network as well, so we stick to what makes Facebook unique.

Monday: Understanding Facebook Advertising Destinations

On most display ad inventory, a click on the ad takes you away from the domain the content is hosted on and delivers you to the website of the advertiser. With Facebook you also have the option of delivering the visitor to your Facebook page. This could be a corporate brand page, event, destination tab, or even a Facebook app.

Where you send clickers depends entirely on the goal of your campaign. Sending them to your website enables better tracking and transaction capability. Remaining within Facebook allows greater social interaction and amplification of your topic, product, or brand. Often advertisers who are used to search engine marketing (SEM) and have a well-optimized funnel prefer to send users offsite, while those looking to generate brand awareness and maximize conversation and interactivity may choose to stay within the Facebook walled garden.

If you send visitors to your site, we recommend a dedicated landing page, highly targeted to the users and including the greater social and sharing functionality that Facebook users are predisposed to using.

Another thing to consider is that users who stay on Facebook continue to make money for Facebook through further ad impressions and clicks, so Facebook incentivizes advertisers to opt for an internal destination, and research shows that Facebook often deeply discounts costs for ads that point internally rather than externally.

Tuesday: When to Use Facebook Advertising

Facebook display advertising can be a somewhat radical departure for those accustomed to search-based text ads because it's not only a different format and targeting approach but also a different mindset. Impressions tend to be higher, and CTRs tend to be lower. Facebook tries to shift focus away from those traditional online metrics by partnering with Nielson and ComScore to develop gross rating points that emulate traditional advertising metrics.

Since Facebook has such a vast number of users, it can certainly provide a broad reach. However, it can also be useful when you aim to reach a specific segment of users by demographic or specific interest. It can be great for those looking to receive feedback from that targeted demo or build a community around a product, service, or brand.

If your target is actually an app, event, video, or page on Facebook itself, it is a no-brainer to promote it on Facebook. The targeting options are better and it's usually very cost-effective.

Because the demographic information is self-supplied by Facebook users, it tends to be of much higher accuracy than data inferred from more traditional sources. Although an algorithm may infer that a user is interested in the band Iron Maiden because they visited a web page about them, there are a number of scenarios where this is a false-positive. Perhaps it was a friend using the computer, an unrelated search that happened to lead to that page, or even research for a paper on medieval torture devices. However, a person who lists Iron Maiden as a musical interest is almost certainly a true fan.

Wednesday: The Ad Format and Where It Shows

While we focus on the IAB standard ad formats in the previous chapters, Facebook has formats that are unique to this medium. Facebook designates three primary ad categories that can be a little confusing because often the distinctions are subtle (and fluid). We cover the main ones here, but these often change in this rapidly evolving environment, so we suggest checking the Facebook Ads help center for the latest offerings (http://j.mp/DisplayBook4).

Premium Ads

Premium ads are inventory that runs in the best, most valuable locations on Facebook. Value is determined with respect to engagement, time spent, and overall quality of interaction. It tends to include the home page (with newsfeed) as well as profile and logout pages.

One advantage of the premium ads is they are interactive and can incorporate social actions such as a like, event RSVP, or even a request for a product sample. These actions are taken within the ad itself and the user doesn't leave the site. The action taken is indicated in the ad as well and adds to the user's social graph profile.

Premium ads also offer demographic targeting, guaranteed delivery, the highest share of voice on the page, and the pages with the most traffic on the site. Facebook internal studies claim premium ads are 80 percent more likely to be remembered than standard ads and drive 40 percent higher engagement and a significant increase in purchase intent. The catch is that they are available only via insertion orders (not self-serve) and currently require a monthly minimum spend of over $50,000. They also are not available for CPC, only a CPM billing model. There are six premium ad types:

Standard premium ad These don't include the interactions or generate organic stories on the rest of the site as the ads that include engagement do. These ads link to external sites and take the user away from Facebook. They are essentially a standard market-place ad but with premium placement.

Premium like ad This popular and effective ad unit encourages users to like a brand or product by pointing out which of their friends have also liked it, offering a kind of social proof to encourage engagement with the ad. If none of the user's friends have liked the ad, it simply shows the total number of people across all of Facebook that have like the brand, which can also provide social proof, albeit far less powerful.

Premium poll ad As the name suggests, the interaction of this ad isn't to like the brand but simply to offer the user's opinion in a poll. It asks a question and offers a list of avail-able responses (Figure 12.24). When the response is selected, the ad changes to reveal how other users have answered the poll. A further click indicates how their friends have voted. These ads also result in wall stories on the page of the brand, which are then published in the news feeds of the people who have liked the brand.

Figure 12.24 Premium poll ad

Premium event ad These ads detail upcoming events and allow users to invite other users to it (Figure 12.25). The ad expands after a user responds, which allows users to invite their friends along with a custom message. The RSVP interaction can then show in news feeds of friends.

Figure 12.25 Premium event ad

Premium sampling ad These ads are somewhat rare but can be effective in the right scenario. When users click the ad, it expands to allow them to enter their physical mailing address to have the selected product shipped to their residence.

Premium video comment ad This is a video ad that allows additional interaction by enabling users to leave comments or like a video without leaving the page or disrupting video play. The comments that the user's friends have made appear below the ad, increasing interest and trust of the ad and brand. When users comment or like, it is public and can thus appear in the news feeds of their friends (Figure 12.26).

Figure 12.26 Premium video comment ad

Marketplace Ads

Marketplace ads are the standard display ads that are ubiquitous on the right-hand column of pages throughout Facebook. They often allow users to interact with the ads, such as liking, without leaving the current page. While they don't include the faces of friends, they do include names as social context.

They are available through the self-service interface or API and are demographically targeted. They offer both CPC and CPM bidding (unlike premium ads, which are only CPM), although most advertisers opt for CPC for this type of ad.

They include a page title of up to 35 characters (25 for standard ad) and body copy up to 90 characters. The included image is 99×72 pixels and auto-resizes if needed. Close crops are best to ensure that the image is visible and clear at such a small size (Figure 12.27).

Figure 12.27 A marketplace ad

Marketplace ads fall into four main categories that differ primarily by their destination when clicked:

Marketplace standard ad These ads are capable of linking offsite to an external landing page.

Marketplace like ad These ads are best used to drive traffic and engagement to a Facebook page.

Marketplace app ad These ads drive engagement to the Facebook app being promoted.

Marketplace event ad These ads drive awareness and engagement with an event.

Sponsored Stories

Sponsored stories are a type of advertising that is fairly unique to Facebook and has become extremely popular due to their high levels of engagement. To work well, all performance display ads depend on some type of highly relevant targeting method. Sponsored stories rely on the idea that when users hear about a brand from their friends, they are more than twice as likely to interact.

Sponsored stories allow regular posts (or any action) from friends or pages on Facebook to be highlighted via paid ads on the right-hand column in addition to the newsfeed. They don't require any creative to be uploaded because they are generated from actions taken by users.

Advertisers have a choice of which engagements are highlighted, but they cannot edit any part of the ad. Sponsored stories are also available to run in marketplace locations, alongside marketplace ads. The type of actions can be page likes, page post likes (such as a particular photo album), app used, app shares, check-ins, or domain story (such as someone hitting the Like button on your website). An example of a check-in can be seen in Figure 12.28 and an app used in Figure 12.29.

Like premium marketplace ads, sponsored stories also have a premium option where they are the only piece of sponsored content on the page.

Figure 12.28 A sponsored check-in story

Figure 12.29 A sponsored app used story

Thursday: Targeting Options

Targeting options in Facebook are per ad, so it's actually possible to have multiple ads within a campaign with different targeting for each. However, for reporting and optimization purposes, it's best to split campaigns by audience.

Location

Facebook uses geolocation based on IP address to determine a user's location. Users may also be targeted by a current address if they have provided that information in their profile, regardless of their current location. Advertisers can target based on country, state/province, city, and zip code (United States only).

Demographic

Facebook offers age and gender targeting that is highly accurate. For ages, you can require strictly obeyed age ranges or let Facebook show ads outside the targeted range but at a discount. For example, if you select 18–35 but a person just had a 36th birthday, they can still be served an ad under the broad age match, but at a discounted rate.

Interests

You can target narrow audiences by using terms they have entered on their pro-files under interests, education, job titles, activities, groups, or even pages they have liked. Facebook suggests terms it considers similar or relevant to the ones you enter (Figure 12.30).

Similarly, if you mark a topic with a hash (#), Facebook targets a broader audi-ence that has expressed interest in a similar topic. For example, #Sailing includes interests such as offshore sailing and sailboat racing, whereas sailing without a hash requires the word *sailing* to appear in the profile.

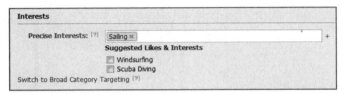

Figure 12.30 Precise interest targeting

You can also switch to broad interest targeting, which offers a taxonomy of top-ics to browse rather than typing in your own terms. You can browse and add topics you feel define relevant audiences. You can also use a combination of broad and precise topics, which requires audiences to be part of *both* interests. For example, you can tar-get users whose interests include both traveling and sailing.

Connections on Facebook

Connections target users based on connections to your brand, such as people who have become a fan of your page, RSVP'd to your event, used your app in the last 30 days, or are a member of your group (Figure 12.31).

Figure 12.31 Targeting by Connection

If you are targeting users who you know have expressed an interest in your brand, you may select "Only people who are fans of...." However, if your goal is to reach out to new audiences that are not yet familiar with your brand, you may prefer "Only people who are *not* fans of...."

Advanced targeting allows admins to targets users who are connected/not connected to specific pages, events, or apps. Additionally, you can extend your reach in a controlled way by targeting *friends* of fans of your page. This can be combined with the prior connection targeting to either include or exclude those who are already fans of the page. This type of targeting has the advantage of personalizing the ad with the names of friends who are connected, which can be very powerful.

Advanced Demographics

Advanced demographics goes beyond age and gender and addresses other aspects that are fairly unique to Facebook, such as relationship status—which gender users are interested in for friendship, dating, a relationship, or networking—and language (Figure 12.32).

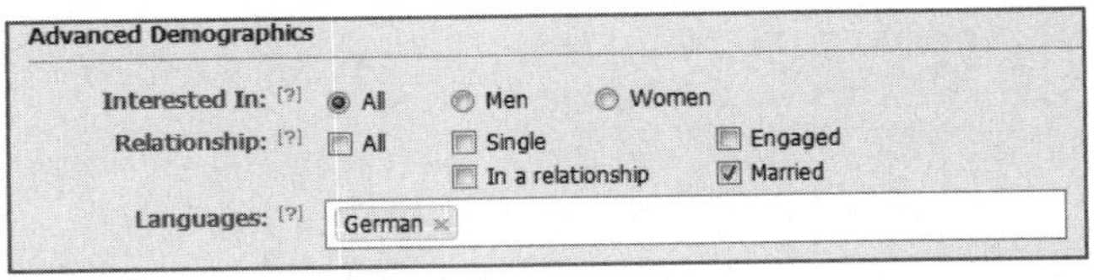

Figure 12.32 Advanced demographics

Education and Work

Education and workplaces can be valuable information for advertisers. Specific schools and majors can be targeted using the College Grad or In College drop-downs. You can also select specific workplaces, but this can result in a very narrow audience. Leave it blank unless you have a specific reason to use it (Figure 12.33).

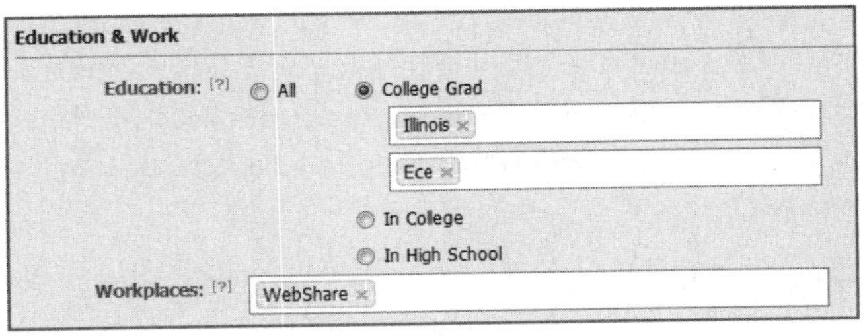

Figure 12.33 Education and work targeting

Friday: Setting Your Pricing and Choosing between CPC and CPM

Campaign budgets can be set by either a daily budget or a lifetime budget, which allows you to set the maximum you want to spend over the entire campaign. You can run the campaign for a specific period or continuously from today on (Figure 12.34). The continuous option requires a daily budget instead of a lifetime budget.

Pricing is based on an auction model. Just as with AdWords, advertisers set the maximum price they are willing to pay, but the actual price paid is usually less.

Bids are either on a CPM or on a CPC basis. CPC is more popular and used when the intent is to drive action rather than mere awareness. The minimum bid price is $0.01. CPM bidding is used in premium ads or when awareness is the primary goal. The minimum bid price is $0.02. You can also use the bid that Facebook suggests.

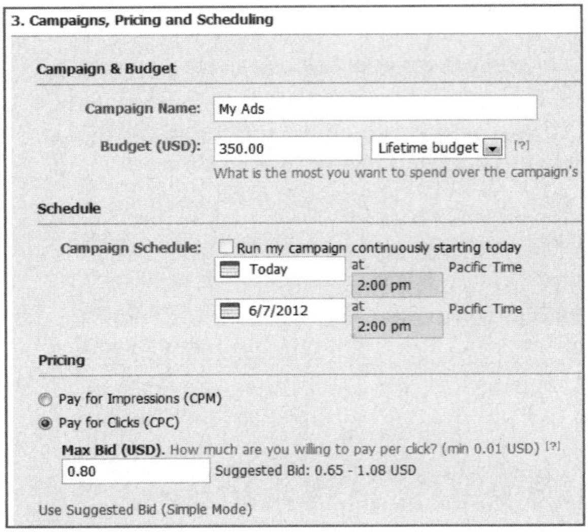

Figure 12.34 Pricing and scheduling options

Week 36: Launch and Measure Facebook Campaigns

As with any other online campaign, Facebook Ads lend themselves to iterative improvement, and there are several tools at our disposal to provide insights and data to guide that process. This is especially important for Facebook sponsored stories because the social interactions of the users with your brand can't be planned in advance and can provide some of the most effective ads.

Monday: Launching Your Facebook Campaign

Today we look at how to get started.

Pre-Campaign Planning

Some of the most important steps to determine the success of a campaign are done before you begin creating the ads. The first critical step is to understand your goals and success metrics for the campaign. Is this primarily to drive awareness? Interaction on your Facebook page? Conversions on your site?

The second step is to understand the audience you are attempting to reach. Although the first step in the Facebook workflow is to define the ad creative itself, this is backwards. First you need to define the audience and how to target that audience. *Then* you tailor the creative to fit the audience you can target. Mentally plan your audiences—which demographics? Which interests? Geographies? Languages? Education?

Setting Up the Campaigns

Navigate to www.facebook.com/ads to create an Ads account. You must have a Facebook account to sign up for an Ads account. From that page, simply click the green Create An Ad button at the top right.

Select the destination landing page for people who click your ad—either within Facebook or your site. Choose your ad type and then fill in the rest with a placeholder until you select your audience targeting options. Select your targeting options as discussed last week, and then go back and update your ad creative.

Some Best Practices

Facebook ads are relatively small, so make sure you focus the ad text and make it easy to read. Just as on other networks, a strong call to action is important.

Images follow the same guidelines laid out earlier in the book, but the sizes are usually very small. This usually means you should crop tightly and severely limit the number of elements in the image. Distracting and attention grabbing remains paramount because there are many compelling items competing for user's attention on a newsfeed. The high number of impressions and repeat traffic means that ad fatigue is a constant problem, so consider changing ad creative often.

Users tend to prefer to stay on Facebook rather than being taken to an external landing page. When possible, use the interaction elements that don't even take the user to another page on Facebook but let them remain on the current page. If you do send traffic to an external page, use custom landing pages to maintain scent and avoid an abrupt change in context.

Try not to target too narrowly. Not all targeting options are required, and using all options may result in a narrow audience with a limited reach. This is particularly true of the precise interest options. Use the reach estimation tool on the right-hand side to make sure you understand the effect of a given option on your overall audience. Similarly, don't target too broadly or you risk blowing your budget on irrelevant exposure. Use the same techniques discussed earlier in the book: hone in on a valuable audience and expand reach through look-alikes and connection targeting.

As always, monitor performance and optimize. For response-driven campaigns, CTR is a good metric of how well you are targeting and creating interesting ads. But don't compare your CTR on Facebook to another medium like a Google search; rather, use CTR to compare audiences and creatives within Facebook. Constantly test new creatives and be aware of creative wearout as you expand your reach and have a mixture of new and old audiences.

Tuesday: The Ads Manager

Once your ads are running, you can manage and evaluate them from the Ads Manager (www.facebook.com/ads/manage). The ad-specific metrics live here, while the info on pages is housed in Facebook Insights. The Ads Manager reports on the performance of your ads for the last 28 days by default and is considered by Facebook to be real time (Figure 12.35). To access additional timeframes, you must export the data from the tool.

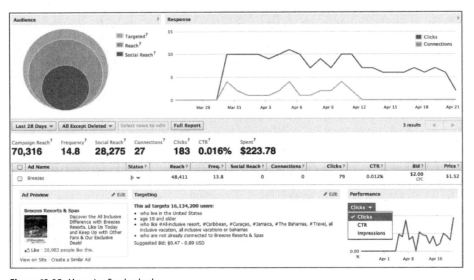

Figure 12.35 Managing Facebook ads

In addition to the standard ad metrics like CPC, clicks, cost, and so forth, it provides info on key metrics focused on people and specific to Facebook:

Targeted audience The theoretical reach (number of people) of your ads and sponsored stories, based on the current targeting settings.

Reach The number of unique people who see this ad during the dates selected. This is different from raw impressions, which overcounts people who see your ad multiple times.

Social reach Similar to reach, but specifically the number of people who see your ad with the names of their friends who like your page, RSVP to your event, or use your app. If you're not advertising a page, event, or app, social reach doesn't apply to your ad.

Frequency The average number of times a unique user within your reach sees your ad or sponsored story.

Connections The number of people who like your page, RSVP to your event, or install your app within 24 hours of seeing an ad. If you don't have a page, event, or app, you don't have connections data.

Wednesday: Facebook Insights Information

For advertisers who send traffic to Facebook pages instead of external pages, Facebook Insights (www.facebook.com/insights) can provide valuable information about how that page performs. The primary benefits of Insights are to determine which content is most valuable to your audience, understand the overall page performance, and adjust the manner in which you publish to optimize impact. Facebook Insights provides information about your pages in three main categories.

Likes

The Likes tab (formerly known as the Fans tab) helps you understand who your fans are and how you acquired them. It includes demographics (gender and age) as well as city-level geography and language (Figure 12.36).

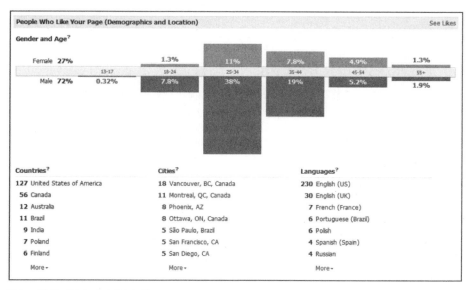

Figure 12.36 Gaining insight into likes

For advertisers, there is a critical component nearly hidden at the bottom of the page: Like Sources (Figure 12.37). This segments out the total likes into all the sources that led to the like, which can help you better understand which channels are performing.

Like Sources[7]

63,163	On Page, News Feed, or Ticker
35,216	Ads and Sponsored Stories
751	Facebook Recommendations
630	Mobile
356	Third–Party Applications
246	Page Likes Another Page
216	Timeline Edit
14	Page Browser

Figure 12.37 Segmenting sources of likes

Reach

The Reach tab (Figure 12.38) has several interesting reports that shed light on who you are reaching with your page content and the channel that reached them. The bar chart indicates gender and age. Geography and language are also indicated, as on the Likes tab.

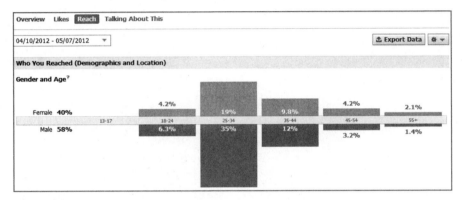

Figure 12.38 Understanding the demographics of reach

Below that, the Reach graph (Figure 12.39) indicates how people reached the page and segments sources by organic, paid, and viral. Organic users saw the post in their newsfeed or ticker or on the page itself. Paid users saw the post from a paid ad, such as a sponsored story or marketplace ad. Finally, viral users saw the post in a story published by a friend.

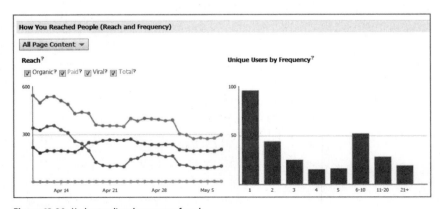

Figure 12.39 Understanding the sources of reach

The frequency graph shows the number of people who have seen content about your page in the last seven days, with a histogram detailing the number of times they saw it during that time. So approximately 100 people saw the content once, and just over 50 saw it 6 to 10 times.

Talking About This

The Talking About This tab provides information about people who are talking about your page. This activity is recorded when someone performs the following activities:

- Likes your page
- Likes, comments on, or shares your page post
- Posts to your wall
- Answers a question you've asked
- Responds to your event
- Mentions your page
- Tags your page in a photo
- Checks into or recommends your place

You also get geo and demographic info breakdowns in this report. Like the former tabs, it includes a histogram for gender and age as well as a breakdown by city. Near the bottom of the page, graphs show the Talking About This metric and Viral Reach (Figure 12.40).

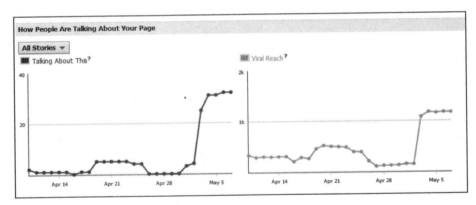

Figure 12.40 Talking About This tab graphs

Thursday: Using the Power Editor

Compared to many of the display ad networks and exchanges, Facebook's interface can make it difficult to operate large-scale or multiple account ad campaigns. While many third-party tools have sprung up recently to help ease the burden, Facebook has also released its own free tool called the Power Editor, which can vastly improve your efficiency when creating and optimizing campaigns. The primary advantages of the tool are as follows:

- Massive time-savings are realized when you're working on large or multiple campaigns.
- Analysis and optimization are possible from within the app because critical stats and performance information are part of the data set.
- It's MS Excel's best friend. For those that prefer to work in Excel, it allows easy copy and paste and is designed to handle edits made in Excel and copied back in.
- It's backward compatible with the Bulk Editor.

This tool replaces the old Bulk Editor and extends its functionality. It is not a stand-alone application but rather a Google Chrome app. To install it, click the Power Editor tab on the left side of the Ads Manager while running the Google Chrome browser. It prompts you to initially download your accounts into the editor.

A drop-down on the left lets you access each account, and a list below that enumerates the campaigns associated with each account. The tabs on top allow you to evaluate and edit the ads, campaigns, and images that belong to the account. You make the actual changes to the creative and targeting options in the workspace below.

While making bulk changes is the primary selling feature, you can also perform analysis. Figure 12.41 shows the additional metrics you can display and export. They are somewhat hidden in the Options › Settings drop-down. You also need to click the Stats drop-down to specify the data range you wish to examine.

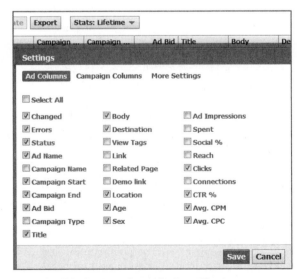

Figure 12.41 Performing analysis within Power Editor is easy.

You can create a new campaign (Create Ad) or start with an existing campaign (Duplicate). You can also create new campaigns by exporting from Power Editor into Excel via the Export button. The key is to delete the existing Campaign/Ad ID and Campaign/Ad Name fields in Excel, leave the IDs blank, and provide a new name. If you are creating new ads for the same campaign as the original, leave the campaign info untouched but provide a new ad ID. Create a new row for each campaign/ad and upload back into the tool via the Bulk Import button.

As noted earlier, creative wearout is an issue. One great use of Power Editor is to duplicate a campaign and use all the old ads but provide a new image for each one. To do that, follow these steps:

1. Export the campaign you wish to use as the base.
2. In Excel, copy and paste all of the existing rows just under the original rows, but delete all of the ad IDs, ad names, campaign IDs, and campaign names.
3. Assign a new ad name and campaign name (but leave the ID fields blank), taking care to make sure the names are both descriptive and unique.
4. Upload the file back to the Power Editor
5. Bulk import images via the Bulk Import button. (Handy tip: You can use a compressed file of multiple images.)
6. Select the new campaign, and using the Workspace, apply the appropriate new image to the news ads from your uploaded campaign.

Make sure you upload your changes via the Upload button. A plus sign or arrow appears next to the newly created or edited ads after uploading. If you don't like the changes, simply highlight the relevant ads/campaigns and click Revert Changes.

Here are some additional tips:

- One advantage of using a good, consistent naming convention is that you can do things like easily pause all ads that match. For example, if your ads follow the common naming format of: {product}_{GEO}_{Gender}_{Age}, such as AnalyticsPremium_SoCal_M_25F35, then it would be easy to pause all of the ads targeting SoCal by a search for that term. Then just highlight the ads that match and pause them at once.
- Never change the ad ID or campaign ID. It's okay to leave them or delete them (leave blank) since the system will match existing ones or create new ones for blank IDs.
- An Excel template with full column descriptions and example fields can be downloaded from http://j.mp/facebooktemplate.

Friday: Integrating with Google Analytics

For many advertisers, Facebook ads, sponsored stories, pages, and other interactions on the site are simply a means to an end. And that end is a conversion back on the advertiser's website. Like any other traffic source, Facebook traffic to the site is best analyzed via a web analytics package, such as the free Google Analytics. Because social media is such an important activity, there is a set of rapidly evolving reports dedicated to just traffic from those sources.

Unfortunately, some of the most powerful Google Analytics reports are derived from the Analytics Social Data Hub, which Facebook has not (at the time of this writing) yet allowed their advertisers' data to be integrated into. You can check the current list of social data partners here:

```
https://developers.google.com/analytics/devguides/socialdata/
```

However, there are still many techniques and reports you can take advantage of within Google Analytics to evaluate your social efforts. And the good news is that for ads that link directly to your website from Facebook, you can capture essentially everything you need to know.

Sources and Conversions

First and foremost, you want to understand what traffic is being sent to your site from Facebook and how well it's performing. To see the value that social media of all types deliver to your site, click Traffic Sources › Social › Overview to see the Social Value page (Figure 12.42). This illustrates the number of visits as well as value of the visits from social sources, including both last click conversions (ones that happened during that visit) and assisted conversions (the user reached the site via social media, but the conversion happened later).

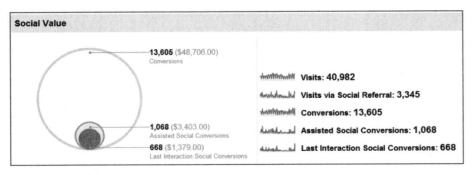

Figure 12.42 Social overview reports

Clicking the Sources report on the left navigation provides more information on which social channels (such as Facebook) are responsible for driving traffic to your site.

Clicking Conversions shows similar data, but it's based on the conversion performance of each channel (Figure 12.43). In this case you can see that Facebook was responsible for traffic that ultimately drove over $50,000 in conversions, of which $35,000 happened on the first visit.

Social Network	Assisted Conversions	Assisted Conversion ↓ Value	Last Interaction Conversions	Last Interaction Conversion Value	Assisted / Last Interaction Conversions
Facebook	3,786	$52,459.99	2,060	$35,629.99	1.84
reddit	502	$7,048.04	284	$4,053.24	1.77
YouTube	378	$6,675.90	141	$13,124.55	2.68
Twitter	372	$4,856.27	117	$1,975.21	3.18
Tumblr	140	$1,515.61	66	$700.08	2.12
Google+	42	$355.38	36	$742.41	1.17
Pinterest	25	$332.99	6	$59.49	4.17
StumbleUpon	20	$236.86	4	$16.98	5.00

Figure 12.43 Conversions by social network

It's often said that while search engine queries tend to be lower-funnel activities (closer to the point when a user is ready to buy), social media is more about awareness (upper funnel). The idea is that the awareness eventually leads to a purchase. So one very interesting question to ask in your analysis is whether or not your ads have a high assist ratio. The far right column in Figure 12.43 shows the assist ratio, which is the number of times a source sent traffic that was an assisted conversion divided by the number of times it was a last interaction conversion. In other words, you can see that Google+ sent traffic to the site that converted 42 times, 36 of which were on that same visit, which is an assist ratio of just 1.17. Meanwhile, StumbleUpon brought 20 conversions, of which only 4 converted on that initial visit, which results in an assist ratio of 5.00. From this you can see that StumbleUpon tends to bring upper-funnel/awareness users. Facebook is in the middle, with an assist ratio of 1.84 for this site. What is Facebook's conversion ratio for your site?

For all of this social tracking to work, Google must be able to determine the source of the traffic. For Facebook ads, you can specifically tag your destination URLs with campaign tracking parameters. This is a great time to go back to Chapter 9, "Month 6: Launch and Measure Your Campaign's Performance," week 23, and review the section on campaign tracking and tagging.

To compare individual Facebook campaigns, click Traffic Sources › Sources › Campaigns and evaluate how your Facebook campaigns compare against each other and other advertising sources. You can even compare properly tagged ad creatives by selecting a primary dimension of Ad Content.

Social Plug-Ins

In addition to visits (and subsequent conversions) from Facebook, you can track some activities that happen on your pages due to the social plug-ins. For example, you can track when someone uses the Facebook code to like your page. Keep in mind, this is not liking when they are already on Facebook but rather clicking the Like button while they are on your page reading your content.

To record the like within Google Analytics, use code to track the event and create a callback to Google's code when the like occurs. A sample of that code is as follows:

```
FB.Event.subscribe('edge.create', function(targetUrl) {
  _gaq.push(['_trackSocial', 'facebook', 'like', targetUrl]);
});
```

You can do the same for unlikes:

```
FB.Event.subscribe('edge.remove', function(targetUrl) {
  _gaq.push(['_trackSocial', 'facebook', 'unlike', targetUrl]);
});
```

Also for shares, and so forth:

```
FB.Event.subscribe('message.send', function(targetUrl) {
  _gaq.push(['_trackSocial', 'facebook', 'send', targetUrl]);
});
```

To see these actions in Google Analytics, view the Social Plug-Ins report (Figure 12.44).

Social Source and Action	Social Actions ▾ ↓	Social Actions
1. ■ social-facebook : like	26	3.41%
2. ■ social-facebook : recommend	17	2.23%

Figure 12.44 Facebook social plug-in report

Facebook Visitor Flow

Another valuable analysis of Facebook traffic is to understand how it moves through your site and where it drops off. This is easily accomplished in a powerful yet intuitive report called the Social Visitors Flow. View this report to see all social media traffic sources. To examine just Facebook, click the Facebook segment and select View Only This Segment. This creates a visitor flow similar to the one shown in Figure 12.45. From there you can highlight individual paths, such as how visitors move from Facebook and ultimately end up at the careers section of the site. Another useful examination is to understand the pattern of drop-offs (site abandonments) for Facebook users versus your other traffic sources.

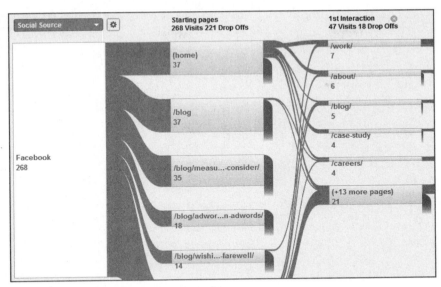

Figure 12.45 Facebook traffic via the Social Visitors Flow report

We've just scratched the surface here with the analysis that can be done via the social media reports in Google Analytics. Because nearly all of the reports are interactive to some degree, spend time really stepping through each of them and really understanding how your Facebook ads and sponsored stories are performing for your site and how Facebook stacks up against the other display ad inventory driving traffic to your site.

Glossary

This glossary lists acronyms, terms, vocabulary, and jargon that appear in or are directly relevant to the chapters of this book. It is not a comprehensive dictionary of online advertising terminology.

algorithm A set of computer instructions to take inputs, perform calculations on those inputs, and then create the desired output. For example, there are several algorithms that can sort a list of numbers from smallest to largest. The credit scoring algorithms used by lenders take inputs about an individual's credit history and determine a score. Search engines use algorithms to determine the best web pages to display in the search results and to determine which keywords best describe the content and meaning of a page.

ad creative The actual commercial advertisement that is displayed to the user. This may include text as ad copy, images, video, audio, or any combination of the above.

ad group In Google AdWords, an ad group is a collection of ad creatives and their associated targeting and bidding properties. For example, an ad group may hold keywords to target, specific sites for placement, or both. Bid prices within the ad group may be set by the bidder for individual keywords or placements.

ad position The position on a web page at which an ad appears relative to competing ads. On Google networks, this is known as AdRank and is based on the results of the auction. Higher-ranking ads generally appear toward the top and lower-ranking ads toward the bottom.

ad exchange A technology platform analogous to a stock exchange that facilitates the buying and selling of online advertising inventory from multiple ad networks in a single auction. The exchange provides automated auction-based pricing and real-time bidding and buying. Examples include Right Media (Yahoo), CONTEXTWEB (independent), and DoubleClick Ad Exchange (Google).

ad server/ad serving A specialized web server that manages and delivers ad creative to a user's screen. Ad servers are usually operated by a publisher directly or by a third party and often provide tracking and analytics data.

attribution modeling A way to allocate credit for an action, conversion, or revenue when multiple ad views or site visits precede the success event. For example, if a visitor views a display ad, subsequently performs a search, and finally clicks an email link just before completing a purchase, a last click attribution model gives 100 percent revenue credit to the last interaction (email link), while a linear model divides the revenue evenly among all touch points.

audience targeting A method of deciding where to show ads based on the expected behavioral, geographic, psychographic, or demographic attributes of expected viewers. Audience targeting generally observes these attributes using anonymous data or data that it not personally identifiable.

banner ad An image ad, most often of rectangular shape, although it can take many forms.

B2B/B2C Business-to-business/business-to-consumer. A description for sites based on whether they primarily target consumer or business customers.

behavioral targeting A method of deciding where to show ads based on the previous online behavior of targeted users—such as viewing a particular page, filling out a form, or making a purchase. Advertising systems gather behavioral data using anonymous cookies.

bid The amount an advertiser is willing to pay for a given ad impression or click in an online auction.

bid management software Software that helps advertisers manage and optimize their advertising bids. It often includes features to automate bidding via rules/conditions or performance-based algorithms. The software generally interfaces directly with publishers or networks through an application programming interface (API).

branding/brandlift/brand awareness Advertising metrics that focus on awareness of a brand rather than a direct response. A set of key branding metrics, such as consumer recall, may be predetermined and measured to study the impact of an ad campaign on the brand.

campaign A collection of advertising elements centered around an idea or product. In Google AdWords, campaigns can contain multiple ad groups.

click fraud/invalid clicks Click fraud occurs in online advertising when a person or automated computer program simulates a user clicking an ad. The goal of click fraud is generally to generate revenue for the publisher or drive up costs for competitive advertisers. Google uses the term *invalid clicks* in lieu of the more common click fraud.

content network The previous name of the Google Display Network. *See GDN.*

contextual ads Text and image ads served on web pages (other than search results pages) and selected for the relevance of their content and meaning to the advertiser's goals.

conversion rate The percentage of visits where users exhibit a behavior designated by the advertiser as a conversion—such as submitting a form, completing a purchase, or viewing a video. Not to be confused with click-through rate (CTR).

CPA Cost per acquisition (also known as cost per action or cost per conversion). Total advertising costs for a specified set of ads divided by the total number of conversions resulting from those ads.

CPC Cost per click (also known as pay per click). A type of performance-driven advertising where the advertiser is not charged based on impressions but rather when a user clicks the ad.

CPM Cost per mille (thousand). While CPC bid prices are per click, CPM prices are per 1,000 impressions. For example, a $20 CPM indicates that the price to reach 2,000 users is $40.

CTR Click-through rate. The percentage of times users click an ad after being shown an impression.

de-duplication The term overall refers to eliminating duplicate entries in data sets. In the context of advertising, it's most often used to describe avoidance of paying for the same audience or traffic twice. For example, in a CPA based on view-throughs, if a visitor sees the same ad through different networks, each network can claim they are owed the CPA for a single conversion. *See attribution modeling.*

DSP Demand side platform (also known as buy side optimizers or buy side platforms). A single system for media buyers to access ad exchanges and networks and sell side platforms, often with the ability to do real-time bidding.

direct response A type of marketing where the advertiser interfaces directly with the end user to elicit an action of some kind, such as a purchase, registration, or download. It is typically contrasted with marketing intended to raise brand awareness or drive traffic to retailers, distributors, or resellers.

Display Network *See GDN.*

eCPM Effective cost per mille (thousand). A way of assigning an equivalent CPM value to a CPC ad; calculated as CPC × CTR (or QS) × 1000. Google uses this to compare CPM and CPC ads to determine their ad positions when they compete in the same auction.

frequency capping A technology that allows advertisers to limit the number of times a specific ad is shown to the same user.

geotargeting Targeting (or excluding) users based on their estimated location. Relevant to both desktop and mobile data services.

GDN Google Display Network. Nearly all of the sites in the Google network that display ads on pages that are not search engine results (ads on search results pages are part of the Search Network, not the Display Network). It includes sites that are part of the AdSense program, YouTube, the DoubleClick AdExchange, Gmail, and other

Google properties. It displays text, image, video, and rich media formatted ads that can be targeted through keywords, placements, or audiences. Formerly called the Content Network, its name change acknowledges that content/contextual keyword targeting is not its only targeting option.

Google Search Network The Search Network consists of Google Search (Google.com) and search partner sites, such as Google Maps, ask.com, netscape.com, amazon.com, and more.

impression One potentially billable display of an ad to a user. Ad servers may record a new impression each time the ad is displayed (even to the same user), but some ad servers can be configured not to count page reloads, automated page loads not requested by a person, and other activities that the advertiser and publisher have agreed not to count.

impression share The percentage of the times an advertiser's ad is shown out of the total opportunities in which it was eligible to be shown. Eligibility includes all targeting settings and approval status.

interstitial ads Ads that are loaded on top of a content page but don't necessarily load a new page with a unique URL. They often act as a bridge between two pages or hide content until a user takes an action (such as viewing or interacting with an ad). Also known as modals, transition ads, intermercial ads, and splash pages.

inventory The available ad space for sale by a publisher.

JavaScript (JS) A client-side language used to extend static HTML and provide enhanced user interfaces and dynamic websites. JavaScript tags are used extensively for ad delivery and measurement.

KPIs Key performance indicators. Metrics and calculations specific to an individual organization to help it measure performance against that organization's defined goals.

landing page The first page a user visits when clicking an ad or link. While it often is, it does not necessarily have to be a purpose-built page (a site's home page is often the top landing page).

LSI Latent semantic indexing is a type of natural language processing that attempts to understand the meaning and themes of the words on a page by using contextual clues. Google uses it extensively to go beyond simple keyword matching and determine which ads are relevant to the theme and meaning of a given page, particularly those opted into the AdSense program. An example is using the fact that "GM" and "car" are keywords on the same page to infer that the word "Malibu" refers to the car made by Chevrolet, not the city in California.

negative keywords Terms used to exclude search queries and themes that the advertiser doesn't want to bid on.

organic listings Links on search engine results pages that appear not as paid ads but as relevant search results.

persona A fictional character created by marketers or user experience professionals to describe one type of user expected to interact with their page or product. Personas are used to represent various market segments and often embody demographic, psychographic, and behavioral characteristics.

PII Personally identifiable information. Unlike the unique but anonymized IDs commonly found in online browser cookies, PII can be used to uniquely identify an actual person. Examples include names, email addresses, Social Security numbers, and postal addresses.

personalization Modifying content to attempt to more closely match the preferences or behaviors of users based on previous observation. Examples include highlighting products related to those previously viewed or including page content related to prior search engine queries. Closely related to behavioral targeting.

placement targeting A targeting option that allows advertisers to select individual sites, sections of a site, and pages of a site in the GDN to display their ads. Unlike contextual targeting, this type of targeting does not use keywords.

Quality Score A metric—used by Google, Yahoo, and MSN—that combines a variety of factors to measure how relevant an advertiser's keyword is to its ad text and to a user's search query. It is closely related to a keyword's performance and largely based on CTR. In general, a high Quality Score means that your keyword will trigger ads in a higher position and at a lower cost per click (CPC).

retargeting Retargeting (also known as remarketing or behavioral retargeting) is a form of online advertising by which ads are delivered to consumers based on their previous behavior, such as a site visit or shopping cart abandonment.

ROAS Return on ad spend. Return as a proportion of ad costs, computed as

(gross revenue – ad costs) / ad costs

ROI Return on investment. Ad measurement tools often (incorrectly) use ROI interchangeably with ROAS, but ROI includes total investment, not just ad spend.

RTB Real-time bidding. An automated process through which ad inventory is evaluated, bid prices determined, and ads purchased and served in real time on a per-impression basis.

SEM Search engine marketing. A vague term that originally referred to any marketing optimization on search engines but recently has referred primarily to paid search and even display (non-search) advertising.

SEO Search engine optimization. Despite the broader name, in practice this refers almost exclusively to optimization of organic (non-paid) search listings. *See SEM.*

SERP Search engine results page.

share of voice Share of voice. *See impression share.*

sponsored listings Paid advertisements on a search engine results page (SERP). Contrast with organic listings.

tracking pixel HTML code that transmits information to a server, usually via a single-pixel image. These are generally used for the purpose of tracking online user activity, such as web analytics or completion of a conversion process.

unique visitor Contrasted with the visits metric, which includes multiple visits by the same person, this metric counts each unique person once, regardless of the number of repeat visits. Repeat visits via the same browser are easily detected, but tracking unique visitors across multiple devices requires more sophisticated techniques such as user logins or third-party measurement techniques, such as those employed by ComScore.

vertical A vertical (also known as an industry vertical) is a category of businesses operating in a similar product area or with similar service offerings. Examples may include travel-related businesses, digital camera manufacturers, and accounting services.

Index

A

A/B landing page testing, 375–376
About.com
    evaluating placements on, 141, 290
    placement research for, 130
    relevance optimization for, 338–339
accidental competition, 77
accuracy, ad, 222–223
action, user
    as direct response goal, 62–65
    qualifying, 381, 386
    upper vs. lower sales funnel, 479
    see also calls to action; clicks
ActionScript 1-3 codes, 218–219
ad creatives. *see* creatives, ad
ad exchange, 483
ad groups
    for ad optimization, 335
    adding placements to, 136–137
    adding to campaigns, 126
    in AdWords account, 111
    Analytics reports for, 301–302
    creating, 123, 181–190
    custom combinations, 389–390
    defined, 483
    exclusions, 150–152
    expanding reach of, 124–125, 341–343
    for LinkedIn campaigns, 450
    organizing, 141–152
    remarketing lists, 387–388
    setting manual bids for, 165
    shared targeting with campaign, 147–148
    specificity in, 115, 343
    uploading ads to, 188–190
ad industry, historic, 40–41, 278
Ad Planner. *see* DoubleClick Ad Planner
Ad Rank, 93, 94
ad rotation, 177–178, 358
ad scheduling
    in AdWords, 112
    how to use, 174–176
    limitations of, 177
    organizing, 143
    time zones and, 155
ad server/serving, 483
ad slot placement, 107
AdMeld, 44
AdMob, 44

Adobe Creative Suite, 88
Adobe/Omniture SiteCatalyst, 407
Ads Manager (Facebook), 472–473
AdScape, 44
AdSense. *see* Google AdSense
advanced segments
    AdWords, 173–181
    branded keyword focus, 304
    defined, 71
    demographic targeting, 469
    Display Ad Builder, 240–242
    sample, 71–72
    to test landing pages, 399
advertisements
    cost of, as market research, 275
    delivery of, 143
    optimizing, 334–336
    paired with landing pages, 193–195
    restricted, 225
    resubmitting, 227
    as solutions, 74–76
    uploading to ad groups, 188–190
    see also creatives, ad; image ads; text ads;
        video ads
advertisers vs. publishers, 40
Advertising.com, 19
AdWords. *see* Google AdWords
AdWords Editor, 126
AdWords for Video
    call-to-action overlays, 261
    metrics for, 251
    as new interface, 247
    overview of, 254–255
AdWords Video Ads, 247
algorithms, 483
All Video Campaigns, 254
Amazon
    Kindle, 212
    One-Click patent, 372
    tablets, 163
analysis options
    customer feedback, 412–415
    for forms, 419–424
    heuristic evaluations, 426
    visual, 416–419
    see also Google Analytics
analyst, data, 89–90
analytic tags
    of ad creatives, 298–299

for data collection, 23
on LinkedIn, 455
to refine ad targeting, 57
Analytics, Google. *see* Google Analytics
Analytics Social Data Hub, 478
Android, 44
any touch attribution, 35
APIs, 318, 320
Applied Semantics, 45
Ash, Tim, 377
assisted conversions
analyzing, 333
from Facebook, 479
as performance metric, 68, 69
report, 314–315
attention maps, visual, 417–418
attribution
defined, 483
as direct response goal, 32–35
in multi-funnel conversion, 312–315
auctions
AdWords, 93–95, 280
LinkedIn, 458–459
audience
adding to ad groups, 185
catering copy to, 202
engagement, 259, 265
LinkedIn, 441
non-captive, 252–253
optimizing, 339–341
retention tracking, 264
see also users
audience targeting
ad optimization for, 334–336
in Ad Planner, 131
adding ad group audiences, 185
adjusting bids for, 344–345
for broad and specific reach, 433–435
campaign separation for, 149
data evaluation for, 332
defined, 55, 483
via Facebook, 467–469, 471, 472
as GDN option, 22
via Google TV, 267, 269
how to use, 108–110
and inference, 324
via LinkedIn, 461
via look-alike modeling, 345–347, 350
New vs. Returning report, 305
power of, 55
see also remarketing/retargeting
authority, questioning, 89
automatic placements
bid adjustments for, 344
defined, 21
how to use, 139

performance report, 294
promoted to managed, 289, 344
auto-tagging, 285, 299

B

back-end programmers, 88
Banana Republic, 372
banner ads
as companions to video, 246, 248, 256
defined, 484
destination aligned with, 203
history of, 40
popularity of, 24
rich media vs., 217, 231
on Yahoo!, 18
banner blindness, 14
behavioral targeting. *see* audience targeting
Benway, Jan Panero, 14
bids
on the Ad Exchange, 53
adjusting
ad group, 341–343
ad scheduling, 175–176
keyword and placement level, 343–344
bidding style, 164–171
as budget part, 97
on competitors trademark, 224
CPC
auction, 93–95
automatic and enhanced, 166–167
for direct response goals, 279
manual, 164–165
defined, 484
GDN options, 91
via keyword, 46
LinkedIn options, 439, 447
managed placement, 289
management software, 484
overrides, 165
real-time bidding (RTB), 41–42
relevance as informing, 115
ROI as informing, 279
starting, 165
suggested, 123–124
video options, 256
billing
for AdWords, 98–100
for engaged views, 259
for Google TV ads, 266
for LinkedIn campaigns, 454–455
for pay-per click advertising, 4–6
for video ads, 247, 252, 259
Blogger, 48
blogs, 49
Bloomberg, 267

bounce rate
   defined, 305
   as good display metric, 333
   recording pre-campaign, 275
   reports, 305–306
   testing, 407
   for video ads, 250
brand channels, 260
branding
   in AdWords, 38
   as competitive advantage, 36–38
   connections, 468
   defined, 484
   and direct traffic reports, 303–304
   via display advertising, 10
   goals, 62, 67–71
   market share measures, 73–74
   measuring, 309–327
   plus calls to action, 196
   social media impacts on, 70
   success metrics for, 71–74, 308–309
   traffic correlations, 327
   via video ads, 250
   on YouTube, 258, 259
Breeze, James, 207
Breezes Resorts, 15–16
broad reach targeting
   in AdWords, 113
   via Google TV ads, 266
   refining campaigns for, 149–150
browsers, Internet
   load time, 363–364
   market share of top, 73
   targeting devices with, 163
budgets
   campaigns limited by, 341–342
   Facebook campaign, 469–470
   how Google spends ad, 97–98
   LinkedIn options, 447–448
   planning, 90–93
   separating search and display, 142
   setting AdWords, 164, 171–173
buffer remarketing lists, 393
business-to-business (B2B) advertising
   defined, 484
   image ads for, 230–231
   on LinkedIn, 438

C

calls, phone, 295
calls to action
   clear landing page, 368–371
   fast-loading, 363–364
   in image ads, 195–197, 203
   styling, 364

   in video ads, 250, 253, 259
   YouTube overlays, 261
campaigns, advertising
   dedicated landing pages for, 374
   defined, 484
   defining objectives in, 27–30
   implementer, 85–86
   measuring impacts of, 38, 60
   online experimental, 198
   optimization tools, 57
   organizing, 141–152
   planning future, 132
   process of successful, 83–85
   separating search and display, 141–144, 161–162
   statistics, 23
see also display campaigns; search campaigns
car ads, 197–198
Card, Stuart, 192
Cardinal Path
   advanced segment sample, 71
   advice on forms, 368
   CPA bidding, 169
   home path, 397
   Straker, Michael, 202–203
   see also Seminars for Success
carriers, 163
Catalogs.com, 407
causal relationships, inferred, 324
CBS Media Labs, 266
CBS Sports, 267
channels, YouTube, 260, 270
checkout friction, 372
Chi, Dr. Ed, 192
Clayton, Mat, 320
click fraud, 484
clicks
   as campaign metric, 277
   initial, 333
   report on free, 294
   social media-sourced, 315–316
   visits as unmatched with, 297
clickstream analytics, 411–412
clickTAG code, 218
ClickTale, 417, 421
click-through rates
   ad optimization for, 336
   in AdWords auction, 93–94
   as campaign metric, 278
   data accumulation on, 275–276
   defined, 484
   on LinkedIn, 459
   as Quality Score metric, 367
   in ROI calculation, 281
   as search campaign focus, 330
click-to-play video ads, 247
clutter, webpage, 373–374

CNN, 267
cognitive psychology, 204–214
color
    for user distraction, 195
    visual tones, 201
comments, audience, 265
communication skills, 87
company targeting, 446
Compete.com, 74
competitive advantages
    data analysis for, 285
    differentiation and, 35
    identifying, 79–81
competitors
    bidding on trademarks, 224
    Competition and Approximate CPC, 122
    excluding, 50
    identifying, 76–78
    keyword, 103, 119
    market share of, 73–74
completions, video ad, 250
confidence intervals
    data collection for, 276
    formulas, 354
    testing to determine, 358
confidence levels
    formulas, 354
    sample test of, 276
    setting value on, 356
    testing to determine, 358
connections, tracking, 468
content, ad
    analyzing performance of, 298–299
    prohibited by Google, 225
    prohibited by LinkedIn, 444
Content Network, 8, 484
contextual ads, 484
contextual targeting
    in ad group setup, 181–183
    campaign optimization for, 338–339
    choosing relevant keywords for, 114
    Contextual Targeting Tool, 123–126, 165
    by Google AdWords, 11, 21
    how to use, 102–104
    via keywords, 54
    negative keywords in, 152
    and retargeting, 380
    shift away from, 380
    specificity in, 115
contrast, 204–205
Conversion Optimizer
    ad scheduling limits with, 177
    how to use, 168–171
conversion rate
    analyzed by time, 291–292
    defined, 66, 484
    expected, 355

    recording pre-campaign, 274
    in ROI calculation, 279, 282
    sample size for testing, 353–357
conversion tracking
    in AdWords, 23, 66, 286, 333
    code. *see* tracking code
    Conversion Optimizer tool for, 5–6
    data needs for, 350
    for enhanced CPC bids, 167
    from Facebook, 479
    in Google Analytics, 286
    of multi-channel engagement, 312–314
    for ROI calculation, 282
conversions
    assisted. *see* assisted conversions
    audience targeting to increase, 55
    bidding based on, 92
    as campaign metric, 278
    forms as hindering, 368
    goal of increased, 61
    vs. impressions, 272
    metrics to measure, 66
    offline, 310, 392
    optimizing for, 177
    performance report, 292–293
    traffic balanced with, 138
    from video ads, 250
cookies
    CRM integration and, 393
    disabled, 297
    DoubleClick, 383–384
    and Google's privacy policy, 110
    purpose of, 12, 22
    retargeting function of, 55–56
copy
    experimentation with, 364–365
    how human eyes read, 205
    for LinkedIn ads, 444
    requirements, 220–221
    testing landing page, 371
    tips on, 202–203
    for TV ads, 269
Coremetrics, 333
Coriolis effect, 353
Corning glass, 231
correlation, data, 324
cost
    as campaign metric, 278
    of dedicated landing pages, 374
    in ROI calculation, 281–282
cost per acquisition (CPA)
    as bid option, 91
    bidding how-to, 168–171
    DCO assumptions on, 351
    defined, 484
    in pay-per click advertising, 5
cost per action (CPA), 279

cost per click (CPC)
  approximating, 120
  auction, 93–95, 280
  bids
    automatic, 166
    in bidding options, 91
    vs. CPM, 96–97
    LinkedIn, 447
    manual, 164–165
  calculating ROI for, 279
  as campaign metric, 278
  defined, 484
  enhanced, 166–167
  on Facebook, 470
  history of, 40–41
  how Adwords manages, 91–92
  in pay-per click advertising, 4–5
  in ROI calculation, 281, 282
cost per conversion (Cost/Conv)
  as campaign metric, 66, 278
  in ROI calculation, 283
cost per thousand (CPM)
  as bid option, 91, 92–93
  bidding how-to, 167–168
  defined, 484
  on Facebook, 470
  LinkedIn bids for, 447
  in pay-per click advertising, 5
  vs. CPC bids, 96–97
Crazy Egg, 418–419
creatives, ad
  added to ad group, 188
  analyzing
    in AdWords, 23
    for approval by Google, 233
    campaign tagging, 298–299
    in Google Analytics, 337
    of video ads, 254
  in campaign process, 84
  cognitive psychology for, 204–214
  Creative Specs Database, 216
  defined, 483
  Display Ad Builder for, 235–243
  experimentation with, 246, 363–365
  graphic designers of, 88
  image size in, 130
  landing page correlation, 194
  in maintaining scent, 192
  real-time generation of, 42
  split-testing, 352–353
  wearout of, 472, 477
  YouTube video options, 260
credibility, 365
cross-channel integration, 394
custom combinations
  for audience targeting, 22

  as remarketing tool, 392
  when to use, 388–390
customer relationship management (CRM), 393
customer service, 29, 413
customers
  competitive analysis as, 77
  defining and finding, 81–83
  feedback from, 412–415
  new, 61
  solving the problems of, 74–76

D

data
  polluted, 300
  tagging non-Google ads, 299–301
data collection
  action based on, 334
  for Ad Planner, 126
  aggregating social, 324
  and analysis, 23, 87
  analysts, 89–90
  for budgeting, 173
  confidence in, 275–276
  for Conversion Optimizer, 170
  by Facebook, 463
  on forms, 420
  inaccurate, 421–422
  for marketing accountability, 17
  personally identifiable, 221, 222, 444
  separate search and display, 144
  and sharing, 285
  of social interactions, 317–321
  for split testing, 358–359
  for starting bids, 165
  to tailor digital advertising, 3–4
  third-party, 109
  to track advertising value, 31
  waiting for, 274
dayparting, 174, 268
deception, user, 221, 444
decision-making, 90
de-duplication, 484
delivery, ad
  rotation and frequency capping, 177–178
  separating campaigns for, 143
Delta, 196
demand side platforms (DSPs), 41–42, 485
demographic metrics
  for ad optimization, 335
  in AdWords, 293
  from Facebook, 322
  from social media sites, 320–321
  in YouTube Analytics, 263
demographic targeting
  advanced, 469

via Facebook, 463, 467
on LinkedIn, 446
desktops, targeting, 163
destination URL, 293
developers, 88–89
device targeting
    as AdWords feature, 112
    with Google Keyword Tool, 118
    how to use, 162–163
    organizing campaigns by, 145
differentiation
    as competitive advantage, 35, 36
    identifying competitive, 79–80
    images to highlight, 208
    between paid and free ads, 458
    script, 269
digital advertising
    accountability in, 17, 279
    data collection to tailor, 3–4
    defining objectives in, 26–38
    direct response, 32–35
    efficiency of, 5
    forms of, 4–6
    networks commonly used for, 18
    search vs. display, 6–13
    of "solution" to a "problem", 13–16
direct competition, 77
direct response advertising
    attribution as measure of, 32–35
    CPC bid model, 279
    defined, 485
    goals for, 62–65
    metrics important in, 308
    on YouTube, 259
Direct Traffic report, 302
DIRECTV, 267
Dish Network. see Google Display Network
dislikes. audience, 265
Display Ad Builder
    ad creation, 237–240
    advanced options, 240–242
    benefits/drawbacks, 235–236
    personalizing, 242–243
    templates, 251
    themes and filters, 236–237
display advertising
    ad types and formats, 23–26
    advertiser/publisher landscape, 41–45
    benefits of, 9–11
    campaign goals, 60–73
    defining objectives in, 26–38
    Google Keyword Tool use, 117
    Google rules for, 220–222
    history of, 41
    keywords, 103–104

major players in, 18–19
targeting, 11–13
technology powering, 41–42
Display Campaign Optimizer (DCO)
    analysis by, 5–6
    how to use, 350–351
    for placements, 171
display campaigns
    account setup, 154–163
    ad groups
        creating, 181–190
        reports, 301
        shared targeting, 147–148
    ad review process, 233–235
    advanced settings, 173–181
    analysis options, 295–309, 333
    Analytics reports for, 296–297
    bid style and budget, 164–173
    calculating ROI for, 280–284
    clear goals for, 227–228
    with constrained budget, 341–343
    exclusions, 150–152
    expanding, 345–350
    on Facebook, 462–470
    Google TV, 265–272
    impression optimization, 330
    launch, 274–285
    on LinkedIn. see LinkedIn
    metrics. see metrics, performance
    naming tips, 156, 298, 301
    negative keywords in, 188
    optimizing. see optimization, campaign
    parameters, 155–156
    segregated by performance, 337
    split-testing experiments, 359–361
    starting video, 254, 255–257
Display Networks tab, 331
distraction, user
    via calls to action, 196
    as campaign goal, 13–16
    via font and color, 195
    graphics to enhance, 199–200
distribution, TV, 268
dMarc Broadcasting, 44
Dollar Shave Club, 253
DoubleClick Ad Exchange
    access for AdWords advertisers, 53
    accessed with LinkedIn ads, 461
    defined, 21
    as GDN source, 20
DoubleClick Ad Planner
    for demographics, 335
    how to use, 126–133
    for placements
        plus Placement Tool, 135

research of, 345–350
usefulness of, 12
on YouTube, 262–263
site profile, 131
topic targeting in, 431–432
DoubleClick for Advertisers (DFA)
defined, 53
for multi-channel measuring, 314
as strategy tool, 295
DoubleClick for Publishers (DFP), 53
downloads, 29
drill-down options
into ad groups, 289
to add audiences, 185
to add keywords, 182
to add placements, 184
AdWords hierarchy, 330
in campaign reports, 301
customizing, 307
Drop report, ClickTale, 421
dubious practices, 226

E

e-commerce
calculating ROI for, 279
checkout friction, 372–373
as a goal, 28, 63
image ads for, 228–229
overview report, 304
eCPM (effective cost per mille), 485
editing, video, 258, 270
education targeting, 469
educational videos, 260
email
checking, 2
Gmail, 46–47
retargeting, 381
emotional appeals, 80
engagement, user
measuring, 312
reports on, 306
tracking social, 317–319
in video ads, 253
via YouTube, 259
Engagement report (YouTube), 265
entertainment, video ads as, 253, 260
errors, form, 368
ESPN, 267
eSurveysPro, 414
event ads, Facebook, 464
exclusions
audience, 187–188
in bulk, 160
of competitors, 50

defining, 150–152
with Google Keyword Tool, 119
importance of, 12
keyword, 121
placement, 140, 186–187
from remarketing lists, 392
of topics, 432–433
underperforming placements, 331–333
expandable ads
CPC billing for, 26
Display Ad Builder templates, 241
experience, evaluating user, 424–427
experiment code, 399
experimentation/testing
with ad copy, 203
calls to action tests, 369
campaign split testing, 359–361
ease of online, 198
eye-tracking, 417
form tests, 369
Google Analytics Content Experiments, 395–404
importance of, 363, 369
of landing pages, 394–395
of LinkedIn ads, 459
to maximize budget, 341–343
multivariate, 376–377, 395
with Optimizely, 404–411
sample size for, 354
user testing, 424–425
value of failure, 275
Eye-Fi, 312–313
eyes
guiding, 199
movement tracking, 207–209

F

Facebook
campaigns
Analytics integration, 478–481
budgets, 469–470
destinations, 462
editing, 475–477
formats of, 463–467
Insights info, 473–475
launching, 470–472
managing, 472
targeting options, 467–469
demographic metrics, 320
as display ad forum, 18
measuring branding on, 73
and ReadWriteWeb, 412
social media tracking from, 322
targeting options, 13
tracking code, 318

Facebook Insights, 322, 473–475
Facebook Marketing: An Hour a Day (Smith and Treadaway), 462
favorites, audience, 265
feature differentiation, 36, 79
feedback, user, 412–415
feeds
    embedded display ads in, 51
    user interaction with, 28–29
filming video ads
    editing, 270
    importance of quality, 268, 269–270
    outsourcing production, 270–271
    script, 269
    tips for, 257–258
filters
    audience (Ad Planner), 128
    content (Ad Planner), 129
    Content Experiment warnings, 399
    in Display Ad Builder, 237
    effect on Analytics data, 297
    ideas (Google Keyword Tool), 119
    inline, 304
    placement (Ad Planner), 130
    Placement Tool, 134–135
    to track Google review, 234–235
    for website exclusion, 339–340
Find My Sample Size, 356
first touch attribution, 35
Flash
    distraction techniques, 209
    effectiveness of, 215
    as incompatible with iOS, 26, 163, 426
    requirements, 218–220
    tracking, 301
FluidSurveys, 414
focus groups, 427
focus points, visual, 206–210
fonts, 201–202
ForeSee, 413
formats
    analyzing ad, 365
    Display Ad Builder, 235–243
    Facebook ad, 463–467
    GDN supported, 215–216
    LinkedIn, 442–443
forms
    advice for online, 367–368
    analyzing, 419–424
Forrester, 372
Fox News, 268
Free Clicks report, 251
FreeOnlineSurveys, 414
frequency
    analysis, 293

capping, 177–178, 392, 485
    on Facebook campaigns, 472, 475
front-end programmers, 88

G

GEICO, 374
geographic targeting
    absent from Google TV, 266
    by AdWords, 111
    defined, 485
    by Facebook, 467
    by LinkedIn, 445
    performance report, 293–294
Gmail, 46–47
goals
    analysis as dependent on, 302
    assigning value to, 30–31
    in Content Experiments, 399
    for CPA bidding, 169
    defining, 60–73
    evaluating placements by, 138
    for Facebook campaigns, 470
    for Google TV ads, 269
    importance of clear, 227–228
    for LinkedIn campaigns, 440–441, 460
    in Optimizely results, 409–411
    optimizing website for, 365
    remarketing, 390
    types of advertising, 28–30
    for YouTube ads, 259–260
Godin, Seth, 62
Google
    ad review process, 233–235
    brand values, 224
    budget spending by, 97–98
    contextual targeting update 2012, 115–116
    landing page metrics, 366–367
    policies and guidelines, 225–227
    privacy stance of, 110, 225
    reach of, 383
Google Account
    setup, 154
    time zone of, 177
Google AdSense
    as ad option expansion, 40
    content pairing by, 48–50
    defined, 44
    for mobile apps, 50–51
    reach of, 20
    relevance sorting by, 45–46
Google AdWords
    accessing Display Network via, 7
    account setup, 154–155

Ad Planner exports to, 132–133
billing options, 98–100
budget allocation, 172
budget spending, 97–98
campaign metrics
 commonly reported, 277–278
 for direct response goals, 65–67
 evaluation, 6, 330–331
 view through conversions, 38
data collection, 275
defined, 44
as an industry revolution, 278
linked to Google Analytics, 284–285, 288, 296
organizing account, 145–152
Placement Tool, 133–137
PPC model, 4–5
reach, relevance, and ROI, 20–23
remarketing with, 55, 382–388
reports, 285–295
targeting via, 11, 111
traffic analysis in, 333
TV ad campaigns, 265–272
video ads, 246–252
Google Analytics
advanced segmentation, 71
AdWords integration, 284–285, 288
analysis options, 23, 295–309
campaign-level report, 296–297
Content Experiments, 395–404
conversion tracking, 286
defined, 44
Facebook integration, 478–481
ignorance of upper-funnel phase, 312
importance of using, 296
LinkedIn integration, 455–458
to measure TV ad success, 271–272
post-click evaluation in, 333
separating data for, 144
test integration, 407–408
traffic tracking, 68–70
Google Display Network
ad campaign overview, 56–57
defined, 8, 485
Dimensions tab, 291–295
formats supported by, 216
vs. Google Search Network, 7–9
history of, 41
properties on, 46–48
reasons to focus on, 19–23
reports, 289
scope of, 5, 44
targeting, 161
Google Finance, 47
Google Insights for Search, 73
Google Keyword Tool, 117–123

Google Maps, 48
Google Search Network
 defined, 8, 485
 geotargeting on, 157
 targeting the, 160–161
Google Voice, 295
Google Webmaster Tools, 225
Google+, 178–181
Google's Insights for Search, 38, 326
graphic designers, 88
graphic elements
 calls to action, 368–371
 landing page clutter, 373
 requirements for, 220–221
 using effective, 199–202
Green Bay Packers, 107
group targeting, 446

H

Harris Interactive polls, 30
heuristic evaluations, 426
Hilton, 352
Homepage Takeover, 52
HTML5, 26
Hulu
 ad viewing options, 248
 cost per viewing completion, 246

I

image ads
 cognitive psychology in, 204–214
 copy for, 202–203
 defined, 24–25
 on Facebook, 471
 in feeds, 52
 graphic elements, 199–202
 imports into AdWords, 232–233
 industry rules, 215–227
 on LinkedIn, 439, 442–443
 science behind appealing, 192–214
 uploading to ad groups, 190
images
 effective use of small, 445
 enticing, 197–199
 visual analysis of, 412–415
implementation, plan, 84
implementer, campaign, 85–86
impressions
 budget as limiting, 341–342
 as campaign metric, 277
 vs. conversions, 272
 defined, 485

as a goal, 29
lost to budget limits, 172
in ROI calculation, 281
share of, 485
tracking, 295
of video ads, 250
inconsequential competition, 77
in-display video ads, 261–262
InFocus, 36, 37, 213
information architecture, 426
information dissemination, 29
informational videos, 260
in-search video ads, 261
in-slate ads, 248–249
in-stream ads, 247–248
Intel, 75–76
intent, user, 6, 371
interaction, user
with ads, 202, 295
free click report, 294
phone calls, 295
on social networks, 28–29
tracking onsite socializing, 317–319
on websites, 68–70
Interactive Advertising Bureau (IAB)
click metric from, 277
current formats, 215–216
future formats, 217–218
Interactive Marketing Units (IMUs), 215–216
interest, tracking user
on Facebook, 463, 468
via look-alike modeling, 346–349
Internet Protocol (IP) address, 156
Internet use
on airlines, 2
content consumption trends, 10
hub and spoke surfing, 192
potential customer habits, 82
interstitial ads, 485
invalid clicks, 484
inventory, 485
InVideo ads, 249
Invite Media, 44
iPerceptions 4Q, 413
Ipsos, 266

J

JavaScript
for Content Experiments, 400
conversion tracking via, 286
defined, 485
remarketing code as, 386
Jet Blue, 70
JMP, 230

job title targeting, 446
JOHNSON's Baby Shampoo, 37

K

Kampyle, 413, 415
Kawaja, Terence, 42
keywords
in ad group setup, 181–183
adjusting bids for, 343–344
bidding on, 7
branded, 71, 304
campaign optimization by, 338–339
changing, 183
choosing relevant, 114–126
competitive analysis via, 77
for display campaign targeting, 103–104
expanding groups of, 124–125
Google Keyword Tool, 117–123
individual performance of, 115–116
negative, 152, 188, 486
for search campaign targeting, 102–103
targeting via, 8, 11, 54
to track brand impacts, 38
for YouTube video ads, 262
Kindle, 212
KISSinsights, 413
Klout.com, 322
KPIs (key performance indicators), 486

L

Landing Page Optimization: The Definitive Guide to Testing and Tuning for Conversions (Ash), 377
landing pages
checking/improving Quality Score, 366–367
creation of, 84, 365–377
dedicated, 374, 462
defined, 365–366, 486
enticing imagery for, 197–199
for Facebook campaigns, 471
incomplete load, 297
performance report, 293, 301
testing
LinkedIn, 460
skills, 377
split-, 375–376
tools for, 394–395
tips for effective, 367–374
use analysis, 309, 334
Lane, David M., 14
language targeting
via AdWords, 160

defined, 111
with Google Keyword Tool, 119
organizing campaigns by, 145
laptops, targeting, 163
last touch attribution, 35
launch, ad campaign
AdWords, 274–285
in campaign cycle, 85
on Facebook, 470–472
on LinkedIn, 448–452
launch, product, 259
layout, 364
lead generation
assigning dollar values to, 310–312
as direct response goal, 28, 64–65
image ads for, 229–230
in LinkedIn, 453, 461
Leaf, Nissan, 259
legal issues
illegal ads, 221
trademark laws, 223–224
lighting, for video ads, 257
like ads, 464
likes, audience
on Facebook, 473
on YouTube, 265
LinkedIn
ad formats, 442–443
ad placements, 439–440
Ads tool, 438
Audience Network, 461
bids/budgets, 447–448
campaign launch, 448–452
campaign optimization, 458–460
as display ad forum, 18, 438–448
Google Analytics link, 455–458
Help Center, 462
interface use, 452–455
targeting options, 13, 445–446, 450
when to advertise on, 440–442
listing service, 78
location targeting
adding/excluding within, 158
benefits of, 111
with Google Keyword Tool, 118
how Google performs, 156–158
via map view, 158–159
organizing campaigns by, 145
radius targeting, 159–160
login/usage, 29
logos, 445
look-alike modeling, 345–347, 350
loss, net, 284
LSI (latent semantic indexing), 486
LUMA Partners, 42

M

Macy's Express Checkout, 372
maintaining scent, 192–195, 374
malware, 225
managed placements
in ad group setup, 183–185
bid adjustments for, 343
defined, 21, 54
editing, 185
promoting automatic to, 139–141, 289
management, project, 86
Manber, Udi, 45
Manfrotto, 304
map view, 158–159
market research
ad spend as, 275
cost of, 165
staff performing, 86–87
tests based on, 363
market segmentation, 82
market share, 73–74
marketing
art of, 362
competitive advantage as basis for, 35
digital, 4–6
on Facebook, 462
questions on forms, 421
search engine, 2–6
marketplace ads, 466
markets, new, 61
Matching RegExp field, 304
Max Profitable CPA, 280
Mays, Billy, 211
Mazda, 197, 198
media plans, 132
Medscape, 231
metrics, performance
Analytics reports, 295–309
for branding goals, 65–67, 71–74
vs. competitors, 76
confidence intervals, 275–276
for correlation/causation, 324–327
for display campaigns, 333
evaluating, 330–331
for Facebook campaigns, 472–473
GDN Dimensions tab, 291–295
GDN reports, 289–290
in Google Keyword Tool, 119
importance of understanding, 274
for LinkedIn campaigns, 454, 460
measured over time, 65
most common, 277–278
sample size for, 353–357
"soft", 38, 309–312
for TV campaigns, 271–272

for video ads, 250–252
    YouTube Analytics, 263–265
micro-conversions, 312
microphones, 258
Microsoft Advertising, 18
Mixcloud, 320
mobile devices
    Display Ad Builder ads, 241–242
    downloads, 30
    sites/apps for, 50–51
    targeting, 112, 163
moderation skills, 427
Motorola Mobility, 44
Multi-Channel Funnels (MCF) report, 68, 313
multiple touch attribution, 35
multivariate testing, 376–377

N

negotiation, 90
net profit/loss, 284
networks
    analyzing all, 306
    display, 41
    DoubleClick, 44, 53–54
    Google, 383
    LinkedIn, 438
    managing TV ads, 268
    organizing campaigns by, 145
    reached by Google TV, 267
    social media tracking by, 322–323
    tagging data from, 299–301
Nevada Commission on Tourism, 384
New York Times, 106
newsletter signups, 28
Next-Gen Keyword Contextual Targeting, 116
Nike, 363
Nissan, 259
notifications
    AdWords, 330
    LinkedIn, 455

O

operating systems, targeting, 163
OpinionLab, 413
optimization, campaign
    of ads, 334–336
    of audience, 339–341
    as data-reliant, 274
    landing pages for, 365
    on LinkedIn, 458–460
    metrics evaluation, 330–331
    search vs. display, 330
    via testing

of ads, 358–361
    of sample size, 354–357
Optimizely, 395, 404–411
Orabrush, 259, 271
order fulfillment, 372–373
organic listings, 486
organic searches
    analyzing traffic from, 311
    blocking malware from, 225
    branding correlations with, 327
    competitors revealed by, 77, 78
    as end-stage conversion, 278, 313
    as lower sales funnel, 479
    +1 annotations of, 178
    reports on, 304
    video ad interaction from, 265
    vs. viral traffic, 320
organization, 86
outbound clicks, 30
The Owned Agency, 257

P

page/ad impressions, 29
pay-per-click advertising (PPC), 4–6
people, images of, 206–210, 365, 445
performance metrics. *see* metrics, performance
perks, offering, 80
persona, 486
personalization, 486
personally identifiable information
    defined, 486
    harvesting of, 222
    phishing for, 221
    as prohibited by LinkedIn, 444
personas, customer, 81–82
persuasion, 90
Pew Internet & American Life Project, 2
phishing, 221
phone calls, 28
Pirolli, Peter, 192
placement evaluation
    for context, 137
    and exclusion, 331–333
    measures, 138–139
    and optimization, 335
    in ROI calculation, 279
    of underperformers, 334
    volume/specificity balance, 138
Placement Tool, AdWords, 133–137, 262
placements
    in ad group setup, 183–185
    adjusting bids, 343–344
    by AdWords, 21, 133–137
    automatic and managed, 139–141

campaign separation by, 337–338
excluding, 151, 186–187
expanding, 345–350
finding effective, 126–141
how to use, 104–107
on LinkedIn, 439–440
managing, 54
performance reports for, 289
researching specific, 130
sorting options, 136
targeting via, 12, 486
viewing sample, 125–126
YouTube video, 262
playback location reports, 264
plays, video ad, 250
+1 annotations, 179–180
poll ads, Facebook, 464
positioning, ad, 483
positioning, brand. *see* branding
PostRank, 324
Power Editor, Facebook, 475–477
premium Facebook ads, 463–465
prices, competitive, 36, 79
privacy
    addressing concerns on, 372
    advertiser policies, 55
    Google policy on, 110, 226
    and retargeting, 393
problem solving
    display advertising as, 13–16
    emulating customers', 77
    as goal of marketing, 74–76
    video ads as, 258
product benefits
    demonstrating, 211–214
    rules about realistic, 221
product launch, 259
product retargeting, 381
product showcase ads, 26, 240
professionals, business, 438
profit, net, 284
program targeting, 268
programmers, 88–89
Promoted Video, 261
psychology, 87, 204–214
publishers
    access to Ad Exchange, 53
    vs. advertisers, 40
    competitor exclusion by, 50
    formats supported by, 215–216
    YouTube, 258

Q

qualitative feedback, 412–415
quality of product, 79

Quality Score
    calculation of, 94
    defined, 486
    improving landing page, 366–367
    relevance-based, 122–123, 183
    as search campaign focus, 330
    specificity as increasing, 115
query string parameters, 299–300, 456, 479

R

radius targeting, 159–160
reach
    of AdWords remarketing, 383
    broad, 149–150, 266, 433
    broad and specific, 112–114
    expanded with ad group bids, 341–343
    of Facebook, 463, 472
    of Google AdWords, 20
    look-alike modeling to improve, 345–347
    performance report, 293
    tab (Facebook), 474
    topic targeting to increase, 428
ReadWriteWeb, 412
real-time bidding (RTB), 41–42
relevance
    of ad by audience, 334
    of ads for LinkedIn, 442
    of Google AdWords, 21
    Google rules for, 220–221
    how Google determines, 45, 115–116
    keyword, 103, 183
    optimizing for, 130
    Quality Score as based on, 122–123
    traffic balanced with, 138
remarketing/retargeting, 380–394
    in AdWords, 382–384
    of audience, 109, 340–341
    best practices, 390–394
    by competitors, 78
    defined, 486
    effectiveness of, 350
    forms of, 380–382
    GDN tools for, 56–57
    to increase conversion rate, 55
    in LinkedIn, 461
    lists
        by audience interest, 347–349, 350
        custom combinations, 388–390
        defined, 22
        as high performing, 340
        how to create, 385–388
        separating campaigns for, 150
    solutions, 19
reputation management, 259
research, ad campaign, 84

resources, identifying, 83–86
return on investment (ROI)
    ad scheduling as boosting, 175
    in budget management, 172
    calculating, 278–284
    defined, 486
    with Google AdWords, 23
reviews, 30
rich media ads
    benefits of, 231–232
    defined, 26
Rising Stars, 217–218
ROAS (return on ad spend), 486
Rokenbok, 259
rotation, ad, 177–178
RSS feeds, 51
RTB (real-time bidding), 487
Rule of Seven, 14

S

safety, user, 221
sales channels, 314
sales funnel
    back end tracking of, 31
    and calls to action, 364
    improvements, 334
    increasing traffic into, 61
    maintaining scent in, 192–195, 374
    multi-channel, 312–315
    soft sells to initiate, 442
    upper, 28, 333, 479
sales videos, 260
sample size, 353–357, 361
Sample Size Calculator Tool, 355
sampling ad, Facebook, 465
ScrubsAndBeyond.com, 33–34
search advertising
    contextual targeting in, 102
    display vs., 6–8
    Google Keyword Tool, 117
    history of, 40–41
    identifying competition in, 78
    retargeting for, 380
    sites serving, 8
    time limitation in, 9
search campaigns
    negative keywords in, 188
    Quality Score focus of, 330
search engines
    Google's 2012 contextual targeting update,
        115–116
    Google's relevance sorting, 45
    marketing via, 2–6
    YouTube as, 258

searches, keyword
    local trends, 120–121
    tracking monthly, 120
    volume and seasonality, 122
seasonality
    Conversion Optimizer does not serve, 170
    of keyword searches, 122
    sorting campaigns by, 148–149
secure sites, 226, 372
Secure Sockets Layer (SSL), 226
SEM (search engine marketing), 487
Seminars for Success
    attention map of homepage, 416–418
    direct response goals for, 63
    as recommended, 296
    sample success metrics for, 66–67
    sample test of, 404–405
    signups to, 65
    visual analytics at, 416–419
SEO (search engine optimization), 487
SERP (search engine results page), 487
share of voice, 487
sharing, video, 265
signups, 65
Silly Putty, 62
sitewide placement, 105
"Slap Me for Good Videos", 257–258
Smith, Mari, 462
Smith, Thomas, 13–14
Social Data Hub, 324
social networks
    brand impact from, 70–71, 73
    catering ads to, 334
    Google+, 178–181
    as initial sales channel, 314
    interaction with, 28–29
    LinkedIn, 438, 458
    metrics, 315–321, 324
    retargeting, 381
    tracking leads from, 68
social plug-ins, 480
soft metrics, 38, 309–312
software downloads, 226
solutions, marketing, 13–16, 74–76
sorting options, 136
Southwest Airlines, 36
specific reach targeting, 114
split-testing ads
    for campaign optimization, 358–361
    creatives, 352–353
    interpreting results, 361–362
split-testing landing pages, 375–376
spokespeople, 258
sponsored listings, 466–467, 487
SportsCardForum.com, 105
SpotMixer, 248

spyware, 225
standard premium ads, 464
starring placements, 136
statistical significance
 finding, 357–358
 importance of sample size to, 354
 in split test results, 361
statistics, ad campaign, 23
steady video, 257
Stevenson, Seth, 268
Stone, Charlie, 257–258
Straker, Michael, 202–203
strategy, remarketing, 390
style, 201
subscribers, 265
subsection placement, 106
Successful Advertising (Smith), 13–14
surfing, web, 192
SurveyGizmo, 415
SurveyMonkey, 415
surveys, 38, 414–415

T

tablets, targeting, 163
Talking About This tab, 475
Target.com, 50, 193–194
targeting
 via AdWords, 21–22
 broad and specific reach, 112–114
 campaign strategies, 54–56
 competitive advantage, 80
 display ad, 11
 Facebook options, 467–469
 keyword-based bidding, 46
 on LinkedIn, 442, 445–446, 450
 multi-faceted, 428–429
 options, 55, 102–114
 search vs. display, 142–143
 via video ads
  options for, 255, 256
  precision of, 253
  on TV, 266
  on YouTube, 262
 see also audience targeting; contextual targeting;
  placements; remarketing/retargeting
technology, 41–42
Teracent, 44
testing. *see* experimentation/testing
text ads
 defined, 24
 in feeds, 51
 on LinkedIn, 439, 442–443
 uploading to ad groups, 188–190
thematic organization
 of campaigns, 146–149

to improve Quality Score, 183
 for performance testing, 362
themes, reinforcing, 193
third-party retargeting, 382
time
 of conversion rate tests, 356
 data analysis by, 291–292, 332
 spent browsing, 363–364
 spent on forms, 423
TNT, 267
Top Conversion Paths, 69, 70, 314
topic targeting
 in Ad Planner, 432–433
 adding/editing, 429–431
 for broad and specific reach, 433–435
 in combination, 428–429
 defined, 12, 22, 116
 to increase reach, 428
 as refinement option, 110
tracking code
 AdWords vs. Analytics, 286
 for audience targeting, 108
 clickTAG, 218
 defined, 487
 for demographics, 320–321
 on Facebook campaigns, 479–480
 Flash, 301
 installing, 85, 286–288
 for onsite social engagement, 317–319
 in Twitter links, 316
trademark laws, 223–224
traditional advertising, 6
traffic, website
 analyzing, 333
 attracting the right, 60–61
 balanced with relevance/conversion, 138
 branding correlations with, 327
 cost of, 281–282
 Direct Traffic report, 302
 engaged, 306
 LinkedIn reports, 456–457
 measuring, 38
 mediums, 298
 new vs. returning, 68, 305
 pre-campaign metrics on, 274–275
 segregating campaigns by, 337–339
 testing, 399
 tracking sources, 264, 297–298, 478
 value assessment of, 310
Traffic Allocation, 405–406
transparency, 226, 290
TravelNevada.com, 384
Treadaway, Chris, 462
trends, 309–310
TrueView
 billing model, 246

in-search and in-display ads, 261–262
in-slate ads, 249
in-stream ads, 248
payment for click-to-play, 247
success metrics, 251
see also AdWords for Video
TV
campaigns, 265–272
as historic video ad forum, 252
measuring campaign success, 271–272
metrics for correlation, 325
program targeting, 268
Twiddy, Ross, 415
Twiddy & Company Realtors, 415
Twitter
measuring branding on, 73
social media tracking from, 322, 323
as source of clicks, 316
tracking code, 318

U

unique visitors, 487
United Airlines, 70
URLs
attaching query string parameters to, 299, 456,
479
builder, 300
in direct traffic reports, 303
performance report, 293
rewrites, 399
to track Twitter sources, 316–317
usability analysis, 424
users
active, 6
addressing concerns of, 372–373
attention map, 416–418
banner blindness in, 14
behavioral targeting of, 22, 55, 324
evaluating experience of, 424–427
feedback from, 412–415
filtering, for placements, 128–129
Google rules to protect, 221–222
interface time with, 9, 202
LinkedIn, 438
LinkedIn tab, 453–454
objectives for action by, 27–28
pre-campaign metrics for, 274–275
retargeting, 381–382
segments, testing, 396
tracking
interests of, 108, 346–349
reach and frequency, 293
segmented, 319–320
see also audience

V

value assessment
of advertising goals, 30–31
for CPA bidding, 169
by Google, 224
of lead generation, 65, 310–312
of product branding, 38
for signups, 65
of social sharing sites, 69
value per click (VPC), 280
ValueClick Media, 19
Verizon
FiOS, 267
image ad samples, 194–195
verticals, 487
ViaMedia, 267
video ads
AdWords options, 246–252
bids by viewing trends, 246
click-to-play, 247
defined, 25–26
evaluating performance of, 250–252
filming. *see* filming video ads
how to create, 252–258
options for, 52–53
requirements for, 220–221
on TV via AdWords, 265–272
viewer choice in, 248–249
YouTube, 258–265
video comment ads, Facebook, 465
views, webpage, 275
Views reports (YouTube), 263–264
view-through conversion, 66
virtual private network (VPN), 156
vision, maintaining, 86
visitors, unique, 487
visits
analyzing
attention map, 417
Facebook, 480–481
via Google Analytics, 295, 296
importance of, 85
by time, 175
from branded keywords, 71
clicks as unmatched with, 297
vs. competitors, 76
cookies installed during, 108
leading to micro-conversions, 312
as performance metric, 274–275
retargeting non-converting, 384
Sites Also Visited list, 346
from TV campaigns, 271, 272
visual contrast, 204–205
Volvo, 37

INDEX ■

W

Walmart, 36
web pages
    ad location on, 137
    clutter, 373–374
    Content Experiments, 395–397
    exclusion filters for, 339–340
    installing Optimizely on, 408–409
    managing placements by, 141
websites
    ad placement on, 12, 137–138
    Ad Planner profiles of, 131, 132
    affinity research, 345–347
    interaction with, 68–70, 319
    pre-campaign metrics for, 274–275
    retargeting solutions, 381, 385–386
    secured, 226
    YouTube, 258
white space, 200
Wieden, Dan, 363
Wieden + Kennedy, 363
Wi-Fi, 163
WIRED magazine, 196
workplace targeting, 469
Wright, James, 62

X

Xerox, 192

Y

Yahoo!, 18
Yellow Pages, online, 78
YouTube
    AdWords as reaching, 246
    brand channels, 260
    brand impacts from, 70
    partners, 247
    social media tracking from, 322, 323
    video ads on
        via GDN, 25–26
        how to create, 258–265
        InVideo, 249
        opportunity of, 52
    video source files on, 254, 256, 270
YouTube Analytics, 263
YouTube Insight, 263

Z

Zoom Zoom campaign, 197

GET A LEG UP

You've read the book. Now take the next step:

Learn to master Google AdWords and Analytics from
the same experts Google trusts to train its clients.

Google approved Cardinal Path training courses can pay for themselves in less than a week:

- Save money: eliminate ad-spend waste
- Increase reach: attract more highly-targeted customers
- Boost conversion rates, profits and your career!

For upcoming dates and locations, visit: **training.cardinalpath.com/book**

Your competitors have taken these courses. Can you afford not to?